Linguistic Anthropology

Blackwell Anthologies in Social & Cultural Anthropology (ASCA)

Series Editor: Parker Shipton, Boston University

Drawing from some of the most significant scholarly work of the 19th and 20th centuries, the *Blackwell Anthologies in Social and Cultural Anthropology* series offers a comprehensive and unique perspective on the ever-changing field of anthropology. It represents both a collection of classic readers and an exciting challenge to the norms that have shaped this discipline over the past century.

Each edited volume is devoted to a traditional subdiscipline of the field such as the anthropology of religion, linguistic anthropology, or medical anthropology; and provides a foundation in the canonical readings of the selected area. Aware that such subdisciplinary definitions are still widely recognized and useful – but increasingly problematic – these volumes are crafted to include a rare and invaluable perspective on social and cultural anthropology at the onset of the 21st century. Each text provides a selection of classic readings together with contemporary works that underscore the artificiality of subdisciplinary definitions and point students, researchers, and general readers in the new directions in which anthropology is moving.

Published Volumes

1. *Linguistic Anthropology: A Reader, Second Edition*
   Edited by Alessandro Duranti
2. *A Reader in the Anthropology of Religion, Second Edition*
   Edited by Michael Lambek
3. *The Anthropology of Politics: A Reader in Ethnography, Theory, and Critique*
   Edited by Joan Vincent
4. *Kinship and Family: An Anthropological Reader*
   Edited by Robert Parkin and Linda Stone
5. *Law and Anthropology: A Reader*
   Edited by Sally Falk Moore
6. *The Anthropology of Development and Globalization: From Classical Political Economy to Contemporary Neoliberalism*
   Edited by Marc Edelman and Angelique Haugerud
7. *The Anthropology of Art: A Reader*
   Edited by Howard Morphy and Morgan Perkins
8. *Feminist Anthropology: A Reader*
   Edited by Ellen Lewin
9. *Ethnographic Fieldwork: An Anthropological Reader*
   Edited by Antonius C. G. M. Robben and Jeffrey A. Sluka
10. *Environmental Anthropology: A Historical Reader*
    Edited by Michael R. Dove and Carol Carpenter
11. *Anthropology and Child Development: A Cross-Cultural Reader*
    Edited by Robert A. LeVine and Rebecca S. New

Linguistic Anthropology
A Reader

Edited by
Alessandro Duranti

Second Edition

A John Wiley & Sons, Ltd., Publication

This edition first published 2009

Blackwell Publishing was acquired by John Wiley & Sons in February 2007. Blackwell's publishing program has been merged with Wiley's global Scientific, Technical, and Medical business to form Wiley-Blackwell.

Registered Office
John Wiley & Sons Ltd, The Atrium, Southern Gate, Chichester, West Sussex, PO19 8SQ, United Kingdom

Editorial Offices
350 Main Street, Malden, MA 02148-5020, USA
9600 Garsington Road, Oxford, OX4 2DQ, UK
The Atrium, Southern Gate, Chichester, West Sussex, PO19 8SQ, UK

For details of our global editorial offices, for customer services, and for information about how to apply for permission to reuse the copyright material in this book please see our website at www.wiley.com/wiley-blackwell.

Library of Congress Cataloging-in-Publication Data

Linguistic anthropology : a reader / edited by Alessandro Duranti. —2nd ed.
p. cm.—(Blackwell anthologies in social and cultural anthropology)
Includes bibliographical references and index.
ISBN 978-1-4051-2633-5 (hardcover : alk. paper)—ISBN 978-1-4051-2632-8 (pbk. : alk. paper)
1. Anthropology linguistics. I. Duranti, Alessandro. II. Series.
P35.L48 2009
306.4′4089—dc22

2009000845

A catalogue record for this book is available from the British Library.

Set in 9/11 pt Sabon
by SPi Publisher Services, Pondicherry, India
Printed in Singapore

1 2009

Contents

Acknowledgments to the Second Edition

Special thanks to the students and colleagues who provided feedback on the first edition of this Reader and to the wonderful staff at Wiley-Blackwell for their assistance and patience in the preparation of this second edition. The undergraduates in my lower division course, "Culture and Communication" at UCLA, have played an especially important role for my own understanding of what might be done to make linguistic anthropology more relevant to their lives (the choice of some of the new chapters in this edition took this goal into consideration). Several of my resourceful and insightful graduate students, among them Robin Conley, Jennifer Guzman, and Anjali Browning, assisted me in rethinking the selection of articles to be included. Anjali and Jennifer also helped me formulate the study questions at the end of each chapter – a new feature of this edition. Any shortcomings in the final choice of articles, suggested readings, and study questions remain of course my own.

Preface to the Second Edition

The first edition of this Reader is only seven years old and yet so much has happened in linguistic anthropology and related fields in the meantime that I could not resist making some changes for a second edition. Taking into consideration my own experience in using the Reader and the feedback from instructors and students, I decided to maintain the division of the Reader into four parts, but to expand the range of topics and issues explored within them. This new edition introduces eight new chapters (5, 6, 9, 10, 11, 17, 19, and 21) that cover topics such as language and ethnicity, style, genre and intertextuality, political debates, the language of hip hop, language change and its ideological implications, the construction of expertise through multi-media communication and manipulation, and language and sexuality. The new title of Part I – "Ideal and Real Speech Communities" – takes inspiration from the new chapter by Leung, Harris, and Rampton on the problematic notion of "native speaker" in the context of TESOL classes in Great Britain. The recognition of the vast range of linguistic competence exhibited by new immigrants in European countries helps us reframe the topics presented in the other chapters of Part I, each of which can be read as a reformulation or expansion of John Gumperz's notion of speech community (Chapter 1).

The subtitle of Part II has been changed to read "Events, Genres, and Narratives" in order to highlight the inclusion of four new chapters that discuss the performance of language in artistic performance, political arenas, and everyday contexts. Theoretically, the new chapters recognize the importance of three units of analysis in linguistic anthropology: ways of speaking (a notion explicitly connected by Dell Hymes to "style" and to Whorf's notion of "fashions of speaking"), genre, and narrative. In each case, the understanding of language as a domain of performance suggests new ways of connecting language use to the exercise of power as well as to the resistance that speakers may try to exert (a major theme presented in Chapter 9 by Charles Briggs and Richard Bauman as well as in all of the chapters in Part IV). Chapter 10 on the language of contemporary political debates in the US (based on my coverage of a political campaign in California) and Chapter 11 on the language of Rap and Hip Hop music by H. Samy Alim also provide a small but significant sample of the new ethnographic contexts chosen by linguistic anthropologists to gather linguistic data, test their theories, and challenge previous findings.

Part III on language socialization and literacy practices has remained unchanged even though the field continues to grow as attested to by the bourgeoning of new books and collections on the topic. Three of the four chapters in Part III are "classic" articles that need to be on everyone's list of essential reading. Chapter 12 by Elinor Ochs and Bambi B. Schieffelin is the programmatic article that was responsible for the definition and launching of the field of language socialization within anthropology and linguistics. The subsequent chapter by Susan Philips was the first ethnographic account of the impact of primary socialization on secondary socialization among minority children in the US; and Shirley Brice Heath's ground-breaking study of the socialization to literacy in three communities represented in Chapter 14 has remained a model for anyone interested in the connection between home and school. In the fourth contribution to Part III, Chapter 15, Patricia Baquedano-López extends the notion of language socialization to literacy events in Sunday school classes for children of new immigrants, offering a model of how to study the role of grammatical framing in the narrative construction of social and ethnic identity.

Part IV includes three new articles. The comparative and distinctly theoretical chapter by Judith Irvine and Susan Gal on language differentiation is one of the most cited articles within the recent and still growing literature on language ideology (also represented in Chapters 16 and 20); Charles Goodwin's multimodal discussion of what he calls "professional vision" provides us with an original perspective on the proceedings of a much discussed and controversial trial on police exercise of force in the 1990s while expanding the notion of "language" to include visual communication and material culture; and finally Don Kulick's concluding chapter on the meaning of "no" in cases involving requests for sex unmasks the cultural assumptions of language use and the difficulty speakers experience trying to overcome those hidden assumptions.

A new feature of this second edition is the Study Questions that are now at the end of each chapter (which replace the more limited number of study questions provided at the beginning of each part in the first edition).

The Suggestions for Further Reading have also been expanded considerably in scope and number. Even though the books cited cannot fully represent the now vast literature on almost every topic having to do with language as a cultural practice, they provide a good start for anyone interested in exploring the themes and issues touched upon in the individual chapters. They also help balance whatever shortcomings some readers might find in the specific choices I have made, which were inevitably guided by my own theoretical and methodological preferences.

The success of the first edition of this Reader in a competitive market (there are other excellent readers on "language and culture" or related areas of interest) has made me realize that linguistic anthropology – the smallest of the four original subfields of US and Canadian anthropology – continues to exert a considerable attraction not only within anthropology at large but also within a range of distinct disciplines and research paradigms that include qualitative and quantitative sociolinguistics, applied linguistics, communication studies, education, sociology of language, comparative literature, media studies, classics, and cultural studies. It is from these intersections that the field is likely to gain theoretical and empirical strength in the years to come. I hope that the articles gathered in this edition will help continue the dialogue with those in other disciplines while participating in the shaping of new generations of researchers and informed policy-makers. Language plays a crucial role in our private and public life. We can never grow tired of searching for a better understanding of such a role.

Alessandro Duranti
Fall 2008

Linguistic Anthropology: History, Ideas, and Issues

Alessandro Duranti

1 Introduction[1]

We are born with the ability to learn languages. However, the contexts in which we learn them, the manner in which we use them, and the extent to which they help or hinder us in achieving our goals is culturally mediated. If we want to understand the role of languages in people's lives, we must go beyond the study of their grammar and venture into the world of social action, where words are embedded in and constitutive of specific cultural activities such as telling a story, asking for a favor, greeting, showing respect, praying, giving directions, reading, insulting, praising, arguing in court, making a toast, or explaining a political agenda.

Linguistic anthropology is one of many disciplines dedicated to the study of the role of languages (and the language faculty) in these and the many other activities that make up the social life of individuals and communities. To pursue such an agenda, researchers have had to master the intricate logic of linguistic systems – e.g. their grammars – and document the activities in which those systems are used and reproduced through routine and yet highly creative acts. The articles collected in this Reader are a representative sample of the best scholarship in this tradition. They should give readers a clear sense of what it means to study language in a way that often starts from utterances but always looks for the cultural fabric within which such utterances are shaped and meanings are produced.

When Dell Hymes put together what could be easily recognized as the first comprehensive Reader in linguistic anthropology (Hymes 1964d), he included writings whose authors would not have defined themselves as linguistic anthropologists (e.g. Marcel Mauss, Antoine Meillet, Claude Lévi-Strauss, Roger Brown, Leonard Bloomfield). Such an editorial decision was not just a declaration of interdisciplinarity; it was also the reconstitution of a field (or subfield) relying on any solid piece of work that could give a sense of (i) the importance of language(s) for an understanding of culture and society and (ii) the relevance of cultural and social phenomena for an understanding of language(s). Looking for articles to include in this Reader, I found myself in a very different situation. Since Hymes's 1964 collection there has been such a wealth of research and writing in linguistic anthropology that, although I would have liked to include articles by authors from other fields whose work has been influential to our discipline – the linguist Roman Jakobson and the sociologist Erving Goffman are the first two names that come to mind – it became very difficult to include such authors without excluding an even greater number that have recently helped to define linguistic anthropology as a discipline with its own unique vision of language structures and language practices. What is this unique vision? In what follows I will try to provide a brief overview of the field beginning with a discussion of two names that are often used as synonyms for linguistic anthropology, namely, anthropological linguistics and sociolinguistics. I will suggest that the difference between the names "linguistic anthropology" and "anthropological linguistics" has to do with different histories, professional identities, and theoretical interests. In the case of linguistic anthropology vs. sociolinguistics, I will argue that, although in the 1960s and 1970s they were thought of as one field, they have moved further apart since that time. Despite continuous cross-fertilization and sharing of topics (especially "gender and language"), sociolinguistics and linguistic anthropology constitute at the moment two related but separate research enterprises. The rest of this introductory chapter provides a brief overview of the history of linguistic anthropology in the United States (section 3); a discussion of linguistic relativity (section 4), which was until the 1960s the major theoretical issue in the discipline; a discussion of the four areas of research represented in this Reader (sections 5, 6, 7, and 8); and some final comments that connect the past with the foreseeable future (section 9).

2 What's in a Name? Linguistic Anthropology, Anthropological Linguistics, and Sociolinguistics

In contemporary academic and scientific discourse, the name "linguistic anthropology" coexists with a number of other names that are often understood to be synonyms for the same intellectual enterprise. The two most common variants are "anthropological linguistics" and "sociolinguistics"[2] (with "ethnolinguistics" being a distant third within the United States[3]). Although it could be argued that this semantic ambiguity has helped construct a loosely tied community of scholars – many of whom might have been intellectually isolated within the boundaries of larger disciplines such as linguistics and anthropology – there are some differences that have emerged over the years. An understanding of such differences will help us further define the discipline represented by the articles included in this Reader.

2.1 Anthropological linguistics and linguistic anthropology

There is linguistics, there is linguistics in anthropology, and there is linguistic anthropology, but if we wish our terms to have unambiguous and pertinent reference, there is no anthropological linguistics.

(Teeter 1964: 878)

Whether or not there is in fact a field called "anthropological linguistics," there is no question that the term often functions as a synonym for linguistic anthropology, both within and outside the United States. This is, for example, the way it is used in William Bright's series *Oxford Studies in Anthropological Linguistics*, which includes books that cover classic topics in the study of language and culture such as sound symbolism (Nuckolls 1996) and new theoretical perspectives such as language ideologies (Schieffelin, Woolard, and Kroskrity 1998). From the point of view of its scope, the series could have been called "Oxford Studies in Linguistic Anthropology." The same could be said about William Foley's *Anthropological Linguistics: An Introduction*, which has chapters on many of the topics and approaches represented in this Reader. Foley's (1997: 3) definition of anthropological linguistics ("that subfield of linguistics which is concerned with the place of language in its wider social and cultural context, its role in forging and sustaining cultural practices and social structures") is close to the one given in this introduction (see above) and even closer to the one given in my *Linguistic Anthropology*,[4] with one exception. Foley sees the field he is describing as a subfield of linguistics, whereas I see it as a subfield of anthropology. This difference can be explained at least in part by the different intellectual climates in which we work – Foley teaches in a linguistics department in Australia and I teach in an anthropology department in the United States. Australian linguistics was strongly influenced in the 1970s and 1980s by (mostly British) scholars who were committed to a view of language as a social tool (e.g. Halliday 1973, 1978) and to fieldwork among Australian Aborigines with the goal of producing comprehensive and sophisticated reference grammars (e.g. Dixon 1972, 1977). This intellectual heritage has meant that linguistics in Australia has been less directly affected than linguistics in the USA by the so-called "Chomskian revolution," whose followers since the 1960s have pursued and encouraged "autonomous" models of grammar and discouraged the study of cultural or sociological dimensions of language (Chomsky 1965, 1986, 1995; Newmeyer 1980, 1986).

The linguists in Australia who are still concerned with the documentation and preservation of Australian aboriginal languages live in an academic climate that is, at least in some respects, similar to the one found in the USA (and Canada) at the end of the nineteenth century and the beginning of the twentieth century, when the documentation of American Indian languages and cultures was the intellectual project through which anthropology – with material support from a very interested party, the US government – became a profession (Darnell 1998a; Stocking 1974; Voegelin 1952) (see section 3).[5] It was in that intellectual climate that Alfred Kroeber and Edward Sapir matured and, through them, that an entire new generation of scholars was formed, including Harry Hoijer, Carl Voegelin, Benjamin Lee Whorf, Mary Haas, and Morris Swadesh. These researchers – like Bright and Foley today – thought of themselves primarily as linguists and thus it is not surprising to know that in the 1950s several of them chose the name "anthropological linguistics" for their work (Haas 1953, 1977; Hoijer 1961; Voegelin and Harris 1952).[6] Their main concerns were (i) the documentation of grammatical structures of American Indian languages and other indigenous languages without writing,[7] (ii) language as the medium through which myths and historical narratives could take form,[8] and (iii) the use of language as a window on culture (understood as worldview or

Weltanschauung). These goals were pursued by studying nomenclatures and taxonomies (of animals, plants, types of disease, kinship terms, color terms) – an area that eventually developed into ethnoscience (e.g. Conklin 1962; Frake 1969; Goodenough 1956, 1965; Lounsbury 1969) – genetic relations among languages (e.g. through the comparative method), the impact of culture on language (e.g. euphemisms, taboo words, sacred or respectful terms) or of language on culture, in various versions of linguistic relativity (see section 4). Overall, from the point of view of teaching, linguists working within anthropology departments in the first half of the twentieth century saw themselves as in charge of training graduate students from other subfields (cultural anthropology in particular) to use linguistic data for their research. It was this goal that justified what Voegelin and Harris called "technical linguistics":

> The importance of relating anthropological training to technical linguistics is that the latter brings to the former a few necessary but not too difficult techniques for exploring culture. Cultural studies without linguistic consideration tend to be narrowly sociological rather than broadly anthropological. On the other hand, ethnolinguistic studies essayed by anthropologists innocent of technical linguistic training tend to be amateurish. (Voegelin and Harris 1952: 326)

It was only in the 1960s that this view was revised and the subfield moved from a position of "service" to the rest of anthropology to one of independence. Two projects that instigated this new professional identity were Charles Ferguson and John Gumperz's (1960) investigation of dialect variation and language contact in South Asia[9] (see section 2.2) and Dell Hymes' call for an "ethnography of speaking" (Hymes 1962), soon renamed "ethnography of communication" (Hymes 1964c).[10] It was in those years that Hymes proposed to use the name "linguistic anthropology" – which had been first introduced in the late 1870s (see section 3) but not quite adopted by the practitioners – to designate a distinctly anthropological approach to the study of language:

> Put in terms of history and practice, the thesis is that there is a distinctive field, linguistic anthropology, conditioned, like other subfields of linguistics and anthropology, by certain bodies of data, national background, leading figures, and favorite problems. In one sense, it is a characteristic activity, the activity of those whose questions about language are shaped by anthropology. Its scope is not defined by logic or nature, but by the range of active anthropological interest in linguistic phenomena. Its scope may include problems that fall outside the active concern of linguistics, and *always it uniquely includes the problem of integration with the rest of anthropology*. In sum, linguistic anthropology can be defined as *the study of language within the context of anthropology*. (Hymes 1964a: xxiii) (emphasis in the original)

This programmatic statement had at least two concerns: (i) to keep the study of language as a central part of the discipline of anthropology (instead of letting it "slip away" to the numerous linguistics departments that were being established in the 1960s); and (ii) to broaden the concept of language beyond the narrow interest in grammatical structures. However, despite the birth of sociolinguistics in the 1960s (see section 2.2) and discourse analysis in the 1970s (Brown and Yule 1983; Givón

1979; Schiffrin 1994; Stubbs 1983), the situation has not changed much since Hymes's statement. In the USA and elsewhere, many anthropologists still take language for granted, as if it were a transparent medium for culture, relegating it to the role of what Tedlock (1983) called "a postcard from the field," and mainstream linguistics continues to be fundamentally concerned with grammars rather than with speakers, with *forms in isolation* rather than *forms in relation* to the context of their use. Of course, as Hymes himself noted, "[o]n general intellectual principle, of course, nothing linguistic is alien to anthropology" (Hymes 1964a: xxiii). For one thing, the description of previously undocumented languages is still relevant to the anthropological enterprise because, as Franz Boas and Bronislaw Malinowski reminded us, it is impossible to understand a community without an understanding of the language(s) used by its members.[11] It is also true that linguistic reconstruction, for example through the comparative method, can be a useful tool for archaeology and historical anthropology (e.g. Kirch 1984; McConvell and Evans 1997). It is only in this broad sense of linguistics as always relevant to the general anthropological enterprise (because language *is* culture) that we can make sense of the title of Joseph Greenberg's (1968) *Anthropological Linguistics: An Introduction.*[12] The book introduces the study of phonology, morphology, language change, and potential synchronic and diachronic universals. But linguistic anthropology as practiced today and represented in this Reader is more than grammatical description and historical reconstruction, and it is also more than collection of texts, regardless of whether those texts were collected in one's office or under a tent. It is the understanding of the crucial role played by language (and other semiotic resources) in the constitution of society and its cultural representations. To pursue this goal, linguistic anthropologists have ventured into the study of everyday encounters, language socialization, ritual and political events, scientific discourse, verbal art, language contact and language shift, literacy events, and media. To the extent to which anthropology can offer the intellectual and institutional support for such a broad research program, it makes sense to use, as Hymes proposed, the name "linguistic anthropology" for such an enterprise. A great part of the research discussed by Foley (1997) was in fact done by scholars who see themselves as working within an anthropological paradigm rather than within a linguistic one and for this reason tend to call themselves linguistic anthropologists.[13] On the other hand, should linguistics revise its theoretical and analytical horizon to include in the center a notion of language that is more than grammar and an interest in speakers as more than producers of linguistic forms, scholars like Bright and Foley might see their dream of a truly *anthropological* linguistics realized.

2.2 Sociolinguistics and linguistic anthropology

Sociolinguistics was born in the early 1960s as the study of linguistic forms in relation to the social context of their use. Both the types of phenomena studied and the methods used for their study varied, depending on the researchers involved. For example, Charles Ferguson and John Gumperz (1960) were interested in understanding language contact through qualitative methods involving work with informants, informal observations, and (sometimes) questionnaires (e.g. Blom and Gumperz

1972). Starting a few years later, William Labov was interested in providing an empirical basis for the study of language change that could start from actual language use in urban communities. He pursued this goal by developing a method for the study of speech in social context based on statistical analysis of a large corpus of data extracted from recorded interviews.[14] In collaboration with Joshua Waletzky, Labov also developed an analysis of the syntax and structural organization of elicited narratives (Labov and Waletzky 1966) that became very influential in a number of fields (see the contributions in Bamberg 1997).

The different methodological orientation and theoretical goals produced distinct schools of research on language use, but the term "sociolinguistics" has survived, with various qualifiers doing the work of acknowledging some differences among approaches. Thus, Labov-style sociolinguistics has been known as "quantitative," "macro," or "urban," whereas Gumperz-style sociolinguistics has been called "qualitative," "micro," or "interactional."[15] In part due to the collaboration between Gumperz and Hymes in the 1960s (while Hymes was at the University of California at Berkeley[16]), the term "sociolinguistics" was used to cover a wide range of approaches, including some distinctively anthropological and sociological perspectives. For example, such collections as Bright's (1966) *Sociolinguistics: Proceedings of the UCLA Sociolinguistics Conference, 1964* and Gumperz and Hymes's (1972) *Directions in Sociolinguistics: The Ethnography of Communication* include quantitatively oriented studies of language variation and language change in urban settings (e.g. Labov 1966a, 1972b), correlational studies between language forms and speakers' social status (e.g. Ervin-Tripp 1972a, 1972b; Friedrich 1966), specific guidelines for the ethnographic descriptions of language use within a community (e.g. Hymes 1966, 1972a), componential analysis (e.g. Tyler 1972), ethnoscience (e.g. Frake 1972), ethnomethodology (e.g. Garfinkel 1972), and conversation analysis (Schegloff 1972). Until the 1970s, ethnographic studies of language were considered part of sociolinguistics, as implied in Dell Hymes' *Foundations in Sociolinguistics: An Ethnographic Approach* (1974a).[17] Since then, however, the situation has changed considerably.

Despite Hymes's renewed attempt, especially through his long tenure as the founding editor of the journal *Language in Society*, to keep sociolinguistics and linguistic anthropology under the same umbrella, or at least not to draw any sharp boundaries, since the mid-1980s there has been an increasing separation between the two subdisciplines. Except for the occasional chapter on "Language and Culture" or on "The Ethnography of Communication,"[18] textbooks and edited books in sociolinguistics tend to focus almost exclusively on either quantitatively oriented studies of mostly urban speech communities or studies of patterns of language use and language change that are attentive to sociological variables (especially social status and gender) and pragmatic dimensions (e.g. politeness), but are not informed by anthropological theory or methods (e.g. ethnography). In parallel sign of incipient separatism, recently published textbooks in linguistic anthropology and anthropological linguistics dedicate very little or no space at all to sociolinguistic theories and methods (e.g. Duranti 1997b; Foley 1997; Hanks 1996; Palmer 1996; Salzmann 1993).

The roots of this separation are both methodological and theoretical. Most sociolinguists – especially quantitatively oriented ones – continue to use today the same methodology introduced by Labov in the 1960s, that is, they typically rely on statistical analysis of data collected through interviews. There is no question that through these methods sociolinguists have produced an impressive body of work which can tell us a great deal about the internal dynamics of speech communities and the relevance of social class, sex, and age for a number of linguistic phenomena, most typically (and most effectively) dialect variation and sound change in progress. At the same time, these methods and some of the theoretical implications of sociolinguistic research are problematic for many linguistic anthropologists. First, the treatment of sociological concepts such as social class, sex, gender, race, and generation as independent variables is not universally accepted in the social sciences, anthropology in particular. From the 1980s there has been a considerable amount of writing devoted to the cultural construction of these sociological categories (Gal 1992, 1995). This literature is ignored by most quantitative sociolinguists. Second, the definition of context as a constantly changing frame that needs reference to speech itself as one of its constitutive elements (e.g. Duranti and Goodwin 1992) is usually absent from quantitative sociolinguistic studies. Third, the exclusive reliance on the interview as the only reliable method for recording spontaneous speech is viewed with suspicion by most linguistic anthropologists, who see speaking as an interactional achievement. Over thirty years of research on conversational exchanges[19] and on the speech patterns that ensue from those exchanges have taught us that speakers are constantly engaged in the business of fashioning their speech for their interlocutors and that stories rarely have only one author in conversation.[20] The texts collected by sociolinguists tend to be (or be presented as) monologic. Questions and feedback channel responses by fieldworkers are often left out of transcripts together with other features of the interaction (e.g. pauses, false starts) that do not seem relevant to the study of phonological features (e.g. deletion of final consonant). And yet, some of these features are considered important by linguistic anthropologists and other researchers who believe in the co-construction of narrative accounts and the importance of the mutual monitoring that goes on in any encounter.

On the other hand, it would be naïve not to recognize that, in turn, many studies within linguistic anthropology do not match the kind of scientific standards aimed at by sociolinguists, not simply because of linguistic anthropologists' tendency toward qualitative as opposed to quantitative analysis – with the common strategy of discussing only a few examples and then generalizing from them – but because many of the studies within linguistic anthropology, as most of those within its closest sibling, cultural anthropology, are based on data that are not easily accessible for counter-arguments or independent testing. This lack of accessibility is due to a number of factors, including (i) the anthropological tradition of working in isolated small communities or in communities that require considerable time and financial investment for anyone else to go and collect additional data, and (ii) the lack of shared corpora, in part due to ethical considerations (see Duranti 1997b: 119–21) and in part to the unwillingness of researchers to expose their data to the scrutiny of others without the proper contextualization, which would be very difficult to provide without knowing how the data might be used by others. If one rejects the idea that talk alone (whether in a recording or in a transcript) constitutes "the data," the entire idea of sharing "a corpus" becomes problematic.

These methodological, analytical, and theoretical differences are reinforced by the institutional separation due to the tendency for sociolinguists to work in departments of linguistics or foreign language and for linguistic anthropologists to work in departments of anthropology. The result is a separation that is by no means beneficial to either one of the two fields, especially for training new scholars. Linguistic anthropologists could certainly benefit from the systematic attention to broad patterns of variation in linguistic forms and social networks that characterizes contemporary sociolinguistic research. Sociolinguists, in turn, could take more advantage of ethnographic methods and the theoretical concerns regarding the cultural construction of social categories of participants (e.g. ethnicity, race, gender). One domain of inquiry where there has been some exchange between sociolinguists and linguistic anthropologists is the study of gender differences (see section 8). Although it is difficult to say whether this convergence will provide a model to be emulated in other research areas, it does show that a concentration on issues (e.g. is men's and women's language different and if so why? how is gender made to count in an interaction?) can draw together researchers who are usually kept apart by methodological and epistemological differences.[21]

3 The Birth of Linguistic Anthropology in the United States

If one were asked to name the one work which has been of greatest importance and influence in the development of American anthropology, it could scarcely be any other than Powell's "Indian Linguistic Families of America North of Mexico," published in the Seventh Annual Report of the Bureau of Ethnology fourteen years ago.

Kroeber 1905: 579

The inclusion of linguistic anthropology as an integral part of mainstream anthropology – the "four field approach"[22] – is a phenomenon that is unique to the USA – as opposed to European countries like Great Britain for example[23] – and must be understood within the context of the research program under which anthropology became a profession in the USA, namely, the documentation of North American indigenous cultures. In this (largely government-sponsored) project, the study of American Indian languages played a major role. Under the auspices first of the Smithsonian Institution (founded in 1846) and later of the Bureau of Ethnology (founded in 1879 and later renamed Bureau of American Ethnology [BAE]), the documentation of indigenous languages spoken north of Mexico became an important part of the work pursued by anthropologists in private and public institutions.

The person who more than anyone else helped organize, direct, and find funds for the survey of American Indian languages in North America in the second part of the nineteenth century was the founder of the BAE, John Wesley Powell (1834–1902). A natural scientist who retrained as a geologist and saw an obvious connection between the study of the land and the cultural tradition of its inhabitants (Darnell 1998a: 25), Powell believed that languages could be an excellent instrument for classifying cultures and he employed linguists and other scholars to collect as much material as possible on American Indian languages (e.g. word lists, myths, descriptions of ritual life). On the basis of this material, those employed by the BAE worked on linguistic classifications and tried to organize the surveyed languages in families

(Powell 1880). It is then not surprising that what is perhaps the oldest use of the term "linguistic anthropology" is found in the 1st Annual Report of the Bureau for 1879–1880 (published in 1881), in a section prepared by Otis T. Mason (1838–1908), a curator of artifacts at the Bureau who also became fascinated by linguistic classifications (Darnell 1998a: 38–9; Mason 1900). With the establishment of the American Anthropological Association (see note 25), there began a period of intense interest in linguistic matters in American anthropology, as shown by the numerous articles that provide grammatical descriptions, classifications, texts, and notes on nomenclatures (almost exclusively on American Indian languages[24]) in the first issues of the official organ of the Association, the *American Anthropologist*.[25] For example, in Volume 2 (1900), we find John R. Swanton's "Morphology of the Chinook Verb," Albert S. Gatschet's "Grammatical Sketch of the Catawba Language," and Franz Boas' "Sketch of the Kwakiutl Language." By Volume 7 (1905), the articles on linguistic topics and issues had risen to ten.

Despite the importance of Powell and the BAE, however, it is Franz Boas who is credited with transforming what was originally an almost exclusive interest in classification of American Indian languages (largely based on word lists) into a systematic study of their grammatical structures. Boas, who taught himself linguistic analysis, set the standards that were to be followed by subsequent generations of scholars through his own grammatical descriptions and his editorial work on the *Handbook of American Indian Languages* published in 1911 (Jakobson 1944; Stocking 1974; Voegelin 1952).[26] His "Introduction" to that volume was a major departure from the perspective on non-Indo-European languages that was popular at the time.

Boas argued that there was no necessary correlation between a given language and a given race or between a given language and a given culture. This claim constituted an implicit rejection of Powell's goal of using Native American languages for ethnic classification (Boas was also skeptical of genetic classification of considerable time depth and more inclined toward acculturation as an explanation for linguistic and cultural change[27]). At the same time, Boas, certainly influenced by eighteenth- and nineteenth-century German philosophical tradition, agreed with Powell that language plays a crucial role in culture and should be studied by ethnologists: "If ethnology is understood as the science dealing with the mental phenomena of the life of the peoples of the world, human language, one of the most important manifestations of mental life, would seem to belong naturally to the field of work of ethnology..." (Boas 1911: 63). This perspective had methodological implications, one of the most important of which was that ethnographic fieldwork should be done using the native language of the people one wanted to study instead of speaking through an interpreter or using a lingua franca (e.g. a pidgin). Since he saw the categories formed in or through language as unconscious, Boas believed that languages provided excellent material for the study of cultural phenomena (Hymes 1964b: 7–9; Stocking 1974).[28]

In addition to being interested in language as a window on the human mind, Boas was also committed to a theoretical understanding of grammatical systems, their differences and similarities. He identified the sentence (as opposed to the word) as the fundamental unit for expressing ideas in any language[29] and listed a number of grammatical categories that are likely to be found in all languages. His criticism of some common prejudices about American Indian languages (and implicitly of other languages of the people who were then called "primitive") helped to establish scientific standards for linguistic investigation. He stressed the importance of making orthographic conventions and analytical categories appropriate for the languages under investigation instead of uncritically extending categories originally developed for the study of ancient European languages. Boas argued against the then commonly held idea that speakers of American Indian languages are less accurate in their pronunciation than speakers of Indo-European languages. Repeating an argument first made in his 1889 article "On Alternating Sounds," Boas argued that this is a false perception due to the difficulty that linguistically unsophisticated listeners had in making the phonetic distinctions that are relevant in these languages. While stressing that different languages may classify the world differently, Boas also cautioned against interpreting the lack of certain linguistic forms as evidence of the lack of abstract thought or ability to generalize (Boas 1911; Lévi-Strauss 1966).

> Thus the Indian will not speak of goodness as such, although he may very well speak of the goodness of a person... It is, however, perfectly conceivable that an Indian trained in philosophic thought would proceed to free the underlying nominal forms from the possessive elements, and thus reach abstract forms strictly corresponding to the abstract forms of our modern languages. (Boas 1911: 65)

Thus, while continuing to use the term "primitive languages," as in vogue at the time,[30] Boas in fact showed that such languages were by no means primitive.[31]

Unlike Powell (1880), Boas did not see the different types of morphological patterns (e.g. word formation) in the world languages along an evolutionary scale, especially not one that ended with English at the top. Instead, in his investigation of grammatical structure, vocabulary, and poetry in American Indian languages, Boas found support for an underlying unity of the human mind (Boas 1911, 1925; Hymes 1999: 87; Lucy 1992a: 11–17).

This general stance toward aboriginal languages was restated by his students. For example, Edward Sapir started his 1933 entry "Language" for the *Encyclopedia of the Social Sciences* with a statement that echoes the Boasian view of human languages:

> The gift of speech and a well ordered language are characteristic of every known group of human beings. No tribe has ever been found which is without language, and all statements to the contrary may be dismissed as mere folklore. There seems to be no warrant whatever for the statement which is sometimes made that there are certain people whose vocabulary is so limited that they cannot get on without the supplementary use of gesture so that intelligible communication between members of such a group becomes impossible in the dark. The truth of the matter is that language is an essentially perfect means of expression and communication among every known people. Of all aspects of culture, it is a fair guess that language was the first to receive a highly developed form and that its essential perfection is a prerequisite to the development of culture as a whole. (Sapir [1933] 1949a: 7)

The obvious implication is that language is the most sophisticated cultural system available to human societies and to their members, and, therefore, there can be no anthropology without the study of language.

4 Linguistic Relativity

The first major theoretical issue that occupied linguistic anthropologists was linguistic relativity. The interest in this issue was born out of a marriage between an idea and an encounter. The idea is the nineteenth-century Romantic association between a language and the "spirit" (German *Geist*) of a nation or the language and the worldview (*Weltanschauung*) of its speakers. The encounter was with the languages of the indigenous peoples of the Americas and the other continents (re)discovered or conquered by Europeans. The subsequent attempt by missionaries, travelers, and linguists to describe those languages (Salmon 1986) highlighted the difficulty in translating and in adapting grammatical categories originally developed for Indo-European languages (Cardona 1976; Haas 1977). Boas's cultural relativism was extended to (or perhaps inspired by) his linguistic relativism:

> As is well known, Boas's most important theoretical contribution to the study of linguistics was his promulgation of the concept of linguistic relativism, that is, that each language had to be studied in and for itself. It was not to be forced into a mold that was more appropriate to some other language. Side by side with this was his insistence on seeing the language as a whole. (Haas 1978b: 195)

The efforts to find analytical categories that could adequately describe the grammatical structures of non-Indo-European languages resulted in the realization that languages have quite different ways of encoding information about the world and our experience of it. One possible inference from these observations on linguistic diversity was that languages are arbitrary systems and one cannot predict how they will classify the world (linguistic relativism). Another inference was that languages would develop distinctions and categories that are needed to deal with the reality surrounding the people who speak them (linguistic functionalism). A third inference was that the different conceptual systems represented in different languages would direct their speakers to pay attention to different aspects of reality, hence, language could condition thinking (linguistic relativity). An earlier version of this last view is found in the posthumous *Linguistic Variability and Intellectual Development* by the German diplomat and linguist Wilhelm von Humboldt (1767–1835):

> Each tongue draws a circle about the people to whom it belongs, and it is possible to leave this circle only by simultaneously entering that of another people. Learning a foreign language ought hence to be the conquest of a new standpoint in the previously prevailing cosmic attitude of the individual. In fact, it is so to a certain extent, inasmuch as every language contains the entire fabric of concepts and the conceptual approach of a portion of humanity. But this achievement is not complete, because one always carries over into a foreign tongue to a greater or lesser degree one's own cosmic viewpoint – indeed one's personal linguistic pattern. (von Humboldt [1836] 1971: 39–40)

As shown in this passage, von Humboldt's view was that the conceptual world represented in each language is *sui generis* and as such incommensurable with the worlds represented in other languages. This makes the perfect acquisition of a foreign language impossible unless speakers are willing and able to leave behind the ways of thinking acquired through their first language (competent multilingual speakers – of which there are millions in the world – would then be people who can successfully switch from one worldview to another). About a hundred years later, Edward Sapir expressed a very similar view:[32]

> Language is not merely a more or less systematic inventory of the various items of experience which seem relevant to the individual, as is so often naïvely assumed, but is also a self-contained, creative symbolic organization, which not only refers to experience largely acquired without its help but actually defines experience for us by reason of its formal completeness and because of our unconscious projection of its implicit expectations into the field of experience. [...] Such categories as number, gender, case, tense, mode, voice, "aspect" and a host of others, many of which are not recognized systematically in our Indo-European languages, are, of course, derivative of experience at last analysis, but, once abstracted from experience, they are systematically elaborated in language and are not so much discovered in experience as imposed upon it because of the tyrannical hold that linguistic form has upon our orientation in the world. (Sapir [1931] 1964: 128)

Sapir's ideas had a profound impact on Benjamin Lee Whorf (1897–1941), a chemical engineer who worked as an insurance inspector while pursuing a number of intellectual quests, including linguistics (see Carroll 1956; Lucy 1992a: 24). After Sapir moved to Yale from Chicago in the Fall of 1931, Whorf attended Sapir's courses and became part of the cohort of Sapir's students (Carroll 1956; Darnell 1990). Soon after, he started to study Hopi, the language through which he was able to best articulate his views on the relation between linguistic patterns and thinking (Whorf 1938, 1941, 1956a). The frequent use of the term "Sapir–Whorf Hypothesis," as a synonym for linguistic relativity comes from the intellectual association between Sapir's and Whorf's ideas on the role of linguistic patterns on thinking and acting in the world (see Koerner 1992 for a review of the literature generated by this "hypothesis"). The term "Sapir–Whorf Hypothesis," however, is misleading.[33] The two scholars never worked out a joint statement about the relation between language and thought, and a close analysis of their writings shows some important differences, including the different conceptual level reached by the two scholars (Lucy 1992a). Furthermore, for some time Whorf's name was more closely associated with that of Dorothy Lee than with that of Sapir (e.g. Lee 1944).[34]

The "tyrannical hold" of linguistic forms, as expressed in the passage quoted above, was perhaps for Sapir a way of articulating a number of insights he had developed on the relation between language, culture, and personality. Two of them in particular are recurrent in his writing and his teaching (as reconstructed by Judith Irvine in Sapir 1994). One was the realization of what he saw as a fundamental paradox of human life, namely, the need that each individual has to use a shared and predefined (we could say "public") code in expressing what are subjectively different experiences. The other was the arbitrary (i.e. non-natural) character of linguistic structures, which makes them the most advanced type of cultural forms – a basic theme of Sapir's 1927 article "The Unconscious Patterning of Behavior in Society." The two insights inform the idea expressed in his lectures that language "is one of the most patterned, one of the most culturalized, of habits, yet that one, above all others, which is supposed capable of articulating our inmost feelings" (Sapir 1994: 55).

The comparative study of typologically different languages (e.g. English and Chinese) shows that the specific properties of linguistic systems cannot be explained functionally given that what is obligatory in one language (e.g. the distinction between singular and plural nouns) may be optional in another. In order to make sense of the way in which each language has its own (arbitrary) logic, Sapir compared the logic of grammars to the logic of artistic codes: "Every language is itself a collective art of expression. There is concealed in it a particular set of esthetic factors – phonetic, rhythmic, symbolic, morphological – which it does not completely share with any other language" (Sapir 1921: 225). For Sapir, then, just as we cannot easily give functional explanations of aesthetic forms and aesthetic taste, we cannot easily give a functional explanation (e.g. in terms of communicative needs) for why languages behave the way they do.[35] Linguistic rules are usually unconscious but with an internal coherence (Lucy 1992a: 23). It is this coherence that makes it difficult for individual speakers to enter the logic of the linguistic system and alter it to their liking. Sapir ([1927] 1949a) illustrates this point with the marking of plural in English. There seem to be no functional reasons for the use of plural with nouns that are accompanied by numerals. Hence, why do English speakers need to say *five men* instead of **five man*? For Sapir, it is a question of aesthetic taste (or, as he says in the following quote, "feeling"): "English, like all of the other Indo-European languages, has developed a feeling for the classification of all expressions which have a nominal form into singulars and plurals" (Sapir 1949b: 550). On the other hand, in languages like Chinese, where nouns are not marked for number, if there is a need for being specific, numerals (e.g. words for "five," "ten") and quantifiers (e.g. "all," "several") can be added.

Cross-linguistic comparison then reveals the arbitrary nature of the grammatical distinction between singular and plural and its taken-for-granted necessity in the minds of those speakers of languages that do have such an obligatory feature. Sapir, however, never developed a conceptual apparatus for testing the implications of these observations.

Whorf started out sharing several of the basic positions held by Sapir on the nature of linguistic classification, but he went on to develop his own conceptual apparatus and his own version of linguistic relativity. This apparatus included the important distinction between *overt* and *covert* grammatical categories (Whorf 1956b; Duranti 1997b: 58–9; Lucy 1992a: 26–31). Overt categories are marked in the morphology of the word or in accompanying words. For example, in Spanish, gender is an overt category because it is usually given by the ending of the noun (e.g. *-o* vs. *-a*) or by a number of accompanying elements, e.g. the article (*el* vs. *la*). In English, instead, gender tends to be a covert category that is made explicit only under particular circumstances. When someone says, "I met a neighbor at the store," we don't have a way of inferring the gender of the neighbor. But if a personal pronoun is used next, we will know, without asking, whether the friend in question is a man or a woman ("I met a neighbor at the store. She was buying French wine"). The distinction between overt and covert was a precursor of Chomsky's (1965) distinction between "surface" and "deep" structure[36] and it carried an important implication for cultural analysis because it underscored that conceptual distinctions are made in languages even when no overt signs of them can be recognized. What is overt, explicit in one language may not be in another. The analyst's task is to uncover the hidden cultural logic of the linguistic system and ascertain whether this logic has implications for thinking or acting in the world.

The statement that comes the closest to being a hypothesis about the relationship between language and thought is Whorf's "linguistic relativity principle," according to which "users of markedly different grammars are pointed by their grammars toward different types of observations and different evaluations of extremely similar acts of observation, and hence are not equivalent as observers but must arrive at somewhat different views of the world" (Whorf 1956b: 221). The same essay in which this principle is stated contains the much quoted – and later criticized – comparison of the conceptualization of time in Hopi and SAE (Standard Average European) and the English example of the wrong inference produced by the use of the word *empty* in describing drums that had previously contained gasoline. Whorf explains that the lack of contents described by *empty* is interpreted by English speakers as implying that the drum is no longer dangerous, whereas in effect it is more dangerous than when full because it contains explosive vapor (see Lucy 1992a: 50 for a clear diagram that illustrates the inference process).

Whorf's "linguistic relativity principle" generated a considerable amount of research mostly by linguistic anthropologists and psycholinguists from the 1940s to the 1960s (see Lucy 1992a). In the 1960s, in conjunction with the rise of cognitive science and other research paradigms aimed at linguistic and cognitive universals, Whorf's claims underwent a period of harsh criticism, which culminated on the one hand with Brent Berlin and Paul Kay's (1969) claim that there are cross-linguistic universals in the elaboration of color coding across a large number of languages[37] and on the other with the reanalysis of Hopi tense and aspect and the correction of some of Whorf's original claims, including the one that Hopi does not have a future tense (Malotki 1983; P. Lee 1991, 1996). During the same period, there arose a misguided view of linguistic relativity, which continues into the present, as pertaining to differences among languages in number of words for the "same" concept. Thus, the (questionable) claim that Eskimo dialects have more words for *snow* than English dialects (see Martin 1986 for a criticism of this claim) was believed to be evidence of different thinking patterns between Eskimo and English speakers. Rather than talking about "habitual thought" being directly influenced by lexical choices or grammatical patterns, Whorf was focusing on how a way of thinking may arise *by analogy* with "fashions of speaking" (a term later echoed by Hymes's [1974b] "ways of speaking").

Among the new efforts to test, reframe, and extend Whorf's original intuitions, John Lucy's (1992b) comparison of the performance of speakers of Yucatec and speakers of English in a series of cognitive tasks has been so far the most successful within an experimental paradigm. Starting from the observation that English marks plural overtly and obligatorily on a wide range of noun phrases, whereas Yucatec usually does not mark plural and when it does, it is optional, Lucy hypothesizes that English speakers should habitually attend to the number of various objects more than Yucatec speakers do, and for more types of referents. The results of his experiments support his hypothesis. Another hypothesis was built on the use and distribution of classifiers (these are nouns or particles that many languages employ to encode information on the type of category represented by a given noun). Yucatec nouns that take a plural marker need to be accompanied by a classifier. Thus, whereas in English one can say *three men* (numeral + noun), in Yucatec, one must say "numeral (*óos*) + human classifier (*túul*) + man (*máak*)." This constraint is similar to the one for so-called mass nouns in English (e.g. *sugar, cotton, zinc*), which also need classifiers to be modified by a numeral. One cannot say **two cottons*, but must say *two balls of cotton* (Lucy 1992b: 73). From these observations Lucy inferred that many English lexical items presuppose a unit as part of their meaning and for this reason no classifier is needed, whereas Yucatec lexical items do not presuppose a unit. The unit presupposed by English lexical nouns referring to inanimate objects tends to be the form or shape of the object (Lucy 1992b: 89). Yucatec nouns, instead, have no such presupposed unit and their meaning implies types of substance or material composition. For example, in Yucatec the same word *che'* "wood" is used to form words referring to objects like trees, sticks, and boards, which are of different shapes but are made out of wood substance. This is a different lexical strategy from the one adopted in English, where objects of the same substance (wood) but different shapes are referred to with different lexical items, e.g. *tree, stick, board, table, shelf*.[38] From these considerations, Lucy (1992b: 89) hypothesized that "*English speakers should attend relatively more to the shape of objects* and *Yucatec speakers should attend relatively more to the material composition of objects* in other cognitive activities" (emphasis in the original). This hypothesis was tested with a series of tasks involving recognition and recollection of pictures where the number of items (people, animals, tools) and various substances (corn, firewood, rock) varied. The results demonstrated that indeed English speakers and Yucatec speakers differ in how they categorize and recall different types of referents. For example, English speakers tend to group objects in terms of common shape whereas Yucatec speakers tend to group them in terms of common substance (e.g. wood, water). "These patterns suggest that the underlying lexical structures associated with the number marking in the two languages have an influence on the nonverbal interpretation of objects" (Lucy 1992b: 157).[39]

4.1 Extensions of linguistic relativity

Over the years, the original conceptualization of linguistic relativity has often been reformulated or extended to new research questions. For example, Hymes (1966) expanded the notion of linguistic relativity to include not only the ways in which linguistic structure may influence our experience of the world but also the ways in which cultural patterns, for example, specific cultural activities, can influence language use and determine the functions of language in social life. This second type of linguistic relativity draws attention to the uses of language and the cultural values associated with such uses. Communities can be shown to differ in the ways in which they use and value names, silence, or the telling of traditional stories and myths.

Another line of research that expands on the notion of linguistic relativity is represented by Michael Silverstein's notion of **metapragmatic awareness**, that is, the ability that speakers have to talk about the pragmatics of their language use. This concept draws from and extends the discussion of the unconscious nature of linguistic knowledge found in the writings of Boas, Sapir, and Whorf. Silverstein formulated a hypothesis about three specific features of language structure, which, depending on their value, can either favor or hinder native speakers' ability to interpret the pragmatic force of specific linguistic forms (Silverstein 1981) [this volume] – hence, they are indicators of metapragmatic awareness. The three features are: (i) unavoidable referentiality (i.e. whether the linguistic expression unambiguously identifies one and only one referent); (ii) continuous segmentability (i.e. whether the pragmatic meaning is expressed by a discrete and continuous linguistic segment, e.g. a word, a single suffix, an entire phrase), and (iii) relative presupposing vs. creative quality (e.g. the extent to which the linguistic expression in question presupposes the existence of a given relation, status, act or instead helps constitute that relation, status, act by being used).[40]

In addition to being used to talk about the limits of native speakers' intuitions on the force of their utterances, the same categories can also provide the foundations for a cultural critique of the ways in which certain language philosophers described and classified the social acts performed by speech. In his article "Cultural Prerequisites to Grammatical Analysis," Silverstein (1977) argues that even philosophers are not immune to the limits of metapragmatic awareness and have tended to focus on those effects of language that can be explicitly represented by linguistic expressions. For example, the "things done by language" – or speech acts – identified by the philosopher J. L. Austin (1962, 1975) are the acts that can be described by (referential) expressions such as *I promise that, I declare that, I order you to*... etc. In other words, Silverstein argues that "promising" is recognized as a possible speech act because it is lexicalized (through the word *promise*) and can be articulated in a sentence that involves the speaker as the agent of the act and an embedded clause. But there are plenty of social acts done through language that cannot be easily named by such referential expressions and therefore may not be as easily accessible to native speakers' consciousness. These phenomena have consequences for social scientists' ability to use members' intuitions in their research, and therefore they should be taken into consideration by social and cultural anthropologists who rely on the natives' intuitions in their interpretations of interactions or texts (see also B. Lee 1997; Silverstein 2001; Silverstein and Urban 1996).

Another extension of this work is found in the burgeoning field of language ideologies, which investigates the impact of speakers' beliefs about their language (and other languages) on language structure and language use (Kroskrity 2000b; Schieffelin, Woolard, and Kroskrity 1998; Woolard & Schieffelin 1994). In this perspective, speakers' search for an ideal common language (e.g. "the Standard") that can unite a nation or any other aggregate is viewed as a phenomenon quite similar to the working hypothesis of those linguists who want to limit their study of language to an ideal homogeneous speech community, ignoring the variation found at all levels of language use (see section 5).

In most of the earlier studies on linguistic relativity – at least up to the 1960s – language was fundamentally taken as a taxonomic system whereby speakers classify the experiential world (the objects and people around us, our actions and emotions) into distinct (and arbitrary) units. In testing whether language "guides" speakers' understanding of the world, researchers assumed that linguistic expressions (i) can be easily identified and isolated from the stream of behaviors within which they are routinely embedded in social action, and (ii) constitute an autonomous system that can be studied on its own, without regard for the other semiotic resources that typically coexist with them, and contribute to their meaning. A different approach is pursued by those researchers who have recently stressed the importance of looking at how speaking is part of a broader array of activities. These include at a micro-interactional level the semiotic exploitation of the human body, e.g. through gestures (Haviland 1996; Levinson 1996, 1997), and of the material artifacts with which humans surround themselves (C. Goodwin 1996a, 1997).

5 Communicative Competence and the Speech Community

While Hymes (1962, 1964c) was launching his call for an ethnographic study of language use across speech communities, a new theoretical paradigm was being established in linguistics: generative grammar. This was primarily due to the writing of Zellig Harris's student Noam Chomsky, who, after attacking behaviorist conceptions of language (Chomsky 1959) and American structuralism (Chomsky, Halle, and Lukoff 1956),[41] went on to propose a mentalistic model of grammar, to be understood as "concerned with discovering a mental reality underlying actual behavior" (Chomsky 1965: 4). This mentalistic perspective was foremost expressed by Chomsky's distinction between **competence** (knowledge of language) and **performance** (use of language) and his research strategy to focus exclusively on the study of competence, conceived of as an idealized system:

> Linguistic theory is concerned primarily with an ideal speaker-listener, in a completely homogeneous speech-community, who knows its language perfectly and is unaffected by such grammatically irrelevant conditions as memory limitations, distractions, shifts of attention and interest, and errors (random or characteristic) in applying his knowledge of the language in actual performance. This seems to me to have been the position of the founders of modern general linguistics, and no cogent reason for modifying it has been offered. (Chomsky 1965: 3–4)

Furthermore, for Chomsky, the focus on competence meant that the study of performance had to be postponed, until a full description of competence could be available.[42]

After praising Chomsky's approach for shifting the conceptualization of language from an independent object to a human capacity, Hymes argued that the distinction between competence and performance presented a number of problems: "The term 'competence' promises more than it in fact contains. Restricted to the purely grammatical, it leaves other aspects of speakers' tacit knowledge and ability in confusion, thrown together under a largely unexamined concept of 'performance'" (Hymes

1971a: 55). Starting from a commonsense notion of competence, Hymes held that speakers are "competent" not only when they have the knowledge of grammatical rules but also when they have the knowledge of how to use them appropriately. Furthermore, language acquisition could not be restricted to the process of acquiring knowledge of grammatical rules given that in acquiring a language, "a child becomes able to accomplish a repertoire of speech acts, to take part in speech events, and to evaluate their accomplishment by others" (Hymes 1972b: 277) [this volume]. To be a member of a particular community, one must know when to speak and when not to speak, how to be polite, how to request or offer collaboration, how to sound calm, surprised, interested, concerned, and so forth. Finally, not all members of the speech community have access to the same knowledge or to the same repertoire (Gumperz 1964). Not everyone knows how to deliver a lecture or how to understand a clinician's diagnosis. Rather than focus on the innate aspects of linguistic competence – the phylogenetic correlate of the observed human universal capacity for language acquisition – Hymes shifted the focus to the diversity that is apparent when we study how language is used in social life. Instead of ignoring differences for the sake of creating a homogeneity that can be more easily accessed through a scientific method, Hymes assumed that an anthropological program for the study of language must start from the assumption of heterogeneity (Duranti 1997b: chapter 3). He defined "an ethnography of speaking" as "a theory of speech as a system of cultural behaviour; a system not necessarily exotic, but necessarily concerned with the organization of diversity" (Hymes 1971b: 51).

By proposing an alternative research paradigm, Hymes replaced Chomsky's notion of competence as tacit (typically unconscious) knowledge of grammatical rules with the notion of **communicative competence**, which includes both tacit knowledge and ability to use language (Hymes 1972b: 282). This new notion of competence is analytically tied to new units of analysis. Instead of sentences, researchers are required to look at acts, situations, events (Hymes 1972a). This change for Hymes "entails social description (ethnography)" (Hymes 1971b: 52). In philosophy and cognitive science, it is perfectly acceptable to talk about acts (Searle 1965, 1969) or situations (Barwise and Perry 1983) without having to engage in the systematic observation and documentation of actual behavior (ethnography). In contrast, for Hymes the study of language as social action commits the researcher to ethnography. This commitment locates the notion of communicative competence within the field of anthropology at large. The revision of the notion of competence also implies a new way of thinking about performance, first of all giving it a positive rather than a negative definition (anything left after competence) and, second, tying it to aesthetic dimensions of speaking (see section 6).

In his criticism of Chomsky's "ideal speaker-hearer" and of the assumption of homogeneity as a necessary precondition for linguistic analysis, Hymes was by no means alone. Starting in the 1960s, sociolinguists like Labov demonstrated again and again that even within monolingual communities, there is a considerable amount of linguistic variation and that such variation correlates with social stratification (Labov 1966a, 1966b, 1972b, 1972c). The notion of "ideal speaker" is then questionable on empirical and theoretical grounds (Labov 1972c). While Labov stressed the importance of thinking of a large metropolitan area like New York City as a single speech community – based on speakers' shared norms for evaluating variation – Gumperz was motivated by his own work on multilingualism to look for analytical concepts that could help him make sense of the ability that speakers have to shift from one language, dialect, or style to another and the variation found in the access speakers have to various linguistic resources. The notion of **repertoire** (Gumperz 1964) was meant to account for the range of varieties speakers had access to, and the notion of **linguistic community** (Gumperz [1962] 1968b), later renamed **speech community** (Gumperz 1968a [this volume]), was meant to account for the boundaries of what should be studied as a unit.[43] People routinely switch within a predictable range of linguistic **varieties**, a general term that covers language, dialect, style, and register:[44]

> A variety is any body of human speech patterns which is sufficiently homogeneous to be analyzed by available techniques of synchronic description and which has a sufficiently large repertory of elements and their arrangements or processes with broad enough semantic scope to function in all normal contexts of communication. (Ferguson & Gumperz 1960: 3)

At the same time, variation is not simply determined by the situation and there are limits to what the analyst can predict (Blom and Gumperz 1972). A series of studies addressed the issue of language choice in multilingual communities. In looking at which language was spoken by whom to whom and when, researchers were trying to come up with hypotheses about language choice that could give us hints about the causes of language change (Romaine 1995; Sankoff 1980). Gal's study of declining bilingualism in a small Austrian town connects the abandonment of Hungarian and the resulting German monolingualism of young women to their rejection of peasant life and values and their embracing of an industrial economy (Gal 1978, 1979).

Within the United States, the study of language variation and of the differences between standard and non-standard dialects carried out by urban sociolinguists gave educators the tools to avoid racial stereotypes based on prejudice and ignorance of linguistic matters. The work of Labov on the logic of Non-Standard English was particularly influential in helping define Black English Vernacular (BEV) as a dialect of English with its own distinct phonological and syntactic rules (some of which are in fact similar to other non-standard dialects of English) (Labov 1969, 1972a). The attitudes toward BEV (or AAVE, that is, African American Vernacular English) by members of the black community were then left unanalyzed. Marcyliena Morgan's discussion of the views expressed within the African American speech community was at the same time an attempt to encourage sociolinguists to face the consequences of their own scientific efforts and an occasion to look at the language ideology of African Americans, tying it to the history of race relations within the United States (Morgan 1994a [this volume], 1994b; Rickford 1997, 1999).

The attention paid to different types of variation within multilingual communities eventually led Gumperz to concentrate on the mechanisms through which speakers signal to each other how to interpret what they are saying (e.g. what the hearer should pay attention to, how the speaker feels about something). He referred to these mechanisms as **contextualization cues**. They are linguistic features that can operate at different levels of the linguistic system involving intonation, rhythm, lexical selection, organization of information in an utterance or in a stretch of discourse, or language or dialect selection (Gumperz 1977, 1982a, 1992). When contextualization cues are missed or misread, communication is in trouble. Since the early 1980s, miscommunication based on different ways of communicating has been known among linguistic anthropologists as **crosstalk**, a term originally invented by T. C. Jupp and used as a title for a well-known BBC program centered around Gumperz's work on miscommunication between British speakers and South Asian immigrants (Jupp, Roberts, and Cook-Gumperz 1982). Gumperz's work has been extended to a number of areas, including miscommunication between genders (Maltz and Borker 1982; Tannen 1990).

Despite the fact that scholars like John Gumperz had been working on language contact since the late 1950s, it was not until the 1980s that linguistic anthropologists became intellectually engaged with the issue of heterogeneity. This shift was partly due to the difficulty in ignoring the linguistic effects of new and massive immigration and the globalization of economic markets. At the same time, there were new intellectual sources that allowed a reconceptualization of "language"; among them the writings of Mikhael Bakhtin were particularly influential (Bakhtin 1981, 1984, 1986; Vološinov 1973). In his analysis of the novel, Bakhtin (1981: 261) argued that investigators are confronted with a variety of coexisting styles, which represent different "voices" (the author's, the characters'). It is through these voices that language as a fundamentally stratified and differentiated code, what he called **heteroglossia** (Russian *raznorecie*), can enter the novel – as well as everyday talk (Lucy 1993). In this perspective the notion of a unitary language is not just a working hypothesis, as proposed by Chomsky, but an ideological stance. Rather than homogeneity, we find differentiation, which on the one side creates ... inequality among speakers and on the other it allows for subtle aesthetic effects (through the juxtaposition of multiple voices and coexisting varieties). This work inspired a number of linguistic anthropologists including Jane and Kenneth Hill (1986), whose notion of **syncretic language** to describe language use and language ideology among Mexicano (Nahuatl) speakers is informed by some of Bakhtin's writings. Along similar lines, Duranti and Ochs (1997) coined the term **syncretic literacy** for activities that are informed by teaching and learning strategies that draw from different cultural traditions. The main idea behind this notion is the belief that when different cultural systems meet, it is rarely the case that one simply replaces the other. As pointed out by Hanks (1986, 1987) for the Maya, as soon as contact takes place, any pre-existing indigenous tradition is bound to be affected by the new tradition proposed (or imposed) by the newcomers.

Until recently, linguistic anthropologists thought of communities as entities constituted by daily face-to-face interaction. This is in part due to the fact that most anthropologists worked in small rural communities. Even those who worked in the city tended to concentrate on a relatively small territory, such as a neighborhood or a block. Some even worked with isolated individuals or families who did not know each other. These fieldworkers often acted as if their subjects were isolated from the rest of the world, that is, as if there were no connection or communication with parties who were not physically present or as if such parties were not important or relevant. The situation has started to change in recent years, as some researchers have become interested in the role played by media and new technologies in the daily life of speakers all over the world and the impact of media on everyday communication. For example, Debra Spitulnik (1998a, 1998b, 1999) has analyzed the role of the audience in recontextualizing the messages produced by national and local radio in Zambia, providing a rich documentation of linguistic transfer and transformation from media discourse to popular (and everyday) discourse. Equally important has been the work on the use (and abuse) of new technologies for guiding interpretation of reality through what Charles Goodwin (1994) calls "professional vision" (see section 8).

6 A Focus on Performance

The reframing of the notion of competence came with a rethinking of the notion of performance. Chomsky's view of performance was guided by two assumptions. The first was that to speak of performance meant to speak of perception and production. The second was that the scientific method requires us to ignore performance because it is subject to "memory limitations, distractions, shifts of attention and interest, and errors (random or characteristic)" (Chomsky 1965: 3). Hymes revised and extended Chomsky's notion of performance to include something more than the behavioral record of what speakers do when they talk. For Hymes, as for folklorists and aesthetic anthropologists, performance is a realm of social action, which emerges out of interaction with other speakers, and as such it cannot be described in terms of individual knowledge (Hymes 1972b: 283 [this volume]). Rather than thinking about performance as a residual category – that is, whatever is left after having defined what constitutes competence – Hymes (1981: 81–2) underscored the positive and creative nature of performance (see also Duranti 1997b: 14–17). Instead of reducing our ability to generalize about language, the view of speakers as performers allows us to broaden the analytical horizon of language use in a number of ways.

First, it recognizes a different notion of creativity from the one emphasized by Chomsky's notion of grammar, which must be able to produce a potentially infinite set of sentences on the basis of a finite set of rules. The creativity of performance refers to the ability (and sometimes necessity) to adapt speech to the situation or the situation to speech, as well as the ability to extend, manipulate, and reframe meanings in ways that are related to or identical to what we call poetic language. Metaphors abound in all kinds of speech situations – much of what we say cannot be taken to be "literal" – and both child and adult conversation is full of parallelism and other poetic devices.[45] If it is true, as argued by Friedrich (1986), that there is a poet in each of us, one of the goals of any serious study of language use implies not only the identification of the special features that go into great verbal art and performance but also the discovery of the creative aspects of language in everyday talk. Contrary to popular belief, even scientists are not immune to the creative power of linguistic metaphors and other poetic devices; in fact they routinely rely on them in their problem-solving activities. In their study of a physics laboratory in the USA, Ochs, Gonzales, and Jacoby (1996) found that physicists discussing experiments involving changes in temperature that bring about changes of "states" (e.g. from "paramagnetic" to "domain") attribute human qualities to physical entities, for example, producing utterances like "this system has no knowledge of that system." At other times the physicists' language suggests a blend of different identities: the researchers use personal pronouns (*I, you*) with predicates that refer to change of states undergone by particles: "When I come down I'm in the domain state." In this construction, the speaker (the physicist) appears to assume the identity of a physical entity, producing a semantically ungrammatical sentence. And yet, it is through the use of such supposedly impossible sentences that scientists are able to think creatively.

Second, the view of speakers as performers also recognizes individuals' unique contribution to any given situation and to the evolution of any linguistic tradition. This has been difficult to do within formal linguistics because the emphasis (from Saussure to Chomsky) has been on the linguistic system – often described in terms of context independent rules – rather than on what specific speakers do with language in specific situations. Both the structuralist linguistics of the first half of the twentieth century and the rationalist (mostly synchronic) paradigm of formal linguistics, which started in the 1960s, favored linguistic forms over their users because of the fear that a focus on individual performance detracts from the ability to generalize. This has allowed researchers to improve their descriptions of the formal properties of languages but has revealed very little about individual differences and the role of individuals in linguistic change. As pointed out by Barbara Johnstone (1996: 19), "[t]hinking about language from the perspective of the individual requires a pragmatics that deals centrally with newness and idiosyncrasy rather than a pragmatics in which conventionality is the focus."

Third, the focus on performance singles out those situations in which speakers are accountable not only for *what* they say but also, and sometimes predominantly, for *the way* in which they say it (Bauman 1975 [this volume], 1977; Hymes 1975, 1981). This perspective unites a concern with the aesthetic dimensions of speaking with their social and political implications.[46] The identification of a good leader with a good orator is common enough around the world to suggest that evaluation of the way in which a message is delivered enters into and informs political judgment. Furthermore, the speaker's commitment to an audience is only one side of a complex relationship that must be understood as crucial for the shaping of messages and meanings (Duranti 1993; Hill and Irvine 1993; Streeck 1980, 1994).

Fourth, the focus on performance recognizes the role of the audience in the construction of messages and their meanings (Duranti and Brenneis 1986; Graham 1995) and the complexity underlying the apparent simplicity of the distinction between speaker and hearer (Goffman 1981; Hymes 1972a). This is a point that has been at the center of a number of recent and not-so-recent enterprises, including hermeneutics (e.g. Gadamer 1976), Bakhtin's dialogism (see above), Goffman's strategic interactionism (Goffman 1959, 1963, 1971), and conversation analysis (Goodwin and Heritage 1990). The challenge for contemporary researchers is to provide sound empirical results that can test, inform, and refine abstract theoretical positions. Despite the recurrent emphasis on dialogue and intertextuality, relatively few researchers have actually looked at spontaneous verbal interaction in everyday life, where most of the "text" of our social life is constructed. For example, Marjorie

H. Goodwin's (1990b) study of teenage boys' and girls' talk in a Philadelphia neighborhood in the early 1970s remains unsurpassed for empirical rigor, depth of documentation, and ability to provide us with solid generalizations about narrative structure and argumentation in natural settings.

The role of the audience is but one of the aspects of context that linguistic anthropologists have been eager to capture (Goodwin and Duranti 1992). As demonstrated by the work of Gumperz, Labov, and others, at any given time, speakers may have at their disposal not just one or more codes (for example, English as opposed to English and Korean) but a vast range of registers, genres, routines, activities, expressions, accents, prosodic and paralinguistic features (e.g. volume, tempo, rhythm, voice quality). The choices available to speakers are a repertoire acquired through life experiences and subject to change through the life cycle, and partly due to one's social network (L. Milroy 1987; Milroy and Milroy 1992), including the effects of schooling, profession, and a person's special interests. The concern for the role of the audience and for the construction of messages across speakers, turns, and channels makes us question the view of speaking as merely the expression of an individual's intentions (Du Bois 1993; Duranti 1988, 1993; Moerman 1988; Rosen 1995). If we take a socio-historical approach, we must agree with Bakhtin (1981: 294) that "[l]anguage is not a neutral medium that passes freely and easily into the private property of the speaker's intentions; it is populated – overpopulated – with the intentions of others. Expropriating it, forcing it to submit to one's own intentions and accents, is a difficult and complicated process." Furthermore, our original intentions must be constantly updated by the effect we produce on our interlocutors, the knowledge we have of their background knowledge (C. Goodwin 1979, 1981; Heritage 1990/91), and their willingness or ability to go down the interpretive path we have sketched up thus far. For example, when an audience treats as humorous something that was meant to be serious, the speaker must confront a difficult choice: whether to reclaim his original interpretive key ("this is meant to be serious") or adapt ("this is meant to be funny"). A focus on performance makes us particularly aware of the relative control that we as speakers have on what Hymes (1972a) (borrowing the term from Birdwhistell) called the "key" of our messages. By moving into the realm of performance, we must face the fact that interpretation of what we say is always a joint production.

7 Language Acquisition and Language Socialization

Chomsky's hypothesis that the language faculty is innate and that the universal properties of languages can be studied and described in terms of grammatical rules (to be written using the formalism of generative grammar) inspired a new generation of psychologists to venture into the study of language acquisition. One way to test Chomsky's hypothesis about the innate quality of Universal Grammar (UG) was to go into great depth in the analysis of one language and find out what information is lacking in the linguistic input but necessary for a child to make generalizations and thus formulate rules for interpreting and producing speech. This was the strategy first followed by Chomsky himself, who, throughout the 1960s and 1970s, felt fully entitled to talk about language universals by working exclusively on English.[47] Another approach was to study the acquisition of as many languages as possible to see what common patterns (e.g. in the order of what is acquired, in the mistakes that children make, in their successes) they display. One of the first and most ambitious projects in this direction was the collaborative effort by psychologists, linguists, and anthropologists at the University of California at Berkeley in the mid-to late 1960s that produced *A Field Manual for Cross-Cultural Study of the Acquisition of Communicative Competence* (Slobin 1967).[48] Dan Slobin had studied at Harvard and MIT with a number of prominent linguists and psychologists, including Noam Chomsky, Roman Jakobson, Jerome Bruner, and Roger Brown. Soon after he was hired at Berkeley, he became part of a reading and discussion group that first included Susan Ervin-Tripp, John Gumperz, Erving Goffman, John Searle, and Dell Hymes, and by 1966 had also expanded to their graduate students. Prompted by Slobin's talk about language universals and his review of the existing literature on child language acquisition across languages, the group adopted Hymes' notion of communicative competence and mapped out an ambitious plan for the cross-cultural study of language acquisition. It was an attempt to merge experimental methods (from psychology) and ethnographic methods (from anthropology) and thus bring together Chomsky's cognitivism with the ethnographic approach promoted by Gumperz and Hymes.

Armed with the Field Manual, students took off for their field sites and came back after a year with lots of data and lots of questions. These early attempts at the cross-cultural study of language acquisition encountered a considerable number of problems, mostly due to the fact that it was difficult, if not impossible, to carry out the planned experiments in the field. Even the mere observation of adult–child interactions was at times highly problematic due to local expectations about how children should behave when a stranger enters the domestic space (Schieffelin 1979a: 75; Ochs 1988: 1–2). The discussion of these problems at Berkeley produced a new awareness of the issues involved in the extension of a paradigm developed to work with white middle-class families (where one caretaker, usually the mother, attends one or two children) to speech communities with a different social organization (sibling caregiving, extended family) and different beliefs about children and their relationship with adults. Taking into consideration these limitations, Slobin decided to reframe the enterprise in terms of cross-*linguistic* rather than cross-*cultural* comparison and organized a collaborative effort with colleagues in other countries to study language acquisition of English, Italian, Serbo-Croatian, and Turkish. Concentrating on linguistic dimensions that seemed to be fruitful for developmental psycholinguistic analysis, Slobin and his colleagues avoided the issue of the impact of culture on language acquisition by homogenizing the sample, that is, by working only with children of literate, professional, and urban parents (Slobin, personal communication).[49]

Two studies that more fully realized the goal of studying the acquisition of communicative competence in non-Western communities were done by Bambi B. Schieffelin and Elinor Ochs, who were aware of the work done in Berkeley but had received their training at different universities.[50] In both cases, the task was approached with a different and, in some respects, richer set of intellectual and human resources than those of the earlier fieldworkers who had tried to implement the model of the Field Manual.

Both Schieffelin and Ochs had previous fieldwork experience (in Papua New Guinea and in Madagascar respectively), had already collected child language data, and were not isolated from other researchers during their fieldwork. In 1975, Schieffelin returned to Mount Bosavi, Papua New Guinea, where she had been in 1967–8 with Edward L. Schieffelin (he was also with her in 1975–7 working on spirit mediums). In 1976, they were joined by ethnomusicologist Steven Feld who carried out a dissertation project on music and emotions (Feld 1982). As Schieffelin acknowledged in her dissertation (1979b) and in her 1990 book *The Give and Take of Everyday Life: Language Socialization of Kaluli Children*, the interaction with the other two anthropologists played an important role in her study of Kaluli culture. Equally important was the training she had previously received from Lois Bloom at Columbia University. By the time she went to Bosavi, Schieffelin knew how to carry out a longitudinal study and was familiar with the existing literature on child language acquisition.

Elinor Ochs had written a dissertation on oratory in Madagascar (Keenan 1974) and had been teaching in the linguistics department at the University of Southern California since 1974. Her earlier work based on the video recording of the interaction between her own twins encouraged her to venture into the study of child language.[51] In the summer of 1978, Ochs went to a (Western) Samoan village to carry out a longitudinal study of children's acquisition of Samoan. With her were two graduate students, Martha Platt and myself. Platt followed and documented the acquisition of three of the six children in the acquisition and socialization study (Platt 1982). I concentrated on adult grammar and language use across contexts (Duranti 1981, 1994).

Ochs and Schieffelin, who had met in 1974 and collaborated on a number of articles together, went to the field with very similar goals:

> The goal of my research in Papua New Guinea was the description of the development of communicative competence in a small-scale, nonliterate society.... The first endeavor. ..was to determine and describe the significant, recurring situations and interactions in the everyday life of Kaluli children. I needed to know the pattern of their daily activities, how and by whom they were organized (or not organized), who was responsible for feeding them, settling disputes between them, and where, when, and how these children regularly interacted with adults and other children. Initially these questions were partially answered through extensive observations of children over entire days and by interviewing adults for their views on what was going on and why. Both my actual observations and what the Kaluli themselves said about things helped formulate the first ethnographic accounts of what Kaluli children do all day and with whom they do it. (Schieffelin 1979a: 78)

> In making sense out of what people are saying and in speaking in a sensible fashion themselves, children relate linguistic forms to social situations. Part of their acquired knowledge of a linguistic form is the set of relations that obtain between that form and social situations, just as part of their acquired knowledge of a social situation includes the linguistic forms that define or characterize it. (Ochs 1988: 2)

As discussed earlier (see section 5), the acquisition of communicative competence was always meant to be a crucial area of study in the type of linguistic anthropology proposed by Gumperz and Hymes in the 1960s (see Sherzer and Darnell 1972).

However, the two longitudinal studies by Ochs and Schieffelin were the first to fully integrate an interest in the acquisition of grammar and the acquisition of other cultural patterns. The publication of their joint article "Language Acquisition and Socialization: Three Developmental Stories and Their Implications" (Ochs and Schieffelin 1984 [this volume]) – written in 1981, during a period spent at the Research School of Pacific Studies at the Australian National University[52] – set up the basic theoretical framework for what then became the field of language socialization. Starting from a definition of language socialization as (i) the process of getting socialized *through* language and (ii) the process of getting socialized *to* language, Ochs and Schieffelin re-examined prior work on language acquisition as embedded in culturally specific expectations about the role of children and adults in society. For example, they used their discovery that neither the Kaluli nor the Samoans have a register corresponding to what linguists call **baby talk** (Ferguson 1964) and psycholinguists call-**Motherese** (Newport 1976) not only to argue that (*pace* Ferguson 1978) baby talk is *not* universal,[53] but also that its presence or absence is tied to the presence or absence of other forms of accommodation to children and to local conceptualizations of children and their place in society.

Their work inspired others to look at the cultural implications of talk to children and by children in other societies. For example, Don Kulick adopted a language socialization perspective in his study of language shift in the village of Gapun in Papua New Guinea, where children are growing up speaking Tok Pisin instead of their parents' first language, Taiap, the local vernacular. Kulick argued that macro-sociological factors such as migration, assimilation, and the formation of a nation-state are not sufficient to explain the abandonment of the vernacular by these children and that we need to look at the daily practices of language use to understand "the conceptions that people have about language, children, the self" (Kulick 1992: 17; see also Ochs and Schieffelin 1995).

Ochs and Schieffelin assumed that socialization is a never-ending process that starts at birth (or even earlier) and continues throughout the life span. This perspective extends the notion of language socialization to language-mediated peer-interaction, apprenticeship and everyday cognition, literacy activities, language contact, and cross-cultural encounters.[54] Elizabeth Mertz's study of the ways in which Law School students are taught how to read a text and argue its potential interpretations is a good example of how institutions and professional organizations socialize adults into **entextualization** – the process of transforming experience into text – and **recontextualization** – the process of making texts relevant to the ongoing situation[55] (Mertz 1996).

8 The Power of Language

There are two main strategies for analyzing the relationship between language and culture. One is to start from linguistic forms (e.g. words or parts of words, intonational contours, syntactic constructions, conversational routines) and then try to discover what those forms accomplish in social interaction or, more generally, in the construction of everyday life. This strategy has often been used to discuss the expression of respect or politeness (Agha 1994; Brown and Levinson 1978, 1987).

The other strategy is to start from a particular cultural construct (e.g. gender, power, race, ethnicity, disability, conflict, emotions) or social process (e.g. socialization, marginalization, conflict, healing, advertising, play, verbal performance) and then try to find out how specific linguistic forms participate in (or constitute) such constructs or processes.

Much of the work on linguistic relativity (see section 4) can be thought of as part of the first method. Linguistic forms, either because of their arbitrary nature (for Sapir) or because of their implicit worldview (for Whorf), are seen as constraints on the ways in which individual speakers as members of speech communities perceive reality or are able to represent it. Silverstein's work on metalinguistic and metapragmatic awareness (see section 4.1) can be seen as an extension of this tradition in that it provides a framework for thinking about the power of specific linguistic forms to reveal or to hide (from speakers' consciousness) their indexical value, that is, their dependence or ability to impact upon reality.

Maurice Bloch's (1975a) "Introduction" to *Political Language and Oratory in Traditional Society* represents another trend within this tradition. Bloch argued that the very form of traditional political oratory, especially the routinized formulae used to express respect toward tradition and politeness toward leaders, provides a frame-work for the unconscious acceptance of authority and the status quo. For Bloch, formalized speech – as opposed to conversation – restricts the range of possible questions and possible answers and therefore limits freedom of expression and any real challenge of authority. Although the category of formalization he used was later criticized (Irvine 1979 [this volume]; Brennels and Myers 1984), Bloch's ideas made it possible to rethink the power of language on human action and strengthen the ties between political anthropology and linguistic anthropology.[56]

The argument of the power of language over mind and society was also present in the discussion of the impact of the invention of literacy. Jack Goody and Ian Watt (1962) argued that alphabetic writing had a crucial role in the development of Western civilization. This role was accomplished by transforming oral messages into a permanent record and thus introducing the practice of "history" (as opposed to "myths" or "legends") and by helping the "change from mythical to logico-empirical modes of thought" (Goody and Watt [1962] 1968: 43). A number of empirical studies were designed to test Goody and Watt's hypotheses about the impact of alphabetic writing on cognitive abilities and social change (Kingten, Kroll, and Rose 1988; Olson and Torrance 1991; Street and Besnier 1994). Eventually, most linguistic anthropologists have come to share Scribner and Cole's (1981) view that there are different types of literacy and that many of the earlier generalizations were conflating differences, including the difference between literacy as an isolated, autonomous activity and literacy as embedded in other activities and in institutions, for example, schools or state bureaucracies.[57] Goody's "autonomous model" of literacy was also criticized by Brian Street (1984) who proposed an "ideological model" of literacy, that is, a perspective that links writing practices to power structures in a society (e.g. establishment of authority, access to institutional resources, wealth). He also stressed the importance for ethnographic studies of literacy, based on "detailed, indepth accounts of actual practice in different cultural settings" (Street 1993: 1).

Within linguistic anthropology, the interest in literacy revived an earlier interest in schooling and classroom interaction (Cazden, John, and Hymes 1972) and Shirley Brice Heath's (1983) groundbreaking study of home literacy activities in three communities in the United States had a tremendous influence on future research. On the basis of extensive observation and documentation of the various ways in which children from different communities were engaged with written texts, Heath argued that earlier experiences within the family and the community have an impact on a child's ability to succeed in a school system whose model of literacy events is based on the same principles that guide reading and writing in white middle- (and upper-middle) class families. The study of literacy merged with language socialization and has since been an important part of linguistic anthropology, with an ever-expanding set of issues and dimensions, including the relation between literacy and the formation of class, gender, racial, and ethnic identities (Collins 1995).

The technological revolution of the 1980s and 1990s extended the notion of literacy so that now we easily talk about "video literacy" or "computer literacy." Within linguistic anthropology, a growing number of researchers have been using these new technologies for documenting and analyzing social interaction (Duranti 1997b: chapter 5). It is now common practice to use the latest audio-visual technology to store, retrieve, and code verbal behavior. Just as the invention of the portable audio tape recorder revolutionized the study of talk – it is difficult to imagine the birth of sociolinguistics without the portable tape recorder – the more recent digital innovations have opened up the possibility of a different type of linguistic anthropology. Analysts can now study in great detail the simultaneous operations that produce and make possible any stretch of talk.[58] Through new kinds of **inscription** (Ricoeur 1981: 198) these tools allow us to see (as opposed to only hear) talk as collaboratively produced by participants with the help of a number of semiotic resources, including the human body, the built environment, and a variety of material artifacts and tools. These technological innovations also came with a rethinking of the notion of "context," which is no longer understood as an independent variable (e.g. a speaker's social status) or a given backdrop against which to analyze linguistic forms, but as the product of specific ways of behaving. Participants in an interaction are constantly and mostly implicitly preoccupied with defining the context against which their actions should be interpreted. The analyst's job is to reconstruct such a process of contextualization (Goodwin and Duranti 1992: 3–4) while being conscious of the fact that analysis itself is a form of contextualization. The power to frame events and provide a preferred interpretation is both within the interaction (as negotiated by the participants) and outside of it, as researchers (and other "experts") frame the event in order to produce an analysis of it.

In this, the work of Michel Foucault on the institutionalization of madness and other forms of social control over deviance and transgression was very important in alerting social scientists to the power of observation, documentation, and classification, as well as to their participation in social control and surveillance (e.g. Foucault 1979, 1980, 1984). Albeit coming from a different tradition (the study of face-to-face interaction), Charles Goodwin's notion of **professional vision** is a recent contribution to a related issue: the power that certain interpretive procedures have to convince an audience. Goodwin analyzes three practices used by experts: "(1) *coding*, which transforms phenomena observed in a specific setting into the objects of knowledge that animate the discourse of a profession; (2) *highlighting*, which makes specific phenomena in a complex perceptual field salient by marking them in some fashion; and (3) *producing and articulating material representations*" (C. Goodwin 1994: 607, emphasis in the original). One of the events analyzed by Goodwin was the televised proceedings of one of the most widely watched criminal trials of the twentieth century, in which four police officers from the Los Angeles Police Department were accused of using excessive force against an African American motorist, Mr Rodney King. Goodwin argues that the prosecutors lost the case[59] because they treated the video of the beating (which had originally caused public outrage when broadcast on television) as a *natural* object, whose content would be self-explanatory. The defense, instead, treated the video tape as a document in need of interpretation and employed experts who used the three practices mentioned above to socialize the jury to see the actions recorded as justifiable.

One of the ways in which a community dominates another, or some members of a community dominate other members, is by determining the acceptable ways of speaking. For this reason linguists have long been interested in the process that defines a variety as the Standard and in its use by the dominant class to maintain control (Bloomfield 1935; Labov 1970; Baugh 1999; Rickford 1999). Standardization is common in the formation of a nation-state and is a weapon by the central government against linguistic minorities. A classic study of this process is Bruce Mannheim's (1991) reconstruction of the rise of Quechua to the status of the standard language of the Inka Empire (in Southern Peru) after the Spanish invasion, in the sixteenth century. Minority languages, however, are not always dominated by the majority language as shown by Kathryn Woolard's (1989) research in Barcelona, where a national minority language (Catalan), spoken by the ethnic group that has economic control in the region, is the "high prestige" language and the nation's Standard (Castilian) is the "low prestige" language.

In their efforts to connect the details of language use in everyday life with the political and economic institutions and processes that allow for those details to be interpreted and be either effective or futile, linguistic anthropologists have relied on a number of theorists and concepts from other fields. I will mention two theorists here: Antonio Gramsci and Pierre Bourdieu. For Gramsci, as he wrote in his "Prison Notebooks" (*Quaderni del carcere*), it is not sufficient for a dominant class to rule through state institutions such as the legal system, the police, and the military. It must also succeed at imposing its own intellectual and moral standards, possibly and more effectively through persuasion. Gramsci's notion of **hegemony** was meant to capture the ability that a ruling class has to build consensus through the work of all kinds of intellectuals (e.g. managers in industrial societies, priests in feudal societies) who give the rest of the population a political, intellectual, and moral direction (Gramsci 1971, 1975; Williams 1977). These ideas have been adopted – sometimes critically, other times not – by linguistic anthropologists and other students of language use to illuminate the processes through which a group or class manages to impose its own view of what constitutes the prestige dialect (Standard English vs. African-American English), the prestige language (e.g. English vs. Spanish, Spanish vs. Mexicano), or even the prestige accent (Philips 1998: 215–16; Woolard 1985). By being interested in language use and more generally communication, of course, linguistic anthropologists cannot but be interested in the inequality that characterizes speakers' ability to control different linguistic varieties, whether they are recognized "languages" or registers (e.g. the way in which doctors or lawyers talk) (Hymes 1996). The focus on inequality, however, has been only recently conceptualized through a direct concern with the relationship between language and political economy (Gal 1989). In this endeavor, the work of French sociologist Pierre Bourdieu has been influential, especially his notions of **habitus** and **cultural capital**. Bourdieu's notion of habitus is related to Gramsci's notion of hegemony in that it is an unconscious set of dispositions that are connected to and recursively activated by participation in specific activities or practices. But the concept of habitus also has the meaning of "regulated improvisations" (only apparently an oxymoron) and is more easily related to socialization and the study of language as a practice that draws from and maintains traces of a variety of social sources and "voices" (Bakhtin 1981). Bourdieu's notion of cultural capital – which includes not only aesthetic taste but also linguistic skills – allows us to think of linguistic varieties as having a "value" within a "market" (Bourdieu 1982, 1985; Gal 1989; Woolard 1985). William Hanks' study of sixteenth-century texts produced by native Maya officials takes advantage of these insights in making sense of how both old and new conventions were drawn upon in the production of "boundary genres," that is, ways of organizing texts and expressing ideas that "derived from a fusion of Spanish and Maya frameworks" (Hanks 1987: 677).

It is this interest in the heterogeneity of texts and their political implications that characterizes some of the most recent contributions in linguistic anthropology. Jane Hill's (1998 [this volume]) study of Mock Spanish by government officials and the media is an example of this trend, which combines a long-standing interest in language contact (e.g. borrowings, code-switching) and linguistic creativity with a more recent interest in the use of language in the construction, maintenance, and challenging of racial stereotypes and ethnic division within a society (see also Baugh 1999; Mendoza-Denton 1999; Rampton 1995a, 1995b; Spears 1999; Urciuoli 1991; Wodak and Reisigl 1999; Zentella 1997).

After a pre-feminist era in which scholars were mostly interested in uncovering the logic of the encoding of sex differences in languages (e.g. Sapir 1929), the first generation of feminist linguists – as pointed out by Bucholtz (1999) – concentrated on the oppressive implications of ordinary speech (e.g. R. Lakoff 1973) and on the differences between men's speech and women's speech (e.g. West and Zimmerman 1983), whereas the second generation became preoccupied with trying to explain why there were communication problems between men and women. Borrowing from Gumperz's concept of interethnic miscommunication, some researchers suggested that miscommunication between men and women was due to the fact that the two groups belong to different cultures (Maltz and Borker 1982; Tannen 1990). A more recent trend of studies has adopted the view that gender is constructed and interacts with other identities (Anzaldúa 1987, 1990; Bucholtz, Liang, and Sutton 1999; Eckert and McConnell-Ginet 1992a, 1992b; Hall and Bucholtz 1995; Mendoza-Denton 1996). The role of language in helping establish gender identity is part of a broader range of processes through which membership in particular groups is activated, imposed, and sometimes contested through the use of linguistic forms that do not simply index "woman" vs. "man" or "feminine" vs. "masculine," but activate stances or perform speech acts that are associated with a particular gender (Ochs 1992, 1996). This constructivist and interactional view of gender (and more generally identity) has been more open to the integration of verbal communication with other semiotic practices within the lived space of human interaction (M. H. Goodwin 1999; Goodwin and Goodwin 2000 [this volume]; Sidnell 1997).

9 Conclusions

What needs to be clearly seen by anthropologists, who to a large extent may have gotten the idea that linguistics is merely a highly specialized and tediously technical pigeonhole in a far corner of the anthropological workshop, is that linguistics is essentially the quest of MEANING.

Whorf 1956a:73

In order to have a better sense of the future of a discipline, we need to have a better sense of its past. When we look back at our history, we learn a number of important lessons, including the following.

1 The basic assumption of linguistic anthropology is that to understand the meaning of linguistic messages one must study them within the contexts in which they are produced and interpreted. This commitment to contextualized language is supported by a number of units of analysis that go beyond the word, the sentence, and the notion of language as an ideal system to include speech communities, speech events, activities, and acts as well as the notions of register and variety.

2 The different names used for referring to the study of language in/and/as culture (e.g. linguistic anthropology, anthropological linguistics, sociolinguistics) can be made sense of by a historical overview of the methods, goals, and academic affiliation of the researchers involved (section 2). The term "anthropological linguistics" reveals a strong identification with the discipline of linguistics as opposed to anthropology and a "service" mentality, that is, a view of linguistics as a tool for training social or cultural anthropologists to do fieldwork. The term "linguistic anthropology" – used as early as 1880 but more widely adopted only in the 1960s – places the enterprise squarely within the field of anthropology and starts from an understanding of speaking as an activity that has its own cultural organization, to be studied by means of a combination of linguistic (read "structuralist") analysis and ethnographic methods. As discussed in section 2.2, in the 1960s and 1970s the term "sociolinguistics" served as a cover term for a variety of approaches to the study of language in context which included quantitative studies of variation within and across communities and ethnographic studies of verbal genres and speech events (e.g. the ethnography of communication). However, contemporary sociolinguistics and linguistic anthropology seem directed toward separate paths (with the possible exception of the study of gender, where there is more communication across methodological and theoretical boundaries). Despite an earlier convergence of interests (language variation, the role of context), most contemporary linguistic anthropologists

subscribe to a constructivist view of social categories (e.g. gender, status) and thus reject the sharp separation between dependent and independent variables found in sociolinguistics, especially in its quantitatively oriented research. The reliance on interviews as the primary source for data collection is still a defining feature of sociolinguistic surveys whereas linguistic anthropologists tend to record spontaneous verbal interaction across a range of situations.

3 What we presently call linguistic anthropology started out in the 1880s as an attempt to document and describe aboriginal North American languages and as such it coincided for about seventy years with descriptive, historical, and (to a lesser extent) theoretical linguistics (section 3). That tradition continues through those linguists who carry out fieldwork in geographical areas (e.g. Australia, Papua New Guinea, the Amazon) where there are still languages that have not been properly described (e.g. Foley 1986; Dixon and Aikhenvald 1999) or who try to document and help revive languages that are considered endangered (Dorian 1993, 1994; Grenoble and Whaley 1998; Hale et al. 1992). Theoretically, there is also continuity between Boas' original plan (and his diffusionism) and some of the more recent work on linguistic diversity and the relationship between the spread of languages and the spread of populations (e.g. Nichols 1992, 1995a, 1995b; Nichols and Peterson 1996).

4 The earlier encounters with American Indian languages sparked an interest in what a language could reveal about a people's view of the world, while an increased understanding of the complexities of linguistic forms and their organization in systems (e.g. grammars) suggested the possibility of constraints on speakers' ability to see the world "with the naked eye." Since to be a full participant in a community, a person needs to be a speaker of the language(s) spoken in that community, in some way our interaction with the animate and inanimate world around us is always mediated through language(s). Sapir's and Whorf's ideas on these issues inspired a series of empirical and theoretical studies around the issue of "linguistic relativity" (section 4). Some of the themes found in Sapir's and Whorf's work have been recently reframed within a number of new enterprises, including the work on metapragmatics and language ideology (section 4.1).

5 The study of language as a cultural resource has motivated the extension of Chomsky's cognitive notion of "competence" to include socio-cultural knowledge, i.e. Hymes' notion of communicative competence. The interest in language contact and language variation produced an awareness of the role played by the community in providing guidance and meaning for language use and language choice. In the future, the notion of community is likely to expand to include aggregates that are not defined by face-to-face communication and take into consideration the impact of old (print) and new media (radio, television, computers) on language use and linguistic standards.

6 Since the 1960s there has been a shift from an interest in what language encodes (reference, denotation) to what language does (performance) (see section 6). This shift has fostered an interest in the social and cultural organization of linguistic activities (e.g. speech acts, speech events) and the subtle ways in which linguistic forms are existentially connected with the situations in which they are used and the people who use them (indexicality). Verbal performance has been shown to

have a cultural organization of its own, which needs to be studied by researchers who are able to combine the ethnographic methods practiced by socio-cultural anthropologists with the structuralist methods practiced by linguists (based on the documentation of actual language use).

7 The developmental dimension of the study of competence and communities has been developed in the field of language socialization (see section 7), which looks at the impact of cultural expectations and social interaction on the acquisition of language and at the role of language in creating competent and productive members of society.

8 As the most complex symbolic system developed by the species *Homo sapiens*, language has the power to convince, seduce, obscure, highlight, frame, and reframe social reality. Contemporary linguistic anthropology uses a variety of analytical tools and concepts to examine the power of language in a wide range of social situations. Social categories that used to be studied separately, e.g. race, class, and gender, are now analyzed as interdependent. While paying attention to the local and global context of communication, it is the moment-by-moment construction of "texts" – broadly defined – that is emphasized in the effort to uncover the mechanisms and resources that make the meaning of human action, words included, possible, interpretable, and consequential.

NOTES

1 Special thanks to the people who helped me become a better historian of my discipline by providing invaluable recollections, references, clarifications, and corrections: Regna Darnell, John Gumperz, Dell Hymes, Paul Kroskrity, Dan Slobin, William Foley, Mary Bucholtz, Elinor Ochs, Bambi B. Schieffelin, and Laura Nader. I would also like to thank Vincent Barletta and Sarah Meacham for detailed comments on the first draft of this chapter and Tracy Rone for her suggestions and editorial advice. My second draft benefited from very detailed comments by Dell Hymes, who was particularly generous with factual and theoretical corrections to my representation of the history of the field. I remain, of course, solely responsible for any remaining errors, misrepresentations, or omissions.

2 A good example of apparent free variation among the different terms is Stephen Murray's *American Sociolinguistics: Theory Groups* (1998), which alternates from one term to the other usually without warning. For example, although the title of the book promises a study of "sociolinguistics," its first sentence reads: "This study of postwar anthropological linguistics in North America . . ." (p. 1). Particularly puzzling is the choice of the term "ethnolinguistics" for describing the work by John Gumperz and his students at the University of California at Berkeley in the 1980s (Murray: chapter 9), given Gumperz's preference for either "the ethnography of communication" (in his collaboration with Hymes) or "sociolinguistics" (see n. 15).

3 Except for a brief period in the 1940s and 1950s (e.g. Garvin and Riesenberg 1952; Voegelin and Harris 1945), the terms "ethnolinguistic" and "ethnolinguistics" have been more popular in European circles than in the USA (see Duranti 1997b: 2; Hymes 1971a: 48). A notable exception in recent years is Paul Kroskrity's monograph on the Arizona Tewa speech community where the term "ethnolinguistics" is used in the more restricted

sense of "native metalinguistics" (Kroskrity 1993: 34). This perspective was later developed in the study of language ideologies (see Woolard and Schieffelin 1994; Schieffelin, Woolard, and Kroskrity 1998; Kroskrity 2000a, 2000b).

4 "Simply stated, in this book linguistic anthropology will be presented as *the study of language as a cultural resource and speaking as a cultural practice*. As an inherently interdisciplinary field, it relies on and expands existing methods in other disciplines, linguistics and anthropology in particular, with the general goal of providing an understanding of the multifarious aspects of language as a set of cultural practices, that is, as a system of communication that allows for interpsychological (between individuals) and intrapsychological (in the same individual) representations of the social order and helps people use such representations for constitutive social acts" (Duranti 1997b: 2–3).

5 My interpretation of the situation in Australia was largely confirmed by Foley during a recent exchange over electronic mail. On December 21, 1999, he wrote: "I think you're right about my being influenced by the Australian situation in which in most universities there are close connections between linguistics and anthropology. Due to the fieldwork emphasis, most departments of linguistics here regard some anthro expertise as essential. Fieldwork is greatly devalued in linguistics in the US, that's true, but to the extent that it is important in some departments, e.g. Berkeley [where Foley received his Ph.D. in linguistics], there is a niche for anthropological linguistics, albeit often unrealized. I suppose my own ideological position is that yes, anthropological linguistics is an integral part of linguistics, however how much hegemonic forces at work in the discipline have worked to and largely have sidelined it. That is the current situation, I agree, but things change, hegemonies don't last forever, and I would deplore any redefinition of linguistics which would actually help to institutionalize the current situation."

6 A thorough reconstruction of the history of the relationship between linguistics and anthropology in the first half of the twentieth century is well beyond the scope of this chapter. Valuable information regarding Edward Sapir's relationship with anthropology and linguistics and the impact that this relationship had on his students is provided by Regna Darnell's historical reconstructions (1990, 1998b). Regarding Sapir's association with the Yale linguistics department while chairing the anthropology department, Darnell (1998b: 362) wrote: "Sapir encouraged his linguistic students to take their degrees in linguistics rather than anthropology. This was in line with the increasing autonomy of linguistics from anthropology signaled by the establishment of the Linguistic Society of America and its journal *Language* after 1925. At Chicago, Sapir's failure to establish flexible working relations with Carl Buck in classical philology effectively restricted anthropological linguists to working in anthropology."

Moreover, the linguistics that Sapir wanted his students to learn was not anthropological in the sense proselytized by Boas. The "first Yale school" in linguistics developed around Sapir and the advanced graduate students he brought with him from Chicago, with Morris Swadesh, Stanley Newman, and Mary Haas as the core, later joined by Charles Hockett, George Trager, Benjamin Whorf, Charles Voegelin, Zellig Harris, George Herzog, and others..."

Darnell's reconstruction is supported by David Sapir (1985), who suggested that his father had a much stronger identification with linguistics than with anthropology: "Sapir considered himself a linguist. He thought of himself as only accidentally an anthropologist" (D. Sapir 1985: 291).

7 For example, Harry Hoijer (1961: 10) defined anthropological linguistics as "an area of research which is devoted in the main to studies, synchronic and diachronic, of the languages of the people who have no writing."

8 I owe the articulation of this second goal to Dell Hymes's comments on an earlier draft of this chapter.

9 Ferguson and Gumperz originally approached their research as part of linguistics, as shown by the following quote: "No great effort is made to carry the interpretation far afield from linguistics, but each of the studies contains suggestive material for the approaches of other disciplines in the study of contemporary South Asia" (Ferguson and Gumperz 1960: 1).

10 See Murray (1998: 96–8, 101–3, and passim) for a useful historical reconstruction of this period, but beware of his occasionally inaccurate terminology. For example, Murray (1998: 98) refers to Ferguson and Gumperz (1960) as "the first exemplar of what would be dubbed 'the ethnography of speech.'" But "the ethnography of speech" is not the name of a school or paradigm and Gumperz has never used it (John Gumperz, personal communication). The terms that are found in the literature are "the ethnography of speaking" (Hymes 1971b; Bauman and Sherzer 1975) and "the ethnography of communication" (Gumperz and Hymes 1964).

11 "Linguistics without ethnography would fare as badly as ethnography would without the light thrown on it by language" (Malinowski 1920: 78). For Boas's position, see section 3.

12 Greenberg's vision of linguistics was also important to anthropological linguists because it was comparative-typological and provided an alternative to the Chomskian paradigm, as made evident in the following statement by Mary Haas (1978a: 121–2): "Concentration on one's own language somehow seems to lead to the conclusion that there is a universal grammar that can be deduced from one's own language. Now this is certainly not a new idea but the very one that Boas and his followers had been at such pains to dispel. Fortunately it has not become for us necessary to fall back into the beliefs of the pre-Boasian period. Instead in recent years there has been another kind of linguistic activity, standing somewhat aside from both the Bloomfieldian and the Chomskian paradigms, which has come to the rescue in this impasse. The activity referred to has been the work of Joseph H. Greenberg and his staff at Stanford University on language typology and language universals. Clearly such a project cannot be pursued by limiting it to the perusal of grammars of languages written by authors who are native speakers thereof. Indeed for the purposes of a universal project, the more languages for which information can be obtained the better. Happily, then, there is now a renewed interest in all kinds of languages spoken near and far and it is by necessity accepted that information on most of them may have to be supplied through field work done by nonnative speakers. Consequently, there has been a renewal of interest in field work."

13 This is particularly true of Foley's (1997) Part V "The Ethnography of Speaking" (chapters 13–18). The one topic treated by Foley that does not include research by linguistic anthropologists is chapter 2, "The Evolution of Language." This topic has not been a subject of interest within linguistic anthropology in recent years. Agha (1997) is a rare exception.

14 "The most detailed contributions [on the relation between language and society] have come from the anthropologists working in Southeast Asia. However, for the study of the complex communities of the United States and Western Europe, it appears that

quantitative methods are required" (Labov 1966b: 23). The implicit reference here is to Ferguson and Gumperz (1960) and Gumperz (1958), both of which are mentioned by Labov earlier (Labov 1966b: 21).

15 "Interactional sociolinguistics" is the title of Gumperz's Cambridge University Press series, which includes contributions by Gumperz himself (Gumperz 1982a), Jenny Cook-Gumperz (1986), some of his former students (Brown and Levinson 1987; Gumperz 1982b; Tannen 1989), discourse analysts (Schiffrin 1987), and conversation analysts (Drew and Heritage 1992).

16 See Murray (1998: 100–3).

17 This view is confirmed in an earlier publication, where Hymes defines the ethnography of speaking as "a particular approach" within sociolinguistics, understood as "an area of research that links linguistics with anthropology and sociology" (Hymes 1971b: 47).

18 For example, Wardhaugh (1986), out of 16 chapters, dedicates one (chapter 16) to "Language and Culture" and another to "Ethnography and Ethnomethodology." Ralph Fasold, in the second volume of his *Introduction to Sociolinguistics*, includes one chapter on "The Ethnography of Communication" (1990: chapter 2).

19 The work on conversation was pioneered by sociologists Harvey Sacks, Emanuel A. Schegloff and Gail Jefferson in the 1960s and has since expanded its influence on a number of disciplines, among them pragmatics (e.g. Levinson 1983), child language studies (e.g. McTear 1985; Ochs and Schieffelin 1983), and grammatical analysis (e.g. Ford 1993; Ochs, Schegloff, and Thompson 1996). For a discussion of conversation analysis from the point of view of linguistic anthropology, see Duranti (1997b: chapter 8).

20 The literature on this subject is vast. It includes methodologically oriented studies such as Briggs (1986) and a voluminous body of empirical research on conversation that shows how speakers are constantly monitoring and adapting their speech according to the type of recipients they are interacting with (e.g. Duranti and Brenneis 1986; C. Goodwin 1981; Schegloff 1972, 1986), detailed discussion of how stories in conversation are typically co-authored (e.g. Capps and Ochs 1995; Goodwin 1986; Mandelbaum 1987a, 1987b, 1989; Ochs 1997; Ochs and Capps 1996), and the role of interaction in the shaping of grammar itself (Ochs, Schegloff, and Thompson 1996; Silverstein 1997).

21 As often in history, the efforts of a few individuals who manage to win a minimal institutional support can make a difference. A good example is the interdisciplinary enterprise known as the Berkeley Women and Language Group, which started in 1985 with a small conference organized by Sue Bremner, Noelle Caskey, Elisabeth Kuhn, and Birch Moonwomon. In 1992, a second conference was held with about 80 papers and over 300 participants (Hall, Bucholtz, and Moonwomon 1992). The group held three other large conferences (every other year) with a rotating group of facilitators, until the fall of 1999 when it was disbanded. Its legacy is expected to be continued at Stanford university as the International Gender and Language Association (IGALA).

22 The four fields are archaeology, biological anthropology (formerly "physical"), linguistic anthropology (formerly "linguistics" or "philology"), and sociocultural anthropology (formerly "ethnology"). The Boasian conceptualization of anthropology as a four field discipline is often contested today given the recent multiplication of subdisciplines and the internal debate regarding the goals of anthropological research and the limit of the Boasian, holistic approach.

23 Hillary henson convincingly argued that, despite the influence of Bronislaw Malinowski's work on British anthropology, "[i]n the period from about 1920 until 1960, British social anthropologists paid no serious attention to language" (Henson 1974: 119). For a review of anthropology departments in Canada, with some data on linguistic anthropology in that country, see Darnell (1998c).

24 A notable exception is a series of articles by William Edwin Safford on Chamorro, one of the two major languages spoken in the Philippines.

25 The *American Anthropologist* was started in 1888 as the organ of the Anthropological Society of Washington, which relinquished it in 1899 when the founders of the American Anthropological Association (AAA) asked to use the same name for the AAA journal. Since the AAA did not officially start until 1902, the journal predates the Association (the first meeting was held in 1901).

26 "Bureau members did *collect* considerable bodies of linguistic material, but prior to Boas' time they *published* relatively little in the way of extended grammatical analysis. And despite all this material, despite decades of speculation on the "incorporating" or "polysynthetic" character of American Indian languages, the amount of detailed and systematic study of specific Indian languages which would stand professional scrutiny – at least as far as Franz Boas and Edward Sapir were concerned – was virtually nil" (Stocking 1974: 458–9) (emphasis in the original). Although Stocking gives Boas credit for his important role in the planning and editing of the *Handbook*, he rejects Voegelin's (1952) claim that Boas should be considered the author or co-author of most of the grammatical sketches contained in it.

27 Boas was a strong believer in the power of acculturation and some of the articles collected in Boas (1940) contain statements that reveal his aversion to hasty genetic classification for American Indian languages. For example, in an article originally published in 1920, he wrote: "In other words, the whole theory of an 'Ursprache' for every group of modern languages must be held in abeyance until we can prove that these languages go back to a single stock and that they have not originated, to a large extent, by the process of acculturation" (1940: 217).

28 "The great advantage that linguistics offer in this respect is the fact that, on the whole, the categories which are formed always remain unconscious, and that for this reason the processes which lead to their formation can be followed without the misleading and disturbing factors of secondary explanations, which are so common in ethnology, so much so that they generally obscure the real history of the development of ideas entirely" (Boas 1911: 70–1).

29 This idea is the linguistic equivalent of the position held in logic by Gottlob Frege, Ludwig Wittgenstein, and others that meaning is not to be found in words but in propositions (the distinction made by English-speaking philosophers between "sentence" and "proposition" is vacuous in German, where the term *Satz* has been used to mean "proposition" or "sentence").

30 This practice continued for several decades, in concomitance with the reference to "primitive society" and "primitive culture." For example, the 1931–2 catalog for the graduate program in anthropology at Yale, which is very likely to have been written by Sapir (Darnell 1998b: 363), mentions "primitive linguistics" (which could not possibly mean "a primitive form of linguistics" but "a linguistic study of primitive languages"). The belief that anthropological linguists study "primitive communities" is unfortunately

still found in some circles, as shown by the following definition of anthropological linguistics in David Crystal's *Dictionary of Linguistics*: "A branch of LINGUISTICS which studies language variation and use in relation to human cultural patterns and beliefs, as investigated using the theories and methods of anthropology. For example, it studies the way in which linguistic features may identify a member of *a (usually primitive) community* with a social, religious, occupational or kinship group. . . ." (Crystal 1997: 20) (emphasis mine).

31 See also Hill (1964) and the Editor's "General comments and references" after Hill's article (Hymes 1964d: 89).

32 It is not clear whether Sapir actually read von Humboldt, although there were several ways for him to be exposed to von Humboldt's ideas, for example, through Boas (see Drechsel 1988).

33 For example, Hill and Mannheim (1992: 383) argue that the term "hypothesis" is not appropriate in this case: "We maintain that 'linguistic relativity' as proposed by Boas, Sapir, and Whorf is not a hypothesis in the traditional sense, but an axiom, a part of the initial epistemology and methodology of the linguistic anthropologist. Boas, Sapir, and Whorf were not relativists in the extreme sense often suggested by modern critics."

34 Dell Hymes, personal communication.

35 The second part of the twentieth century saw the establishment of a strong functional tradition in linguistics that tries to explain grammatical forms in terms of communicative needs or discourse functions (e.g. Hopper and Thompson 1980; Givón 1989; Hopper and Traugott 1993). Somewhat paradoxically, the argument in favor of the non-functional, autonomous nature of linguistic forms has been pursued not by linguistic anthropologists but by formal grammarians who have shown little or no interest in the relationship between language and culture.

36 This connection is not acknowledged by Chomsky, who prefers to trace ancestry within the French rationalist tradition (Chomsky 1966) rather than admitting any link to Whorf, whose basic approach he harshly criticized in the context of an unflattering introduction to Adam Schaff's (1973) *Language and Cognition*: "My impression is that Schaff vastly over-estimates the quality of the material that ethnolinguistics can provide. It sheds no discredit on the anthropological linguist, who is faced with problems of vast complexity and scope, to point out that the evidence that he can provide is of an altogether superficial sort" (Chomsky 1973: ix).

37 For a revision of the original theory of "basic color terms," see Kay and Maffi (2000). For a criticism of the model, see Lucy and Shweder (1979) and Levinson (2000).

38 This is the same phenomenon illustrated by Boas's (1911: 25) example of the distinct lexical items through which English expresses the shapes of WATER: *lake, river, brook, rain, dew, wave, foam.*

39 A similar line of work on linguistic relativity has been pursued since the early 1990s by researchers at the Max Planck institute for Psycholinguistics under the direction of Stephen Levinson, who launched a comparative study of the ways in which space is conceptualized across typologically different languages (Levinson 1992). A programmatic paper by Gumperz and Levinson (1991) was followed by a conference where a number of linguists, anthropologists, and psychologists reopened the discussion of linguistic relativity that had been almost forgotten (Gumperz and Levinson 1996).

40 For an interesting use of this classification, see Merlan and Rumsay (1991: 97–8).

41 For an appraisal of Chomsky's ability to redirect American linguistics, see Murray (1993: chapter 9) and Newmeyer (1980, 1986).

42 "There seems to be little reason to question the traditional view that investigation of performance will proceed only so far as understanding of underlying competence permits" (Chomsky's 1965: 10). Despite the considerable amount of research on language use within quantitative sociolinguistics, linguistic anthropology, discourse analysis, and conversation analysis, Chomsky's position has not changed on this issue over the years, as shown by the following statement: "it would be unreasonable to pose the problem of how Jones [a typical speaker of English] decides what he does, or how he interprets what he hears in particular circumstances. But highly idealized aspects of the problem are amenable to study" (Chomsky 1995: 18).

43 "We will define [linguistic community] as a social group which may be either monolingual or multilingual, held together by frequency of social interaction patterns and set off from the surrounding areas by weaknesses in the lines of communication. Linguistic communities may consist of small groups bound together by face-to-face contact or may cover large regions, depending on the level of abstraction we wish to achieve" (Gumperz 1968b: 463). For a recent critique of the notion of "speech community," see Silverstein (1996a).

44 On the term "variety," see Hudson (1980); on dialect and contact among dialects, see Trudgill (1986); on register, see the essays in Biber and Finegan (1994); on speech communities, see Romaine (1982).

45 See Goodwin and Goodwin (1987), G. Lakoff (1987), Lakoff and Johnson (1980), Ochs and Schieffelin (1983), Sapir and Crocker (1977), Silverstein (1984, 1997), Wilce (1998).

46 See Briggs and Bauman (1992), Beeman (1993), Caton (1990), Du Bois (1986), Keane (1997), Keating (1998), Keil and Feld (1994), Kuipers (1990), Palmer and Jankowiak (1996), Sherzer (1983, 1990), Yankah (1995).

47 "A valid observation that has frequently been made (and often, irrationally denied) is that a great deal can be learned about U[niversal]G[rammar] from the study of a single language, if such study achieves sufficient depth to put forth rules or principles that have explanatory force but are underdetermined by evidence available to the language learner. Then it is reasonable to attribute to UG those aspects of these rules or principles that are uniformly attained but underdetermined by evidence" (Chomsky 1982: 6).

48 The following recounting of the Berkeley project owes a great deal to personal correspondence with Dan Slobin, who generously provided me with a historical account of his involvement in the design of a cross-cultural/cross-linguistic study of language acquisition.

49 These efforts culminated in a number of articles on universals of language acquisition (Slobin 1973, 1982, 1985a, 1985b) and a series of edited volumes that included acquisition studies by linguists, psycholinguists, and linguistic anthropologists.

50 In 1975 Bambi Schieffelin was a PhD student in anthropology at Columbia University, where she had received an MA in developmental psychology under the direction of Lois Bloom. Before and after her fieldwork, Schieffelin spent time at Berkeley, first preparing for fieldwork and then writing her dissertation on Kaluli language acquisition (Schieffelin 1979b). In 1979–80, after completing her dissertation under Bloom's supervision, she had a postdoctoral fellowship in developmental psychology at the University of California at Berkeley, taught a course with Dan Slobin, and participated in the group he led on the cross-linguistic study of language acquisition. Elinor Ochs (formerly Elinor O. Keenan)

received her Ph.D. in anthropology in 1974 from the University of Pennsylvania, where she studied with Dell Hymes (her primary advisor), Ward Goodenough, and David Sapir.

51 The reader for her first seminars at USC on children's discourse became the basis for *Developmental Pragmatics*, the first collection of essays Ochs edited with Schieffelin (Ochs & Schieffelin 1979). Ochs and Schieffelin's earlier joint papers were later collected in Ochs & Schieffelin (1983).

52 They were part of a Working Group on Language and Cultural Context organized by Roger Keesing that included Penelope Brown, Alessandro Duranti, John B. Haviland, Stephen Levinson, Judith Irvine, Edward Schieffelin, Michael Silverstein, and Robert Van Valin.

53 This discovery is still ignored by psychologists who continue to write as if baby talk and Motherese are universals (e.g. Gopnik, Meltzoff, and Kuhl 1999) and it is even difficult to accept for linguistic anthropologists who worked in societies where adults do modify their speech to infants. Blount (1995), for example, first concludes that one cannot take Ochs's findings as conclusive because the youngest child in her corpus was 19 months old (Blount 1995: 560) and then tries to explain the Samoan data (which he had previously dismissed) and some of his own findings on the Luo by extending the notion of accommodation to include accommodation to the local cultural model, suggesting that even when parents do not accommodate to children, they are in fact accommodating, because they are adapting to their own cultural model: "In one sense, the form of Samoan and Luo parental speech behavior could also be viewed as accommodative, since it was selected to be consistent with and thus to model the appropriate language interaction with children, appropriate according to cultural expectations. In other words, the absence of salient linguistic markers in Samoan parental speech does not mean that no accommodation is made to the child's linguistic interactive capacity. To the contrary, the speech appears, in fact, to be tailored to the cultural definition of the child and thus consistent with the broader cultural parameters" (Blount 1995: 561). This position stretches the notion of accommodation to such an extent that it becomes difficult to see its value.

54 On peer-interaction, see M. H. Goodwin (1990b, 1999), Goodwin and Goodwin (1987); Schlegel (1998); on apprenticeship and everyday cognition, see Lave (1988, 1990), Lave and Wenger (1991), Rogoff (1990), Rogoff and Lave (1984), Scribner (1984); on literacy activities, see Besnier (1995), Heath (1983), Kuipers (1998: chapter 6), Scribner and Cole (1981), Street (1984); on language contact and linguistic syncretism, see Errington (1998), Hill and Hill (1986), Kulick (1992), Zentella (1997).

55 There is now a considerable amount of work on the transformation of experience in text or entextualization; see for example Briggs and Bauman (1992), Capps and Ochs (1995), Ochs and Capps (1996), Silverstein and Urban (1996).

56 Some scholars independently argued that the use of formal language can be used to restrict the choices that a person of higher rank has (e.g. Duranti 1992b; E. Goody 1972; Irvine 1974).

57 There is also a considerable amount of published research on the differences between spoken and written language, e.g. Tannen (1982), Biber (1988).

58 See Duranti (1992a), C. Goodwin (1981), Goodwin and Goodwin (1992, 2000), M. H. Goodwin (1990a, 1995), Woolard (1998).

59 Two of the police officers were convicted of violating Mr King's civil rights at a second, federal, trial.

REFERENCES

Agha, A. (1994). Honorification. *Annual Review of Anthropology, 23*: 277–302.

Agha, A. (1997). "Concept" and "Communication" in Evolutionary Terms. *Semiotica, 116* (2–4): 189–215.

Anzaldúa, G. (1987). *Borderlands / La Frontiera: The New Mestiza*. San Francisco: Spinsters/ Aunt Lute.

Anzaldúa, G. (1990). How to Tame a Wild Tongue. In R. M. Ferguson, T. Trinh Minh-ha Geve, and C. West (eds.), *Out There: Marginalization and Contemporary Cultures* (pp. 203–11). New York: The New Museum of Contemporary Art/MIT Press.

Austin, J. L. (1962). *How to Do Things with Words*. Oxford: Oxford University Press.

Austin, J. L. (1975). *How to Do Things with Words* (2nd edn.), J. O. Urmson and Marina Sbisà, editors. Cambridge, MA: Harvard University Press.

Bailey, B. (1997). Communication of Respect in Interethnic Service Encounters. *Language in Society, 26*(3): 327–56.

Bailey, B. (2000). Communicative Behavior and Conflict between African-American Customers and Korean Immigrant Retailers in Los Angeles. *Discourse & Society, 11*(1): 87–108.

Bakhtin, M. M. (1981). *The Dialogic Imagination: Four Essays*. Edited by M. Holquist, translated by C. Emerson and M. Holquist. Austin: University of Texas Press.

Bakhtin, M. M. (1984). *Problems of Dostoevsky's Poetics*. Edited and translated by C. Emerson. Introduction by Wayne C. Booth. Minneapolis: University of Minnesota Press.

Bakhtin, M. M. (1986). *Speech Genres & Other Late Essays*. Translated by Vern W. McGee. Austin: University of Texas Press.

Bamberg, M. (ed.) (1997). Oral Versions of Personal Experience: Three Decades of Narrative Analysis. *Journal of Narrative and Life History*, 7(1–4) (Special Issue).

Barwise, J., and Perry, J. (1983). *Situations and Attitudes*. Cambridge, MA: MIT Press.

Baugh, J. (1999). *Out of the Mouths of Slaves. African American Language and Educational Malpractice*. Austin: University of Texas Press.

Bauman, R. (1975). Verbal Art as Performance. *American Anthropologist, 77*: 290–311.

Bauman, R. (1977). *Verbal Art as Performance*. Rowley, MA: Newbury House.

Bauman, R., and Sherzer, J. (eds.) (1975). The Ethnography of Speaking. *Annual Reviews, 4*: 95–119.

Beeman, W. O. (1993). The Anthropology of Theater and Spectacle. *Annual Review of Anthropology, 22*: 369–93.

Berlin, B., and Kay, P. (1969). *Basic Color Terms: Their Universality and Evolution*. Berkeley: University of California Press.

Besnier, N. (1995). *Literacy, Emotion, and Authority: Reading and Writing on a Polynesian Atoll*. Cambridge: Cambridge University Press.

Biber, D. (1988). *Variation Across Speech and Writing*. Cambridge: Cambridge University Press.

Biber, D., and Finegan, E. (eds.) (1994). *Sociolinguistic Perspectives on Register*. New York: Oxford University Press.

Bloch, M. (1975a). Introduction. In M. Bloch (ed.), *Political Language and Oratory in Traditional Society* (pp. 1–28). London: Academic Press.

Bloch, M. (1975b). *Political Language and Oratory in Traditional Society.* London: Academic Press.

Blom, J.-P., and Gumperz, J. J. (1972). Social Meaning in Linguistic Structures: Code-Switching in Norway. In J. J. Gumperz and D. Hymes (eds.), *Directions in Sociolinguistics: The Ethnography of Communication* (pp. 407–34). New York: Holt, Rinehart, and Winston.

Bloomfield, L. (1935). *Language.* London: Allen & Unwin.

Blount, B. G. (1995). Parental Speech and Language Acquisition: An Anthropological Perspective. In B. G. Blount (ed.), *Language, Culture, and Society. A Book of Readings* (pp. 551–66). Prospect Heights, IL: Waveland.

Boas, F. (1889). On Alternating Sounds. *American Anthropologist, 2 (o.s.):* 47–53.

Boas, F. (1900). Sketch of the Kwakiutl Language. *American Anthropologist,* 2(4): 708–21.

Boas, F. (1911). Introduction. In F. Boas (ed.), *Handbook of American Indian Languages* (Vol. BAE-B 40, Part I). Washington, DC: Smithsonian Institution and Bureau of American Ethnology.

Boas, F. (1925). Stylistic Aspects of Primitive Literature. *Journal of American Folk-Lore, 38:* 329–39.

Boas, F. (1940). *Race, Language, and Culture.* New York: The Free Press.

Bourdieu, P. (1982). *Ce que parler veut dire.* Paris: Fayard.

Bourdieu, P. (1985). *Distinction: A Social Critique of the Judgement of Taste.* Cambridge, MA: Harvard University Press.

Brenneis, D. L., and Myers, F. (eds.) (1984). *Dangerous Words: Language and Politics in the Pacific.* New York: New York University Press.

Briggs, C. L. (1986). *Learning How to Ask: A Sociolinguistic Appraisal of the Role of the Interview in Social Science Research.* Cambridge: Cambridge University Press.

Briggs, C. L., and Bauman, R. (1992). Genre, Intertextuality, and Social Power. *Journal of Linguistic Anthropology,* 2(2): 131–72.

Bright, W. (ed.) (1966). *Sociolinguistics: Proceedings of the UCLA Sociolinguistics Conference, 1964.* The Hague: Mouton & Co.

Brown, G., and Yule, G. (1983). *Discourse Analysis.* Cambridge: Cambridge University Press.

Brown, P. (1993). Gender, Politeness, and Confrontation in Tenejapa. In D. Tannen (ed.), *Gender and Conversational Interaction* (pp. 144–62). New York: Oxford University Press.

Brown, P., and Levinson, S. C. (1978). Universals in Language Usage: Politeness Phenomena. In E. N. Goody (ed.), *Questions and Politeness Strategies in Social Interaction* (pp. 56–311). Cambridge: Cambridge University Press.

Brown, P., and Levinson, S. C. (1987). *Politeness: Some Universals in Language Usage.* Cambridge: Cambridge University Press.

Bucholtz, M. (1999). Bad Examples: Transgression and Progress in Language and Gender Studies. In M. Bucholtz, A. C. Liang, and L. A. Sutton (eds.), *Reinventing Identities: The Gendered Self in Discourse* (pp. 3–24). New York: Oxford University Press.

Bucholtz, M., Liang, A. C., and Sutton, L. A. (eds.) (1999). *Reinventing Identities: The Gendered Self in Discourse.* New York: Oxford University Press.

Capps, L., and Ochs, E. (1995). *Constructing Panic: The Discourse of Agoraphobia.* Cambridge, MA: Harvard University Press.

Cardona, G. R. (1976). *Introduzione all'etnolinguistica.* Bologna: Il Mulino.

Carroll, J. B. (1956). Introduction. In J. B. Carroll (ed.), *Language, Thought, and Reality: Selected Writings of Benjamin Lee Whorf* (pp. 1–34). Cambridge, MA: MIT Press.

Caton, S. C. (1990). *"Peaks of Yemen I Summon": Poetry as Cultural Practice in a North Yemeni Tribe*. Berkeley: University of California Press.
Cazden, C. B., John, V. P., and Hymes, D. (eds.) (1972). *The Functions of Language in the Classroom*. New York: Teachers College Press.
Chomsky, N. (1959). Review of *Verbal Behavior* by B. F. Skinner. *Language, 35*, 26–58.
Chomsky, N. (1965). *Aspects of the Theory of Syntax*. Cambridge, MA: MIT Press.
Chomsky, N. (1966). *Cartesian Linguistics*. New York: Harper & Row.
Chomsky, N. (1973). Introduction to Adam Schaff's *Language and Cognition*. New York: McGraw-Hill.
Chomsky, N. (1982). *Lectures on Government and Binding: The Pisa Lectures* (2nd edn.). Dordrecht: Foris.
Chomsky, N. (1986). *Knowledge of Language: Its Nature, Origin and Use*. New York: Praeger.
Chomsky, N. (1995). *The Minimalist Program*. Cambridge, MA: MIT Press.
Chomsky, N., Halle, M., and Lukoff, F. (1956). On Accent and Juncture in English. In M. Halle, H. Lunt, and H. MacLean (eds.), *For Roman Jakobson: Essays on the Occasion of His Sixtieth Birthday* (pp. 65–80). The Hague: Mouton.
Collins, J. (1995). Literacy and Literacies. *Annual Review of Anthropology, 24*: 75–93.
Conklin, H. C. (1962). Lexicographical Treatment of Folk Taxonomies. In F. W. Household and S. Saporta (eds.), *Problems in Lexicography*. Bloomington: Indiana University Research Center in Anthropology, Folklore, and Linguistics.
Cook-Gumperz, J. (ed.) (1986). *The Social Construction of Literacy*. Cambridge: Cambridge University Press.
Crystal, D. (1997). *A Dictionary of Linguistics and Phonetics* (4th edn.). Oxford: Blackwell.
Darnell, R. (1990). *Edward Sapir: Linguist, Anthropologist, Humanist*. Berkeley: University of California Press.
Darnell, R. (1998a). *And Along Came Boas: Continuity and Revolution in Americanist Anthropology*. Amsterdam/Philadelphia: John Benjamins.
Darnell, R. (1998b). Camelot at Yale: The Construction and Dismantling of the Sapirian Synthesis, 1931–39. *American Anthropologist, 100*(2): 361–72.
Darnell, R. (1998c). Toward a History of Canadian Departments of Anthropology: Retrospect, Prospect and Common Cause. *Anthropologica, 40*: 153–68.
Dixon, R. M. W. (1972). *The Dyirbal Language of North Queensland*. Cambridge: Cambridge University Press.
Dixon, R. M. W. (1977). *A Grammar of Yidin*. Cambridge: Cambridge University Press.
Dixon, R. M. W., and Aikhenvald, A. Y. (eds.) (1999). *The Amazonian Languages*. Cambridge: Cambridge University Press.
Dorian, N. (1993). A Response to Ladefoged's Other View of Endangered Language. *Language, 69*(3): 575–9.
Dorian, N. C. (1994). Purism vs. Compromise in Language Revitalization and Language Revival. *Language in Society, 23*(4): 479–94.
Drechsel, E. J. (1988). Wilhelm von Humboldt and Edward Sapir: Analogies and Homologies in Their Linguistic Thoughts. In W. Shipley (ed.), *In Honor of Mary Haas: From the Haas Festival Conference on Native American Linguistics* (pp. 225–64). Berlin: Mouton de Gruyter.
Drew, P., and Heritage, J. (eds.) (1992). *Talk at Work*. Cambridge: Cambridge University Press.
Du Bois, J. (1986). Self-Evidence and Ritual Speech. In W. Chafe and J. Nichols (eds.), *Evidentiality: The Linguistic Coding of Epistemology* (pp. 313–36). Norwood, NJ: Ablex.

Du Bois, J. W. (1993). Meaning Without Intention: Lessons from Divination. In J. Hill and J. Irvine (eds.), *Responsibility and Evidence in Oral Discourse* (pp. 48–71). Cambridge: Cambridge University Press.

Duranti, A. (1981). *The Samoan Fono: A Sociolinguistic Study.* Pacific Linguistics Monographs, Series B. Vol. 80. Canberra: Australian National University, Department of Linguistics, Research School of Pacific Studies.

Duranti, A. (1988). Intentions, Language and Social Action in a Samoan Context. *Journal of Pragmatics, 12*: 13–33.

Duranti, A. (1992a). Language and Bodies in Social Space: Samoan Ceremonial Greetings. *American Anthropologist, 94*: 657–91.

Duranti, A. (1992b). Language in Context and Language as Context: The Samoan Respect Vocabulary. In A. Duranti and C. Goodwin (eds.), *Rethinking Context: Language as an Interactive Phenomenon* (pp. 77–99). Cambridge: Cambridge University Press.

Duranti, A. (1993). Intentionality and Truth: An Ethnographic Critique. *Cultural Anthropology, 8*: 214–45.

Duranti, A. (1994). *From Grammar to Politics: Linguistic Anthropology in a Western Samoan Village.* Berkeley and Los Angeles: University of California Press.

Duranti, A. (1997a). Indexical Speech Across Samoan Communities. *American Anthropologist, 99*(2): 342–54.

Duranti, A. (1997b). *Linguistic Anthropology.* Cambridge: Cambridge University Press.

Duranti, A., and Brenneis, D. (1986). The Audience as Co-Author. Special Issue of *Text* (6–3): 239–347.

Duranti, A., and Goodwin, C. (eds.) (1992). *Rethinking Context: Language as an Interactive Phenomenon.* Cambridge: Cambridge University Press.

Duranti, A., and Ochs, E. (1997). Syncretic Literacy in a Samoan American Family. In L. Resnick, R. Säljö, C. Pontecorvo, and B. Burge (eds.), *Discourse, Tools, and Reasoning: Situated Cognition and Technologically Supported Environments* (pp. 169–202). Heidelberg: Springer-Verlag.

Eckert, P., and McConnell-Ginet, S. (1992a). Think Practically and Look Locally: Language and Gender as Community-Based Practice. *Annual Review of Anthropology, 21*: 461–90.

Eckert, P., and McConnell-Ginet, S. (1992b). Communities of Practice: Where Language, Gender, and Power All Live. In K. Hall, M. Bucholtz, and B. Moonwomon (eds.), *Locating Power. Proceedings of the Second Berkeley Women and Language Conference* (Vol. 1, pp. 89–99). Berkeley: Berkeley Women and Language Group, University of California.

Eckert, P., and McConnell-Ginet, S. (1999). New Generalizations and Explanations in Language and Gender Research. *Language in Society, 28*: 185–201.

Errington, J. J. (1998). *Shifting Languages: Interaction and Identity in Javanese Indonesia.* Cambridge: Cambridge University Press.

Ervin-Tripp, S. (1972a). On Sociolinguistic Rules: Alternation and Co-occurrence. In J. J. Gumperz and D. Hymes (eds.), *Directions in Sociolinguistics: The Ethnography of Communication* (pp. 213–50). New York: Holt, Rinehart, and Winston.

Ervin-Tripp, S. (1972b). Sociolinguistic Rules of Address. In J. B. Pride and J. Holmes (eds.), *Sociolinguistics* (pp. 225–40). Harmondsworth: Penguin Books.

Fasold, R. (1990). *The Sociolinguistics of Language.* Oxford: Oxford University Press.

Feld, S. (1982). *Sound and Sentiment: Birds, Weeping, Poetics, and Song in Kaluli Expression.* Philadelphia: University of Pennsylvania Press.

Ferguson, C. (1964). Baby Talk in Six Languages. *American Anthropologist, 66*(6), 103–14.

Ferguson, C. A. (1978). Talking to Children: A Search for Universals. In J. H. Greenberg (ed.), *Universals of Human Language* (pp. 205–24). Stanford: Stanford University Press.

Ferguson, C. A., and Gumperz, J. J. (eds.) (1960). *Linguistic Diversity in South Asia: Studies in Regional, Social and Functional Variation* (Vol. 26). Indiana University Research Center in Anthropology, Folklore, and Linguistics: International Journal of American Linguistics.

Fletcher, P., and MacWhinney, B. (eds.) (1995). *The Handbook of Child Language.* Oxford: Blackwell.

Foley, W. (1986). *The Papuan Languages of New Guinea.* New York: Cambridge University Press.

Foley, W. A. (1997). *Anthropological Linguistics: An Introduction.* Malden, MA: Blackwell.

Ford, C. (1993). *Grammar in Interaction: Adverbial Clauses in American English Conversations.* Cambridge: Cambridge University Press.

Foucault, M. (1979). *Discipline and Punish: The Birth of the Prison.* New York: Random House.

Foucault, M. (1980). *Power/Knowledge: Selected Interviews & Other Writings 1972–1977.* Edited by Colin Gordon; translated by Colin Gordon, Leo Marshall, John Mepham, and Kate Soper. New York: Pantheon.

Foucault, M. (1984). The Birth of the Asylum. In P. Rabinow (ed.), *The Foucault Reader* (pp. 141–68). New York: Pantheon Books.

Frake, C. O. (1969). The Ethnographic Study of Cognitive Systems. In S. A. Tyler (ed.), *Cognitive Anthropology* (pp. 28–41). New York: Holt, Rinehart, and Winston.

Frake, C. O. (1972). "Struck by Speech": The Yakan Concept of Litigation. In J. J. Gumperz and D. Hymes (eds.), *Directions in Sociolinguistics: The Ethnography of Communication* (pp. 106–29). New York: Holt, Rinehart, and Winston.

Friedrich, P. (1966). Structural Implications of Russian Pronominal Usage. In W. Bright (ed.), *Sociolinguistics: Proceedings of the UCLA Sociolinguistics Conference, 1964* (pp. 214–59). The Hague: Mouton & Co.

Friedrich, P. (1986). *The Language Parallax: Linguistic Relativism and Poetic Indeterminacy.* Austin: University of Texas Press.

Gadamer, H.-G. (1976). *Philosophical Hermeneutics.* Translated by David E. Linge. Berkeley: University of California Press.

Gal, S. (1978). Peasant Men Can't Get Wives: Language Change and Sex Roles in a Bilingual Community. *Language in Society, 7*: 1–16.

Gal, S. (1979). *Language Shift. Social Determinants of Linguistic Change in Bilingual Austria.* New York: Academic Press.

Gal, S. (1989). Language and Political Economy. *Annual Review of Anthropology, 18*: 345–67.

Gal, S. (1992). Language, Gender, and Power: An Anthropological Perspective. In K. Hall, M. Bucholtz, and B. Moonwomon (eds.), *Locating Power. Proceedings of the Second Berkeley Women and Language Conference* (Vol. 1, pp. 153–61). Berkeley: Berkeley Women and Language Group, University of California.

Gal, S. (1995). Language, Gender, and Power. An Anthropological Review. In K. Hall and M. Bucholtz (eds.), *Gender Articulated: Language and the Socially Constructed Self* (pp. 169–82). New York: Routledge.

Garfinkel, H. (1972). Remarks on Ethnomethodology. In J. J. Gumperz and D. Hymes (eds.), *Directions in Sociolinguistics: The Ethnography of Communication* (pp. 301–24). New York: Holt, Rinehart, and Winston.

Garvin, P. L., and Riesenberg, S. H. (1952). Respect Behavior in Ponape: An Ethnolinguistic Study. *American Anthropologist, 54*: 201–20.

Gatschet, A. S. (1899). "Real," "True," or "Genuine," in Indian Languages. *American Anthropologist, 1*: 155–61.

Givón, T. (ed.) (1979). *Syntax and Semantics*, Vol. 12, *Discourse and Syntax*. New York: Academic Press.

Givón, T. (1989). *Mind, Code, and Context: Essays in Pragmatics*. Hillsdale, NJ: Lawrence Erlbaum Associates.

Goffman, E. (1959). *The Presentation of Self in Everyday Life*. Garden City, NY: Doubleday.

Goffman, E. (1963). *Behavior in Public Places: Notes on the Social Organization of Gathering*. New York: Free Press.

Goffman, E. (1971). *Relations in Public: Microstudies of the Public Order.* New York: Harper & Row.

Goffman, E. (1981). *Forms of Talk*. Philadelphia: University of Pennsylvania Press.

Goodenough, W. H. (1956). Componential Analysis and the Study of Meaning. *Language, 32*: 195–216.

Goodenough, W. H. (1965). Rethinking "Status" and "Role": Toward a General Model of the Cultural Organization of Social Relationships. In M. Banton (ed.), *The Relevance of Models for Social Anthropology* (pp. 1–24). London: Tavistock.

Goodwin, C. (1979). The Interactive Construction of a Sentence in Natural Conversation. In G. Psathas (ed.), *Everyday Language: Studies in Ethnomethodology* (pp. 97–121). New York: Irvington Publishers.

Goodwin, C. (1981). *Conversational Organization: Interaction Between Speakers and Hearers*. New York: Academic Press.

Goodwin, C. (1986). Audience Diversity, Participation and Interpretation. *Text, 6*(3), 283–316.

Goodwin, C. (1994). Professional Vision. *American Anthropologist, 96*(3), 606–33.

Goodwin, C. (1995). Seeing in Depth. *Social Studies of Science, 25*, 237–74.

Goodwin, C. (1996a). Practices of Color Classification. *Ninchi Kagaku (Cognitive Studies: Bulletin of the Japanese Cognitive Science Society), 3*(2): 62–81.

Goodwin, C. (1996b). Transparent Vision. In E. Ochs, E. A. Schegloff, and S. A. Thompson (eds.), *Interaction and Grammar* (pp. 370–404). Cambridge: Cambridge University Press.

Goodwin, C. (1997). The Blackness of Black: Color Categories as Situated Practice. In L. Resnick, R. Säljö, C. Pontecorvo, and B. Burge (eds.), *Discourse, Tools, and Reasoning: Situated Cognition and Technologically Supported Environments* (pp. 111–40). Heidelberg: Springer-Verlag.

Goodwin, C., and Duranti, A. (1992). Rethinking Context: An Introduction. In A. Duranti and C. Goodwin (eds.), *Rethinking Context: Language as an Interactive Phenomenon* (pp. 1–42). Cambridge: Cambridge University Press.

Goodwin, C., and Goodwin, M. H. (1992). Assessments and the Construction of Context. In A. Duranti and C. Goodwin (eds.), *Rethinking Context: Language as an Interactive Phenomenon* (pp. 147–89). Cambridge: Cambridge University Press.

Goodwin, C., and Heritage, J. (1990). Conversation Analysis. *Annual Reviews of Anthropology, 19*: 283–307.

Goodwin, M. H. (1990a). Byplay: Participant Structure and the Framing of Collaborative Collusion. In B. Conein, M. D. Fornel, and L. Quéré (eds.), *Les Formes de La Conversation* (Vol. 2, pp. 155–80). Paris: CNET.

Goodwin, M. H. (1990b). *He-Said-She-Said: Talk as Social Organization among Black Children*. Bloomington, IN: Indiana University Press.

Goodwin, M. H. (1995). Co-Construction of Girls' Hopscotch. *Research on Language and Social Interaction, 28*: 261–82.

Goodwin, M. H. (1998). Games of Stance: Conflict and Footing in Hopscotch. In S. Hoyle and C. T. Adger (eds.), *Language Practices of Older Children* (pp. 23–46). New York: Oxford University Press.

Goodwin, M. H. (1999). Constructing Opposition within Girls' Games. In M. Bucholtz, A. C. Liang, and L. A. Sutton (eds.), *Reinventing Identities: The Gendered Self in Discourse* (pp. 388–409). New York: Oxford University Press.

Goodwin, M. H., and Goodwin, C. (1987). Children's Arguing. In S. Philips, S. Steele, and C. Tanz (eds.), *Language, Gender, and Sex in Comparative Perspective* (pp. 200–48). Cambridge: Cambridge University Press.

Goodwin, M. H., and Goodwin, C. (2000). Emotion within Situated Activity. In N. Budwig, I. C. Uzgirls, and J. V. Wertsch (eds.), *Communication: An Arena of Development* (pp. 33–53). Stamford, CT: Ablex.

Goody, E. (1972). "Greeting", "begging", and the Presentation of Respect. In J. S. La Fontaine (ed.), *The Interpretation of Ritual* (pp. 39–71). London: Tavistock.

Goody, J., and Watt, I. (1962). The Consequences of Literacy. *Comparative Studies in Society and History, 5*: 304–26.

Goody, J., and Watt, I. (1968). The Consequences of Literacy. In J. Goody (ed.), *Literacy in Traditional Society* (pp. 27–68). Cambridge: Cambridge University Press.

Gopnik, A., Meltzoff, A. N., and Kuhl, P. K. (1999). *The Scientist in the Crib: Minds, Brains, and How Children Learn*. New York: William Morrow.

Graham, L. R. (1995). *Performing Dreams: Discourses of Immortality among the Xavante of Central Brazil*. Austin: University of Texas Press.

Gramsci, A. (1971). *Selections from the Prison Notebooks*. Edited and translated by Quintin Hoare and Geoffrey Nowell Smith. New York: International Publishers.

Gramsci, A. (1975). *Gli intellettuali e l'organizzazione della cultura*. Roma: Editori Riuniti.

Greenberg, J. H. (1968). *Anthropological Linguistics: An Introduction*. New York: Random House.

Grenoble, L. A., and Whaley, L. J. (eds.) (1998). *Endangered Languages: Current Issues and Future Prospects*. Cambridge: Cambridge University Press.

Gumperz, J. J. (1958). Dialect Differences and Social Stratification in a North Indian Village. *American Anthropologist, 60*: 668–82.

Gumperz, J. J. (1964). Linguistic and Social Interaction in Two Communities. *American Anthropologist, 66*(6), 137–53.

Gumperz, J. J. (1968a). The Speech Community. *International Encyclopedia of the Social Sciences* (pp. 381–6). New York: Macmillan.

Gumperz, J. J. (1968b). Types of Linguistic Communities. In J. A. Fishman (ed.), *Readings in the Sociology of Language* (pp. 460–72). The Hague: Mouton.

Gumperz, J. J. (1977). Sociocultural Knowledge in Conversational Inference. In M. Saville-Troike (ed.), *Georgetown University Round Table on Languages and Linguistics 1977*. Washington, DC: Georgetown University Press.

Gumperz, J. J. (1982a). *Discourse Strategies*. Cambridge: Cambridge University Press.

Gumperz, J. J. (ed.) (1982b). *Language and Social Identity*. Cambridge: Cambridge University Press.

Gumperz, J. J. (1992). Contextualization and Understanding. In A. Duranti and C. Goodwin (eds.), *Rethinking Context: Language as an Interactive Phenomenon* (pp. 229–52). Cambridge: Cambridge University Press.

Gumperz, J. J., and Hymes, D. (1964). The Ethnography of Communication. *American Anthropologist*, 66, 6, *part II*.

Gumperz, J. J., & Hymes, D. (1972). *Directions in Sociolinguistics: The Ethnography of Communication*. New York: Holt, Rinehart, and Winston.

Gumperz, J. J., and Levinson, S. (1991). Rethinking Linguistic Relativity. *Current Anthropology, 32*: 613–23.

Gumperz, J. J., and Levinson, S. C. (eds.) (1996). *Rethinking Linguistic Relativity.* Cambridge: Cambridge University Press.

Haas, M. (1953). Sapir and the Training of Anthropological Linguistics. *American Anthropologist, 55*: 447–9.

Haas, M. R. (1977). Anthropological Linguistics: History. In A. F. C. Wallace (ed.), *Perspectives in Anthropology 1976* (pp. 33–47): A Special Publication of the American Anthropological Association.

Haas, M. R. (1978a). The Study of American Indian Languages: A Brief Historical Sketch. In *Language, Culture, and History: Essays by Mary R. Haas*. Selected and Introduced by Anwar S. Dil (pp. 110–29). Stanford, CA: Stanford University Press.

Haas, M. R. (1978b). Boas, Sapir, and Bloomfield: Their Contribution to American Indian Linguistics. In *Language, Culture, and History: Essays by Mary R. Haas*. Selected and Introduced by Anwar S. Dil (pp. 194–206). Stanford, CA: Stanford University Press.

Hale, K., Krauss, M., Watahomigie, L. J., Yamamoto, A. Y., Craig, C., Jeanne, L. M., and England, N. C. (1992). Endangered Languages. *Language, 68*(1): 1–62.

Hall, K., and Bucholtz, M. (eds.) (1995). *Gender Articulated: Language and the Socially Constructed Self*. New York: Routledge.

Hall, K., Bucholtz, M., and Moonwomon, B. (eds.) (1992). *Locating Power. Proceedings of the Second Berkeley Women and Language Conference*. Berkeley: Berkeley Women and Language Group, University of California.

Halliday, M. A. K. (1973). *Explorations in the Functions of Language*. London: Arnold.

Halliday, M. A. K. (1978). *Language and Social Semiotic: The Social Interaction of Language and Meaning*. Baltimore, MA: University Park Press.

Hanks, W. F. (1986). Authenticity and Ambivalence in the Text: A Colonial Maya Case. *American Ethnologist, 13*(4): 721–44.

Hanks, W. F. (1987). Discourse Genres in a Theory of Practice. *American Ethnologist, 14*(4): 668–92.

Hanks, W. F. (1990). *Referential Practice: Language and Lived Space Among the Maya*. Chicago, IL: University of Chicago Press.

Hanks, W. F. (1993). Notes on Semantics in Linguistic Practice. In C. Calhoun, E. LiPuma, and M. Postone (eds.), *Bourdieu: Critical Perspectives* (pp. 139–55). Cambridge: Polity.

Hanks, W. F. (1996). *Language and Communicative Practices*. Boulder, CO: Westview.

Haviland, J. B. (1996). Projections, Transpositions, and Relativity. In J. J. Gumperz and S. C. Levinson (eds.), *Rethinking Linguistic Relativity* (pp. 271–323). Cambridge: Cambridge University Press.

Heath, S. B. (1983). *Ways with Words: Language, Life and Work in Communities and Classrooms*. Cambridge: Cambridge University Press.

Henson, H. (1974). *British Social Anthropologists and Language: History of Separate Development*. Oxford: Clarendon Press.

Heritage, J. (1990/91). Intention, Meaning and Strategy: Observations on Constraints on Interaction Analysis. *Research on Language and Social Interaction, 24*: 311–32.

Hill, A. A. (1964). A Note on Primitive Languages. In D. Hymes (ed.), *Language in Culture and Society: A Reader in Linguistic Anthropology* (pp. 86–9). New York: Harper & Row.

Hill, J. H. (1998). Language, Race, and White Public Space. *American Anthropologist, 100*: 680–9.

Hill, J. H., and Hill, K. C. (1986). *Speaking Mexicano: Dynamics of a Syncretic Language in Central Mexico*. Tucson: University of Arizona Press.

Hill, J. H., and Irvine, J. T. (eds.) (1993). *Responsibility and Evidence in Oral Discourse*. Cambridge: Cambridge University Press.

Hill, J. H., and Mannheim, B. (1992). Language and World View. *Annual Review of Anthropology, 21*: 381–406.

Hoijer, H. (1961). Anthropological Linguistics. In C. Mohrmann, A. Sommerfelt, and J. Whatmough (eds.), *Trends in European and American Linguistics 1930–1960* (pp. 110–25). Utrecht and Antwerp: Spectrum Publishers.

Hopper, P. J., and Thompson, S. A. (1980). Transitivity in Grammar and Discourse. *Language, 56*: 251–99.

Hopper, P. J., and Traugott, E. C. (1993). *Grammaticalization*. Cambridge: Cambridge University Press.

Hudson, R. A. (1980). *Sociolinguistics*. Cambridge: Cambridge University Press.

Hymes, D. (1962). The Ethnography of Speaking. In T. Gladwin and W. C. Sturtevant (eds.), *Anthropology and Human Behavior* (pp. 13–53). Washington, DC: Anthropological Society of Washington. (Reprinted in J. A. Fishman (ed.), *Readings in the Sociology of Language*, pp. 99–138. The Hague: Mouton, 1968.)

Hymes, D. (1964a). General Introduction. In D. Hymes (ed.), *Language in Culture and Society: A Reader in Linguistics and Anthropology* (pp. xxi–xxxii). New York: Harper & Row.

Hymes, D. (1964b). Introduction to Part I. In D. Hymes (ed.), *Language in Culture and Society: A Reader in Linguistic Anthropology* (pp. 3–14). New York: Harper & Row.

Hymes, D. (1964c). Introduction: Toward Ethnographies of Communication. In J. J. Gumperz and D. Hymes (eds.), *The Ethnography of Communication* (pp. 1–34). Washington, DC: American Anthropologist (Special Issue).

Hymes, D. (ed.) (1964d). *Language in Culture and Society: A Reader in Linguistic Anthropology*. New York: Harper & Row.

Hymes, D. (1966). Two Types of Linguistic Relativity. In W. Bright (ed.), *Sociolinguistics* (pp. 114–67). The Hague: Mouton.

Hymes, D. (ed.) (1971a). *Pidginization and Creolization of Languages*. Cambridge: Cambridge University Press.

Hymes, D. (1971b). Sociolinguistics and the Ethnography of Speaking. In E. Ardener (ed.), *Social Anthropology and Language* (pp. 47–93). London: Tavistock.

Hymes, D. (1972a). Models of the Interaction of Language and Social Life. In J. J. Gumperz and D. Hymes (eds.), *Directions in Sociolinguistics: The Ethnography of Communication* (pp. 35–71). New York: Holt, Rinehart, and Winston.

Hymes, D. (1972b). On Communicative Competence. In J. B. Pride and J. Holmes (eds.), *Sociolinguistics* (pp. 269–93). Harmondsworth: Penguin.

Hymes, D. (1974a). *Foundations in Sociolinguistics: An Ethnographic Approach*. Philadelphia: University of Pennsylvania Press.

Hymes, D. (1974b). Ways of Speaking. In R. Bauman and J. Sherzer (eds.), *Explorations in the Ethnography of Speaking* (pp. 433–51). Cambridge: Cambridge University Press.

Hymes, D. (1975). Breakthrough into Performance. In D. Ben-Amos and K. S. Goldstein (eds.), *Folklore: Performance and Communication* (pp. 11–74). The Hague: Mouton.

Hymes, D. (1981). *"In Vain I Tried to Tell You": Essays in Native American Ethnopoetics*. Philadelphia: University of Pennsylvania Press.

Hymes, D. (1996). *Ethnography, Linguistics, Narrative Inequality*. Bristol, PA: Taylor & Francis.

Hymes, D. (1999). Boas on the Threshold of Ethnopoetics. In L. P. Valentine and R. Darnell (eds.), *Theorizing the Americanist Tradition* (pp. 84–107). Toronto: University of Toronto Press.

Irvine, J. T. (1974). Strategies of Status Manipulation in Wolof Greeting. In R. Bauman and J. Sherzer (eds.), *Explorations in the Ethnography of Speaking* (pp. 167–91). Cambridge: Cambridge University Press.

Irvine, J. T. (1979). Formality and Informality in Communicative Events. *American Anthropologist, 81*(4): 773–90.

Jakobson, R. (1944). Franz Boas' Approach to Language. *International Journal of American Linguistics, 10*: 188–95.

Johnstone, B. (1996). *The Linguistic Individual: Self-Expression in Language and Linguistics*. New York: Oxford University Press.

Jupp, T. C., Roberts, C., and Cook-Gumperz, J. (1982). Language and the Disadvantage: The Hidden Process. In J. J. Gumperz (ed.), *Language and Social Identity* (pp. 232–56). Cambridge: Cambridge University Press.

Kay, P., and Maffi, L. (2000). Color Appearance and the Emergence and Evolution of Basic Color Lexicons. *American Anthropologist, 101*: 743–60.

Keane, W. (1997). *Signs of Recognition: Powers and Hazards of Representation in an Indonesian Society*. Berkeley: University of California Press.

Keating, E. (1998). *Power Sharing: Language, Rank, Gender and Social Space in Pohnpei, Micronesia*. Oxford: Oxford University Press.

Keenan, E. O. (1974). Conversation and Oratory in Vaninankaratra Madagascar. Unpublished Ph.D. dissertation, University of Pennsylvania.

Keil, C., and Feld, S. (1994). *Music Grooves*. Chicago, IL: University of Chicago Press.

Kingten, E. R., Kroll, B. M., and Rose, M. (eds.) (1988). *Perspectives on Literacy*. Carbondale and Edwardsville: Southern Illinois University Press.

Kirch, P. V. (1984). *The Evolution of Polynesian Chiefdoms*. Cambridge: Cambridge University Press.

Koerner, E. F. K. (1992). The Sapir–Whorf Hypothesis: A Preliminary History and a Bibliographical Essay. *Journal of Linguistic Anthropology, 2*(2): 173–98.

Kroeber, A. L. (1905). Systematic Nomenclature in Ethnology. *American Anthropologist, 7*: 579–93.

Kroskrity, P. V. (1993). *Language, History, and Identity: Ethnolinguistic Studies of the Arizona Tewa*. Tucson: University of Arizona Press.

Kroskrity, P. V. (1998). Arizona Tewa Kiva Speech as a Manifestation of a Dominant Language Ideology. In B. B. Schieffelin, K. Woolard, and P. Kroskrity (eds.), *Language Ideologies* (pp. 103–22). New York: Oxford University Press.

Kroskrity, P. V. (2000a). Regimenting Languages: Language Ideological Perspectives. In P. V. Kroskrity (ed.), *Regimes of Language: Ideologies, Politics and Identities* (pp. 1–34). Santa Fe, NM: School of American Research Press.

Kroskrity, P. V. (ed.) (2000b). *Regimes of Language: Ideologies, Politics and Identities*. Santa Fe, NM: School of American Research Press.

Kuipers, J. C. (1990). *Power in Performance: The Creation of Textual Authority in Weyewa Ritual Speech*. Philadelphia: University of Pennsylvania Press.

Kuipers, J. C. (1998). *Language, Identity, and Marginality in Indonesia: The Changing Nature of Ritual Speech on the Island of Sumba*. Cambridge: Cambridge University Press.

Kulick, D. (1992). *Language Shift and Cultural Reproduction: Socialization, Self, and Syncretism in a Papua New Guinean Village*. Cambridge: Cambridge University Press.

Labov, W. (1996a). Hypercorrection by the Lower Middle Class as a Factor in Linguistic Change. In W. Bright (ed.), *Sociolinguistics* (pp. 84–113). The Hague: Mouton.

Labov, W. (1966b). *The Social Stratification of English in New York City*. Arlington: Center for Applied Linguistics.

Labov, W. (1969). The Logic of Nonstandard English. In J. Alatis (ed.), *Georgetown Monographs on Language and Linguistics* (Vol. 22, pp. 1–44). Washington, DC: Georgetown University Press.

Labov, W. (1970). *The Study of Nonstandard English*. Champaign, IL: National Council of Teachers.

Labov, W. (1972a). *Language in the Inner City: Studies in the Black English Vernacular*. Philadelphia: University of Pennsylvania Press.

Labov, W. (1972b). On Mechanism of Linguistic Change. In J. J. Gumperz and D. Hymes (eds.), *Directions in Sociolinguistics: The Ethnography of Communication* (pp. 512–38). New York: Holt, Rinehart, and Winston.

Labov, W. (1972c). *Sociolinguistic Patterns*. Philadelphia: University of Pennsylvania Press.

Labov, W., and Waletzky, J. (1966). Narrative Analysis: Oral Version of Personal Experience. In J. Helm (ed.), *Essays on the Verbal and Visual Arts: Proceedings of the 1996 Annual Spring Meeting of the American Ethnological Society* (pp. 12–44). Seattle: University of Washington Press.

Lakoff, G. (1987). *Women, Fire, and Dangerous Things: What Categories Reveal About the Mind*. Chicago, IL: Chicago University Press.

Lakoff, G., and Johnson, M. (1980). *Metaphors We Live By*. Chicago, IL: Chicago University Press.

Lakoff, R. (1973). Language and Women's Place. *Language in Society, 2*: 45–80.

Lave, J. (1988). *Cognition in Practice*. Cambridge: Cambridge University Press.

Lave, J. (1990). The Culture of Acquisition and the Practice of Understanding. In J. W. Stigler, R. A. Shweder, and G. Herdt (eds.), *Cultural Psychology: Essays on Comparative Human Development* (pp. 309–27). Cambridge: Cambridge University Press.

Lave, J., and Wenger, E. (1991). *Situated Learning: Legitimate Peripheral Participation*. Cambridge: Cambridge University Press.

Lee, B. (1997). *Talking Heads: Language, Metalanguage, and the Semiotics of Subjectivity*. Durham, NC: Duke University Press.

Lee, D. (1944). Linguistic Reflection of Wintu Thought. *International Journal of American Linguistics, 10*: 181–7.

Lee, P. (1991). Whorf's Hopi Tensors: Subtle Articulation in the Language/Thought Nexus? *Cognitive Linguistics, 2*(2): 123–47.

Lee, P. (1996). *The Whorf Theory Complex: A Critical Reconstruction*. Amsterdam: John Benjamins.

Lévi-Strauss, C. (1966). *The Savage Mind*. Chicago, IL: Chicago University Press.

Levinson, S. C. (1983). *Pragmatics*. Cambridge: Cambridge University Press.

Levinson, S. C. (1992). Primer for the Field Investigation of Spatial Description and Conception. *Pragmatics, 2*(1): 5–47.

Levinson, S. C. (1996). Relativity in Spatial Conception and Description. In J. J. Gumperz and S. C. Levinson (eds.), *Rethinking Linguistic Relativity* (pp. 177–202). Cambridge: Cambridge University Press.

Levinson, S. C. (1997). Language and Cognition: The Cognitive Consequences of Spatial Description in Guugu Yimithirr. *Journal of Linguistic Anthropology, 7*(1): 98–131.

Levinson, S. C. (2000). Yelî Dnye and the Theory of Basic Color Terms. *Journal of Linguistic Anthropology, 10*(1).

Lounsbury, F. G. (1969). The Structural Analysis of Kinship Semantics. In S. A. Tyler (ed.), *Cognitive Anthropology* (pp. 193–212). New York: Holt, Rinehart, and Winston.

Lucy, J. A. (1992a). *Grammatical Categories and Cognition: A Case Study of the Linguistic Relativity Hypothesis*. Cambridge: Cambridge University Press.

Lucy, J. A. (1992b). *Language Diversity and Cognitive Development: A Reformulation of the Linguistic Relativity Hypothesis*. Cambridge: Cambridge University Press.

Lucy, J. A. (ed.) (1993). *Reflexive Language: Reported Speech and Metapragmatics*. New York: Cambridge University Press.

Lucy, J. A., and Shweder, R. A. (1979). Whorf and His Critics: Linguistic and Nonlinguistic Influences on Color Memory. *American Anthropologist, 81*: 581–615.

Malinowski, B. (1920). Classificatory Particles in the Language of Kiriwina. *Bulletin of the School of Oriental and African Studies, 1*: 33–78.

Malotki, E. (1983). *Hopi Time: A Linguistic Analysis of the Temporal Concepts in the Hopi Language*. Berlin: Mouton.

Maltz, D. N., and Borker, R. A. (1982). A Cultural Approach to Male–Female Miscommunication. In J. J. Gumperz (ed.), *Language and Social Identity* (pp. 196–216). Cambridge: Cambridge University Press.

Mandelbaum, J. (1987a). Couples Sharing Stories. *Communication Quarterly, 35*(4): 144–71.

Mandelbaum, J. (1987b). Recipient-driven Storytelling in Conversation. Unpublished PhD dissertation, The University of Texas at Austin.

Mandelbaum, J. (1989). Interpersonal Activities in Conversational Storytelling. *Western Journal of Speech Communication, 53*(2): 114–26.

Mannheim, B. (1991). *The Language of the Inka since the European Invasion*. Austin: University of Texas Press.

Martin, L. (1986). Eskimo Words for Snow: A Case Study in the Genesis and Decay of an Anthropological Example. *American Anthropologist, 88*: 418–23.

Mason, O. T. (1900). The Linguistic Families of Mexico. *American Anthropologist, 2*: 63–5.

McConvell, P., and Evans, N. (eds.) (1997). *Archaeology and Linguistics: Aboriginal Australia and Global Perspective*. Melbourne: Oxford University Press.

McTear, M. (1985). *Children's Conversation*. Oxford: Blackwell.

Mendoza-Denton, N. (1996). "Muy Macha": Gender and Ideology in Gang-Girls' Discourse about Makeup. *Ethnos, 1–2*: 47–63.

Mendoza-Denton, N. (1999). Sociolinguistics and Linguistic Anthropology. *Annual Review of Anthropology, 28*: 375–95.

Merlan, F., and Rumsay, A. (1991). *Ku Waru: Language and Segmentary Politics in the Western Nebilyer Valley, Papua New Guinea*. Cambridge: Cambridge University Press.

Mertz, E. (1996). Consensus and Dissent in U.S. Legal Opinions: Narrative Structure and Social Voices. In C. L. Briggs (ed.), *Disorderly Discourse: Narrative, Conflict, and Inequality* (pp. 135–57). New York: Oxford University Press.

Milroy, L. (1987). *Language and Social Networks* (2nd edn.). Oxford: Blackwell.

Milroy, L., and Milroy, J. (1992). Social Network and Social Class: Toward an Integrated Sociolinguistic Model. *Language in Society, 21*: 1–26.

Moerman, M. M. (1988). *Talking Culture: Ethnography and Conversation Analysis*. Philadelphia: University of Pennsylvania Press.

Morgan, M. M. (1994a). The African-American Speech Community: Reality and Sociolinguists. In M. M. Morgan (ed.), *Language and the Social Construction of Identity in Creole Situations* (pp. 121–48). Los Angeles: Center for Afro-American Studies, UCLA.

Morgan, M. M. (1994b). Theories and Politics in African American English. *Annual Review of Anthropology, 23*: 325–45.

Murray, S. O. (1993). *Theory Groups and the Study of Language in North America*. Amsterdam and Philadelphia: John Benjamins.

Murray, S. O. (1998). *American Sociolinguistics: Theorists and Theory Groups*. Amsterdam and Philadelphia: John Benjamins.

Newmeyer, F. J. (1980). *Linguistic Theory in America: The First Quarter Century of Transformational Generative Grammar*. New York: Academic Press.

Newmeyer, F. J. (1986). Has There Been a "Chomskian Revolution" in Linguistics? *Language, 62*(1): 1–18.

Newport, E. (1976). Motherese: The Speech of Mothers to Young Children. In N. J. Castellan, D. B. Pisoni, and G. R. Potts (eds.), *Cognitive Theory* (Vol. 2). Hillsdale, NJ: Lawrence Erlbaum.

Nichols, J. (1992). *Linguistic Diversity in Space and Time*. Chicago, IL: University of Chicago Press.

Nichols, J. (1995a). Diachronically Stable Structural Features. In H. Anderson (ed.), *Historical Linguistics 1993: Selected Papers from the 11th International Congress of Historical Linguists, Los Angeles, 16–20 August, 1993* (pp. 337–55). Amsterdam: John Benjamins.

Nichols, J. (1995b). The Spread of Language around the Pacific Rim. *Evolutionary Anthropology, 3*: 206–15.

Nichols, J., and Peterson, D. A. (1996). The Amerind Personal Pronouns. *Language*, 72(2): 336–71.

Nuckolls, J. B. (1996). *Sounds like Life: Sound-symbolic Grammar, Performance, and Cognition in Pastaza Quechua*. Oxford: Oxford University Press.

Ochs, E. (1988). *Culture and Language Development: Language Acquisition and Language Socialization in a Samoan Village*. Cambridge: Cambridge University Press.

Ochs, E. (1992). Indexing Gender. In A. Duranti and C. Goodwin (eds.), *Rethinking Context: Language as an Interactive Phenomenon* (pp. 335–58). Cambridge: Cambridge University Press.

Ochs, E. (1996). Linguistic Resources for Socializing Humanity. In J. J. Gumperz and S. C. Levinson (eds.), *Rethinking Linguistic Relativity* (pp. 407–37). Cambridge: Cambridge University Press.

Ochs, E. (1997). Narrative. In T. van Dijk (ed.), *Discourse as Structure and Process* (pp. 185–207). London: Sage.

Ochs, E., and Capps, L. (1996). Narrating the Self. *Annual Review of Anthropology, 25*: 19–43.

Ochs, E., Gonzales, P., and Jacoby, S. (1996). "When I Come Down I'm in the Domain State": Grammar and Graphic Representation in the Interpretive Activity of Physicists. In E. Ochs, E. A. Schegloff, and S. A. Thompson (eds.), *Interaction and Grammar* (pp. 328–69). Cambridge: Cambridge University Press.

Ochs, E., Jacoby, S., and Gonzales, P. (1994). Interpretive Journeys: How Physicists Talk and Travel through Graphic Space. *Configurations*, *2*(1): 151–71.

Ochs, E., Schegloff, E. A., and Thompson, S. A. (eds.) (1996). *Interaction and Grammar.* Cambridge: Cambridge University Press.

Ochs, E., and Schieffelin, B. B. (1979). *Developmental Pragmatics*. New York: Academic Press.

Ochs, E., and Schieffelin, B. B. (1983). *Acquiring Conversational Competence*. Boston: Routledge & Kegan Paul.

Ochs, E., and Schieffelin, B. B. (1984). Language Acquisition and Socialization: Three Developmental Stories and Their Implications. In R. A. Shweder and R. A. LeVine (eds.), *Culture Theory: Essays on Mind, Self, and Emotion* (pp. 276–320). Cambridge: Cambridge University Press.

Ochs, E., and Schieffelin, B. B. (1995). The Impact of Language Socialization on Grammatical Development. In P. Fletcher and B. MacWhinney (eds.), *The Handbook of Child Language* (pp. 73–94). Oxford: Blackwell.

Olson, D. R., and Torrance, N. (eds.) (1991). *Literacy and Orality.* Cambridge: Cambridge University Press.

Palmer, G. B. (1996). *Toward a Theory of Cultural Linguistics*. Austin: University of Texas Press.

Palmer, G. B., and Jankowiak, W. R. (1996). Performance and Imagination: Toward an Anthropology of the Spectacular and the Mundane. *Cultural Anthropology, 11*(2): 225–58.

Philips, S. U. (1998). Language Ideologies in Institutions of Power. In B. B. Schieffelin, K. Woolard, and P. Kroskrity (eds.), *Language Ideologies* (pp. 211–25). New York: Oxford University Press.

Platt, M. (1982). Social and Semantic Dimensions of Deictic Verbs and Particles in Samoan Child Language. University of Southern California, unpublished PhD dissertation.

Powell, J. W. (1880). *Introduction to the Study of Indian Languages, 2nd edition*. Washington, DC.

Rampton, B. (1995a). *Crossing: Language and Ethnicity among Adolescents*. London: Longman.

Rampton, B. (1995b). Language Crossing and the Problematisation of Ethnicity and Socialisation. *Pragmatics*, *5*(4): 485–515.

Rickford, J. R. (1997). Unequal Partnership: Sociolinguistics and the African American Speech Community. *Language in Society, 26*(2): 161–98.

Rickford, J. R. (1999). *African American Vernacular English*. Malden, MA: Blackwell.

Ricoeur, P. (1981). *Hermeneutics and the Human Sciences*. Cambridge: Cambridge University Press.

Rogoff, B. (1990). *Apprenticeship in Thinking*. New York: Oxford University Press.

Rogoff, B., and Lave, J. (1984). *Everyday Cognition: Its Development in Social Context*. Cambridge, MA: Harvard University Press.

Romaine, S. (1982). *Sociolinguistic Variation in Speech Communities*. New York: Edward Arnold.

Romaine, S. (1995). *Bilingualism* (2nd edn.). Oxford: Blackwell.

Rosen, L. (ed.) (1995). *Other Intentions*. Santa Fe, NM: School of American Research.

Salmon, V. (1986). Effort and Achievement in Seventeenth-Century British Linguistics. In T. Bynon and F. R. Palmer (eds.), *Studies in the History of Western Linguistics* (pp. 69–95). Cambridge: Cambridge University Press.

Salzmann, Z. (1993). *Language, Culture, and Society: An Introduction to Linguistic Anthropology*. Boulder, CO: Westview.

Sankoff, G. (1980). *The Social Life of Language*. Philadelphia: University of Pennsylvania Press.

Sapir, D. (1985). Introducing Edward Sapir. *Language in Society, 14*(3): 289–97.

Sapir, E. (1921). *Language*. New York: Harcourt, Brace & World.

Sapir, E. (1927). The Unconscious Patterning of Behavior in Society. In E. S. Dummer (ed.), *The Unconscious: A Symposium* (pp. 114–42). New York: Knopf.

Sapir, E. (1929). Male and Female Forms of Speech in Yana. In S. W. J. Teeuwen (ed.), *Donum Natalicium Schrijnen* (pp. 79–85). Nijmegen-Utrecht.

Sapir, E. (1933). Language. *Encyclopaedia of the Social Sciences* (pp. 155–69). New York: Macmillan.

Sapir, E. (1949a). Language. In D. G. Mandelbaum (ed.), *Selected Writings of Edward Sapir in Language, Culture and Personality* (pp. 7–32). Berkeley and Los Angeles: University of California Press.

Sapir, E. (1949b). The Unconscious Patterning of Behavior in Society. In D. G. Mandelbaum (ed.), *Selected Writings of Edward Sapir in Language, Culture and Personality* (pp. 544–59). Berkeley and Los Angeles: University of California Press.

Sapir, E. (1964). Conceptual Categories in Primitive Languages. In D. Hymes (ed.), *Language in Culture and Society* (p. 128). New York: Harper & Row.

Sapir, E. (1994). *The Psychology of Culture: A Course of Lectures*. Reconstructed and edited by Judith T. Irvine. Berlin: Mouton de Gruyter.

Sapir, J. D., and Crocker, J. C. (eds.) (1977). *The Social Uses of Metaphor*. Philadelphia: University of Pennsylvania Press.

Schaff, A. (1973). *Language and Cognition*. Translated by Olgierd Wojtasiewicz. New York: McGraw-Hill.

Schegloff, E. A. (1972). Sequencing in Conversational Openings. In J. J. Gumperz and D. Hymes (eds.), *Directions in Sociolinguistics: The Ethnography of Communication* (pp. 346–80). New York: Holt, Rinehart, and Winston.

Schegloff, E. A. (1986). The Routine as Achievement. *Human Studies*, 9: 111–51.

Schieffelin, B. B. (1979a). Getting It Together: An Ethnographic Approach to the Study of the Development of Communicative Competence. In E. Ochs and B. B. Schieffelin (eds.), *Developmental Pragmatics* (pp. 73–110). New York: Academic Press.

Schieffelin, B. B. (1979b). How Kaluli Children Learn What to Say, What to Do, and How to Feel: An Ethnographic Study of the Development of Communicative Competence. Unpublished PhD dissertation, Columbia University.

Schieffelin, B. B. (1990). *The Give and Take of Everyday Life: Language Socialization of Kaluli Children*. Cambridge: Cambridge University Press.

Schieffelin, B. B., and Ochs, E. (1986). Language Socialization. In B. J. Siegel, A. R. Beals, and S. A. Tyler (eds.), *Annual Review of Anthropology* (pp. 163–246). Palo Alto: Annual Reviews, Inc.

Schieffelin, B. B., Woolard, K., and Kroskrity, P. (eds.) (1998). *Language Ideologies: Practice and Theory*. New York: Oxford University Press.

Schiffrin, D. (1987). *Discourse Markers*. Cambridge: Cambridge University Press.

Schiffrin, D. (1994). *Approaches to Discourse*. Oxford: Blackwell.

Schlegel, J. (1998). Finding Words, Finding Meanings: Collaborative Learning and Distributed Cognition. In S. M. Hoyle and C. T. Adger (eds.), *Kids Talk: Strategic Language Use in Later Childhood* (pp. 187–204). New York: Oxford University Press.

Scribner, S. (1984). Studying Working Intelligence. In B. Rogoff and J. Lave (eds.), *Everyday Cognition: Its Development in Social Context* (pp. 9–40). Cambridge, MA: Harvard University Press.

Scribner, S., and Cole, M. (1981). *Psychology of Literacy*. Cambridge, MA: Harvard University Press.

Searle, J. R. (1965). What is a Speech Act? In M. Black (ed.), *Philosophy in America* (pp. 221–39). London: George Allen & Unwin.

Searle, J. R. (1969). *Speech Acts: An Essay in the Philosophy of Language*. Cambridge: Cambridge University Press.

Sherzer, J. (1983). *Kuna Ways of Speaking: An Ethnographic Perspective*. Austin: University of Texas Press.

Sherzer, J. (1990). *Verbal Art in San Blas: Kuna Culture through its Discourse*. Cambridge: Cambridge University Press.

Sherzer, J., and Darnell, R. (1972). Outline Guide for the Ethnographic Study of Speech Use. In J. J. Gumperz and D. Hymes (eds.), *Directions in Sociolinguistics: The Ethnography of Communication* (pp. 548–54). New York: Holt, Rinehart, and Winston.

Sidnell, J. (1997). Organizing Social and Spatial Location: Elicitations in Indo-Guyanese Village Talk. *Journal of Linguistic Anthropology*, 7(2): 143–65.

Silverstein, M. (1976). Shifters, Linguistic Categories, and Cultural Description. In K. H. Basso and H. A. Selby (eds.), *Meaning in Anthropology* (pp. 11–56). Albuquerque: University of New Mexico Press.

Silverstein, M. (1977). Cultural Prerequisites to Grammatical Analysis. In M. Saville-Troike (ed.), *Linguistics and Anthropology: Georgetown University Round Table on Languages and Linguistics 1977* (pp. 139–51). Washington, DC: Georgetown University Press.

Silverstein, M. (1979). Language Structure and Linguistic Ideology. In P. R. Clyne, W. F. Hanks, and C. L. Hofbauer (eds.), *The Elements: A Parasession on Linguistic Units and Levels* (pp. 193–247). Chicago, IL: Chicago Linguistic Society.

Silverstein, M. (1981). *The Limits of Awareness. Sociolinguistic Working Paper No. 84*. Austin: Southwest Educational Development Laboratory.

Silverstein, M. (1984). On the Pragmatic "Poetry" of Prose: Parallelism, Repetition, and Cohesive Structure in the Time Course of Dyadic Conversation. In D. Schiffrin (ed.),

Meaning, Form, and Use in Context: Linguistic Applications (pp. 181–99). Washington, DC: Georgetown University Press.

Silverstein, M. (1996a). Encountering Language and Languages of Encounter in North American Ethnohistory. *Journal of Linguistic Anthropology, 6*(2): 126–44.

Silverstein, M. (1996b). Monoglot "Standard" in America: Standardization and Metaphors of Linguistic Hegemony. In D. Brenneis and R. H. S. Macaulay (eds.), *The Matrix of Language: Contemporary Linguistic Anthropology* (pp. 284–306). Boulder, CO: Westview.

Silverstein, M. (1997). The Improvisational Performance of Culture in Realtime Discursive Practice. In R. K. Sawyer (ed.), *Creativity in Performance* (pp. 265–312). Greenwich, CT: Ablex.

Silverstein, M. (2001). The Limits of Awareness. In A. Duranti (ed.), *Linguistic Anthropology: A Reader* (pp. 382–401). Malden, MA: Blackwell.

Silverstein, M., and Urban, G. (eds.) (1996). *Natural Histories of Discourse*. Chicago, IL: University of Chicago Press.

Slobin, D. I. (ed.) (1967). *A Field Manual for Cross-Cultural Study of the Acquisition of Communicative Competence*. Berkeley: Language Behavior Research Laboratory, University of California.

Slobin, D. I. (1973). Cognitive Prerequisites for the Development of Grammar. In C. A. Ferguson and D. I. Slobin (eds.), *Studies of Child Language Development* (pp. 175–208). New York: Holt, Rinehart, and Winston.

Slobin, D. I. (1982). Universal and Particular in the Acquisition of Language. In W. Deutsch (ed.), *Language Acquisition: The State of the Art* (pp. 128–72). Cambridge: Cambridge University Press.

Slobin, D. I. (1985a). The Crosslinguistic Evidence for the Language-making Capacity. In D. I. Slobin (ed.), *The Crosslinguistic Study of Language Acquisition*, Vol. 2: *Theoretical Issues* (pp. 1157–256). Hillsdale, NJ: Lawrence Erlbaum.

Slobin, D. I. (ed.) (1985b). *The Crosslinguistic Study of Language Acquisition* (Vol. 1). Hillsdale, NJ: Lawrence Erlbaum.

Spears, A. K. (ed.) (1999). *Race and Ideology: Language, Symbolism, and Popular Culture*. Detroit: Wayne State University Press.

Spitulnik, D. (1998a). Anthropology and Mass Media. *Annual Review of Anthropology, 22*: 293–315.

Spitulnik, D. (1998b). The Language of the City: Town Bemba as Urban Hybridity. *Journal of Linguistic Anthropology, 8*(1): 30–59.

Spitulnik, D. (1999). Mediated Modernities: Encounters with the Electronic in Zambia. *Visual Anthropology Review, 14*(2): 63–84.

Stocking, G. W. (1974). The Boas Plan for the Study of American Indian Languages. In D. Hymes (ed.), *Studies in the History of Linguistics: Traditions and Paradigms* (pp. 454–83). Bloomington: Indiana University Press.

Streeck, J. (1980). Speech Acts in Interaction: A Critique of Searle. *Discourse Processes, 3*: 133–54.

Streeck, J. (1994). Gesture as Communication II: The Audience as Co-author. *Research on Language and Social Interaction, 27*: 239–67.

Streeck, J., and Hartge, U. (1992). Previews: Gestures at the Transition Place. In P. Auer and A. di Luzio (eds.), *Contextualization of Language* (pp. 135–58). Amsterdam: John Benjamins.

Street, B. V. (1984). *Literacy in Theory and Practice*. Cambridge: Cambridge University Press.

Street, B. V. (ed.) (1993). *Cross-Cultural Approaches to Literacy*. Cambridge: Cambridge University Press.

Street, B. V., and Besnier, N. (1994). Aspects of Literacy. In T. Ingold (ed.), *Companion Encyclopedia of Anthropology: Humanity, Culture, and Social Life* (pp. 527–62). London: Routledge.

Stubbs, M. (1983). *Discourse Analysis*. Oxford: Blackwell.

Swanton, J. R. (1900). Morphology of the Chinook Verb. *American Anthropologist*, 2(2): 199–237.

Tannen, D. (ed.) (1982). *Spoken and Written Language: Exploring Orality and Literacy.* Norwood, NJ: Ablex.

Tannen, D. (1989). *Talking Voices: Repetition, Dialogue, and Imagery in Conversational Discourse*. Cambridge: Cambridge University Press.

Tannen, D. (1990). *You Just Don't Understand: Women and Men in Conversation*. New York: William Morrow and Co.

Tedlock, D. (1983). *The Spoken Word and the Work of Interpretation*. Philadelphia: University of Pennsylvania Press.

Teeter, K. V. (1964). "Anthropological Linguistics" and Linguistic Anthropology. *American Anthropologist, 66*: 878–9.

Trudgill, P. (1986). *Dialects in Contact*. Oxford: Blackwell.

Tyler, S. A. (1972). Context and Alternation in Koya Kinship Terminology. In J. J. Gumperz and D. Hymes (eds.), *Directions in Sociolinguistics: The Ethnography of Communication* (pp. 251–69). New York: Holt, Rinehart, and Winston.

Urciuoli, B. (1991). *Exposing Prejudice: Puerto Rican Experiences of Language, Race, and Class*. Boulder, CO: Westview.

Voegelin, C. F. (1952). The Boas Plan for the Presentation of American Indian Languages. *Proceedings of the American Philosophical Society, 96*: 439–51.

Voegelin, C. F., and Harris, Z. S. (1945). Linguistics in Ethnology. *Southwestern Journal of Anthropology, 1*: 455–65.

Voegelin, C. F., and Harris, Z. S. (1952). Training in Anthropological Linguistics. *American Anthropologist, 54*: 322–7.

Vološinov, V. N. (1973). *Marxism and the Philosophy of Language*. Translated by Ladislav Matejka and I. R. Titunik. New York: Seminar Press. (First published 1929 and 1930.)

von Humboldt, W. ([1836] 1971). *Linguistic Variability and Intellectual Development*. Translated by George C. Buck and Frithjof A. Raven. Philadelphia: University of Pennsylvania Press.

Wardhaugh, R. (1986). *An Introduction to Sociolinguistics*. Oxford: Blackwell.

West, C., and Zimmerman, D. H. (1983). Small Insults: A Study of Interruptions in Cross-Sex Conversation between Unacquainted Persons. In B. Thorne, C. Kramarae, and N. Henley (eds.), *Language, Gender and Society* (pp. 102–17). Rowley, MA: Newbury House.

Whorf, B. L. (1938). Some Verbal Categories of Hopi. *Language, 14*: 275–86.

Whorf, B. L. (1941). The Relation of Habitual Thought and Behavior in Language. In L. Spier, A. I. Hallowell, and S. S. Newman (eds.), *Language, Culture, and Personality: Essays in Honor of Edward Sapir* (pp. 75–93). Menasha, WI: Sapir Memorial Publication.

Whorf, B. L. (1956a). Grammatical Categories. In J. B. Carroll (ed.), *Language, Thought, and Reality: Selected Writings of Benjamin Lee Whorf* (pp. 87–101). Cambridge, MA: MIT Press.

Whorf, B. L. (1956b). Linguistics as an Exact Science. In J. B. Carroll (ed.), *Language, Thought, and Reality: Selected Writings of Benjamin Lee Whorf* (pp. 220–32). Cambridge, MA: MIT Press.

Whorf, B. L. (1956c). The Relation of Habitual Thought and Behavior to Language. In J. B. Carroll (ed.), *Language, Thought, and Reality: Selected Writings of Benjamin Lee Whorf* (pp. 134–59). Cambridge, MA: MIT Press.

Wilce, J. M. (1998). *Eloquence in Trouble: The Poetics and Politics of Complaint in Rural Bangladesh*. New York: Oxford University Press.

Williams, R. (1977). *Marxism and Literature*. Oxford: Oxford University Press.

Wodak, R., and Reisigl, M. (1999). Discourse and Racism: European Perspectives. *Annual Review of Anthropology, 28*: 175–99.

Woolard, K. A. (1985). Language Variation and Cultural Hegemony: Toward an Integration of Sociolinguistic and Social Theory. *American Ethnologist, 12*: 738–48.

Woolard, K. A. (1989). *Double Talk: Bilingualism and the Politics of Ethnicity in Catalonia*. Stanford, CA: Stanford University Press.

Woolard, K. A. (1998). Simultaneity and Bivalency as Strategies in Bilingualism. *Journal of Linguistic Anthropology, 8*(1): 3–29.

Woolard, K. A. and Schieffelin, B. B. (1994). Language Ideology. *Annual Review of Anthropology, 23*: 55–82.

Yankah, K. (1995). *Speaking for the Chief: Okeyame and the Politics of Akan Royal Oratory*. Bloomington: Indiana University Press.

Zack, N., Shrage, L., and Sartwell, C. (eds.) (1998). *Race, Class, Gender, and Sexuality: The Big Questions*. Malden, MA: Blackwell.

Zentella, A. C. (1997). *Growing Up Bilingual: Puerto Rican Children in New York*. Oxford: Blackwell.

Part I

Ideal and Real Speech Communities

Introduction

In the 1950s the pioneer work of John Gumperz and Charles Ferguson on linguistic diversity in South Asia shifted the focus in linguistic anthropology from thinking about "language" as a unitary and coherent system to a set of "varieties" that share a sufficient number of phonological or grammatical features, which they considered to be either mutually intelligible or to be "connected by a series of mutually intelligible varieties." Once variation not only among individuals but also among groups within the same community came to be accepted as quite common, there arose the need to think about varieties not simply in terms of different grammatical systems but also in terms of their use in everyday life. It was in this context that the term "speech community" was introduced. As demonstrated in the first chapter by John Gumperz, ever since the 1960s linguistic anthropologists have assumed that, for speakers to be able to acquire and use particular linguistic skills, they must be members of a community within which those skills are practiced and transmitted. Furthermore, as argued by Marcyliena Morgan in Chapter 2, for a truly anthropological understanding of a speech community and its members' communicative competence, we need to go beyond the description of language use and include an analysis of how speakers value the different language varieties in their speech repertoire. The notion of speech community is furthered expanded and refined by recent work on media-generated discourse. An example of this new research trend is provided in Chapter 3, where Debra Spitulnik reveals some of the subtle ways in which media discourse in Zambia is adopted and transformed in everyday life. However, as shown in Chapter 4 by Benjamin Bailey, we cannot assume that those who communicate with one another on a regular basis should be considered members of the same speech community or share the exact same strategies or interpretive principles. A detailed analysis of service encounters between members of two groups who each accuses the other of behaving with a lack of "respect" allows us to examine the role of divergent verbal strategies in the production of conflict. Finally, in Chapter 5, Constant Leung, Roxy Harris, and Ben Rampton provide a critical examination of the ways in which schools evaluate and categorize second-language learners which shows that the very notion of "native speaker" is loaded with assumptions that are not adequate for the realities of contemporary multicultural and multilingual communities.

SUGGESTIONS FOR FURTHER READING

For a general introduction to contemporary theories, concepts, and issues in the study of language: D. Crystal (1987), *The Cambridge Encyclopedia of Language*, Cambridge: Cambridge University Press (an excellent resource for non-specialists); for quick reference on anthropological perspectives on language matters, see A. Duranti (ed.) (2001), *Key Terms in Language and Culture*, Malden: MA: Blackwell (a collection of 75 entries on linguistic concepts, issues, and theories, written by leading experts, with recommended readings for each entry).

A good synthesis of Gumperz's work on multilingualism is: J. J. Gumperz (1982), *Discourse Strategies*, Cambridge: Cambridge University Press. See also J. J Gumperz and J. Cook-Gumperz (eds.) (1982), *Language and Social Identity*, Cambridge: Cambridge University Press. An important book that inspired some of the more recent work on multilingual communities is B. Anderson (1991), *Imagined Communities: Reflections on the Origin and Spread of Nationalism*, rev. edn., London and New York: Verso. For a review of speech communities and language varieties within the USA, see E. Finegan and J. R. Rickford (eds.) (2004), *Language in the USA: Themes for the Twenty-first Century*, Cambridge: Cambridge University Press.

Important methodological considerations on how to conduct interviews that take into consideration the points made in the chapters in Part I can be found in C. L. Briggs (1986), *Learning How to Ask: A Sociolinguistic Appraisal of the Role of the Interview in Social Science Research*, Cambridge: Cambridge University Press.

A useful review of the work on bilingual communities, code switching, and the communicative competence of bilingual children is S. Romaine (1995), *Bilingualism* (2nd edn.), Oxford: Blackwell; see also Josiane F. Hamers and Michel H. A. Blanc (2000), *Bilinguality and Bilingualism*, Cambridge: Cambridge University Press.

The literature on the African American speech community is vast, starting with William Labov's (1972) ground-breaking *Language in the Inner City: Studies in the Black English Vernacular*, Philadelphia: University of Pennsylvania Press, and continuing with numerous important contributions including: John Baugh (1983), *Black Street Speech: Its History, Structure, and Survival*, Austin: University of Texas Press; John R. Rickford (1999), *African American Vernacular English*, Malden, MA: Blackwell; Geneva Smitherman (2000), *Talkin That Talk: Language, Culture and Education in African America*, New York: Routledge; Sonja L. Lanehart (2001), *Sociocultural and Historical Contexts of African American English*, Amsterdam: Benjamins; Marcyliena Morgan (2002), *Language, Discourse and Power in African American Culture*, Cambridge: Cambridge University Press; Lisa J. Green (2002), *African American English: A Linguistic Introduction*, Cambridge: Cambridge University Press; Walt Wolfram and Erik R. Thomas (2002), *The Development of*

African American English, Oxford: Blackwell; Samy H. Alim (2004), *You Know My Steez: An Ethnographic and Sociolinguistic Study of Styleshifting in Black American Speech Community*, Durham, NC: American Dialectical Society and Duke University Press; L. Jacobs-Huey (2006), *From the Kitchen to the Parlor: Language and Becoming in African American Women's Hair*, Oxford: Oxford University Press.

Contributions in book form to the study of media discourse tend to come from outside of anthropology, from such fields as ethnomethodology, conversation analysis, sociolinguistics, and discourse analysis: A. Bell (1991), *The Language of News Media*, Cambridge, MA: Blackwell; N. Fairclough (1995), *Media Discourse*, London: Edward Arnold Fair; A. Bell and P. Garrett (eds.) (1998), *Approaches to Media Discourse*, Oxford: Blackwell; P. L. Jalbert (ed.) (1999), *Media Studies: Ethnomethodological Approaches*, Lanham, NY: University Press of America; S. Clayman and J. Heritage (2002), *The News Interview: Journalists and Public Figures on the Air*, Cambridge: Cambridge University Press; M. Macdonald (2003), *Exploring Media Discourse*, London: Arnold; A. Tolson (2006), *Media Talk: Spoken Discourse on TV and Radio*, Edinburgh: Edinburgh University Press; A. O'Keefe (2006), *Investigating Media Discourse*, London: Routledge; S. Johnson and A. Ensslin (eds.) (2007), *Language in the Media: Representations, Identities, Ideologies*, London: Continuum.

On the topic of interethnic encounters, race, ethnicity, and language, in addition to the books listed in other parts of this collection (e.g., on African American English), see A. K. Spears (ed.) (1999), *Race and Ideology: Language, Symbolism, and Popular Culture*, Detroit: Wayne State University Press; R. Scollon and S. W. Scollon (2001), *Intercultural Communication: A Discourse Approach*, Malden, MA: Blackwell; Benjamin H. Bailey (2002), *Language, Race, and Negotiation of Identity: A Study of Dominican Americans*, New York: LFB Scholarly Publishing LLC; S. F. Kiesling and C. B. Paulston (eds.) (2004), *Intercultural Discourse and Communication: The Essential Readings*, Malden, MA: Blackwell.

A number of themes in the chapter by Leung, Harris and Rampton are developed further in R. Harris (2006), *New Ethnicities and Language Use*, Basingstoke and New York: Palgrave; Rampton's work on what he calls "crossing" has revolutionized our views of native speakers and second-language learners; see B. Rampton (1995), *Crossing: Language and Ethnicity among Adolescents*, London: Longman; for a different perspective on linguistic innovation and loss, see Nancy Dorian (ed.) (1989), *Investigating Obsolescence: Studies in Language Contraction and Death*, Cambridge: Cambridge University Press.

The issue of minority languages and speech communities is discussed in a number of books, including S. May (2001), *Language and Minority Rights: Ethnicity, Nationalism and the Politics of Language*, London: Longman; C. L. Schmid (2001), *The Politics of Language: Conflict, Identity and Cultural Pluralism in Comparative Perspective*, Oxford: Oxford University Press.

1

The Speech Community

John J. Gumperz

Although not all communication is linguistic, language is by far the most powerful and versatile medium of communication; all known human groups possess language. Unlike other sign systems, the verbal system can, through the minute refinement of its grammatical and semantic structure, be made to refer to a wide variety of objects and concepts. At the same time, verbal interaction is a social process in which utterances are selected in accordance with socially recognized norms and expectations. It follows that linguistic phenomena are analyzable both within the context of language itself and within the broader context of social behavior. In the formal analysis of language the object of attention is a particular body of linguistic data abstracted from the settings in which it occurs and studied primarily from the point of view of its referential function. In analyzing linguistic phenomena within a socially defined universe, however, the study is of language usage as it reflects more general behavior norms. This universe is the speech community: any human aggregate characterized by regular and frequent interaction by means of a shared body of verbal signs and set off from similar aggregates by significant differences in language usage.

Most groups of any permanence, be they small bands bounded by face-to-face contact, modern nations divisible into smaller subregions, or even occupational associations or neighborhood gangs, may be treated as speech communities, provided they show linguistic peculiarities that warrant special study. The verbal behavior of such groups always constitutes a system. It must be based on finite sets of grammatical rules that underlie the production of well-formed sentences, or else messages will not be intelligible. The description of such rules is a precondition for the study of all types of linguistic phenomena. But it is only the starting point in the sociolinguistic analysis of language behavior.

Grammatical rules define the bounds of the linguistically acceptable. For example, they enable us to identify "How do you do?" "How are you?" and "Hi" as proper American English sentences and to reject others like "How do you?" and "How you are?" Yet speech is not constrained by grammatical rules alone. An individual's choice from among permissible alternates in a particular speech event may reveal his family background and his social intent, may identify him as a Southerner, a Northerner, an urbanite, a rustic, a member of

For permission to publish copyright material in this book, grateful acknowledgment is made to: J. J. Gumperz (1968), "The Speech Community," *International Encyclopedia of the Social Sciences*. New York: Macmillan, pp. 381–6.

the educated or uneducated classes, and may even indicate whether he wishes to appear friendly or distant, familiar or deferential, superior or inferior.

Just as intelligibility presupposes underlying grammatical rules, the communication of social information presupposes the existence of regular relationships between language usage and social structure. Before we can judge a speaker's social intent, we must know something about the norms defining the appropriateness of linguistically acceptable alternates for particular types of speakers; these norms vary among subgroups and among social settings. Wherever the relationships between language choice and rules of social appropriateness can be formalized, they allow us to group relevant linguistic forms into distinct dialects, styles, and occupational or other special parlances. The sociolinguistic study of speech communities deals with the linguistic similarities and differences among these speech varieties.

In linguistically homogeneous societies the verbal markers of social distinctions tend to be confined to structurally marginal features of phonology, syntax, and lexicon. Elsewhere they may include both standard literary languages, and grammatically divergent local dialects. In many multilingual societies the choice of one language over another has the same signification as the selection among lexical alternates in linguistically homogeneous societies. In such cases, two or more grammars may be required to cover the entire scope of linguistically acceptable expressions that serve to convey social meanings.

Regardless of the linguistic differences among them, the speech varieties employed within a speech community form a system because they are related to a shared set of social norms. Hence, they can be classified according to their usage, their origins, and the relationship between speech and social action that they reflect. They become indices of social patterns of interaction in the speech community.

Historical Orientation in Early Studies

Systematic linguistic field work began in the middle of the nineteenth century. Prior to 1940 the best-known studies were concerned with dialects, special parlances, national languages, and linguistic acculturation and diffusion.

Dialectology

Among the first students of speech communities were the dialectologists, who charted the distribution of colloquial speech forms in societies dominated by German, French, English, Polish, and other major standard literary tongues. Mapping relevant features of pronunciation, grammar, and lexicon in the form of *isoglosses*, they traced in detail the range and spread of historically documented changes in language habits. Isoglosses were grouped into bundles of two or more and then mapped; from the geographical shape of such isogloss bundles, it was possible to distinguish the *focal areas*, centers from which innovations radiate into the surrounding regions; *relic zones*, districts where forms previously known only from old texts were still current; and *transition zones*, areas of internal diversity marked by the coexistence of linguistic forms identified with competing centers of innovation.

Analysis along these lines clearly established the importance of social factors in language change. The distribution of rural speech patterns was found to be directly related to such factors as political boundaries during the preceding centuries, traditional market networks, the spread of important religious movements, etc. In this fashion dialectology became an important source of evidence for social history.

Special parlances, classical languages

Other scholars dealt with the languages of occupationally specialized minority groups, craft jargons, secret argots, and the like. In some cases, such as the Romany of the gypsies and the Yiddish of Jews, these parlances derive from foreign importations which survive as linguistic islands surrounded by other tongues. Their speakers tend to be bilinguals, using their own idiom for in-group communication and the majority language for interaction with outsiders.

Linguistic distinctness may also result from seemingly intentional processes of distortion. One very common form of secret language, found in a variety of tribal and complex societies, achieves unintelligibility by a process of verbal play with majority speech, in which phonetic or grammatical elements are systematically reordered. The pig Latin of English-speaking schoolchildren, in which initial consonants are transferred to the end of the word and followed by "-ay," is a relatively simple example of this process. Thieves' argots, the slang of youth gangs, and the jargon of traveling performers and other occupational groups obtain similar results by assigning special meanings to common nouns, verbs, and adjectives.

Despite their similarities, the classical administrative and liturgical languages – such as the Latin of medieval Europe, the Sanskrit of south Asia, and the Arabic of the Near East – are not ordinarily grouped with special parlances because of the prestige of the cultural traditions associated with them. They are quite distinct from and often unrelated to popular speech, and the elaborate ritual and etiquette that surround their use can be learned only through many years of special training. Instruction is available only through private tutors and is limited to a privileged few who command the necessary social status or financial resources. As a result, knowledge of these languages in the traditional societies where they are used is limited to relatively small elites, who tend to maintain control of their linguistic skills in somewhat the same way that craft guilds strive for exclusive control of their craft skills.

The standard literary languages of modern nation-states, on the other hand, tend to be representative of majority speech. As a rule they originated in rising urban centers, as a result of the free interaction of speakers of a variety of local dialects, became identified with new urban elites, and in time replaced older administrative languages. Codification of spelling and grammar by means of dictionaries and dissemination of this information through public school systems are characteristic of standard-language societies. Use of mass media and the prestige of their speakers tend to carry idioms far from their sources; such idioms eventually replace many pre-existing local dialects and special parlances.

Linguistic acculturation, language shift

Wherever two or more speech communities maintain prolonged contact within a broad field of communication, there are crosscurrents of diffusion. The result is the formation of a *Sprachbund*, comprising a group of varieties which coexist in social space as dialects, distinct neighboring languages, or special parlances. Persistent borrowing over long periods creates within such groups similarities in linguistic structure, which tend to obscure pre-existing genetic distinctions; a commonly cited example is the south Asian subcontinent, where speakers of Indo-Aryan, Dravidian, and Munda languages all show significant overlap in their linguistic habits.

It appears that single nouns, verbs, and adjectives are most readily diffused, often in response to a variety of technological innovations and cultural or religious trends. Pronunciation and word order are also frequently affected. The level of phonological and grammatical pattern (i.e., the structural core of a language), however, is more resistant to change, and loanwords tend to be adapted to the patterns of the recipient language. But linguistic barriers to diffusion are never absolute, and in situations of extensive bilingualism – two or more languages being regularly used in the course of the daily routine – even the grammatical cores may be affected.

Cross-cultural influence reaches a maximum in the cases of pidgins and creoles, idioms combining elements of several distinct languages. These hybrids typically arise in colonial societies or in large trading centers where laborers torn out of their native language environments are forced to work in close cooperation with speakers of different tongues. Cross-cultural influence may also give rise to language shift, the abandonment of one native tongue in favor of another. This phenomenon most frequently occurs when two groups merge, as in tribal absorption, or when minority groups take on the culture of the surrounding majority.

Although the bulk of the research on speech communities that was conducted prior to 1940 is historically oriented, students of speech communities differ markedly from their colleagues who concentrate upon textual analysis. The latter tend to treat languages as independent wholes that branch off from uniform protolanguages in accordance with regular sound laws. The former, on the other hand, regard themselves primarily as students of behavior, interested in linguistic phenomena for their broader sociohistorical significance. By relating dialect boundaries to settlement history, to political and administrative boundaries, and to culture areas and by charting the itineraries of loanwords in relation to technical innovations or cultural movements, they established the primacy of social factors in language change, disproving earlier theories of environmental or biological determinism.

The study of language usage in social communities, furthermore, revealed little of the uniformity ordinarily ascribed to protolanguages and their descendants; many exceptions to the regularity of sound laws were found wherever speakers of genetically related languages were in regular contact. This led students of speech communities to challenge the "family-tree theory," associated with the neogrammarians of nineteenth-century Europe, who were concerned primarily with the genetic reconstruction of language history. Instead, they favored a theory of diffusion which postulates the spread of linguistic change in intersecting "waves" that emanate from different centers of innovation with an intensity proportionate to the prestige of their human carriers.

Thus, while geneticists regarded modern language distribution as the result of the segmentation of older entities into newer and smaller subgroups, diffusionists viewed the speech community as a dynamic field of action where phonetic change, borrowing, language mixture, and language shift all occur because of social forces, and where genetic origin is secondary to these forces. In recent years linguists have begun to see the two theories as complementary. The assumption of uniformity among protolanguages is regarded as an abstraction necessary to explain existing regularities of sound change and is considered extremely useful for the elucidation of long-term prehistoric relationships, especially since conflicting short-term diffusion currents tend to cancel each other. Speech-community studies, on the other hand, appear better adapted to the explanation of relatively recent changes.

Language Behavior and Social Communication

The shift of emphasis from historical to synchronic problems during the last three decades has brought about some fundamental changes in our theories of language, resulting in the creation of a body of entirely new analytical techniques. Viewed in the light of these fresh insights, the earlier speech-community studies are subject to serious criticism on grounds of both linguistic and sociological methodology. For some time, therefore, linguists oriented toward formal analysis showed very little interest. More recent structural studies, however, show that this criticism does not affect the basic concept of the speech community as a field of action where the distribution of linguistic variants is a reflection of social facts. The relationship between such variants when they are classified in terms of usage rather than of their purely linguistic characteristics can be examined along two dimensions: the *dialectal* and the *superposed*.

Dialectal relationships are those in which differences set off the vernaculars of local groups (for example, the language of home and family) from those of other groups within the same, broader culture. Since this classification refers to usage rather than to inherent linguistic traits, relationships between minority languages and majority speech (e.g., between Welsh and English in Britain or French and English in Canada) and between distinct languages found in zones of intensive intertribal contact (e.g., in modern Africa) can also be considered dialectal, because they show characteristics similar to the relationship existing between dialects of the same language.

Whereas dialect variation relates to distinctions in geographical origin and social background, superposed variation refers to distinctions between different types of activities carried on within the same group. The special parlances described above form a linguistic extreme, but similar distinctions in usage are found in all speech communities. The language of formal speechmaking, religious ritual, or technical discussion, for example, is never the same as that employed in informal talk among friends, because each is a style fulfilling particular communicative needs. To some extent the linguistic markers of such activities are directly related to their different technical requirements. Scientific discussion, for instance, requires precisely defined terms and strict limitation on their usage. But in other cases, as in greetings, forms of address, or choosing between "isn't" and "ain't," the primary determinant is the social relationship between speakers rather than communicative necessity. Language choice in these cases is limited by social barriers; the existence of such barriers lends significance to the sociolinguistic study of superposed variation.

This distinction between dialectal and superposed varieties obviates the usual linguistic distinction between geographically and socially distributed varieties, since the evidence indicates that actual residence patterns are less important as determinants of distribution than social interaction patterns and usage. Thus, there seems to be little need to draw conceptual distinctions upon this basis.

Descriptions of dialectal and superposed variation relate primarily to social groups. Not all individuals within a speech community have equal control of the entire set of superposed variants current there. Control of communicative resources varies sharply with the individual's position within the social system. The more narrowly confined his sphere of activities, the more homogeneous the social environment within which he interacts, and the less his need for verbal facility. Thus, housewives, farmers, and laborers, who rarely meet outsiders, often make do with only a narrow range of speech styles, while actors, public speakers, and businessmen command the greatest range of styles. The fact that such individual distinctions are found in multilingual as well as in linguistically homogeneous societies suggests that the common assertion which identifies bilingualism with poor scores in intelligence testing is in urgent need of re-examination, based, as it is, primarily on work with underprivileged groups. Recent work, in fact, indicates that the failure of some self-contained groups to inculcate facility in verbal manipulation is a major factor in failures in their children's performances in public school systems.

Attitudes to language choice

Social norms of language choice vary from situation to situation and from community to community. Regularities in attitudes to particular speech varieties, however, recur in a number of societies and deserve special comment here. Thieves' argots, gang jargons, and the like serve typically as group boundary maintaining mechanisms, whose linguistic characteristics are the result of informal group consensus and are subject to continual change in response to changing attitudes. Individuals are accepted as members of the group to the extent that their usage conforms to the practices of the day. Similar attitudes of exclusiveness prevail in the case of many tribal languages spoken in areas of culture contact where other superposed idioms serve as media of public communication. The tribal language here is somewhat akin to a secret ritual, in that it is private knowledge to be kept from outsiders, an attitude which often makes it difficult for casual investigators to collect reliable information about language distribution in such areas.

Because of the elaborate linguistic etiquette and stylistic conventions that surround them, classical, liturgical, and administrative languages function somewhat like secret languages. Mastery of the conventions may be more important in gaining social success than substantive knowledge of the information dispensed through these languages. But unlike the varieties mentioned above, norms of appropriateness are explicit in classical languages; this permits them to remain unchanged over many generations.

In contrast, the attitude to pidgins, trade languages, and similar intergroup media of communication tends to be one of toleration.

Here little attention is paid to linguistic markers of social appropriateness. It is the function of such languages to facilitate contact between groups without constituting their respective social cohesiveness; and, as a result, communication in these languages tends to be severely restricted to specific topics or types of interaction. They do not, as a rule, serve as vehicles for personal friendships.

We speak of *language loyalty* when a literary variety acquires prestige as a symbol of a particular nationality group or social movement. Language loyalty tends to unite diverse local groups and social classes, whose members may continue to speak their own vernaculars within the family circle. The literary idiom serves for reading and for public interaction and embodies the cultural tradition of a nation or a sector thereof. Individuals choose to employ it as a symbol of their allegiance to a broader set of political ideals than that embodied in the family or kin group.

Language loyalty may become a political issue in a modernizing society when hitherto socially isolated minority groups become mobilized. Their demands for closer participation in political affairs are often accompanied by demands for language reform or for the rewriting of the older, official code in their own literary idiom. Such demands often represent political and socioeconomic threats to the established elite, which may control the distribution of administrative positions through examination systems based upon the official code. The replacement of an older official code by another literary idiom in modernizing societies may thus represent the displacement of an established elite by a rising group.

The situation becomes still more complex when socioeconomic competition between several minority groups gives rise to several competing new literary standards, as in many parts of Asia and Africa, where language conflicts have led to civil disturbances and political instability. Although demands for language reform are usually verbalized in terms of communicative needs, it is interesting to observe that such demands do not necessarily reflect important linguistic differences between the idioms in question. Hindi and Urdu, the competing literary standards of north India, or Serbian and Croatian, in Yugoslavia, are grammatically almost identical. They differ in their writing systems, in their lexicons, and in minor aspects of syntax. Nevertheless, their proponents treat them as separate languages. The conflict in language loyalty may even affect mutual intelligibility, as when speakers' claims that they do not understand each other reflect primarily social attitudes rather than linguistic fact. In other cases serious linguistic differences may be disregarded when minority speakers pay language loyalty to a standard markedly different from their own vernacular. In many parts of Alsace-Lorraine, for example, speakers of German dialects seem to disregard linguistic fact and pay language loyalty to French rather than to German.

Varietal distribution

Superposed and dialectal varieties rarely coincide in their geographical extent. We find the greatest amount of linguistic diversity at the level of local, tribal, peasant, or lower-class urban populations. Tribal areas typically constitute a patchwork of distinct languages, while local speech distribution in many modern nations takes the form of a dialect chain in which the speech of each locality is similar to that of adjoining settlements and in which speech differences increase in proportion to geographical distance. Variety at the local level is bridged by the considerably broader spread of superposed varieties, serving as media of supralocal communication. The Latin of medieval Europe and the Arabic of the Near East form extreme examples of supralocal spread. Uniformity at the superposed level in their case, however, is achieved at the expense of large gaps in internal communication channels. Standard languages tend to be somewhat more restricted in geographical spread than classical languages, because of their relationship to local dialects. In contrast to a society in which classical languages are used as superposed varieties, however, a standard-language society possesses better developed channels of internal communication, partly because of its greater linguistic homogeneity and partly because of the internal language loyalty that it evokes.

In fact, wherever standard languages are well-established they act as the ultimate referent that determines the association of a given local dialect with one language or another. This may result in the anomalous situation in which two linguistically similar dialects spoken on different sides of a political boundary are regarded as belonging to different languages, not because of any inherent linguistic differences but because their speakers pay language loyalty to different standards. Language boundaries in such cases are defined partly by social and partly by linguistic criteria.

Verbal repertoires

The totality of dialectal and superposed variants regularly employed within a community make up the *verbal repertoire* of that community. Whereas the bounds of a language, as this term is ordinarily understood, may or may not coincide with that of a social group, verbal repertoires are always specific to particular populations. As an analytical concept the verbal repertoire allows us to establish direct relationships between its constituents and the socioeconomic complexity of the community.

We measure this relationship in terms of two concepts: *linguistic range* and *degree of compartmentalization*. Linguistic range refers to internal language distance between constituent varieties, that is, the total amount of purely linguistic differentiation that exists in a community, thus distinguishing among multilingual, multidialectal, and homogeneous communities. Compartmentalization refers to the sharpness with which varieties are set off from each other, either along the superposed or the dialectal dimension. We speak of compartmentalized repertoires, therefore, when several languages are spoken without their mixing, when dialects are set off from each other by sharp isogloss bundles, or when special parlances are sharply distinct from other forms of speech. We speak of fluid repertoires, on the other hand, when transitions between adjoining vernaculars are gradual or when one speech style merges into another in such a way that it is difficult to draw clear borderlines.

Initially, the linguistic range of a repertoire is a function of the languages and special parlances employed before contact. But given a certain period of contact, linguistic range becomes dependent upon the amount of internal interaction. The greater the frequency of internal interaction, the greater the tendency for innovations arising in one part of the speech community to diffuse throughout it. Thus, where the flow of communication is dominated by a single all-important center – for example, as Paris dominates central France – linguistic range is relatively small. Political fragmentation, on the other hand, is associated with diversity of languages or of dialects, as in southern Germany, long dominated by many small, semi-independent principalities.

Over-all frequency in interaction is not, however, the only determinant of uniformity. In highly stratified societies speakers of minority languages or dialects typically live side by side, trading, exchanging services, and often maintaining regular social contact as employer and employee or master and servant. Yet despite this contact, they tend to preserve their own languages, suggesting the existence of social norms that set limits to freedom of intercommunication. Compartmentalization reflects such social norms. The exact nature of these sociolinguistic barriers is not yet clearly understood, although some recent literature suggests new avenues for investigation.

We find, for example, that separate languages maintain themselves most readily in closed tribal systems, in which kinship dominates all activities. Linguistically distinct special parlances, on the other hand, appear most fully developed in highly stratified societies, where the division of labor is maintained by rigidly defined barriers of ascribed status. When social change causes the breakdown of traditional social structures and the formation of new ties, as in urbanization and colonialization, linguistic barriers between varieties also break down. Rapidly changing societies typically show either gradual transition between speech styles or, if the community is bilingual, a range of intermediate varieties bridging the transitions between extremes.

REFERENCES

Barth, Frederik (1964). Ethnic Processes on the Pathan-Baluch Boundary. Pages 13–20 in *Indo-Iranica: Mélanges présentés à Georg Morgenstierne, à l'occasion de son soixante-dixième anniversaire*. Wiesbaden (Germany): Harrassowitz.

Bernstein, Basil ([1958] 1961). Social Class and Linguistic Development: A Theory of Social Learning. Pages 288–314 in A. H. Halsey et al. (eds.), *Education, Economy, and Society*. New York: Free Press; first published in Volume 9 of the *British Journal of Sociology*.

Bloomfield, Leonard ([1933] 1951). *Language*. Rev. edn. New York: Holt.

Brown, Roger W. (1965). *Social Psychology*. New York: Free Press.

Gumperz, John J., and Hymes, Dell H. (eds.) (1964). The Ethnography of Communication. *American Anthropologist* New Series 66, no. 6, part 2.

Halliday, Michael A. K., McIntosh, Angus, and Strevens, Peter ([1964] 1965). *The Linguistic Sciences and Language Teaching*. Bloomington: Indiana University Press.

Haugen, Einar I. (1956). *Bilingualism in the Americas: A Bibliography and Research Guide*. University, Ala.: American Dialect Society.

Haugen, Einar I. (1966). *Language Conflict and Language Planning*. Cambridge, Mass.: Harvard University Press.

Hertzler, Joyce O. (1965). *A Sociology of Language*. New York: Random House.

Hymes, Dell H. (ed.) (1964). *Language in Culture and Society: A Reader in Linguistics and Anthropology*. New York: Harper.

Jespersen, Otto ([1925] 1964). *Mankind, Nation and the Individual, From a Linguistic Point of View*. Bloomington: Indiana University Press; first published as *Menneskehed, nasjon og individ i sproget*.

Kurath, Hans (ed.) (1939–1943). *Linguistic Atlas of New England*, 3 vols. and a handbook. Providence, R.I.: Brown University Press.

Labov, William (1966). *The Social Stratification of English in New York City*. Arlington: Center for Applied Linguistics.

Passin, Herbert (1963). Writer and Journalist in the Transitional Society. Pages 82–123 in Conference on Communication and Political Development, Dobbs Ferry, NY, 1961, *Communications and Political Development*. Edited by Lucian W. Pye. Princeton University Press; contains a discussion of the relationship of national languages to political development.

Weinreich, Uriel (1953). *Languages in Contact: Findings and Problems*. New York: Linguistic Circle of New York.

STUDY QUESTIONS

1 How does Gumperz define the speech community?
2 Which speech community or communities do you belong to? How do you know (i.e., what are the criteria you used in your assessment)?
3 Gumperz distinguishes between dialectal and superposed variation. Provide a concise definition and examples of each based on your own life experience of linguistic variation.
4 How is language loyalty defined and discussed in the article? Is it relevant to your own life (at home, in college, in the workplace)?
5 What constitutes the verbal repertoire of a speech community? What features or dimensions can be used to describe it? Describe your own verbal repertoire.

2

The African-American Speech Community: Reality and Sociolinguists[1]

Marcyliena Morgan

One of the more persistent challenges in creole language studies and sociolinguistics in general is to determine the extent and ways in which information or linguistic facts gathered from a particular speech community can, in some way, benefit that community. This challenge is directly related to what Labov (1982) identifies as the two questions most frequently put to linguists by the public: "What is linguistics about?" and "What is it good for?" How linguists address these questions is often more important to the speech community under study than the linguistic information that has been assembled. For the most part, sociolinguistic training focuses on the identification and analysis of linguistic variation compared to sociological variables such as ethnicity, class, age, and gender. Training does not stress the identification and incorporation of intragroup language norms and values – and often considers these subjects as falling outside the realm of sociolinguistics.[2] Consequently, language plans and policies that may be theoretically sound from a linguistic perspective do not necessarily address the speech community's notion of language as a reflection of social reality, especially theories concerning language and identity, power and loyalty. Such shortcomings often lead to the reconstitution of hegemonic theories that marginalize culturally different speech communities. Once sociolinguistic theories privilege the standard variety as the "norm" in relation to competing varieties, the intent of both language plans and planners becomes suspect, and speakers sense that linguistics may be dangerous to the health of their speech community. One of the clearest examples of the conflict that can result from excluding a community's language ideology (cf. Schieffelin et al. 1998) from language planning and policy comes from African-American English (AAE), a variety often characterized as surrounded by a history of controversy.[3]

For permission to publish copyright material in this book, grateful acknowledgment is made to: M. Morgan (1994), "The African-American Speech Community: Reality and Sociolinguistics," in M. Morgan (ed.), *Language & the Social Construction of Identity in Creole Situations*. Los Angeles: Center for Afro-American Studies, UCLA, pp. 121–48.

Sociolinguistics and Language Planning and Policy in the African-American Speech Community

Beginning in the mid-1960s and for a decade thereafter, many dialectologists and creolists devoted considerable attention to the historical development and linguistic description of AAE.[4] These linguists, most notably, Bailey (1969, 1971), Dillard (1968, 1972), Stewart (1968), Labov (1972), Wolfram (1969), and Fasold (1969, 1972), presented their research in a political climate that included, on the one hand, the expression of African-American pride and identity and, on the other, reactions to the charge that African-American culture and language is deviant and deficient.[5] Few linguists of the day could remain silent when asked: "What is Black English? What is it good for?" Their nearly unanimous response to attacks from educational and psychological quarters was that AAE, while different from American English (AE), is as logical and as capable of representing intelligent ideas as any other language or dialect.[6] Linguists addressed the misinformed and often racist arguments by educating students of linguistics as well as members of the educational establishment on the system and structure of AAE. Their opinions and research results appeared in introductory language and linguistics texts under the heading of "cultural difference" or "cultural diversity."[7]

A decade later, texts on the language education of African-American children appeared again. The contributors to these anthologies, many of whom are members of the African-American community, presented arguments, plans, and proposals that they believed represented their community's language, educational, and cultural interests. In contrast to earlier arguments for the legitimacy of AAE within the national landscape, publications such as Smitherman (1981a) and Brooks (1985) focused on the educational system's continuing failure to incorporate knowledge of AAE into curriculum in ways that benefit the education of African-American children. This state of affairs provoked Smitherman (1981b) to conclude that the bottom line in language-policy debates about AAE is the fate of Black children as victims of miseducation.

The volumes written on the language and education of African Americans reflect the tremendous effort expended over the past 20 years in proving that society in general, and the educational system in particular, should respect AAE and its speakers. Yet, the most dissident and serious obstacle to the implementation of these efforts has been the African-American community itself (Baugh 1983b). Although their rejection has been characterized as self-hate by Stewart (1975), it is partly due to the failure of sociolinguists to incorporate the language and educational values and beliefs of the African-American community within language and education plans. While examples of conflicts between the community and linguists have existed since the 1970s,[8] the following discussion will focus on two specific proposals that resulted in conflict: the King case, which ended in 1979, and a study conducted by William Labov (1985) on the divergence of African-American and white dialects. These two highly publicized events are of great interest for three reasons. First, they were discussed extensively within both the linguistic and African-American communities. Second, the proposals were popularly interpreted as representing two opposite views on the significance of AAE. Finally, despite the fact that each proposal incorporated different views on the function of AAE in education, both plans were rejected by significant segments of the African-American community.

Martin Luther King Junior Elementary School versus the Ann Arbor School District Board

In 1977, the legal case filed on behalf of the children of the Martin Luther King Junior Elementary School against the Ann Arbor School District Board (USDC Eastern District of Michigan Southern Division Civil Action No. 7–71861) charged that school officials had placed African-American children in learning-disabled and speech-pathology classes and held them at low grade levels because of language, cultural, and class differences. Geneva Smitherman (1981a, 1981b), the linguist most centrally involved in the case, described the Martin Luther King School as an institution that subscribed to liberal goals and philosophies but was unable to reconcile either its practice regarding cultural and class biases or its ignorance of cultural differences and values. Though the suit's initial legal arguments considered the problem of cultural and class bias on the part of the school, the presiding judge determined that children are not protected from that particular form of prejudice in education under the US Constitution. Instead, citing section 1703(f) of the 1974 Equal Education Opportunity Act, which guarantees that race, color, sex, national origin, or language barrier cannot impede equal education, the judge decided that the case would focus on the question of the children's language. The expert witnesses on AAE included J. L. Dillard and William Labov (both of whom participated in the defense of Black English in the early 1970s), as well as other linguists and scholars from psychology and education.[9] On July 12, 1979, two years after the initial lawsuit was filed, presiding Judge Charles W. Joiner ruled that there is a substantial difference between AAE and AE and that to ignore the existence of AAE in the education of African-American youth constituted failure on the part of the school district to provide equal education under the law. In his written opinion on the 1979 King case, Judge Joiner described AAE as a language variety spoken by 80 percent of the African-American community, which is part of, but different from, the English used in schools. Labov (1982) describes the consensus reached by linguists on the nature and origin of AAE as follows:

a. The Black English vernacular is a subsystem of English with a distinct set of phonological and syntactic rules that are now aligned in many ways with the rules of other dialects.
b. It incorporates many features of Southern phonology, morphology and syntax; Blacks in turn have exerted influence on the dialects of the South where they have lived.
c. It shows evidence of derivation from an earlier Creole that was closer to the present-day Creoles of the Caribbean.
d. It has a highly developed aspect system, quite different from other dialects of English, which shows a continuing development of its semantic structure. (p. 192)

Judge Joiner then ruled that the Ann Arbor school district must help its teachers recognize the home language (AAE) of the students and to use that knowledge in their attempts to teach reading skills in Standard English (p. 41).

As mentioned earlier, Smitherman (1981a, 1981b) was critically aware that the issues concerning the King case were not only about the language variety spoken by the children. Rather, the intolerance toward AAE also embodies a bias against the cultural, political, and social reality it represents. Along with having to contend with the justice system's refusal to recognize the connection between language, culture, and class, Smitherman was also confronted with the "broad misinterpretations and gross distortions" that surrounded the press reporting of the case. Headlines from the African-American press included: "Judge to Hear the 'Black Slang' Case," "Black English Must Go!," "Black English Would Doom Blacks to Fail," "Black English Is Silly."

The perversive manner in which the press reported the case was partly responsible for the community's suspicious reaction to the final verdict. In particular, the African-American middle class considered the King case a threat to freedom and believed it would encourage segregation. June Brown (1979), a popular African-American columnist for the *Detroit News*, reduced the issues and intent of the actual ruling on the case to insipid self-interest on the part of scholars and teaching professionals. Though Brown acknowledged in her series of articles on the case that ineffective reading and teaching methods were important issues, she concluded:

> The court should not order Black children into a separate program because the facts do not support the need for one ... As for

> whites understanding Blacks, many white teachers in inner city schools understand "Black English" clearly and do outstanding jobs in teaching Black kids ... Whites can understand just as much "Black English" as they want to.

Though representing a different constituency, Samuel 17X (1975), writing in the *Bilalian News*, the newspaper of the Nation of Islam, supported Brown's suspicions. He refers to AAE as "slave speech" and quotes a Chicago Southside street observer: "That old Black English thing is just a shrewd Black ... hustler's game to make a job for himself as a counselor or teacher in some slick educational program."

The Divergence of Black and White Dialects

Considering the misrepresentation and misinterpretations surrounding the King case, it is not surprising that vocal and influential members of the African-American community suspected that the ruling was a trick to continue oppression through miseducation by teaching AAE in the schools. Yet, some ten years later, when Labov (1985) argued for the importance of Standard English in the education of African-American children, the community showed little support for either his theories or his concern that continued language divergence leads to educational failure.

In 1985, the results of the National Science Foundation (NSF) project conducted by William Labov on "The Influence of Urban Minorities on Linguistic Change" were widely reported by the international and national print and electronic media.[10] According to Vaughn-Cooke (1987), at least 157 domestic and foreign newspapers reported on the findings of the study and their implications. News items appeared in the *New York Times*, and all the major news programs and talk shows described the study's findings. The NSF project maintained that African Americans in Philadelphia are not participating in the vernacular changes that are going on in other dialect varieties of the city. Instead, Labov and Harris (1986) discovered that in Philadelphia and other Northern cities, the speech pattern of African Americans was developing in its own direction and was becoming increasingly more different from the speech of whites in the same communities.[11] The reason for divergence from white social dialect varieties, according to Labov and Harris (1983: 2), is that "there is a close parallel between residential segregation and linguistic segregation, and between residential segregation and educational failure." Labov proposed to address the problem of increasing language divergence by developing a program for language arts in the integrated classroom.

The results of Labov's (1985) study, as well as his intent to put sociolinguists' understanding of language difference to use, were not unanimously embraced by linguists. A special issue of the *Journal of American Speech* (Butters 1987), which was devoted to the controversy, reveals considerable disagreement over the claims made by Labov (1987), Bailey and Maynor (1987), and others on the divergence of AAE from AE. Vaughn-Cooke (1987), perhaps the most outspoken of the African-American linguists, assailed Labov and referred to his study as poorly investigated, "flawed and misguided," and ultimately detrimental to the education of African-American children.[12]

In the same publication, Arthur Spears (1987) questioned another aspect of Labov's findings as reported in a news release from the University of Pennsylvania, dated 15 March 1985. The release in part read:

> These language differences have contributed to widespread educational failure in the inner-city schools. ... And the problem seems to be getting worse over time rather than better. Labov believes that language division has been caused by decreasing personal contact between Blacks and whites. The most effective way for Black children to learn other dialects of English in addition to their own dialects is through greater interaction with whites. ... The mass media, including television and radio, have had little influence on the speech patterns of Blacks or any other group.

Spears (1987) considered the above release enigmatic because it linked the acquisition of AE to racial integration. He reasoned that linguistic divergence could not result from the lack of integration, as the 1985 study argues, since AE is spoken by middle-class African Americans. Spears concluded that lack of opportunity for African-American youth is the likely cause of Labov's (1985) findings.

As some linguists found exceptions to various aspects of Labov's (1985) results and educational proposals, the speech community concurred. Considering the position taken by the middle class on the King case, perhaps the most surprising reaction to the divergence controversy appeared in Kenneth M. Jones's September 1986 article in *EM: Ebony Man*, a middle-class publication devoted to African-American men. In this article, Jones maintained that many sociolinguists simply did not understand the community's notion of pride or power. He argued that AAE is the language variety of choice throughout the African-American community and cites language use in rap and hip-hop music as an example of the expressive character and "African beat" inherent in African-American speech styles. In the Jones article Spears explains, "Generally everybody thought that all Black people wanted to do was assimilate. So when we found divergence, the reason had to be social isolation ... we hadn't had the chance to be around whites, so we haven't learned their ways."

Though *EM* exalts AAE, it does not argue for its exclusive use within or outside of the community, but rather for verbal dexterity or code switching. Kenneth Jones (1986) qualifies his position with quotes from several African-American artists and linguists.

> "The requirement that you be verbally dexterous is one of your admission fees to Black culture," Redmond adds. For this very reason, certain elements of the Black community lash out against "talking proper." "If your language shifts are extreme," observes Dr. Scott, "the Black community interprets that as your being pretentious or unnatural. In other words, you are trying to be something you are not."(p. 69)

EM's final appraisal of the speech community's notion of AAE is enmeshed in a sense of African identity: "Former President of Senegal Leopold Senghor once said that Africans abhor the straight line. We speak in rhythms and blues. Our speech is African and our speech is American. Our speech is inevitable" (K. Jones 1986, 69).

In the King case, the African-American middle class responded with hostility to the proposal that AAE should be considered a valid language alternative in education settings. In fact, Carl Rowan, a radio personality and newspaper columnist, referred to AAE as "ghetto language" in his syndicated column ("Rowan Report," RR 12 and 13, 14 and 15 August 1979), while some African-American newspapers like the *Chicago Defender* called the whole case "phony." Yet, *EM* (K. Jones 1986) bristles at the notion that AE is as essential as Labov (1985) suggests or that integration with whites is important in order to speak AE. Instead, Jones invokes an African continuum and then focuses on the beauty of African-American language. These two perspectives, while opposing, reflect how language, identity, culture, and social reality interact and are reflected within the African-American community. The dialogue on AAE has and continues to focus on two fundamental issues that constitute the symbolic and ideological context in which it is used: the history and function of AAE within the speech community and its function in relation to AE.

Perspectives of African-American English

The African-American speech community operates according to an intricate integration of language norms and values associated with the symbolic and practical functions of AAE and AE. The complexities of this system are aptly illustrated by the author Langston Hughes (Smitherman, 1977) in his use of "the voice of the community," Jesse B. Simple.[13]

SIMPLE: Do you want me to talk like Edward R. Murrow?

JOYCE: No! But when we go to formals I hate to hear you saying, for example, "I taken" instead of "I took." Why do colored people say, "I taken" so much?

SIMPLE: Because we are taken – taken until we are undertaken, and, Joyce, baby, funerals is high!

Simple's explanation of *taken*, which is neither questioned nor disputed by Joyce, represents the speech community's view of the nature of AAE (cf. Smitherman 1977). It historicizes an African-American linguistic reality that was framed by the public use of language, a use that accommodated dominant racist and class ideology and discourse concerning African Americans while indirectly resisting it. Thus, for Simple, *taken* can refer to being taken from Africa and cheated in life and death through social injustice. Though Simple's expression of the community's social and historical reality is accepted without question, his grammar, as Joyce attests, is not. It is in this sense that AAE reflects language as a symbol of "actual social life ... a multitude of concrete worlds ... of bounded verbal-ideological and social belief systems" (Bakhtin 1981: 288).

Until the 1970s, the African-American community was composed of different social classes that lived and interacted within racially segregated institutions and geographical areas (Drake and Cayton 1945; Wilson 1978; Dillingham 1981). As a speech community, it has been characterized by anthropologists, folklorists, and literary critics as an oral culture (Kochman 1972; Abrahams 1976) with a tradition of "talk" (discourse) about language use (Morrison 1981; Gates 1988). Because of the community's social-class mixing, this "talk" has included both formal and informal uses and understanding of language and its importance in representing social reality, history, and identity.

As the language and education debates discussed above raged in academic institutions, their implications were extensively examined among African-American scholars and community activists in popular, theoretical, and research journals.[14] Poets, writers, and musicians all contributed to the developing positions that were often framed by a particular understanding of Africans before US slavery. AAE was discussed from three related perspectives: (1) in terms of its "expressive" African character, (2) as a symbol of resistance to slavery and oppression and, the opposite view, (3) as an indicator of a slave "mentality" or consciousness.

In the first conception of AAE, the indigenous languages of Africa are considered to be symbolic of African culture, identity, and power. Africans of the diaspora, who speak their native languages, are described in terms of their enslavement and forced learning of English, which represents the language of oppression and domination and thus a symbol of their loss of power and identity. In an earlier work, Harrison (1972: 53) described the situation: "After a lifetime of speaking their own native tongues they [Africans in slavery] were forced to learn English so that they would be able to communicate, not *among* themselves but *with* their masters." Yet, both community and institutional scholars argue that the essence of the language and therefore the culture survived. For instance, K. Jones (1986, 69) cites writer Halima Toure, who notes: "We were together in the slave quarters and in the fields. Communication between Blacks and the overseer was usually conducted by one person. It wasn't necessary for all the slaves to deal with the slave master." Harrison (1972) lambastes linguists' tendency to ignore the African ancestry of AAE and the multiple realities of the African-American experience.

> Until recently, linguists had placed the colloquial expressions used on the block, without properly being advised by their African roots, into a category of non-language, a form of speech given toward immature usages. There had been a consensus of opinion that the common language of Black people was static, since to those unattuned to the communicative context, the words seemed never to develop or advance in meaning. Black language is anything but static; it receives its dynamism from the constant change of a context which influences the spoken word, giving it new meaning and a wide latitude of expression. (p. 52)

Some, like Burgest (1973, 14), attach metaphysical significance to African continuity and suggest that "many Africans have a psyche ... which prevents the admission of the foreign racist destructive language from entering into their system. ..." Writer Eugene Redmond, as reported in *EM* (K. Jones 1986: 69), concludes: "We talk in English but think in African. We actually speak English with an African accent."

Thus the African identity, whether idealized or historically situated, is firmly established in this argument as the foundation of AAE. As Langston Hughes (1957) might have argued, African language style was the thing not "taken" but transformed. While community discussions of the existence of AAE are often explained in terms of an African continuity, proof of a linguistic genealogy is not a requisite. Rather, the discussion recognizes that the language behavior of African Americans is different from that of whites and similar to that of Africans in Africa and the diaspora. This attention to African identity and AAE has been addressed by African-American linguists such as Taylor (1975) and Smitherman (1977), as well as writers such as Baldwin (1979), Morrison (1981), and Redmond (1986). Rather than focus on the details or particulars of the historical origins of AAE, they attend to the ways in which the social and political conditions of slavery and Jim Crow laws affected the language and identity of a people.[15] This issue is represented by the commonly asked question: Does AAE represent resistance to slavery or a slave mentality?

The resistance theory of AAE is based on the function, nature, and importance of indirect speech and ambiguity in African-American speech. Morgan (1989, 1991, 1993a) argues that a counterlanguage emerged during slavery that was based on African systems of communication. Smitherman (1977) describes the context that necessitated this language strategy.

> The condition of servitude and oppression contributed to the necessity for coding or disguising English from the white man. Since slaves were forced to communicate in the white man's tongue, they had to devise ways of running it down that would be powerful and meaningful to the Black listener, but harmless and meaningless to any whites who might overhear their rap. (p. 47)

This counterlanguage was a conscious attempt on the part of US slaves and their descendants to represent an alternative reality through a communication style based on ambiguity, irony, and satire.[16]

Indeed counterlanguage, as a language choice, is at the heart of "talk" surrounding African-American speech. Its existence is apparent in lexical usage throughout the community (cf. Holt 1972; Levine 1977; Smitherman 1977), and it is the basis of much of the lexical creativity found in hip-hop and rap as well as the source of indirection used in socially conscious hip-hop and rap styles (Morgan 1993b). In addition to support for counterlanguage styles, when the syntactic and phonological characteristics of African-American speech – for example, camouflaged forms like *come* (Spears 1982) and stressed *been* as an anterior marker (Rickford 1973) – are discussed in terms of norms, function, or meaning, there is little or no dispute in terms of AAE's importance or significance as an intragroup communication system. In contrast, when AAE is discussed in reference to contexts or domains identified with AE usage, serious disagreement can develop.

Both addressing and redressing issues associated with slavery are the purview of many African-American nationalist groups. While all of these groups consider African heritage incontrovertible, they do not support the notion that AAE sustains an African origin. In 1975, the article by Samuel 17X became the source of heated debate in the African-American community. Because he insisted that during slavery English functioned to maintain a subservient relationship between master and slave, Samuel 17X maintained that AAE is a symbol of that oppressive relationship and therefore argued against its use.

> One fact is that "Black English" is a language which emanates from slavery. It is a slave mentality and a slave's way of thinking. If we spoke a certain type language during slavery, then by continuing to speak that language we are transmitting the legacy of slavery, its culture, thinking, and reality on which that language is based.

In a dialogue with the *Bilalian News* about their position on AAE (or Bilalian English), Ernie Smith (1976) argued against Samuel 17X's interpretation.

> Now what can be more indicative of a "slave mentality" and a "slave's way of thinking" than a Bilalian [African American] who is sycophant and so obsequiously enamored with the language of his Euro-American slave masters that he publicly reveres their language, and finds it necessary to denigrate the Bilalian language as a "sloppy language" which reflects "sloppy thinking"? (p. 6)

The tension that emerges from AAE as a complex sign of both resistance and oppression problematizes Bakhtin's (1981) notion of language use reflecting multiple concrete worlds. Indeed, the discussion historicizes AAE as a dual sign and mediates discourse concerning which position best reflects the essence of the African-American experience (cf. Vološinov 1973). Yet, it is only within the context of African-American language norms and values that AAE is a cultural sign representing the experiences, norms, and values of the community. For AAE speakers outside the community and in contact with dominant discourse that attempts to control and marginalize their existence, AAE becomes a political sign of solidarity and resistance. This rise to counterhegemonic sign occurs when confronted with the "ideal" language variety and "citizenship standard": AE.

American English

The language "legitimacy" of African Americans who seek citizenship rights has been a recurring issue in American society (Frazier 1968; Mitchell-Kernan 1972; Winfrey 1987). Yet, as Mitchell-Kernan (1972) demonstrates in her classic study of African-American attitudes toward AAE and AE, the interplay between "good" English and AAE is extremely complex because both are considered crucial to improve life chances. Those who choose to accommodate the demands of non-African-American society and use AE exclusively risk losing community membership and, as Mitchell-Kernan (1972) warns, earning a pariah status that can lead to abuse. Indeed, there is a pejorative variety of English referred to as "talking white."[17]

> Speaking good and proper English becomes equivalent to "light skinned," and "good (straight like whites') hair." It is not foreign for Blacks to have suffered condescension from other Blacks for not being able to master the "King's English." By the same token, it is in the experiences of the "good (white) English user" to have received "compliments" from whites like, "you don't talk like the rest of them," insinuating that you are different and "better" because you speak more like whites. The inability to master the language becomes equated with being "uneducated," "deprived," "disadvantaged." In other words, Black is defined from its racist perspective. (Burgest 1973: 41)

The above depiction focuses on AE as a racially identified variety and as symbolic of a culture that considers its norms and values a model for all others and exercises power and control over life chances. Consequently, through language, mono-AE speakers constitute a reality that excludes the language and cultural values of the wider African-American community. As a result, AE can be symbolic of historical oppression and the annihilation of African consciousness and resistance when it is used in contexts where AAE is normally spoken. Because AE plays a political role in African-American life, only those who celebrate African heritage and identity have the authority to talk about the politics of its use without being castigated for trading identities. The *Bilalian News* (1975), though severely criticized, could launch a provocative discussion about AAE without fear of censure because the Nation of Islam's ideological foundation was based on an African heritage and the necessity of competing for and achieving power within and in spite of dominant ideology. Likewise, the "Graffiti" column of the January 1990 issue of *Essence* magazine (a publication that celebrates

African-American culture) stressed the importance of achieving success in both school and the "white working world" by reminding its readers to say *ask* instead of *ax* and *specific* instead of *pacific*.[18] In contrast, *Newsweek* magazine's "My Turn" column chronicled Rachel Jones's experience as a mono-AE speaker in the African-American community. Jones (1986) describes her childhood as difficult because of hounding by other children with questions like "Why do you talk like you're white?" In defending her pariah status, Jones insists "I don't think I talk white, I think I talk right."

As discussed above, in the African-American speech community, disputes regarding language choice revolve around how those living under slavery and later social and economic discrimination viewed their reality. Since social reality is constructed via language here, two questions emerge (Berger and Luckman 1966; Smitherman 1991). The first question is whether AAE signifies the resistance to an imposed definition of personhood that constructs African Americans as dependent "others" who rely on those of European ancestry for recognition and existence. The second is whether AAE represents acquiescence and participation in the imposed definition. These questions are essential to understand attitudes toward both AAE and AE. The first question focuses on the ways in which Africans sought to forge an identity within slavery by employing generalized African norms of communication to establish an antisociety with AAE as counterlanguage. The second question accepts the designation of "Other" and AE as the vehicle with which one can transcend the noncitizenship status of "different" and become the model of good and humanity and, therefore, citizen. Within this framework, monolingual AE in intragroup interaction symbolizes self-hate regarding an African-American identity and an exaltation of European values. Thus, in terms of language choice, AE is the only variety that one can choose to speak, while AAE is a variety that one may *choose not* to speak. Consequently, AE is a symbol of both the speaker's desire to be accepted by whites as well as a symbol of accomplishment toward life goals. This problematic is played out on many levels.

It is into this complicated and often volatile debate that sociolinguists have entered. In an attempt to right perceived wrongs that have been inflicted on the African-American community by educational policies and psychological theories of deficit, sociolinguists have inadvertently focused on the very aspects of AAE that are most symbolic and significant to the community itself. To fully comprehend the motivations and ideology that influence sociolinguistic theories about the function of AAE, it is useful to further explore three general methodological and theoretical issues: (1) how speech community membership is determined; (2) the symbolic function of education; and (3) the role of speech styles and events.

The African-American Speech Community: Race Consciousness, Class Consciousness, and Education

It is impossible to provide a simple definition of the African-American speech community, or any urban speech community. This is true not only because of its complicated history and countless attacks designed to elicit compliance within a hegemonic system based on race, class, and gender hierarchies, but also because the community expands and contracts across class and geographic lines. Considering its complexity, it is not surprising that one source of criticism of linguistic plans and proposals can be traced to early descriptions of the African-American speech community and what constitutes membership. Confusion regarding who speaks AAE began in the late 1960s with the pronouncement from creolists and dialectologists that "eighty percent of all Black people speak Black English" (Dillard 1972: 229). In rendering his legal decision in the King case, Judge Joiner referred to 80 percent of African-American speakers of AAE. The 80 percent theory emerged during the deficit/difference debates in an attempt to identify African Americans in terms of culture, history, and language, and to decide whose rights, therefore, must be protected. It is based on the notion that AAE is spoken by the working class and at least 80 percent of all African Americans are working class.

Unfortunately, this theory does not attach cultural significance to AAE and excludes age differences, context, group, individual variation, and African-American systems of class and status distinctions. To further complicate matters, because vernacular AAE has been defined as hip, male, adolescent, street, or gang-related speech, nonvernacular speech is described as weak, lame, or white (Labov 1972). Those who do not fit the model of the vernacular-idealized speaker (the 20 percent) are therefore, according to this sociolinguistic paradigm, not African American or, to put it in modern terms, not the "authentic Other." Gilyard (1991) provides a particularly critical portrayal of the issues in relation to Labov's (1972) chapter, "The Linguistic Consequences of Being a Lame." As the above discussion of the cultural and political significance of AAE and AE reveals, sociolinguists have constituted speech community membership and style in ways that reinscribe the dominant society's interpretation of AAE as a sign of poverty and oppression. The apparent confusion over what constitutes speech community membership is analogous to the difficulty that sociologists have in describing the relationship between class and racial consciousness in the African-American community.

Because the community has historically been denied access to traditional indicators of the dominant social class – housing, employment, occupation – how the community assigns class and status remains open to question. An analytical problem emerges because in order for class differences to exist, "a population must differentiate to a minimum extent with respect to an attribute before that attribute can serve as a basis for invidious distinction" (Glenn 1963: 665). In his analysis of the basis of social prestige found in 16 studies of the African-American community between 1899 and 1960, Glenn (1963) found that in all but one case, African Americans considered education more important in determining class and status than income and occupation. These findings corroborated Drake and Cayton's (1945) earlier classic study of Chicago's African-American community, in which they found that during the 1940s, advanced education virtually secured membership at the top of the Black social hierarchy of Chicago.[19] Though the community was composed of members who earned large incomes, the exclusion from typical middle-class occupations meant that earned income did not play a significant role as a class indicator since it was secured through nontraditional means.

In 1978 and later in 1987, Wilson argued that in the African-American community, class consciousness is becoming more important than race in determining life chances. One consequence of the change is that African-American middle and working classes are becoming more stratified. If Wilson is correct, it would explain Labov's (1985) contention that racial integration is necessary since, following Wilson's theory, middle-class African Americans lose their racial identity and take on the characteristics of middle-class whites. However, Dillingham (1981: 432) argues that in an ethnically stratified society it is more feasible that subjective feelings of ethnic group or racial identification become more powerful determinants of behavior than objective assessments of socioeconomic status. In a study of three hundred African Americans, Dillingham (1981) found that contrary to Wilson's (1978) analysis, the higher the class of the respondent, the higher the racial consciousness. Other studies (Ginzberg 1967; Kronus 1970; Sampson and Milam 1975) also report that middle-class African Americans have a positive attitude toward the lower class and continue to feel an obligation to their race due to their more privileged position. In fact, during my research (Morgan 1989, 1991, 1993b) I have had numerous discussions about class and race with middle-class African Americans. None of them equate being middle class with an absence of African-American culture and values. They argue that the street culture (as defined by sociologists) is integral to the community, and they object to any attempt to identify it as either representative or separate. Thus, though the representation of class may be changing in the African-American community – and quite likely the significance of education as an indicator of social class – racial consciousness continues to be an important indicator of community membership.

Recent studies on language in context have revealed the extent to which AAE functions to signal community membership and solidarity across class lines. The importance of functioning within multiple contexts is accentuated by the use of AAE among those middle-class African Americans who were not socialized in the speech community, as well as by the use of AE by rap and hip-hop artists who were (Morgan 1993b). In the first instance, there is a developing trend among upper middle-class African-American students attending elite college campuses to use lexical, phonological, and grammatical features of AAE in both formal and informal contexts (cf. Baugh 1987). DeBose (1992) and Spears (1988) report that in their research on language use among working- and middle-class African-American adults, both AAE and AE are used in informal mixed-class conversations, regardless of the class of the speaker. In addition, Morgan (1993b) reports that the hip-hop community, whose membership is based on the ability to represent the truth about life in the city by using "real" street AAE (reflecting current usage), relies on both AE and AAE grammar and phonology, and AAE lexical and morphological style (dope rhymes).

The tendency of sociolinguists to include some segments of the African-American community and exclude others extends beyond class to gender. With few exceptions (Mitchell-Kernan 1971; Goodwin 1990; Morgan 1989, 1991) research on discourse and verbal genres has highlighted male-centered activities and male sexual exploits. As a consequence, African-American women are either erased from the urban landscape because of their purported linguistic conservatism or portrayed as willing interlocutors and audiences for the plethora of street hustler raps and misogynistic boasting reported by researchers. Since the speech community, in this case, is viewed as a monistic entity, a specific speech event is often presented as a generalized norm rather than characteristic of a particular style or genre.[20] Kochman (1981, 75) is emblematic of this problem with his statement, "In Black culture it is customary for Black men to approach Black women in a manner that openly expresses a sexual interest, while in white culture it is equally customary for 'respectable' women to be offended by an approach that presumes sexual interest and availability." Kochman contends that this form of "rapping" is a norm, though his assumptions are mainly based on male self-reporting of street culture and street observations.[21]

The fallout that results from this rendering is, once again, both the African-American community's rejection of research on AAE and accusations from linguists of community self-hate. The extent of this problem was revealed in a conflict at the University of Wisconsin's (Beloit) Rock County Center regarding an assigned reading by Kochman (1981, 1990) in an introductory anthropology text.[22] The dispute began when, after reading the chapter entitled "Race, Culture and Misunderstanding," an African-American woman taking the course called her mother at work and asked "Mom, what's a pimp eye?" (Ostrander 1990). Following is one of the many examples of African-American male and female interactions included in the reading.

> In one street rap a young man says to a woman of about 20, who is walking by in tight shorts:
>
> MALE: What's happenin', fox?
> FEMALE: Nothing.
> MALE: You mean with all that you got ain't nothin' happenin'?
> FEMALE: Get lost nigger.
> MALE: Come here you funky bitch.
> FEMALE: What the hell do you want?
> MALE: I want some leg baby.

Ostrander (1990) reported the mother's outrage: "The reading portrays us like a bunch of animals. ... It takes the very worst things about a Black person – or any person – and makes it out like all Blacks act that way." The Reverend Floyd Prude added, "You can use all sorts of adjectives – disgusting, appalling, derogatory, demeaning – they all apply. I wouldn't want that kind of thing to be taught in school. What if this is a person's only contact with Afro-Americans?"

The *Beloit* dispute resulted in the university's removal of the text (Kochman 1990) and a promise from the publisher to reevaluate the chapter's inclusion in the text's next edition. While these actions may have placated the community in this particular instance, the dispute also proved provocative because it elicited an argument from both the mother and minister that was not disguised as a subjective plea for self-representation but rather a demand that the language styles purported to describe the African-American community represent the entire social field. The examples favored by Kochman (1981) denoted African-American verbal genres as "others" because they were evaluated according to white middle-class cultural norms. They imply that street behavior is typical (normal) and the African-American community is sexually charged, with women "ready" for sex and not worthy of respect and men, at least when they talk to women, in constant pursuit of it. Women, from the linguists' perspective, can be either wild (because they speak like men) or frigid (because they don't).

Conclusion

Members of society construct and communicate meanings through language. In this sense, language does not use its users but is employed by active agents to represent, invoke, symbolize, and even embellish concrete situations that arise from multiple realities (Vološinov 1973; Bakhtin 1981). For the African-American community, AAE is multiply constructed as a variety and in relation to AE.

The preceding discussion argues that choosing AAE or AE invokes alternative cultural, social, and linguistic home environments (Duranti and Goodwin 1992) and therefore ideologies. For African-American speech community members, AAE is a language choice that (1) is influenced by African culture, (2) is a symbol of African-American identity, and (3) may function as a counterlanguage. There is disagreement over whether syntactic and phonological features of AAE represent resistance to oppression or the proof of domination. Correspondingly, there is dispute over whether exclusive use of AE represents a break with slave mentality and movement toward empowerment or a break with African tradition and identity. Because of the many-faceted ways in which speech situations are constituted, on the one hand, the community fully supports AE in schools since it is both an alternative choice within the speech community and the language of education and formal settings. On the other hand, it also considers AAE a variety that should not be denigrated since it too is a grammatical and communicative alternative, though not the language of education.

Once the King case was reduced to proving AAE was sufficiently different from AE to impede learning, the concern of the community was that the children needed AE, "the language of education," in order to receive an education. Likewise, once Labov (1985) seemed to question socializing tendencies among African Americans with his argument for social and language intergration, the community became concerned that his position did not value the multisituated nature of African-American life.

When linguistic facts or descriptions are gathered without acknowledging the ideological precepts inherent in both the disciplinary activity and the attempt to assign significance through plans and policies, linguistics as a science perpetuates the prevailing dominant ideology that language study is objective and neutral (cf. Joseph and Taylor 1990). Under these circumstances, linguistics cannot "do good" for any subordinated group. AAE is a resilient language variety whose emergence flourished under historical conditions that required concealment of the belief that African-American self-identity included a sense of history, pride, emotion, and intelligence as complex as that experienced by other human beings. As the modern urban landscape continues its drift away from cultural enactments, which marginalize those who do not embody dominant cultural practices, AAE's dual value and use as both a cultural and counterhegemonic sign within the African-American community in particular and urban society in general may actually increase.

NOTES

1 This paper was completed while I was a fellow at the University of California's Humanities Research Institute at Irvine. I am especially appreciative of the discussions I've had with Valerie Smith, Kobena Mercer, Anthony Brown, Jon Cruz, Raul Fernandez, Lindon Barrett, Marta Sanchez, Jeffrey Belnap, Sarah Banet-Weiser, Karen Christian, and Heartha Wong. Earlier versions of this paper benefited from the input of Alessandro Duranti, Salikoko Mufwene, Bambi Schieffelin, two anonymous reviewers, and students in my African-American-English class it UCLA.

2 This essay recognizes the distinction between the definition of the speech community used by quantitative sociolinguists and that used by those also involved in the ethnography of speaking (Gumperz and Hymes 1972). Sankoff (1974, 45) has argued that it is possible to combine the two methodologies and writes of "the desire of sociolinguists for their results to have some sociocultural validity." In fact, as this essay demonstrates, sociolinguists have had a profound influence on movements for the educational equality of African Americans. However, until recently, it was Sankoff's (1974: 45) second observation that sociolinguists should "attempt to define categories that are socially meaningful to the people whose linguistic behavior is being investigated" that was left wanting. Rickford (1985, 1986) provides a detailed analysis of the problem, as well as an example of how other theoretical models can be employed.

3 Some linguists (e.g., Bailey and Maynor 1989) actually continue the controversy when they reintroduce categorical stereotypes by assigning equal historical value to racist phenotype arguments (thick lips) and linguistic arguments.

4 Except for direct quotes, or to remain consistent with the publications under discussion, the name African-American English will be used instead of Black English or Black vernacular English. American English (AE) will be used except in those cases where class, ethnicity, region, gender, or age are considered constitutive of the language variety.

5 Earlier, one widely popularized educational theory promoted by Bereiter and Engleman (1966), Jensen (1969), and others was that AAE itself was deficient and produced deficient thinking. The work of William Labov (1972) and others effectively argued that AAE was not deficient but different from AE in systematic ways.

6 The history of sociolinguists' association with the education of African-American children has been discussed in detail in Baratz (1973) and Baugh (1983a, 1983b).

7 These include the edited collections: Johanna DeStephano (1973), *Language, Society and Education: A Profile of Black English*, Ralph Fasold and Roger Shuy (1970), *Teaching Standard English in the Inner City*, and Joan Baratz and Roger W. Shuy (1969), *Teaching Black Children to Read.*

8 The Standard English as a Second Dialect (SESD) teaching method (Stewart 1964, 1965; Allen 1967; Lin 1965, etc.) was not warmly accepted. Nor were dialect readers such as those of the Board of Education, City of Chicago (1966, 1968). When Stewart (1975, 117) introduced AAE dialect reading material into the language arts curriculum of the Florida school system, the response of the community was "These were bad language, bad materials. This bad language shouldn't be put in the schools."

9 The list of King case witnesses is as follows: Geneva Smitherman, professor of speech communication and director of the Center for Black Studies, Wayne State University; Daniel N. Fader, professor of English language and literature, University of Michigan; Jerrie Scott, assistant professor of English and linguistics, University of Florida; William Labov, professor of linguistics, University of Pennsylvania, with a secondary appointment in psychology and education; J. L. Dillard, assistant professor of

languages, Northwestern State University, Natchitoches, Louisiana; Gary Simpkins, director of social health services and chief of mental health, Watts Health Foundation; Richard Bailey, professor of English, University of Michigan; Ronald Edmonds, member of faculty, Harvard Graduate School of Education; Kenneth Haskins, president, Roxbury Community College.

10 For example, see: *The New York Times* article by Williams Stevens (March 14, 1985, A14), "Black and Standard English Held Diverging More"; the "CBS Evening News"; *The Baltimore Sun* (March 18, 1985); and 157 domestic and foreign newspapers (as reported by Vaughn-Cooke 1987: 13).

11 While the linguistic details of the study from which his argument is based are not the subject of this chapter, it is important to note that Labov's current evidence appears in four studies (D. Sankoff 1986) that examine specific phonological and morphological features. In addition, a separate study by Bailey and Maynor (1987) supports Labov's claim that AAE is becoming less like white speech. Bailey and Maynor examine the use of invariant *be* in the speech of older adults and young children in east-central Texas and conclude that the younger generation uses this form more frequently in specific environments than the older generation. They go even further than Labov and consider the younger generation's use an "innovation" since they believe it is not prevalent in the speech of older speakers. They argue not only that Black and white speech forms are diverging, but also that older and younger AAE speakers actually represent two separate speech communities.

12 Both Rickford (1987) and Wolfram (1987), in the same volume, support most of Vaughn-Cooke's claims.

13 This particular excerpt is cited by Smitherman (1977: 167–9). Hughes was a popular African-American newspaper columnist who wrote for the *Chicago Defender* in the 1950s. The *Defender* was widely read by all segments of the community, and it was often referred to as "the Black Bible" since it played a significant role in encouraging Northern migration, civil rights, and racial pride. Hughes's character, Jesse B. Simple, was developed shortly after World War II. The philosophy and exploits of Simple, who was based in Harlem, were hotly contested by all segments of the community because of the character's working-class values.

14 An entire issue of the *Journal of Black Studies* (1979) was devoted to AAE. In addition, African-American linguists have debated which name (e.g., Ebonics) best reflects both its African origin and development in the United States (cf. Mufwene 1992).

15 There is some discussion that the destruction of AAE will aid those who are intent on destroying African-American people and culture because it will destroy the African character as well as the ability to surreptitiously communicate.

16 For detailed discussion on the similarities, see Levine (1977). Even the literary critic Joyce (1987) refers to the need to "speak in such a way that the master does not grasp their meaning" while writing in scholarly journals.

17 The terms "good English," "talking white," "talking proper," and "talking good" are widely reported in literature on the African-American speech community (Mitchell-Kernan 1972; Spears 1988). More recently, these terms were used interchangeably during a lively talk show discussion/debate under the topic of Black English (Winfrey 1987).

18 The inclusion of these words in *Essence* magazine identifies them as marked by AAE speakers and the object of discussion in the speech community irrespective of social class and region.

19 Gregory (1992) also reveals the importance of education in distinguishing class in the late 1970s in an African-American community in Queens. Landry (1987, 104) assigns even more significance to education but for different reasons. By the mid-1970s, he says, a college education could mean securing middle-class

occupations: "Eighty percent of Black males and 60 percent of Black females from middle-class families who remained in the middle-class had attended college. ... Education was at last beginning to pay off for Blacks – if it could be acquired."

20 Henley (1995) provides a detailed critique of the problem of ethnicity and gender issues in sociolinguistic inquiry.

21 *Rapping* means many things including talk. This complicates the problem, since male–female talk can include a rap. But rap is also associated with asking for a date, which, at least at the time of this publication, does not necessarily include sex. See Smitherman (1977) for a fuller discussion of the uses of rap.

22 The reading by Thomas Kochman appeared in the seventh edition of an anthropology text entitled *Conformity and Conflict*, edited by Spradley and McCurdy (Kochman 1990). It was taken from his 1981 text, *Black and White Styles in Conflict.*

REFERENCES

Abrahams, Roger (1976). *Talking Black*. Rowley, MA: Newbury.

Abrahams, Roger, and John Szwed (1983). *After Africa: Extracts from the British Travel Accounts and Journals of the Seventeenth, Eighteenth and Nineteenth Centuries Concerning the Saves, Their Manners and Customs in the British West Indies.* New Haven, CT: Yale University Press.

Allen, Virginia (1967). Teaching Standard English as a Second Dialect. *Teachers College Record.* Reprint. In *Linguistic-cultural Differences and American Education* (special anthology issue), *The Florida FL Reporter* 7: 1.

Ash, Sharon, and John Myhill (1983). Linguistic Correlates of Inter-ethnic Contact. Manuscript, Department of Linguistics, University of Pennsylvania.

Bailey, Beryl Loftman (1969). Language and Communication Styles of Afro-American Children in the United States. The *Florida FL Reporter* 7: 46, 153.

Bailey, Beryl (1971). Towards a New Perspective in Negro English Dialectology. In *Readings in American Dialectology*, ed. Harold B. Allen and Gary N. Underwood. New York: Appleton-Century-Crofts.

Bailey, Guy, and Natalie Maynor (1987). Decreolization? *Language in Society* 16: 449–73.

Bailey, Guy, and Natalie Maynor (1989). The Divergence Controversy. *American Speech* 64(1): 12–39.

Bakhtin, M. M. (1981). *The Dialogic Imagination.* Austin: University of Texas Press.

Baldwin, James (29 July 1979). If Black English isn't a Language, Then Tell Me, What Is? *New York Times.*

Baratz, Joan (1973). Language abilities of Black Americans. In *Comparative Studies of Blacks and Whites in the United States*, ed. Kent S. Miller and Ralph Mason Dreger. New York: Seminar Press.

Baratz, Joan, and Roger W. Shuy (eds.) (1969). *Teaching Black Children to Read.* Washington, DC: Center for Applied Linguistics.

Baugh, John (1983a). A Survey of Afro-American English. *Annual Review of Anthropology* 12: 335–54.

Baugh, John (1983b). *Black Street Speech: Its History, Structure and Survival.* Austin: University of Texas Press.

Baugh, John (1987). The Situational Dimension of Linguistic Power. *Language Arts* 64: 234–40.

Bereiter, Carl, and Seigfried Engelman (1966). *Teaching Disadvantaged Children in the Preschool.* Englewood Cliffs, NJ: Prentice-Hall.

Berger, Peter, and Thomas Luckman (1966). *The Social Construction of Reality.* Harmondsworth: Penguin.

Brooks, Charlotte K. (ed.) (1985). *Tapping Potential: English and Language Arts for the Black Learner.* Urbana, IL: National Council of Teachers of English.

Brown, June (1 July 1979). Black English – Poor Excuse for Incorrect Use of Language. *Detroit News*, pp. 1B, 4B.

Burgest, David R. (1973). The racist use of the English language. *Black Scholar* (September): 37–45.

Butters, Ronald R. (ed.) (1987). Are Black and White Vernaculars Diverging? Papers from the NWAVE XIV panel discussion. *American Speech* 62: 3–80.

Dandy, Evelyn (1991). *Black Communications: Breaking Down the Barriers*. Chicago, IL: African American Images.

DeBose, Charles (1992). Codeswitching: Black English and Standard English in the African-American Linguistic Repertoire. *Journal of Multilingual and Multicultural Development*, 131 (1–2): 157–67.

DeStephano, Johanna (ed.) (1973). *Language, Society and Education: A Profile of Black English*. Worthington, OH: Charles A. Jones.

Dillard, J. L. (1968). Non-Standard Dialects – Convergence or Divergence? *The Florida FL Reporter* 6: 9–10, 12.

Dillard, J. L. (1972). *Black English*. New York: Random House.

Dillingham, Gerald (1981). The Emerging Black Middle Class: Class Conscious or Race Conscious? *Ethnic and Racial Studies* 4(4): 432–51.

Drake, St. Clair, and Horace Cayton (1945). *Black Metropolis*. New York: Harcourt, Brace.

Duranti, Alessandro, and Charles Goodwin (1992). *Rethinking Context: Language as an Interactive Phenomenon*. Cambridge: Cambridge University Press.

Fasold, Ralph (1969). Tense and the Form *be* in Black English. *Language* 45: 763–76.

Fasold, Ralph (1972). *Tense-marking in Black English*. Washington, DC: Center for Applied Linguistics.

Fasold, Ralph, and Roger Shuy (eds.) (1970). *Teaching Standard English in the Inner City*. Washington, DC: Center for Applied Linguistics.

Frazier, E. Franklin (1968). *On Race Relations*. Chicago, IL: University of Chicago Press.

Gates, Jr., Henry Louis (1988). *The Signifying Monkey: A Theory of African-American Literary Criticism*. Oxford: Oxford University Press.

Gilyard, Keith (1991). *Voices of the Self: A Study of Language Competence*. Detroit: Wayne State University Press.

Ginzberg, Eli (1967). *The Middle Class Negro in a White Man's World*. New York: Columbia University Press.

Glenn, Norval (1963). Negro Prestige Criteria: A Case Study in the Bases of Prestige. *American Journal of Sociology* 68(6): 645–57.

Goodwin, Marjorie (1990). *He-Said-She-Said: Talk as Social Organization among Black Children*. Bloomington: Indiana University Press.

Graff, David, William Labov, and Wendell Harris (1983). Testing Listeners' Reactions to Phonological Markers of Ethnic Identity: A New Method for Sociolinguistic Research. Manuscript.

Graffiti. *Essence*, January 1990.

Gregory, Steven (1992). The Changing Significance of Race and Class in an African American Community. *American Ethnologist* 19 (2): 255–74.

Gumperz, John, and Dell Hymes (1972). *Directions in Sociolinguistics: The Ethnography of Communication*. New York: Holt, Rinehart, and Winston.

Harrison, Paul Carter (1972). *The Drama of Nommo*. New York: Grove Press.

Henley, Nancy (1995). Ethnicity and Gender Issues in Language. In *Bringing Cultural Diversity to Feminist Psychology*, ed. H. Landrine. Washington, DC: American Psychological Association.

Holt, Grace (1972). Inversion in Black Communication. In *Rappin' and Stylin' Out*, ed. Thomas Kochman. Urbana, IL: University of Illinois Press.

Hughes, Langston (1957). *Simple Stakes a Claim*. New York: Rinehart.

Hymes, Dell (1974). *Foundations in Sociolinguistics – An Ethnographic Approach*. Philadelphia: University of Pennsylvania.

Jensen, Arthur (1969). How Much Can We Boost IQ and Scholastic Achievement? *Harvard Educational Review* 39(1): 1–123.

Jones, Kenneth (1986). Blacktalk: The Controversy and Color of Black Speech. *Ebony Man* 9: 68–9.

Jones, Rachel (27 December 1986). My Turn. *Newsweek*.

Joseph, John, and Talbot J. Taylor (1990). *Ideologies of Language*. London: Routledge.

Joyce, Joyce (1987). The Black Canon: Reconstructing Black American Literary Criticism. *New Literary History* 18(2): 335–44.

Kochman, Thomas (ed.) (1972). *Rappin' and Stylin' Out: Communication in Urban Black America*. Urbana, IL: University of Illinois Press.

Kochman, Thomas (1981). *Black and White Styles in Conflict*. Chicago, IL: University of Chicago Press.

Kochman, Thomas (1990). Race, Culture and Misunderstanding. In *Conformity and Conflict – Readings in Cultural Anthropology*, ed. David W. Spradley and James P. McCurdy. Glenview, IL: Scott, Foresman.

Kronus, Sidney (1970). Some Neglected Aspects of Negro Class Comparisons. *Phylon* 31(4): 359–71.

Labov, William (1972). *Language in the Inner City: Studies in the Black English Vernacular*. Philadelphia: University of Pennsylvania Press.

Labov, William (1982). Objectivity and commitment in linguistic science: The case of the Black English trial in Ann Arbor. *Language in Society* 11: 165–202.

Labov, William (1985). The Increasing Divergence of Black and White Vernaculars: Introduction to the Research Reports. Typescript, Department of Linguistics, University of Pennsylvania.

Labov, William (1987). Are Black and White Vernaculars Diverging? Papers from the NWAVE XIV panel discussion, ed. Ronald R. Butters. *American Speech* 62: 5–12, 62–74.

Labov, William, and Wendell Harris (1986). Defacto Segregation of Black and White Vernaculars. In *Diversity and Diachrony*, ed. D. Sankoff. Amsterdam: John Benjamins.

Landry, Bart (1987). The *New Black Middle Class*. Berkeley: University of California Press.

Levine, Lawrence (1977). *Black Culture and Black Consciousness*. Oxford: Oxford University Press.

Lin, San-Su C. (1965). *Pattern Practice in the Teaching of Standard English to Students with a Non-standard Dialect*. New York: Teachers College, Columbia University.

Mitchell-Kernan, Claudia (1971). *Language Behavior in a Black Urban Community* (Working Paper 23). Berkeley, CA: Language Behavior Research Laboratory.

Mitchell-Kernan, Claudia (1972). On the Status of Black English for Native Speakers: An Assessment of Attitudes and Values. In *Functions of Language in the Classroom*, ed. Courtney Cazden, Vera P. John, and Dell Hymes. New York: Teachers College Press.

Morgan, Marcyliena (1989). From Down South to Up South: The Language Behavior of Three Generations of Black Women Residing in Chicago. PhD diss., University of Pennsylvania.

Morgan, Marcyliena (1991). Indirectness and Interpretation in African American Women's Discourse. *Pragmatics* 1(4): 421–51.

Morgan, Marcyliena (1993a). The Africanness of Counterlanguage among Afro-Americans. In *Africanisms in Afro-American Language Varieties*, ed. Salikoko Mufwene. Athens: University of Georgia Press.

Morgan, Marcyliena (1993b). In Search of the Hip Hop Nation: Language and Social Identity. Paper read at the Humanities Research Institute, University of California, Irvine.

Morrison, Toni (1981). "The Language Must Not Sweat": A Conversation with Toni Morrison. By Thomas LeClair. *New Republic*, 21 March 1981.

Mufwene, Salikoko (1992). Ideology and Facts on African American English. *Pragmatics* 2 (2): 141–68.

Mufwene, Salikoko (n.d.). African-American English. In *The Cambridge History of the English Language*. Vol. 6, *History of American English*, ed. John Algeo.

Myhill, John, and Wendell Harris (1983). The Use of the Verbal *-s* Inflection in BEV. Manuscript.

Ostrander, Kathleen (12 February 1990). Text called demeaning to Blacks. *Beloit Daily News*.

Pickford, Ruth (1956). American Linguistic Geography: A Sociological Appraisal. *Word* 12: 211–33.

Redmond, Eugene (1986[1973]). *In a Time of Rain and Desire: New Love Poems*. East St Louis, IL: Black River Writers.

Rickford, John (1975). Carrying the New Wave into Syntax: The Case of Black English BIN. In *Analyzing Variation in Language*, ed. R. Fasold and R. Shuy. Washington, DC: Georgetown University Press.

Rickford, John (1985). Ethnicity as a Sociolinguistic Boundary. *American Speech* 60: 99–125.

Rickford, John (1986). The Need for New Approaches to Social Class Analysis in Sociolinguistics. *Language and Communication* 6(3): 215–21.

Rickford, John (1987). Are Black and White Vernaculars Diverging? Papers from the NWAVE XIV panel discussion, ed. Ronald R. Butters. *American Speech* 62: 55–62, 73.

Samuel 17X (22 October 1975). Analysts Warn about Pitfalls of "Black" English. *Bilalian News*.

Sampson, William, and Vera Milam (1975). The Intraracial Attitudes of the Black Middle-Class: Have They Changed? *Social Problems* 23(2): 151–65.

Sankoff, David (ed.) (1986). Defacto Segregation of Black and White Vernaculars. In *Diversity and Diachrony*. Amsterdam: John Benjamins Publishing Co., 1–24.

Sankoff, Gillian (1974). A Quantitative Paradigm for the Study of Communicative Competence. In *Explorations in the Ethnography of Speaking*, ed. R. Bauman and J. Sherzer. Cambridge: Cambridge University Press, 18–49.

Schieffelin, B. B., K. A. Woolard, and P. V. Kroskrity (eds.) (1998). *Language Ideologies: Practice and Theory*. New York: Oxford University Press.

Smith, Ernie (1976). Personal correspondence to Brother Lawrence X.

Smitherman, Geneva (1977). *Talkin and Testifyin: The Language of Black America*. Boston: Houghton Mifflin.

Smitherman, Geneva (ed.) (1981a). *Black English and the Education of Black Children and Youth – Proceedings of the National Invitational Symposium on the King Decision*. Detroit: Harpo Press.

Smitherman, Geneva (1981b). What Go Round Come Round: King in Perspective. *Harvard Educational Review* 1: 40–56.

Smitherman, Geneva (1991). What is Africa to Me? Language, Ideology and African American. *American Speech* 66: 115–32.

Spears, A. (1982). The Black English Semi-auxiliary Auxiliary *Come*. *Language* 58: 850–72.

Spears, Arthur (1987). Are Black and White Vernaculars Diverging? Papers from the NWAVE XIV panel discussion, ed. Ronald R. Butters. *American Speech* 62: 48–55, 71–2.

Spears, Arthur (1988). Black American English. In *Anthropology for the Nineties: Introductory Readings*, ed. Johnetta Cole. New York: The Free Press.

Spradley, James P., and David W. McCurdy (eds.) (1990). *Conformity and Conflict: Readings in Cultural Anthropology*. Glenview, IL: Scott, Foresman/Little, Brown Higher Education.

Stewart, William (1964). Urban Negro Speech: Sociolinguistic Factors Affecting English Teaching. In *Social Dialects and Language Learning*, ed. Roger Shuy. Urbana, IL: National Council of Teachers of English.

Stewart, William (1965). Foreign Language Teaching Methods. In *Quasi-foreign Language Situations in Non-standard Speech and the Teaching of English*, ed. W. A. Stewart. Washington, DC: Center for Applied Linguistics.

Stewart, William (1968). Continuity and Change in American Negro Dialects. *The Florida FL Reporter* 6: 3–4, 14–16, 18.

Stewart, William (1975). Teaching Blacks to Read against Their Will. In *Linguistic Perspectives on Black English*, ed. Philip A. Luelsdorff, 107–32. Germany: Verlag Hans Carl Regensburg.

Taylor, Orlando (1975). Black Language and What To Do about it. *Ebonics: The True Language of Black Folks*, ed. R. Williams. St. Louis: Institute of Black Studies.

Vaughn-Cooke, Fay (1987). Are Black and White Vernaculars Diverging? Papers from the NWAVE XIV panel discussion, ed. Ronald R. Butters. *American Speech* 62: 12–32, 67–70.

Vološinov, V. N. (1973). *Marxism and the Philosophy of Language*, translated by Ladislav Matejka and I. R. Titunik. New York: Seminar Press (original work published 1929, 1930).

Williams, R. (ed.) (1975). *Ebonics: The True Language of Black Folks*. St Louis: Institute of Black Studies.

Willie, Charles (1989). *Caste and Class Controversy on Race and Poverty: Round Two on the Wilson/Willie Debate*. New York: General Hall.

Wilson, Julius (1978). *The Declining Significance of Race*. Chicago, IL: University of Chicago Press.

Wilson, Julius (1987). *The Truly Disadvantaged*. Chicago, IL: University of Chicago Press.

Winfrey, Oprah (19 November 1987). Standard and "Black" English. "The Oprah Winfrey Show." New York: Journal Graphics, Inc.

Wolfram, Walter (1969). *A Sociolinguistic Description of Detroit Negro Speech*. Washington, DC: Center for Applied Linguistics.

Wolfram, Walter (1987). Are Black and White Vernaculars Diverging? Papers from the NWAVE XIV panel discussion, ed. Ronald R. Butters. *American Speech* 62: 40–8, 73–4.

STUDY QUESTIONS

1. Use the 1979 King case and the National Science Foundation study by Labov to describe the controversy about African American English (AAE) discussed in Morgan's article.
2. What are the three perspectives on AAE that Morgan identifies?
3. What does it mean to say that AAE can be seen as a "counterlanguage"?
4. How are African American attitudes toward monolingual speakers of American English (AE) described in the article?
5. What is the role of class consciousness in attitudes toward AAE?

3

The Social Circulation of Media Discourse and the Mediation of Communities

Debra Spitulnik

Nothing begins from zero, and this is especially true when it comes to the mass mediation of communities that are large, shifting, and somewhat intangible, like those that extend across cities, regions, and nations. When we look at the communications that emanate from mass media, we see that, like most other forms of speaking, they are preceded and succeeded by numerous other dialogues and pieces of language that both implicate them and render them interpretable. Such is the social life of language – as an abundance of scholars have repeatedly argued – to be imbricated in innumerable webs of connection with other utterances (Bakhtin 1981, 1986; Foucault 1972), indexically linked to past and future speech events (Bauman and Briggs 1990: 64; Irvine 1996; Silverstein 1976), and vitally entangled with the ongoing practices of everyday life (Hanks 1996).

In this article, I would like to explore how such cross-linkages of language in use – what have come to be called relations of intertextuality (following Bakhtin; cf. Briggs and Bauman 1992) – factor into the mediation of communities. Undertaking this task requires a return to the older and very complex question of what constitutes a speech community. It also leads us into the relatively new terrain of investigating the actual processes of intertextuality, for example, questions about the transportability of speech forms from one context to another and the conditions that enable their decontextualization and recontextualization (Bauman and Briggs 1990; Briggs and Bauman 1992; Lucy 1993; Silverstein and Urban 1996).

The specific problem to be examined here concerns the social circulation of media discourse in Zambian popular culture. We will consider several cases in which phrases and discourse styles are extracted from radio broadcasting and then recycled and reanimated in everyday usage, outside of the contexts of radio listening. As Urban has argued, such social circulation of discourse is essential for the existence of every society or culture because it creates a kind of "public accessibility" that is vital for the production of shared meaning (Urban 1991: 10, also 27, 191). Relations of intertextuality are elemental in this process,

For permission to publish copyright material in this book, grateful acknowledgment is made to: D. Spitulnik (1996), "The Social Circulation of Media Discourse and the Mediation of Communities," *Journal of Linguistic Anthropology* 6(2): 161–87.

according to Urban (1991: 20), because shared meanings result from the construing of interconnections across different instances of publicly accessible discourse. While Urban focuses on how social circulation leads to public accessibility, much of the material considered here exhibits somewhat of a reverse direction – where the widespread availability of the communication form itself creates possibilities for social circulation.[1]

The discussion below demonstrates that, because of their extensive accessibility and scope, mass media can serve as both reservoirs and reference points for the circulation of words, phrases, and discourse styles in popular culture.[2] In addition, it explores how mass media – as ongoing, high-status, public communication forms – have the potential to magnify and even create the "socially charged life" of certain linguistic forms (Bakhtin 1981: 293). Thus as confirmation of Gumperz's early insight that "mass media and the prestige of their speakers tend to carry idioms far from their sources" (1971: 223), we will see how radio's impact on everyday language extends from the introduction of single lexical items and catchphrases to the shifting of semantic fields and the modeling of discourse styles. And finally, the analysis below makes some broader linguistic and cultural generalizations about both the kinds of media discourse that circulate and the kinds of conditions that enable this circulation.

The implications of the social circulation of media discourse for questions about speech communities are far-reaching and go beyond Gumperz's (1971) important points about their impact on language change. First, it provides evidence that particular kinds of social situations and social institutions have greater weight than others in establishing the sociolinguistic significance of certain linguistic forms (Bourdieu 1991; Gal 1989; Gumperz 1971; Irvine 1987; Kroskrity 1992). For example, in some societies, the dominant site for producing normative standards for linguistic usage might be political oratory, while in other societies it might be television newscasting. This has relevance for thinking about the constitution of speech communities, because it suggests that there is a correlation between social scale and the type of communication modality that dominates the mediation of community. Along these lines, one question that definitely merits much more exploration is whether *mass* communication itself is a necessary precondition for the construction of community in large-scale societies (Anderson 1983; Habermas 1989). This seems inherently to be the case, since public accessibility means something quite different in large-scale societies than in small-scale societies.

Second, it leads to a series of questions concerning the definition of the speech community and its applicability to large-scale societies. For example, does it even make sense to speak of a speech community across the nation-state when there is no one common language? When we are talking about millions of people who may never know or interact with one another, how do we handle questions about density of communication, frequency of interaction, and shared linguistic knowledge – three key features that figure prominently in various definitions of the speech community and that seem to be a prerequisite for the kind of discursive mediation of society described by Urban? While these three criteria have been challenged (or just abandoned) in recent work, along with the general utility of the speech community concept itself, I believe that they are relevant in important and interesting ways for thinking about the social and linguistic effects of mass mediated communication and that they merit another look.[3] For example, in large-scale societies, a high frequency of interaction and density of communication do occur in a vertical sense – that is, the dominant directionality of mass media – even if they do not occur in a lateral sense – that is, the typical (or idealized) directionality of face-to-face communication. Thus people have frequent interactions or *frequent acts of consumption* with certain media forms, even if they do not directly interact with other users of the same media. Similarly, there is a density of communication in the sense that there is *large-scale exposure* to a common communication form, such as simultaneous listening to a radio drama or a newscast. And finally, as suggested earlier, questions concerning the production of shared linguistic knowledge, while greatly vexed, can be productively reworked to include analysis of how certain institutions provide *common linguistic reference points*.

Mediating Communities

These various features – common reference points, frequency of consumption, common exposure, simultaneity – are not adequate, however, to ensure that mass media will contribute to the formation of a community (speech or otherwise) in large-scale societies. The mass mediation of large-scale societies requires that some *experience* of belonging and mutuality be generated as well. Anderson's notion of the imagined community is useful in this regard, because it provides a model of a community where members may not all know one another but all share an idea of belonging to a collectivity, that is, "in the minds of each lives the image of their communion" (1983: 15). While Anderson's work has been criticized for its idealized model of a fairly homogeneous, egalitarian, and equally believed in community (Bhabha 1994; Gal 1995; Spitulnik 1994a), it is still extremely valuable because it demonstrates how linguistic practices create possibilities for shared identities to be imagined.

For example, Anderson (1983: 33–6) discusses how, through both definite description and generic reference (naming *familiar* places and invoking *types* of places and *types* of persons), the eighteenth-century novel constructed a sense of a shared world, a common social and cultural milieu that belonged to both author and reader and to a collective readership. In contrast to the book, the newspaper enabled such simultaneous mass consumption of an identical communication form to occur on a daily basis, as modern man's "substitute for morning prayers" (Anderson 1983: 39). Anderson argues that these new communication forms helped to create the feeling of belonging to a shared but anonymous community of fellow readers.

These insights into the mass mediation of communal identity are important because they point out how community and belonging are indexically constructed in texts. The major drawback of Anderson's work, however, is that it overemphasizes the power of vertical modes of communication at the expense of *lateral* communication. For example, we learn little about the practices of consumption and even less about what people are saying to each other about their experiences of consumption. Instead, reminiscent of the earlier "hypodermic" models of media effects and media power (see Spitulnik 1993), there is a privileging of a one-way directionality from a mass communication form to the masses, who supposedly receive it and consume it. The implicit assumption is that, as soon as this mass-produced communication form (e.g., a novel or a newspaper) is distributed, it is simultaneously participated in and almost *automatically* produces a feeling of a shared collectivity because of specific textual features.

While textual acts of asserting or indexing collective identity are important, they do not guarantee that this identity actually corresponds to anything at the experiential level. Production is only half of the picture. We need also to factor in what is happening at the levels of reception and lateral communication, such as the social circulation of media discourse outside of contexts of direct media consumption. I suggest in the following that the repeating, recycling, and recontextualizing of media discourse is an important component in the formation of community in a kind of subterranean way, because it establishes an indirect connectivity or intertextuality across media consumers and across instances of media consumption. Returning to the earlier discussion about speech communities, then, this indicates that even for large-scale societies, it is possible to speak of a density of communication and frequency of interaction in a lateral sense. That is, there can be a density and frequency of common communications and cross-linkages, mediated in a *transitive* fashion by mass media, without a high density or frequency of direct comunication between all members of a society.

Public Words and the Semiotics of Circulation

The social circulation of media discourse provides a clear and forceful demonstration of how media audiences play an *active* role in the interpretation and appropriation of media texts and messages. It is possible to investigate these processes in semiotic terms, and recent work on genre and performance theory offers a very valuable starting point. For example, of the many important semiotic questions that Bauman and Briggs (1990; Briggs and Bauman 1992) raise in their discussions of decontextualized (decentered) and recontextualized (recentered) discourse, three are particularly pertinent for studying the circulation of media discourse: How are decontextualization and recontextualization possible? What does the recontextualized text bring with it from its earlier context(s) (e.g., what kind of history does it carry with it)? What formal, functional, and semantic changes does it undergo as it is recentered? (Bauman and Briggs 1990: 72–5; Briggs and Bauman 1992: 141 ff.).

The following analysis of how media language is recontextualized, reinterpreted, and played with in everyday discourse, focuses specifically on the recycling of radio expressions such as program titles, broadcasters' trademark phrases, and broadcasters' turn-taking routines. These phrases are in English and ChiBemba, two of the country's most widely spoken lingua francas and two of the eight languages that are sanctioned for use on national radio (Spitulnik 1992).[4] The data on recycled media discourse considered here stem from dialogue that I either participated in or overheard during ethnographic research in the capital city of Lusaka and in the semi-urban/semirural provincial capital of Kasama; it was not elicited and was not studied systematically across a structured sample population. The data on media discourse stem from listening notes on and recordings of radio broadcasts from the three channels of Radio Zambia – Radio 1, Radio 2, Radio 4 – which are part of the Zambia National Broadcasting Corporation (ZNBC). The linguistic significance of radio in Zambia is substantial because it is the most widely consumed medium in the country, it is a primary site for exposure to English, and it is the only widespread mass communication form that uses Zambian languages.[5] Furthermore, given the fact that Radio Zambia is a centralized state-run monopoly with simultaneous national transmission (i.e., there is no regional broadcasting), the same broadcasts are accessible to the entire national population at the same time and, thus, allow for the possibility of producing a degree of shared linguistic knowledge across a population of roughly 9.1 million.

As we investigate the semiotics of how this radio discourse circulates, four basic issues will concern us: (1) the inherent reproducibility and transportability of radio phrases; (2) the "dialogic [or intertextual] overtones" (Bakhtin 1986: 92) that are carried over into the new context of use; (3) the formal, functional, and semantic alterations that occur in the recontextualization; and (4) the degree to which knowledge of the original radio source is relevant for understanding the recycled phrase. We will see, for example, that many recycled radio phrases have a formal "prepared-for detachability" (Bauman and Briggs 1990: 74), which enables them to be circulated in particular ways in everyday discourse. We will also see that there is a degree of semantic open-endedness and flexibility that fosters an ease of recontextualization and that people actively exploit this semantic flexibility to create their own meanings for radio-derived discourse.

Overall, the cases considered here exemplify how radio is a source and reference point for phrases and tropes which circulate across communities. Many of these are so well-known and standardized that knowledge of them is virtually essential for one to be considered a communicatively competent member of a particular society or subculture. As such, they are part of what can be termed a society's (or a subculture's) "public words." Public words, understood in this sense, are nothing particularly new to the world or to linguistic anthropologists, and they exist in societies of all scales and scopes. They are standard phrases such as proverbs, slogans, clichés, and idiomatic expressions that are remembered, repeated, and quoted long after their first utterance. Some public words are anonymous and unattributable, for others the sources may be well or vaguely known and perhaps even invoked. Often, these public words are condensations or extracts from much longer speech events, and when used, they may function metonymically to index the entire frame or meaning of the earlier speech situation (Basso 1990a, 1990b; Urban 1991). In the United States such words are the stuff of popular culture, endlessly recycled and renewed by mass media, politicians, culture critics, bumper stickers, and the young and trendy. Examples include: "Make my day," "Been there," "Big brother (is watching)," "The buck stops here," "Beam me up (Scotty)," "Play it again, Sam," and "Hasta la vista, baby."[6]

While linguistic anthropology has tended to focus on the analysis of narrative, oratory, ritual speech, and other very well bounded and easily identifiable speech genres, little has been said about the smaller, scattered pieces of formulaic language, for example, the public words of street signs, graffiti, and political parties, or the popular extracts from radio, film, and the world of advertising. I argue here that tuning into these smaller genres or "minor media" (Fischer and Abedi 1990: 335 ff.) is one productive avenue for beginning an analysis of the linguistic intertextuality of contemporary societies. Further, I suggest that for large-scale societies from the city to the nation and even the global village, the pervasive connections among these smaller genres (and between them and the larger genres) is actually a key constitutive and integrating feature of what can be called a community.

Recycling Metapragmatic Discourse

Many of the public words inspired by Zambian broadcasters are actually more than just single expressions; they are interactional routines and, in particular, dyadic exchanges that are about the communication event itself. Radio broadcasters are faced with the fairly unique condition of having to generate and maintain an ongoing flow of communication in the absence of a face-to-face context and within the constraints of an entirely aural medium. As with telephone communication or other modes of radio use (e.g., in the taxi-driving profession), cues such as gaze and gesture are simply not available for assessing whether the channel is open and working or whether one's intended interlocutor is listening. Because of these particular contextual constraints, several types of metapragmatic discourse are extremely pervasive in radio broadcasting.[7] Many of these expressions constitute broadcasters' channel-monitoring and turn-taking routines. Other types are designed explicitly to build audience expectations and involvement. For example, broadcasting requires title announcements and other framing devices to demarcate what would otherwise be a continuous flow of voices and sound. The frequent practices of entitling and announcing function as important contextualization cues about what listeners should expect; they also serve as key signposts for listeners who have fluctuating attention or who enter into a speech event that is already underway.

Metapragmatic discourse is not the only kind of discourse which is recycled from the realm of radio into contexts of face-to-face communication, but it is readily seized upon. Why is this so? This is an open question and certainly one that requires more extensive research. Three explanations are proposed here as the most likely candidates. First, as Silverstein (1992: 67 ff.) has argued, metapragmatic discourse has a particular kind of *transparency of both form and function*. Because it explicitly serves to frame and orchestrate communication, it tends to be more subject to awareness and segmentation than other linguistic forms (Silverstein 1976: 49 f., 1992, 1993). Second, since metapragmatic discourse is speech about speaking, it is easily transferable to other speech contexts. For example, in many of the cases considered below, the significant feature that enables the decontextualization and recontextualization of metapragmatic discourse is its *general applicability* to virtually any kind of dyadic exchange. And third, I suggest that the detachability and the repeatability of a given radio expression can be fueled by the medium itself, as it lends *prominence* to the phrase, for example, through frequent occurrence or through association with colorful personalities, heightened drama, or humorous moments. It is especially in these latter cases that the transportability of a radio phrase is driven by the specific connotations that it has in the original context. This is illustrated in our first example.

Checking the Channel

Nearly all national broadcasting in Zambia emanates from the capital city of Lusaka, but every Monday through Friday four hours of broadcasting on Radio 2 (one of the English-language channels) are handled by the Kitwe studios in the Zambian Copperbelt region. When the Lusaka broadcaster is getting ready to "cross over to the Kitwe studios," that is, hand over operations to the Kitwe-based broadcaster, he or she may say: "Kitwe, are you there?," "Kitwe, can you hear me?," or "Hello, Kitwe?" If all goes smoothly, the Kitwe-based broadcaster responds affirmatively, with greetings, thanks, and good-byes to the Lusaka broadcaster. If the connection is not good, however, several awkward seconds of airtime may be spent checking the channel, with the Lusaka-based broadcaster repeating the meta-pragmatic phrases: "Hello, hello?," "Kitwe, are you there?," "Kitwe, can you hear me?," or "Hello, Kitwe?" This scenario is rather common at ZNBC (temporary linkup failures occur almost weekly), and thus it is no surprise that the Kitwe crossover itself can serve as an analogy for temporarily failed communication, as illustrated in the following vignette.

One day I was shopping in a very large and crowded Lusaka store, and I noticed a woman trying to get the attention of a friend standing in the next aisle. She was whispering loudly in the friend's direction, "Hello, hello? Hello?" The friend didn't respond, and the woman, a bit embarrassed over drawing attention to herself while still not able to attract the friend, laughed and shouted, "Hello, Kitwe?" This definitely got the attention of the friend, as well as several other customers, who were clearly amused by this clever allusion to the bungled ZNBC communication link.[8]

How is the recontextualization of a radio phrase made possible in this comic scene? Primarily, the successful recycling of "Hello Kitwe?" rests on the transposition of two basic components of the original radio event: (1) the existence of two interlocutors at different locales (Lusaka : Kitwe :: aisle 1 : aisle 2), and (2) uncertainty about the existence of a shared channel. Furthermore, knowledge of the original radio source is essential for understanding the recycled expression. "Kitwe" is not a personal name; it is the place-name for a city on the Zambian Copperbelt. On radio, "Kitwe" metonymically functions as the proper name of the broadcaster and/or studio based in the city of Kitwe. In the context of a Lusaka store, however, there is no obvious link between an individual shopper and the name "Kitwe." Unless, of course, one understands it, within the vocative construction, as an echoing of the well-known radio scenario. "Kitwe" then becomes a name for a person who is hard of hearing.[9] The remarkable humor here is further enhanced by the fact that the sequence "Hello, hello? Hello, Kitwe? Kitwe, can you hear me?" *has no other context* besides the famous radio interaction. The entire expression is uniquely identified with its context of occurrence, and this identification is what triggers the parodic mood that results from the expression's unusual displacement.

Turn-Taking Routines

While the previous example represents what may be a single, idiosyncratic, instance of radio-discourse recycling – and one that I just happened to overhear in an urban store – there are numerous cases of recycled radio phrases that have become fairly ordinary and that occur in a wide range of social contexts. One of these is the title of the popular radio program *Over to You*, which runs in six different languages and which has been running in English for over 30 years.[10] In this program a team of two broadcasters alternate as disc jockeys and signal the handing over of speaker role by uttering the phrase "Over to you." One broadcaster is based in the Lusaka studios, and the other is in the Kitwe studios. The program features musical selections, many of which are listeners' requests accompanied by their dedications and greetings, and the witty exchange between the two broadcasters. In the show, uttering "Over to you" creates an opening for the transfer of speaker role, in which the co-DJ will select a song or read a listener's letter.

In the Zambian-language programs, the title and turn-taking phrase is phonologically assimilated from English: *Ovata yu* (ChiNyanja) and *Ofata yu* (ChiBemba).[11] The phrase's assimilation into Zambian culture is also evidenced by the completeness of its linguistic assimilation. In many usages, especially among speakers who do not know English, the phrase functions as a Zambian-language expression with no connotations of foreign origin.

As with the successful recycling of "Hello, Kitwe?," the use of "Over to you" outside the context of radio requires that certain components of the original radio event also be in place. There must be another person to assume the speaker role, and there must be an expectation that the other speaker perform in some way. Four brief ethnographic examples illustrate this usage.

In a ChiBemba speaking context during a traditional Bemba marriage preparation ceremony, one of the prominent elder women who had been leading a series of songs in ChiBemba addressed a group of women sitting on the opposite side of the room: "Ofata yu," she said, expecting that the addressees would select and lead the next song. In an analogous, but more "modern" and urban setting in Lusaka, I witnessed the use of the idiom again in the context of song turn-taking among women instructors/advisors. This was at a prewedding "Kitchen party," an event that merges the traditional wedding preparations with the European-derived bridal shower. In this case, the family and the elder women were upper-class and highly fluent speakers of English. The ceremonial songs were in ChiBemba, but the turns were signaled with the English "Over to you." I came across yet another example of the phrase's use in the context of women singing during a practice session of a Seventh-Day Adventist choral group. After finishing an English-language song that she had selected and led, the leader of the singing group handed the hymn book to one of her colleagues and said, "Over to you."

A final instance of the use of this expression occurred on a letter that I received from a neighbor in Kasama. Written along the bottom of an envelope addressed to me and handed to me by the writer, a 14-year-old girl, was the phrase "Over '2' you, D.S." The young girl, whom I had just met a few days earlier, was very interested in becoming my pen pal and was hoping that she might be able to visit me in the United States. Her written recontextualization of the radio idiom added a special flair to the hand-delivered envelope, as it both foregrounded and played with the form of the phrase. The symbol 2 took the place of its homonym *to*, and this deviation was acknowledged with quotation marks. In addition, my personal initials were appended to the construction in a form analogous to the way that radio disc jockeys identify themselves and each other. This cleverly elaborated on the transposition of the radio speech event to the context of personal letter writing, and further indexed the young girl's conversancy with the latest trends in popular expressions.

Returning to our questions about the semiotics of circulation, what is transported in the recentering of "Over to you" (and its variants) is the basic discourse format of turn exchange *combined with* a performance format in which the animation of a different genre is embedded. The data here suggest that the phrase is primarily tied to the turn-taking contexts of song choice and letter-reading/writing, both of which are elemental in the radio program. But to what degree is knowledge of the radio source crucial for understanding "Ofata you" and "Over to you" in these contexts? For the most part, these phrases have filtered into popular usage, and attributability to a radio source is not as necessary for interpretability as it is with the phrase "Hello, Kitwe." It is only in the final example that knowledge of the radio program really enhances the interpretation of the utterance. Here, the radio context is invoked with special written flourishes such as abbreviations and quotation marks. The message on the envelope is interpretable without knowledge of its intertextuality with the radio program and disc-jockey nicknames, but awareness of these links is crucial for a full appreciation of the form and its potential currency for a young girl writing to acquire an American pen pal.

"Getting It" from Radio

Many of the popular phrases inspired by radio broadcasting have a distinctive kind of symbolic value because of their association with the medium, which itself is a site of innovation, word play, and colorful drama. Young Zambians, in particular, closely attend to the linguistic nuances of radio and creatively poach from radio discourse to make their own trendy formulations. The following example of recontextualized metapragmatic discourse illustrates how such processes work and raises larger questions about the media-external forces that propel the recycling of media language.

When a ChiBemba broadcaster is handing over operations to another broadcaster or when a live reporter is linked in from an outside location, the following exchange may occur on air:[12]

(1) *Mwaikata* line?	"Do you have the line?"
Ninjikata	"I've got (it)."

The verb root *-ikata* means "hold," "grasp," or "catch"; thus this interchange refers to the grasping of a transmission link. Among young Zambians, however, the radio-derived phrase "*Mwaikata* line?" has been transformed into a popular slang expression that focuses on the successful relay of the *message* rather than the successful link up of the physical *channel*:

(2) *Waikata* line?	"Do you understand?"
	"Do you get me?"

In addition to this semantic shift, the original radio phrase also undergoes a formal change as it is recontextualized. The expressions in (1) and (2) differ in the second-person form. The radio utterance in (1) utilizes the second-person plural form (*mu-*, assimilated as *mw-*) in reference to single addressees. This polite usage (V of T/V) is mandatory for radio announcers in such contexts. In the slang usage in (2), however, the second-person singular form (*u-*, assimilated as *w-*) is more appropriate for single addressees as it connotes familiarity and informality.

Linguistic evidence suggests that the recyclability of the radio expression "*Mwaikata* line?" as "*Waikata* line?" is supplemented, or even motivated, by two other key factors that are external to the original radio context: (1) other usages of the verb *-ikata* within Zambian popular culture and (2) the existence of a more general paradigmatic set of slang expressions for "getting it." Regarding the first factor, the verb *-ikata* features prominently in idioms of relay (both channel relay and message relay) during musical performances, for example, in the imperative phrase "ikata, ikata" "grab, grab". This phrase occurs as part of a chorus or transition point where one musician is inviting another musician to come in, that is, to seize the beat or to take the opportunity to do a special solo. Such musical relays are analogous to the announcer relay in (1), where one performer hands over the stage to another. During a performance, "ikata, ikata" "grab, grab" can also be an exhortation to the listeners to "get it" or "dig it." Here, the meaning is more analogous to that of the slang usage (2), which focuses on addressee's comprehension or engagement.

The second motivating factor outside of the realm of radio – the existence of other related slang expressions for "getting it" – also raises an important question about the cosmopolitan connotations of recontextualized radio phrases. Significantly, the slang phrase "Waikata line?" joins a host of other nearly synonymous code-mixed expressions within Zambian youth culture such as:

(3) *Na*u*get*a*?*	"Do you$_{[sg]}$ get (me/it)?"
*Namu*get*a?*	"Do you$_{[pl]}$ get (me/it)?"
*Nau*dig*a?*	"Do you$_{[sg]}$ dig (me/it)?"
*Namu*dig*a?*	"Do you$_{[pl]}$ dig (me/it)?"

In these popular phrases, the English verbs *get* and *dig* have been morphologically incorporated as ChiBemba verb roots. They are inflected with the present perfect tense (*na-*), the second-person singular or plural subject markers (*u-*, *mu-*), and the indicative suffix (*-a*). But they are not phonologically assimilated (the consonants *g* and *d* would undergo devoicing), and thus they retain the indexical link with their fashionable English counterparts "Do ya get me?" and "Do you dig it?" The recontextualized radio phrase is not therefore an isolated linguistic innovation; it participates in a more general pattern of similar expressions for interpersonal rapport within Zambian youth culture.

These two motivating factors highlight the critical fact that radio is not the be-all and end-all for putting a phrase into motion. Indeed, they generate a crucial modification of Gumperz's important observation that "mass media and the prestige of their speakers tend to carry idioms far from their sources" (1971: 223), one that is consistent with other principles of diachronic linguistics. Specifically, we see here that the social circulation of media discourse is often propelled by other (media-external) linguistic lines of influence of many different orders (e.g., structural, pragmatic, sociolinguistic, paradigmatic, analogic, ideological, etc.) that must be accounted for as well.

This point then leads us to a final question, about the sociolinguistic significance of the codeswitching in the expressions "Mwaikata line?" and "Waikata line?". How does this factor into the processes of recycling media discourse? In Zambia, as well as in many parts of the world, the strategic use of codeswitching has the potential to function as "a sign of social distinction or urbanity" (Kashoki 1978b: 94; also see Gumperz 1982 and Myers-Scotton 1993). It is important to note, however, that not all codeswitching is necessarily trendy or exceptional. It may be a relatively normal and unmarked feature of urban speech (Swigart 1994), or it may be fairly ordinary as in utterance (1): "Mwaikata line?" Here, in the context of a ChiBemba broadcast, the usage of *line* is motivated by a lexical gap and is thus more a case of borrowing than of codeswitching. *Line* is simply a technical word imported from the realm of modern utilities, for example, electricity, telephone, water, sanitation, and broadcasting. By contrast, the blend of ChiBemba and English in (2) is more marked and unusual. Indeed, it is the basic index of the expression's trendiness. This sociolinguistic difference between (1) and (2) thus demonstrates how recentered radio phrases may also undergo subtle functional changes in addition to semantic and formal ones.

Entitling and Naming

Radio program titles constitute another form of metapragmatic discourse which – comparable to the various interpersonal expressions discussed above – has a high degree of transparency of form and function. Titles also have a certain prominence derived from frequent repetition and their placement within the flow of broadcasting. As stated earlier, titles function as announcing, captioning, or (re)framing devices. They are designed for reproducibility and recognizability, and these factors render them particularly available for recontextualization in popular usage.

Even *within* broadcasting, program titles are recycled from other sources. For example, nearly all English-language program titles on Radio Zambia (as well as most program formats) derive from Western sources such as the BBC and the VOA: for example *Main News Bulletin, The Breakfast Show, Up-to-Date, The World of Sport*, and *Sports Roundup*.[13] Most Zambian language program titles are also indebted to other external sources, and many are strikingly intertextual. For example, the ChiBemba advice program *Kabuusha Taakolelwe Boowa* takes its name from a well-known Bemba proverb meaning "the asker was not poisoned by a mushroom." The program has, in turn, become the source of coinage for the occupational title *kabuusha* "advisor". Another advice program, *Baanacimbuusa* "Women Advisors," has as its source the name for the ritual leaders of the Bemba girls' initiation ceremony. And in an interesting twist on origins, the title of the comic drama series *Ifyabukaaya* ("Things That Are Familiar" or "Things from Around Here") derives its name from a ChiBemba reader constructed for basic literacy during the colonial period by the White Fathers missionaries.

In short, virtually all radio titles represent a reanimation or invocation of another source or another genre. The larger point, then, is that radio programs themselves represent a range of recyclings, transpositions, and cannibalizations of other discourse genres. Moreover, this inherent intertextuality of radio itself seems to be a dynamic contributing factor in the recycling of radio words outside of broadcasting and the ease with which they circulate and become recontextualized. In popular usage, radio titles are transported to everyday situations as labels for speech events, experiences, and even personality types. As we saw in the case of "Over to you," a radio program title is used to caption a component of a speech event, namely, the handing over of a turn. The following example illustrates how a program title can also become the title of a personal experience.

One evening about 7 o'clock, my neighbor returned home from selling buns at the market, and I asked her how her day went. Using the title of a ChiBemba radio program, she sighed, "Ah mayo, 'Imbila ya Bulanda' " [Oh dear, "News of Suffering"]. One of the most popular programs on Radio Zambia, *Imbila ya Bulanda* airs virtually every day and serves as a primary vehicle for individuals to send messages announcing illnesses, deaths, and funerals. Here, my neighbor was using the radio program title to entitle the events of her day. She went on to explain how all the places at the market were filled when she went there at 5:30 a.m., and how she unsuccessfully tried to maneuver for a spot. She was forced to return later in the afternoon and finally did manage to find a place to sell her baked goods, but the day had been very long and exhausting.

Analogous to the Kitwe example above, this recycling injects a bit of humor into the situation through a marked contrast with the expression's original context. The phrase "imbila ya bulanda" is unmistakably welded to the popular program that features news of death and illness; so virtually any utterance of it outside this context intertextually invokes the program. By recontextualizing the phrase as a caption for her day, my neighbor did indeed exploit the functional force of the phrase to announce that a tale of woe was forthcoming. But since these events were far less serious than those announced on radio, her entitling was hyperbolic and lent an ironic humor to the tale, which after all, had a happy ending.

In addition to providing a common public source for ways of entitling situations and experiences, media can also be a source for proper names and names of types of people (table 3.1). These humorous modes of naming and labeling exhibit elements of what is a very pervasive kind of playful, ironic kind of public verbal culture in Zambia which is not limited to any particular age, locale, or language (Spitulnik 1994b). They also illustrate how active audience interpretations enter into the mediated construction of a world of familiar people, social types, and locales, as described by Anderson (1983). Some of the particular examples shown here are urban and youth based, and others are ones that originated in urban-youth slang but are now more widely used.[14] The meaning and derivation of most items in table 3.1 are self-evident, but the first two need some explanation.[15]

The labeling of party vigilantes as "By Air Boys" in the late 1980s essentially began with a television advertisement for Zambian Airways. The ad pictures a smiling customer sitting in a disembodied plane seat floating across the sky, while the announcer talks about the pleasure of

Table 3.1 Innovative names derived from media sources

Name	*Meaning*	*Media source*
By Air Boys	political-party vigilantes	TV commercial
Chongololo	pretentious, European-like Zambian	radio program
BaSix Koloko	people from the Northwestern Province (the ones whose newscasts start at 6 a.m.)	radio newscasts
Dallas City	the Lusaka neighborhood of Kabwata (an upper-middle-class residential area)	TV show *Dallas*
Hawaii	women's dorms at Copperbelt University ("because the ladies there live like they are at a resort")	TV show *Hawaii Five-O*
Ninja	50-kwacha bill (the highest currency denomination in the late 1980s)	foreign movies

traveling "by air" with Zambia Airways. This striking image of the floating customer was then applied to the way that the party vigilantes remove illegal traders from local marketplaces.[16] Once discovered without the proper papers, the marketeer is lifted on both sides and is suddenly whisked away by the vigilantes while still in a sitting position, much like the man in the ad who somehow floats across the screen while seated in a chair.

The story of *chongololo* also illustrates the creative reworking of a media name that imports distinctive imagery from the original source. The Wildlife Conservation Society of Zambia and Bata Shoe Company sponsor a children's program entitled *Chongololo* ("centipede" in ChiNyanja), which is produced in ChiNyanja, ChiBemba, and English. This educational program features two or three adult hosts who discuss the habits and habitats of Zambian wildlife. Interspersed with their comments, fictional outings, and the sound effects of wild animals are songs about animals sung by a chorus of children. Listeners can become members of the Chongololo Radio Club of the Air by submitting their answers to the question "Why is it so important for us to conserve nature?" In all three languages, the program opens and closes with the children's chorus singing their theme song in English:

> *Chongololo*, it's our favorite club.
> *Chongololo*, it's the club we love.
> Come and join us on this show, and you'll have lots of fun.
> Learn about the living things [*clap*] under the sun.[17]

In popular Zambian slang, *chongololo* has become a term for Zambians who try to speak like Europeans. The English-language program is hosted by a British male who is typically joined by two Zambian females, all of whom speak with a slow and deliberate British Received Pronunciation (RP) accent. The Zambian children on the program also speak this form of English very well for their ages (roughly 8 to 12 years old) and thus sound particularly precocious and privileged. Even in the ChiBemba and ChiNyanja programs, this is reflected in the English theme song. One young Zambian explained to me:

> *Chongololo* is a word for Zambians who try to adopt a foreign accent so that to a Zambian they sound like they are Europeans, while Europeans on the other hand fail to understand what they say. ... [University of Zambia] students say, "They speak in tongues."

A less affected form of Zambian English (with a phonology closer to that of Zambian languages) is preferred by most Zambians, even by those who are highly educated and frequently exposed to the English of Europeans and Americans. For example, a 20-year-old student at a technical training college walked into the dormitory common room to watch the television news (which is always in English) and declared in ChiNyanja:

> *Ah, lelo niza nvelako* news *cifukwa si achongololo amene azabelenga.* [Oh, today I'm going to listen to the news because it's not the chongololos reading it.]

The young man clearly approved of the pronunciation of the two newscasters; presumably if they had spoken like chongololos, he would have walked out.

Not only is the Zambian chongololo guilty of having a fake accent, but he or she is also guilty of going to the extreme in mimicking European dress and behavior. This takes on class dimensions, as one university student told me, "A chongololo is the child of an *apamwamba* [upper class person]." Another put it more extremely: " 'Chongies' are victims of bourgeois capitalist ideology. They speak with American accents."[18] The negative behavior of the chongololo thus extends beyond a verbal style of "speak[ing] in tongues" to include the desire for a bourgeois lifestyle that is beyond the reach of most Zambians. Indeed, the actual content of the *Chongololo* program itself – observing birds in nature, appreciation of the world of insects, tourism within Zambia, and concern with wildlife preservation – emblematizes this essentially un-Zambian outlook.

What kinds of semiotic processes are at work in this recontextualization of a program title as a personal stereotype? First, there are certain formal linguistic conditions that support it. Analogous to the Kitwe example, this recontextualization is based on both metonymy and the existence of a shared lexical category (proper name). The program name *Chongololo* is also the club name, and club members – or people like them – are metonymically designated as *chongololos* or *chongies*. In addition, the recycling imports several features of the original radio context into its negative connotations: the mode of speaking, upper-class leisure activities, and a Western-oriented outlook. Moreover, the very concept of the radio program *as a club* that can be joined furthers the implicit critique that the show and the chongololo represent an exclusive sector of Zambian society. The Chongololo Radio Club of the Air, as a club for chongololos, in essence constitutes a distinct speech community where members share a common norm of English language usage (i.e., RP). The point of contention, and what motivates the negative stereotype, is whether this speech community has the rightful claim to also represent the linguistic community of English within Zambia. While the program's speakers do adhere to a "culture of the standard" (Silverstein 1987) and view themselves as exemplifying proper English usage – particularly as they are guided by a male British program host – most Zambians reject this as a model for how Zambians should speak English.

Poaching from Personalities

In contrast to the *Chongololo* show, numerous other radio programs provide very attractive models of speech styles which are emulated and invoked in more positive ways. In many cases, these styles and linguistic innovations are actually the trademarks of a particular radio personality. The uniqueness of such radio personalities is to a great degree built upon this verbal creativity, a creativity that is at the same time relatively predictable since it is recognizable as a personal style. In many instances this very reputation and visibility is what subsequently propels the adoption of broadcasters' linguistic innovations within popular culture (see Gumperz 1971: 223). Some of these recycled innovations retain the indexical link to the individual broadcaster's speech style, and others have been absorbed more widely into popular usage. In the following we look at a few examples of this popular adoption of broadcasters' speech innovations and habits.

Dennis Liwewe, Zambia's most famous sports announcer, is renowned for his fast speech, innovative descriptions, and dramatic delivery. His broadcasts are almost always in English, and his mode of speaking has become a model and a reference point for certain phrasings, even beyond the area of sports. For example, one very common Liwewe phrase during football (soccer) games combines the word *situation* with one or two numbers:

(4) It's a one-zero situation.
(5) Bwalya comes into the Zaire zone. It's a one-two situation.

In utterance (4), *situation* refers to the score. A one-zero situation is thus a score of one to zero. In (5), *situation* refers to the *positions* on the playing field. That is, there is one offensive player – Bwalya on the Zambian team – moving in against two defensive players in the Zaire zone.

Zambians have picked up on this usage of *situation* and have applied it outside the realm of sports, to refer to contexts where some numerical quantity is involved. For example, I was at the University of Zambia snack bar, and a young man had been at the counter trying to get some matches to light a cigarette. He was unsuccessful and walked back to his friend, saying:

(6)	*Ifya*matches, zero situation	"Things [boxes] of matches, zero situation." "About the matches, zero situation."

The "zero situation" in this case is the unavailability of matches. While one might interpret *situation* here as meaning "predicament," it also has a sense analogous to the sports-specific forms in (4) and (5), as "score" or "position."

The young man came up empty-handed in the search for matches; he thus failed to score and found that nothing was in position.

The recycling of the Liwewe formula "[number(-number)] situation" outside of sports talk is highly marked as creative language use. While recontextualized, it still retains an important indexical link back to its original source. This is not just a link of attribution, that is, the identification of Liwewe as the originator of the expression, but one that carries the broader associations of a "Liweweism," a phrasing that is dramatic, lively, and somewhat hyperbolic in the manner of the famous Liwewe.[19] The usage of ChiBemba-English code-mixing in (6) lends an additional air of trendiness to the expression.

Other examples of linguistic innovations stemming from specific radio personalities include the words *get* and *dig* as idioms for "understand" that, as discussed earlier, have been incorporated into the code-mixed slang expressions "Naugeta?" (Do ya get me?) and "Namudiga?" (Do you dig it?). These words emanate from the most popular Radio Zambia DJs, who are themselves recyclers, as they extract popular American and British slang from song lyrics while exhorting their listeners, talking up the records, and making segues between selections. Many DJs also exemplify the pronunciations characteristic of informal American English usage (for example, strongly nasalized "gonna," "wanna," and "ya know"), and these expressions circulate quite widely among Zambian youths. The following excerpt from Radio 4 disc jockey Leonard Kantumoya, also known as "The Groove Maker" or "The GM," illustrates some of these media sources of urban slang:

Ah, when you hear the GM playing instrumentals and keeping a little quiet, you just know the hour is about to arrive and I'm about to *hit the road* for home, because I see my good friend Swidden Hangaala is already in.
He's *dug* in already and he's trying to *dig* in even further. [*Laughs*.]
He's *gonna* sweep me out of my DJ saddle.
[Radio 4, February 3, 1989, emphasis added]

With this kind of fast-paced, exciting style, Zambian DJs play a pivotal role in introducing an English-language vocabulary that speaks to the mood and tempo of the modern condition. Contemporary Zambian English is replete with such words and idioms, many of which are not restricted to subcultural usage and many of which have origins as far back as the 1940s. Some of the most popular of these are the words *jive, jazz, super, live, nonstop, beat*, and *rap*. In this sense, radio – in conjunction with popular music that is often the original site of such vocabulary – has played a key role not only in introducing new lexical items but in structuring an entire semantic field that denotes excitement and entertainment.

Broadcasters' Recyclings: The Case of Personal Titles

The preceding discussion has touched on several instances where media professionals themselves recontextualize and reanimate phrases that originate in other contexts, for example, program titles that stem from indigenous oral traditions and Western media sources, and disc-jockey speech registers that draw from popular song lyrics and the styles of DJs heard on foreign stations. In this sense, not only does radio serve as a model of normative language use and as a springboard for linguistic innovations within popular culture, it is also a dynamically intertextual site in which an existing repertoire of public words is continually being modified and elaborated upon. This section examines one final case of broadcasters' recyclings, one that illustrates the possibilities of political parody within broadcasting.

All radio disc jockeys have at least one nickname that they regularly use; most of these are boasts of some sort, and many are creative twists on political titles or other titles associated with high status. For example, the late Peter Mweemba went by the name "Brother PM," a combination of his personal initials and an American-derived term for solidary males.[20] In the Zambian context, this coinage is particularly striking, because PM also designates the third highest ranking politician in the country, the Prime Minister.[21] As he cultivated his own style of casual and trendy familiarity,

Brother PM played off the fact that the real PM is surrounded by the exact opposite: an aura of extreme deference and seriousness. Exploiting the full force of this contrast, ZNBC management actually orchestrated the meeting of Brother PM and the real PM on national radio, by inviting the then-Prime Minister to preside over the inauguration of a new radio channel. Peter Mweemba was the DJ on duty:

Right, this is your DJ, Brother PM,
behind the microphone hoping you're ready for us,
as we bring it to you, the biggest and best on FM stereo.
Right, in just a few minutes' time from now,
the Right Honorable Prime Minister, Kebby Musokotwane
will be walking into Radio Mulungushi stereo studio,
to officially switch on Radio Mulungushi.
[Radio 4, February 1, 1989]

After the Prime Minister inaugurates the new radio channel, Peter Mweemba interviews him at length about the role of broadcasting. In the exchange, the two address each other as "Right Honorable Prime Minister" and "Peter." Later in the interview, Mweemba personalizes the discussion and focuses on the musical tastes of the Prime Minister. The PM is asked if he has any favorites to request, and by the end of the interview, he is integrated like any other avid radio listener into the popular radio format of the deejayed greeting/request program:

Well, before I spin your records, Right Honorable Prime Minister,
finally, any special greetings to your friends and family?
I realize you are a national leader;
so I suppose there are one or two people you'd like to say hello to.

Of course, the integration is not really complete. Mweemba does not refer to himself as "Brother PM" during this exchange, nor would we expect the real PM to use this phrase. Moreover, the list of people whom the Prime Minister wishes to greet and thank is rather unusual. He first greets his wife, then his "colleagues in Cabinet," the Zambian people, and finally the President.

In an interesting twist on both Peter Mweemba's innovation and another political abbreviation, the broadcaster Margaret Phiri uses the initials "MP" as her DJ trademark. In common parlance, MP designates a Member of Parliament. Phiri is a rather low-key broadcaster and does not really play up the political connotations of her nickname. Many listeners feel that she rather uncreatively copied Mweemba's model. Behind this, however, are some basic gender differences and expectations about speaking styles. Projecting a strong lively personality on national airwaves and, especially, the playfulness and boasting that is inherent in many DJ nicknames (e.g., "The Sweet Sensation" and "The Man with the Longest Queue in Town") is deemed more appropriate for Zambian men and less appropriate for Zambian women.

One popular radio DJ who is constantly promoting himself and coining new phrases is Leonard Kantumoya ("The Groove Maker" or "The GM"). Behind the microphone, Kantumoya talks quite a lot and often uses American slang (circa 1970), as illustrated above. The wordplay, or abbreviation play, in his nickname builds on the fact that, in Zambia, GM is one of the most pervasive labels for the highest-ranking office in business and industry: the general manager. Using another abbreviation, Kantumoya dubs his music "PPS" (People Pleasing Sounds). PPS with GM is somewhat of a mixed metaphor (or mixed bureaucracy), but it is amusing in any case as it invokes the well-known title "Provincial Political Secretary."[22]

In their recontextualizations of these abbreviations designating bureaucratic structures and high offices, Zambian broadcasters display a distinctive sense of humor. They never directly refer to the original source of their nicknames; they only allude to it. But like political leaders and top level bureaucrats, they are, in their own realm, at the controls. They are in charge of spinning the records and making the announcements. In terms of their pragmatic structure, such DJ nicknames are most apt as uniquely identifying radio trademarks or signatures, because they already have a built-in definiteness. The initials themselves presuppose the existence of a specific nonabbreviated form, and these nonabbreviated forms specifically designate the holder of a particular office or position.

As recyclings of tropes of the nation-state, these DJ nicknames illustrate a more general point about the public sphere in Zambia. The knowledge of acronyms and abbreviations is an important part of communicative competence in Zambia, and this is essentially part of the postcolonial legacy.[23] For example, in modern-day Zambia the most prominent positions, institutions, and interests – from government offices and state services to multinational corporations and foreign donor agencies – are designated by a proliferation of acronyms such as UNZA, TAZARA, ZESCO, INDECO, ZNBC, DANIDA, SIDO, FTJ, KK, PM, MP, GM, and DG.[24] What appears to be a virtual alphabet soup for the uninitiated is actually a very concrete mapping and populating of the public sphere. With their own initials, Brother PM, MP, and the GM thus index not only their conversancy and sense of humor about this public sphere but also their unique membership in it: to be initialed in this way is to have a uniquely identifying description and to be counted among the ranks of the nation's leading figures.

Conclusion

This article has attempted to open up a relatively unexplored area of research at the intersection of language and culture, by investigating the social circulation of media discourse and its implications for the mediation of communities. I have argued that broadcasting functions as a common reservoir and reference point for various kinds of linguistic innovations in Zambia, ranging from the subcultural to the mainstream, from the fleeting to the perduring, and from the parodic to the mundane. Radio is a source for lexical coinage (e.g., *chongies* and *kabuusha*), idiomatic expressions (e.g., "Waikata line?"), and distinctive modes of verbal interaction (e.g., "Over to you"). It is also a resource for innovative tropes and analogies: for example, *BaSix Koloko* (The Six o'Clockers) as a name for members of ethnic groups whose newscasts begin daily at 6 a.m., or "Hello, Kitwe" as an address form for someone who is hard of hearing.

In addition to documenting these processes, I have made some broader semiotic generalizations about the types of media discourse that circulate and the types of conditions that enable this circulation. For example, metapragmatic discourse and, in particular, various kinds of interpersonal routines and framing devices are readily seized upon in creative reworkings of media language. I have proposed that features such as transparency of form and function and prominence (via frequent repetition or association with dramatic moments) create a "prepared-for detachability" (Bauman and Briggs 1990: 74) that enables such discourse to be circulated across communities. I have also suggested that the language of proper names and definite description (including place-names, nicknames, and abbreviations), as well as generic names for social types, figure importantly in socially circulating media discourse, because they function to locate and populate a shared world, much in a manner analogous to the processes described by Anderson (1983) in reference to the eighteenth-century novel. And finally, I have suggested that these processes of circulation operate within a much larger context of a very dynamic verbal culture which itself is playful, ironic, and highly intertextual.

Addressing the thorny question of the construction of communities is a much more difficult task than discovering the various semiotic and cultural conditions that propel the social circulation of media discourse. I have claimed that mass media provide common reference points for the production of shared linguistic knowledge and that the social circulation of media discourse is just one case of the subtle linguistic connections that exist across populations that stretch over regional and national boundaries. I have proposed that criteria such as frequency of media consumption and large-scale exposure to a common media source enter into this equation and that the speech community concept can be productively refined by including these features.

As the cases considered here have intimated, the communities mediated by radio broadcasting are several. Since media discourse is not uniformly accessible or even uniformly seized upon and interpreted in the same ways, all kinds of outcomes are possible. In some instances the social circulation of media discourse occurs at the subcultural level (e.g., "Waikata line?" among urban youths), and in some instances it is more general (e.g., "Imbila ya Bulanda" and "Ofata yu"). Still other instances may be highly idiosyncratic, as suggested by the case of "Hello, Kitwe." Further research into the sociolinguistic distribution of recycled media discourse across age, gender, class, locale, and language is really required to answer such questions about communities more concretely.

One enduring issue throughout the discussion has been how to characterize the status of these phrases that circulate across and through mass media and popular culture. Following other work in linguistic anthropology (Bauman and Briggs 1990; Briggs and Bauman 1992; Lucy 1993; Silverstein and Urban 1996), I have attempted in each case to specify the various formal conditions on, and functional effects of, such recontextualized speech. In comparison to the better-known speech genres (e.g., narrative, oratory, ritual speech, and reported speech) that feature in such studies, many of the media fragments considered here exhibit (1) a much greater mobility through various social contexts, and (2) a peculiar built-in detachability and reproducibility, as stated above. As they thread through different contexts of use, giving people their own voices and aesthetic pleasures, such public words hearken to speakers and contexts which are in some ways larger than life. Indeed, it is this transportability, or detachability, that allows public words to seem to have lives of their own yet also be fibers of connection across various social situations and contexts.

While some scholars might attribute this circulation of media discourse more generally to the inherent nature of mass media and/or to a postmodern condition, I would challenge this. It may be true that the postmodern condition is characterized by an unprecedented fascination with icons, images, slogans, jingles, and other mass-produced objects that mass media disseminate and produce (Baudrillard 1983; Harvey 1989; Hebdige 1988; Jameson 1984). But the various practices that characterize active audiences such as media poaching and intertextuality (Certeau 1984; Jenkins 1992) do not seem to be particularly new. The evidence here suggests that recycling media discourse and even the existence of such "detachables" are part of a much more general process of language use, or social life of language, which intersects (but precedes) the postmodern, pop-culture era, and the advent of mass media as widespread, public communication forms. In fact, it seems equally the case that the radio recyclings discussed here are not really exemplars of a postmodern condition per se, but rather they are evidence of the more general heteroglossic nature of language. To quote Bakhtin:

> [T]here are no "neutral" words and forms – words and forms that can belong to "no one"; language has been completely taken over, shot through with intentions and accents. For any individual consciousness living in it, language is not an abstract system of normative forms but rather a concrete heterglot conception of the world. All words have a "taste" of a profession, a genre . . . a particular person, a generation, an age group, the day and hour. Each word tastes of the contexts in which it has lived its socially charged life. (1981: 293)

As a far-reaching, ongoing, public communication form – which is itself a constant reanimator – radio broadcasting has the potential to magnify, and even create, this "socially charged life" of certain linguistic forms. I have suggested here that the study of media discourse in popular culture is one such avenue for examining the dynamism and mobility of language, and that this mobility (and mobilizability) has far-reaching implications for both language change and the construction of public cultures and speech communities which are vibrant and creative.

NOTES

Acknowledgements. The primary research for this article was carried out in 1988–90, supported by Fulbright-Hays and NSF fellowships, and facilitated by the Institute for African Studies (now INESOR) at the University of Zambia. I would like to extend my sincere thanks to these institutions. I am also grateful to the Spencer Foundation and the University Research Committee at Emory University for supporting various stages of this work. I am deeply indebted, as well, to many colleagues who have offered their valuable input at various writing stages, including, but not limited to, Mark Auslander, Misty Bastian, James Collins, Jane Hill, Bruce Knauft, Ben Lee, John Lucy, Mwelwa Musambachime, Bradd Shore, Michael Silverstein, and the anonymous reviewers for the *Journal of Linguistic Anthropology.*

1 As an adjective, *public* is used here (following Urban) in a fairly neutral sense to connote wide distribution and a general openness and availability. This definition contrasts in important ways with definitions of the noun *public,* or *the public*, as an ideological construct concerning state–citizen relations or corporation–consumer relations (Calhoun 1992; Gal 1995: 417 f.; Gal and Woolard 1995; Spitulnik 1994a). For discussions of how these two are linked, that is, how public availability of certain communication forms figures into the ideological construction of publics, see Gal and Woolard 1995 and Spitulnik 1994a, 1994b.

2 For electronic media, the semantics of the term *broadcast* (which originated from the realm of agriculture) encapsulates this important sense of widespread distribution.

3 See Irvine 1987 for a discussion of the history of the speech community concept and its various definitions, revisions, shortcomings, and merits. Probably the most strongly debated issues concern the importance of shared knowledge of a linguistic code, including shared knowledge of norms for usage and interpretation (Gumperz 1971) and the related emphasis on the homogeneity of the speech community. For example, several scholars have pointed out that linguistic and sociolinguistic knowledge is not evenly shared across communities (Irvine 1987; Parkin 1994), despite a dominant ideology of sharedness in many cases (Silverstein 1987). In contrast, the criteria of density and frequency of interaction have been omitted, more than debated, perhaps because of their problematic nature for large-scale societies and their behaviorist connotations stemming from Bloomfield, the originator of the speech community concept.

4 ChiBemba is the name for the language of the Bemba people, BaBemba, who constitute roughly 19 percent of Zambia's national population (Kashoki 1978a). More than half of the nation's 9.1 million inhabitants speak ChiBemba (56 percent of the national population, according to Kashoki 1978a), and at least one-quarter speak English (26 percent according to Kashoki 1978a, and 45 percent according to Claypole and Daka 1993). Approximately 69 percent of all national radio broadcasting is in English, and 6 percent is in ChiBemba (Spitulnik 1992).

5 According to a national media survey conducted in 1991, 57 percent of all Zambians own a working radio, 74 percent listen at least once per week, and 63 percent listen daily or almost daily. By sharp contrast, only 17 percent own TVs and 30 percent view TV at least once a week (Claypole and Daka 1993: 63–4).

6 For a discussion of this last phrase, see Hill 1993 [and this volume].

7 Metapragmatic discourse is speech that is about the communication context or about the functions of language in context: for example, "Here's what I want to tell you . . . ," "I didn't hear what you just said," and "Stop lecturing me." As speech about speaking, metapragmatic discourse functions to both regiment and frame the interpretation of the ongoing speech event (Silverstein 1976, 1993).

8 Media discourse about mistakes and failures is a common target of comic recycling. For example, ZNBC radio and TV frequently broadcast public service announcements for the national electric company regarding temporary power outages. The phrase "Any inconvenience caused is deeply regretted" is a standard feature of such announcements and can be humorously recast in other speech contexts. For an example on the World Wide Web, see Ranjit Warrier's rendering of the Zambian English version as "Any inconvenience caused is diply regraitted" in reference to his homepage's possibly strange appearance through non-Netscape browsers (Warrier 1996b).

9 The complex humor of this exchange is even more elaborate for those who know the etymology of the place-name "Kitwe" in Lamba, the language indigenous to the Copperbelt region. Kitwe is an abbreviation of a Lamba expression for "big ear." The place was named after an historical event involving an elephant.

10 In the late 1980s, versions of *Over to You* aired on Thursdays in Luvale, on Saturdays in English and ChiLunda, and on Sundays in ChiBemba, ChiNyanja, and ChiTonga.

11 Further investigation is required to determine the precise morpheme boundaries in these assimilated phrases. My representation is based on a hypothesis that the first three syllables are one word and that *you* is analyzed as a demonstrative pronoun for third-person singular, in an analogy with *yu* (ChiNyanja) and *uyu* (ChiBemba) "this person," "her," "him."

12 In the examples, italicized words are ChiBemba (unless otherwise noted), and non-italicized words are English.

13 Further examples of foreign-derived titles on Radio Zambia include *This Is My Song, My Old Favorites, Yours for the Asking*, and other titles based on fill-in-the-blank formulas such as *X's Corner (Children's Corner, Women's Corner,* and *Poet's Corner*) and *X's Magazine (Women's Magazine)*.

14 More specific sociolinguistic questions about the significance of each form remain open for further research, since their usage and distribution were not systematically studied.

15 In addition to these more innovative names, Zambian media are also a popular source for personal names, for example, names for newborns and names that teenagers adopt for themselves. During the late 1980s the names Jeff and Pam were very popular, as they derived from the American television series *Dynasty* and *Dallas* running on TV-Zambia.

16 At the time, the party vigilantes were members of the country's ruling (and sole) party, the United National Independence Party (UNIP).

17 The closing song substitutes the last two verses with: "Now it's time to say goodbye to our friends far and near. Before we go let's give our wildlife a great big cheer. Yeah!"

18 This quote points to the difficulty in precisely defining the chongololo accent. In the radio program the broadcasters' accents are RP, and the children's accents approximate this. But outside of radio, many forms of non-Zambian English count as chongololo accents, including ones that sound like a blend of American and British varieties. As one reviewer of this article noted, the perception that chongies have American accents may be linked, via ideological pressures, to the identification of speakers as "capitalists."

19 Liwewe's most famous phrase is his characteristic wild yell, "It' a goooooooooaaal!!!" For an electronic poaching of this, see Warrier 1996a.

20 Peter Mweemba's use of *brother* has several possible connotations and may stem from idioms of Christian brotherhood and/or from African-American usage.

21 Political positions and rankings have changed somewhat under the current Chiluba government. At the time of fieldwork, during the one-party system, the secretary-general of the ruling party ranked second after the Zambian president.

22 During the period of one-party rule, this was the title for the second-highest government position at the provincial level.

23 The creative poaching of such abbreviations, acronyms, and state slogans is pervasive in Zambia and throughout much of Africa (Mbembe 1992; Spitulnik 1994b). One example of this is illustrated by the renderings of the abbreviation "IFA," which is on the front of the large Zambian army trucks manufactured by the IFA company (of the former East Germany). Because these vehicles are involved in so many fatal road accidents, the name is interpreted as designating "International Funeral Association/Ambassadors," or *inifwa* "death."

24 Respectively, these stand for University of Zambia, Tanzania-Zambia Railway, Zambia Electric Supply Corporation, Industrial Development Corporation, Zambia National Broadcasting Corporation, Danish International Development Agency, Small Industries Development Organisation, Frederick T. J. Chiluba (the current president), Kenneth Kaunda (the former president), Prime Minister, Member of Parliament, General Manager, and Director General.

REFERENCES

Anderson, Benedict (1983). *Imagined Communities: Reflections on the Origin and Spread of Nationalism*. London: Verso.

Bakhtin, Mikhail M. (1981[1934–35]). Discourse in the Novel. In *The Dialogic Imagination: Four Essays*. Michael Holquist and Caryl Emerson, trans.; Michael Holquist, ed., pp. 259–422. Austin: University of Texas Press.

Bakhtin, Mikhail M. (1986[1952–53]). The Problem of Speech Genres. In *Speech Genres and Other Late Essays*. Vern W. McGee, trans.; Caryl Emerson and Michael Holquist, eds., pp. 60–102. Austin: University of Texas Press.

Basso, Keith H. (1990a[1984]). "Stalking with Stories": Names, Places, and Moral Narratives among the Western Apache. In *Western Apache Language and Culture*, pp. 99–137. Tucson: University of Arizona Press.

Basso, Keith H. (1990b[1988]). "Speaking with Names": Language and Landscape among the Western Apache. In *Western Apache Language and Culture*, pp. 138–73. Tuscon: University of Arizona Press.

Baudrillard, Jean (1983[1978]). The Implosion of Meaning in the Media. In *In the Shadow of the Silent Majorities*. Paul Foss, Paul Patton, and John Johnston, trans, pp. 95–110. New York: Semiotext(e).

Bauman, Richard, and Charles L. Briggs (1990). Poetics and Performance as Critical Perspectives on Language and Social Life. *Annual Review of Anthropology* 19: 59–88.

Bhabha, Homi (1994). *The Location of Culture*. New York: Routledge.

Bourdieu, Pierre (1991[1982]). *Language and Symbolic Power*. Gino Raymond and Matthew Adamson, trans.; John B. Thompson, ed. Cambridge, MA: Harvard University Press.

Briggs, Charles L., and Richard Bauman (1992). Genre, Intertextuality, and Social Power. *Journal of Linguistic Anthropology* 2: 131–72; reproduced in Chapter 9 of this Reader.

Calhoun, Craig (ed.) (1992). *Habermas and the Public Sphere*. Cambridge, MA: MIT Press.

Claypole, Andrew, and Given Daka (1993). Zambia. In *Global Audiences: Research in Worldwide Broadcasting 1993*. Graham Mytton, ed., pp. 59–70. London: John Libbey.

Certeau, Michel de (1984). *The Practice of Everyday Life*. Steven Rendall, trans. Berkeley: University of California Press.

Fischer, Michael M. J., and Mehdi Abedi (1990). *Debating Muslims: Cultural Dialogues in Postmodernity and Tradition*. Madison: University of Wisconsin Press.

Foucault, Michel (1972[1971]). The Discourse on Language. In *The Archaeology of Knowledge and the Discourse on Language*, pp. 215–37. Rupert Swyer, trans. New York: Harper & Row.

Gal, Susan (1989). Language and Political Economy. *Annual Review of Anthropology* 18: 345–67.

Gal, Susan (1995). Language and the "Arts of Resistance." *Cultural Anthropology* 10: 407–24.

Gal, Susan, and Kathryn A. Woolard (eds.) (1995). Constructing Languages and Publics. Theme issue. *Pragmatics* 5(2).

Gumperz, John J. (1971[1968]). The Speech Community. In *Language and Social Context*. Pier P. Giglioli, ed., pp. 219–31. New York: Viking Penguin.

Gumperz, John J. (1982). *Discourse Strategies*. Cambridge: Cambridge University Press.

Habermas, Jürgen (1989). *The Structural Transformation of the Public Sphere*. Thomas Burger, trans. Cambridge, MA: MIT Press.

Hanks, William F. (1996). *Language and Communicative Practices*. Boulder, CO: Westview.

Harvey, David (1989). *The Condition of Postmodernity: An Enquiry into the Origins of Cultural Change*. Cambridge, MA: Blackwell.

Hebdige, Dick (1988). *Hiding in the Light: On Images and Things*. London: Comedia.

Hill, Jane H. (1993). Hasta La Vista, Baby: Anglo Spanish in the American Southwest. *Critique of Anthropology* 13: 145–76.

Irvine, Judith T. (1987). Domains of Description in the Ethnography of Speaking: A Retrospective on the "Speech Community." In *Performance, Speech Community, and Genre*, pp. 13–24. Working Papers and Proceedings of the Center for Psychosocial Studies, 11. Chicago, IL: Center for Psychosocial Studies.

Irvine, Judith T. (1996). Shadow Conversations: The Indeterminacy of Participant Roles. In *Natural Histories of Discourse*. Michael Silverstein and Greg Urban, eds, pp. 131–59. Chicago, IL: University of Chicago Press.

Jameson, Fredric (1984). Postmodernism, or the Cultural Logic of Late Capitalism. *New Left Review* 146: 53–92.

Jenkins, Henry (1992). *Textual Poachers: Television Fans and Participatory Culture*. London: Routledge.

Kashoki, Mubanga E. (1978a). The Language Situation in Zambia. In *Language in Zambia*. Sirarpi Ohannessian and Mubanga E. Kashoki, eds., pp. 9–46. London: International African Institute.

Kashoki, Mubanga E. (1978b). Lexical Innovation in Four Zambian Languages. *African Languages/Languages Africaines* 4: 80–95.

Kroskrity, Paul V. (1992). Arizona Tewa Kiva Speech as a Manifestation of Linguistic Ideology. *Pragmatics* 2: 297–309.

Lucy, John A. (ed.) (1993). *Reflexive Language: Reported Speech and Metapragmatics*. New York: Cambridge University Press.

Mbembe, Achille (1992). The Banality of Power and the Aesthetics of Vulgarity. *Public Culture* 4(2): 1–30.

Myers-Scotton, Carol (1993). *Social Motivations for Codeswitching*. Oxford: Clarendon Press.

Parkin, David (1994). Language, Government and the Play on Purity and Impurity: Arabic, Swahili and the Vernaculars in Kenya. In *African Languages, Development and the State*. Richard Fardon and Graham Furniss, eds., pp. 227–45. London: Routledge.

Silverstein, Michael (1976). Shifters, Linguistic Categories and Cultural Description. In *Meaning in Anthropology*. Keith H. Basso and Henry A. Selby, eds., pp. 11–55. Albuquerque: University of New Mexico Press.

Silverstein, Michael (1987). *Monoglot "Standard" in America*. Working Papers and Proceedings of the Center for Psychosocial Studies, 13. Chicago, IL: Center for Psychosocial Studies.

Silverstein, Michael (1992). The Indeterminacy of Contextualization: When Is Enough Enough? In *The Contextualization of Language*. Peter Auer and Aldo di Luzio, eds., pp. 55–76. Amsterdam: John Benjamins.

Silverstein, Michael (1993). Metapragmatic Discourse and Metapragmatic Function. In *Reflexive Language: Reported Speech and Metapragmatics*. John A. Lucy, ed., pp. 33–58. New York: Cambridge University Press.

Silverstein, Michael, and Greg Urban (eds.) (1996). *Natural Histories of Discourse*. Chicago, IL: University of Chicago Press.

Spitulnik, Debra (1992). Radio Time Sharing and the Negotiation of Linguistic Pluralism in Zambia. *Pragmatics* 2: 335–54.

Spitulnik, Debra (1993). Anthropology and Mass Media. *Annual Review of Anthropology* 22: 293–315.

Spitulnik, Debra (1994a). Radio Culture in Zambia: Audiences, Public Words, and the Nation-State. PhD dissertation, University of Chicago.

Spitulnik, Debra (1994b). Radio Cycles and Recyclings in Zambia: Public Words, Popular Critiques, and National Communities. *Passages* 8: 10, 12, 14–16.

Swigart, Lee (1994). Cultural Creolisation and Language Use in Post-Colonial Africa: The Case of Senegal. *Africa* 64(2): 75–89.

Urban, Greg (1991). *A Discourse-Centered Approach to Culture*. Austin: University of Texas Press. Warrier, Ranjit (1996a). Memories from Zambia. Electronic document. http://www.latech. edu/~ranjitw/memory.html

Warrier, Ranjit (1996b). Ranjit Warrier's Home Page. Electronic document. http:// www. latech.edu:80/~ranjitw/index.html

STUDY QUESTIONS

1 In what ways does Spitulnik's study of media discourse help redefine the notion of speech community as discussed in the two preceding chapters (by Gumperz and Morgan respectively)?
2 Using the examples provided by Spitulnik in the chapter, provide an argument for each of the following statements: (a) some kinds of phrases seem easier to transport from the media context to everyday contexts; (b) some aspects (e.g., implications) of the meaning of the media phrases are altered in the transposition; (c) knowledge of the original radio source is important for being able to understand the meaning of the phrases in new contexts.
3 Drawing on your own experience, provide examples of transfer from media discourse into everyday discourse. What do those examples tell you about your peer group? What do they tell you about your beliefs and values?
4 What does the *Chongololo Program* represent linguistically and ideologically for most Zambians?
5 Define "intertextuality," "recontextualization," and "recycling" based on Spitulnik's use of the terms. Provide some examples for each.

4

Communication of Respect in Interethnic Service Encounters

Benjamin Bailey

Conflict in face-to-face interaction between immigrant Korean retail merchants and their African American customers has been widely documented since the early 1980s. Newspapers in New York, Washington, DC, Chicago, and Los Angeles have carried stories on this friction; and the 1989 movie *Do the Right Thing* depicted angry confrontations of this type. By the time that the events of April 1992 – referred to variously as the Los Angeles "riots," "uprising," "civil disturbance" or, by many immigrant Koreans, *sa-i-gu* "April 29" – cast a media spotlight on such relations, there had already been numerous African American boycotts of immigrant Korean businesses in New York and Los Angeles; politicians had publicly addressed the issue; and academics (e.g. Ella Stewart 1989 and Chang 1990) had begun to write about this type of friction.

There are multiple, intertwined reasons for these interethnic tensions in small businesses. An underlying source is the history of social, racial, and economic inequality in American society. In this broader context, visits to any store can become a charged event for African Americans. Thus, according to Austin (1995: 32):

> Any kind of ordinary face-to-face retail transaction can turn into a hassle for a black person. For example, there can hardly be a black in urban America who has not been either denied entry to a store, closely watched, snubbed, questioned about her or his ability to pay for an item, or stopped and detained for shoplifting.

Specific features of small convenience/liquor stores, such as the ones studied here, exacerbate the potential for conflict. Prices in such stores are high, many customers have low incomes, and the storekeepers are seen by many as the latest in a long line of economic exploiters from outside the African American community (Drake and Cayton 1945; Sturdevant 1969; Chang 1990, 1993). Shoplifting is not uncommon, and the late hours and cash basis of the stores make them appealing targets for robbery. Nearly all the retailers interviewed had been robbed at gunpoint; this had led some to do business from behind bulletproof glass, making verbal interaction with customers difficult.

In this socially, racially, and economically charged context, subtle differences in the

For permission to publish copyright material in this book, grateful acknowledgment is made to: B. Bailey (1997), "Communication of Respect in Interethnic Service Encounters," *Language in Society* 26(3): 327–56.

ways that respect is communicated in face-to-face interaction are of considerable significance, affecting relationships between groups. This article documents how differences in the ways that immigrant Korean storekeepers and African-American customers communicate respect in service encounters have contributed to mutual, distinctively intense feelings of disrespect between the two groups, and serve as an ongoing source of tension. These contrasting practices for the display of politeness and respect are empirically evident in the talk and behavior that occur in stores, and the negative perceptions that result are salient in interviews of retailers and customers alike.

Respect

The issue of "respect" in face-to-face encounters has been stressed both in the media and in academic accounts of relations between African Americans and immigrant Korean retailers. Ella Stewart (1991: 20) concludes that "respect" is important for both groups in service encounters:

> Both groups declared rudeness as a salient inappropriate behavior. The underlined themes for both groups appear to be respect and courtesy shown toward each other. Each group felt that more respect should be accorded when communicating with each other, and that courtesy should be shown through verbal and nonverbal interaction by being more congenial, polite, considerate, and tactful toward each other.

Such analysis suggests that good intentions are all that is required to ameliorate relationships: each group simply has to show more "respect and courtesy" to the other. However, the data presented in this article suggest that, even when such good intentions seem to be present, respect is not effectively communicated and understood. The problem is that, in a given situation, there are fundamentally different ways of showing respect in different cultures. Because of different conventions for the display of respect, groups may feel respect for each other, and may continuously work at displaying their esteem – yet each group can feel that they are being disrespected. This type of situation, in which participants communicate at cross-purposes, has been analyzed most notably by Gumperz 1982a, b, 1992 regarding intercultural communication, though not regarding respect specifically.

The communication of respect is a fundamental dimension of everyday, face-to-face interaction. As Goffman says (1967: 46), "the person in our urban secular world is allotted a kind of sacredness that is displayed and confirmed by symbolic acts." These symbolic acts are achieved, often unconsciously, through the manipulation of a variety of communicative channels including prosody, choice of words and topic, proxemic distance, and timing of utterances. Gumperz 1982a, 1992 has shown how cultural differences in the use of such contextualization cues – at levels ranging from the perception and categorization of sounds to the global framing of activities – can lead to misunderstandings in intercultural communication. The focus of this article is the ways in which constellations of interactional features can communicate (dis)respect in service encounters.

The intercultural (mis)communication of respect between African American customers and immigrant Korean retailers is particularly significant for interethnic relations because behavior that is perceived to be lacking in respect is typically interpreted as actively threatening. Thus, according to Brown and Levinson (1987: 33), "non-communication of the polite attitude will be read not merely as the absence of that attitude, but as the inverse, the holding of an aggressive attitude." When conventions for paying respect in service encounters differ between cultures, as they do between immigrant Koreans and African Americans, individuals may read each other's behavior as not simply strange or lacking in social grace, but as aggressively antagonistic.

Brown and Levinson posit a classification system for politeness practices that is useful for conceptualizing the contrasting interactional practices of immigrant Korean retailers and African-American customers. Following Durkheim 1915 and Goffman

1971, they suggest two basic dimensions of individuals' desire for respect: NEGATIVE FACE wants and POSITIVE FACE wants. Negative face want is "the want of every 'competent adult member' that his actions be unimpeded by others," while positive face want is "the want of every member that his wants be desirable to at least some others" (Brown and Levinson: 62). Stated more simply, people do not want to be imposed on (negative face want); but they do want expressions of approval, understanding, and solidarity (positive face want). Because the labels "positive" and "negative" have misleading connotations, I use the word INVOLVEMENT to refer to positive politeness phenomena, and RESTRAINT to refer to negative politeness phenomena. These terms denote the phenomena to which they refer more mnemonically than the terms POSITIVE and NEGATIVE.

Strategies for paying respect include acts of "involvement politeness" and acts of "restraint politeness." Involvement politeness includes those behaviors which express approval of the self or "personality" of the other. It includes acts which express solidarity between interactors – e.g. compliments, friendly jokes, agreement, demonstrations of personal interest, offers, and the use of in-group identity markers. Data from store interactions show that these acts are relatively more frequent in the service encounter talk of African Americans than of immigrant Koreans.

Restraint politeness includes actions which mark the interactor's unwillingness to impose on others, or which lessen potential imposition. These strategies can include hedging statements, making requests indirect, being apologetic, or simply NOT demanding the other's attention to begin with. Restraint face wants are basically concerned with the desire to be free of imposition from others, where even the distraction of one's attention can be seen as imposition. Behaviors that minimize the communicative demands on another – e.g. NOT asking questions, NOT telling jokes that would call for a response, and NOT introducing personal topics of conversation – can be expressions of restraint politeness or respect. Such acts of restraint are typical of the participation of immigrant Korean store-owners in service encounters.

Methods

Fieldwork for this study took place in Los Angeles between July 1994 and April 1995. Data collection methods included ethnographic observation and interviewing in immigrant Korean stores, interviews with African Americans outside of store contexts, and videotaping of service encounters in stores.

I made repeated visits to six stores in the Culver City area, five in South Central, and two in Koreatown. Visits to stores typically lasted from one-half hour to two hours; with repeated visits, I spent over 10 hours at each of three stores in Culver City and one in South Central, and over five hours in one Koreatown store.

Service encounters in two immigrant Korean stores, one in Culver City and one in Koreatown, were videotaped for a total of four hours in each store. Video cameras were set up in plain view, but drew virtually no attention, perhaps because there were already multiple surveillance cameras in each store. The tapes from the Koreatown store are used for the current study because the Culver City store had no Korean customers and a lower proportion of African-American customers. During the four hours of taping in this Koreatown store, there were 12 African-American customers and 13 immigrant Korean customers.

The encounters with African-American customers were transcribed using the conventions of conversation analysis (Atkinson and Heritage 1984),[1] resulting in over 30 pages of transcripts. The encounters in Korean were transcribed by a Korean American bilingual assistant according to McCune–Reischauer conventions, and then translated into English. Transcription and translation of Korean encounters were accompanied by interpretation and explanation – some of which was audiorecorded – by the bilingual assistant while watching the videotapes. In addition, the storekeeper who appears throughout the four hours of videotape watched segments of the tapes and gave background information on some of the customers appearing in the tapes, e.g. how regularly they came to the store. Transcripts of encounters in Korean comprise over 25 pages.

Service Encounter Interaction

In the following sections, I first consider the general structure of service encounters as an activity, delineating two types: SOCIALLY MINIMAL VS. SOCIALLY EXPANDED service encounters. Second, I consider the characteristics of convenience store service encounters between immigrant Koreans, presenting examples from transcripts that show socially minimal service encounters to be the common form. Third, I consider the characteristics of service encounters between immigrant Korean storekeepers and African-American customers, using transcripts of two such encounters to demonstrate the contrasting forms of participation in them.

Merritt (1976: 321) defines a service encounter as:

> an instance of face-to-face interaction between a server who is "officially posted" in some service area and a customer who is present in that service area, that interaction being oriented to the satisfaction of the customer's presumed desire for some service and the server's obligation to provide that service. A typical service encounter is one in which a customer buys something at a store ...

Service encounters in stores fall under the broader category of institutional talk, the defining characteristic of which is its goal-orientation (Drew and Heritage 1992a). Levinson (1992: 71) sees the organization, or structure, of such activities as flowing directly from their goals: "wherever possible I would like to view these structural elements as rationally and functionally adapted to the point or goal of the activity in question, that is the function or functions that members of the society see the activity as having."

The structural differences between Korean–Korean service encounters and those with African-American customers that will be described below suggest that the two groups have different perceptions of the functions of such encounters. Even when goals are seen to overlap, participants in intercultural encounters frequently utilize contrasting means of achieving those goals (Gumperz 1992: 246). Although African-American customers and immigrant Korean shopkeepers might agree that they are involved in a service encounter, they have different notions of the types of activities that constitute a service encounter and the appropriate means for achieving those activities.

The service encounters involving immigrant Koreans and African Americans that are transcribed in this article took place in a Koreatown liquor store between 3 p.m. and 7 p.m. on a Thursday in April 1995. The store does not use bulletproof glass, and from the cash register one has an unobstructed line of sight throughout the store. The cashier is a 31-year-old male employee with an undergraduate degree from Korea; he attended graduate school briefly, in both Korea and the US, in microbiology. He has been in the US for four years and worked in this store for about three and a half years.

Service encounters in this corpus vary widely both in length and in the types of talk they contain. They range from encounters that involve only a few words, and last just seconds, to interactions that last as long as seven minutes and cover such wide-ranging topics as customers' visits to Chicago, knee operations, and race relations. More common than these two extremes, however, are encounters like the following, in which an immigrant Korean woman of about 40 buys cigarettes:

CASH: *Annyŏng haseyo.*
"Hello/How are you?" ((Customer has just entered store.))
CUST: *Annyŏng haseyo.*
"Hello/How are you?"
CUST: *Tambae!*
"Cigarettes!"
CASH: *Tambae tŭryŏyo?*
"You would like cigarettes?" ((Cashier reaches for cigarettes under counter.))
CASH: *Yŏgi issŭmnida.*
"Here you are." ((Cashier takes customer's money and hands her cigarettes; customer turns to leave.))
CASH: *Annyŏnghi kaseyo.*
"Good-bye."
CUST: *Nye.*
"Okay."

The basic communicative activities of this encounter are: (a) greetings or openings, (b) negotiation of the business exchange, and (c) closing of the encounter.

Greetings, as "access rituals" (Goffman 1971: 79), mark a transition to a period of heightened interpersonal access. In these stores, greetings typically occur as the customer passes through the doorway, unless the storekeeper is already busy serving another customer. Greetings in these circumstances include *Hi, Hello, How's it going, How are you?* – or, in Korean, *Annyŏng haseyo* "Hello/How are you?"

The second basic activity is the negotiation of the business transaction, which includes such elements as naming the price of the merchandise brought to the counter by the customer, or counting out change as it is handed back to the customer. While explicit verbal greetings and closings do not occur in every recorded encounter, each contains a verbal negotiation of the transaction. The negotiation of the business exchange can be long and full of adjacency pairs (Schegloff and Sacks 1973) – involving, e.g., requests for a product from behind the counter, questions about a price, repairs (Schegloff et al. 1977), and requests or offers of a bag. Merritt calls these adjacency pairs "couplets," and she gives a detailed structural flow chart (1976: 345) that shows the length and potential complexity of this phase of a service encounter.

The third and final activity of these encounters, the closing, often includes formulaic exchanges: *See you later, Take care, Have a good day,* or *Annyŏnghi kaseyo* "Goodbye." Frequently, however, the words used to close the negotiation of the business exchange also serve to close the entire encounter:

CASH: One two three four five ten twenty ((Counting back change.))
CASH: (Thank you/okay)
CUST: Alright.

This type of encounter – limited to no more than greetings/openings, negotiation of the exchange, and closings – I call a SOCIALLY MINIMAL service encounter. The talk in it refers almost entirely to aspects of the business transaction, the exchange of goods for money; it does not include discussion of more sociable, interpersonal topics, e.g. experiences outside the store or the customer's unique personal relationship with the storekeeper.

However, many service encounters do NOT match this socially minimal pattern. SOCIALLY EXPANDED service encounters typically include the basic elements described above, but also include activities that highlight the interpersonal relationship between customers and storekeepers. These socially expanded encounters are characterized by practices that increase interpersonal involvement, i.e. involvement politeness strategies such as making jokes or small-talk, discussing personal experiences from outside the store, and explicitly referring to the personal relationship between customer and storekeeper.

The initiation of a social expansion of a service encounter is evident in the following excerpt. The African-American customer has exchanged greetings with the Korean owner and cashier of the store; the cashier has retrieved the customer's habitual purchase, and begins to ring it up. The customer, however, then reframes the activity in which they are engaged, initiating (marked in boldface) a new activity – a personable discussion of his recent sojourn in Chicago – which lasts for several minutes.

CASH: That's it?
CUST: Tha:t's it ((Cashier rings up purchases.)) ((1.5))
CUST: I haven't seen you for a while
CASH: hehe Where you been
CUST: Chicago. ((Cashier bags purchase.))
CASH: Oh really?

The customer's comment *I haven't seen you for a while* instantiates and initiates a new type of activity and talk. The discussion of the customer's time in Chicago is a fundamentally different type of talk from that of socially minimal service encounters. Specifically, it is characterized by talk that is not directly tied to the execution of the business transaction at hand, but rather focuses on the ongoing relationship between the customer and storekeeper. Discussing the customer's trip to Chicago both indexes this personal relationship and, at the same time, contributes to its maintenance.

Such sharing of information helps constitute social categories and co-membership. To quote Sacks (1975: 72):

> Information varies as to whom it may be given to. Some matters may be told to a neighbor, others not; some to a best friend, others, while they may be told to a best friend, may only be told to a best friend after another has been told, e.g., a spouse.

In introducing talk of his trip to Chicago, the customer asserts solidarity with the cashier: they are co-members of a group who can not only exchange greetings and make business exchanges, but who can also talk about personal experiences far removed from the store.

This type of talk, which indexes and reinforces interpersonal relationships, distinguishes socially expanded service encounters from minimal ones. My data contain a wide range of such talk which enhances personal involvement. Specific practices include, among many others, talk about the weather and current events (*Some big hotel down in Hollywood, all the windows blew out*), jokes (*I need whiskey, no soda, I only buy whiskey*), references to commonly known third parties (*Mr. Choi going to have some ice?*), comments on interlocutors' demeanor (*What's the matter with you today?*), and direct assertions of desired intimacy (*I want you to know me.*)[2] Through their talk, customers and retailers create, maintain, or avoid intimacy and involvement with each other. These individual service encounters – an everyday form of contact between many African Americans and immigrant Koreans – are fundamental, discrete social activities that shape the nature and tenor of interethnic relations on a broader scale.

Service Encounters between Immigrant Koreans

Before examining immigrant Korean interaction with African Americans, I consider service encounters in which the customers as well as the storekeepers are immigrant Koreans. These Korean–Korean interactions provide a basis for comparison with African American encounters with Koreans. If, for example, the taciturnity and restraint of retailers in their interaction with African Americans were due solely to racism, one would expect to find retailers chatting and joking with their Korean customers and engaging in relatively long, intimate conversations.

In fact, the retailers in Korean–Korean encounters display the same taciturn, impersonal patterns of talk and behavior that they display with African-American customers, even in the absence of linguistic and cultural barriers. The Korean–Korean interactions are even shorter and show less intimacy than the corresponding interactions with African-American customers. Ten of the 13 service encounters with immigrant Korean customers were socially minimal, while only 3 of the 12 encounters with African Americans were socially minimal. Unlike their African-American counterparts, immigrant Korean customers generally do not engage in practices through which they could display and develop a more personal relationship during the service encounter, e.g. making small talk or introducing personal topics. The example of a Korean woman buying cigarettes, transcribed above, is typical of encounters between Korean merchants and customers. Racism or disrespect are not necessarily reasons for what African Americans perceive as distant, laconic behavior in service encounters.[3]

I have no recorded data of service encounters involving African-American store-owners with which to compare these encounters with immigrant Korean ones. I did, however, observe many interactions between African-American customers and African-American cashiers who were employed in stores owned by immigrant Koreans. Interactions between customers and such African-American cashiers were consistently longer, and included more social expansions and affective involvement, than the corresponding encounters with immigrant Korean cashiers in the same stores.

Of the three socially expanded service encounters among immigrant Koreans, two involve personal friends of the cashier from contexts outside the store, and the third is with a child of about 10 years who is a regular customer at the store. According to Scollon and Scollon (1994: 137), the communicative behavior that East Asians display toward those whom they know and with whom they have an ongoing personal relationship ("insiders") differs drastically from the behavior displayed toward those in relatively anonymous service encounters ("outsiders"):

> One sees quite a different pattern [from "inside" encounters] in Asia when one observes "outside" or service relationships. These are the situations in which the participants are and remain strangers to each other, such as in taxis, train ticket sales, and banks. In "outside" (or nonrelational encounters) one sees a pattern which if anything is more directly informational than what one sees in the West. In fact, Westerners often are struck with the contrast they see between the highly polite and deferential Asians they meet in their business, educational, and governmental contacts and the rude, pushy, and aggressive Asians [by Western standards for subway-riding behavior] they meet on the subways of Asia's major cities.

In my data, service encounter communicative behavior among Korean adults could be predicted by the presence or absence of personal friendship from contexts outside the store. Socially expanded encounters with immigrant Korean adults occurred only when those adults were personal friends of the cashier, with whom he had contact outside the store. The cashier did not have a relationship with the child customer outside the store; but criteria for expanding encounters with children, and the nature of the expansions, may be different than for adults. In this case, the social expansion included a lecture to the child on the necessity of working long hours, and the child formally asked to be released from the interaction before turning to go.

Even in socially expanded service encounters among adult Korean friends, interlocutors may at times display a relatively high degree of restraint. For example, in the following segment, the cashier encounters a former roommate whom he has not seen in several years, who has by chance entered the store as a customer. The cashier and this customer had shared an apartment for two months in Los Angeles, more than three years prior to this encounter, and the customer had later moved away from Los Angeles.

When the customer enters the store, he displays no visible surprise or emotion at this chance encounter with his former roommate. He initially gives no reply to the cashier's repeated queries, "Where do you live?", and gazes away from the cashier as if nothing had been said. After being asked five times where he lives, he gives a relatively uninformative answer, "Where else but home?"

CASH: *Ŏ:!*
"He:y!" ((Recognizing customer who has entered store. Cashier reaches out and takes customer's hand. Customer pulls away and opens cooler door.)) ((3.0))
CASH: *Ŏdi sarŏ*
"Where are you living?"
CASH: *Ŏ?*
"Huh?" ((7.0))
CASH: *Ŏdi sarŏ.*
"Where are you living?" ((.5))
CASH: *Ŏdi sarŏ.*
"Where are you living?" ((Cashier and customer stand at the counter across from each other.)) ((2.5))
CASH: *Ŏ?*
"Huh?" ((Customer gazes at display away from cashier. Cashier gazes at customer.))
CASH: *Ŏdi sarŏ::*
"C'mon, where are you living?" ((1.0))
CUST: ( )
CASH: *Ŏ?*
"Huh?" ((Cashier maintains gaze toward customer; customer continues to gaze at display.)) ((7.0))
CASH: *Ŏdi sanyanikka?*
"So, where are you living?" ((3.0))
CUST: *Ŏdi salgin, chibe salji.*
"Where else, but home?" ((1.0))
CASH: *Ŏ?*
"Huh?"
CASH: *Chibi ŏdi nyago?*
"So where is your house?"

In this opening segment of transcript, the cashier has asked the customer six times where he lives – 10 times if the follow-up *Huh?'s* are included. The customer does not reveal to his former roommate where he lives, even as he stands three feet away from him, directly across the counter.

The customer's initial unresponsiveness in this encounter is striking by Western standards of conversational cooperation (Grice 1975). The cashier, however, does not seem to treat the customer's behavior as excessively uncooperative, e.g. by becoming angry or demanding an explanation for his interlocutor's lack of engagement. A Korean-American consultant suggested that the customer's restraint was a sign not of disrespect, but of embarrassment (perhaps regarding his lack of career progress), which could explain the cashier's relative patience with uninformative responses.

This apparent resistance to engagement, however, is precisely the type of behavior cited by African Americans as insulting, and as evidence of racism on the part of immigrant Korean storekeepers:

> When I went in they wouldn't acknowledge me. Like if I'm at your counter and I'm looking at your merchandise, where someone would say "Hi, how are you today, is there anything I – " they completely ignored me. It was like they didn't care one way or the other.
>
> They wouldn't look at you at all. They wouldn't acknowledge you in any way. Nothing. You were nobody... They'd look over you or around you. (46-year-old African American woman)
>
> ... to me, many, not all, many of them perceive Blacks as a non-entity. We are treated as if we do not exist. (50-year-old African American male gift shop owner)

The customer's reluctance to acknowledge the cashier verbally or to respond to his questions – and the cashier's lack of anger at this – indicate that, at least in some situations, relatively dispassionate and impassive behavior is not interpreted by Koreans as insulting or disrespectful.

The taciturnity of the customer in this interaction, and of immigrant Korean storekeepers and customers more generally, is consistent with descriptions of the importance of *nunch'i* among Koreans – roughly "perceptiveness", "studying one's face", or "sensitivity with eyes" (M. Park 1979; Yum 1987). It is a Korean interactional ideal to be able to understand an interlocutor with minimal talk, to be able to read the other's face and the situation without verbal reference. Speaking, and forcing the interlocutor to react, can be seen as an imposition: "to provide someone with something before being asked is regarded as true service since once having asked, the requester has put the other person in a predicament of answering 'yes' or 'no'" (Yum 1987: 80).

This ideal, of communicating and understanding without talk, is present in the two most important religio-philosophical traditions of Korea – Confucianism and Buddhism. Confucian education stresses reading and writing, rather than speaking. Talk cannot be entirely trusted and is held in relatively low regard:

> To read was the profession of scholars, to speak that of menials. People were warned that "A crooked gem can be straightened even by rubbing; but a single mistake in your speech cannot be corrected. There is no one who can chain your tongue. As one is liable to make a mistake in speech, fasten your tongue at all times. This is truly a profound and urgent lesson..." (Yum 1987: 79)

In Buddhism, communication through words is generally devalued: "there is a general distrust of communication, written or spoken, since it is incomplete, limited, and ill-equipped to bring out true meaning" (Yum 1987: 83). Enlightenment and understanding in Korean Buddhism is achieved internally, unmediated by explicit utterances: "The quest for wordless truth – this has been the spirit of Korean Buddhism, and it still remains its raison d'être" (Keel 1993: 19).

The data from service encounters presented here suggest that this cultural ideal, of understanding without recourse to words, exists not only in religio-philosophical traditions, but may extend in certain situations to ideals of behavior in everyday face-to-face interaction.

Service Encounters between Immigrant Koreans and African Americans

As noted above, the service encounters with African-American customers are characterized by more personal, sociable involvement and talk than the Korean–Korean encounters. While social expansions with Korean adult customers occurred only with personal friends of the cashier from contexts outside the store, only one of the nine African-American customers in socially expanded encounters was friends with the cashier outside the store context.

Although the encounters with African Americans are longer and in many ways more intimate than the corresponding ones with Korean customers, close examination reveals consistently contrasting forms of participation in the service encounters. Overwhelmingly, it is the African-American customers who make the conversational moves that make the encounters more than terse encounters focusing solely on the business transaction. Repeatedly, African-American customers, unlike the immigrant Korean storekeepers and customers, treat the interaction not just as a business exchange, but as a sociable, interpersonal activity – by introducing topics for small-talk, making jokes, displaying affect in making assessments, and explicitly referring to the interpersonal relationship between cashier and customer.

Immigrant Korean retailers in these encounters are interactionally reactive, rather than proactive, in co-constructing conversation. Videotaped records reveal, for example, repeated instances where African-American customers finish turns when discussing issues not related to the business transaction, and then re-initiate talk when no reply is forthcoming from the storekeepers. African-American customers carry the burden of creating and maintaining the interpersonal involvement.

When immigrant Korean storekeepers do respond to talk, many responses display an understanding of referential content of utterances – but no alignment with the emotional stance, of the customer's talk, e.g. humor or indignation. Consider the reaction to ASSESSMENTS, i.e. evaluative statements that show one's personal alignment toward a phenomenon (Goodwin and Goodwin 1992). These are not met by storekeepers with second-assessments of agreement. When they do respond to assessments with affect, e.g. smiling at a customer's joke and subsequent laughter, their displayed levels of affect and interpersonal involvement are typically not commensurate with those of the customers.

The relative restraint of storekeepers in interaction with African-American customers is not only a function of cultural preference for socially minimal service encounters and situated, interactional restraint; it also reflects limited English proficiency. It is more difficult to make small-talk, to joke, or to get to know the details of a customer's life if communication is difficult. Restraint politeness can be expressed by NOT using the verbal channel, i.e. silence; but involvement politeness requires more complex verbal activities – e.g. using in-group identity markers, showing interest in the other's interests, and joking.

The phonological, morphological, and syntactic differences between Korean, an Altaic language, and English, an Indo-European one, make it difficult to achieve fluency, and store-owners have limited opportunities for study. Even among those who have been in America for 20 years, many cannot understand English spoken at native speed, and many express embarrassment about speaking it because of limited proficiency.[4]

Videotaped records of interaction do NOT reveal constant hostility and confrontations between immigrant Korean retailers and African-American customers; this finding is consistent with many hours of observation in stores. Some relationships, particularly those between retailers and regular customers, are overtly friendly: customers and storekeepers greet each other, engage in some small-talk, and part amicably. Observation and videotape do not reveal the stereotype of the inscrutably silent, non-greeting, gaze-avoiding, and non-smiling Korean storekeepers which were cited by African Americans in media accounts and in interviews with me. However, videotaped records do reveal subtle but consistent differences between African Americans and immigrant Koreans in the forms of talk and behavior in service encounters. These differences, when interpreted through culture-specific frameworks, can contribute to and reinforce pejorative stereotypes of store-owners as unfriendly and racist, and of customers as selfish and poorly bred.

In the following section I detail these differences in interactional patterns in transcripts of two socially expanded service encounters. The first interaction is with a middle-aged African-American man who is a regular at the store. The cashier was able to identify him immediately on videotape in a follow-up interview; he said that the customer had been coming to the store two or three times a week for at least three and a half years. This encounter shows notably good and comfortable relations, typical of encounters with regular customers, but at the same time it displays the asymmetrical pattern of involvement described above. The second interaction is a much longer one that occurs with a 54-year-old customer who is new to the area and the store, and who may be under the influence of alcohol at the time. Contrasting forms of participation are particularly evident in this second interaction.

Encounter 1

In this interaction, a neatly dressed African-American man in his 40s, carrying a cellular phone, comes into the store to buy a soda and some liquor. He is a regular at the store, but at the time of videotaping he had been away in Chicago for a month. The cashier is behind the counter, and the store-owner is standing amid displays in the middle of the store. The store-owner, about 40, has been in America for 20 years. He received his undergraduate degree from the University of California, Los Angeles; he studied math and computer science, he told me, because his English was not good enough for other subjects. He is more outgoing and talkative with customers than most of the storekeepers of his age, or older, who were observed.

Following greetings, the customer begins to treat the activity not just as a business transaction, but as an opportunity to be sociable, e.g. by introducing personal narratives about his long absence from Los Angeles and his experiences in Chicago:

((Customer enters store and goes to soda cooler.))
CUST: [Hi]
OWN: [How ar]e you?
((Customer takes soda toward cash register and motions toward displays.)) ((7.5))
CUST: Wow you guys moved a lot of things around
CASH: Hello:, ((Cashier stands up from where he was hidden behind the counter.))
CASH: Heh heh
CASH: How are you? ((Cashier retrieves customer's liquor and moves toward register))
CUST: What's going on man? ((Cashier gets cup for customer's liquor.)) ((.8))
CUST: How've you been?
CASH: Sleeping
CUST: eh heh heh ((1.8))
CASH: That's it?
CUST: That's it ((Cashier rings up purchases.)) ((1.5))
CUST: I haven't seen you for a while
CASH: hehe Where <u>you</u> been
CUST: Chicago. ((Cashier bags purchase.))
CASH: Oh really?
CUST: [yeah]
CASH: [How] long?
CUST: For about a <u>month</u> ((1.2))
CASH: How's there.
CUST: Co:l'!
CASH: [Co:ld?]
CUST: [heh] heh heh heh
OWN: Is Chicago cold?
CUST: u::h! ((lateral headshakes)) ((1.4)) man I got off the plane and walked out the airport I said "<u>Oh</u> shit."
CUST: <u>heh heh heh</u>
OWN: I thought it's gonna be nice spring season over there
CUST: Well not now this is about a month– I been there– I was there for about a month but you know (.) damn ((lateral headshakes))
((Customer moves away from cash register toward owner.)) ((1.4))
CUST: Too co:l'
CUST: I mean this was really cold
OWN: (They have snowy) season there
CUST: I've known it to snow Easter Sunday ((.))
CUST: Alright this Sunday it'll be Easter ((.))

CUST: I've seen it snow Easter Sunday ((15-second discussion, not clearly audible, in which the owner asks if there are mountains in Chicago, and the customer explains that there are not.))
CUST: See th– this– California weather almost never changes.
CUST: ((Spoken slowly and clearly as for non-native speaker.)) back there it's a seasonal change, you got fall, winter, spring
OWN: mm hm
CUST: You know
CUST: But back there the weather sshhh ((lateral headshake))
CUST: It's cold up until June
CUST: I mean these guys like they– they wearing lon:g john:s from September until June
OWN: (It's hot season, June)
CUST: He– here it's hot, but there it's ((lateral headshake))
CUST: (Really) ((Customer moves toward exit.))
OWN: Kay [see you later]
CUST: [see you later]
CUST: Nice talking to you

Although this customer has come into the store to buy a soda and liquor, he also displays interest in chatting, particularly about his sojourn in Chicago and the climate there. After the initial greetings, he comments on how much the store displays have changed: *Wow you guys moved a lot of things around.* This comment is consistent with the fact that he's been away; it provides an opening for a reply such as *We moved those a long time ago*, or another such comment that would display acknowledgment that the customer hasn't been in the store for some time. But neither cashier nor owner responds to his comment. The customer's use of the present perfect tense (*How've you been?*) – as opposed to present tense (*How are you?* or *How ya doing?*) – draws attention to the fact that he hasn't had contact with these storekeepers for a period of time beginning in the past and ending as he speaks; again this invites discussion of the fact that he hasn't been to the store for an unusually long time. The cashier answers the question *How've you been?* with *Sleeping*, treating it as referring to the present. The English present perfect tense is expressed with a past tense form in Korean, and may have led the cashier to interpret the question as a form of present tense.

The cashier places the customer's habitually preferred liquor on the counter without the customer's requesting the item. In doing so, the cashier, without talk, shows that he knows the customer, at least his business exchange habits. As the cashier rings up the purchase, the customer again uses the present perfect tense, indexing his relatively long absence from the store, commenting: *I haven't seen you for a while.* This comment not only indexes his long absence from the store, but draws the cashier into conversation. The comment is typically made by a person who has remained in one place while another has left and come back. In this case there is no indication that the cashier has been away. In fact, as an immigrant Korean working in a liquor store, he probably spends 80 or more hours a week in the store, up to 52 weeks each year.

The customer's seeming reversal of roles – speaking as if the cashier, rather than he, had been away – has the function, however, of drawing the cashier into conversation. The customer does not simply introduce the topic he wants to discuss; he compels the cashier to ask him about the topic. If the customer had simply stated, *I've been in Chicago for a month and it was cold*, his audience could simply have nodded and acknowledged it. Instead the speaker chooses an interactional strategy that compels a question from his interlocutors, increasing interpersonal involvement.

The customer's delivery displays a relatively high level of affective personal involvement: he uses profanity (*Oh shit*), falsetto voice, hyperbole (*they wearing long johns from September until June*), elements of African American English syntax (*they wearing*) and phonology (*col'*), and relatively high-volume laughter. The cashier and owner, however, do not display such a high level of affective personal involvement in the interaction, even through channels which are not dependent on linguistic proficiency. They do not laugh during the encounter, for example, and the owner is looking down unsmiling when the customer recounts his reaction (*Oh shit*) when getting off the plane in Chicago.

This disparity in levels of personal involvement is particularly apparent as the customer makes repeated assessments that display his alignment toward the weather in Chicago. According to Goodwin and Goodwin (1992: 166):

> this alignment can be of some moment in revealing such significant attributes of the actor as his or her taste and the way in which he or she evaluates the phenomena he or she perceives. It is therefore not surprising that displaying congruent understanding can be an issue of some importance to the participants.

Assessments provide a locus for interlocutors to show a common understanding and orientation through verbal and/or non-verbal markers of agreement with the assessment. Even when an individual has little knowledge of the referent of an assessment, positive response to the assessment will show emotional understanding and alignment with the assessor.

Explicit practices for displaying this alignment are highly developed among African Americans in the interactional pattern of "call-and-response," in which one actor's words or actions receive an immediate, often overlapping, response and confirmation from others (Smitherman 1977). Call-and-response marks involvement and congruent understanding with explicit vocal and non-verbal acts. Responses that overlap the caller's action are not seen as disrespectful interruptions, but rather as a means of displaying approval and of bringing caller and responder closer together.

While most often studied in formal performances – e.g. concerts, speeches, or sermons – relatively animated back-channel responses also characterize everyday talk of (and particularly among) many African Americans. Smitherman (1977: 118) points out that differing expectations and practices of back-channel responses can lead to the breakdown of interethnic communication:

> "call-response" can be disconcerting to both parties in black–white communication ... When the black person is speaking, the white person ... does not obviously engage in the response process, remaining relatively passive, perhaps voicing an occasional subdued "Mmmmmmhhm." Judging from the white individual's seeming lack of involvement, the black communicator gets the feeling that the white isn't listening ... the white person gets the feeling that the black person isn't listening, because he "keeps interrupting and turning his back on me."

In the encounter under consideration, the storekeepers display little reaction to the customer's assessments – much less animated, overlapping responses. The customer makes repeated assessments of the extreme cold of Chicago, e.g. *Co:l'!; Oh shit; damn; Too col'; this was really cold; back there the weather sshhh; it's cold up until June; they wearing lon:g john:s from September until June*; and *there it's* [lateral headshake]. The cashier smiles at the customer's *Oh shit* and immediately succeeding laughter, but other assessments get no such show of appreciation. The owner's responses to these dramatic assessments tend toward checks of facts: *Is Chicago cold?; I thought it's gonna be nice spring season over there*; and *It's hot season, June*. The Korean storekeepers show little appreciation for the cold of Chicago, thereby failing to align themselves and display solidarity with the customer making these assessments.

Following two of these assessments (*co:l'* and *I got off the plane and walked out the airport I said "Oh shit"*), the customer laughs. According to Jefferson (1979: 93):

> Laughter can be managed as a sequence in which speaker of an utterance invites recipient to laugh and recipient accepts that invitation. One technique for inviting laughter is the placement, by speaker, of a laugh just at completion of an utterance, and one technique for accepting that invitation is the placement, by recipient, of a laugh just after onset of speaker's laughter.

The customer's laughter following his utterances matches this pattern precisely, but cashier and owner do not accept the invitation to laugh. Not only do they fail to accept the invitation to laugh, but the owner actively declines the invitation to laugh. He does this not through silence, which would allow the speaker to pursue recipient laughter further, but by responding to the customer's laughter with serious talk of facts, i.e. the temperature in Chicago: *Is Chicago cold?* and *I thought it's gonna be nice spring season over there.* As Jefferson says:

> In order to terminate the relevance of laughter, recipient must actively decline to laugh. One technique for declining a post-completion invitation to laugh is the placement of speech, by recipient, just after onset of speaker's laughter, that speech providing serious pursuit of topic as a counter to the pursuit of laughter.

The owner's response to the customer's invitation to laugh serves as an effective counter to the invitation.

Finally, the customer's comment upon leaving (*Nice talking to you*) suggests his attitude toward this service encounter: it wasn't just an encounter about doing a business transaction, it was a time to enjoy talking personally and make connections to people. Such an attitude is consistent with observations and videotaped records, which show African-American customers consistently engaging in a relatively high degree of sociable, interpersonal interaction in service encounters.

The customer's parting comment, *Nice talking to you*, has no equivalent in Korean. The closest expression might be *sugo haseo*, which has a literal meaning close to "Keep up the good work," but is used to mean "Thank you and goodbye." Reference to work may serve as a more appropriate social currency ("Keep up the good work") than reference to talk ("Nice talking to you"), consistent with cultural ideals of relative taciturnity in service encounters.

This asymmetrical pattern of interaction occurs despite apparent attempts by both parties to accommodate to the perceived style or linguistic proficiency of the other. Both cashier and owner, for example, make repeated inquiries about the customer's trip to Chicago (*How long?; How's there*) and the weather there (*Is Chicago cold?; They have snowy season there*). Showing interest in one's interlocutor's interests is a basic form of involvement politeness (Brown and Levinson 1987: 103), and one that is absent in the encounters between immigrant Koreans that do not involve intimate friends or children. The cashier and owner are adopting a relatively involved style. The customer also appears to adapt his speech behavior to his interlocutors, in this case for non-native speakers. He explains and repeats his assessments after they draw no second-assessment of agreement (*I've known it to snow on Easter Sunday ... Alright this Sunday it'll be Easter ... I've seen it snow Easter Sunday*); and he shifts to a slow and enunciated register to explain the seasonal weather of Chicago (*back there it's a seasonal change, you got fall, winter, spring*). Thus both parties accommodate to the other, narrowing differences in communication patterns; but the accommodation is not necessarily of the type or degree that can be appreciated by the other, to result in a more synchronous, symmetrical interaction.

Encounter 2

This second encounter of a Korean immigrant shop-owner and cashier with an African-American customer is much longer, lasting about 7 minutes, with distinct episodes – including two instances when the customer moves to the exit as if to leave, and then returns to re-initiate conversation. Five excerpts from the encounter are presented and discussed.

The customer's talk and communicative behavior are in sharp contrast to that of immigrant Korean customers. He not only engages in interactional practices that increase interpersonal involvement, e.g. talk of personal topics; he also explicitly states that he wants the storekeepers to know him, and he pledges extreme solidarity with them – e.g. he tells them to call him to their aid if their store is threatened in future "riots." His interaction with the storekeepers suggests that he has different ideas about the relationship between customers and storekeepers than do immigrant Koreans, and different ideas about the corresponding service encounter style.

This customer's explicit expressions of solidarity and intimacy with the storekeepers are matched with an interactional style that includes many of the characteristics – e.g. relatively high volume, volubility, and use of profanity – that immigrant Korean retailers have characterized as disrespectful (Ella Stewart 1989, 1991; Bailey 1996). While this customer's interactional style is "emotionally intense, dynamic, and demonstrative" (Kochman 1981: 106), relative to most of the African-American customers at this Koreatown store, it shares many features with the style regularly observed in stores in low-income South Central Los Angeles.

The customer, a male in his 50s, has visited the store just once before, the previous night. He is accompanied by his nephew, who does not speak during the encounter. The customer is wearing a warm-up suit and has sunglasses resting on top of his head. His extreme expressions of co-membership with the storekeepers as he talks to them, along with the jerkiness of some of his arm motions, suggest that he may have been drinking. It is not uncommon for customers at mom-and-pop liquor stores to display signs of alcohol use when they are at the store. This customer's speech is not slurred, however, and he does not appear to be unsteady on his feet.

This new customer arrives at the store speaking to his nephew at relatively high volume. The encounter proceeds as a socially minimal service encounter until the African-American customer, following the pattern described above, reframes the activity by introducing a personal topic from outside the store context (his recent move to the area) and referring to his personal relationship with the cashier:

((Customer arrives talking to his companion, who is later identified as his nephew.))
CUST: () thirty-seven years old (in this) ass
CUST: Motherfucker ((1.0))
CASH: Hi ((Customer approaches counter)) ((.2))
CUST: How's it going partner? euh ((Cashier nods.)) ((1.0))
CUST: You got them little bottles?
CASH: (eh) ((Customer's gaze falls on the little bottles.)) ((3.5))
CUST: One seventy-fi:ve! ((Customer gazes at display of bottles.)) ((2.0))
CUST: You ain't got no bourbon? ((1.2))
CASH: No: we don't have bourbon ((1.0))
CUST: I'll get a beer then.
CUST: ((turns to nephew)) What would you like to drink? what do you want? ((Customer selects beverages and brings them to the cash register.)) ((7.5))
CASH: Two fifty ((Cashier rings up purchase and bags beer.)) ((4.5))
CUST: I just moved in the area. I talked to you the other day. You [remember me]?
CASH: [Oh yesterday] last night
CUST: Yeah
CASH: [(O:h yeah)] ((Cashier smiles and nods.))
CUST: [Goddamn, shit] [then you don't–]
OWN: [new neighbor, huh?] ((Customer turns halfway to the side toward the owner.))
CUST: Then you don't <u>know</u> me
CASH: [(I know you)] ((Cashier gets change at register.))
CUST: [I want you to <u>know</u>] me so when I walk in here you'll know me. I smoke Winstons.
Your son knows me
CASH: [Ye::ah]
CUST: [The yo]ung guy
CASH: There you go ((Cashier proffers change.))
CUST: [Okay then]
CASH: [Three four] five ten ((Cashier steps back from counter.))

The interaction with the storekeepers proceeds as a socially minimal service encounter until the customer volunteers personal information about himself (*I just moved in the area*) and raises the history of his relationship with the cashier (*I talked to you the other day. You remember me?*) Although the cashier shows that he remembers the customer (*Oh yesterday, last night*), the customer continues as if the cashier didn't know or remember him. The customer's *goddamn, shit... then you don't know me* is spoken at high volume, but with a smile, suggesting humor rather than anger.

Though the cashier acknowledges having seen the customer before, his turns are oriented toward completing the transaction. Except for the words *last night*, his acknowledgments of this customer's history with the store (*Oh yeah, I know you, Yeah*) are spoken in overlap with the customer's words, and only in response to the customer's assertions.

The customer does not acknowledge it when the cashier shows that he remembers him. Perhaps the recognition does not count when it requires prompting (*Then you don't* <u>*know*</u> me), but rather must be done immediately and spontaneously. The customer then explicitly states that he wants the cashier and the owner to know him (he moves his gaze back and forth between them): *I want you to* <u>*know*</u> *me so when I walk in here you'll know me. I smoke Winstons. Your son knows me*. This customer is concerned with the storekeepers "knowing" him: he wants them to know him now and on future store visits, and he finds it worth noting that one of the other employees (*your son*), already knows him.

Knowing a customer's habitual purchases and brand preferences (e.g. Winstons) is one way of "knowing" the customer, and storekeepers frequently ready a customer's cigarettes or liquor without being asked; minimally, this customer wants to be known in this way. Subsequent talk, however, suggests that "knowing" him will involve a more personal, intimate relationship, and one that involves specific types of talk and behavior.

The data presented here suggest that immigrant Korean retailers and African-American customers have differing notions of what it means to "know" someone in a convenience store context, and differing ideas about the kinds of speech activities entailed by "knowing" someone in this context. Different ideas about what it means to know someone may apply not just to service encounters, as described above, but to any encounter between relative strangers. Thus M. Park (1979: 82) suggests that, by Western standards, Koreans are restrained and impersonal with those who are not intimate friends or part of a known group:

> The age-old cliché, "Koreans are the most courteous people in the East" is rather rightly applied only to inter-personal interaction among ingroups or hierarchical groups. Koreans tend to be [by Western standards] impolite or even rude when they interact with outgroups like outsiders or strangers. Everyone outside the ingroup is likely to be treated with curiosity or caution or even a bit of suspicion...

It may be difficult for these storekeepers to extend what for them is an intimate communicative style to a relative stranger.

In America, many communicative activities – e.g. greetings, smiles, and small-talk – occur in interactions both with friends and with relative strangers. The communicative style extended to both strangers and friends relatively emphasizes the expression of casual solidarity and explicit recognition of personal details.

> Personal treatment in American life includes use of the first name, recognition of biographical details and acknowledgements of specific acts, appearances, preferences and choices of the individual. Cultural models are given by salesmen and airline hostesses. Their pleasant smiles, feigned and innocuous invasions of privacy, "kidding" and swapping of personal experiences constitute stereotypes of personal behavior ... Signs of friendship, the glad handshake, the ready smile, the slap on the back ... have become part of the normal way of behavior. (Edward Stewart 1972: 55, 58)

Everyday speech behavior among strangers in America includes practices that would be reserved for talk among relative intimates in Korea.

Such differing assumptions about appropriate communicative style in service encounters, and about the relationship between customer and server, may underlie the contrasting forms of participation in the encounter under consideration. When the customer states that he wants the storekeepers to know him, the cashier's *Yeah* and subsequent *There you go*, as he hands back change, fail to engage the topic of knowing the customer. The cashier is reframing the activity as a business transaction, specifically the closing of the business negotiation component, and perhaps the entire encounter. The return and counting of change (*There you go; Three four five ten*) is used in many service encounters as a way of closing not only the business negotiation, but also the entire interaction.

The customer, however, does not treat this as the end of the encounter. Instead, he treats this as a time to discuss details of his life outside the store:

CUST: And then I– I've got three months to be out here.
CASH: How's [here] ((Cashier steps back from counter and gazes down.))
CUST: [I'm going] to school
CASH: How's here
CUST: I'm going to– (.2) locksmith school
CASH: Oh really
CUST: Yeah. so after that– because I had a (.) knee operation ((Customer rolls up pant leg to show scars.)) ((4.2))
CUST: I had a total knee so my company is retiring my– old black ass at fifty-four ((Customer smiles and gazes at owner.)) ((.6))
OWN: (mmh) ((Owner shakes his head laterally and gazes away from the customer.))
CUST: And they give me some money
CASH: Huh ((Cashier bares his teeth briefly in a smile.))
CUST: So I'm spending my money at your store on liquor heh heh heh heh hah hah hah hah hah ((Customer laughs animatedly, turning toward the owner who does not smile, but who continues lateral headshakes as he takes a few steps to the side.))
OWN: You still can work?

The business exchange has been completed, and the customer initiates discussion of a series of personal topics. He volunteers how long he will be in Los Angeles, what he is doing there, details of his medical history, and his current employment status. He goes so far as to roll up his pant-leg to show the scars from his knee replacement operation. He has said that he wants these storekeepers to "know" him, and he's giving them some of the information they need to know him. In doing so he is treating them as co-members of an intimate group, i.e. the circle of people who can see his knee scars, even though by some standards they are virtual strangers. The customer is treating the social distance between himself and the storekeepers as small; his interactional style increases involvement between him and the storekeepers.

The cashier's talk displays some interest in the interaction, e.g. his initial query *How's here* displays understanding of the customer's statement (*I've got three months to be out here*) and invites further comment. The customer, however, does not answer the question. The nonstandard form *How's here* (for "How do you like it here?") may not have been understood by the customer, and comprehension may have been further hindred by the cashier's nonverbal actions. During the first *How's here*, the cashier's arm is in front of his face, and his gaze is not on the customer; during the second, he's shifting his weight to lean on a counter to the side. The even intonation contour of *How's here* may also prevent the customer from realizing that a question is being asked. Even when a storekeeper expresses involvement in an interaction, his or her limited English proficiency may prevent the customer from understanding the expression of interest.

The customer concludes this introduction with a joke that stresses the humorous nature of his relationship with the liquor store owners: he is sharing the proceeds from his disability payments with them. His smile and laughter at this situation are an invitation to his audience to share in his laughter (Jefferson 1979). The store-owner and cashier fail to join in this laughter; the cashier displays a fleeting, stiff smile, and the owner none at all. Not only do cashier and owner fail to accept the invitation to laughter, but as in the previous encounter, the owner, through his subsequent question, ACTIVELY DECLINES the invitation to laughter. His question *You still can work?* is a serious pursuit of a topic that effectively counters the customer's pursuit of laughter. The question proves his comprehension of the customer's prior talk, but displays no affective alignment or solidarity with the customer's humor. Even though the store-owner can understand the referential content of the words, he does not participate in the interactional activity of laughing – the preferred response to the customer's laughter.

It is also, of course, possible that the owner is displaying a dispreferred response because he does NOT want to display alignment: perhaps he thinks that people take advantage of social programs when they could support themselves through their own work – a sentiment voiced in interviews with immigrant Korean retailers in a variety of forms. This active declination to laugh, however, also occurs in my data during talk about morally less sensitive topics, e.g. the weather, with both African-American and Korean customers; this suggests a pattern of declining invitations to laughter that is unrelated to personal opinions about the topic at hand.

In the next two minutes of talk and interaction (not transcribed here), the customer gets change for a five-dollar bill, and then explains to the owner that his former employer doesn't want him to work for fear that they would have to redo his knee operation if he resumed work. The customer takes his bag of purchases from the counter, and moves to the door as if to leave (the owner says *See ya*); but he stops in the doorway, then re-enters the store to resume talking. He discusses the exact amount of money he receives per month for his disability, compares it to the amount of money he made previously, and reiterates that if he goes to work now, his disability benefits will be cut off.

In the next segment, transcribed below, the customer explains that he is being retrained for a new job. He begins to depart, and then once again returns from the threshold of the exit door to re-initiate talk:

CUST: So I gotta get another trade. Just like if you get hurt in the liquor store business, you gotta go get another trade. So I gotta go get another trade. For them to pay me the money. So I'm gonna get another trade. But then like– after I get another trade they pay me (a sum) a lump sum of money? And I'm gonna do what I wanna do. ((.8))
CUST: They only gonna give me about sixty or seventy thousand. ((1.4))
CUST: Plus– my schooling– ((1.0))
CUST: So:– I got to take it easy for a little bit. ((Customer moves toward exit.))
CUST: That's why I'm gonna buy enough of your liquor (so I can take it)
OWN: Alright, take care
CUST: Okay ((Customer pauses in doorway.))

This segment is characterized by dramatically asymmetrical contributions to the interaction. Not only does the customer do most of the talking, but there is a noticeable absence of response to his statements. He gives up his turn at talk five times in this short segment, but receives a verbal response only once. The customer only gets verbal collaboration, in this segment, in leaving the store – which suggests that these storekeepers may be more proficient at closing interactions with customers than they are at sociable, personal discussion with them.

The lack of verbal response to the customer's talk is particularly noteworthy because he is making statements that invite easy responses. The fact that he's going to get a lump sum of money and *do what I wanna do* makes relevant such questions as: *How much are you going to get?* or *What are you going to do when you get the money?* The amount of money he's going to get (*sixty or seventy thousand*) similarly invites comment, e.g. *That's great*, or *That's a lot of money*, or again, *What are you going to do with it?* The customer's *Plus my schooling* invites questions about the details of the schooling, beyond the fact (stated earlier) that it's locksmith school. The customer's reference to buying *enough of your liquor* also provides an opening for storekeeper recognition of his patronage, e.g. *We appreciate your business*. The silence of the storekeepers displays restraint, but not interest or involvement.

The immigrant Korean storekeepers' lack of overt response to the customer's talk forms a stark contrast with the African-American pattern of call-and-response described above. Smitherman (1977: 108) emphasizes the importance of responding to a speaker, regardless of the form of the response: "all responses are 'correct'; the only 'incorrect' thing you can do is not respond at all." By this standard, the storekeepers' lack of response is inappropriate.

In the next segment, although the customer has once again moved to the door, and the owner has said goodbye, the customer re-enters the store and more talk follows. After learning the storekeepers' names, the customer invokes the events of April 1992. He tells the store-owners that he will come to their aid if they have problems in the future, and goes on to discuss his philosophy of race relations:

CUST: What's your name? ((Customer re-enters store and approaches the owner.))
OWN: Han Choi ((.6))
CUST: Han? ((Customer shakes hands with the owner.)) ((1.2))
CUST: What's your name? ((Customer shakes cashier's hand.))
CASH: Shin
CUST: Chin?
CASH: No, [Shin]
CUST: [Okay] (.) Shin?
CASH: Yeah
OWN: What's yours (then)?
CUST: Larry
OWN: Larry
CUST: I'm a gangsta from Chicago, Larry Smith. Anybody fuck with you, this black– I seen them riots and things and they was fucking up with the Korean stores and the– and the what's his name stores? And I was in Vietnam and everything like that
OWN: [(Our) neighbors friendly (here)]
CUST: [Well-(.) well let me] tell you something– nobody fuck with your store, if I catch 'em making fuck with your store (.) you just ca:ll me: dow:n
OWN: Alright
CUST: I:'ll fuck 'em up ((Customer reaches out and shakes the owner's hand; the owner's arm is limp and he is pulled off balance by the handshake.)) ((.8))
CUST: Because I believe in people not Koreans, not Blacks, not Whites, not this, I believe in people. ((.4))
CUST: Right there. ((Customer taps the owner on the chest twice, in rhythm with the two words *right there*))

The customer, who has created and emphasized solidarity with the storekeepers throughout their interaction, continues to reinforce his solidarity and co-membership with them. After learning their names and shaking their hands – an act of physical intimacy – he makes two explicit assertions of solidarity.

His initial assertion of solidarity is dramatic: he promises with high volume and affect that he will respond to their call for help, and "fuck up" anyone who is harming them or their store. He has seen the havoc of Los Angeles in April 1992 on TV; but he is a Vietnam veteran, so he has the capacity to deal with such events. The storekeepers' enemies are his enemies; he and the storekeepers are co-members of an intimate group, a group whose members will risk harm to protect each other.

He reiterates this sentiment of solidarity by explaining his readiness to act on their behalf based on his personal philosophy: *Because I believe in people not Koreans, not Blacks, not Whites*. Social distance between him and these storekeepers is low; race is not a barrier. He emphasizes his intimacy with the store-owner by tapping him on the chest, once more making physical contact, and citing this specific store-owner as an example of the people in whom he has faith.

Following the segment transcribed above, there are two minutes of talk (not transcribed here) during which the customer discusses his beliefs about the basic sameness of people, regardless of race, and his criticisms of those who make society racist. The customer utters more than 10 words for each of the store-owner's words during this period. The service encounter comes to an end with the following turns:

((The customer speaks with high volume and animation, and sounds almost angry during these penultimate two turns. He is gesticulating so strongly that his sunglasses become dislodged from atop his head and he has to reposition them as he talks.))

CUST: Okay what I'm saying is (.) if you throw five kids (in the middle of the floor) and don't tell them what they are nothing like that they just grow up to be people ((.))
CUST: They don't even know (.) that they Black. they don't even know they Korean they don't know that they White they don't know this and that. It have to be an old person like you or me, George Washington and all these motherfuckers. Martin Luther King and all these motherfuckers.
((The customer has begun moving toward the exit. His vocal register shifts suddenly

to one of low volume and affect for his final turn. He gazes first at the owner and then the cashier as he waves goodbye.))
CUST: Anyway– have a good day.
OWN: Later ((Customer turns and exits.))

As this interaction progresses, the storekeepers become more and more reticent while the customer becomes more and more outspoken. Although the customer has dominated the talk throughout the interaction, his volume and affect level get higher as it progresses, and he holds the floor an ever higher proportion of the time. In the final two minutes of talk, the customer is literally following the owner from place to place in the store, leaning over the shorter man, and repeatedly touching him on the chest as he makes his points.

This asymmetry in participation occurs despite apparent efforts at accommodation by both customer and storekeepers. Thus the storekeepers ask more questions that display interest in the customer – *How's here; You still can work?* – than they ask of non-intimate adult Korean customers. The customer adapts his speech for non-natives, e.g. by using an example to explain his job retraining (*Just like if you get hurt in the liquor store business, you gotta go get another trade*); and he introduces a topic that might be of particular interest to them, e.g. Los Angeles civil unrest that could threaten their store. As in the first encounter, however, the mutual accommodation may not be of the degree or type that can be fully appreciated by the other party, or can result in more symmetrical participation in the encounter.

Mismatch in politeness orientations can have a self-reinforcing, spiraling effect that exaggerates differences in politeness style as interaction continues; this can exacerbate misunderstandings and mutual negative evaluations. The more this African-American customer cheerfully talks and stresses his camaraderie with the store-owner, the more the retailer withdraws and declines involvement. This may be a more general phenomenon in interethnic communication. Borrowing a term from Bateson 1972, Tannen (1981: 138) concludes that speakers from backgrounds with contrasting linguistic practices frequently respond to each other in "complementary schismogenetic fashion"; i.e., "the verbal devices used by one group cause speakers of the other group to react by intensifying the opposing behavior, and vice versa."

Since, for many African Americans the nature of good and respectful service encounter relations involves relatively great personal involvement, this customer may be redoubling his efforts to create solidarity as he encounters the retailers' increasing reticence. For the store-owner, the appropriate response to a customer's increasing intimacy may be the silence or avoidance that demonstrates restraint. In this instance, the pattern does not escalate out of control. The owner maintains a degree of engagement, although he appears uncomfortable at times; and the customer does not react as if he is being ignored, although his increasing affect as the interaction proceeds may well be related to the low level of response he gets from the storekeepers.

However, this self-escalating cycle may contribute to confrontations that have occurred elsewhere. Media and informant accounts of confrontations between retailers and African Americans often stress the seeming suddenness with which storekeepers, perceived to be inscrutably impassive, suddenly explode in anger at customers. As customers persist in behaviors that the retailer perceives as invasive, the storekeeper will remain silent; the customer will not know that he or she is doing something that the storekeeper finds inappropriate, and will increase the intensity of the involvement behaviors in reaction to the restraint of storekeepers. When the weight of the trespass against sensibilities becomes too grave, the store-owner will feel justified in lashing out (Kochman 1981: 118, 1984: 206). Conversely, the increasingly restrained behavior of store-owners, as customers express ever-greater friendliness, can lead to customer outbursts and accusations of storekeeper racism. Storekeepers report repeated instances in which customers have suddenly (and to the storekeepers, inexplicably) accused them of being racists.

Conclusion

Divergent practices for displaying respect in service encounter interaction are an ongoing cause of tension between immigrant Korean retailers and their African-American customers. The two groups have different concepts of the relationship between customer and storekeeper, and different ideas about the speech activities that are appropriate in service encounters. The talk of immigrant Koreans focuses almost exclusively on the business transaction at hand, while the talk of African-American customers includes efforts toward more personal, sociable interaction.

The interactional patterns that are apparent in videotaped records are consistent with data that come from dozens of hours of observation in various stores, and from interviews with store-owners, customers, and consultants. The seeming avoidance of involvement on the part of immigrant Koreans is frequently seen by African Americans as the disdain and arrogance of racism. The relative stress on interpersonal involvement among African Americans in service encounters is typically perceived by immigrant Korean retailers as a sign of selfishness, interpersonal imposition, or poor breeding (Bailey 1996).

The focus of this article on miscommunication should not be taken to mean that immigrant Korean merchants and African-American customers can never communicate effectively, or never have friendly relationships. The overwhelming majority of African-American customers and immigrant Korean retailers that I observed get along, and relationships between retailers and regular customers (40–80 percent of the clientele at stores I visited) are often very positive. Retailers often know regular customers' family members and other details of their lives; and many retailers engage in friendly small-talk with such customers, even when limited English proficiency make it difficult. This type of relationship, which often results only after longer contact, can change mutual perceptions, as described by an African-American woman in her 50s:

> I find that they shy away from you until you get to know them. Like this lady, the Korean store, I've been in the neighborhood for years and years, and she's friendly with everybody cause she knows everybody but when they don't know you, they're shy, and you think they're prejudice. They might be, but you just have to get to know them. They're nice people once you get to know them.

This article has focused on one source of interethnic tensions: miscommunication due to cultural and linguistic differences. Socio-historical conditions – e.g. social, economic, and racial inequality – are also clearly sources of tensions between African Americans and immigrant Korean storekeepers. Within a social and historical context, however, there are specific linguistic and cultural practices that can ameliorate or exacerbate tensions between groups. The goal of this essay has been to shed light on communicative processes that can lead to tensions between groups in face-to-face interaction, in the hope that understanding linguistic and cultural bases of difference in communication patterns can make these differences less inflammatory.

NOTES

Initial fieldwork for this research was funded by a Research Institute for Man/Landes Training Grant. Many thanks to Alessandro Duranti for extensive comments on repeated drafts of the UCLA M.A. thesis on which this article is based. Thanks also to Jae Kim, who transcribed and translated the Korean service encounters, and who shared much with me about the language, lives, and perceptions of Korean immigrants in Los Angeles.

1 Transcription conventions are as follows: Speakers are identified with an abbreviation in the far left column, e.g. "Cust" for "Customer," "Cash" for "Cashier," and "Own" for "Owner." A question mark in this column indicates that the speaker's identity is not clear to the tran-

scriber. Descriptions of non-verbal activities are in double parentheses, e.g. ((Customer enters store.)) Note also the following:

((4.3)) Numbers in parentheses indicate the length of time in seconds during which there is no talk. Single parentheses are used for intra-turn silences, double parentheses for silences between turns.

(.) A period in parentheses or double parentheses indicates a stretch of time, lasting no more than two-tenths of a second, during which there is no talk.

: A colon indicates that the preceding sound was elongated in a marked pronunciation.

? A question mark indicates a marked rising pitch.

. A period indicates a marked falling pitch.

() Parentheses that are empty indicate that something was said at that point, but it is not clear enough to transcribe. Parentheses around words indicate doubt about the accuracy of the transcribed material. A slash between words in parentheses indicates alternate possibilities.

hhh *h*'s connected to a word indicate breathiness, usually associated with laughter.

[ ] Brackets enclose those portions of utterances that are spoken in overlap with other talk. The overlapping portions of talk are placed immediately above or below each other on the page.

! An exclamation point indicates an exclamatory tone.

, A comma indicates a marked continuing intonation in the sound(s) preceding the comma.

_ Text that is underlined was pronounced with emphasis, i.e. some combination of higher volume, pitch, and greater vowel length.

' A single apostrophe replaces a letter that was not pronounced, e.g. *col'* for *cold*, when the *d* is not pronounced.

- A hyphen or dash indicates that speech was suddenly cut-off during or after the preceding word.

Transcriptions of Korean data follow Martin et al. (1967: xv).

2 This category includes practices that might seem to vary significantly in degree of intimacy; however, immigrant Koreans do not treat such distinctions as relevant in most encounters with immigrant Korean customers. As described in the section on encounters between immigrant Koreans, small-talk about the weather (for example) does not occur independently of, or more frequently than, talk of more personal matters.

3 This is not meant to deny the role of racism in tensions between African Americans and immigrant Korean retailers. Racism permeates American society; and it provides a cogent explanation for a wide variety of historical, social, and economic phenomena, including behavior in face-to-face interaction. Quotes from store-owners interviewed in other studies (e.g. Ella Stewart 1989; K. Park 1995), attest the blatant racism of some storekeepers. The point here is not that immigrant Korean merchants are or are not racist, but rather that many immigrant Korean interactional practices upon which African-American customers base assumptions of racism are not valid indices of racism, because retailers use identical practices with immigrant Korean customers.

4 The difficulty of mastering English for adult speakers of Korean is suggested by the grammatical interference evident in the following utterance by a storekeeper who had been in Los Angeles over 20 years. When asked where her husband was, she replied: *Husband some merchandise buy* (i.e. "My husband is buying some merchandise.") The subject–object–verb word order of Korean is used, rather than the subject–verb–object word order of English. The present tense form of *buy* is used, rather than present progressive; this parallels Korean usage, in which the present tense form of action verbs can indicate

present progressive meaning. The possessive pronoun *my* is elided, since it would be understood from context in Korean (Lee 1989: 90).

REFERENCES

Atkinson, J. Maxwell, and Heritage, John (1984) (eds.) *Structures of Social Action: Studies in Conversation Analysis*. Cambridge and New York: Cambridge University Press.

Austin, Regina (1995). Moving Beyond Deviance: Expanding Black People's Rights and Reasons to Shop and to Sell. *Penn Law Journal* 30: 30–4.

Bailey, Benjamin (1996). Communication of Respect in Service Encounters between Immigrant Korean Retailers and African-American Customers. MA thesis, University of California, Los Angeles.

Bateson, Gregory (1972). *Steps to an Ecology of Mind*. New York: Ballantine.

Brown, Penelope, and Levinson, Stephen (1987). *Politeness: Some Universals in Language Usage*. Cambridge and New York: Cambridge University Press.

Chang, Edward (1990). New Urban Crisis: Korean–Black Conflicts in Los Angeles. Dissertation, University of California, Berkeley.

Chang, Edward (1993). Jewish and Korean Merchants in African American Neighborhoods: A Comparative Perspective. *Amerasia Journal* 19: 5–21.

Drake, St. Clair, and Cayton, Horace (1945). *Black Metropolis: A Study of Negro Life in a Northern City*. New York: Harper & Row.

Drew, Paul, and Heritage, John (1992a). Analyzing Talk at Work: An Introduction. In Drew and Heritage (eds.), pp. 3–65.

Drew, Paul, and Heritage, John (1992b) (eds.) *Talk at Work: Interaction in Institutional Settings*. Cambridge and New York: Cambridge University Press.

Duranti, Alessandro, and Goodwin, Charles (1992), (eds.) *Rethinking Context: Language as an Interactive Phenomenon*. Cambridge and New York: Cambridge University Press.

Durkheim, Emile (1915). *The Elementary Forms of the Religious Life*. London: Allen & Unwin.

Goffman, Erving (1967). The Nature of Deference and Demeanor. In his *Interaction Ritual: Essays on Face-to-Face Behavior*, pp. 47–95. New York: Pantheon.

Goffman, Erving (1971). *Relations in Public: Microstudies of the Public Order*. New York: Basic Books.

Goodwin, Charles and Goodwin, Marjorie H. (1992). Assessments and the Construction of Context. In Duranti and Goodwin (eds.), pp. 147–90.

Grice, Paul (1975). Logic and Conversation. In Peter Cole and Jerry Morgan (eds.), *Syntax and Semantics*, 3: 41–58. New York: Academic Press.

Gumperz, John (1982a). *Discourse Strategies*. Cambridge and New York: Cambridge University Press.

Gumperz, John (1982b) (ed.). *Language and Social Identity*. Cambridge and New York: Cambridge University Press.

Gumperz, John (1992). Contextualization and Understanding. In Duranti and Goodwin (eds.), pp. 229–52.

Jefferson, Gail (1979). A Technique for Inviting Laughter and its Subsequent Acceptance/Declination. In George Psathas (ed.), *Everyday Language: Studies in Ethnomethodology*, pp. 79–96. New York: Irvington.

Keel, Hee-Sung (1993). Word and Wordlessness: The Spirit of Korean Buddhism. *Korea Journal* 33: 11–19.

Kochman, Thomas (1981). *Black and White Styles in Conflict*. Chicago, IL: University of Chicago Press.

Kochman, Thomas (1984). The Politics of Politeness: Social Warrants in Mainstream American Public Etiquette. *Georgetown University Roundtable on Languages and Linguistics* 1984: 200–9.

Lee, Hyon-Bok (1989). *Korean Grammar*. Oxford and New York: Oxford University Press.

Levinson, Stephen (1992). Activity Types in Language. In Drew and Heritage (eds.), pp. 66–100.

Martin, Samuel, et al. (1967). *A Korean–English dictionary.* New Haven, CT: Yale University Press.

Merritt, Marilyn (1976). On Questions Following Questions (In Service Encounters). *Language in Society* 5: 315–57.

Park, Kyeyoung (1995). The Re-invention of Affirmative Action: Korean Immigrants' Changing Conceptions of African Americans and Latin Americans. *Urban Anthropology* 24: 59–92.

Park, Myung-Seok (1979). *Communication Styles in Two Different Cultures: Korean and American.* Seoul: Han Shin.

Sacks, Harvey (1975). Everyone Has to Lie. In Mary Sanches and Ben Blount (eds.), *Sociocultural Dimensions of Language Use*, pp. 57–79. New York: Academic Press.

Schegloff, Emanuel, Jefferson, Gail, and Sacks, Harvey (1977). The Preference for Self-correction in the Organization of Repair in Conversation. *Language* 53: 361–82.

Schegloff, Emanuel, and Sacks, Harvey (1973). Opening up Closings. *Semiotica* 7: 289–327.

Scollon, Ron, and Scollon, Suzanne Wong (1994). Face Parameters in East–West Discourse. In Stella Ting-Toomey (ed.), *The Challenge of Facework*, pp. 133–58. Albany: State University of New York Press.

Smitherman, Geneva (1977). *Talkin' and Testifyin': The Language of Black America.* Boston: Houghton Mifflin.

Stewart, Edward (1972). *American Cultural Patterns.* Chicago, IL: Intercultural Press.

Stewart, Ella (1989). Ethnic Cultural Diversity: An Interpretive Study of Cultural Differences and Communication Styles between Korean Merchants/Employees and Black Patrons in South Los Angeles. MA thesis, California State University, Los Angeles.

Stewart, Ella (1991). Ethnic Cultural Diversity: Perceptions of Intercultural Communication Rules for Interaction between Korean Merchants/Employees and Black Patrons in South Los Angeles. Paper presented to the 19th Annual Conference of the National Association for Ethnic Studies at California State Polytechnic University, Pomona, CA.

Sturdevant, Frederick (1969) (ed.), *The Ghetto Marketplace.* New York: Free Press.

Tannen, Deborah (1981). New York Jewish Conversational Style. *International Journal of the Sociology of Language* 30: 133–49.

Yum, June-Ock (1987). Korean Philosophy and Communication. In D. Lawrence Kincaid (ed.), *Communication Theory: Eastern and Western Perspectives*, pp. 71–86. San Diego: Academic Press.

STUDY QUESTIONS

1 What does Bailey say about how respect is communicated or miscommunicated?

2 Illustrate with examples the meaning of the terms "restraint politeness" and "involvement politeness." Use examples from the article and from your own experience in service encounters.

3 Describe the difference between what Bailey calls "socially minimal" and "socially expanded" service encounters.

4 What did Bailey learn about the interactional style of Koreans and African Americans in Los Angeles?

5 Why do you think that Bailey included an analysis of how Korean customers interacted with the Korean clerks? What is the contribution of this analysis to the argument he makes about communication between the Koreans and African Americans in his study?

5

The Idealised Native Speaker, Reified Ethnicities, and Classroom Realities

Constant Leung, Roxy Harris, and Ben Rampton

TESOL (Teaching English to Speakers of Other Languages) practice within the schooling sector in England has been mainstreamed.[1] Historically this represents a major advance in terms of pedagogical relevance and equality of access, but our current research (Rampton, Harris, and Leung, 1997) and our recent experience in working with teachers have suggested that mainstreaming itself has generated a number of new and unresolved issues in relation to language use, ethnicity, and social identity. This chapter seeks to advance a number of propositions.

1 Socially and ideologically inspired conceptualisations of the language learner and the associated language pedagogies in England over the past 40 years are no longer adequate to cope with the range of what are termed *bilingual learners*[2] typically encountered in classrooms, particularly in urban settings.
2 Some of the recent developments in cultural theory assist a critical analysis of the prevailing thinking. They also contribute to an understanding of the changing nature of the linguistic formation and social identity of the bilingual learner and of the resulting need to develop an expanded notion of TESOL pedagogy.
3 In the specific arena of language, little development of such an expanded pedagogy is possible without displacing conventional notions of the *native speaker* of English (what we label here *the idealised native speaker*). This can be accomplished by asking about the language expertise, language inheritance, and language affiliation of all learners of English in the classroom (Rampton, 1990), regardless of the language attributed to them.
4 Language use and notions of ethnicity and social identity are inextricably linked. Because of this, specific attention must be paid to the way that many bilingual learners actively construct their own patterns of language use, ethnicity, and social identity. These patterns can often be in strong contradiction to the fixed patterns and the reified ethnicities attributed to bilingual learners by many of those attempting to develop effective TESOL pedagogies.

For permission to publish copyright material in this book, grateful acknowledgment is made to: C. Leung, R. Harris, and B. Rampton (1997), "The Idealised Native Speaker, Reified Ethnicities, and Classroom Realities," *TESOL Quarterly* 31: 543–60.

The current historical moment of profound change and flux is not a time for the pronouncement of grand strategies or solutions but rather an opportunity to engage in open analysis and questioning as a first step towards a better understanding of some of the problems encountered in classrooms and the possible development of an expanded and more responsive TESOL pedagogy. We stress that in this article we are writing specifically of the English urban context, although we hope that some of what we say will have a resonance for colleagues working on TESOL questions in major urban centres in other locations.

Background and Prevailing Assumptions about TESOL in England

An important element in understanding both the historic and current TESOL context in England is the nature of the post-1945 inward migration of peoples and languages. Martin-Jones (1989) characterises these migrations as principally of people entering England as either migrant workers or refugees. At the same time she sees a significant divide between those entering from other parts of Europe and those entering from former colonies and third-world nations. Historically, it has been the latter who have had the greatest interaction with TESOL policy and practice in England – people who migrated to England in relatively large numbers from India, Pakistan, Bangladesh, the Caribbean, Hong Kong, East Africa (principally Kenya, Tanzania, and Uganda), West Africa (mainly Nigeria and Ghana), Vietnam, Ethiopia and Eritrea, Somalia, and Cyprus (see Peach 1996), bringing with them languages such as Panjabi, Urdu, Gujerati, Hindi, Bengali and Sylheti, Cantonese and Hakka Chinese, Caribbean Creoles, Yoruba, Twi, Cypriot Greek and Turkish, Kurdish, Tigrinya, Amharic, and Somali (see Alladina and Edwards 1991; Inner London Education Authority 1989).

Space constraints prohibit a detailed critical analysis of the historical development and limitations of TESOL in England (see Leung 1993, 1996; Leung, Harris, and Rampton 1997; Rampton 1985, 1988; Rampton, Harris, and Leung 1997). At present, however, TESOL practitioners urgently need to take account of social and demographic changes that pose troubling questions about the ways in which TESOL pedagogy classifies and conceptualises the large numbers of bilingual learners who are the children and grandchildren of the migrants of the 1950s, 1960s, 1970s, and 1980s. A highly significant factor has been the historical racism and disdain for the peoples and languages emanating from former English colonies and third-world countries. Over the past 40 years, this attitude has tended to lead to TESOL approaches bounded at first by overtly assimilationist approaches (Department of Education and Science 1971) and then, after assimilationism was dropped as an official approach (Swann 1985), by a tendency not to take a proper account of the complexities of language learning and language use in contemporary multiethnic urban settings. (For a fuller discussion of the tenets of the current practice, see Edwards and Redfern 1992.) In fact, we would summarize the current configuration of L2 education goals and practices in England in terms of three implicit assumptions:

1 That linguistic minority pupils are, by definition, bilingual, having an ethnic minority language at home while at school they are learning and using English.
2 That these pupils' language development needs can be understood and categorised broadly in the same way; that is, there is a universal L2 learner phenomenon, which, since the 1960s and despite the mainstreaming initiative, has been conceptualised as someone learning English as a social and linguistic outsider; and:
3 That there is an abstracted notion of an idealised native speaker of English from which ethnic and linguistic minorities are automatically excluded.

In fact, we agree with Garcia's (1996) conclusion from North American experience that for many teachers

> it has become necessary to cope with a process of change whereby the ethnolinguistic identity of children is itself

> undergoing rapid change....The greatest failure of contemporary education has been precisely its inability to help teachers understand the ethnolinguistic complexity of children, classrooms, speech communities, and society, in such a way as to enable them to make informed decisions about language and culture in the classroom. (p. vii)

In the next section, we try to explore approaches to this complexity that might be more productive.

Contemporary Realities of TESOL

To adjust to the complex realities of contemporary urban multilingualism, we would suggest at least three strategies. First, it is worth attending closely to recent developments in cultural theory and research that offer ways of accommodating patterns of change in language use and social identity. Second, educators need to address the actual rather than the presumed language use, ethnicity, and culture of the bilingual learner. And third, they need to draw on the first two strategies to develop more specific, precise, and differentiated English language pedagogies, spanning a range of practice from the pupil who is a recent arrival and early English user to the pupil who is a settled bilingual in the mainstream class. In the process, teachers will need to engage properly with the hitherto unresolved (and now virtually invisible) issues surrounding the language needs of speakers of Creole-influenced language and Black English. The question of similarities and differences in L2-and Creole-influenced language continues to be unresolved in the English educational literature.[3] One reason why this is important is that in recent years the English-born children of other settled migrant minority groups, like their Caribbean-descended peers from an earlier period, have become much more difficult to separate into clearly bounded ethnic and linguistic categories that neatly divide them from ownership of English ethnicity, standard English, and local urban vernacular Englishes. (See Voices from the Classroom below for some evidence of the salience of this observation in the contemporary multiethnic classroom.)

Developments in Cultural Theory

One of the key questions addressed in an innovative way in British cultural studies is this: At what point are the people involved in migration to be considered as a permanent and integral part of the host nation and not as part of a kind of permanent "otherness"? For TESOL, this question is important for curriculum organisation and for classroom pedagogy because it paves the way for a better understanding of two further challenging questions:

1 Why do many bilingual learners, especially those in adolescence, actively seek to escape the essentialising linguistic and ethnic categories within which their English language teaching takes place?
2 What are ESOL teachers to do when the actual language use and language expertise of the young learners whom they daily observe confound the commonsense, fixed, and clearly bounded notions of language and ethnicity?

We would suggest that TESOL practitioners who wish to make progress with these and allied questions have much to gain from studying the thinking emanating from cultural theory and research in the late 1980s and early 1990s. Bhabha (1994), for instance, in a detailed theoretical treatment, gives an insight into the ways in which particular ethnic groups come to be constructed into a permanent otherness: "An important feature of colonial discourse is its dependence on the concept of 'fixity' in the ideological construction of otherness" (p. 66). Meanwhile, Gilroy (1987) analyzes the processes in the British nation-state that construct notions of Englishness or Britishness that permanently exclude certain minority groups. He identifies the role played by what he calls *ethnic absolutism*, a perspective that "views nations as culturally homogeneous communities of sentiment" (pp. 59–61). As Hall (1988) suggests, members of minority groups are not simple inheritors of fixed identities, ethnicities, cultures, and languages but are instead engaged in a continual collective and individual process of making, remaking, and negotiating these elements, thereby constantly constructing dynamic new ethnicities.

Writing more specifically of language, Hewitt (1991) identifies the significant ways in which urban youth participate in the "destabilisation of ethnicity" (p. 27) in their routine language use. He further suggests that an important but often overlooked part of their language use is what he describes as a local multiethnic vernacular, a community English. This language use is "the primary medium of communication in the adolescent peer group in multi-ethnic areas" (p. 32). There is also relevance in the associated notion of *language crossing*, which involves the use of minority languages by members of ethnic out-groups (e.g., Creole used by White and Asian adolescents or Panjabi used by Whites and African Caribbeans – see Rampton 1995, 1996). Among other things, crossing draws attention to the existence of many cross-ethnic friendships, to the fact that "there can be a strong interest in minority languages by majority group peers," and to the reality that "adolescents do not necessarily require *all* members of their peer group to speak *all* its languages with *equal* proficiency" (Rampton 1995: 328). It also emphasises the intractable problems associated with the term *native speaker* in relation to the speaking of English.

It is not necessary to accept these contributions in their entirety in order to argue for their potential relevance. This is neatly and vividly illustrated in an article by a multilingual Indian-born teacher about himself and his British-born son (Hallan 1994).

> As a British person I have lived 33 of my 40 years in England. So I should not have been surprised when, on a recent educational visit to the USA, I was constantly referred to as "our English guest" or "our English visitor." I was amazed at how much they admired my English accent and confused when, on a formal occasion, I received the compliment: "you English always dress so well."
>
> I was puzzled because in all my 33 years in England nobody had ever referred to me in those terms. In England I am always referred to as Indian. Why was my "Englishness" so prominent in the USA and so unrecognised here?.... The real surprise came last Christmas when, having left at the age of seven, I returned to India for a holiday.... My eight year old son, who is not fluent in Panjabi, suddenly found himself in an environment that he did not fully comprehend, where customs and traditions were not always familiar. There was a different emphasis on food, particularly towards vegetarianism, and fast food was a rarity. He was constantly looking for the "safe" and familiar. The street games played by the children of his age were new to him and, as he spoke little Panjabi and no Hindi, and they spoke only Hindi and no English, it was clear from day one that to stay within the bounds of the safe, he would be spending most if not all of his stay, with me and my parents or with other English speakers. He spent his spare time watching English language broadcasts on cable TV, MTV and BBC Asia, and after the first few days he was missing his Big Mac, chips and bacon sandwiches, and he was bored.
>
> In my son I was witnessing an amplification of my "Englishness" and a reduction of my "Indianness." As he was only fluent when communicating in English, it was no surprise when some of my relatives began to call him "*Angrez*" – the "Englishman." But here lies the dilemma experienced by English people whose parents originate from outside Europe, particularly those who do not have a white skin and therefore do not "blend in" with most of the British population. In England he is seen as an outsider, an Indian, but in India he is seen as an outsider, the "*Angrez*." So where does his ethnic identity lie, and what epithet correctly describes his ethnicity? (pp. 14–15)

Cultural theorists provide theoretical frameworks that help clarify phenomena like this. For instance, Mercer (1994) is one of many writers to redeploy the concept of *diaspora* to show that many people in minority groups in Britain can retain both real and imaginary global African, Asian, Caribbean, and other affiliations, combining them with definite

British identities. His notion of "emerging cultures of hybridity, forged among the overlapping African, Asian and Caribbean diasporas" (p. 3) could also help make sense of what this teacher and his son have been experiencing. As Mercer further observes, "in a world in which everyone's identity has been thrown into question, the mixing and fusion of disparate elements to create new, hybridized identities points to ways of surviving, and thriving, in conditions of crisis and transition" (pp. 4–5).[4]

Voices from the Classroom: Making Sense of Experience

In contemporary English urban environments, issues like these are commonly exemplified in the lived linguistic and cultural experience of young bilingual and multilingual learners. This is illustrated in the following written extracts, drawn from some 13- and 14-year-old pupils in one class of a London secondary school in 1996.[5]

> M. T. (female): I've lived in London all my life. The two main languages that I speak everyday are English and Gujarati.... When I was little I went to India. My mum's family were teaching me how to speak standard Gujarati, but I was too young and not interested. Now I am 13 I wish I had learnt how to speak proper Gujarati. Now at school I learn German. I can read, write, listen and speak German o. k., better than my home language Gujarati where I can only understand and speak it....I don't like speaking it (Gujarati) a lot mainly because I can speak English better. I have to speak Gujarati with my mum – sometimes when I don't know how to say a thing or object in Gujarati, I say the word in English, but with a Gujarati accent... my dad is always telling me to speak proper English so that I don't get in the habit of speaking slang all the time.
>
> A. T. (female): When I was young I was unable to speak another language like Hindi. My mother spoke to me all the time in Hindi hoping that I would pick it up, but however hard I tried to speak it, I did it all wrong and I was only able to understand. But when I went to India I felt really awkward. There all the children all spoke in Hindi and I was the only one who spoke English and so with me being young I had to fit in. I had felt so left out. I was only there for a month.
>
> N. K. (female): My first language is English. I read, write, speak and think in English. I also speak Gujarati because my mum and dad are Gujarati first language speakers. At home we mostly speak English, but my mum speaks to me in Gujarati, and I answer back in English which is common.... My own language style is using a lot of slang and not enough Standard English. I have tried to speak Standard English... but I can't. I can't because I am used to speaking slang.... In Gujarati I can only speak a few sentences and words. I only know some numbers and none of the alphabet in Gujarati.... People said that I should try to speak proper English not slang or cockney. My parents say that my English is not that good because I speak too much slang.
>
> D. C. (female): I was born in London. I speak Gujarati and English. My mother tongue is Gujarati but I mainly speak English. I can understand other languages such as Panjabi, Urdu and Hindi but I can't speak, read or write them. I can speak Gujarati and English fluently, but there are some words in Gujarati which I can't pronounce. I also can't read or write Gujarati. I've tried learning Gujarati but I can't seem to remember it. I have been learning German for nearly 3 years. I can read, write and speak, but there are still lots of things I don't know. I've been speaking Gujarati for all my life but I still can't read or write it... when I'm with my friends I speak London English including slang.
>
> P. M. (male): My family religion is Sikh. My Mum was born in Nairobi, Kenya, and came to this country when she was three years old. My Dad was born in Madras, India, and came to this country when he was twenty years old. I myself was born in England.... As I started out in High School, I had to develop a cockney accent of speaking in order too fit in with the rest of my friends. I kept on speaking London

> English to the point where I spoke it naturally.... When I'm with my mates you'll hear me say things like "easy" or "awight" instead of "hello"...or "send it here" instead of "pass it here," or "nasty" instead of "disgusting"...or "laters" instead of "bye" or "bad" or "wicked" instead of "cool," or "gwan there" instead of "well done," and "relax" instead of "don't worry".... When I'm speaking to people like my uncle on my dad's side of the family and my grandparents I speak Punjabi... people in my class think of me as normal, whereas my parents think that I talk like a "Gangsta."

> S. K. (female): I know Punjabi, Urdu, Swahili, German, English and Arabic. I can speak Punjabi perfectly and understand it very well. I know a lot of German, and I know how to speak it, and understand it and write it mainly. I know Arabic very little but can write a little bit of it. I know how to speak, write and understand English.

The pupils quoted above were attempting to describe, indirectly and delicately, the difference between their experience and the linguistic and ethnic categories imposed on them. Hall (1992) perceives that perhaps

> everywhere, cultural identities are emerging which are not fixed, but poised, *in transition* between different positions; which draw on different cultural traditions at the same time; and which are the product of those complicated cross-overs and cultural mixes which are increasingly common in a globalised world. (p. 310)

Along with the concept of transition, Hall presents that of *translation*, which

> describes those identity formations which cut across and intersect natural frontiers, and which are composed of people who have been dispersed forever from their homelands. Such people retain strong links with their places of origin and their traditions, but they are without the illusion of a return to the past. They are obliged to come to terms with the new cultures they inhabit, without simply assimilating to them and losing their identities completely. They bear upon them the traces of the particular cultures, traditions, languages and histories by which they were shaped. The difference is that they are not and will never be *unified* in the old sense, because they are irrevocably the product of several interlocking histories and cultures, belong at one and the same time to several "homes" (and to no one particular "home"). People belonging to such *cultures of hybridity* have had to renounce the dream or ambition of rediscovering any kind of "lost" cultural purity, or ethnic absolutism. They are irrevocably *translated*.... They are the products of the new *diasporas* created by the post-colonial migrations. They must learn to inhabit at least two identities, to speak two cultural languages, to translate and negotiate between them. Cultures of hybridity are one of the distinctly novel types of identity produced in the era of late-modernity, and there are more and more examples of them to be discovered. (p. 310)

The relevance of Hall's ideas stands out in these pupils' writing.

- M. T. has experienced family support in developing her bilingualism but has rejected it. On the other hand, she depicts both her schooled German and her schooled English as languages in which she has a dramatically higher level of competence than she does in Gujarati, her supposed mother tongue.
- A. T. demonstrates what is true for many other bilingual learners in the class, namely, that she feels "other," a linguistic and cultural outsider, not in relation to the English language and Britain but in relation to the Hindi language and India. At the same time she nevertheless retains a definite relationship with both Hindi and India. In this example the notion of *diaspora* is particularly useful.
- N. K. seems to claim only a minimum attachment to her family language; even when it is spoken to her she has neither the desire nor the level of competence to

sustain a spoken response in it. This pattern was characteristic of several of her classmates. Like many other pupils, she identified her usual language use as slang. Are she and her colleagues referring to Hewitt's (1991) local multiethnic vernacular or community English?

- P. M.'s parents' different birthplaces and his own birthplace raise the question of what ethnic category he would be classified under. In his language use, he clearly places Panjabi in a relatively restricted domain while demonstrating his identification and comfort with London English and a kind of Black London English with Jamaican Creole undertones. This situation may link into Hewitt's local multiethnic vernacular as well as Rampton's concept of language affiliation (to which we will later return).
- S. K. would be defined by the school as having Panjabi as her mother tongue, but she claims no literacy in it (see also D. C.). In fact, like a lot of other pupils at the school, she seems to feel that curriculum languages – here German – are rated more highly, and the fragility of describing her as a Panjabi-English bilingual is demonstrated elsewhere in her writing when she illustrates her discussion with examples that include confident German sentences alongside the full Arabic alphabet, Gujarati script, Gujarati sentences, and Swahili expressions.

These pupils seem to be struggling to understand the impact on themselves and their families of the processes that Hall describes, and the discovery of these processes by their teachers may well be an urgent prerequisite to the development of more sophisticated pedagogic strategies. Certainly, when approached with sensitivity, these students were perfectly willing to assist the enquiring teacher in gaining a better understanding of the effects of global social change on language use. But what kind of school language policy planning and pedagogy could exist for pupils with this kind of capability? Of course, the examples just cited contain all the weaknesses associated with self-report, and we have no room here for more than a brief, oversimplified discussion. Even so, this class is not highly atypical[6] and yields enough evidence to show that there are serious problems with current routine practices in the education of bilingual learners. Such pupils are frequently attributed a kind of romantic bilingualism and turned into reified speakers of community languages, and in the process their ethnicities are also reified.

Such then is the mismatch between the realities of urban multilingualism and the educational classification of students' language identities and backgrounds. On the other side are the prevailing views of English.

The Swann Committee (1985) and National Curriculum documents (from 1988 to date) officially accept ethnic and linguistic diversity in society, but they nevertheless insist on cultivating English as the universal medium defining the nation-state and as a principal instrument for achieving social cohesion. In doing so, the population of England is for practical purposes cast as a homogenous community with one language and one culture. According to Anderson (1991), this situation is typical of the way a nation comes to be artificially constructed as an imagined community, and one dimension can be seen in the way bilinguals are taught as if only one English mattered. This English is seen as the province of the idealised native speaker, something that he or she already possesses and that the outsider imperfectly aspires to. A more accurate picture of English language realities in Britain emerges from scholars whose work is more empirically oriented.

> The British education system rests on the assumption that teachers and pupils will use the grammar of standard English. However, the majority of British children are speakers not of standard English but of a non-standard variety of English (a dialect), and this has been recognized as posing extremely important problems concerning language in education. (Cheshire, Edwards, and Whittle 1993: 54)

This view is endorsed in a recent piece of empirical national research in England, which concluded that a minimum of 68 percent of 11- to 16-year-olds did not habitually use only standard English speech forms (Hudson and Holmes, 1995). The following piece of writing shows an attempt to write in standard English by a White, monolingual English-speaking 7-year-old child.

> We find a car wive grnsu on it...aw no they cacht us. they wolt to the dunjoon. We hewd aw bref...wen we opoed awe iys we was in the diynjoon...we slept in the dungeon for friy nights...we only had 10 pans left. We fand 10,000 Pans on the strit Pavmot...we was wocen olog the rode... John basht into the wole...we got att... they ran away they was nevu to bey sene a gen...Tony foth for a minit...Tony foth we can put a are money in the bank (Harris, 1995)

> [We found a car with guns on it...oh no they caught us. They walked to the dungeon. We held our breath...when we opened our eyes we were in the dungeon... we slept in the dungeon for three nights... we only had 10 pounds left. We found 10,000 pounds on the street pavement... we were walking along the road...John crashed into the wall...we got out...they ran away they were never to be seen again... Tony thought for a minute...James thought we can put all our money in the bank.]

Reasons of focus and space prohibit a full analysis, but the key point is that even so-called native speakers do not necessarily use standard forms. In the example above, the child is showing that the language use he finds most natural is in fact London English and not standard English.

These findings, we would suggest, are true not only for those pupils of White British descent but also for a large proportion of the descendants of the migrant groups to whom we have been referring. Either many of the pupils defined as bilingual learners are most comfortable linguistically with either a local urban spoken English vernacular, or, alternatively, a nonstandard variety of this kind serves as their first spoken entry into English in the local community context. This reflects

> the obliteration of pure language forms deriving from a single cultural source, evident in some inner city areas (in the U.K.) and...the diasporic distribution of communicative forms which, whilst generated from and based in local communities, nevertheless reach out and extend lines of connection in a global way. The local penetration and mixing of language forms evident in some urban settings in the U.K. should, in fact, be seen perhaps as a reflex of the broader linguistic diasporic processes. (Hewitt 1995: 97)

Again, it is important to ask what consideration traditional TESOL pedagogic approaches give to these factors.

Language Expertise, Affiliation, and Inheritance: An Educational Response to Linguistic and Ethnic Diversity

So far, we have suggested that the conceptual frameworks of contemporary TESOL provide little leaverage on the classroom realities created by the linguistic and ethnic composition of the pupil population. This lack of analytic clarity has led both TESOL practitioners and mainstream teachers to feel paralyzed in their ability to respond to pupils' language needs, as seen, for example, in the constant struggle to develop adequate pedagogies for the large numbers of bilingual pupils who are no longer at an early stage of learning English, who have spent a significant proportion of their lives in Britain, and who use everyday colloquial English with ease (often referred to as the *plateau effect*, in which the pupil does not seem to be able to make any further progress in English language development).

In this context, Rampton (1990) offers a framework that may offer one or two ways forward. He suggests that "language education [is seen] as a social activity in which efforts are made to manage continuity, change and the relationship between social groups" (p. 100; also see Rampton 1995: chap. 13). Rampton suggests replacing the terms *native speaker* and *mother tongue* with the notions of *language expertise, language inheritance,* and *language affiliation*. In a slight reworking of Rampton's original formulation, the term *language expertise* refers to how proficient people are in a language; *language affiliation* refers to the attachment or identification they feel for a language whether or not they nominally belong to the social group customarily associated with it; and *language inheritance* refers to the ways in which individuals can be born into a language tradition that is prominent within the family and community setting whether or not they claim expertise in or affiliation to that language. In this scheme, language teachers need to ask whether the learner's relationship with each language thought to exist in that learner's repertoire is based on expertise, on inheritance, on affiliation, or on a combination.

We might expand on this as follows.

Language expertise

What do teachers know about their pupils' ability in each of the posited languages? (Interestingly, although educators have become accustomed to classifying pupils according to stages or levels of putative competence in English (Hester 1996), it is still not standard practice to attempt such an assessment in any rigorous way for their competence in languages other than English.)

This question raises several other issues. For instance, what are the criteria for assessment? Are they based on any explicitly stated, and therefore contestable, language models or norms in all the languages involved?

Language affiliation

Do teachers know anything about their pupils' sense of affiliation to any of the languages allegedly within their repertoire? How might such knowledge about their affective relationship with their languages be used in the classroom and the curriculum?

Language inheritance

Does membership in an ethnic group mean an automatic language inheritance? In the light of our earlier discussion this assumption seems to be unsafe for some pupils. What are the consequences of an inaccurate assumption for curricular provision of community language teaching? Can educators rely on an abstract notion of the benefits of bilingualism when they are working with ethnic/linguistic minority pupils?

The potential value of these questions becomes clear if they are used to outline conventional TESOL assumptions and compare them with the kind of classroom intimated above.

Language expertise

The conventional TESOL assumption is that ethnic minority pupils are beginners or relative newcomers to English (or at any rate lack native-speaker expertise) but that they possess expertise in their home or community language (L1). A related assumption is that the ethnic majority pupil possesses native-speaker expertise in an undifferentiated English (i.e., no distinction is made between standard English and local vernacular Englishes).

In contrast, it is difficult to assume that ethnic majority pupils faced with the complex urban realities sketched in the earlier sections possess expertise in English, especially standard English for academic purposes. A further complication is that many ethnic minority pupils disclaim expertise in their putative L1 (home/community) language (see M. T. and D. C. above). Minority pupils may also claim expertise in English – at least in the same kind of English possessed by their ethnic majority classroom peers.

Language Affiliation

In attempting to adopt a positive approach to bilingualism, conventional contemporary TESOL practice tends not only to attribute expertise in the putative L1 to ethnic minority pupils but also to attribute a high degree of affiliation on the part of these ethnic minority pupils to their home and community languages. This tendency is reflected, for instance, in the standard recommendation that teachers maximise the use of linguistically familiar material to promote pupils' confidence and self-esteem. As one teacher puts it, "Well the Asians are taken care of with E2L. They get a lot of support and of course their culture is strong. They have a number of languages which they use" (Mac an Ghaill 1988: 56). At the same time there is a tendency to assume White monolingual English speakers are automatically affiliated to standard English. The urban realities cast doubt on these certainties. First, a significant number of ethnic minority adolescent pupils demonstrate a weak sense of affiliation to their supposed home/community L1 (see D. C. and M. T. above). In addition, other ethnic minorities may claim affiliation to linguistic varieties that are supposed to be part of the natural inheritance of other ethnic groups (see P. M. above). At the same time a similar tendency is also visible amongst ethnic majority pupils (see, e.g., Hewitt 1986; Rampton 1995). And there is evidence that some white pupils have a weak affiliation with standard English and use nonstandard forms by choice (Hudson and Holmes 1995).

Language Inheritance

An underlying assumption in TESOL practice is that ethnic groups inherit (are born into) language traditions that transcend questions of the actual language use of individuals and collectives; at the same time TESOL practice often assumes that language inheritance is strictly endogamous. This view can be seen in instances when ethnic minority community languages are offered as study options but are only designed for putative L1 speakers. Once again, in the realities of urban multilingualism, a noticeable number of adolescents from both majority and minority ethnic groups do not show a strong allegiance to their supposed linguistic inheritance. Equally, many working-class white youngsters do not show an allegiance to what is supposed to be their linguistic inheritance (standard English). Many pupils of Asian descent may also claim a strong inheritance in relation to English (see A. T. above).

We do not want to suggest that the conventional assumptions are automatically invalid. Indeed some of these assumptions work well with some pupils. But clearly, it is vital to validate all such assumptions against the actualities of a linguistically and culturally diverse classroom.

Future Development

We have attempted to identify the complexities of some of our urban classrooms. A period of open analysis, critical questioning, and working with new ideas in the classroom may lead to more responsive pedagogies. Current knowledge does not warrant the pronouncement of grand strategies or solutions. Certainly, the binary native-speaker-versus-other is increasingly redundant, and the development of more appropriate classroom approaches should be based on a sharper awareness of learners with different needs. But how to classify and organize such pedagogies is an issue that requires a lot more exploration and reflection. One such pedagogy would be readily recognizable to TESOL practitioners – one designed for the learner who is new to the English language and English-speaking cultural contexts.

However, beyond this, other forms of English language pedagogy might be better based on an assumption that most learners, albeit from different starting points, are unfamiliar with the deployment of standard English for academic purposes. This pedagogy might be accompanied by the development of context-sensitive and learning-oriented assessments to establish the degree of expertise an individual pupil possesses in understanding, speaking, reading, or writing any given language.

Finally, it is of the utmost importance that TESOL pedagogy explicitly recognise and address societal inequalities between ethnic and linguistic groups, inequalities that can indeed often lead pupils to respond ambiguously to questions about their linguistic expertise, affiliation, and inheritance. Like Cummins (1996), we are interested in creating a pedagogy that takes genuine account of learners' expertise and identities.

We hope we have shown the importance of developing more effective and more pupil-sensitive classroom and curriculum responses to multilingual urban contexts. Our current research explores ways of constructing such pedagogies, and we hope that this will be continued in the future, both by ourselves and others.

THE AUTHORS

Constant Leung, Roxy Harris, and Ben Rampton teach sociolinguistics, language and culture, and second language acquisition at Thames Valley University, London. Their current research interests include language use across social, cultural, and ethnic boundaries; L2 assessment; and language education policy and practice in multilingual settings.

NOTES

1 Throughout this article, for reasons of legislation and social context, we refer to TESOL in England specifically. Although there might be commonalities among the national TESOL practices within Britain as a whole, we do not claim that our descriptions and arguments are directly applicable to Scotland and Wales.
2 The term *bilingual pupil/learner* is widely used in England as a broad category to refer to pupils who are at various stages of learning English as a second or additional language for studying purposes and who have at least some knowledge and skills in another language or languages already.
3 For discussions of this issue in the Caribbean itself, see Devonish (1986) and Roberts (1988).
4 We emphasize that recognizing notions of hybridity does not in any sense ignore the very real ways in which certain ethnic minority groups suffer specific and systematic societal inequalities on the basis of fixed and ascribed ethnic identities.
5 These data were collected by Harris. Writing was elicited after a taught unit on language and power.
6 Approximately 200 languages (other than English) are spoken by pupils in England (School Curriculum and Assessment Authority, 1996). Most professional estimates suggest that approximately 10 percent of the total school population is bilingual, and the figure is increasing. The percentage of bilingual pupils in individual schools varies; in some urban schools the bilingual intake may be 85 percent (or above). Census information indicates that the number of people in undefined (other) and mixed ethnic categories has been increasing consistently in the past two decades (Owen 1996).

REFERENCES

Alladina, S. and Edwards, V. (1991). *Multilingualism in the English Isles* (Vol. 2). London: Longman.

Anderson, B. (1991). *Imagined Communities*. London: Verso.

Bhabha, H. (1994). *The Location of Culture*. London: Routledge.

Cheshire, J., Edwards, V. and Whittle, P. (1993). Non-standard English and Dialect Levelling. In J. Milroy and L. Milroy (eds.), *Real English: The Grammar of English Dialects in the English Isles* (pp. 53–96). London: Longman.

Cummins, J. (1996). *Negotiating Identities: Education for Empowerment in a Diverse Society*. Ontario: California Association for Bilingual Education.

Department of Education and Science. (1971). *The Education of Immigrants: Education Survey 13*. London: Her Majesty's Stationery Office.

Department of Education and Science. (1995). *English in the National Curriculum*. London: Her Majesty's Stationery Office.

Devonish, H. (1986). *Language and Liberation: Creole Language Politics in the Caribbean*. London: Karia Press.

Edwards, V., and Redfern, A. (1992). *The World in a Classroom*. Clevedon, England: Multilingual Matters.

Garcia, O. (1996). Foreword. In C. Baker, *Foundation of Bilingual Education and Bilingualism* (pp. vii–ix). Clevedon, England: Multilingual Matters.

Gilroy, P. (1991). *There ain't no Black in the Union Jack*. London: Routledge.

Hall, S. (1988). New ethnicities. In A. Rattansi and J. Donald (eds.), *"Race," Culture and Difference* (pp. 252–9). London: Sage/Open University.

Hall, S. (1992). The Question of Cultural Identity. In S. Hall, D. Held, and T. McGrew (eds.), *Modernity and its Futures* (pp. 274–316). Cambridge: Polity/Open University.

Hallan, V. (1994, Autumn). Whose Ethnicity is it Anyway? *Multicultural Teaching*: 14–15.

Harris, R. (1995). Disappearing language. In J. Mace (Ed.), *Literacy, Language and Community Publishing* (pp. 118–44). Clevedon, England: Multilingual Matters.

Hester, H. (1996). The Stages of English Learning: The Context. In *Invitational Conference on Teaching and Learning English as an Additional Language* (pp. 182–87). London: School Curriculum and Assessment Authority. Summarized in *Teaching and Learning English as an Additional Language: New Perspectives* (SCAA Discussion Paper No. 5). (1996). London: School Curriculum and Assessment Authority.

Hewitt, R. (1991) Language, youth and the Destabilisation of Ethnicity. In C. Palmgren, K. Lorgren, and G. Bolin (eds.), *Ethnicity and Youth Culture* (pp. 27–41). Stockholm, Sweden: Stockholm University.

Hewitt, R. (1995). The Umbrella and the Sewing Machine: Trans-culturalism and the Definition of Surrealism. In A. Alund and R. Granqvist (eds.), *Negoliating Identities* (pp. 91–104). Amsterdam: Rodopi.

Hudson, R., and Holmes, J. (1995). *Children's Use of Spoken Standard English*. London: School Curriculum and Assessment Authority.

Inner London Education Authority (ILEA). (1989). *Catalogue of Languages: Spoken by Inner London School Pupils: RS 1262/89*. London: ILEA Research & Statistics.

Lawton, D. (1968). *Social Class, Language and Education*. London: Routledge & Kegan Paul.

Leung, C. (1993). The Coming Crisis of ESL in the National Curriculum. *English Association for Applied Linguistics Newsletter, 45:* 27–32.

Leung, C. (1996). Content, Context and Language. In T. Cline and N. Frederickson (eds.), *Curriculum Related Assessment, Cummins and Bilingual Children* (pp. 26–40). Clevedon, England: Multilingual Matters.

Leung, C., Harris, R., and Rampton, B. (1997). *The Idealised Native Speaker, Reified Ethnicities and Classroom Realities: Contemporary Issues in TESOL* (CALR Occasional Papers in Language and Urban Culture 2). London: Thames Valley University, Centre for Applied Linguistic Research.

Mac an Ghaill, M. (1988). *Young, Gifted and Black*. Milton Keynes, England: Open University Press.

Martin-Jones, M. (1989). Language Education in the Context of Linguistic Diversity: Differing Orientations in Educational Policy Making in England. In J. Esling (ed.), *Multicultural Education Policy: ESL in the 1990's* (pp. 36–58). Toronto, Canada: OISE Press.

Mercer, K. (1994). *Welcome to the Jungle*. London: Routledge.

Owen, D. (1996). Size, Structure and Growth of the Ethnic Minority Populations. In D. Coleman and J. Salt (eds.), *Ethnicity in the 1991 Census: Vol. 1. Demographic Characteristics of the Ethnic Minority Populations* (pp. 87–91). London: Her Majesty's Stationery Office.

Peach, C. (ed.). (1996). *Ethnicity in the 1991 Census* (Vol. 2). London: Her Majesty's Stationery Office.

Rampton, B. (1985). A Critique of Some Educational Attitudes to the English of British Asian Schoolchildren, and their Implications. In C. Brumfit, R. Ellis, and J. Levine (eds.), *English as a Second Language in the UK* (pp. 187–98). Oxford: Pergamon Press.

Rampton, B. (1988). A Non-educational View of ESL in Britain. *Journal of Multilingual and Multicultural Development, 9:* 503–27.

Rampton, B. (1990). Displacing the "Native Speaker": Expertise, Affiliation and Inheritance. *ELT Journal, 44:* 97–101.

Rampton, B. (1995). *Crossing: Language and Ethnicity among Adolescents*. London: Longman.

Rampton, B. (1996). Language Crossing, New Ethnicities and School. *English in Education, 30*(2): 14–26.

Rampton, B., Harris, R., and Leung, C. (1997). Multilingualism in England. *Annual Review of Applied Linguistics, 17:* 224–41.

Roberts, P. (1988). *West Indians and Their Language*. Cambridge: Cambridge University Press.

School Curriculum and Assessment Authority. (1996). *Teaching English as an Additional Language: A Framework for Policy.* London: Author.

Swann Report. (1985). *Education for All.* London: Her Majesty's Stationery Office.

STUDY QUESTIONS

1 In what ways has post-1945 migration to England challenged the very notion of "native speaker"? Is the same analysis applicable to other countries you are familiar with (e.g., the US)? Justify your answer.
2 In what ways are the issues addressed in this chapter connected to and relevant for (a) the notion of speech community; (b) attitudes toward the standard language and one's own dialect; (c) the circulation of media discourse; and (c) communication and miscommunication across ethnic groups?
3 How does the notion of "hybridity" help us understand the experience of the multilingual speakers who participate in TESOL classes?
4 Explain the concepts of "language expertise," "language inheritance," and "language affiliation" using examples of each from the chapter.
5 How do the authors argue that racism and otherness have played a part in the formation of TESOL pedagogies? How have they affected English language learning for students from diverse backgrounds? Extend the authors' argument to other contexts.

Part II

The Performance of Language: Events, Genres, and Narratives

Introduction

A major contribution of linguistic anthropology to the understanding of language as a social activity has been the focus on performance. Whereas most theoretical linguists have studied language abstracted from its contexts of use, linguistic anthropologists have emphasized the need to think about language as an activity which is born out of social life and has consequences for speakers-hearers as members of particular speech communities. This shift in the object of study has created new challenges for researchers, including the issue of finding new units of analysis to add to the established notions used by linguists, which focus exclusively on grammar. In the first chapter of this Part (Chapter 6), Dell Hymes, the founder of the approach known as "the ethnography of speaking," proposes using the notion of speech style in order to rethink the cultural and social significance of alternative ways of "saying the same thing." He argues for the cultural significance of certain features of speaking that are usually left out of grammars even though they play a crucial role in the constitution of social identities and, more generally, of particular "ways of life."

In Chapter 7, Judith Irvine reviews the literature on formality and informality in language use starting from the notion of "event." In her critical review of the four recurring aspects of formality, Irvine focuses on speech events among the Wolof, the Yoruba, the Burundi, the Mursi, and the Ilongots. In each case, she shows that there is a relationship between what researchers have called "formality" and what she calls "political coercion." She also argues in favor of a more nuanced analysis of the specific contexts and functions of speaking that have been traditionally identified with the English term *formality*. In Chapter 8, Alessandro Duranti analyzes speaking in terms of speech exchanges, which are internally composed of speech acts produced by different parties. The study of one of the most common daily rituals, greetings, gives us a chance to think about the extent to which what we do routinely loses its social significance or simply makes it unnoticeable. The simultaneous attention to universal and culture-specific properties of opening salutations provides us with a grid to think about a wide range of occasions in which speakers perform their social identities and reconstitute their social relations within their community.

The notion of "genre" has been one of the most commonly used units of analysis for the study of verbal performance. In Chapter 9, Richard Bauman and Charles Briggs embark on a detailed examination of the ways in which genres have been studied, defined, and deconstructed in anthropology, folklore, and literary studies. They playfully alter Edward Sapir's famous phrase "all grammars leak" to argue that "all genres leak" during actual performance and we must develop ways to describe and explain the gaps between what people are expected to say and what they actually do say in a given cultural and interactional context.

Narratives have always been of interest to anthropologists. In the last few decades, however, there has been a change in the types of narratives that are being studied and in the methods used for their documentation. In addition to the recording of elicited folktales, myths, and other traditional stories, contemporary researchers have been video-taping and transcribing spontaneous narrative activities that emerge in a wider range of contexts, including everyday family interaction (see Chapter 18 in Part IV) and political debates in the US and Europe. Chapter 10, the second chapter by Alessandro Duranti in Part II, shows that political candidates in the US use personal narratives to create a sense of coherence regarding their own lives and moral selves while looking for inconsistencies in the narrative constructions of their opponents.

In Chapter 11, H. Samy Alim introduces a new trend of research into what he calls "Hip Hop Nation Language." He combines attention to the performance aspects of language use (for example, the practice of call-and-response) with the systematic investigation of phonological, syntactic, and lexical features of what other authors call "African American English" (or "African American English Vernacular"). These latter features are those typically studied by quantitative sociolinguists working in urban speech communities. Building on previous contributions by others and on his own fieldwork in the community, Alim proposes a set of defining features of Hip Hop Nation Language and sets up an agenda for future research that is aimed at documenting both continuity and innovation within the African American speech community.

SUGGESTIONS FOR FURTHER READING

Some of Dell Hymes's writings on speech events, genres, and performance are collected in: D. Hymes (1974), *Foundations in Socioliguistics: An Ethnographic Approach*, Philadelphia: University of Pennsylvania Press; D. Hymes (1981), *"In Vain I Tried to Tell You": Essays in Native American Ethnopoetics*, Philadelphia: University of Pennsylvania Press; and D. Hymes, (1996), *Ethnography, Linguistics, Narrative Inequality*, Bristol, PA: Taylor & Francis. An ethnography of language use that puts into practice Hymes's approach is J. Sherzer (1983), *Kuna Ways of Speaking: An Ethnographic Perspective*, Austin: University of Texas Press; see also the articles in R. Bauman and J. Sherzer (eds.) (1989), *Explorations in the Ethnography of Speaking* (2nd edn.), Cambridge: Cambridge University Press.

An important anthropological contribution to the theorization of language as action is found in the second volume of B. Malinowski (1935), *Coral Gardens and Their Magic*, London: Allen & Unwin.

Contributions by linguistic anthropologists to the study of verbal art and performance include: R. Bauman (ed.) (1992), *Folklore, Cultural Performances, and Popular Entertainments*. New York: Oxford University Press; R. Bauman (2004), *A World of Others' Words: Cross-Cultural Perspectives on Intertextuality*, Malden, MA: Blackwell. Ethnographic studies of verbal art include: C. L. Briggs (1988), *Competence in Performance: The Creativity of Tradition in Mexicano Verbal Art*, Philadelphia: University of Pennsylvania Press; J. Errington (1988), *Structure and Style in Javanese: A Semiotic View of Linguistic Etiquette*, Philadelphia: University of Pennsylvania Press; J. Sherzer (1990), *Verbal Art in San Blas: Kuna Culture through its Discourse*, Cambridge: Cambridge University Press; J. Sherzer (2002), *Speech Play and Verbal Art*, Austin: University of Texas Press; D. Tedlock (1983), *The Spoken Word and the Work of Interpretation*, Philadelphia: University of Pennsylvania Press; L. R. Graham (1995), *Performing Dreams: Discourses of Immortality Among the Xavante of Central Brazil*, Austin: University of Texas Press; J. C. Kuipers (1990), *Power in Performance: The Creation of Textual Authority in Weyewa Ritual Speech*, Philadelphia: University of Pennsylvania Press; C. A. Kratz (1994), *Affecting Performance: Meaning, Movement, and Experience in Okiek Women's Initiation*, Washington: Smithsonian Institution Press; J. C. Kuipers (1998), *Language, Identity, and Marginality in Indonesia: The Changing Nature of Ritual Speech on the Island of Sumba*, Cambridge: Cambridge University Press; J. M. Wilce (1998), *Eloquence in Trouble: The Poetics and Politics of Complaint in Rural Bangladesh*, New York: Oxford University Press; R. Finnegan (2007), *The Oral and Beyond: Doing Things with Words in Africa*, Chicago, IL: The University of Chicago Press.

The interaction between language and context is discussed in: A. Duranti and C. Goodwin (eds.) (1992), *Rethinking Context: Language as an Interactive Phenomenon*, Cambridge: Cambridge University Press; M. Silverstein and G. Urban (eds.) (1996), *Natural Histories of Discourse*, Chicago, IL: The University of Chicago Press; A. Agha (2007), *Language and Social Relations*, Cambridge: Cambridge University Press.

Contributions to an anthropological understanding of narratives in everyday life and in ritual events are found in a number of monographs and collections, including: R. Bauman (1986), *Story, Performance, and Event: Contextual Studies of Oral Narrative*, Cambridge: Cambridge University Press; C. L. Briggs (ed.) (1996), *Disorderly Discourse: Narrative, Conflict, and Inequality*, New York: Oxford University Press; C. Mattingly (1998), *Healing Dramas and Clinical Plots: the Narrative Structure of Experience*, Cambridge: Cambridge University Press; S. Slyomovics (1998), *The Object of Memory: Arab and Jew Narrate the Palestinian Village*, Philadelphia: University of Pennsylvania Press; G. Urban (2001), *Metaculture: How Culture Moves through the World*; Minneapolis, MN: University of Minnesota Press; E. Ochs and L. Capps (2001), *Living Narrative: Creating Lives in Everyday Storytelling*, Cambridge, MA: Harvard University Press; B. Rymes (2001), *Conversational Borderlands: Language and Identity in an Alternative Urban High School*, New York: Teachers College Press; D. M. Klapproth (ed.) (2004), *Narrative as Social Practice: Anglo-Western and Australian Aboriginal Traditions*, Berlin and

New York: Mouton de Gruyter. For a discussion of the notion of master narrative and counter-narrative, see M. Bamberg and M. Andrews (eds.) (2004), *Considering Counter-narratives: Narrating, Resisting, Making Sense*, Amsterdam: John Benjamins.

A number of linguistic anthropologists have been influenced by P. Ricoeur (1988), *Time and Narrative*, 3 vols., Chicago, IL: The University of Chicago Press.

There is a long tradition of the study of language and politics in linguistic anthropology, which partly overlaps with the study of verbal performance (see above). Here are some of the most important contributions: R. Paine (ed.) (1981), *Politically Speaking: Cross-Cultural Studies of Rhetoric*, Philadelphia: Institute for the Study of Human Issues; M. Bloch (1975), *Political Language and Oratory in Traditional Society*, London: Academic Press; Donald L. Brenneis and Fred Myers (eds.) (1984), *Dangerous Words: Language and Politics in the Pacific*, New York: New York University Press; C. A. Lutz and L. Abu-Lughod (eds.) (1990), *Language and the Politics of Emotion*, Cambridge: Cambridge University Press; F. Merlan and A. Rumsey (1991), *Ku Waru: Language and Segmentary Politics in the Western Nebilyer Valley, Papua New Guinea*, Cambridge: Cambridge University Press; Alessandro Duranti (1994), *From Grammar to Politics: Linguistic Anthropology in a Western Samoan Village*, Berkeley and Los Angeles: University of California Press; S. F. Harding (2000), *The Book of Jerry Falwell: Fundamental Language and Politics*, Princeton, NJ: Princeton University Press.

The analysis of everyday interaction as performance, including the study of greetings, was stimulated in great part by the work of Erving Goffman on strategic interaction and his use of dramaturgic metaphors: E. Goffman (1959), *The Presentation of Self in Everyday Life*, Garden City, NY: Doubleday; (1963), *Behavior in Public Places: Notes on the Social Organization of Gathering*, New York: Free Press; (1967), *Interaction Ritual: Essays in Face to Face Behavior*, Garden City, New York: Doubleday; (1974), *Frame Analysis: An Essay on the Organization of Experience*, New York: Harper and Row. Goffman's most influential essays on verbal interaction are collected in E. Goffman (1981), *Forms of Talk*, Philadelphia: University of Pennsylvania Press.

Everyday interaction is a central concern in ethnomethodology and conversation analysis. Important books and collections of articles include: H. Garfinkel (1967), *Studies in Ethnomethodology*, Englewood Cliffs, NJ: Prentice-Hall; J. Schenkein (1978), *Studies in the Organization of Conversational Interaction*, New York: Academic Press; G. Psathas (1979), *Everyday Language: Studies in Ethnomethodology*, New York: Irvington Publishers; J. Heritage (1984), *Garfinkel and Ethnomethodology*, Cambridge: Polity; J. M. Atkinson and J. Heritage (1984), *Structures of Social Action: Studies in Conversation Analysis*, Cambridge: Cambridge University Press; M. Moerman (1988), *Talking Culture: Ethnography and Conversation Analysis*, Philadelphia: University of Pennsylvania Press; H. Sacks (1992), *Lectures on Conversation, 2 Vols.*, Cambridge, MA: Blackwell; E. A. Schegloff (2007), *Sequence Organization in Interaction, Vol. 1: A Primer in Conversation Analysis*, Cambridge: Cambridge University Press.

On the language and culture of Rap and Hip Hop music, see: T. Rose (1994), *Black Noise: Rap Music and Black Culture in Contemporary America*, Middletown, CT: Wesleyan University Press; I. Perry (2004), *Prophets of the Hood: Politics and*

Poetics in Hip Hop, Durham, NC: Duke University Press; H. S. Alim (2006), *Roc the Mic Right: The Language of Hip Hop Culture*, London and New York: Routledge; A. Pennycook (2007), *Global Englishes and Transcultural Flows*, London: Routledge; H. S. Alim and A. Pennycook (eds.) (2008), *Global Linguistic Flows: Hip Hop Cultures, Youth Identities, and the Politics of Language*, London: Routledge.

6

Ways of Speaking

Dell Hymes

We start from the speech community conceived as an "organization of diversity"; we require concepts and methods that enable us to deal with that diversity, that organization. The great stumbling block is that the kinds of organization most developed by linguists presuppose the grammar as their frame of reference. (By grammar is meant here the genre of grammars.) Since its invention in classical antiquity, the grammar has been dominated by association with analysis of a single, more or less homogeneous, norm. In earlier periods the choice of norm was determined by social constraints. Linguistics, as grammar, came into existence to dissect and teach just that language, or language-variety, that embodied valued cultural tradition (Homeric Greek, the Sanskrit of the Vedas, the Chinese of the Confucian classics), not just any language; indeed, not any other language at all. The grammar, like the language, was an instrument of hegemony. In recent times the choice of norm has been determined often enough by factors intrinsic to the linguistic task. Although the class background of linguists favors the "standard" of the schools, considerations of simplicity, clarity, fullness, of whatever is advantageous to the linguistic task itself, have also entered. Linguists have often been as decisive as schoolmasters in excluding things. With the schoolmaster, exclusion may have been for reasons of prestige and pedantry; with the linguist, it may most often have been for the sake of a model or an elegant result; but the consequence in relation to the speech patterns of a community as a whole has not been too different. Much of those patterns, when not ignored, can be accommodated only in terms of deviations from the privileged account. It is not revealed in its own right.

Now, if members of a community themselves class certain patterns of speech as deviant, mixtures, marginal, or the like, that is a significant fact; but we do not want to be trapped into having to treat phenomena that way, merely because of the limitations of the model with which we start. Where community members find patterns natural, we do not want to have to make them out to be unnatural.

The available term for an alternative starting point is style. We propose to consider a speech community initially as comprising a set of *styles*. By "style," we do not in the first instance mean one or another of the specific uses to which this protean term has been put, but just

For permission to publish copyright material in this book, grateful acknowledgment is made to: D. Hymes (1974), "Ways of Speaking," in R. Bauman and J. Sherzer (eds.), *Explorations in the Ethnography of Speaking*. Cambridge: Cambridge University Press, pp. 433–51.

the root sense of a way or mode of doing something. We need to use the term neutrally, generally, for any way or mode, all ways and modes.

Recently a way of dealing with speech styles has been made explicit by Ervin-Tripp (1972), building on work of Gumperz (cf. Gumperz 1972: 21). Their achievement fits into the history of achievements with descriptive concepts in linguistics. That history can be seen as one of the successive discovery of concrete universals, such that language could be described in terms relevant to a specific system, yet applicable to all; terms, that is, free of bias due to a particular context, and mediating between given systems and general theory, doing justice to both. In phonology, the concepts of the phoneme, and then of distinctive features, have been such. In morphology, the generalizations of the morpheme as a concept for all formatives of a language, and of terms for grammatical categories, processes, and types, were also such. Much of this work was accomplished by Boas, Sapir, Bloomfield, and their students, and depended upon universalizing the range of languages to be described. Recent efforts in syntactic and semantic analysis have had a related aim, pushing the search for universal aspects of grammar to new depths, although sometimes at the expense of specific systems. We have reached a point at which the concept of grammar itself is that which needs to be transcended.

In recent years a number of linguists have recognized this possibility (e.g., Whorf, Firth, Harris, Joos), but their insights have not been systematically followed up. (On this point, and others in this section, cf. Hymes 1970.) Styles have been noted with regard to a variety of bases (authors, settings, groups), but not style itself as the general basis of description. Often enough the notion of style has been invoked ad hoc, simply to save the ordinary grammatical analysis (as often with role and status differences (see Hymes 1970)). Ervin-Tripp has now generalized two principles of modern linguistics, the syntagmatic and the paradigmatic relations, and freed them from dependence on a particular sector of grammar, or on a formal grammatical model. She develops two notions, *rules of co-occurrence*, and *rules of alternation*. The point, obvious after the event, yet novel and liberating, is that one can characterize whatever features go together to identify a style of speech in terms of rules of co-occurrence among them, and can characterize choice among styles in terms of rules of alternation. The first concept gives systematic status to the ways of selecting and grouping together of linguistic means that actually obtain in a community. The second concept frees the resulting styles from mechanical connection with a particular defining situation. Persons are recognized to choose among styles themselves, and the choices to have social meaning. (This is the vantage point from which a variety of phenomena treated separately under headings such as bilingualism, diglossia, standard and non-standard speech, and the like, can be integrated.)

These notions are well exemplified in Ervin-Tripp's study (1972). Here I want to build upon them in the three sections that follow, by considering further their relationship to the description of a speech community: (a) more enters into speech styles than is usually identified linguistically, and (b) the concept of speech styles requires specification and supplementation in an ethnography of speaking. Finally, (c) the notion of style is not just an alternative to the notion of grammar, but has application to grammar itself, as something socially constituted.

The Two Elementary Functions

For nearly half a century American linguists have taken as fundamental to their science the assumption that in a speech community some utterances are the same in form and meaning (Bloomfield 1933: 144; Swadesh 1948: 257 note 11; Postal 1968: 7, 12, 217). The assumption has enabled them to identify relevant differences, as opposed to irrelevant differences, and thus to identify the elementary units in terms of whose relationships a grammar is defined. Built into the assumption has been the corollary that relevant differences were of just one kind. As Bloomfield once put it, when a beggar says "I'm hungry" and a child says "I'm hungry," to avoid going to bed, the linguist is interested just in what is the same in the two utterances, not in what is different. From his standpoint, the utterances count as repetitions. "You're hungry," "he's hungry," "she's hungry," "it's hungry," etc., would count as structurally revealing contrasts, as to grammatical forms. "It's dungaree" (pronounced to rhyme with "hungry") would be a revealing contrast, as to features of sound. "I'm hungary" (pronounced to rhyme with "hungry"), said perhaps by a representative of an east European country, would be an instance of homophony between distinct forms (as in "pair," "pear") and perhaps open up consideration of contextual differentiation, differences between written and spoken forms of the language, and the like. None of this would broach the possibility that utterances of the same forms, in the same order, might be, not repetition, but contrast. Yet there are two standpoints from which utterances may be the same or different in form and meaning.

The second kind of repetition and contrast in language has been demonstrated especially well in the work of Labov in New York City (1966). One line of evidence for his study consisted precisely of the respect in which successive utterances of the same forms, in the same order (from the one point of view) were not repetitions, but in contrast. The presence or absence of *r*-constriction after a vowel in a word, indeed, the degree of *r*-constriction, is variable in New York City speech. The variation is associated with social status, on the one hand, and with context, on the other. In situations of the same degree of self-consciousness persons of different social status will differ in the proportion of *r*-constriction in their speech. Persons of the same social status, indeed, the same person, will differ as between situations of less self-consciousness and more (as between situations of lesser and greater formality in a sense). Labov went to the third floors of department stores, chosen for differences in the social status of their customers and employees, and asked the location of something that he knew was located on the floor above. The clerk would respond with an utterance including "on the fourth floor." Labov would say, "Huh?" or the equivalent, and the clerk would repeat. The proportions of *r*-constriction differed among stores, as anticipated, and also as between first utterance and repetition. There was more *r*-constriction in the second, presumably somewhat more self-conscious, utterance.

There is an import, a meaningfulness, to the differences in *r*-constriction. Persons are judged, and judge themselves, in terms of this among other features of speech. It is not, of course, that such a feature is simply an automatic manifestation of identity. As indicated above, one and the same person will vary. The feature does have a social meaning, such that presence of *r*-constriction is positively valued, and its absence disvalued, in assigning social standing. But the "creative" aspect of language use enters here as well. The *r*-ness of an utterance may spontaneously express the identity of the speaker; and it may express the speaker's attitude toward topic, hearer, or situation. The more *r*-less style may be consciously adopted by a politician to convey solidarity with voters as a "regular" guy.

This is a general fact about such features. Not all babytalk is used by, or to, babies. We have to do with features in terms of which utterances may contrast, features subject to meaningful choice as much as the kinds of features usually described in grammars.

In short, the speech styles of communities are not composed only of the features and elements of ordinary grammar, differently related. Speech styles are composed of another kind of feature and element as well. The competence of members of a community has to do with both kinds.

The two kinds of repetition and contrast, the two kinds of features, could be distinguished as "referential" and "stylistic," and I shall frequently make use of these two terms as shorthand labels. We must be careful not to overinterpret these terms, or any other pair of terms. Both kinds of features are to be understood as elementary *diacritic* features, and as based on two complementary elementary diacritic functions, constitutive of linguistic means. The relevant "referential" difference that makes syllabically identical pronunciations of "hungry" and "dung(a)ree" initially different does no more than differentiate; it does not express any part of the meaning of a state of the stomach (or soul), or of the material of a pair of trousers. Just so the relevant "stylistic" difference between "I'm hungry" with light aspiration, and "I'm hungry" with heavy aspiration of the *h*-, does not of itself express the particular meaning of the contrast.

Difference in aspiration is available as a stylistic feature in English, just because it is not employed as a referential feature. (Unlike Hindi, in which /pil/ and /phil/ would be different forms in the lexicon, they are the same form in the English lexicon, differently expressed.) But difference in aspiration, like vowel length, and other elementary English stylistic features, is just that: elementary. It is available for use, just as the differences between /h/ : /d/, /p/ : /b/, etc., are available for use, diacritically. In one instance its use may be metalinguistic, to clarify a meaning: "I said 'phill,' not 'bill.'" In other instance, it may be used to express attitude – emphasis being employed for the sake of insistence, hostility, admiration, etc. In yet another kind of case, it may be used to qualify the attributes of something talked about, as to just how big, or intense, or the like, something was; such uses verge on the referential meanings of utterances ("It was big, I mean, bi:::g").

This last kind of case should be paired with another. The kinds of meaning we often think of as stylistic, expressive, attitudinal, and the like, are of course frequently encoded in languages in lexicon and grammar. There are words for emotions and tones of voice, and 'expressive' elaborations in morphology and morphophonemics proper (cf. Ullman 1953; Stankiewicz 1954, 1964; Van Holk 1962). When one considers linguistic means from the standpoint of the communication of a given kind of meaning, one finds features of both the "referential" and "stylistic" kind involved. To a very great extent, features of the type here called "referential" are involved in what may be said to be *designative* and *predicative* roles: naming things talked about and stating things about them. Yet what is talked about may be conveyed with aid of stylistic features ("No, not that one, the bi:::g one"), and the logical standing and truth value of sentences may depend crucially on stylistic features (e.g., features which define the sentence as mocking rather than sincere). To a very great extent, features of the type here called "stylistic" are involved in what may be said to be *characterizing* and *qualifying* roles: modifying things talked about and saying how what is said about them is to be taken. Yet, as observed just above, lexical and grammatical ways of accomplishing these purposes exist.

The situation is parallel to that of lexicon in relation to grammar. De Saussure observed that a general theory of language could not be confined to either, because what was done in one language by lexical means was done in another grammatically and conversely. It is the same at a deeper level with the "referential" and "stylistic" vectors of language. Within a given system the features and structures of the two are intertwined, *imbricated*, one might say. From the standpoint of a comparison of systems in terms of functions served by them, both must be considered, or part of the verbal means of a community will be missed, and with it, essential aspects of a general theory.

Consider aspiration, for example. On a referential basis alone, it is not a phonological universal: some languages have it, some do not. On a referential and stylistic basis, quite possibly all languages employ it as a conventional means of expression. Indeed, I venture to speculate that a number of features, not now recognized as universal, will prove to be so, when the stylistic vector of language is taken into account. The initial question about features, then, is whether or not they are conventional means in all communities. It is a *second* question to ask if they serve referential function (as distinct from stylistic). Just because the referential and stylistic use of features is interdependent within individual systems, and because stylistic function is itself universal, the number of features that have stylistic use, when they do not have referential, and that hence are truly universal, is likely to be substantial.

Other candidates for status as linguistic universals include vowel length, reduplication, pitch accent, syllabification, word order, and properties such as a minimal vowel system. In Wasco, for example, a purely phonological analysis, seeking to eliminate redundancy, might arrive at a system of three vowels (i, u, a). Yet one can hardly use Wasco appropriately without employing a vowel primarily serving rhetorical emphasis, low front *ae* (as in English "hat"). Generally phonological analysis, seeking to eliminate redundancy, and to find in languages only systems of differences, discard essential features of communication. A phonological feature, redundant from the standpoint of economically distinguishing words, may yet identify normal or native speech, and contrast with its absence. (Try speaking English without the redundant voicing of nasals [m, n, ng]; a telling case is analyzed in Hymes 1970.) The loan-words with phonological particularities set aside in some 'economical' analyses are still in use in the community. The fewer 'phonemic' (referentially based) vowels a language has, the more likely it is to make use of other vowels for stylistic purposes. In sum, the phonological analyses we need, that will be adequate to the actual phonological competence of persons, will include more than the phonology we usually get.

Notice that the more general approach enables us to reach deeper generalizations in particular cases as well as universally. Linguists have debated for some time as to whether the syllable was necessary, or useful, in the analysis of particular languages. I would suggest that syllabification is an ability that is part of the competence of normal members of every speech community, that it is a universal. Communities will be found to differ, not as to the presence or absence of syllabification, but as to the location of its role. In some communities the syllable will appear fundamental to the usual phonemic analysis; in others it will be found essential to the analysis of certain styles (styles of emphasis and metalinguistic clarity, for example, or of speech play, or verbal art). The debates as to the status of the syllable have been possible only because conceptions of structure, and competence, have been too narrow.

Again, once it is accepted that "headline style" is part of English competence (e.g., "Man bites dog"), it will be found artificial to postulate the presence of articles in underlying English syntax (e.g., "A man bites a dog") as in current approaches derived from Chomsky. The elementary relations will be seen to be between "man", "bite," and "dog," and the presence or absence of article to be a second matter, a matter of the style of the discourse in question. A good deal of trouble has been needlessly wasted, trying to account for the article in English on too narrow a basis.

It is thus in the interest of ordinary linguistics, as well as of sociolinguistics, to recognize the dual nature of the elementary diacritic functions in language.

Structures and Uses

Speech styles, we have said, comprise features and constructions of both kinds (referential and stylistic). Let us now say more about the place of speech styles in the ethnography of speaking. Let us first make a further distinction among kinds of functions in speech. The two elementary diacritic functions are part of what may be generally called *structural functions*, as distinct from *use functions* (following here for convenience the common distinction between language structure and language use). 'Structural' functions have to do with the bases of verbal features and their organization, the relations among them, in short, with the verbal means of speech, and their conventional meanings, insofar as those are given by such relationships. "Use" functions have to do with the organization and meaning of verbal features in terms of nonlinguistic contexts. The two are interdependent, but it is useful to discriminate them. It seems likely that rules of co-occurrence can be considered to have to do with structural functions, and rules of alternation with use functions. The analysis of rules of alternation, in other words, entails the analysis of components of use in context, such as the relevant features of the participants in a speech event, of the setting, the channel, and so forth. (See Hymes 1972 for a heuristic analysis of components of speech events.) The principle of contrast for identification of relevant features, as opposed to repetitions, applies here as well, but the features of the situation are not verbal.

Relations among Structures

Notice that rules of co-occurrence define speech styles in an entirely general, open fashion. The relevant speech styles of a community cannot be arrived at mechanically, for one could note an infinite number of differences and putative co-occurrences. One must discover relevant differences in relation to analysis of context. Doubtless communities differ in the relative importance, or "functional load," of particular contexts, and components of contexts, in the determination of styles. Persons, or personal roles, may be a predominant basis for such determination in one community, not so much in another. So also for contexts of activity, group membership, and institutional settings. There is a parallel here, of course, with the differences among languages in the relative significance of semantic categories as bases for grammatical organization (tense, aspect, mode, person, shape, etc. – cf. Hymes 1961b for a tentative scheme for comparison). Just as with referential, so with social meanings: one must start with a general framework, and expect that certain kinds of meaning will be expressed in every community, even if in different ways or to different degrees of elaboration. Men's and women's roles may be intrusive in ordinary grammar in one case, a dimension of consistently organized styles encompassing a variety of features in another, and but marginally visible in verbal means in yet another. Likewise, the functions of deixis, and of textual cohesion, may differentially involve referential and stylistic features in different communities, and even become the chief principle or dimension of one or another style.

In sum, communities differ in the number and variety of significant speech styles, and in the principal bases of their delimitation. This is one of the important and interesting things about communities, needing to be described and to be connected with its causes in their other characteristics and their histories.

Major speech styles associated with social groups can be termed *varieties*, and major speech styles associated with recurrent types of situations can be termed *registers*. Speech styles associated with persons, particular situations, and genres could be termed simply *personal*, *situational*, and *genre* styles. An adequate set of terms cannot be imposed in advance of case studies, however, but will grow interdependently with them. We can, however, and need to, say something more about the relations among kinds of style and stylistic features.

Let me reiterate that speech styles are not mechanical correlations of features of speech with each other and with contexts. The criterion of a *significant speech style* is that it can be recognized, and used, outside its defining context, that is, by persons or in places other than those with which its typical meaning is associated, or contrasted with relation to the persons and places with one or more other styles. Thus one may determine styles associated with castes, classes, ethnic groups, regions, formality, oratory, sermons, and the like, but one must also notice the use of these styles, or of quotations or selections, or stereotypes of them, to convey meanings by, to, and about other persons and situations. Likewise, one must not confine one's attention in church, say, to the style of the sermon, but also notice the style of the speech before, after, and perhaps during it. There probably are customary linkages in these respects, and they need to be determined. A style defined first of all in terms of a group may be also the style for certain situations, or the style, in fact or aspiration, of certain other persons, certain genres or parts of genres, and so on. Within its defining setting a style may be prominent or obscured in relation to what else goes on. There may be clashes within communities as to the admissibility of certain linkages, or as to prominence or lack of it. (The histories of religion, literature, and the stage have many examples.)

Let me say a little about the scale along which stylistic features must be considered, especially with regard to genres, since the disciplines that study verbal genres – folklore, literature, rhetoric, and stylistics – are major sources of insight for the general linguistics that will incorporate stylistic function. First, stylistic features may simply be present in discourse without defining a significant style. Their presence may simply convey a certain tinge or character, perhaps quite locally. We are likely to consider speech with a great many such effects "colorful" (perhaps too colorful, distractingly or seemingly aimlessly so); relative richness of harmony, as it were, can distinguish verbal as well as musical styles, but it may be an incidental flavoring rather than an organizing principle.

Beyond the fact of the presence of stylistic features are kinds of groupings of such features that do constitute organized use, or define a conventional use of verbal means. Two principal kinds of grouping come to mind. There are the kinds which can be said to color or accompany the rest of what is done, and the kinds which can be said to define recurrent forms. For the first, one can speak of *stylistic modes*, and for the second, of *stylistic structures*.

A principal aspect of *stylistic modes* is a set of modifications entailed in consistent use of the voice in a certain way, as in singing, intoning, chanting, declaiming, etc. Modifications of the visual form of speech, in writing and printing, go here as well. Note well that what count as instances of these things are culturally defined. The modifications that are the basis for considering speech to be in a certain mode are on a continuum with the incidental use of features that has been called coloring just above. A basic problem is to discover the relation of such continua, or variables, to qualitative judgments, such that members of a community categorize speech as the presence of a mode or structure. A lilt in the voice may or may not count as singing; a pleonasm, pronunciation, or technical term may or may not count as formal or learned discourse. Sometimes a single instance is enough to define or frame the rest of what is said. Sometimes the definition is negotiated, and shifting frequencies of features manifest the negotiation, as in a proffered move from formal to informal relationship; sometimes the ranging of features between stylistic poles manifests temporary appeals to the presuppositions of one or another of them.

The importance of these kinds of features, not usually included in grammars or well studied by most linguists, is patent when one confronts masterful oral narrative style, so rich in its use of such features. Until now the printed pages from which most of us know such styles have left such mastery in oblivion, but the experiments of Tedlock in the presentation of Zuni narrative (1972) open a new era. Such features may be essential ingredients of the 'levels' of speech central to the structure of a society. Among the Wolof of Senegal, there is a fundamental, pervasive contrast between "restrained" and "unrestrained" speech. It saliently distinguishes the caste of professional speakers, *griots* and nobles, as two poles, but applies as well to other contrasts of status, as between men and women, adults and children, and even applies to contrast in the conduct of the same person, as between a low and high, petitioner and patron, role. All aspects of verbal means enter into the contrast of modes, but the most striking involve use of the voice. Irvine (MS.) summarizes these dimensions in the accompanying table.

	High	Low
Pitch	Low	High
Quality	Breathy	Clear
Volume	Soft	Loud
Contour	Pitch nucleus last	Nucleus first
Tempo	Slow	Fast

Any aspect of verbal means may be the ingredient of a mode including aspects which a conception of competence as perfection would not lead one to notice at all. In the Senegal community of Kayor the pinnacle of the nobility, the Damel, must make mistakes in minor points of grammar. Correctness would be considered an emphasis on fluency of performance, or on performance for its own sake, that is not appropriate to the highest of nobles (Irvine MS.).

Stylistic structures comprise verbal forms organized in terms of one or more defining principles of recurrence and/or development. They have, so to speak, a beginning and an end, and a pattern to what comes between. What are often called 'minor genres' belong here: riddles, proverbs, prayers, but also minimal verse forms, such as the couplet, and such things as greetings and farewells, where those have conventional organization. It seems best to designate such things as *elementary, or minimal, genres*. (They need not be minor in their importance.)

We must bear in mind that one may sing something that is not a song, and present a song without singing it; that is, *modes* and *structures* are indeed distinct, and their connections problematic, to be discovered in the given case. Moreover, it would be a mistake to assume that the essential principle of a form of speech is always structure, never mode. Most often it is structure, but to generalize would be equivalent to recognizing form in music only insofar as one can identify sonata pattern, rondo, twelve-tone scale, or the like. Delius is a case in point. He did turn to sonata-form works in consequences of the First World War (unfortunately, we never hear recitals or recordings to judge them ourselves), but the works of his in the standard performance repertoire are those in which the secret of organization is his own, and the development inextricable from the handling of harmony and orchestration, i.e., of 'color.' (Musical terminology will prove a great resource for exploration of speech styles, as a matter of fact.)

Both kinds of groupings of features, modes and structures, enter into more complex groupings, which may be designated *complex genres*. Thus Zuni *telapnanne* "tale" can comprise formal speaking delivery, a mode of delivery called "raised up speech," a monotone chant with one auxiliary tone, and passages of conversational looseness (Tedlock, personal communication).

Genres, whether minimal or complex, are not in themselves the 'doing' of a genre, that is, are not in themselves acts, events, performances. They can occur as whole events, or in various relationships to whole events. The structure of an event may encompass preliminaries and aftermaths, may allow only for partial use of a genre, or even just allusion to it, and so forth. And I want to consider performances as relationships to genres, such that one can say of a performance that its materials (genres) were reported, described, run through, illustrated, quoted, enacted. Full performance I want to consider as involving the acceptance of responsibility to perform, to do the thing with acceptance of being evaluated.

Obviously genres may vary, from simple to complex, and from looseness to tightness in what they accommodate, incorporate, permit, as to modes and other genres. The "novel" is an easy example; it may take the form of letters (Richardson's *Pamela*), verse (Pushkin's *Eugen Onegin*), and simulated journalism, among others.

It is tempting to generalize the categories of genre and performance, so that all verbal material is assignable to some genre, and all verbal conduct to some kind of performance. My own hunch is that communities differ in the extent to which this is true, at least in the sense of the prevalence of tightly organized genres, and of evaluated performance (of "being on stage" in speech). If the categories are needed as general descriptive concepts, then the differences can be registered by an additional distinction within each, perhaps *fixed genres*, and *full performance*.

Relations among Uses

The connection between genres and performances is one aspect of the general connection between styles defined in terms of rules of co-occurrence and their uses in contexts in a community. First, recall the proposal that significant speech styles be considered those that can be contrasted in or beyond their initial defining context. The proposal has two complications. The degree to which this is possible may itself be a dimension on which communities differ. Just as speech communities, historical periods, and persons differ in the degree to which they consider appropriate use of words and phrases to be context-specific, so also with stylistic features and structures. A tightly context-bound style may be highly valued. On the other hand, unique structures, stylistic relationships, may emerge in a single event, and be remembered and valued for their qualities. Nevertheless, it would seem that evaluation of the emergent qualities of a single event, and recognition of the appropriateness of a context-specific style, would both presuppose comparison. The comparison may be implicit, rather than observable in the immediate situation, but it would be discoverable by inquiry outside the situation. (From such considerations we see the failure inherent in a conception of sociolinguistics as a method of obtaining "real" data. Realistic, observational data are essential, if styles, many of whose features are unconscious or not producible on demand, are to be studied; but styles involve kinds of underlying competence and judgments based on competence as well.) We need to consider both context-bound styles and emergent properties, in order to deal with stylistic change. One aspect of stylistic change is narrowing or expansion of contextual constraints (rather like spread or contraction of the range of distribution of a phonological or grammatical feature), and another is the imitation or emulation, and consequent conventionalization, of emergent properties. But the central considerations here are that speech styles are not merely observed co-occurrences and correlations, but subject to contrast and choice, and that they are not merely appropriate or inappropriate, but meaningful.

The notion of rules of alternation carries us into the analysis of the contexts of speech styles, but, as noted before, such analysis is ethnographic and sociological as well as linguistic. When the meanings of speech styles are analyzed, we realize that they entail dimensions of participant, setting, channel, and the like, which partly govern their meanings. And analysis of the relevant features of these dimensions is found to implicate more than alternation of speech styles. It subtends norms of verbal conduct, or interaction, in general – things such as rights to turns at talking, acceptable ways of getting the floor, whether more than one voice can be speaking at a time, and so on. (Here again musical terminology is a resource: *ripieno, concertante*, and *ritornello* catch features of some speech events.) And both speech styles and norms of verbal conduct have underlying meanings in common, meanings which involve community attitudes and beliefs with regard to language and speech. The Wolof styles cited above, for example, embody a notion and values fundamental to Wolof society, having to do with "honor" (*kerse*), and with 'one of the most fundamental Wolof cultural assumptions [namely] that speech, especially in quantity, is dangerous and demeaning' (Irvine MS.).

I cannot go into the analysis of norms of verbal conduct, attitudes, and beliefs here, but have sketched some of their dimensions, and some of the evidence of types of speech community in this regard elsewhere (Hymes 1972). Here I can only sketch the place of this part of the ethnography of speaking in relation to the whole, with reference to terminology for the parts.

If one accepts 'ethnography of speaking' as name for the enterprise, still the name refers to the approach, or the field, not to the subject matter itself. One can engage in an ethnography of speaking among the Zuni, but what one studies is not in any usual sense "Zuni ethnography of speaking." (What the Zuni consciously make of speaking is important, but part of the whole.) An ethnography of law among the Zuni studies Zuni law, and an ethnography of speaking studies Zuni speaking. I myself would say: Zuni *ways of speaking*. There are two reasons for this. First, terms derived from "speak" and "speech" in English suffer from a history of association with something marginal or redundant. While linguists have commonly distinguished "speech" from "language" in a way that might seem to serve our purpose, they have commonly taken back with the hand of usage what the hand of definition has offered. In practice, "speech" has been treated as either elegant variation for "language" (thus, Sapir's book *Language* was subtitled "An introduction to the study of speech" and "interaction by means of speech" has been equated with knowledge of a single language by Bloomfield, Bloch, Chomsky, and others), or as a second-class citizen, external to language, mere behavior. (Thus for many writers "act of speech" does not mean a complex social act based on underlying competence extending beyond grammar, but mere physical manifestation.) Indeed, "speech" has been used so much as interchangeable with "language" that Sherzer and Darnell (1972) felt constrained to add "use," and to talk of the analysis of "speech use." I do not myself like "speech use," because I am disturbed by what should be a redundancy, that is, "speech" should indicate use in a positive sense. Nevertheless, it does not, and adequate terms seem to require some joining of the key term that English provides with complements that make it free of the redundant or reductive connotations.

My second reason for favoring *ways of speaking* is that it has analogy with "ways of life," on the one hand, and Whorf's term "fashions of speaking," on the other. The first analogy helps remind anthropologists that the ways of mankind do include ways of speaking, and helps remind linguists that speaking does come in ways, that is, shows cultural patterning. And since Whorf was the first in the American linguistic and anthropological tradition, so far as I know, to name a mode of organization of linguistic means cutting across the compartments of grammar, it is good to honor his precedence, while letting the difference in terms reflect the difference in scope of reference. (Whorf had in mind the usual features of grammars, considered from the standpoint of active life as cognitive styles.)

Our analysis so far would point to ways of speaking as comprising two parts, speech styles and their contexts, or means of speech and their meanings. The limitation of these terms is that they do not readily suggest part of what enters into ways of speaking, namely, the norms of interaction that go beyond choice of style, and the attitudes and beliefs that underlie both. "Contexts" and "meanings" also both leave the focus on "styles" and "means," and seem to deprive the second part of the equality, and relative autonomy, that must be recognized in it. The Ngoni of southern Africa, for example, have maintained their distinctive norms of verbal conduct, while losing their original, Ngoni language; they still consider maintenance of the norms of verbal conduct definitive of being a proper Ngoni. (I owe this example to Sheila Seitel.) It does not seem happy to talk of the maintenance of Ngoni "contexts" or "meanings of means of speech" in this connection. A positive term is wanted. Of the possibilities that have occurred to me, all but one have the defect that they might be taken to imply more than is intended. "Ways of speaking" would serve on this level as well; but contexts are not always sure to differentiate the two senses, especially in the case of a novel terminology, and we need to be clear if we can be. "Patterns of speech/speaking," "forms," "modes" seem to say too much or too little, or to conflict with other uses of the differentiating word. The expression that does not is: *speech economy* (cf. Hymes 1961a). We can then readily distinguish *means of speech* (comprising the features that enter into styles, as well as the styles themselves), and *speech economy.* The pair are parallel in utilizing 'speech,' which may be a mnemonic advantage. The two concepts are of course interrelated, even interdependent (as said, meanings lie in the relationships), and from a thoroughgoing standpoint, the speech economy of a community includes its means of speech as one of the components that enter into its pattern of relationships. The historical autonomy of the two, and the major division of labor in our society between those who study verbal means and those who study conduct, makes the division appropriate.

Consideration of the stylistic component of language, then, has led us to a conception of the ethnography of speaking that can be expressed in the following form:

WAYS OF SPEAKING

Means of speech *Speech economy*

The direction of our discussion so far has been consistently away from grammar toward other things, but grammar itself is not exempt from becoming what those who use it make of it, and hence in some respects a style.

Languages as styles

It is not only in situations of heterogeneity that a constitutive role of social factors can be glimpsed. If we abstract from heterogeneity, and consider only a single language, indeed, only a single grammar, a radically social component still appears. Consider the California Indian language Yokuts, as described by Stanley Newman.[1]

Newman reports that the words he recorded were short, composed of a stem and mostly but one or two suffixes, almost never more than that. Newman noticed, however, that the underlying patterning of the suffixes implied the formal possibility of longer sequences. He reports (1964 (1940): 374):

> An instructive exercise ... was to construct words having four or five suffixes and ask the informant for a translation. Although such words complied with the grammatical rules and could be translated by my informant without any difficulty, they seldom failed to provoke his amusement.

> It was obvious that these words were impossibly heavy and elaborate. To the Yokuts feeling for simplicity they were grammatical monstrosities.

From Newman's account it appears that the longer words were not deviant (not derivatively generated in the sense of Chomsky (1965: 227 note 2). Their interpretation posed no problem at all. They were of the same degree of grammaticalness in a formal sense as shorter sequences, but they were not acceptable. At best they were marginally marked for humor or pomposity, but Newman notes no examples of such use, besides, inadvertently, his own. He goes on to report:

> Although Yokuts words, with the notable exception of the "do" verbs (regarded as the linguistic property of children), tend to sketch only the bare and generalized outlines of a reference, the language possesses syntactic resources for combining words in such a way that its sentences could attain any degree of notional intricacy and richness. A passage of Macaulay's prose, with its long and involved periods, could be translated into grammatically correct Yokuts. But the result would be a grammarian's idle fancy, a distortion of the syntactic idiom of Yokuts. The language is as diffident in applying its means of elaboration in syntax as in suffixation. (p. 376)

The basis of the restraint is a general Yokuts demand for severe simplicity, a value that a colleague finds to underlie Yokuts narrative style as well. Newman contrasts the Yokuts value with an expressive value he finds implicit in English, arguing for the equal validity of each. To the English imagination the Yokuts style appears drab, "but, by the same token, the stylistic features of English cannot appeal to the intuitions of a Yokuts native" (p. 377). He follows Sapir in regarding each language as "like a particular art form in that it works with a limited range of materials and pursues the stylistic goals that have been and are constantly being discovered in a collective quest" (p. 377).

One can object to wording that personifies a language; it is the Yokuts-speaking community that works with a range of materials and pursues stylistic goals. Nevertheless, an important point is clear. If grammar is identified with what is structurally possible (as Newman identifies it in a paragraph summed up by the remark that "It [grammar] tells what a language can do but not what it considers worthwhile doing" [p. 372]), or even with what is possible and transparent (as were Newman's four- and five-suffix words), then the community has drawn a line within the grammatical. On the basis of shared values, common to language and its uses in narrative, the community judges utterances that are formally possible as impossible in speech. This is a creative aspect of language use not taken into account in linguistic discussion, or overridden, the judgments of speakers being sacrificed to the requirements of formal statement. But notice that to get a native speaker to agree to the naturalness of one of Newman's monstrous words would not be to get him to see something he had not previously realized. He realized the grammatical possibility when Newman presented the forms to him. It would be to get him to change his native intuition. In a crucial sense, grammatical Yokuts is not what is possible to the grammar, as a device, but what is possible according to Yokuts norms. Here without intrusion of schools or pedants, we have a normative definition of possible Yokuts that is best described as aesthetic or stylistic in nature. For the Yokuts community, Yokuts is after all in that sense what they make of it.

Notice that the same grammar, as a formal device, is consistent with a drawing of the stylistic line in different places. The place might change over time within the same community. Yokuts judgments of Yokuts utterances would change, but formal grammar would not record it. By the same token, different communities of Yokuts speakers might draw the line in different places. Judgments of utterances would contrast, and again formal grammar not register the difference.

It would seem then that what Yokuts speakers know, their underlying competence, includes a dimension of style in the most essential way. Nothing about special speech styles and specific components of situations is involved; just plain Yokuts, showing that grammar is a matter of community 'should' as well as "could," is inherently normative.

The Yokuts case involves relations among given elements (although one can imagine that such restraint inhibits elaboration of affixes and other machinery, and favors its opposite, as Newman at one point suggests). The content of languages can itself be regarded from the standpoint of style, and again in terms of the exercise of an ability, a creative aspect of language use. Style is not only a matter of features other than referential, or of the selective use of features of both kinds; it also has to do with the selective creation of new materials and letting go of old. As languages change, they do not change wholly randomly, or lose structure in accordance with the second law of thermodynamics. They remain one relatively consistent set of realizations of the possibilities of language, rather than another. And they have the character they do in this regard partly because of choices by their users. It is possible to consider some kinds of change, including sound change, coming about in part because of social meaning associated with features, more prestigeful variants replacing less prestigeful ones. It is possible to consider some changes as coming about in response to internal imbalances and pressures, and to cumulative drifts which make some avenues of change far more tractable than others. But some changes cannot be understood except as changes over time in what users of the language find it most desirable or essential to say. Changes in the obligatory grammatical categories of a language, or in the relative elaboration of these, are such. Sometimes one can find a consistency (a 'conspiracy') in the semantic character of a variety of seemingly unrelated changes and trends. I have tried to show this to be the case for Wasco (Hymes 1961b, section 5), presenting evidence that in recently coined words, in recent changes in affixes marking tense-aspect and post-positions marking case relations, and in trends in the derivation of verb themes, there is common a certain cognitive orientation.

It is important to avoid two misunderstandings. First, to recognize the orientation, or style, is not to project an interpretation upon defenseless material. Not just any trait of the language is entered in evidence, but traits that have recently been brought into being, that represent choices, creative activity, on the part of the community. Second, no inference can be directly made to the minds of speakers. One's evidence is of the result of changes that must have had some psychological reality for those that introduced and accepted them; but evidence independent of the language is needed to demonstrate their psychological reality for a later speaker. In point of fact, it is unlikely that surviving Wasco speakers, all multilingual, and using the language only rarely, would show much evidence. Linguistic relativity in Whorf's sense is dependent on a more fundamental type of relativity, that of the function of linguistic means. Speakers of different generations may provide evidence of a common grammar, but for one the grammar may be only something remembered, for the other the central verbal instrument for handling experience.

It is worth noting that linguistic inference of underlying grammatical knowledge is in the same boat as Whorf's inference of underlying cognitive outlook. Both argue to a capacity or characteristic of users of language from linguistic data alone. The linguistic data are both source and evidence for the claimed characteristics. The criticism of circularity lodged against Whorf attaches to work in grammar which identifies a formal analysis with psychological reality without independent test. (Newman's presentation of constructed words to speakers was informally such a test.)

I am saying that the import of cognitive styles in languages is problematic, needing to be established, not that there is no import (cf. Hymes 1966). The same holds for all speech styles, and means of speech in general. In other aspects of life we recognize that the means available condition what can be done with them. We recognize that the tools available affect what is made without reducing outcomes to tools alone. Somehow there has been a schizophrenic consciousness in our civilization with regard to verbal tools. Some have taken them as determinants of almost everything, others have denied that they determine anything. One suspects a reflection of a long-standing conflict between "idealist" and "materialist" assumptions, language being identified with the "idealist" side, so that to argue for its determinative role was to seem to argue for one philosophical outlook and against another. (Something of this interpretation of matters seems current in the Soviet Union.) For others, it is all right to speak of the great role of language in general, but never of languages in particular. One suspects a resistance to a long-standing tendency to treat some linguistic particularities as inferior, or a reflection of a climate of opinion in which any explicit limitation on mental freedom is resented. Here a statement of position must suffice.

First, it seems inescapably true to me that the means available to persons do condition what they can verbally do, and that these means are in important part historically shaped. Second, such a view is not derogation of differences; what can be done may be admirable.

In this connection, it should be noted that fluent members of communities often enough themselves evaluate their languages as not equivalent. It is not only that one language, or variety, often is preferred for some uses, another for others, but also that there is experience with what can in fact be best done with one or the other. This sort of differential ability has nothing to do with disadvantage or deficiency of some members of a community relative to others. All of them may find, say, Kurdish the medium in which most things can best be expressed, but Arabic the better medium for religious truth. Users of Berber may find Arabic superior to Berber for all purposes except intimate domestic conversation (Ferguson 1966).[2]

But, third, differences in available means and related abilities do exist in ways that pose problems. In some respects the problems are inherent in the human condition, insofar as each of us must be a definite person in a world changing unpredictably and without our consent or control. In other respects problems are inherent only in certain social orders and circumstances, and could in principle be solved. It is my conviction that the requisite social change requires knowledge of actual abilities and activities, and that a linguistics of the sort sketched above can contribute to such knowledge.[3]

NOTES

1 Newman's fine grammar, which exemplifies the mature methods of Sapir, has become the material of a virtual industry since the Second World War, having been restated and restructured in a number of papers and at least one book. The information considered here, however, has not been treated as relevant to linguistic theory, so far as I know – commentary enough on the loss of richness to linguistics with the eclipse of the Sapir tradition, which we must seek to restore.

2 Cf. a European case representative of many: "L'accession rapide de l'élite de la société polonaise à l'humanisme, dans la seconde moitié du 16e siècle, posa de façon aiguë le problème des moyens d'expression. Pour les nouvelles aspirations artisitiques, seul le latin convenait avec ses ressources de vocabulaire, de syntaxe, de métrique et ses qualités d'abondance et de précision, tandis que le polonais demeurait l'apanage d'un univers spirituel médiéval qui n'avait trouvé jusqu'alors qu'une expression fragmentaire et qui commençait tardivement a prendre un essor encore timide. L'auteur analyse les aspects de ce bilinguisme et son évolution jusqu'à la fin du 16e siècle, évolution au cours de laquelle un humanisme créateur a présidé à l'élaboration de la langue littéraire en Pologne" (Backvis 1958). Cf. Jones 1953 on English in the same period.

3 This paper formed the basis of a section in a book on the concept of language which I prepared for the "Key concepts in the social sciences" series published by Harper & Row.

REFERENCES

Backvis, C. (1958). *Quelques rémarques sur le bilinguisme latino–polonais dans la Pologne du XVIe siècle*. Brussels.

Bloomfield, L. (1933). *Language*. New York.

Chomsky, N. (1965). *Aspects of the Theory of Syntax*. Cambridge, Mass.

Ervin-Tripp, S. (1972). On Sociolinguistic Rules: Alternation and Co-occurrence. In Gumperz and Hymes 1972: 213–50.

Ferguson, C. A. (1966). On Sociolinguistically Oriented Surveys. *The Linguistic Reporter* 8 (4): 1–3.

Gumperz, J. J. (1972). Introduction. In Gumperz and Hymes 1972: 1–25.

Gumperz, J. J. and Hymes, D. (eds.) (1972). *Directions in Sociolinguistics: The Ethnography of Communication*. New York.

Hymes, D. (1961a). Functions of Speech: An Evolutionary Approach. In F. Gruber (ed.), *Anthropology and Education*. Philadelphia, pp. 55–83.

Hymes, D. (1961b). On Typology of Cognitive Style in Languages (with examples from Chinookan). *Anthropological Linguistics* 3(1): 22–54.

Hymes, D. (1966). Two Types of Linguistic Relativity. In W. Bright (ed.), *Sociolinguistics*. The Hague, pp. 114–65.

Hymes, D. (1970). Linguistic Theory and the Functions of Speech. *International Days of Sociolinguistics*. Rome, pp. 111–44.

Hymes, D. (1972). Models of the Interaction of Language and Social Life. In Gumperz and Hymes 1972: 35–71.

Irvine, J. T. (MS.). Caste Stereotypes: The Basis for Interaction. For a University of Pennsylvania dissertation in anthropology.

Jones, R. F. (1953). *The Triumph of the English Language*. Stanford, Calif.

Labov, W. (1966). *The Social Stratification of English in New York City*. Washington, DC.

Newman, S. S. (1964) (1940). Linguistic Aspects of Yokuts Style. In D. Hymes (ed.), *Language in Culture and Society*. New York, pp. 372–7.

Postal, P. (1968). *Aspects of Phonological Theory*. New York.

Sapir, E. (1921). *Language*. New York.

Sherzer, J. and Darnell, R. (1972). Outline Guide for the Ethnographic Study of Speech Use. In Gumperz and Hymes 1972: 548–54.

Stankiewicz, E. (1954). Expressive Derivation of Substantives in Contemporary Russian and Polish. *Word* 10: 457–68.

Stankiewicz, E. (1964). Problems of Emotive Language. In T. A. Sebeok, A. S. Hayes and M. C. Bateson (eds.), *Aspects of Semiotics*. The Hague, pp. 239–64.

Swadesh, M. (1948). On Linguistic Mechanism. *Science and Society* 12: 254–9.

Tedlock, D. (trans.) (1972). *Finding the Center: Narrative Poetry of the Zuni Indians*. From performances by Andrew Peynetsa and Walter Sanchez. New York.

Ullman, S. (1953). Descriptive Semantics and Linguistic Typology. *Word* 9: 225–40.

Van Holk, A. (1962). Referential and Attitudinal Constructions. *Lingua* 11: 165–81.

STUDY QUESTIONS

1 How does Hymes's definition of speech community as an "organization of diversity" relate to the themes of the articles in Part I? Why is the notion of "style" used to describe such diversity?

2 What does Hymes mean by his use of the terms "referential" and "stylistic"? Can you give some examples?

3 What is the difference between "structural functions" and "use functions"? How do they relate to one another and to speech styles more generally?

4 Hymes writes that "communities differ in the number and variety of significant speech styles, and in the principal bases of their delimitation." Can you support this generalization by providing examples of styles, stylistic structures, and speech genres from the speech community (or communities) you are familiar with?

5 What are the reasons Hymes provides for his preference of the term "ways of speaking" over other terms? How are "means of speech" and "speech economy" related to "ways of speaking"?

6 Why do you think Stanley Newman's account of his study of the language of the California Indian Yokuts was included? What does it contribute to Hymes's argument?

7

Formality and Informality in Communicative Events

Judith T. Irvine

Formality and its opposite, informality, are concepts frequently used in the ethnography of communication, in sociolinguistics, and in social anthropology to describe social occasions and the behavior associated with them. This paper examines the usefulness of those concepts in description and comparison. What might one mean by *formality*, in terms of observable characteristics of human social interaction? How might formality correspond to the cultural categories with which other peoples describe their own social occasions? Are the relevant distinctions best formulated as dichotomy (as the contrast formality/informality might suggest), or as a continuum ranging between two poles, or as something more complex? Do whatever distinctions we decide are involved in formality/informality apply to every society? Will the same kinds of behavioral differences, or the same kinds of cultural categories, emerge everywhere?

I pose these questions in an attempt to further the development of a more precise analytical vocabulary, particularly for the ethnography of communication, which has perhaps invoked those concepts most often (although their relevance is not limited to that field). We now have a small number of case-history descriptions of ways of speaking in particular speech communities. But the terms in which those descriptions are made are often vague, lacking in explicit analytical content, too close to our own folk categories – inadequate or cross-cultural comparison, or even for description itself. Many anthropologists (and I include myself) have used terms such as formality without defining them or thinking about their definitions, simply assuming that the meanings are clear, when in fact the usages are vague and quite variable.

My object, then, is to give our usages more substance and to explore how they might then better serve cross-cultural comparison. I shall first consider what has been meant by formality and informality in the recent literature – that is, what various authors seem to have intended those terms to describe. The literature I draw upon comes mainly from sociolinguistics and the ethnography of speaking although some works in other fields will be cited as well. I shall then restate these various senses of formality in what I hope is a more explicit fashion and argue for the usefulness of the more detailed formulation for comparison, both within and between speech communities. A third section of the paper attempts a more

For permission to publish copyright material in this book, grateful acknowledgment is made to: J. T. Irvine (1979), "Formality and Informality in Communicative Events," *American Anthropologist* 81(4): 773–90.

extended comparison; it examines the formality of certain social occasions in two African societies, the Wolof and the Mursi, and compares them with a third society, the Ilongots of the northern Philippines. The fourth, and final, section, asks whether the cover term formality remains useful at all.

The last section also considers some broader issues in social theory to which these terms and concepts relate. Actually, this is the larger object of the essay. Refining an analytical vocabulary is not simply a matter of improving the quality of empirical data; the terminology also reflects and incorporates more general assumptions about the nature of the social order. To discuss the descriptive and analytical vocabulary, therefore, is also to address those assumptions.

What Has Been Meant by Formality in the Literature

A look at some recent literature in sociolinguistics, the ethnography of speaking, and related fields (e.g., Gumperz and Hymes 1972; Bauman and Sherzer 1974; Sanches and Blount 1975; Fishman 1968; Bloch 1975; Kirshenblatt-Gimblett 1976; papers in *Language in Society; Working Papers in Sociolinguistics*) suggests three principal senses of formality, which are potentially confused with each other. These different senses have to do with whether the formality concerns properties of a communicative code, properties of the social setting in which a code is used, or properties of the analyst's description.

For instance, many authors use formality in the sense of an increased structuring and predictability of discourse. Here, formality is an aspect of code, such that the discourse is subject to extra rules or some greater elaboration of rules. In this vein, for example, Bricker (1974: 388) and Gossen (1974: 412), both writing on the Maya, and Fox (1974: 73) who writes on the Rotinese, all describe "formal speech" as marked by special structuring – notably redundancy, and syntactic or semantic parallelism. Others have emphasized the predictability of structured discourse; they have argued that a "formal style" reduces the variability and spontaneity of speech (see Joos 1959 and Wolfson 1976). For example, Rubin's (1968) paper on bilingualism in Paraguay discusses formality in terms of limitations on the kinds of behaviors that are acceptable and on the amount of allowable variation (conceived as deviation from a norm).

Other authors use formality/informality as a way of describing the characteristics of a social situation, not necessarily the kind of code used in that situation. The relevant characteristics of the situation may have something to do with a prevailing affective tone, so that a formal situation requires a display of seriousness, politeness, and respect. For instance, Fischer (1972), describing ways of speaking among Trukese and Ponapeans, discusses the use of "respect vocabulary" and "formal etiquette" as displays of politeness marking a formal situation. In Fishman's (1972: 51) discussion of "lecturelike or formal situations," formality seems to be understood as the opposite of levity and intimacy. Ervin-Tripp (1972: 235), too, relates formality to politeness and "the seriousness of such situations." Not all authors agree on just what formality means about a situation, however. Rubin (1968) lists formality as a situational variable separate from "degree of intimacy" and "degree of seriousness." For Labov (1972: 113), formality of situational context is what makes a speaker pay increased attention to his or her speech.

Finally, many authors use formal to refer to a technical mode of description, in which the analyst's statement of the rules governing discourse is maximally explicit. Although most linguists apply this sense of formality (as "explicitness") only to the statements made by an outside observer,[1] some anthropologists also apply it to a people's own analysis of their social order. When Murphy (1971: 159), for instance, speaks of "the formal, conscious models of society held by its members," he refers to those conceptions of society and behavior that informants can present in explicit verbal statements. For other anthropologists the explicit statements need not be verbal; see Leach's (1965: 15–16) discussion of nonverbal ritual as a way in which social structure, or a people's ideas about social structure, are made explicit and "formally recognized."

These three senses of formality have often been merged or interrelated. For example, when formality is conceived as an aspect of social situations, it is common to extend the term to the linguistic varieties used in such situations, regardless of what those varieties happen to be like otherwise. Formal and informal pronouns are a case in point. Their formality lies in what they connote about a social setting in which they are appropriately used; they do not necessarily differ in the number or elaboration of syntactic (or other) rules governing their use.

Some authors go further, blending all three senses of formality and arguing that formal descriptions are most suitable (or only suitable) for the more structured discourse that occurs in ceremoniallike formal situations. Here, one wonders whether it is not just the use of the single term formal for a kind of description, a kind of discourse, and a kind of situation that makes the three appear necessarily related. Discourse that is spontaneous is still rule-governed, as linguists working with syntax have been at pains to point out; indeed, a major effort of linguists in the past 20 years has been to show how and why rules of grammar permit the utterance and comprehension of sentences that have never occurred before. Explicit formulation of those rules cannot, therefore, be limited to specially rigidified or redundant discourse. So, with Halliday (1964), I would seek to avoid confusing the technical sense of formality (explicitness of the observer's description) with senses that concern the behavior and conceptual systems of the people described.

Still, some ways of interrelating different senses of formality are potentially fruitful. Maurice Bloch (1975) has recently argued, for instance, that code structuring and situational formality are causally related, so that increased structuring of discourse necessarily brings about increased politeness and a greater display of respect for a traditional, normative social order (and perhaps a coercive political establishment). That argument has various antecedents in social anthropology, although they are less clearly articulated and do not give particular attention to speech. One such forerunner is Durkheim's conception of ritual, as expressing and confirming the solidarity of the group and constraining the individual to conformity. A related matter, too, is the widespread view in structural-functional anthropology that connects structure with norm and tradition, and with order, coherence, and stability – a view of structure as essentially static.

Bloch's argument is an important one and I shall return to it later. Now, however, the point is that these basic questions about structure and action in discourse can be addressed only if the relevant variables are first disentangled. Arguments that do so (such as Bloch's) are much more useful than those that merely slide from one sense of formality to another, leaving implicit the connection between formal situations and frozen, rigidified speech (or other behavior).

Four Aspects of Formality that Apply Cross-Culturally

Leaving aside questions of causal relationships for now, I will restate, in a more detailed way, what considerations one may have in mind when describing social occasions as formal or informal. A search of some available ethnographic evidence, inadequate as it is for the purpose – and filtered as it is through ethnographers' descriptive vocabularies – suggests that the discourse aspect and the situational aspect of formality should be broken down into finer distinctions. Four different aspects of formality emerge that seem to apply to a wide variety of speech communities, perhaps to all. The four kinds of formality often co-occur in the same social occasion though not always (hence their presentation as separate variables).

Increased code structuring

This aspect of formality concerns the addition of extra rules or conventions to the codes that organize behavior in a social setting. Although I focus on the linguistic, any code (such as dress, gesture, or spatial organization) can, of course, be subject to degrees of structuring. It is important to recognize, however, that a social occasion involves many codes that operate at once, and the degrees of structuring that they variously display may differ. Even within the linguistic code one should distinguish among the various levels of linguistic organization that may be subject to the additional or elaborated structuring, such as intonation (including pitch contour, meter, loudness, and speed of talk), phonology, syntax, the use of particular sets of lexical items, fixed-text sequences, and turn taking. Increased structuring need not affect all these aspects of linguistic organization equally or at the same time.[2] Some speech events formalize different parts of the linguistic system and so cannot be lined up on a simple continuum from informality to formality.

For instance, among the Wolof[3] there are two distinct speech events, *woy* ("praise-singing") and *xaxaar* ("insult sessions"), which differ from ordinary conversations in their structuring of intonational patterns (among other things). But different aspects of intonation are affected. In praise-singing, the pitch contour of utterances is more structured than in ordinary talk but meter remains relatively loose; in insult sessions, meter is strictly regulated (with drum accompaniment), while pitch remains loose. It would be impossible to say that one form of discourse is more formalized than the other, although one could say that both are more formalized than ordinary conversation (and less formalized than some types of religious singing, which structure both pitch and rhythm).

Similarly, among the Yoruba, two speech events, both associated with the Iwi Egungun cult celebrations, formalize different aspects of the discourse (Davis 1976). In one event, speakers use highly structured utterances, often fixed texts, on conventional topics, whereas turn taking among speakers is unpredictable, with much of the interest for the audience residing in the speakers' competition for the floor. In the other type of speech event, turn taking is quite strictly regulated (as though in a play), but the topics can be creative and novel. The formalization of discourse here cannot be thought of as just a progressive rigidifying and restriction on creative potential. Instead, what is involved is a focusing of creativity onto a certain aspect of talk, which is highlighted because other aspects are redundant and predictable.

Code consistency

A second kind of formalization involves co-occurrence rules. At many different levels of linguistic organization and in other avenues of communicative expression as well, speakers select from among alternatives that have contrasting social significance. Co-occurrence rules provide for the extent to which these choices must be consistent. In the kinds of discourse that ethnographers have labeled more formal, consistency of choices (in terms of their social significance) seems to be greater than in ordinary conversation, where speakers may be able to recombine variants to achieve special effects.

For example, among the Wolof, differences of pitch, loudness, and speed of talk (as well as other discourse features) may connote something about the speaker's social rank: high pitch, high volume, and high speed all suggest low social rank, while low pitch, low volume, and a laconic slowness suggest high social rank. Sometimes a speaker can mix choices (e.g., high pitch + low volume + low speed seems to indicate baby talk, used by adults to address infants; for some other mixes and their uses, see Irvine 1974); but in some kinds of discourse – which one might call the more formal – choices for each discourse feature are consistent in their social connotations.

Another example comes from Friedrich's (1972) paper on Russian pronouns. Friedrich notes that usage of the second-person pronouns *ty* and *vy* (for singular addressee) can be consistent or inconsistent with facial expressions. More formal situations are characterized by greater consistency – as opposed to "ironic" uses that combine the pronoun *vy* (usually called the formal pronoun) with a contemptuous expression ("paralinguistic *ty*"). Similarly, Jackson (1974: 63) indicates that among the Vaupés Indians, "language-mixing" – for example, the use of Tuyuka words in a conversation that is syntactically Bará (and Bará in the rest of the lexicon) – is likely to occur only in informal discourse. In settings that she calls "more formal," co-occurrence rules are stricter so that the social connotations of lexicon and syntax are consistent (connotations of long-house and descent-unit identity).

Because many authors describe co-occurrence violations with terms such as *irony, levity, humor*, or *local color*, it appears that some of what is meant by the "seriousness" of formal situations is actually a matter of behavioral consistency and adherence to a set of co-occurrence rules that apply to these situations and not to others. As Ervin-Tripp remarks (1972: 235), co-occurrence rules are especially strict in formal styles of discourse "because of the seriousness of such situations."

But why should co-occurrence rules and "seriousness" be linked? Perhaps the clue lies in the fact that code-switching and code inconsistencies are so often used as distancing devices – ways of setting off a quotation, making a parenthetic aside, mimicking someone, or enabling a speaker to comment on his or her own behavior (see Goffman 1961; Irvine 1974; and the code-switching literature summarized in Timm 1975). By code inconsistency the speaker can detach himself from the social persona implied by one type of usage and suggest that that persona is not to be taken quite "for real"; the speaker has another social persona as well. Code inconsistency, then, may be a process of framing or undercutting one message with another that qualifies it and indicates that in some sense, or from some point of view, it doesn't really count (cf. Bateson 1972; Goffman 1961, 1974). In contrast, the code-consistent message has to count; it has to be taken "seriously" because no alternative message or social persona is provided. Each aspect of the speaker's behavior shows the same kind and degree of involvement in the situation.[4]

Invoking positional identities

A third aspect of formality has to do with the social identities of participants in a social gathering. More a property of the situation than of code *per se*, it concerns which social identity (of the many that an individual might have) is invoked on a particular kind of occasion. Formal occasions invoke positional and public, rather than personal, identities (to use a term proposed by Mead [1937] and applied to speech events by Hymes [1972]).[5] Public, positional identities are part of a structured set likely to be labeled and widely recognized in a society (that is, it is widely recognized that the set of identities exists and that persons X, Y, and Z have them). Personal identities, on the other hand, are individualized and depend more on the particular history of an individual's interactions. They are perhaps less likely to be explicitly recognized or labeled and less likely to be common knowledge in the community at large.

This aspect of formality is involved in what many authors have interpreted as the formal event's emphasis on social distance (as opposed to intimacy) and respect (for an established order of social positions and identities). For example, Albert (1972), writing on the Burundi, distinguishes two speech events that she calls formal and informal visiting. Formal visiting requires an open acknowledgment of differences in social rank, and it usually occurs between persons whose positions are clearly ranked in a publicly known, apparently indisputable sense (such as feudal lord and vassal). Formal visiting is characterized by other aspects of formality as well: special structuring and planning of the discourse; use of formulas; special stance; and "seriousness" (which I take to imply some constraints on topic, intonation, facial expressions, and gestures, and consistency of these with social rank).

Because positional identities and formal (structured) discourse go together in the example just cited, one might suppose that this type of social identity is necessarily invoked by the structuring of discourse and need not be considered an independent variable. But another part of Albert's description suggests otherwise. Here, Albert discusses a speech event she calls "semiformalized quarreling," a "symbolic fight" between persons who represent the bride's and groom's families at a wedding. It seems that the major factor contrasting "semiformalized quarreling" with other (unformalized) quarreling is that the identities of the participants are positional rather than personal. True, enough information is not really given to know whether there are also differences in the organization of discourse in these two kinds of quarrels. But Albert's statement that there is always a great danger that the symbolic fight might become a real fight suggests that the major difference between them lies less in the organization of the discourse than in whether it applies to personal identities.

Of course, societies can be compared as to what social identities are structured in this positional (or formal) sense; and, within a society, communicative events can be compared as to which positional sets are invoked and the scope of the social relations organized in them. For instance, among the Wolof, kinship positions, although publicly known, organize relations among a smaller group of persons than do society-wide identities, such as caste. An individual Wolof man is patrilateral cross-cousin to only a certain group of people, and that identity is relevant only to his interaction with them, whereas his caste identity is relevant to his interaction with everyone. Whether the identities invoked in a Wolof communicative event are society-wide or not has consequences for many aspects of the participants' behavior. It is convenient to say that the wider, or more public, the scope of the social identities invoked on a particular occasion, the more formal the occasion is, in this third sense of the term.

Emergence of a central situational focus

A fourth aspect of formality concerns the ways in which a main focus of attention – a dominant mutual engagement that encompasses all persons present (see Goffman 1963: 164) – is differentiated from side involvements. Probably all conversations display this differentiation to some extent. Jefferson (1972) shows that even ordinary conversations between two persons clearly mark off certain sets of utterances as side sequences and distinguish them from the main, or focal, sequence. When a social gathering has a larger number of participants, however, it may or may not be organized around a central focus of attention that engages, or might engage, the whole group. An American cocktail party, for example, is usually decentralized, with many small groups whose conversations are not meant to concern the gathering as a whole; but a lecture is centralized even if members of the audience mutter asides to each other during the lecturer's performance.

The emergence of a central focus of attention for a social gathering parallels the process of focusing mentioned above for aspects of code. Participation in the central, focal activity is regulated and structured in special ways. For instance, it may be that only certain persons have the right to speak or act in the main sequence, with others restricted to the side sequences. In the main sequence, speech is governed by constraints on topic, continuity, and relevance that do not apply (or not to the same extent) in the side sequences (cf. Ervin-Tripp 1972: 243).

This focusing process can be seen at work in the organization of events at a Wolof naming-day ceremony. Much of the ceremony involves decentralized participation: the guests sit in small groups, chatting and eating. At various points, however, a *griot* (praise-singer) may start shouting bits of praise-poems in an effort to capture the attention of the crowd and establish a focus of attention for his performance. If he succeeds, the situation changes character, altering the patterns of movement and talk for all participants, and bringing caste identities (rather than more personal relations) into the foreground.

Similarly, David Turton (1975), in his writing on the Mursi of southern Ethiopia, distinguishes among three kinds of political speech events according to criteria that seem to resemble this focusing process. Turton calls the difference between "chatting," "discussion," and "debate" in Mursi society a difference in "degree of formality": what the more formal events entail is a process of setting off a single central (onstage) speaker from his audience, by spatial arrangements and verbal cues. Only men of certain age-grades may speak in the main (focal) sequence; other persons are relegated to the audience or to side sequences.[6] In this way, central activities and central actors are differentiated from peripheral activities and actors.

For any society, that only certain kinds of activities and actors will be able to command center stage can be expected. At the least, the activities must be ones that all participants recognize as relevant to them. Because these distinctions are made by the participants themselves in the ways they direct their attention and in the ways they do or do not perform, the organization of a formal occasion must reflect ideas that the participants hold about their own social life. In this sense a people's own analysis of its social order is intrinsic to the emergence of a central situational focus, the fourth aspect of formality, just as it was intrinsic to the explicit labels for, and public knowledge of, positional identities.

A Cross-Cultural Comparison: Wolof, Mursi, and Ilongot Political Meetings

I have suggested that these four aspects of formality may apply universally – that all speech communities may have social occasions that show different degrees of formality according to each of these criteria or combinations of them. These four aspects of formality are useful for comparing communicative events within a given sociocultural system, as the previous examples are meant to illustrate. But how might communities differ with respect to formality and informality in social occasions? For cross-cultural comparison both the similarities and the differences among societies need to be seen in some systematic fashion. Using the definitions of formality here proposed, one can say that speech communities may differ: (a) in the specific details of each variable or aspect of formality (e.g., what social identities are available, or precisely which linguistic phenomena are subject to additional structuring?); (b) in the ways the four aspects of formality combine or are interdependent; (c) in additional factors that correlate with formality in a given community (that is, when formality in one or all aspects is greatest, what other characteristics will the social occasion display in that community?).

To show how such differences might work and what kinds of factors might explain them, I shall compare in more detail two societies, the Wolof and the Mursi (from Turton 1975), with respect to the organization of political discourse and action. Each of these African societies has special speech events concerned with politics, including some events that are more formal than others. In other respects the two societies are quite different. The Wolof have a large-scale, complex organization of castes and centralized political authority, with a strong emphasis on social rank and inequality. The Mursi are a small-scale society, with an acephalous political system, and recognize no fundamental differences in rank other than those based on sex and age.

The comparison between Wolof and Mursi will be supplemented with a comparison with a third society, the Ilongots of the northern Philippines (from Rosaldo 1973), that shows certain resemblances to each of the other two. This part of the discussion will allow me to return to some earlier questions about relations between formality and political coercion.

Wolof and Mursi political speech events

Both the Wolof and the Mursi distinguish more formal political "discussions" or "meetings" (*methe* in Mursi, *ndaje* in Wolof)[7] from casual "chat" about political topics. The more formal events contrast with the chats in all four of the ways that are being discussed.

First, the more formal events show a greater degree of structuring, both in spatial arrangements and in the discourse. Spatially, the Wolof participants are arranged according to rank; within this arrangement the speaker in the focal sequence stands (near the center) while others sit (or stand around the sidelines). The Mursi participants are spatially arranged by age-grades, with the focal speaker standing separately and pacing back and forth. In the discourse, in both societies each speaker opens with conventional phrases. Among the Wolof there are also conventional interjections by griots in the audience, and sometimes special repetitions by griots acting as spokesmen for high-caste speakers.

The more formal events also show greater consistency in the selection among alternative forms in all communicative modes. Among the Wolof, a speaker's movements, gestures, intonation, amount of repetition, and degree of syntactic elaboration are all consistent with his social rank, particularly his caste (and so will differ according to whether he is a griot or a noble, for instance), whereas in informal chatting he might vary one or more of these modes for special purposes. Among the Mursi, although Turton gives few details, it appears that the successful speaker is one who performs in a manner fully consistent with the social image of a wise elder. The speaker's movements should be forceful but he should not show "excitement," repetitiousness, or "unintelligible" enunciation – from which I infer that there are co-occurring constraints on gesture and facial expression, intonation, rapidity of speech, choice of phonological variants, and the organization of his discourse.

In the more formal events in both societies there is a single main focal sequence, in which participation is specially regulated: only certain persons really have the right to speak "on stage," and that right has to do with their publicly recognized social identities. Among the Mursi, these positional identities involve sex and membership in particular age-grades; among the Wolof, they involve generation, caste, and tenure of labeled political offices.

There are, however, some clear differences between formal meetings of the Wolof and of the Mursi, differences that concern the organization and nature of participation among those persons who have the right to speak onstage. One difference lies in the regulation of turn taking. In Wolof meetings turn taking is relatively highly structured; the order of speakers may be announced at the beginning, or there may be a person who acts as a master of ceremonies. That is, there is usually one person who has the right to control the order of speakers in the focal sequence. In Mursi meetings, however, speakers compete for turns, and interruptions are frequent. A speaker may not be able to finish what he wants to say before the audience or another speaker interrupts him.

Another contrast concerns the nature of the speaking roles themselves. Among the Wolof, the more formal a speech event is (according to any of the four criteria, and depending on whether or not the occasion is explicitly concerned with politics), the more likely it is that the speaking roles will divide into complementary sets, associated with high and low social rank. That is, even among those who participate in the main sequence of discourse, participation is differentiated into two asymmetric roles. All levels of linguistic organization show this differentiation. There will always be some participants who speak louder, at higher pitch, with more repetitive and more emphatic constructions (usages that connote low social rank), while other participants speak more softly, at lower pitch, with fewer emphatic constructions, and so on (usages that connote high social rank). This asymmetry of speaking roles is always a concomitant of formality in Wolof speech events. But I call it a concomitant because one would not want to say it is part of a *definition* of formality that might apply cross-culturally, since the Mursi speaking roles, for instance, seem to be more symmetrical. Among the Mursi there are no structured differences among speaking roles at political meetings. Even the behavioral differences between speaker and audience are fewer than among the Wolof because the Mursi audience interrupts and interjects loud comments in a way that the Wolof audience would not.

What aspects of social or political organization, which (as has been noted) are quite different for the two peoples, might be reflected in the differing organization of their formal speech events? One possible explanation for the Wolof asymmetry of speaking roles is that Wolof society shows a greater degree of role differentiation altogether. But that is not a sufficient explanation for a contrast in speech-event organization that is qualitative, not quantitative (asymmetry vs. symmetry, not really as a matter of degree). Rather, I think the explanation lies in the Wolof preoccupation with rank and hierarchy, as opposed to the Mursi outlook, which is more egalitarian – the only structured inequalities being sex and age. The rural Wolof view society as composed of complementary unequal ranks where the upper has a natural right to command the lower.[8] Political decisions are culturally seen as initiated and decreed from above, by a recognized leader; the role of followers is only to advise and consent.

As a result, Wolof village political meetings are convened not for the purpose of decision making but for announcing decisions made from above and answering questions about them. The complementarity of ranks is the source of the asymmetrical speaking roles; the centralization and autocracy of political authority is the source of the master of ceremonies's right to determine the order of speakers. There is no competition among speakers for the opportunity to express opinions, since the expression of opinions and counterarguments is not the purpose of the meeting. Among the Wolof the expression of opinion and the exercise of debate go on in private, as does the leader's decision-making process.

Mursi political meetings, in contrast, are convened for the express purpose of decision making, by consensus, about future collective action. Each man of sufficient age has an equal right to participate in the consensus and to try to influence what consensus will be reached.

From the differences between Wolof and Mursi formal political meetings, however, it is not logical to conclude that political decision making is *actually* despotic among the Wolof and democratic among the Mursi. Wolof leaders need consensus support for their decisions, or their followers may fail to cooperate or may abandon them for other leaders. Conversely, for the Mursi, Turton notes that the decisions arrived at in formal meetings are sometimes such foregone conclusions that they were not reached during the course of the meeting at all. Private lobbying is as much a factor in some Mursi decisions as it is in the Wolof decision-making process.[9]

The differences between Wolof and Mursi formal political meetings do not reflect differences in the actual decision-making process so much as they reflect contrasts between what can be shown onstage and what happens offstage. The formality of the meetings has to do with what can be focused upon publicly; and it is in this sense that formality can often connote a social order, or forms of social action, that is publicly recognized and considered legitimate (regardless of whether political power actually operates through that public, formal social order or not). The organization of these meetings reflects political ideology, therefore, but it does not necessarily reflect political actuality.

Ilongot political meetings

We have seen that the Wolof and Mursi political meetings are both more formal, in all respects, than ordinary conversation about political matters. But is one *kind* of meeting more formal than the other? If so, does the more formal kind place greater restrictions on its participants' political freedom, as Bloch (1975) suggests? These questions are addressed more easily by turning from the Wolof and Mursi to a third society, the Ilongots of the northern Philippines (as described by Rosaldo 1973), among whom both kinds of meetings are found. One Ilongot subgroup holds political meetings that, in certain ways, resemble the Mursi *methe*; another subgroup holds meetings that resemble the Wolof *ndaje*. Many aspects of language and cultural context remain the same for both Ilongot subgroups, however. For this reason, whatever difference the form of the meeting might make should emerge more clearly than it did in the initial comparison of Wolof and Mursi.

According to Rosaldo, the Ilongots are an acephalous, egalitarian society in the process of being incorporated into a larger Philippine national polity that is both more hierarchical and more authoritarian. This process has not affected all Ilongot communities equally, however; it has gone much further among coastal communities than it has inland. Ilongots are divided, therefore, into two subgroups, the "modern" and the "traditional," which contrast in a number of ways (and see themselves as distinct). Among other things, the two subgroups differ in their conceptions of how a political meeting should be organized. Like the Mursi, traditional Ilongots hold meetings in which there is no master of ceremonies. Speakers compete for the floor and interrupt each other frequently. Like the Mursi, too, speaking roles are relatively undifferentiated. Although some men "speak for" others, no one is bound by what another says, and the relevant parties may also speak for themselves. Modern Ilongots, on the other hand, disapprove of interruptions. In their meetings a master of ceremonies calls on speakers one by one; and the people he calls on are "captains," who speak on behalf of their "soldiers" (men from their respective localities). The soldiers, who remain silent, are considered bound to uphold what their captain says. In the regulation of turn taking and differentiation of complementary behavioral roles, therefore, modern Ilongot meetings have come to resemble the Wolof meetings described above.

As among the Wolof, this centralized type of meeting coincides, for the modern Ilongots, with a new ideological emphasis on rank and authority. The connection is surely not accidental. In fact, one of the interesting things about the Ilongot example is its implication that the kinds of political meetings seen among the Wolof and Mursi actually correspond to two very basic kinds of political ideology that are widely found in societies around the world.[10]

But which kind of meeting is more formal? The modern Ilongot meeting has a more centralized focus of attention: only one person speaks at a time, and the differentiation of central from peripheral participants is apparently maintained throughout, unlike the traditional meeting (Rosaldo 1973: 204–5). In one sense, therefore, the modern meeting seems to be the more formal (that is, in terms of the fourth aspect of formality listed in this article). Yet, the opposite is suggested by linguistic aspects of the discourse. Oratory in traditional meetings displays much more linguistic elaboration and redundancy, such as repetitions of utterances and parts of utterances, reduplicative constructions, formulaic expressions, and so on. Modern Ilongot oratory lacks those elaborations although it does have a few stylistic conventions of its own. So, in terms of linguistic structuring (the first aspect of formality), the traditional meeting is the more formal. The Ilongots themselves perhaps recognize that linguistic elaboration when they call modern oratory "straight speech" and traditional oratory "crooked speech." From an analytical perspective, therefore, one could not say that one type of meeting is altogether "more formal" than the other. The two are just formalized in different ways. For the Ilongots, at least, the two ways seem to be complementary (and hence, mutually exclusive). Rosaldo suggests (1973: 220) that much of the linguistic elaboration and redundancy in traditional oratory is a matter of maintaining continuity and relevance in the central sequence of utterances, and keeping that sequence distinct from peripheral discourse. Linguistic elaboration, in other words, is a way of organizing speakers' access to the floor, in the absence of a master of ceremonies; it is his functional equivalent in this respect, and one would not expect to find both extreme linguistic elaboration and extreme centralization in the same communicative event.

Because the various aspects of formality are not maximized on the same social occasions, formality/informality is not a single continuum, at least not for the Ilongots. Therefore, if one type of meeting somehow restricts the political freedom of its participants more than the other, it is not formality in general that brings restrictions, but only one aspect of formality (either centralization of attention or increased structuring of code). That the more elaborated, redundant oratorical style is found, among the Ilongots, in the less authoritarian political system suggests that increased code structuring (the first aspect of formality) is not necessarily an instrument of coercion manipulated by a political leadership. As Rosaldo comments (1973: 222), "Linguistic elaboration, and a reflective interest in rhetoric, belongs to societies in which no one can command another's interest or attention, let alone enforce his compliance." In contrast, the centralization of attention in modern Ilongot meetings, with a master of ceremonies who not only prevents interruptions but determines which persons may be central speakers and which only peripheral, is the more restrictive of political expression, at least for some participants. Defined as peripheral, the Ilongot "soldiers" are not allowed to speak at the meeting at all. Their opportunities for creative statement are virtually nil.

Yet what the Ilongot "soldier" can or cannot do onstage in the meeting tells little about what he might do offstage. That the captain speaks for his men does not show whether he is a tyrant or a mere figurehead. As among the Wolof and Mursi, the formal organization of political meetings among the Ilongots is more directly related to political ideology – conscious models of the way society ought to work, as held by its members – than to the way political decisions are actually made. It is not clear, therefore, that either kind of meeting has a coercive effect on its participants in the long run, although the modern Ilongot meeting does seem to restrict some participants' opportunities for creative expression during the meeting itself.

In sum, the argument that formalizing a social occasion reduces its participants' political freedom can hold true only in limited ways. (a) Only certain aspects of formality (particularly the fourth, centralization of attention) are relevant to it; structuring of the linguistic aspects of the discourse (the first aspect of formality) is less relevant. (b) Not all participants are necessarily affected. (c) Possibly, formalization is coercive only if a society's political ideology, which the formal meeting's organization expresses, is authoritarian. (d) Finally, any restrictions on participation in formal meetings do not necessarily apply to other contexts, which may be the ones where political decision making actually occurs and where political freedom is, therefore, more at issue.

"Formality" as a Concept in Social Theory

Formality and social stasis

The foregoing discussion has concerned relations between formality (of social occasions) and political coercion. But there remains a broader kind of constraint: the force of tradition. Does formalizing a social occasion inevitably tend to reinforce a normative, traditional social order (regardless of whether that tradition prescribes an authoritarian political leadership)? Does formality always imply rigidity, stability, or conservatism?

To address those questions, the various aspects of formality must be distinguished from each other, since formality represents not just one, but several dimensions along which social occasions can vary. Not all aspects of formalization necessarily concern the public social order at all. The structured discourse of poetry, for instance, does not automatically have a special relationship to the social establishment. It need not have a public audience or a public subject matter. Nor do the ways in which the discourse in poetry is structured necessarily have to be traditional ways. If formality in speech events reflects, and in that sense supports, a traditional social system, it is the other aspects of formality that do so, not the structuring of discourse in itself. With the other three aspects of formality, the relation to an established public social system is more evident, since the social occasions that could be called formal in these respects would be those that invoke social identities and modes of participation that are publicly recognized and considered appropriate.

Certainly, these occasions concern the publicly known social system; they may even call attention to it. What is not quite so clear is whether they therefore *reinforce* it. By mentioning a thesis, for instance, one does in a certain sense support it, more than if it were allowed to fall into oblivion; but mentioning it does not mean that one agrees with it. Calling attention to something can also be a way of altering it – as when a rite of passage calls attention to an individual's social identity in order to transform it into another. Some anthropologists have argued that it is the very formality of such ritual occasions, which minimize personal histories and focus on the relevant social relationships, that makes the creative transformation possible (see, for example, Douglas 1966: 77–9).[11]

Now it might be objected that the transformation of social identities that goes on in a rite of passage, although a kind of creativity, is a superficial kind in that it operates only *within* a traditional system. It is not the same thing as change in that system, to which formalization might still be inimical. But formalization can be thought inimical to change only if one has a certain view of the social system to which formal occasions call attention – a view that the social system is monolithic, that the structure of a society prevents its members from conceiving of alternatives, and that all members of society have exactly identical conceptions of the social order. If members' political ideologies, for instance, differ, there can scarcely be a situation in which such differences become more apparent than in formal meetings whose organization, as we saw for the Wolof, Mursi, and Ilongot, is ideologically based. This ideological clash is just what happens among the Ilongots, when people from coastal ("modern") communities and people from inland ("traditional") communities have to hold joint meetings. When, on such an occasion, the Ilongots found they did not agree on how a meeting should be run, assumptions about how and why meetings are organized could not be left unquestioned. They had to be discussed (and, one gathers, some accommodation reached; see Rosaldo 1973: 219). That is, the process of formalization forces the recognition of conflicting ideas and in so doing may impel their change. (There is also, of course, the inverse situation, in which a group with internal conflicts tries to avoid holding the formal meetings that might oblige those conflicts to be faced. Stability and communal harmony are thus achieved by *not* formalizing. See, e.g., the Israeli *moshav* described by Abarbanel 1975: 152.)

The Ilongot example represents an acculturative situation, where the ideational conflict comes about because new ideas are introduced from outside. I do not want to suggest, however, that outside influence is necessary before formalization can induce change. To the extent that ideas about the social order vary according to the social position of those who hold them, any social system will generate differences of opinion, and that is quite apart from the possibility that the ideas themselves might be ambiguous, contradictory, or indeterminate. The point is that formalization does not automatically support stability and conservatism unless the social relations it articulates are fully agreed on by everyone and admit no alternatives. Whether that is the case depends on the particular social relations and on the cultural system in question; it is not implicit in the analytical concept of formality itself.[12]

Is "formality" useful as a cover term?

The various aspects of formality distinguished in this paper concern quite different kinds of social phenomena. Some concern properties of code while others concern properties of a social situation; some focus on observable behavior while others invoke the conceptual categories of social actors. For purposes of description and analysis, all such matters can and should be considered separately. But their separation in a research strategy does not mean that they are all fully independent variables. In fact, they must be interdependent, to the extent that cultural definitions of social situations and social identities must have a behavioral content.

This interdependence is something that social actors can exploit by altering their behavior to bring about a redefinition of the situation and of the identities that are relevant to it. The Wolof griot (praise-singer) who tries to capture the guests' attention at a naming-day ceremony illustrates this process (see the section on the emergence of a central situational focus). If he succeeds in attracting the attention of all the guests, a situation that began as a multifocused gathering coalesces into a single all-encompassing engagement; and, in consequence, positional identities whose scopes are wide enough to include all persons present will be invoked. Normally, caste identities are the relevant ones, especially since the griot is acting in accordance with his own caste specialization. Because high-caste persons in general owe largesse to griots, invoking caste identities places high-caste guests under obligation to reward the praise-singer even if the words of his performance do not mention them. (Some high-caste Wolof report that in the hope that they will not have to pay, they pretend not to notice the griot unless he already has a large audience.)

In this example, the Wolof naming-day ceremony, the third aspect of formality (positional identities) is entailed by the fourth (emergence of a centralized situational focus). In fact, it is reasonable to suppose that centralization is always likely to entail positional identities if a large number of persons are present, because positional identities are the ones that are widely recognized and that organize people on a systematic and broad scale. Similarly, the third aspect of formality is also entailed by the second (code consistency), because the sociolinguistic variants among which the speaker selects usually express categorical, not individual, identities. Complete code consistency would mean, for instance, that a Wolof man who uses an intonational pattern associated with griots (extreme speed, loudness, high pitch) will consistently express griot identity in all other aspects of his behavior as well (syntax, posture, movements, and so on). Little scope would be left for individuality.

Yet, if there are certain ways in which the various aspects of formality are interdependent, there are other ways in which they are not. In the first place, the entailments just mentioned do not seem to be reversible. Thus no. 4 entails no. 3, but no. 3 does not have to entail no. 4. The griot can invoke caste identities even when privately addressing a single high-caste individual, and he can do so simply by declaring, "I am a griot." Although some of his intonational and gestural usages must be consistent with this statement if it is not to sound like a joke, not all of them need be. For instance, his speed of talk might be slow, unlike the rapid tempo normally associated with griots. By such means he can distance himself enough from the griot role to make some personal comment on it, even if he still intends caste identities to define the situation and to suggest his interlocutor's course of action.

Finally, there is no intrinsic reason why code consistency, positional identities, or centralization (no. 2, 3, or 4) should entail a change in the degree of structuring to which a code is subjected (criterion no. 1) or vice versa. Linguistic aspects of discourse in poetry are structured, for instance, but a poem's subject matter can be entirely private. Moreover, code switches and code inconsistencies in poetry are frequent and can contribute significantly to the poem's special effect. The first aspect of formality seems, therefore, to be independent of the other three; and this was also suggested by the Ilongot example, in which the same event cannot maximize both linguistic structuring (formality no. 1) and centralization (formality no. 4).

Is there, after all this, any sense in which all four aspects of formality are related – a sense in which *formality* remains useful as a cover term? I think there is, but it is so general that it is not very useful as an analytical tool. The only thing all four criteria have in common is that all of them concern the degree to which a social occasion is systematically organized. This sense of formality as "degree of organization" has some resemblance to Goffman's (1963: 199) definition of formality/informality as "tightness"/"looseness." The thrust of my argument, however, is that being organized in one way does not necessarily mean being organized in other ways to the same degree or at the same time. In fact, the various ways in which a communicative event is organizable may be complementary or even antithetical, rather than additive.

I suspect, therefore, that it is appropriate in few instances to speak of "formality" generally without specifying more precisely what one has in mind. Otherwise, there is too great a risk of mistaking one kind of formality for another or assuming that kinds of formality are really the same. That an ordinary English word has multiple meanings – as we have seen in its multiple uses in the sociolinguistic literature – does not make those meanings essentially homogeneous, nor should we unwittingly elevate this word's polysemy to a social theory. As Leach has remarked (1961: 27), "We anthropologists ... must reexamine basic premises and realize that English language patterns of thought are not a necessary model for the whole of human society."

NOTES

Acknowledgment. I am indebted to Ben Blount, Dell Hymes, Joel Sherzer, Maurice Bloch, and David Turton for their helpful comments on an earlier version of this paper.

1 The application is made except insofar as the linguist acts as his or her own informant and so combines the roles of observer and subject.

2 Actually, to equate the relevant aspects of code structuring with addition of or elaboration of existing rules presents some problems. The notion seems to apply well enough to examples such as the Wolof insult sessions described in the section *Increased Code Structuring*, because speech rhythms in those sessions must not only conform to the usual metric principles of stress and length in ordinary speech but be further organized to fit a precise and repetitive drum

rhythm. But it is not clear that redundancies of meter, rhyme, or syntactic parallelism in poetry should always be interpreted in terms of addition of rules. For instance, Sherzer's (1974) description of Cuna congress chants proposes that syntactic parallelism and redundancy are achieved by retaining underlying representations, i.e., by *not* following the usual transformational rules that would zero out redundant noun phrases and verb phrases. This suggests that the special aesthetic structure of chants is achieved by using fewer rules, rather than more. Yet, how do the rules of chanting provide for the fact that the usual reductions are not to occur? Is there any assurance that this provision is not best analyzed via extra rules that reinsert the redundant forms, since that analysis might better conform to general principles of markedness (if the chants are to be considered as marked discourse forms)? A similar problem arises for types of Western poetry in which, it is sometimes said, structuring of meter and rhyme is accompanied by syntactic and semantic "poetic licence." This argument suggests that extra structuring in one aspect of the discourse might be accompanied by loosening of structure in another. It is not clear, however, that "licence" is really the appropriate conception of poetic syntax and semantics. The issues here are complex and they reach far beyond the scope of this paper.

3 Since my fieldwork was conducted in rural areas of the Préfecture de Tivaouane, when I speak of "the Wolof" I can, of course, mean only the villages I have myself observed and the extent to which they may be representative of Wolof villages more generally. This caveat is necessary because "Wolof" as an ethnic category now includes a numerous and diverse population, urban as well as rural, elite as well as peasant. I believe my comments here apply to the *Communautés Rurales* (Senegalese rural administrative units) in the core regions of Wolof occupation; they do not necessarily apply to urban Wolof.

4 See Goffman's discussion (1963: 198–215) relating formality/informality to degree of involvement in a situation.

5 Other authors describe a similar distinction in somewhat different terms. Geertz (1966), for example, speaks of the "anonymization of individuals" in ceremonialized interaction.

6 For another example, see Tyler's (1972) paper on the Koya of central India. A number of behavioral differences, including lexical choices, differentiate central from peripheral actors in Koya formal events.

7 The occasions I refer to are public meetings conducted in rural villages or *Communautés Rurales*. Increasingly, Wolof call these meetings by the French term *réunion*, which (in Senegalese usage) distinguishes them more definitively from casual encounters than does the Wolof term *ndaje*.

8 I leave aside the relation of the priesthood (*Imans* and *marabouts*), which ranks highest in a religious sense, to political decision making.

9 On this point, Turton comments (personal communication) that "although the Mursi do indeed see their debates as decision-making procedures, I am less and less convinced that, from the point of view of the outside observer, they should be thus characterized."

10 I do not mean to suggest that these two societal types, if types they are, exhaust all possibilities of political ideology and organized political discussion; our own society probably fits neither. Nor, on the basis of materials presented in this paper, do I propose to match such types to points on an evolutionary scale. That two forms of political discourse have a certain historical relationship among the Ilongots does not mean they will have the same relationship everywhere.

11 See also Firth (1975) on "the *experimental* aspect of [formal] oratory" in Tikopia (emphasis in original). Firth argues that public meetings and formal oratory emerge in Tikopia under conditions of crisis and social change, not during periods of stability. The Tikopia *fono* (formal assembly of titled elders) cannot be dismissed as merely a reactionary reaffirmation of a threatened tradition. It is also a means of publicly exploring important

issues, and a way for Tikopia leaders to find out whether a new proposal is likely to be acceptable (1975: 42–3).

12 Sally Falk Moore (1975: 231) makes a similar point: "It is important to recognize that processes of regularization, processes having to do with rules and regularities, may be used to block change or to produce change. The fixing of rules and regularities are as much tools of revolutionaries as they are of reactionaries. It is disastrous to confuse the analysis of processes of regularization with the construction of static social models."

REFERENCES

Abarbanel, Jay (1975). The Dilemma of Economic Competition in an Israeli Moshav. In *Symbol and Politics in Communal Ideology*. Sally Falk Moore and Barbara Myerhoff, eds., pp. 144–65. Ithaca, NY: Cornell University Press.

Albert, Ethel (1972). Cultural Patterning of Speech Behavior in Burundi. In *Directions in Sociolinguistics*. John Gumperz and Dell Hymes, eds., pp. 72–105. New York: Holt, Rinehart, and Winston.

Bateson, Gregory (1972). *Steps to an Ecology of Mind*. San Francisco: Chandler.

Bauman, Richard, and Joel Sherzer (eds.) (1974). *Explorations in the Ethnography of Speaking*. London: Cambridge University Press.

Bloch, Maurice (ed.) (1975). *Political Language and Oratory in Traditional Society*. New York: Academic Press.

Bricker, Victoria (1974). The Ethnographic Context of Some Traditional Mayan Speech Genres. In *Explorations in the Ethnography of Speaking*. Richard Bauman and Joel Sherzer, eds., pp. 368–88. London: Cambridge University Press.

Davis, Ermina (1976). In Honor of the Ancestors: The Social Context of Iwi Egungun Chanting in a Yoruba Community. Ph.D dissertation, Brandeis University.

Douglas, Mary (1966). *Purity and Danger*. Baltimore: Penguin.

Ervin-Tripp, Susan (1972). On Sociolinguistic Rules: Alternation and Co-occurrence. In *Directions in Sociolinguistics*. John Gumperz and Dell Hymes, eds., pp. 213–50. New York: Holt, Rinehart, and Winston.

Firth, Raymond (1975). Speech-making and Authority in Tikopia. In *Political Language and Oratory in Traditional Society*. Maurice Bloch, ed., pp. 29–44. New York: Academic Press.

Fischer, John (1972). The Stylistic Significance of Consonantal Sandhi in Trukese and Ponapean. In *Directions in Sociolinguistics*. John Gumperz and Dell Hymes, eds., pp. 498–511. New York: Holt, Rinehart, and Winston.

Fishman, Joshua (ed.) (1968). *Readings in the Sociology of Language*. The Hague: Mouton.

Fishman, Joshua (1972). *Sociolinguistics: A Brief Introduction*. Rowley, Mass.: Newbury House.

Fox, James (1974). "Our Ancestors Spoke in Pairs": Rotinese Views of Language, Dialect, and Code. In *Explorations in the Ethnography of Speaking*. Richard Bauman and Joel Sherzer, eds., pp. 65–85. London: Cambridge University Press.

Friedrich, Paul (1972). Social Context and Semantic Feature: The Russian Pronominal Usage. In *Directions in Sociolinguistics*. John Gumperz and Dell Hymes, eds, pp. 270–300. New York: Holt, Rinehart, and Winston.

Geertz, Clifford (1966). *Person, Time and Conduct in Bali: An Essay in Cultural Analysis*. Yale Southeast Asia Program, Cultural Report Series, No. 14. New Haven.

Goffman, Erving (1961). *Encounters: Two Studies in the Sociology of Interaction*. Indianapolis, IN: Bobbs-Merrill.

Goffman, Erving (1963). *Behavior in Public Places*. New York: Free Press.

Goffman, Erving (1974). *Frame Analysis*. New York: Harper and Row.

Gossen, Gary (1974). To Speak with a Heated Heart: Chamula Canons of Style and Good Performance. In *Explorations in the Ethnography of Speaking*. Richard Bauman and Joel Sherzer, eds., pp. 389–413. London: Cambridge University Press.

Gumperz, John, and Dell Hymes (eds.) (1972). *Directions in Sociolinguistics*. New York: Holt, Rinehart, and Winston.

Halliday, Michael (1964). The Users and Uses of Language. In *The Linguistic Sciences and Language Teaching*. Halliday, McIntosh, and Strevens, eds. London: Longmans. (Reprinted in Fishman 1968, pp. 139–69.)

Hymes, Dell (1972). Models of the Interaction of Language and Social Life. In *Directions in Sociolinguistics*. John Gumperz and Dell Hymes, eds., pp. 35–71. New York: Holt, Rinehart, and Winston.

Irvine, Judith (1974). Strategies of Status Manipulation in the Wolof Greeting. In *Explorations in the Ethnography of Speaking*. Richard Bauman and Joel Sherzer, eds., pp. 167–91. London: Cambridge University Press.

Jackson, Jean (1974). Language Indentity of the Colombian Vaupés Indians. In *Explorations in the Ethnography of Speaking*. Richard Bauman and Joel Sherver, eds., pp. 50–64. London: Cambridge University Press.

Jefferson, Gail (1972). Side Sequences. In *Studies in Social Interaction*. David Sudnow, ed., pp. 294–338. New York: Free Press.

Joos, Martin (1959). *The Isolation of Styles*. Monograph Series on Languages and Linguistics 12: 107–13. Washington, DC: Georgetown University. (Reprinted in Fishman 1968, pp. 185–91.)

Kirshenblatt-Gimblett, Barbara (ed.) (1976). *Speech Play*. Philadelphia: University of Pennsylvania Press.

Labov, William (1972). Some Principles of Linguistic Methodology. *Language in Society* 1: 97–120.

Leach, Edmund (1961). *Rethinking Anthropology*. London: Athlone.

Leach, Edmund (1965). *Political Systems of Highland Burma*. Boston: Beacon Press.

Mead, Margaret (1937). Public Opinion Mechanisms Among Primitive Peoples. *Public Opinion Quarterly* 1: 5–16.

Moore, Sally Falk (1975). Epilogue: Uncertainties in Situations, Indeterminacies in Culture. In *Symbol and Politics in Communal Ideology*. Sally Falk Moore and Barbara Myerhoff, eds., pp. 210–39. Ithaca, NY: Cornell University Press.

Murphy, Robert (1971). *The Dialectics of Social Life*. New York: Basic Books.

Rosaldo, Michelle Z. (1973). I Have Nothing to Hide: The Language of Ilongot Oratory. *Language in Society* 2: 193–224.

Rubin, Joan (1968). Bilingual Usage in Paraguay. In *Readings in the Sociology of Language*. Joshua Fishman, ed., pp. 512–30. The Hague: Mouton.

Sanches, Mary, and Ben Blount (eds.) (1975). *Sociocultural Dimensions of Language Use*. New York: Academic Press.

Sherzer, Joel (1974). Namakke, Sunmakke, Kormakke: Three Types of Cuna Speech Event. In *Explorations in the Ethnography of Speaking*. Richard Bauman and Joel Sherzer, eds., pp. 263–82. London: Cambridge University Press.

Timm, L. A. (1975). Spanish-English Code-Switching: El Porqué y How-Not-To. *Romance Philology* 28: 473–82.

Turton, David (1975). The Relationships Between Oratory and the Exercise of Influence Among the Mursi. In *Political Language and Oratory in Traditional Society*. Maurice Bloch, ed., pp. 163–84. New York: Academic Press.

Tyler, Stephen (1972). Context and Alternation in Koya Kinship Terminology. In *Directions in Sociolinguistics*. John Gumperz and Dell Hymes, eds., pp. 251–69. New York: Holt, Rinehart, and Winston.

Wolfson, Nessa (1976). Speech Events and Natural Speech: Some Implications for Sociolinguistic Methodology. *Language in Society* 5: 189–210.

STUDY QUESTIONS

1 What are the four aspects of formality identified by Irvine? Describe how they can be applied to a speech event that you are familiar with.
2 What are the advantages of dividing the concept of formality into separate aspects or properties?
3 What are the problems with the use of the English term *formality* to describe a wide range of sociocultural contexts?
4 Identify several similarities and differences among the three cultural groups discussed by Irvine.

8

Universal and Culture-Specific Properties of Greetings

Alessandro Duranti

There is widespread evidence that greetings are an important part of the communicative competence necessary for being a member of any speech community.[1] They are often one of the first verbal routines learned by children and certainly one of the first topics introduced in foreign language classes. They are also of great interest to analysts of social interaction, who see them as establishing the conditions for social encounters. It is not surprising, then, to find out that there is a considerable number of ethological, linguistic, sociological, and ethnographic studies of greetings. But despite the attention greetings have received in the social sciences, there is to date no generalizable definition of greetings and therefore no systematic way for deciding what qualifies as "greetings" in a particular speech community. Nonetheless, researchers have felt at ease identifying "greetings" in different languages and providing hypotheses about what greetings "do" for or to people. In this article, I suggest that this has been possible due to the widespread belief that greetings are verbal formulas with virtually no propositional content (Searle 1969) or zero referential value (Youssouf et al. 1976). Students of greetings have argued that people are either not believed to "mean" whatever they say during greetings or they are seen as "lying" (see Sacks 1975). In fact, I will argue, these claims are not always tenable. As I will show, not all greetings are completely predictable and devoid of propositional content. Before making such a claim, however, I must establish some independent criteria by which to determine whether a given expression or exchange should qualify as a "greeting." Short of such criteria, critics might always argue that the apparent counterexamples are not greetings at all.

In what follows I first briefly review the existing literature on greetings in a variety of fields and identify some of the factors that contributed to the common belief that greetings are formulas with no propositional content. Then I introduce six criteria for identifying greetings across languages and speech communities. Using these criteria, I go on to identify four types of verbal greetings in one community where I worked, in [formerly Western] Samoa. In discussing the fourth Samoan greeting, the "Where are you going?" type, I will argue that it blatantly violates the common expectation of greetings as phatic,

For permission to publish copyright material in this book, grateful acknowledgment is made to: A. Duranti (1997), "Universal and Culture-Specific Properties of Greetings," *Journal of Linguistic Anthropology* 7(1): 63–97.

predictable exchanges, and I show that it functions as an information-seeking and action-control strategy. Finally, I examine a Samoan expression that has been translated as a greeting in English but seems problematic on the basis of ethnographic information, and I show that, as we would expect, it does not qualify for some of the criteria proposed in this article.

Previous Studies

The literature on greetings can be divided along several methodological and theoretical lines. In what follows, I will briefly review the contribution of human ethologists, ethnographers, conversation analysts, and speech act theorists.

In the ethological tradition, exemplified by Irenäus Eibl-Eibesfeldt's work, greetings are studied as a means to uncovering some of the evolutionary bases of human behavior. By comparing humans with other species and adult–adult interaction with mother–child interaction (Eibl-Eibesfeldt 1977), greetings are defined as rituals of appeasing and bonding that counteract potentially aggressive behavior during face-to-face encounters. The presupposition here is that humans and animals alike live in a permanent, phylogenetically encoded condition of potential aggression (or fear of aggression) and, were it not for such adaptive rituals as greetings, individuals would be tearing each other apart. Fear of aggression is also used by Kendon and Ferber (1973) to explain eye-gaze aversion during certain phases of human encounters – people look away just as primates and other animals do to avoid the threat of physical confrontation – and by Firth (1972) and others to interpret the common gesture of handshake across societies as a symbol of trust in the other. This line of research is characterized by three features: (i) a focus on nonverbal communication (for example, Eibl-Eibesfeldt's 1972 study of the eyebrow flash), which is often analyzed independently of the talk that accompanies it; (ii) the assumption of shared goals between humans and other species; and (iii) the assumption that the same type of greeting behavior will have the same origin, motivation, or explanation across situations. The focus on nonverbal communication has been important in counterbalancing the logocentric tendency of other studies of greetings (see below) and has revealed commonalities across cultures that would have been missed were researchers concentrating exclusively on verbal behavior. The second feature, namely, the assumption that humans and animals share similar goals, presents certain problems. It might be easy to accept that all species share a concern for survival and safety, but it is less easy to believe that the meaning of such a concern could be the same across species. For instance, Firth (1972), Goffman (1971), and others suggested that greetings in all societies are about continuity of relationships, but the representation, conceptualization, and perception of continuity by humans are likely to be much more complex than those found in other species, partly due to the use of human language (Leach 1972). Furthermore, without minimizing the aggressive potential of human psyche and human action, we must remember that there are other things in life besides fighting or avoiding fights. Hence, even if we accept that greeting behavior might have phylogenetically originated from avoidance behavior, we still must demonstrate that such an origin is relevant to the specific context in which a particular greeting is used.

A second set of studies of greetings is ethnographically oriented. These studies tend to be descriptive in nature, focusing on culture-specific aspects of greeting behaviors, but they also share an interest in a few potentially universal dimensions such as the sequential properties of greeting exchanges and the importance of status definition and manipulation. This is particularly true of two classic studies of African greetings: Esther Goody's (1972) comparison of greeting and begging among the Gonja and the Lodagaa – a stratified and an acephalous society respectively – and Judith Irvine's (1974) study of Wolof greetings.

Ethnographically oriented studies tend to highlight the importance of identity definition in greetings. Some of them also reveal the subtle ways in which greetings are connected to or part of the definition of the ongoing (or ensuing) activity. This is especially the case in Caton's (1986) and Milton's (1982) studies, which provide clear examples not only of the religious dimensions of greetings in some societies but also of how what is said during greetings both presupposes and entails a particular type of social encounter (see also Duranti 1992a).

The emphasis on the sequential nature of greeting exchanges is the most important contribution of the work of conversation analysts. Schegloff and Sacks's work on conversational openings and closings, for instance, shows that greetings should not be analyzed as isolated acts but as a series of pairs, adjacency pairs, whereby the uttering of the first part by one party calls for and at the same time defines the range of a possible "next turn" by a second party, the recipient (Sacks 1992; Schegloff 1968, 1986; Schegloff and Sacks 1973). Sacks's (1975) study of "How are you?" as a "greeting substitute" in English provides a stimulating description of the interactional implications of choosing to greet and choosing to answer in a particular way; we learn why answering "fine" has different consequences from answering "lousy," and hence we are provided with a sociological justification for lying. As I will show later, the extension of these insights into another language and a different speech community shows that it is not always as easy to determine what is a greeting "substitute." Nor is it always the case that routinized questions can be easily answered by lying.

Finally, greetings have been analyzed by speech act theorists, who focused on their function as acknowledgment of another person's presence. Searle (1969) and Searle and Vanderveken (1985) proposed to analyze English greetings as an example of the "expressive" type of speech act,[2] aimed at the "courteous indication of recognition" of the other party (Searle and Vanderveken 1985: 216), and Bach and Harnish (1979) classified greetings as "acknowledgments," their reformulation of Austin's "behabitives"[3] and Searle's "expressives." In line with authors in other research traditions, Searle (1969) and Searle and Vanderveken (1985) also assume that greetings have no propositional content, while Bach and Harnish (1979: 51–2) interpret the act of greeting as an expression of "pleasure at seeing (or meeting)" someone. The claim that greetings have no propositional content – or almost zero referential value (Youssouf et al. 1976) – is at least as old as Malinowski's (1923: 315–16) introduction of the notion of "phatic communion," a concept that was originally meant to recast speech as a mode of action, a form of social behavior that establishes or confirms social relations and does not necessarily communicate "new ideas." The problem with the characterization of greetings as "phatic," and hence merely aimed at establishing or maintaining "contact" (Jakobson 1960), is that it makes it difficult to account for differences across and within communities in what people say during greetings. Finally, the view of greeting as an act that displays pleasure might make sense in some contexts and especially in those situations where verbal greetings are accompanied by smiles and other nonverbal as well as verbal displays of positive affect (for example, the English "Nice to see you"), but it might not be generalizable beyond such cases.

The interest in the biological basis of greetings, their social functions, their sequential organization, and their illocutionary force have revealed a number of recurrent properties of greetings and have presented interesting hypotheses about the form and function of greetings. At the same time, the emphasis on the "social functions" of greetings has contributed to the trivialization of what people actually talk about during greetings. If the only or main goal of greeting is to acknowledge another person's presence, what is actually said during a greeting may be seen as socially insignificant. In this article I argue that this lack of consideration of the propositional content of greetings presents considerable empirical problems, and I suggest that we need ethnographically grounded analyses of greeting expressions to solve such problems.

One of the problems in ignoring the content of verbal greetings is that it establishes loose connections between social functions and the talk used to achieve them. As a consequence, differences in what people say can be ignored and we end up supporting the view that "once you've seen a greeting, you've seen them all," a corollary of the more general principle "once you've seen a ritual, you've seen them all." (Hence, why bother with the study of different societies, given that all you need can be found in your own backyard?)

The context for understanding what people say during greetings is nothing more or nothing less than the culture that supports and is supported by the encounters in which greetings occur or that are constituted by them. The method by which such encounters need to be studied must then minimally include (1) ethnography,[4] (2) the recording of what is actually said, and (3) at least a working definition of the phenomenon that is being investigated. Too many of the existing studies of greetings are based either on observation, interviews, or field notes, without the support of film or electronic recording or on recordings without proper ethnographic work (see Duranti 1997a: ch. 5).

The Universality of Greetings

The starting assumption in this study is that we must be open to all kinds of conventional openings in social encounters as potential cases of greetings. Although some speech communities have activity-specific items that are used only for greetings (the American English "hi!" and the Italian "ciao," for example[5]), the existing literature shows that many communities do not have such expressions, and what people say during greetings might be identical to what is being said during other kinds of speech activities, the English "how're you doing?" being an example of such a type. For this reason, to concentrate only on lexical items and phrases exclusively reserved for greetings (or, more generally, salutations) would be tantamount to admitting that many languages do not have greetings or have a much restricted set of types. The criteria provided below are offered as a solution to this problem.

Criteria for Identifying Greetings across Languages

Building on the studies mentioned above and a few others, it is possible to extract a set of six recurring features to be used as criteria for the identification of greetings in a speech community:

1 near-boundary occurrence;
2 establishment of a shared perceptual field;
3 adjacency pair format;
4 relative predictability of form and content;
5 implicit establishment of a spatiotemporal unit of interaction; and
6 identification of the interlocutor as a distinct being worth recognizing.

As it will become apparent in the following discussion, some of these features could be grouped into larger categories. For example, features 3, 4, and 6 cover what is actually said in greetings, whereas features 2, 5, and 6 are reformulations of what other authors have identified as potential functions of greetings. In addition, features 1 and 5 (and in some ways, 2) define the spatial and temporal organization of the exchange. Although future studies may prove the need to regroup or even eliminate some of the distinctions that I am proposing, for the purpose of this article I have chosen to keep the six criteria distinct to ensure a broader spectrum of potentially relevant cases. Finally, I should mention that although both verbal and nonverbal aspects of greeting behavior were taken into consideration in the choice of defining features, later on in the article, I will favor verbal over nonverbal aspects of greetings. This is simply due to my efforts in this case to draw attention to the importance of the specific verbal expressions used in greetings and is not meant to undermine the importance of gestures and motion in the analysis of social encounters, which I have addressed elsewhere (Duranti 1992a) and intend to return to in the future.

Criterion 1: Near-boundary occurrence

Greetings are routinely expected to occur at the beginning of a social encounter, although they may not always be the very first words that are exchanged between parties. This first feature of greetings is related to their potential function as attention-getting devices and their ability to establish a shared field of interaction (see criteria 2 and 5). As defined here, greetings must then be distinguished from closing salutations or leave takings, despite the fact that in some cases the same expression might function as both opening and closing salutation.[6]

Criterion 2: Establishment of a shared perceptual field

Greetings either immediately follow or are constitutive of the interactants' public recognition of each other's presence in the same perceptual field,[7] as shown by the fact that they are usually initiated after the parties involved have sighted each other (Duranti 1992a; Kendon and Ferber 1973). In some cases, making recognition visually available to the other party may constitute the greeting itself (viz., with a toss of the head, a nod, or an eyebrow flash); in other cases, visual recognition is followed by verbal recognition. There are differences, however, in the timing of the verbal exchange vis-à-vis other forms of mutual recognition or verbal interaction. In some cases, talk may be exchanged before the actual greeting takes place. This is the case, for instance, in the Samoan ceremonial greetings (see below), where participants may exchange jokes, questions, or a few brief remarks before starting to engage in what is seen as the official greeting. A possible hypothesis here is that the more formal – or the more institutionally oriented – the encounter, the more delayed the greeting, and that the more delayed the greeting, the more elaborate the language used. Thus we would expect brief and casual opening salutations to occur simultaneously with or at least very close to mutual sighting and long and elaborate greetings to occur after the parties have had a chance to previously recognize each other's presence in some way. One of the most extreme examples of this delayed greeting is the one described by Sherzer (1983) among the Kuna, where a visiting "chief" who has come to the "gathering house" is greeted after he and his entourage ("typically consisting of his wife, his 'spokesman,' and one of his 'policemen,'") have been taken to someone's house to bathe.

> Then they return to the "gathering house," where the visiting "chief" and one of the host village "chiefs," sitting beside one another in hammocks, perform *arkan kae* (literally handshake), the ritual greeting. (Sherzer 1983: 91)

Such chanted greetings are quite extended, including a long sequence of verses that are regularly responded to by the other chief, who chants *teki* "indeed".

Observationally, this property of greetings is a good index of the function of the greeting and the type of context and participants involved. Immediate and short greetings tend to index an ordinary encounter, whereas delayed and long greetings tend to index something special in the occasion, the social status of the participants, their relationships, or any combination of these various aspects.

This idea of greetings as reciprocal recognitions could be an argument in favor of Bach and Harnish's (1979) classification of greetings as "acknowledgments." Greeting would be a response to finding oneself within someone's visual and/ or auditory range – if such a person is a candidate for recognition. As we shall see, the view of greetings as acknowledgments does not imply the acceptance of Bach and Harnish's view of greeting as a universal expression of attitudes or feelings.

Criterion 3: Adjacency pair format

Although it is possible to speak of a "greeting" by one person, greetings are typically part of one or more sets of adjacency pairs (see Schegloff and Sacks 1973), that is, two-part sequences in which the first pair part by one party (A) invites, constrains, and creates the expectation for a particular type of reply by another party (B); see examples 1, 4, and 6 below. The adjacency pair structure makes sense if greetings are exchanges in which participants test each other's relationship (e.g., Are we still on talking terms? Are we still friends? Do I still recognize your authority? Do I still acknowledge my responsibility toward you?). The sequential format of the adjacency pair allows participants to engage in a joint activity that exhibits some evidence of mutual recognition and mutual understanding. The number, utterance type, and participant structure of these pairs vary both within and across communities (see Duranti 1992a: 660–2).[8] For example, some African greetings are organized in several adjacency pairs (Irvine 1974).

If we take the adjacency pair format to be a defining feature of greetings, a one-pair-part greeting – not as uncommon as one might think – would be "defective" or in need of an explanation.

Criterion 4: Relative predictability of form and content

Since what is said during a greeting or part of a greeting exchange is highly predictable compared to other kinds of interactions, researchers have often assumed that greetings have no propositional content and their denotational value (to be assessed in terms of truth) can be largely ignored. Whether people say "hi," "good morning," or "how are you?" has been seen as an index of properties of the context (for example, the relationship between the parties, the nature of the social encounter) rather than as a concern participants manifest toward gaining access to new information about their interlocutors. This aspect of greetings needs to be further qualified in at least three ways. First, it should be made clear that information is exchanged in human encounters regardless of whether there is talk. Even when there is no speech, there are usually plenty of semiotic resources in an encounter for participants to give out information about themselves and make inferences about others. Such semiotic resources are based on or include participants' mere physical presence, their gestures, posture, and movements, their clothes, the objects they carry or the tools they are using. Second, there is information exchanged beyond the propositional content of what is said. For example, prosodic and paralinguistic features are a rich source of cues for contextualization (Gumperz 1992). Finally, even common formulaic expressions can be informative. In fact, if we start from the assumption that what is said and done in any human encounter lives along a formulaic–creative continuum, greetings might simply be interactions that tend to fall toward the formulaic side. We cannot, however, in principle assume that, because greetings are formulaic, (i) they are always completely predictable, (ii) they have no information value, and (iii) participants have nothing invested in the propositional value of what is said. First, the fact of considering an exchange highly routinized does not make its content completely predictable or uninteresting for social analysis, a point well illustrated by Bourdieu's (1977) analysis of gift exchange and Schegloff's (1986) discussion of telephone openings. It is still important to ascertain how participants manage to achieve the expected or preferred outcome. Second, the occurrence of certain routine and highly predictable questions and answers during greetings does not imply that the parties involved do not exchange some new information. Third, whether or not the participants are interested in the information that is being exchanged should be an empirical question and not an unquestioned assumption.

Criterion 5: Implicit establishment of a spatiotemporal unit of interaction

The occurrence of greetings defines a unit of interaction. Sacks (1975) alluded to this feature of greetings by saying that they occur only once in an interaction and that they can constitute a "minimal proper conversation." More generally, greetings clearly enter into the definition of larger units of analysis such as a day at work, different parts of the day with family members, or even extended interactions over several months – for example, when done through electronic mail (Duranti 1986). That the "unit" is something more complex than a continuous stretch of time (e.g., a day) is shown by the fact that two people meeting in two different places during the same day may in fact exchange greetings again. An empirical investigation of when greetings are exchanged throughout a day by a given group of people who repeatedly come into each other's interactional space might provide important clues on how they conceptualize the different space-time zones in which they operate. It might also give us a sense of the relation between natural units (such as a day–night cycle) versus cultural units (such as a meeting).

Criterion 6: Identification of the interlocutor as a distinct being worth recognizing

The occurrence of greetings and the ways in which they are carried out typically identify a particular class of people. Syntagmatically, a greeting item (e.g., English "hello," "hi," "hey, how're you doing," "what's up") might be accompanied by address terms or other context-dependent and context-creating signs that identify participants as belonging to social groups of various sorts. Paradigmatically, the very use of greetings (as opposed to their absence) identifies a group of people as members of the class of individuals with whom we communicate in public or private arenas. That this is more than a tautology may be shown in various ways, including Sacks's (1975) arguments that in English the people we greet with the (substitute) greeting "how are you?" constitute a class he called "proper conversationalists." Even in those societies in which apparently *any* two people entering the same perceptual field would be expected to exchange greetings, distinctions are in fact made. Thus, for instance, among the Tuareg, according to Youssouf et al. (1976: 801), once two people are seen progressing toward one another, the parties *must* meet, and once they have met, they must greet each other. Such moral imperatives, however, must be understood against the background of a social world in which avoiding greeting would be interpreted as a potentially threatening situation:

> The desert people have a history of intertribal warfare and intratribal feuds. If the Targi meets another, or others, in [the desert], the identification of the other – as early as possible – is critically important. For, once another person is sighted on a intersecting trajectory, there is no turning aside ... for that can be interpreted as a sign of either fear or potential treachery and ambush, which invites countermeasures. (Youssouf et al. 1976: 801)

This means that, implicitly, the use of greetings can distinguish between Us and Them, insiders and outsiders, friends and foes, valuable and nonvaluable interactants. For example, in many societies children and servants are not greeted. The absence of greetings then marks these individuals not only as nonproper conversationalists or strangers but also as not worth the attention implied by the use of greetings.

An Empirical Case Study

Any proposal for universal criteria needs empirical investigations to support it. In the rest of this article, I will offer a brief discussion of Samoan greetings as a way of assessing and refining some of the claims made so far. In particular, I will be concerned with two main issues: (i) the relationship between universal features and culture-specific instantiations of such features, and (ii) the distinction between verbal expressions that are greetings and those that, although they might look like potential candidates, are not greetings.

It should be understood that what follows is not an exhaustive study of Samoan greetings. Such a study would require a project expressively designed with the goal of collecting all types of greetings used in Samoan communities;[9] in fact, as far as I know, such a comprehensive project has never been attempted for any speech community. Although the data discussed here are drawn from a range of interactions originally recorded for other purposes, they do contain a considerable number of exchanges that qualify as greetings according to the above mentioned criteria. Furthermore, in using Samoan data, I have the advantage of relying on previous studies of language in context carried out by myself or other researchers.

Four Types of Samoan Greetings

On the basis of the criteria mentioned above, I examined audio- and videotaped data collected in a Samoan community during three periods for a total of a year and a half of fieldwork.[10] I identified four types of exchanges that can qualify as "greetings": (1) *tālofa* greetings; (2) ceremonial greetings; (3) *mālō* greetings; and (4) "where are you going?" greetings.[11] The analysis presented here is also based on my own observation of and participation in hundreds if not thousands of Samoan greeting exchanges.

Before discussing these four types of greetings, I need to mention a few basic facts about the community where I worked; more detailed information on this community may be found in Duranti 1981 and 1994 and in Ochs 1988. (For a more comprehensive ethnography of Samoan social life, see Shore 1982.)

Despite modernization and a considerable amount of syncretism in religious and political practices, members of the Samoan community where I carried out research still hang on to traditional Polynesian values of family relations and mutual dependence. Their society is still divided between titled individuals (*matai*) and untitled ones (*taulele'a*), and the matai are distinguished according to status (chiefs, orators) and rank (high chief, lower-ranking chiefs). Having a title usually comes with rights over land and its products and the duty to participate in decision-making processes such as the political meetings called *fono* (see Duranti 1994). Status and rank distinctions are pervasive in everyday and ceremonial life in a Samoan village. The language marks such distinctions in a number of ways, the most obvious of which is a special lexicon called *'upu fa'aaloalo* "respectful words" used in addressing people of high status and in talking about them in certain contexts (see Duranti 1992b; Milner 1961; Shore 1982). Such words are part of some of the greeting exchanges that I will discuss below.

None of the greetings I discuss qualifies as the most "basic" or unmarked greeting item or exchange in Samoan society. As I will show below, the greeting that is the highest on the "formulaic" end of the formulaic-creative continuum, and hence with the least propositional content, "tālofa," is the rarest in everyday life and hence is an unlikely candidate for the role of the most basic type or the one the other greetings are substituting for.

The tālofa greeting

This greeting can be used in a number of settings, including open and closed areas (for example, either outside or inside a house), whenever two people become visibly and acoustically accessible to each other. Unlike the other Samoan greetings I will discuss below, the tālofa greeting is at times accompanied by handshaking, a gesture likely borrowed from past Western visitors and colonial authorities. In fact, this is a greeting that is today most commonly used with foreigners. Contrary to what was described by Margaret Mead (1928: 14), people from the same village today rarely greet each other with "tālofa" (see Holmes 1987: 112),[12] which is reserved for people who have not seen each other for a while or have never met before (hence its common use with foreigners and guests from abroad). In an hour-long audiotape of an "inspection committee" (*asiasiga*) going around the village and meeting dozens of people, I found three examples of "tālofa." All three examples involve only one member of the inspection committee (Chief S, the highest ranking chief of the group) who initiates the greeting. In one case, "tālofa" was exchanged with a group of chiefs from another village waiting for the bus. Although I have no information on the people who were greeted with "tālofa" in the other two cases, the interaction is not incompatible with the hypothesis that the parties involved had not seen each other for a while or are not very familiar with one another.[13]

Like the expressions used in the other Samoan greetings, *tālofa* may occur by itself or may be accompanied by an address term, either a name or a title, for example, "tālofa ali'i!," or "greetings sir(s)!" Here is an example that shows the adjacency pair format of the greeting and its rather simple AB structure:

(1) [*Inspection, December 1978: While standing outside, the committee members have been interacting with a woman who is inside the house, when Chief S directly addresses another woman from the same family, Kelesia.*]

CHIEF S: tālofa Kelesia!
Hello Kelesia!
(0.2)
KELESIA: tālofa!
Hello!
CHIEF S: ((*chuckles*)) hehe.

Tālofa is homophonous with and probably derived from the expression *tālofa* or *tālofae* – usually pronounced /kaalofa/ and /kaalofae/, respectively[14] (see the appendix) – used to display empathy for someone who is judged to be suffering or under any form of distress (see also Ochs 1988: 173). This other use of the expression *tālofa* is found in the following excerpt from the same transcript, where a member of the inspection committee invites the others to feel sorry for the old woman Litia, who got up at dawn in order to clean her lawn in time for the committee's inspection. As shown by the following comment by Chief S, Tūla'i's sympathy is not shared by everyone else. In the next turn, Chief S proposes, albeit with some hesitation, to fine Litia.

(2) [*Inspection: The orator Tūla'i sees the old woman Litia, here pronounced /Likia/, cutting the grass.*][15]

1 TŪLA'I: kālofa sē ia Likia- 'ua uso pō e-
empathy Voc Emp Litia Perf rise rise night Comp
Hey, feel sorry for Litia. (She) got up at dawn to –
2 CHIEF S: 'ae- 'ae- 'ae- 'ae kakau ga // sala
but but but but ought to fine
But, but, but, but she should be fined.
3 LITIA: e sēsē mātou i le faimea taeao.
Pres wrong we:excl-pl in Art do-thing morning
We shouldn't be doing things in the morning.

This example shows that it is not the occurrence of a particular expression that defines an utterance as a greeting. Whereas in (1) Chief S uses *tālofa* as the first pair part of a greeting exchange with Kelesia, in (2) the orator Tūla'i uses *tālofa* as an attempt to draw sympathy for the old woman Litia (pronounced /Likia/ in line 1) but not to greet her. In fact, the ensuing interaction with Litia does not contain a greeting. In an apparent response to the men's comments, Litia's first turn in line 3 is a negative assessment of her being up and running early in the morning, which could be interpreted as veiled apology.

In his Samoan–English dictionary, G. B. Milner (1966) suggests that *tālofa* is a compound made out of the words *tā* "strike" and *alofa* "love, have compassion." *Ta* could also be the first-person singular, positive-affect pronoun. In this case the long /aa/ (spelled *ā*) would be accounted for by the combination of two consecutive /a/ : *ta* + *alofa* → / taalofa /, originally meaning "(poor) me feels sorry." Although *tālofa* as a greeting does not have the same meaning of *tālofa* as an expression of empathy and therefore looks like a good candidate for a word with very little or no propositional content, specialized for greetings, its rarity in everyday life makes it an unlikely candidate as the unmarked greeting in a Samoan speech community.

The mālō greeting

In my data, this greeting is most commonly used when one party (A) arrives at a site where the other party (B) already is. It has the structure given in (3).

(3) *Mālō-greeting:*
A: mālō (+ intensifier) (+ address + title or name)
B: mālō (+ intensifier) (+ address + title or name)

The word *mālō* has several meanings in Samoan. Its use as an opening salutation is closely related to its use as a compliment or encouragement to people who are working or have just finished doing something (see below).[16] An example of the mālō greeting is provided in (4), from an audiorecording of the "Inspection" tape mentioned above:

(4) [*Inspection: The committee members, including Afoa, a chief, and Tūla'i, an orator, arrive at the orator Taipī's family compound and see Taipī's wife Si'ilima.*]

1 AFOA: MĀLŌ SI'ILIMA!
Congratulations/hello Si'ilima!
2 (0.5)
3 SI'ILIMA: mālō!
Congratulations/hello!
4 (0.5)
5 AFOA: 'ua lelei mea 'uma!
Everything is fine!
[
6 TŪLA'I: māgaia – (0.3)
māgaia le- (0.5)
le fagua: –
Nice – the land looks nice – [17]
7 Si'ilima
Si'ilima
8 (2.5)
9 TŪLA'I: fea le koeaiga?
Where (is) the old man? [. . .]

Here, line 1 contains the first pair part, and line 3 contains the second pair part. In this case, the structure of the exchange is:

(5)
A: mālō + Name (first pair part)
B: mālō (second pair part)

In other cases, we might find more complex turns not only with names but also with titles and intensifiers (e.g., *lava* "much, indeed").

(6) [*Inspection*]

TŪLA'I:	mālō ali'i Faikaumakau!	(mālō + address + title)
	Congratulations, Mr. Faitaumatau!	
FAITAU-MATAU:	mālō lava.	(mālō + intensifier)
	Much congratulations.	

In most cases, the exchange is initiated by the arriving party. This makes sense if we interpret this use of *mālō* as a greeting as an extension of the use of *mālō* as an expression of congratulation to someone who is engaged in a task or has just successfully completed one. In the latter case, called the "*mālō* exchange" in Duranti and Ochs (1986), the first *mālō* recognizes one party's work or activity and the second *mālō* recognizes the role played by the supporter(s) (*tāpua'i*). The second *mālō* in this case is usually followed by the adverb (intensifier) *fo'i* "quite, also," which further underscores the reciprocity of the exchange. Differently from the greeting *mālō*, the complimenting *mālō* typically occurs in the middle of an interaction; hence it does not conform to the first two criteria described above (near-boundary occurrence and establishment of a shared perceptual field). But when the complimenting *mālō* does occur at the beginning of an encounter, it can function as both a compliment and a greeting. An example of this use of *mālō* is provided in excerpt (7), where the woman Amelia surprises the inspecting committee (see the "repair" particle *'oi* in Tūla'i's response) by initiating the interaction with a congratulating "mālō." This *mālō* is followed by the display of the reason for her congratulations, namely, their "inspecting" or "visiting." (*le asiasi* is the nominalization of the predicate *asiasi* "visit, inspect."[18])

(7) [*Inspection*]

AMELIA:	mālō ā le asiasi!
	congratulations Emp Art visit
	Congratulations indeed (for) the inspecting!
TŪLA'I:	'oi / / mālō!
	oh! // congratulations!
CHIEF AFOA:	mālō fo'i.
	Congratulations also (to you).
TŪLA'I:	'ua 'ou iloa::-
	I realize that –
AMELIA:	pulegu'u ma oukou kōfā i le komiki!
	mayor and you-all honorable (orators) in the committee
	(To the) mayor and you honorable (orators) in the committee!
TŪLA'I:	mālō / / lava iā ke 'oe le kigā!
	congratulations Emp to you the mother
	Congratulations indeed to you, the mother (of the family)!
	[. . .]

In this case, the exchange is enacted as a series of reciprocal compliments, as shown by the syntax of the last utterance by Tūla'i: "*mālō* indeed to you, the mother (of the family)!," but it also works as a greeting. This is predictable given that it conforms to the six criteria introduced earlier and no other greeting with Amelia follows.

In 1978, I was told by a Samoan instructor who had taught Peace Corps volunteers not to use *mālō* as a greeting. He, like other adult Samoans with whom I spoke, considered the use of *mālō* as a greeting a relatively recent and degenerate extension of the use of *mālō* as a compliment. (This view is supported by the fact that *mālō* is not mentioned as a greeting in any of the earlier ethnographic accounts.)

How can we explain the extension of the *mālō* from one context to the other? In the mālō greeting, the party who is about to enter another's living space calls out to the other by starting an exchange of mutual support and recognition. Since the other is likely to be busy doing something or to have just finished doing something, *mālō* is an extension of the one used in those contexts in which one party is more explicitly seen as "doing something" and the other as "supporting the other party's efforts." When the mālō exchange is started by the person who is stationary (e.g., inside a house), it could be seen as an extension of a congratulatory act to the newcomer for having made it to the present location, overcoming whatever obstacles he encountered or could have encountered.

In its ambiguous state between a congratulating act and a greeting act, this Samoan greeting shares certain similarities with the English "How are you?" discussed by Sacks (1975) and others. In both cases, we have a greeting item that is not exclusively used for greeting and in fact is imported, as it were, into the greeting exchange from other uses and contexts. In both cases, we have a relative or incomplete ritualization of the term so that it can be still taken "literally." There still is, in other words, some of the force of the mālō compliment in the mālō greeting. At the same time, differently from the English "How are you?," we cannot define the mālō greeting as a "greeting substitute" because there is no other obvious candidate for the same types of situations.

Ceremonial greetings

Ceremonial greetings are typically exchanged when a high status person (e.g., a titled individual [or *matai*], a government official, a minister of the church, a deacon, a head nurse) arrives at what is either foreseen or framed as an official visit or formal event. As discussed in Duranti (1992a), ceremonial greetings (CGs) only take place after the newly arrived party goes to sit down in the "front region" of the house. CGs are the most complex among the four types of Samoan greetings discussed here. They are made of two main parts, a first pair part, the "welcoming," and a second pair part, the "response."

(8)
A: [WELCOMING]
B: [RESPONSE]

Each of these two parts may, in turn, be divided in two major subcomponents, a predicate and an address.

(9)

WELCOMING	RESPONSE
a. Welcoming predicate	a. Responding predicate
b. Address	b. Address

The welcoming predicates recognize the arrival of the new party and welcome him or her into the house. They are the same predicates that in different contexts function as verbs of motion meaning "arrive, come." A list of some such verbs is given in table 8.1, with information relative to the specific social status indexed by each term. Whereas *maliu* and *sosopo* are said to (and imply that the addressee is) an orator (*tulāfale*), the verb *afio* is used with (and implies that the addressee is) a chief (*ali'i*). The deictic particle *mai*, which accompanies all of them, expresses an action toward the speaker or, more precisely, toward the deictic center (see Platt 1982), which in all the cases discussed here is the totality of the shared space already occupied by the welcoming party and defined according to the physical shape of the house (see Duranti 1992a).

The responding predicate exhibits less variation and is often omitted. The address is the most complex part and the one that allows for more variation. It can also be repeated when the speaker differentiates among the addressees:

(10) Address:

a. Address form
b. Generic title
c. Name (specific) title
d. Ceremonial attributes (taken from *fa'alupega*[19])

The address may have up to these four parts. The address form (see table 8.2) shows distinctions similar to the ones found in the welcoming predicates. Some of the forms are in fact nominalizations of those predicates. The distinction between what I call a generic title and a name title is found only in some cases. In the village of Falefā, where I conducted my research, there were two orator title names (Iuli

Table 8.1 Welcoming predicates used during ceremonial greetings (CGs)

Samoan termt	*English translation*	*Social index*
maliu mai	"welcome"	<orator>
sosopo mai	"welcome"	<orator>
afio mai	"welcome"	<chief>
susū mai	"welcome"	<chief or orator>[a]

[a] This particular verb is used with the holders of titles descending from the high chief Malietoa and can be used with either a chief or an orator. It is also the most commonly used term for high status individuals who are not matai, e.g. pastors, school teachers, doctors, government officials. It is thus often used as an "unmarked" term when one is not sure of the social identity of the addressee or when one knows that the addressee does not have a title but wishes to treat him or her with deference. In my living experience in a Samoan village I moved from being addressed with *susū mai* in the earlier stages to more specific terms such as *afio mai* later on in my stay.

Table 8.2 Address forms according to status

Samoan term	*English translation*	*Social index*
lau tōfā	"your honor/highness"	<orator>
lau afioga	"your honor/highness"	<chief>
lau susuga	"your honor/highness"	<chief or orator>

and Moe'ono) that also had a generic title, Matua, which I have elsewhere translated as "senior orator" (Duranti 1981, 1994).

Any of the following combinations were commonly used during CGs and other formal exchanges in addressing the people holding the Iuli or Moe'ono title:

- an address form (*lau tōfā* "your honor")
- address form + generic title (*lau tōfā* + *le Matua* "your honor + the senior orator")[20]
- address form + generic title + name title (*lau tōfā* + *le Matua* + *Iuli* "your honor + the senior orator + Iuli" or *lau tōfā* + *le Matua* + *Moe'ono* "your honor + the senior orator + Moe'ono").

If a person has a *matai* title, the name given at birth (called *igoa taule'ale'a* "untitled name") will not be used in the CG. Only those who do not have a *matai* title – such as pastors, some government officials, and foreigners – might be greeted with the address form followed by the birth name. For example, a pastor whose untitled name is Mareko would be addressed as "lau susuga Mareko" (your honorable Mareko). In this case, the proper name replaces the "name title." If a person does not have a *matai* title and does not hold a religious or administrative office and his name is not known to the welcoming party, a title must be found for the CG to be complete. The title may be borrowed from someone else in the family. (For example, he might be greeted as if he were a titled person to whom he is related; this is a convention used with untitled people when they perform ceremonial roles on behalf of their family, village, or religious congregation.) Other times, an ad hoc "title" is created on the spot based on whatever information about the newcomer is contextually available. For example, people who did not know me personally often referred to me as "the guest from abroad" (*le mālō mai i fafo*). If they saw me filming, I became "the cameraman": *le ali'i pu'e ata*, lit. "the (gentle)man (who) takes pictures."

The adjacency pair structure of the CGs is hard to perceive at first, and these greetings are particularly hard to transcribe because they are typically performed by several people at once and never in unison. This means that the speech of the different participants typically overlaps and interlocks, producing a non-chanted fugue (Duranti 1997b). Here is an example from a meeting of the village council (*fono*). One of the two senior orators in the village, Moe'ono, has just arrived and gone to sit in the front part of the house. The orator Falefā, who is the village "mayor" (*pulenu'u*) and whose house is being used for the meeting, initiates the greeting and is followed by a few other members of the council. (I have here slightly simplified the transcript for expository reasons.)

(11) [*Monday Fono, August 1988; ceremonial greeting of senior orator Moe'ono*]

FALEFĀ: ia'. māliu mai lau kōfā i le Makua
Well. Welcome your highness, the senior orator.
MALAGA: lau kōfā i le Makua
Your highness, the senior orator
(2.0)
?: lau kōfā i le Makua
Your highness, the senior orator
(2.0)
MOE'ONO: ia'. ('e'e ka'ia) le kākou gu'u
Well. ((I) submit to) our village
[
??: (lau kōfā le Ma:kua)
(*Your highness, the senior orator*)
(7.0)
MOE'ONO: mamalu i le- (1.0) susuga a le ali'i pule-gu'u gei
dignity of the – (1.0) highness of Mr. Mayor here
(7.0)

This exchange seems to qualify easily as a greeting, according to the six criteria established above. Like other exchanges I have either witnessed or recorded, this one occurs a little after the newcomer, Moe'ono, has arrived to the house (criterion 1) (but see more on this later). It also defines a shared perceptual field, as defined by the welcoming predicate with its deictic particle *mai* (criterion 2). The greeting is sequentially organized as an adjacency pair (criterion 3). The expressions used in greeting are predictable but not completely so (criterion 4). The exchange establishes the ensuing interaction as a formal one in which public identities will be evoked, in this case, a formal meeting of the village council (criterion 5 (see Irvine, chapter 7 of this volume)). Moe'ono is recognized as a distinct interlocutor (criterion 6). Sometimes, however, other greetings or greeting like items precede or follow the CG. For example, before the CG shown in (11) above, one of the people in the house uses a *mālō* with Moe'ono – although no audible response can be heard – and a few minutes later, Moe'ono himself exchanges *mālō* with an orator who has just come in and has already been greeted with a CG. My hypothesis is that these other greetings or greetinglike exchanges are between different social personae and that they are performing a different kind of work. The CG recognizes the party's positional identity that is judged relevant to the forthcoming activity, typically a formal type of exchange (e.g., a political or business meeting, a ceremonial exchange), and is done between an individual as a representative of a group and a collectivity (the people already in the house).[21] The *mālō* greeting, on the other hand, although it may be addressed to collectivities,[22] usually is a preliminary to short and relatively informal exchanges. Its use projects a sense of immediacy and is a prelude to some business that can be easily dealt with, without even entering the house. Example (12) below reproduces some of the verbal interaction preceding the CG illustrated in (11). Senior orator Moe'ono and the orator Talaitau have arrived at the same time, but only Moe'ono goes to sit in the front region of the house; this transcript starts a few seconds before the one in (11) above and shows that the notion of "acknowledgment" or "recognition" proposed by speech act theorists as the illocutionary force of greetings must be qualified. We need to specify what is being acknowleged. Physical presence? Status? Social role in the ensuing interaction? For example, when we enlarge the context of the CG in (11), we find out that both Moe'ono's physical presence and his status have already been recognized before the CG is produced. After Moe'ono's remark about the presence of the videocamera in lines 5 and 6, the orator Manu'a provides a justification for the presence of the videocamera (lines 13–15), which starts with a formulaic apology (starting with the expression "vaku . . . ") indexing Moe'ono's higher rank. Manu'a might be apologizing for a number of things, including his speaking at all to such a high-status person before proper greetings have been exchanged, his speaking about such nondignified matters as videotaping, or his (and the other matai's) failure to ask for Moe'ono's approval before allowing the camera to be used.[23]

(12) [*Monday Meeting, August 1988*]

1 MOE'ONO: (he) sole!
(Hey) brother!
2 ?: ((to a woman outside)) (ai) suga!
(?) *Sister!*
3 ?: (??)
4 MANU'A: 'e- mālō lava!
Tns- congratulation Emph
Is – hello, hello!
5 MOE'ONO: māgaia ali'i le- lea ke va'ai aku ali'i
Nice sir, the – that I see sir(s),
e fai le pu'ega aka ali'i (o le –)
there are pictures taken sirs (of the –)
[
7 TALAITAU: (?sē)
(?Hey)
8 oi. oi sole!
Uh-oh, brother!
[
9 MOE'ONO: o le kākou fogo ali'i
of our meeting sirs
10 TALAITAU: ai 'o le ā le mea lea ga ili ai le pū a le pulenu'u.
Maybe that's why the horn of the mayor was blown.
[
11 MANU'A: (leai fa'afekai)
(*No thanks.*)
12 (0.7)
13 'e vaku lau kōfā le Makua,
With due respect, your highness the senior orator,
14 (2.0)
15 'o si koe – 'o si koe'iga e sau e pu'e – se aka o (le –)
The dear old ma – the dear old man comes to film (the –)
16 (1.0)
17 ?MOE'ONO: ((Sigh)) haaaa!
Haaaa!
18 MANU'A: o:: –
19 ?: (??lea)
20 (3.0)
21 ??: (??fagu?)
22 ?: (leai!)
(No!)
23 ??: (???)
[
24 MOE'ONO: e lelei kele le ali'i 'o Falefā
Mr. Falefā is very good
25 FALEFĀ: ia'. māliu mai lau kōfā i le Makua
Well. Welcome your highness, the senior orator.

If acknowledgments of physical presence, status, and rank have already been done, the CG, which is started by the orator and mayor Falefā in line 25, must do something more. I suggest that the CG allows the people present to *collectively* recognize Moe'ono's presence *as* the senior orator, someone who has specific rights and duties within the forthcoming event, the meeting of the fono. Conversely, the CG gives Moe'ono the opportunity to recognize the presence and hence future role played by the rest of the assembly. *It is as social actors engaged or about to be engaged in a particular (and to some extent predictable) type of interaction that participants' presence is recognized by means of a CG.*

It is, of course, possible to argue that CGs are not *real* greetings and a distinction should be made between "greetings" and "welcomings," with the CGs being an example of the latter. The translation of the predicates used in the first pair part would support this hypothesis. My experience in this community, however, makes me reluctant to accept this hypothesis. Rather, I would favor seeing CGs as the type of greeting exchange that is appropriate for high-ranking individuals who meet in a closed area, which is likely to be the site for further activities also involving or indexing their positional roles. This position is supported by a number of observations.

In Samoa, I heard high-ranking persons who met on the road, for example, while inside a car, apologize for the improper way in which they find themselves in each other's presence. The expression used is "leaga tātou te feiloa'i i le auala" ([too] bad [that] we meet on the road). This expression was explained to me by a person who had just used it to imply that meeting on the road is not the proper way for high-ranking people to come together. In other words, the implication is "we should have met elsewhere." Where? For instance, at someone's house. If such a meeting had taken place, ceremonial greetings would have been exchanged (as well as food and perhaps gifts). This, to me, indicates that for high-ranking Samoans ceremonial greetings are part of what makes an encounter proper or canonical.

The formality or ritualistic nature of the CGs is not a reason for not considering them greetings. For one thing, such formality is quite common in everyday encounters. As documented by Bradd Shore, Margaret Mead, and other ethnographers, Samoans are used to rapidly shifting, within the same setting, from an apparently casual exchange to a much more formal one, in which fancy epithets and metaphors are used and individuals get addressed with longer names, inside of longer turns at talk. In other words, CGs are much more routine than we might think and, in fact, statistically much more common than the tālofa greeting. In Western Samoa, whenever I went to visit persons of high status, if I entered their house and sat on the floor in the "front region" (see Duranti 1992a, 1994), I would be greeted with a CG. No matter how hard I tried at times to avoid the CG by acting informally and engaging my hosts in conversation, I was rarely able to avoid it. After a few seconds of my arrival, someone would clear his or her voice and start a CG with the usual shifting activity marker *ia'* "well, so." Only kids or young, untitled folks may enter and leave a house without being the target of CGs. Part of this sharp social asymmetry is still at work in the Samoan community in Los Angeles, where young and untitled members of the families I visited are never introduced to me and do not expect to participate in the greeting rituals that in American society often include the youngest children in the family.

The "where are you going?" greeting

When two parties, at least one of whom is ostensibly going somewhere, cross one another's visual field of perception and are close enough for their voices to be heard by one another (the volume of the parties' voices being adjusted proportionally to the physical distance between them), they may engage in what I will call the "where are you going?" greeting:[24]

(13) Scheme of "where are you going?" greeting
1 A: Where are you going?
2 B: I'm going to [goal].

This goal may be either a place or a task.

First, we must recognize that the adjacency pair in the scheme in (13) conforms to the criteria introduced earlier for greetings. It is typically used when party B is seen moving along the road or a nearby path by party A, who is stationary (e.g., inside a house, in front of a store), but it can also be found in cases in which A and B pass each other on the road. Under these circumstances, the initiator usually stops to address the other (moving party), who may or not also stop to respond. (This is different from the Mehinaku greeting discussed in Gregor 1977.)

The greeting may continue with a leave-taking exchange of the following kind:

(14) Leave-taking after "where are you going?" greeting
3 A: Then go.
4 B: I/we go.

The existence of "where are you going?" greetings in Samoan and other languages (see Firth 1972; Gregor 1977; Hanks 1990) suggests that we cannot easily extend to other speech communities Searle's analysis of English greetings as an expressive type of speech act (see above). As may be gathered by an examination of its content, the "where are you going?" greeting is more than an expression of a psychological state. It is an attempt to sanction the reciprocal recognition of one another's presence with some specific requests of information that may or may not receive satisfactory response. Although they are highly predictable and conventional, "where are you going?" greetings force participants to deal with a wide range of issues including an individual's or group's right to have access to information about a person's whereabouts, culture-specific expectations about the ethics of venturing into public space, the force of questioning as a form of social control and hence the possibility of withholding information as a form of resistance to public scrutiny and moral judgment (Keenan 1976). As in the neighboring language of Tokelau (Hoëm 1993: 143, 1995: 29), Samoan speakers who greet with the "where are you going?" question feel that they have the right to an answer, and the question itself is a form of social control. With the last part of the exchange, shown in (14), the questioner formally grants the other party permission to go. The speech act analysis proposed for English greetings, then, cannot be easily extended to these greetings, given that to initiate a "where are you going?" greeting is definitely more than (or different from) a "courteous indication of recognition" (Searle and Vanderveken 1985: 216) or a conventional expression of pleasure at the sight of someone (Bach and Harnish 1979: 51–2). To ask "where are you going?" is a request for an account, which may include the reasons for being away from one's home, on someone else's territory, or on a potentially dangerous path. To answer such a greeting may imply that one commits oneself not only to the truthfulness of one's assertion but also to the appropriateness of one's actions. It is not by accident, then, that in some cases speakers might try to be as evasive as possible. Samoans, for instance, often reply to the "where are you going?" greeting question with the vague "to do an errand" (*fai le fe'au*). Even when they give what appear to be more specific statements such as "I'm going to buy something," "I'm going to wait for the bus," and "I'm going to Apia," speakers are still holding on to their right to release only a minimum amount of information – with bragging being an obvious exception ("I'm going down to the store to buy a five pound can of corn beef for Alesana!"). Just as in the Malagasy situation discussed by Elinor Ochs Keenan (1976), the tendency in these encounters is to violate Grice's (1975) cooperative principle and not to be too informative.

The violation of this principle, however, does not have the same implications discussed by Sacks (1975) regarding the American passing-by greeting "How are you?". In the American case, the common assumption is that the party who asks the question as a greeting is not really interested in an accurate or truthful answer. It is this lack of interest that justifies what Sacks sees as a social justification for "lying." People are expected to provide a positive assessment (*fine, good, okay*) regardless of how they are actually doing or feeling at the moment. In the Samoan case, instead, questioners would like to know as much as possible about the other's whereabouts, and the vagueness in the answer is an attempt by the responding party to resist the information-seeking force of the greeting. Furthermore, the consequences of one's answer are also different. Whereas in the American English greeting substitute "How are you?," as argued by Sacks, a lie is a preferred answer regardless of its truth value, in the case of the Samoan "Where are you going?" greeting, vagueness is conventionally accepted, but violation of truth is potentially problematic if later detected.

That the Samoan "Where are you going?" greeting is, at least in part, about rights and duties, expectations, and possible violations is shown by the fact that, when questioned by someone with higher authority, Samoan speakers might be expected to give more specific answers. Likewise, they might display their uneasiness about a situation in which they have been placed, uneasiness about the very fact of being visible and hence vulnerable to public questioning by someone with authority. This is indeed the case in (15) below. In this example, the inspection committee encounters a group of young men on the road. One of the members of the committee, the orator Tūla'i, recognizes a young man from his extended family and addresses him:

(15) *[Inspection]*

A	1	TŪLA'I:	fea (a)li('i) a alu iai le kou – kegi 'i ukā? *Where (sir) are you going inland with your pals?*
B	2	YOUNG MAN:	sē vage afioga ali'i ma kulāfale mākou ke ō aku 'i ukā *With your permission, honorable chiefs and orators, we are going inland*
	3		e – (0.8) e kapega mai le – (0.2) suāvai – (0.2) – o le Aso Sā. *to – (0.8) prepare the – (0.2) food (0.2) – for Sunday.*
A	4	TŪLA'I:	ia' ō loa ('ā) *Okay, go then,*
B	5	Other man:	(mākou) ō. *(We) go.*

The way in which this exchange is played out illustrates a number of important points about the social organization presupposed by the encounter, as well as the social organization achieved by it. First, the content displays a noticeable status asymmetry between A and B (which is represented by more than one speaker). Despite the relatively polite questioning by orator Tūla'i (the address form "ali'i" he uses does not have the gender and age selectional restrictions as the English "sir" or the Spanish "señor" but does convey some consideration for the person addressed),[25] there is no question that in lines 2 and 3 the young speaker does his best to show appreciation of the specific statuses represented by the members of the inspection committee, since the respectful term /afioga ali'i/ refers to the chiefs in the committee and the term /kulaafale/ refers to the orators. These terms are in contrast with the casual, almost "slang" word /kegi/, a borrowing from the English *gang*, used by the orator Tūla'i in referring to the young man's group. Furthermore, the young man also indicates through his opening remark /vage/, an apologetic expression for an unbecoming (past or future) act (corresponding to the /vaku/ we saw earlier in (12), line 13) that anything he might do or say to such a distinguished audience is likely going to be inappropriate. In fact, even his group's presence in front of the committee may be seen as an inappropriate interference in the chiefs' and orators' actions, or at least in their interactional space. There are some remnants here of possible avoidance relations with people of high *mana* that have been characterized as typical of ancient Polynesia (Valeri 1985).

Despite the conventionality of the exchange, what is said and how it is said is extremely important. The illocutionary point or goal of the greeting is not just "a courteous indication of recognition, with the presupposition that the speaker has just encountered the hearer" (Searle and Vanderveken 1985: 215). Although recognition is certainly involved, the exchange plays out a set of social relations and cultural expectations about where parties should be at a particular time of the day and what they should be doing then, all expressed through an actual exchange of information about the parties' whereabouts. It is the higher status party, that is, the orator Tūla'i in this case, who asks the question. The only thing the young men can do is answer as quickly and as politely as possible and hope for a quick and uneventful exchange. In this interpretive frame, the final granting of permission to go ("ia' ō loa") is also ambiguous between a formulaic closure (corresponding to the English "See you" or "Good-bye") and a meaningful sanction of the young men's goals and destination by a man of higher authority.

Expressions That Are Not Greetings

Given my claim that the six criteria introduced above should allow researchers to identify greetings across languages and communities, it is important to establish whether the same criteria can allow us to exclude words and exchanges that are *not* greetings. A good candidate for such a test is the Samoan term *tulouna* or *tulouga*.[26] In Augustine Krämer's

(1902–3) extensive ethnography of Samoan history and social life, *tulouga* was translated to the German *gegrüsst*, the past participle of the verb *grüssen* "greet." The English version of the German text done by Theodore Verhaaren (Krämer 1994) mirrors the same translation with the English *greeted*. Here is an example from Krämer's book; (16) shows the original, and (17), the English translation. The passage is taken from the beginning part of the *fa'alupega* (ceremonial address of the village of Falefā, which is the site of the exchanges analyzed in this article).

(16)

Tulouga a 'oe le faleatua	Gegrüsst du das Haus von Atua
tulouga a 'oe le 'a'ai o Fonotī	gegrüsst die Stadt des Fonotī
	(Krämer 1902: 277)

(17)

Tulouga a 'oe le faleatua	Greeted you, the house of Atua
tulouga a 'oe le 'a'ai o Fonotī	greeted Fonotī's city
	(Krämer 1994: 360)

The translation of *tulouga* with "greeted" at the beginning of each phrase achieves the goal of mirroring the word order of Samoan (verb first). But the translation is problematic first of all on empirical grounds, given that *tulouga* is not used in any of the ceremonial greetings I described above. For example, *tulouga* is never mentioned in the ceremonial greetings despite the fact that they are quite formal and, as we saw above, include sections of the ceremonial address (*fa'alupega*) of the village, the context in which *tulouga* appears in Krämer's text. Instead, I found *tulouga* (pronounced /kulouga/; see the appendix) in the first speech given during the meetings of the fono. In this context, as I suggested in Duranti 1981, it makes sense to translate it to "acknowledgment" or "recognition";[27]

(18) *[April 7, 1979: first speech of the meeting, by orator Loa]*

LOA: ia'.
Well,
(2.0)
kulouga ia (1.0) a le aofia ma le fogo,
recognition indeed ... of the assembly and the council,
(3.0)
kulouga le viligia ma – kulouga le saukia,
recognition (of) the suffering and – recognition (of) the early arrival,
(2.0)
kulouga Moamoa 'o kua o Lalogafu'afu'a
recognition (of) Moamoa,[28] the back of Lalogafu'afu'a[29]
[...]

The translation of *tulouna* (or *tulouga*) with *recognition* (one might even consider the term *apology*, given its obvious relation to the expression "tulou!" [excuse (me)][30]) is consistent with the description provided in Milner's dictionary:

> Expression used before mentioning important names or titles (esp. when making a speech). It implies that the speaker makes a formal acknowledgement of their importance, expresses his deference and respect for the established order, and apologizes for any offence he might inadvertently give when speaking before the distinguished assembly. (N.B. This expression is used repeatedly in uttering the ceremonial style and address of a social group or village *[fa'alupega]*). (1966: 286–7)

When we match *tulouga* against the six criteria provided above, we find that it matches only two or perhaps three of the criteria for identifying greetings:

(i) It is part of a relatively predictable part of a speech (criterion 4).
(ii) It contributes in part to the establishment of a spatiotemporal unit of interaction (to the extent to which it contributes to clarifying the type of encounter in which it occurs) (criterion 5).
(iii) It identifies the interlocutors as distinct and yet related beings (criterion 6).

But *tulouga* does not qualify according to the three remaining criteria:

(a) It does not occur close to an interactional boundary (criterion 1). Instead, it is used in the middle of a speech.
(b) It does not establish a shared perceptual field (criterion 2). Such a field has already been established by a number of other expressions and rituals.
(c) It is not in the form of an adjacency pair (criterion 3). There is no immediate or obvious response to the particular section of the speech in which the speaker uses *tulouga*.

Conclusions

The analysis of greetings presented here shows that semantic analysis must be integrated with ethnographic information if we want to provide an adequate pragmatic analysis of speech activities within and across speech communities. Whatever greetings accomplish, they do it by virtue of the participants' ability to match routine expressions with particular sociohistorical circumstances. To say that greetings are constituted by formulaic expressions only tells half of the story. The other half is how such formulaic expressions may be adapted to, and at the same time help establish, new contexts.

I have argued that we cannot compare greetings across speech communities unless we come up with a universal definition of what constitutes a greeting exchange. After proposing such a universal definition consisting of six criteria, I have shown that the tendency to see greetings as devoid of propositional content or expressing "phatic communion" is too limiting and, in fact, inaccurate. Greetings are, indeed, toward the formulaic end of the formulaic–creative continuum that runs across the full range of communicative acts through which humans manage their everyday life, but they can also communicate new information to participants through the types of questions they ask and the kinds of answers they produce. My analysis of four different types of Samoan greetings offers an empirical corroboration of the six criteria and proposes some new hypotheses about the work that is done during greetings in human encounters. In particular, I have shown the following:

1 The notion of "greeting substitute" used for English greetings such as "How are you?" may not be extendable to other speech communities. I showed that in Samoan, since no particular greeting can be identified as the most basic or unmarked one, there is no sense in claiming that any of the expressions used in greetings are "greeting substitutes."
2 In certain types of greetings, most noticeably ceremonial ones, recognition has already taken place before greetings are exchanged. This means that "acknowledgment" of another's presence per se cannot be the function of greeting, unless we redefine the notion of "acknowledgment" to make it more culture- and context-specific. For example, physical recognition might have taken place (i.e., participants might be signaling that they have sighted one another), but context-specific social recognition might still be needed; that is, participants need to be acknowledged for what they represent or embody in a particular situation or course of action. The act of greeting, in other words, does not necessarily imply that the speaker has *just* encountered the hearer, as proposed by Searle and Vanderveken (1985: 216), but that the encounter is taking place *under particular sociohistorical conditions* and the parties are relating to one another *as particular types of social personae*. This is the case across a number of greetings. It undermines the possibility of cross-culturally extending speech act theorists' analysis of English greetings as an "expressive" type of speech act aimed at the "courteous indication of recognition" of the other party (Searle and Vanderveken 1985: 216).
3 Contrary to what is assumed by most existing studies of greetings, greetings are not necessarily devoid of propositional content; they can be used to gather information about a person's identity or whereabouts. The Samoan "Where are you going?" greeting, for example, is seeking

information about the addressee and, unlike what is argued by Sacks (1975) about the English "How are you?," in answering the Samoan greeting, a lie is not the "preferred" answer, or at least not preferred by the one who asks the question. The questioner would rather find out as much as possible about the other party's whereabouts. For this reason, the "Where are you going?" greeting can also work as a form of social control and therefore be quite the opposite of Bach and Harnish's (1979: 51–2) view of the act of greeting (in English only?) as an expression of "pleasure at seeing (or meeting)" someone.

NOTES

1 Although the absence of greetings or their relatively rare occurrence in certain societies has been mentioned at times – the classic example being American Indian groups such as the Western Apache studied by Basso (1972), who are said to prefer "silence" during phases of encounters that other groups would find ripe for greetings (see also Farnell 1995) – there is overwhelming evidence at this point that most speech communities do have verbal expressions that conform to the criteria I define in this article, although their use and frequency may vary both across and within communities. (See Hymes's comments about North American Indians in Youssouf et al. 1976: 817 fn. 6.)

2 Although Searle and Vanderveken claim to be discussing the English verb *greet*, as shown by the following quote, they in fact treat *greet* and *hello* as part of the same class:

> "Greet" is only marginally an illocutionary act since it has no propositional content. When one greets someone [but usually one does not greet by using the verb *greet!* A.D.], for example, by saying "Hello," one indicates recognition in a courteous fashion. So we might define greeting as a courteous indication of recognition, with the presupposition that the speaker has just encountered the hearer. (1985: 215–16)

3 Austin defined behabitives as "reactions to other people's behaviour and fortunes and . . . attitudes and expressions of attitudes to someone else's past conduct or imminent conduct" (1962: 159).

4 By *ethnography* I mean here the study of human action within a particular community through participant-observation of spontaneous encounters for the purpose of gaining an understanding of the participants' perspective on what is going on in such encounters. For a review of ethnographic methods applied to the study of verbal interaction, see Duranti (1997a: ch. 4).

5 Italians use *ciao* for both opening and closing salutations.

6 This statement is ambiguous. It should be understood as meaning either one of the following scenarios: (i) in a given speech community, the same verbal expression may be used in both greeting (viz. opening saluation) and leave-taking; or (ii) a greeting item can exhaust the encounter and in that sense function as both an opening and closing expression. An example of the first situation is the word *ciao* as used in Italy. An example of the second situation is the English question "How're you doing?" when it is not followed by an answer.

7 The use of the notion of *perceptual field* allows for the inclusion of visual and auditory access. The issue of technologies that allow for nonreal time communication (writing in general) is left out of the present discussion. (But see Duranti 1986 for a brief discussion of greetings in electronic mail.)

8 Philips (1972: 377) used the notion *participant structure* in referring to structural arrangements of interaction. For the related notion of "participation framework," see Goffman 1981: 226 and M. H. Goodwin 1990.

9 I am avoiding here the term *Samoan society*, given the existence of many

communities around the world where Samoan is regularly spoken, including two independent countries, (formerly Western) Samoa and American Samoa, each of which with different kinds of language policies and language practices, including different levels of bilingualism.

10 July 1978–July 1979, March–May 1981, August 1988.

11 As I said earlier, these four types of greetings do not exhaust the typology of Samoan greetings. There is at least one more possible candidate, the informal "'ua 'e sau?" (Have you come?), said to someone who has just come into the house. (For a similar greeting in Tikopia, see Firth 1972.) The lack of personal experience with this greeting and the absence of examples of this greeting in my data have prevented me from including it in the discussion. One of the reviewers also suggested the expression *uā* as an abbreviation of the same greeting.

12 It is possible of course that the use of this greeting has changed over the years and that Mead witnessed an earlier usage of the term.

13 The laughter that follows excerpt (1) could be interpreted as an index of the awkwardness of the exchange under the present circumstances.

14 Although I have no quantitative data at this moment to support such a statement, I must mention that the greeting *tālofa* is one of the few Samoan terms that can be pronounced with the initial /t/ even in the "bad speech" pronunciation (see the appendix); in other words, it does not necessarily change to /kālofa/ even in those contexts in which all other /t/ sounds disappear. This feature of *tālofa* might be related to its common use with foreigners.

15 For abbreviations used in interlinear glosses, see the appendix.

16 This meaning makes the Samoan *mālō* related to the homophonous Tongan term *mālō*, meaning "(to be) laudable, worthy of thanks or praise" as well as "thank you" (Churchward 1959: 325), and to the Hawaiian *mahalo* "thanks, gratitude, to thank" (Pukui and Elbert 1986: 218).

17 Given the different word order of English and Samoan, it is impossible to adequately reproduce here the pauses in the English translation. Samoans say "is nice the land" rather than "the land is nice." This explains why many examples of repairs are in the predicate phrase.

18 Samoan distinguishes in this case between *le asiasi* "the inspecting/visiting" and *asiasiga* "the visit/inspection" or the "visiting/inspecting party".

19 What I call "ceremonial attributes" here are parts of the *fa'alupega* "ceremonial style of address" for people of high status or their entire community. (There is a *fa'alupega* of the entire country.) They include metaphorical expressions that identify particular titles and their connections to ancestors, places, and important events in Samoan history. See Duranti 1981, 1994; Mead 1930; and Shore 1982. Krämer 1902–3 (and 1994) contains all the *fa'alupega* as known at the time of his study.

20 Syntactically, the name of the title may be simply juxtaposed next to the addressed term, as in "lau kōfā le Makua," or be linked to it with an oblique preposition (e.g. *'i/i* or *'iā/iā*), as in "lau kōfā i le Makua" (literally, "your honor from the senior orator"). The word *kōfā* also means "opinion (of a chief)." Orators are expected to present the position of their chief.

21 It is also possible to have CGs exchanged between two groups, for example, when two or more individuals arrive simultaneously. In these cases, however, the individuals, especially when their number is low, are each addressed within the same extended CG (Duranti 1997b).

22 Here is an example of a response by an individual to all the members of the inspection committee:

TŪLA'I: mālō (Timi)! // (?)
TIMI: mālō (1.0) afioga i ali'i – ma failāuga!
(3.0) *Congratulations (1.0) honorable chiefs – and orators!*

TŪLA'I: 'ua lē faia lou lima iga 'ua 'ē ka'oko!
You haven't done your hand [i.e., played cards] since you've been operated on [i.e., you've gotten a tattoo]!

23 This third hypothesis makes this exchange similar to another one that took place a decade earlier, when another matai spoke on my behalf to explain to the Moe'ono of those days – the father of the person holding the Moe'ono title in this interaction – what I was writing on my notebook (see Duranti 1992b: 91–2).

24 Given its context of use, this type of exchange is the most difficult to catch on tape unless the researcher carefully plans the use of the audiorecorder or videocamera having in mind this type of greeting. Given that the decision to systematically study greetings was made after returning from the field, although I witnessed and participated in hundreds if not thousands of these exchanges, I have very few clear and reliable "where are you going" greetings in my corpus. Despite this limitation, however, I think that some hypotheses may be made about their organization and in particular about the importance of their propositional content.

25 The term *ali'i*, which historically comes from the Polynesian term for "chief" (Proto-Polynesian *aliki*), maintains in Samoan this meaning for the higher-ranking *matai*. In (15), instead, it is used as a separate address form. It may also be used like a title in English and other Indo-European languages: for example, before a first name (*ali'i Alesana* "Mr. Alesana") and as a descriptor (*le ali'i lea* "this gentleman/fellow"). In contemporary Samoa, the term does not have restrictions in terms of age, gender, or animacy. Thus *ali'i* may be used with a young child, a woman (e.g. *ali'i Elenoa* "Ms. Elinor"), or even an object (*le ali'i lea* can mean "that person" or "that thing"). Such a variety of uses makes it difficult to provide a translation of its use in the first line of (15), but it is clear that it should be understood as showing some form of respect, however minimum, of the addressee's social persona. It contrasts, for instance, with the informal address terms *sole* (for male recipients) and *suga* (for female recipients), which may be translated with English terms such as *lad*, *brother*, or *man* and *lassie*, *sister*, or *girl*, respectively (see example (12), line 2).

26 The alternative spelling and pronunciation is probably due to hypercorrection resulting from the sociolinguistic variation between *n* ([n]) and *ng* ([ŋ]) (see Duranti 1990; Duranti and Ochs 1986; Hovdhaugen 1986; Shore 1982).

27 The English *acknowledgment* parallels the way in which *tulouga* is sometimes used by Samoan speakers, who seem to treat it as a nominalization as well. For example, in example (18), the first *tulouga* is followed by a genitive phrase "a le aofia ma le fogo" (of the assembly and the council).

28 Moamoa is the name of the *malae* "ceremonial green" of the village of Falefā.

29 Lalogafu'afu'a is the name of the malae of the village of Lufilufi, the capital of the subdistrict of Anoama'a East where Falefā is located. The spatial metaphor "the back of" is meant to convey the idea that the people of Falefā are expected to support and protect the people of Lufilufi.

30 "Tulou!" (Excuse me!) is commonly used to excuse oneself for inappropriately entering the interactional space occupied by others (Duranti 1981).

REFERENCES

Austin, J. L. (1962). *How to Do Things with Words*. Oxford: Oxford University Press.

Bach, Kent, and Robert M. Harnish (1979). *Linguistic Communication and Speech Acts*. Cambridge, MA: MIT Press.

Basso, Keith (1972). "To Give Up on Words": Silence in Western Apache Culture. In

Language and Social Context. P. P. Giglioli, ed., pp. 67–86. Harmondsworth: Penguin Books.

Bourdieu, Pierre (1977). *Outline of a Theory of Practice*. Richard Nice, trans. Cambridge: Cambridge University Press.

Caton, Steven C. (1986). Salam Tahiyah: Greetings from the Highlands of Yemen. *American Ethnologist* 13: 290–308.

Churchward, C. Maxwell (1959). *Tongan Dictionary*. Tonga: Government Printing Press.

Duranti, Alessandro (1981). *The Samoan Fono: A Sociolinguistic Study*. Pacific Linguistics Monographs, Series B, 80. Canberra: Australian National University, Department of Linguistics, Research School of Pacific Studies.

Duranti, Alessandro (1986). Framing Discourse in a New Medium: Openings in Electronic Mail. *Quarterly Newsletter of the Laboratory of Comparative Human Cognition* 8(2): 64–71.

Duranti, Alessandro (1990). Code Switching and Conflict Management in Samoan Multiparty Interaction. *Pacific Studies* 141: 1–30.

Duranti, Alessandro (1992a). Language and Bodies in Social Space: Samoan Ceremonial Greetings. *American Anthropologist* 94: 657–91.

Duranti, Alessandro (1992b). Language in Context and Language as Context: The Samoan Respect Vocabulary. In *Rethinking Context: Language as an Interactive Phenomenon*. A. Duranti and C. Goodwin, eds., p. 77–99. Cambridge: Cambridge University Press.

Duranti, Alessandro (1994). *From Grammar to Politics: Linguistic Anthropology in a Western Samoan Village*. Berkeley and Los Angeles: University of California Press.

Duranti, Alessandro (1997a). *Linguistic Anthropology*. Cambridge: Cambridge University Press.

Duranti, Alessandro (1997b). Polyphonic Discourse: Overlapping in Samoan Ceremonial Greetings. *Text* 17(3): 349–81.

Duranti, Alessandro, and Elinor Ochs (1986). Literacy Instruction in a Samoan Village. In *Acquisition of Literacy: Ethnographic Perspectives*. B. B. Schieffelin and P. Gilmore, eds., pp. 213–32. Norwood, NJ: Ablex.

Eibl-Eibesfeldt, Irenäus (1972). Similarities and Differences between Cultures in Expressive Movements. In *Non-Verbal Communication*. R. A. Hinde, ed., pp. 297–312. Cambridge: Cambridge University Press.

Eibl-Eibesfeldt, Irenäus (1977). Patterns of Greetings in New Guinea. In *New Guinea Area Languages and Language Study*, vol. 3. S. A. Wurm, ed., pp. 209–47. Canberra: Australian National University, Department of Linguistics, Research School of Pacific Studies.

Farnell, Brenda (1995). *Do You See What I Mean?: Plains Indian Sign Talk and the Embodiment of Action*. Austin: University of Texas Press.

Firth, Raymond (1972). Verbal and Bodily Rituals of Greeting and Parting. In *The Interpretation of Ritual: Essays in Honour of A. I. Richards*. J. S. La Fontaine, ed., pp. 1–38. London: Tavistock.

Goffman, Erving (1971). *Relations in Public: Microstudies of the Public Order*. New York: Harper and Row.

Goffman, Erving (1981). *Forms of Talk*. Philadelphia: University of Pennsylvania Press.

Goodwin, Marjorie Harness (1990). *He-Said-She-Said: Talk as Social Organization among Black Children*. Bloomington: Indiana University Press.

Goody, Esther (1972). "Greeting", "Begging", and the Presentation of Respect. In *The Interpretation of Ritual*. J. S. La Fontaine, ed., pp. 39–71. London: Tavistock.

Gregor, Thomas (1977). *The Mehinaku: The Drama of Everyday Life in a Brazilian Indian Village*. Chicago, IL: University of Chicago Press.

Grice, H. P. (1975). Logic and Conversation. In *Syntax and Semantics*, vol. 3, *Speech Acts*. P. Cole and N. L. Morgan, eds., pp. 41–58. New York: Academic Press.

Gumperz, John J. (1992). Contextualization and Understanding. In *Rethinking Context*. A. Duranti and C. Goodwin, eds., pp. 229–52. Cambridge: Cambridge University Press.

Hanks, William F. (1990). *Referential Practice: Language and Lived Space among the Maya*. Chicago, IL: University of Chicago Press.

Hoëm, Ingjerd (1993). Space and Morality in Tokelau. *Pragmatics* 3: 137–53.

Hoëm, Ingjerd (1995). A Sense of Place: The Politics of Identity and Representation. Doctoral thesis, University of Oslo.

Holmes, Lowell D. (1987). *Quest for the Real Samoa: The Mead/Freeman Controversy and Beyond*. South Hadley, MA: Bergin and Garvey.

Hovdhaugen, Even (1986). The Chronology of Three Samoan Sound Changes. In *Papers from the Fourth International Conference on Austronesian Linguistics*. P. Geraghty, L. Carrington, and S. A. Wurm, eds., pp. 313–33. Pacific Linguistics, Series C, 93–4. Canberra: Research School of Pacific Studies, Australian National University.

Irvine, Judith (1974). Strategies of Status Manipulation in Wolof Greeting. In *Explorations in the Ethnography of Speaking*. R. Bauman and J. Sherzer, eds., pp. 167–91. Cambridge: Cambridge University Press.

Jakobson, Roman (1960). Closing Statement: Linguistics and Poetics. In *Style in Language*. T. A. Sebeok, ed., pp. 398–429. Cambridge, MA: MIT Press.

Keenan, Elinor Ochs [Also see Ochs, Elinor] (1976). The Universality of Conversational Postulates. *Language in Society* 5: 67–80.

Kendon, Adam, and Andrew Ferber (1973). A Description of Some Human Greetings. In *Comparative Ecology and Behaviour of Primates*. R. P. Michael and J. H. Crook, eds., pp. 591–668. London: Academic Press.

Krämer, Augustine (1902–03). *Die Samoa-Inseln*. Stuttgart, Germany: Schwertzerbartsche.

Krämer, Augustine (1994). *The Samoa Islands. An Outline of a Monograph with Particular Consideration of German Samoa*, vol. 1. Theodore Verhaaren, trans. Honolulu: University of Hawaii Press.

Leach, Edmund (1972). The Influence of Cultural Context on Non-Verbal Communication in Man. In *Non-Verbal Communication*. R. Hinde, ed., pp. 315–47. Cambridge: Cambridge University Press.

Malinowski, Bronislaw (1923). The Problem of Meaning in Primitive Languages. In *The Meaning of Meaning*. C. K. Ogden and I. A. Richards, eds., pp. 296–336. New York: Harcourt, Brace and World.

Mead, Margaret (1928). *Coming of Age in Samoa*. New York: William Morrow.

Mead, Margaret (1930). *Social Organization of Manu'a*. Honolulu, HI: Bishop Museum Press.

Milner, G. B. (1961). The Samoan Vocabulary of Respect. *Journal of the Royal Anthropological Institute* 91: 296–317.

Milner, G. B. (1966). *Samoan Dictionary: Samoan–English English–Samoan*. London: Oxford University Press.

Milton, Kay (1982). Meaning and Context: The Interpretation of Greetings in Kasigau. In *Semantic Anthropology*. D. Parkin, ed., pp. 261–77. London: Academic Press.

Ochs, Elinor [Also see Keenan, Elinor Ochs] (1985). Variation and Error: A Sociolinguistic Study of Language Acquisition in Samoa. In *The Crosslinguistic Study of Language Acquisition*. D. I. Slobin, ed., pp. 783–838. Hillsdale, NJ: Erlbaum.

Ochs, Elinor (1988). *Culture and Language Development: Language Acquisition and Language Socialization in a Samoan Village*. Cambridge: Cambridge University Press.

Philips, Susan U. (1972). Participant Structures and Communicative Competence: Warm Springs Children in Community and Classroom. In *Functions of Language in the Classroom*. C. B. Cazden, V. P. John, and D. Hymes, eds., pp. 370–94. New York: Columbia Teachers Press.

Platt, Martha (1982). Social and Semantic Dimensions of Deictic Verbs and Particles in Samoan Child Language. PhD dissertation, University of Southern California.

Pukui, Mary Kawena, and Samuel H. Elbert (1986). *Hawaiian Dictionary. Hawaiian–English English–Hawaiian*. Revised and enlarged edn. Honolulu: University of Hawaii Press.

Sacks, Harvey (1975). Everyone Has to Lie. In *Sociocultural Dimensions of Language Use*. M. Sanches and B. G. Blount, eds., pp. 57–80. New York: Academic Press.

Sacks, Harvey (1992). *Lectures on Conversation*, vol. 1. Cambridge, MA: Blackwell.

Sacks, Harvey, Emanuel A. Schegloff, and Gail Jefferson (1974). A Simpler Systematics for the Organization of Turn-Taking for Conversation. *Language* 50: 696–735.

Schegloff, Emanuel (1968). Sequencing in Conversational Openings. *American Anthropologist* 70: 1075–95.

Schegloff, Emanuel (1986). The Routine as Achievement. *Human Studies* 9: 111–51.

Schegloff, Emanuel A., and Harvey Sacks (1973). Opening Up Closings. *Semiotica* 8: 289–327.

Searle, John R. (1969). *Speech Acts: An Essay in the Philosophy of Language*. Cambridge: Cambridge University Press.

Searle, John R., and Daniel Vanderveken (1985). *Foundations of Illocutionary Logic*. Cambridge: Cambridge University Press.

Sherzer, Joel (1983). *Kuna Ways of Speaking: An Ethnographic Perspective*. Austin: University of Texas Press.

Shore, Bradd (1982). *Sala'ilua: A Samoan Mystery*. New York: Columbia University Press.

Valeri, Valerio (1985). *Kingship and Sacrifice*. Chicago, IL: University of Chicago Press.

Youssouf, Ibrahim Ag, Allen D. Grimshaw, and Charles S. Bird (1976). Greetings in the Desert. *American Ethnologist* 3: 797–824.

Appendix

Transcription conventions

All Samoan examples are taken from transcripts of spontaneous interactions recorded by the author in Western Samoa at different times between 1978 and 1988. In the transcripts presented in the article, I adopt the conventions introduced by Gail Jefferson for conversation analysis (see Sacks et al. 1974), with a few modifications.

[*Inspection*]	A name in brackets before the text of an example refers to the name of the transcript.
Tūla'i:	Speakers' names (or general descriptors) are separated from their utterances by colons.
?:	A question mark instead of a name indicates that no good guess could be made as to the identity of the speaker.
??:	Repeated question marks indicate additional unidentified speakers.
?Tūla'i:	A question mark before the name of the speaker stands for a probable, but not safe, guess.
(2.5)	Numbers between parentheses indicate length of pauses in seconds and tenths of seconds.
[	A square bracket between turns indicates the point at which overlap by another speaker starts.
//	Parallel slashes are an alternative symbol indicating point of overlap.
=	The equal signs indicate that two utterances are latched immediately to one another with no pause.
=[	The equal signs before a square bracket between turns signals that the utterance above and the one below are both latched to the prior one.
(I can't do)	Talk between parentheses represents the best guess of a stretch of talk which was difficult to hear.
(??)	Parentheses with question marks indicate uncertain or unclear talk of approximately the length of the blank spaces between parentheses.
(())	Material between double parentheses provides extralinguistic information.
[...]	An ellipsis between square brackets indicates that parts of the original transcript or example have been omitted or that the transcript starts or ends in the middle of further talk.
o::	Colons, single or double, indicate lengthening of the sound they follow.

Abbreviations in interlinear glosses

Art = article; Comp = complementizer; Emp = emphatic particle; excl = exclusive; incl = inclusive; Perf = perfective aspect marker; pl = plural (as opposed to singular or dual); Pres = present tense; Voc = vocative particle.

"Good speech" and "bad speech"

Samoan has two phonological registers, called by Samoans *tautala lelei* "good speech" and *tautala leaga* "bad speech." "Good speech" is strongly associated with Christianity, written language (e.g., the Bible), and Western education (Duranti and Ochs 1986; Ochs 1988; Shore 1982). It is thus required of children and adults most of the time in the schools and during church services and most church-related activities. "Bad speech" is used in everyday encounters in the homes, at the store, or on the road and is also characteristic of most formal contexts in which traditional speech-making is used, including the ceremonial greetings discussed in this article. There is also a considerable amount of shifting between these two registers (Duranti 1990; Ochs 1985, 1988). All the examples reproduced here are given with the pronunciation originally used by the speakers, which is usually "bad speech." When discussing words or phrases in the text of the article, I have usually used "good speech," unless I am referring to words actually used by people, in which case I put them between obliques to frame them as different from traditional orthography, e.g. /lau kōfā/ and /fogo/ instead of *lau tōfā* and *fono*, respectively. This means that the same word may be found in two different versions: for example, the expression *tulouga* is /kulouga/ in the transcript of a speech in a fono in which it was used. I followed standard Samoan orthography: the letter *g* stands for a velar nasal ([ŋ]). The apostrophe (') stands for a glottal stop ([?]).

STUDY QUESTIONS

1 What are the six universal properties of greetings proposed by Duranti?
2 What are the four types of Samoan greetings identified by Duranti?
3 Using the six universal features of greetings and drawing from the analysis of Samoan greetings provided in this chapter, can you give a description of the types of greetings used in the speech community you are the most familiar with?
4 Based on the discussion provided by Duranti, assess whether what people say while greeting each other in your speech community is completely predictable and redundant or carries instead new information.

9

Genre, Intertextuality, and Social Power

Charles L. Briggs and Richard Bauman

Why devote an article to the subject of genre? It must be admitted from the outset that genre engenders a number of possible objections when presented as an analytic tool for the study of speech. Like such notions as *text*, *genre* strikes some practitioners as too global and fuzzy a concept to be of much use to detailed formal and functional analysis. Its association with literary theory and critical practice may similarly suggest that it is not likely to be illuminating with respect to either "everyday conversation" or "ordinary" linguistic processes. It is generally used, after all, in *classifying* discourse; typological tasks are often rejected by empiricists and anti-positivists alike, and some researchers will find it difficult to believe that the use of broad empirical categories is likely to be of much use to fine-grained analysis of particular social interactions. Beyond these issues, all of us know intuitively that generic classifications never quite work: an empirical residue that does not fit any clearly defined category – or, even worse, that falls into too many – is always left over.

In defending our chosen topic, we could point out that the concept of genre (with or without the label) has played a role in linguistic anthropology since at least the time of Boas. Generic classifications helped set the agenda for research on Native American languages. The study of genre was later boosted by ethnoscience, structuralism, the ethnography of speaking, and the performance-centered approach to verbal art. The recent popularity of Bakhtin's translinguistics and new perspectives on emotion and gender have similarly accorded new cachet to generic investigation. The first part of our article will thus be devoted to a critical discussion of the place of genre within linguistic anthropology.

As will become apparent in the second part, our goal is not to defend the concept or to claim that it should occupy a more central role in linguistic anthropology. We will rather argue that its nature and significance have been misconstrued in certain fundamental ways by proponents and critics alike. Although the same could be said of research on genre in folkloristics and literary theory as well as in linguistic anthropology, these areas lie beyond the scope of this article. This misapprehension has contributed to the ambivalent reception that the concept has received and its periodic

For permission to publish copyright material in this book, grateful acknowledgment is made to: C. L. Briggs and R. Bauman (1992), "Genre, Intertextuality, and Social Power," *Journal of Linguistic Anthropology* 2: 131–72.

movements in and out of scholarly fashion. We will argue that grasping the complex intertextual relations that underlie genre, along with the way these relations are closely linked to social, cultural, ideological, and political-economic factors, can offer insight into why studies of genre have proved to be so problematic. We hope to be able not only to provide a more solid foundation for investigations of genre, but also to show how research on generic intertextuality can illuminate central issues in linguistic anthropology.

The Boasian Tradition

As we have noted, genre – as term and as concept – has achieved currency in contemporary linguistic anthropology largely under the stimulus of the ethnography of speaking, performance-centered approaches to verbal art, and the work of Mikhail Bakhtin. To be sure, the foundations of this interest in genre were laid much earlier, principally at the points of convergence between linguistic anthropology and the adjacent discipline of folklore, in which the generic shaping and classification of oral forms has been a fundamental concern. In particular, generic issues (though not the term) played a certain operational role in the Americanist tradition of Boas and his intellectual heirs, although the concept was seldom the focus of critical examination in their work. Given the centrality of texts in the Boasian tradition, rooted in the philological foundations of Boasian anthropology, discrimination among orders of texts was at times seen to be a necessary task, at least for certain purposes.

The most prominent use of generic distinctions in the Boasian line occurs in the organization of text collections. Perusal of these collections, however, reveals that the grouping of texts within their pages is frequently quite ad hoc, without discussion of the conceptual basis of the respective sections. Sapir, for example, in his classic collection *Wishram Texts*, writes only that "the arrangement of the texts under the heads of Myth, Customs, Letters, Non-Mythical Narratives, and Supplementary Upper Chinookan Texts, is self-explanatory and need not be commented upon" (1909: xii). The distinction between myths and tales or historical narratives attributed by Boas to North American cultures generally had some effect in shaping text collections (see, e.g., Reichard 1947), but other sorting principles, such as grouping by informant (see, e.g., Reichard 1925), may also be found. One noteworthy feature of Americanist text collections in the Boasian tradition is the frequent inclusion of a corpus of "ethnological narratives" (e.g., Sapir and Hoijer 1942) or "ethnographic texts" (e.g., Jacobs 1959), generic rubrics that reflect the Boasian predisposition toward cultural information in entextualized packages. This genre brings into special relief the way in which generic categories and textual forms are cocreated by the ethnographer and the consultant (see Briggs 1986).

Boas's own work displays a marked ambivalence about the usefulness of generic categories. On the positive side, he does suggest the need to record the full array of verbal genres because of their varying "stylistic peculiarities" (1940c[1917]: 200), in tacit recognition that discourse form is a significant patterning principle in the organization and distribution of linguistic structure, and he does direct attention to the presence or absence of particular verbal genres in a culture's repertoire as a means of testing (generally, debunking) universalistic theories of the origin and development of literature (1940c[1917]: 209). Overall, however, Boas treats generic distinctions with varying degrees of care and precision. In certain instances, he displays a tendency to use generic designations rather casually. In the opening paragraphs of "The Development of Folk-Tales and Myths" (1940b[1916]: 397), for instance, folktales and myths are first separated terminologically, then (apparently) merged under the general rubric of *tales*, after which (again apparently) *folk-tales* becomes the cover term.

If this is an instance of casual sliding across a range of terms, there are other points at which the absence of clear generic distinctions in Boas's writings rests on a more principled foundation. In his comparative investigations of the narrative repertoires of North American peoples, Boas discovered that particular themes and motifs might diffuse, with some degree of independence, to combine and recombine with other elements in a variety of shifting ways. In larger scope, by whatever criteria one might employ to make generic distinctions between myth and folktale, for example, Boas perceived that there is "a continual flow of material from mythology to folk-tale and *vice versa*" (1940b[1916]: 405). Boas's distrust of various attempts to discriminate between narrative genres was further bolstered by his perception that such distinctions did not remain consistent for specific narratives across group boundaries; once again, by whatever criteria the distinction was attempted, narratives that were clearly genetically related might appear in one group's repertoire to belong to one class, and in the neighboring group's repertoire, to another. Hence, Boas attributed the "somewhat indefinite" use of the terms *myth* and *folk-tale* to "a lack of a sharp line of demarcation between these two classes of tales" (1940a[1914]: 454). Boas's critique of generalized, a priori, analytical genre definitions rests on a substantive test of a particular kind: it is not their productiveness in delimiting categories of cultural forms within cultures that is at issue, but their inconsistency in capturing genetically related cultural items across cultures that renders them of questionable usefulness for Boas's purposes.

There is, however, one basis for discriminating between myths and folktales to which Boas is prepared to accord a degree of legitimacy and productiveness – this is a distinction purportedly "given by the Indian himself" (1940a [1914]: 454). "In the mind of the American native," Boas writes,

> there exists almost always a clear distinction between two classes of tales. One group relates incidents which happened at a time when the world had not yet assumed its present form, and when mankind was not yet in possession of all the arts and customs that belong to our period. The other group contains tales of our modern period. In other words, tales of the first group are considered as myths; those of the other as history. [1940a(1914): 454–5]

Concerning this purportedly local distinction, Boas reminds us that here, too, historical and comparative investigations reveal movement between the two classes, and thus from his "analytical" point of view, this way of sorting out narrative genres is no better founded than those devised by scholars. It does, however, have the advantage of corresponding "to concepts that are perfectly clear in the native mind. Although folktales and myths as defined in this manner must therefore still be studied as a unit, we have avoided the introduction of an arbitrary distinction through our modern cultural point of view, and retained instead the one that is present in the minds of the myth-telling people" (1940a[1914]: 455).

Several elements are significant here. First, observe that Boas attributes the distinction between myth and folktale that he outlines to American Indians generally; he never finds it necessary or useful to explore the distinction directly and in detail in any given Native American culture. Rather, he generalizes broadly and summarily, remaining far more centrally interested in those particularistic historical and comparative investigations that require that "folk-tales and myths ... still be studied as a unit" (1940a[1914]: 455).

A further point that is especially worthy of attention is Boas's repeated insistence on how "perfectly clear in the mind of the Indian" is the distinction between myths and historical tales. One wonders at the basis for Boas's assurance in this regard, especially in light of his observation that "historical tales may in the course of time become mythical tales by being transferred into the mythical period, and that historical tales may originate which parallel in the character and sequence of their incidents mythical tales" (1940a[1914]: 455). Apparently, Boas did not encounter – or chose to disregard – instances in which his consultants saw particular narratives as generic hybrids or as categorically ambiguous. Nevertheless, the distinction drawn by Boas between analytical genres and local categories represents an early invocation of a persistent issue in linguistic anthropology and adjacent disciplines.

Among Boas's students, one who stands out for his considered attention to the problematics of genre is Paul Radin. Radin's most significant contribution is his "Literary Aspects of Winnebago Mythology" (1926), which takes its opening frame of reference from Boas but departs from Boas's approach in markedly important ways. Radin begins by observing that "it has been frequently pointed out that many Indian tribes divide their myths into two groups, one coinciding in the main with our category of myth proper, and the other with that of our semi-historical legend or novelette," noting that "the two types are set off from one another by objective differences in style," some of which are defined in terms of linguistic elements and structures (1926: 18). Noting that "this distinction between myth (*waika*) and the tale (*worak*) is very strong and every tale is classified by them in one or another category" (1926: 18), Radin might seem to be casting his account in the mold provided by Boas. Even here, however, the Winnebago case demands qualification of the general schema, as being "at variance with all conventional ethnological classifications: an origin story, being regarded as accounting for true happenings, must fall into the category of the 'tale'" (1926: 21). Radin is thus clearly concerned, as Boas and others appeared not to be, with locally defined generic discriminations, adding to the preceding one still others, having to do with occasions of use and dramatis personae.

The most striking discovery that flows from Radin's attentiveness to Winnebago bases for discriminating among orders of narrative is the availability of a third classificatory possibility, "a mixed category, the 'myth-tale'" (1926: 18). So much for Boas's "perfect clarity." Radin goes on to elaborate:

> The differentiation between a myth and a tale can be made, then, for the Winnebago on several counts, none of them mutually exclusive, and the proper classification of any one story is sometimes therefore a question of the weighting of several factors. ... In any case it is clear that whenever we encounter a story of what might be called a mixed type, we can never be certain what weighting of the various factors will seem proper to the Winnebago, and, in consequence, to what category the story will be assigned. [1926: 21–2]

Now, although Radin might seem to be conceding an inability to disentangle the various bases employed by the Winnebago for assigning a given narrative to one or another category, his insight is far stronger than that. What he is saying, rather, although in preliminary and partial terms, is that generic categories represent flexible social resources in two senses: (1) the selection of one or another basis for categorization will depend upon situational factors, and (2) the generic calibration of a narrative, by combining within it features characteristic of contrasting types, will likewise depend upon situational and strategic factors, such as clan politics. To the best of our knowledge, however, this remarkable insight was never significantly exploited beyond this essay, by Radin or anyone else, for the next half-century.

Formal Definitions of Genre

Outside the Boasian tradition of linguistic anthropology, but convergent with it in certain respects, was a small line of scholarship devoted to the formulation of structural definitions of oral genres. Thomas Sebeok, in his classic article, "The Structure and Content of Cheremis Charms" (1964[1953]), cites the stylistic analysis of folklore texts by Boas and some of his students (e.g., Radin, Reichard) among other lines of structural analysis, but identifies his own analysis most centrally with symbolic logic and the morphological analysis of the Russian formalist folklorist, Vladímir Propp. Propp's influential study is well known and has been the subject of much critical discussion; there is no need to recapitulate his argument here, beyond noting that Propp offers his analysis of fairy tale morphology as the basis of a hypothetical *definition* of the genre (1968[1928]: 9), an element missing from the Americanist line of formal stylistic analysis. "Much in the sense in which Vladímir Propp argued that all fairy tales are uniform in structure," Sebeok argues, "one is compelled to recognize that every Cheremis incantation belongs to the same structural type" (1964 [1953]: 363).

Sebeok describes his analytical strategy as follows: "Our analytical procedure will be an application of binary opposition as a patterning principle: that is, we shall repeatedly divide sequences dichotomously until the ultimate constituents are reached" (1964 [1953]: 360). The charm is thus divided by sections, sentences, clauses, and actor-action phrases, the ultimate contrastive constituents, the relationships between which are rendered in symbolic logic notation to yield the defining structure of the genre.

In a supplement to the original version of the article, published in 1964, Sebeok adds to his morphological analysis of the Cheremis charm an examination of its poetic style. Although charm structure is invariant in defining the genre, "each text is marked by a unique set of features which impart to it a certain particularity and concreteness or – to borrow a label from literary criticism – texture. An extremely interesting fact about the data is this: that striking symmetries are found to characterize each message no less than the work itself" (1964 [1953]: 363). The contrast is thus between "general structure" and "individual texture." Sebeok goes on to analyze the structure of a charm text in terms of syllabic patterns and phonological and syntactic parallelism. There is structure at both levels, but morphological structure defines the entire genre, whereas textual structures organize individual texts. The assignment of priority to morphological structure over textural patterns has significant implications: it is an analytical, not an ethnographic, operation. How Cheremis people conceive of the genre, what features define or characterize it in their understanding and practice, remains outside the purview of Sebeok's analysis.

Like Sebeok, Alan Dundes draws his inspiration from the work of Propp in insisting on the primacy of morphological analysis in the study of folklore genres. For Dundes, the determination of morphological structure opens the way to the investigation of many folkloristic problems of which one is genre definition (Georges and Dundes 1963: 111). Again, like Sebeok (and Propp), Dundes sees morphological structure as the locus of invariance in folklore forms, but although he acknowledges the variant nature of style or texture, he places more emphasis on content as a variant element: "Content may vary, but form is relatively stable" (1965: 127; see also 1964: 25, 53). Dundes's focus on "variability within a given frame" (1964:25) leads him to employ such linguistic models as Pike's tagmenic analysis (Dundes 1964) and Hockett's topic-comment analysis (Georges and Dundes 1963) in his structural explorations.

There is a certain ambiguity in Dundes's writings on the structural definition of genre. At times, he advances structural analysis as the basis of genre definition itself: "An immediate aim of structural analysis in folklore is to define the genres of folklore" (Georges and Dundes 1963: 111; see also Dundes 1964: 105). At other times, however, he points up the inadequacy of a reliance on morphological structure alone. Among the conclusions he draws in *The Morphology of North American Indian Folktales* (1964), for example, is the following:

> Another conclusion suggested by the present analysis is the confirmation of the notion that myth and folktale are not structurally distinct genres. In fact, morphologically speaking, myths and folktales are one and the same. This means that the distinction between them is wholly dependent upon content criteria or totally external factors, such as belief and function. [1964: 110]

In general, then, Dundes's writings raise another persistent problem in regard to genre definition, namely, what feature(s) constitute a sufficient or adequate basis for defining a genre: morphological structure, content, belief, function, and so on?

Much the same problem arises in Charles T. Scott's *Persian and Arabic Riddles: A Language-Centered Approach to Genre* (1965), another attempt at the formal definition of genre. Scott goes to striking lengths – even contortions – to confine his analysis within the disciplinary boundaries of linguistics, but is ultimately forced to concede the inadequacy of this approach. At the end of his monograph Scott essays a "definition of the riddle genre that is recognized as being incomplete":

> The riddle is defined as a grammatical unit of discourse, externally distributed within a matrix of longer discourse or of

> nonverbal behavior, and internally composed of two obligatory utterance-level units, between which there obtains a partially obscured semantic fit. (1965: 74)

What makes the definition incomplete is that the matrix of longer discourse, or of nonverbal behavior in which the genre occurs, is left undescribed because that is the province of anthropology. Scott concludes then, that

> linguistic units alone are not sufficient to provide a complete definition of a literary genre. They are relevant to a description of the internal composition of a genre, which is a necessary component of a definition. However, a description of the nonverbal matrix within which the genre is distributed is a further necessary component of a definition, and linguistics cannot provide this description. It is in these terms that we support an earlier assertion ... that the linguist, within the restrictions of his discipline, is compelled to take an incomplete and unsatisfactory position with respect to literature. (1965: 74)

Genre in the Ethnography of Speaking

With the emergence of the ethnography of speaking in the early 1960s, as we have suggested at the beginning of this article, genre assumes a significant place in the repertoire of concepts in linguistic anthropology (Philips 1987). Neither the term nor the concept figures in Dell Hymes's pioneering essay, "The Ethnography of Speaking" (1962), although the significance of genre is anticipated in Hymes's considerations of speech events and linguistic routines. Genre is mentioned only in passing in Hymes's "Toward Ethnographies of Communication" (1964), but this article likewise adumbrates the later frames of reference in terms of which Hymes locates genre within the conceptual and analytical framework of the ethnography of speaking. In the 1967 article, "Models of the Interaction of Language and Social Setting," genre achieves a clear place in the program, which is subsequently expanded and elaborated in a range of further programmatic essays. In general terms, Hymes's writings offer three complementary perspectives on genre: (1) genre as category or type of speech act or event; (2) genre as a nexus of interrelationships among components of the speech event; and (3) genre as a formal vantage point on speaking practice. Taken all together, Hymes's writings (1967, 1972a, 1972b, 1974, 1975a, 1975b) offer a rich and ramified framework for the exploration of genre, but the scope and focus of this article require that we limit our discussion to selected points.

One significant issue addressed by Hymes has to do with the scope or comprehensiveness of genre as an organizing factor in the speech economy of a community. At first, Hymes suggests that "it is heuristically important to proceed as though all speech has formal characteristics of some sort as manifestation of genres; and it may well be true" (1972a: 65). Elsewhere, it is genres and speech acts that jointly constitute the domain of ways of speaking (1972b: 50). Later, in "Ways of Speaking" (1974), this position is hedged: "It is tempting to generalize the [category] of genre ... so that all verbal material is assignable to some genre. ... My own hunch is that communities differ in the extent to which this is true, at least in the sense of tightly organized genres" (1974: 443–4). From this vantage point, then, the task becomes one of discovering what portion of the speech economy is generically organized, what portion escapes generic regimentation, and why.

This question is further underscored in substantive terms through the juxtaposition of related ethnographic accounts by Gary Gossen and Brian Stross. Consistent with the perspective of the ethnography of speaking, Gossen (1972, 1974) approaches the speech genres of the Chamula people of highland Chiapas as locally constituted and systemically interrelated, in powerful contrast to the scholarly tradition of reliance on a priori, universalistic, Western-based analytical genres, atomistically defined and etically applied.[1] Some Chamula genres may be analogous to Western ones, but the categories and their organization are ultimately fundamentally different. In discriminating the Chamula system of generic categories, Gossen employs the structural-semantic analytical techniques of ethnoscience, which encouraged the exploration of lexicalized category systems, to discover the comprehensive taxonomic organization of the Chamula domain of *sk'op kirsano* 'people speech', from the everyday to the most highly formalized and densely meaningful genres. As speaking is a cultural focus in Chamula, the cultural organization of this generic taxonomy is complex and resonant, encompassing interrelated and isomorphic formal, functional, situational, social organizational, axiological, ethical, and cosmological principles. The categorical elucidation of Chamula ways of speaking thus offers a powerful vantage point on Chamula culture and society in general. Gossen's analysis underscores the productiveness of a systemic ethnographic perspective as against a focus on selected or privileged genres (e.g., myth) alone, or on mere generic inventories (as in Shimkin 1964[1947]).

As illuminating as Gossen's analysis may be, though, it also displays the limitations of a rigorously taxonomic classificatory perspective on genre. Some of the most salient limitations may be highlighted by comparing Gossen's work and that of Brian Stross on the neighboring Tenejapa Tzeltal (1974). Gossen's taxonomy of Chamula genres of verbal behavior carries the taxonomic organization down to fifth level taxa. In discussing his methodology, Gossen acknowledges that first, second, and third level taxa represent "general agreement" among his six male informants, who ranged in age from 18 to 60. Informants did not agree with the same degree of consistency on fourth and fifth level taxa, although if fewer than half did not agree on the definition of a category and its placement in the system, it was not included in his considerations. The resultant schema yields an organizing framework of great order and powerful integration, a succinct view of Chamula language, society, and culture as an integrated system. But what of the kinds of people's speech concerning which there was only limited agreement or consistency – or none at all?

This messy underside of people's speech is what draws the attention of Brian Stross in his analysis of Tenejapa Tzeltal labels for kinds of speaking (1974). The Tenejapa Tzeltal, as noted, are neighbors of the Chamula in highland Chiapas, speakers of a related Mayan language. Stross finds a four-level taxonomy of kinds of *k'op* 'speech' that is quite similar to the one discovered by Gossen. He goes on, however, to record 416 additional terms in the Tzeltal metalinguistic lexicon – not an exhaustive and finite list, but simply as many terms as he managed to collect before giving up the elicitation process. Moreover, he gives us some of the rules for generating additional acceptable terms within this highly productive metalinguistic system. The important point is that his informants could not agree upon the assignment of these terms to superordinate categories. Stross, then, offers us a category system that is open, ambiguous, flexible, disorderly: "The Tzeltal domain of speaking is in fact an open system with fuzzy boundaries. ... As such it is highly adaptable to change in the social environment and must be seen as constantly evolving" (1974: 213). Taken together, Gossen's and Stross's explorations reveal genre systems in their contrasting capacities as spheres of order and as open-ended spheres of expressive possibility. The counterposition of the two investigations must also raise questions concerning the isomorphism of generic systems and other aspects of culture. Whereas Gossen's analysis highlights strong structural correspondences, the amorphous openness and flexibility revealed by Stross calls into question what the overall fit might be.

In establishing the place of genre in the conceptual repertoire of the ethnography of speaking, one important task has been to articulate the relationship between genre and other core concepts and units of analysis, such as speech act, speech event, and speech style. This task represents another prominent concern in Hymes's programmatic essays. Like many other issues, this one emerged into focus in stages. In one early formulation, Hymes blurs distinctions in stating that "by Genres are meant categories or types of speech act and speech event" (1967: 25). Elsewhere, however, he articulates several bases for distinguishing among these units of analysis. As early as 1964, Hymes suggests that "from one standpoint the analysis of speech into acts is an analysis of speech into instances of genres. The notion of genre implies the possibility of identifying formal characteristics traditionally recognized" (1972a: 65). That is to say, in these terms, the notion of speech act focuses on speaking in its guise as social action, whereas the concept of genre directs attention to the routinized, conventionalized organization of formal means, on the formal structure of language beyond the sentence (1972b: 48). This is not merely an analytical distinction; local conceptions of the organization of the domain of speaking may be articulated in terms of categorical systems of speech acts as well as of genres (see Abrahams and Bauman 1971).

If genre affords a formal vantage point on speech acts, speech styles offer a formal vantage point on genre. Building upon the work of Susan Ervin-Tripp (1972), Hymes (1974) develops a concept of speech styles as organized in terms of relations of co-occurrence and alternation:

> One can characterize whatever features go together to identify a style of speech in terms of rules of co-occurrence among them, and can characterize a choice among styles in terms of rules of alternation. The first concept gives systematic status to the ways of selecting and grouping together of linguistic means that actually obtain in a community. The second concept frees the resulting styles from mechanical connection with a particular defining situation. (1974: 434)

Significant speech styles may be associated with social groups (varieties), recurrent types of situations (registers), persons (personal style), specific situations (situational styles), and genres (genre styles). Genre styles, then, are constellations of co-occurrent formal elements and structures that define or characterize particular classes of utterances. The constituent elements of genre styles may figure in other speech styles as well, establishing indexical resonances between them. Additionally, particular elements may be abstracted from recognized generic styles and employed in other discursive settings to endow them with an indexical tinge, a coloration, of the genres with which they are primarily associated and the social meaning that attaches to them, as when students perceive an instructor to be "preaching at them" in a classroom lecture. In a related manner, a subset of diacritical generic features may be combined with those that characterize another genre to effect an interpretive transformation of genre, a phenomenon that Hymes terms "metaphrasis" (1975a). Finally, elementary or minimal genres – irreducible generic structures – may combine in a variety of ways into complex, incorporative genres, as is widely noted of African oratory, for example, or riddle ballads. Considered in these terms, genres may be seen as conventionalized yet highly flexible organizations of formal means and structures that constitute complex frames of reference for communicative practice.

Greg Urban, in his study, "The Semiotics of Two Speech Styles in Shokleng" (1984a), develops this line of analysis in especially suggestive ways. The two speech styles featured in Urban's essay are in fact generic styles, one associated with origin-myth narration and the other with ritual wailing. Extending the principle of co-occurrence, Urban notes that "speech styles are inherently indexical, since their use co-occurs with some other entity, namely, the context or subject matter" (1984a: 313). He goes on to offer a close semiotic analysis of origin-myth narration and ritual wailing that elucidates the webs of interrelationship that link them to other ways of speaking in Shokleng and to explore the communicative capacities of generic speech styles more broadly.

Hymes's observation that attention to rules of alternation organizing choices among speech styles "frees the resulting styles from mechanical connection with a particular defining situation" (1974: 434) implicates the relationship between genres and speech events. The casual merger of genres and speech events in the early literature of the ethnography of speaking soon yielded to the documentation and analysis in the field-based literature of the transferability of genres from their primary situational contexts of use to other speech events as well as to the differential mobilization of particular genres in a range of events.

Joel Sherzer, for example, traces the various contexts in which *ikarkana*, or curing texts, figure in San Blas Kuna culture, from the primary magical uses for curing, disease prevention, improving abilities, and general control of the spirit world to the rehearsal of an *ikar* by specialists, the teaching and learning of an *ikar*, and the chanting of an *ikar* for entertainment on festive occasions, each of which is marked by formal and functional differences (Sherzer 1983: 118–20). In a similar vein, Alessandro Duranti explores the formally and functionally contrastive uses of the Samoan genre of oratory, called *lauga*, in ceremonial events (especially rites of passage) and in a type of political meeting called *fono*. Sherzer's and Duranti's analyses establish that the generic specification of the *ikar* or *lauga* cannot be accomplished by the examination of texts alone, but resides rather in the interaction between the organization of the discourse and the organization of the event in which it is employed; the ways and degrees to which a genre is grounded in, or detachable from, events is to be discovered.

The Kuna and Samoan examples raise one further point, also adumbrated by Hymes in various writings. The most salient difference identified by Duranti between *lauga* in the *fono* and *lauga* in other ceremonial events has to do with performance. The ceremonial *lauga* "is the socially recognized domain of 'performance' par excellence" (1984: 235), in the sense of a display of verbal virtuosity, whereas the *lauga* in the *fono* is delivered and received in a very different, more instrumentally oriented mode. Likewise, the *ikar* as featured in festive occasions is framed primarily as virtuosic performance, in practicing as rehearsal, in teaching as demonstration, and so on. These cases, then, highlight the variable relation of genres to performance and to other frames. That this line of inquiry has been pursued most fully in relation to performance (Bauman 1977b; Hymes 1975a) is understandable in light of the long-standing centrality of artistic "literary" forms in the study of genre more generally. Most significant here is the recognition that not every doing of even the most poetically marked genres is framed as performance, or as full performance, in the sense of the assumption of accountability to an audience for a display of virtuosity, subject to evaluation for the skill and effectiveness with which the display is accomplished.

Of recent work in the exploration of genre in linguistic anthropology, William Hanks's essay, "Discourse Genres in a Theory of Practice" (1987), stands out as the most direct and critical attempt to synthesize a conception of genre and to offer a comprehensive framework for its investigation. Although the contributions of the ethnography of speaking are fundamental to Hanks's treatment of genre, his analytical framework is most immediately a synthesis of Mikhail Bakhtin's sociological poetics and Pierre Bourdieu's theory of practice. In marked contrast to conceptions of genre – formalist and otherwise – in which genre is a structural property of texts. Hanks conceives of genre as an orienting framework for the production and reception of discourse. In Hank's perspective, "The idea of objectivist rules is replaced by schemes and strategies, leading one to view genre as a set of focal or prototypical elements, which actors use variously and which never become fixed in a unitary structure" (1987: 681). Generic structures and functions, which are normatively specified in formalist and eufunctional approaches, "become problematic achievements in a practice-based framework" (1987: 681). More specifically, Hanks defines genres as "the historically specific conventions and ideals according to which authors [in Bakhtin's sense of authorship as the production of utterances] compose discourse and audiences receive it. In this view, genres consist of orienting frameworks, interpretive procedures, and sets of expectations that are not part of discourse structure, but of the ways actors relate to and use language" (1987: 670).

The principle of historic specificity is especially important; it builds into the notion of genre the recognition of historical emergence and change (see also Hymes 1975a), again in radical contrast to treatments of genres as timeless, fixed, unitary structures. In Hanks's framework, genres occupy a dual relationship to historically situated action. Genres are at the same time the ideational outcomes of historically specific acts and among the constituting, transposable frames of reference in terms of which communicative action is possible; they are thus open to innovation, manipulation, and change (1987: 671, 677). Hanks goes on to offer a penetrating elucidation in terms of form-function-meaning interrelationships of the emergence and transformation of genres of sixteenth-century Maya discourse as part of the emergence of new, hybrid forms of discourse under rapidly changing colonial conditions. Here, the "stylistic, thematic, and indexical schemata" (1987: 668) that constitute a range of available generic orienting frameworks become resources for the shaping of new discursive practice.

The Problematics of Genre

On the basis of the foregoing survey of perspectives on genre in linguistic anthropology, let us attempt to abstract and summarize the principal issues, problems, and ways of thinking about them that have characterized the field in order to establish a frame of reference for the discussion that follows.

One of the most central and persistent approaches to genre is from the vantage point of classification. Here, in its most basic terms, genre serves as a way of making categorical discriminations among discursive forms, which may be conceived of in textual terms, as verbal products, or in practice-based terms, as ways of speaking (and writing). The scope of genre, its range of applicability, varies among approaches. The term may be limited to "literary" forms, as forms of verbal art, or it may be extended to encompass a broader range of discursive forms, including, potentially, the entire domain of verbal production. Likewise, genre may be reserved for named categories of discourse, or, alternatively, all discursive forms may be taken to be generically regimented. The latter view, that there is no speaking without genre, may be stated axiomatically, as given, or hypothetically, as to be discovered.

The use of genre as a classificatory concept does not necessarily imply self-conscious attention to classification itself as an intellectual problem. Indeed, much work in the field tends to treat each generic category atomistically. Some significant work, however, has been devoted to the systemic organization of generic classifications, from the vantage point of either scientific taxonomy or the ethnographic investigation of locally constructed classification systems. The former, it is worth noting, fosters a conception of generic categories as necessarily mutually exclusive, consistent with the canons of scientific taxonomy, while the latter more often reveals generic categories that overlap and interpenetrate in a range of complex ways, or aspects of verbal production that are resistant to orderly categorization. Implicated here as well, of course, is the etic-emic distinction – a priori, analytical, universalistic categories, usually labeled in Western terms, versus locally constituted classification systems, employing local labels, which are to be discovered.

The criteria employed to define genres have included a wide range of features, ultimately taking in everything that people have considered significant about discourse: form, function or effect, content, orientation to the world and the cosmos, truth value, tone, social distribution, and manner or contexts of use. Definitional efforts in linguistic anthropology, however, are distinguished by the centrality of formal patterns, whether as the sole basis of definition or in relation to function, content, or context. The most significant dimension of contrast among formal perspectives on genre distinguishes those approaches that identify the formal organization of genre as an immanent, normative, structuring property of texts from those that view generic form as a conventionalized but flexible and open-ended set of expectations concerning the organization of formal means and structures in discursive practice. The latter view tends to raise the emergent properties of discursive organization to parity with the socially given, normative dimensions of generic structure.

Finally, we would register the very broad contrast between those approaches to genre that treat genre as a problem in its own right and those that explore the interrelationships that link genre to other terms, concepts, and sociocultural factors. Within linguistic anthropology in particular, one line of inquiry has concerned itself with the relationship between genre and other sociolinguistic organizing principles, especially speech acts, speech events, speech styles, and frames. In broader anthropological compass, investigators have analyzed dimensions of interrelationship between genres or genre systems and other cultural domains, such as ethics and cosmology, or other social structures, such as institutions or systems of social relations.

Whatever the focus of inquiry may be, however, the broadest contrast that characterizes understandings of genre in linguistic anthropology (and, we might add, in adjacent disciplines) sets off those approaches that constitute genre as an orderly and ordering principle in the organization of language, society, and culture from those that contend with the elements of disjunction, ambiguity, and general lack of fit that lurk around the margins of generic categories, systems, and texts. In the section that follows, we offer in exploratory terms a perspective on genre that brings the fuzzy fringes of genre to the center of the intellectual enterprise.

Generic Intertextuality

The preceding discussion suggests that genre has been under-theorized in linguistic anthropology. Beyond the fact that it has been put to a wide range of analytic and descriptive uses, practitioners have generally simply assumed that they and their audiences know what genres are and what makes them work. We suggest that this general failure to examine critically the nature of genres and to devote sufficient attention to their limitations as tools for classifying discourse is motivated in part by the persistence of the orientation toward genre laid out by Aristotle in the *Poetics*. Aristotle (Telford 1961: 1–2) suggested that to distinguish such types as epic or tragedy we must discern three elements of "the composite whole" of a given work: (1) the formal means by which an object is imitated, (2) the objects which are imitated, and (3) the manner of imitation (first-person narration, third-person narration, or acting). Although a great deal of discussion has centered on questions of mimesis and representation and on the *differentia specifica* of particular genres, Aristotle's emphasis on genre as dealing with works in terms of the way that features of their global construction place them within poetic types has endured.

We noted above that Bakhtin's work has stimulated a rethinking of, and a new emphasis on, genre in linguistic anthropology and other fields. His characterization of genre is particularly rich in that it sees linguistic dimensions of genres in terms of their ideologically mediated connections with social groups and "spheres of human activity" in historical perspective (1986: 65). By drawing attention to "complex" genres that "absorb and digest" other generic types, Bakhtin challenged the notion that genres are static, stylistically homogeneous, and nonoverlapping units (of which more later). In spite of the many advances he made in this area, however, Bakhtin's own definitions of genre are strikingly similar to Aristotle's: An early work, *The Formal Method in Literary Scholarship*, suggests that "genre is the typical totality of the artistic utterance, and a vital totality, a finished and resolved whole" (Bakhtin and Medvedev 1985[1928]: 129), while one of his last essays, which focused specifically on "speech genres," suggests that genres are "certain relatively stable thematic, compositional, and stylistic types of utterances" (1986: 64). Like Aristotle and his followers, Bakhtin laments the failure of researchers "to meet the fundamental logical requirement of classification: a unified basis" (1986: 64). In spite of the profound shift he effects in the theoretical placement of genre, Bakhtin thus casts genre as a tool for both classifying texts and grasping their textual structure by looking in each case for a "unified" set of generic features.

The basic question here concerns the manner in which discourse is seen as "containing" structure, form, function, and meaning. Since Jakobson has played such a key role in shaping how linguistic anthropologists (inter alia) approach poetics, let us examine what he considers to be the proper analytic focus. In concluding his classic "Concluding Statement: Linguistics and Poetics," Jakobson (1960: 365) argues for a strict distinction between the study of invariants and variables in poetic patterning, on the one hand, and concern with variability in the "recitation" of a particular poetic work, on the other. He cites the "sage memento" of

Wimsatt and Beardsley in arguing that "there are many performances of the same poem – differing among themselves in many ways. A performance is an event, but the poem itself, if there *is* any poem, must be some kind of enduring object" (1960: 365–6, emphasis in original). Jakobson makes it clear that the study of performance will not inform our understanding of the "enduring object," and it is accordingly not useful "for the synchronic and historical analysis of poetry" (1960: 365).

To be sure, the last 20 years have witnessed a shift in orientation from *text* to *performance*, with the latter term drawing researchers' attention to both social and poetic dimensions of the assumption of accountability to an audience for a display of virtuosity, subject to evaluation (Bauman 1977b; Hymes 1975a). Although concern with performance has helped shift researchers' focus from the "enduring object" to the process of poetic production and reception, this change runs the risk of simply drawing the analytic drawstrings wider – to encompass the relationship between linguistic and social or cultural dimensions of a given interaction – rather than questioning the equation of poetics with immanent features of particular discursive acts. Not only is the focus too narrow, but it lies in the wrong place as well.

Intertextual Strategies and Genre

An initial clue that can help us build an alternative approach to the study of genre – and of poetics and performance in general – is provided by Bakhtin's view of intertextuality. Kristeva neatly captures the contrasting basis of Bakhtin's thinking along these lines:

> Bakhtin was one of the first to replace the static hewing out of texts with a model where literary structure does not simply *exist* but is generated in relation to *another* structure. What allows a dynamic dimension to structuralism is his conception of the "literary word" as an *intersection of textual surfaces* rather than a point (a fixed meaning), as a dialogue among several writings: that of the writer, the addressee (or the character), and the contemporary or earlier cultural context. [Kristeva 1980: 64–5, emphasis in original]

Two facets of this characterization are crucial. First, structure, form, function, and meaning are seen not as immanent features of discourse but as products of an ongoing process of producing and receiving discourse. Second, this process is not centered in the speech event or creation of a written text itself, but lies in its interface with at least one other utterance.

Bakhtin's interest in a "translinguistics" that is vitally concerned with intertextuality has clearly provided part of the force that lies behind the recent interest in reported speech evident in linguistic anthropology and other fields.[2] A number of works have pointed to the way that intertextual relationships between a particular text and prior discourse (real or imagined) play a crucial role in shaping form, function, discourse structure, and meaning; in permitting speakers (and authors) to create multiple modes of inserting themselves into the discourse; and in building competing perspectives on what is taking place.

We would argue, similarly, that genre cannot fruitfully be characterized as a facet of the immanent properties of particular texts or performances. Like reported speech, genre is quintessentially intertextual. When discourse is linked to a particular genre, the process by which it is produced and received is mediated through its relationship with prior discourse. Unlike most examples of reported speech, however, the link is not made to isolated utterances, but to generalized or abstracted models of discourse production and reception.[3] When genre is viewed in intertextual terms, its complex and contradictory relationship to discourse becomes evident. We suggest that the creation of intertextual relationships through genre simultaneously renders texts ordered, unified, and bounded, on the one hand, and fragmented, heterogeneous, and open-ended, on the other. Each dimension of this process can be seen from both the synchronic and the diachronic perspective.

Viewed synchronically, genres provide powerful means of shaping discourse into ordered, unified, and bounded texts. As soon as we hear a generic framing device, such as "once upon a time," we unleash a set of expectations regarding narrative form and content. Animals may talk and people may possess supernatural powers, and we anticipate the unfolding of a plot structure that involves, as Propp (1968[1928]) showed us long ago, an interdiction, a violation, a departure, the completion of tasks, failure followed by success, and the like. The invocation of genre thus provides a textual model for creating cohesion and coherence, for producing and interpreting particular sorts of features and their formal and functional relations all the way from particular poetic lines to the global structure of the narrative. We would like to call attention not simply to the structural effects but to the process itself – the generation of textuality or, as we referred to it in an earlier work, entextualization (Bauman and Briggs 1990).

When viewed in diachronic or, as Bakhtin put it, vertical perspective,[4] generic intertextuality provides a powerful means of ordering discourse in historical and social terms. Genres have strong historical associations – proverbs and fairy tales have the ring of the traditional past, whereas electronic mail (E-mail) is associated with the ultramodern. Genres also bear social, ideological, and political-economic connections; genres may thus be associated with distinct groups as defined by gender, age, social class, occupation, and the like. Invoking a genre thus creates indexical connections that extend far beyond the present setting of production or reception, thereby linking a particular act to other times, places, and persons. To draw on the terminology we used earlier, generic features thus foreground the status of utterances as recontextualizations of prior discourse. Even when the content of the discourse lacks a clear textual precedent, generic intertextuality points to the role of recontextualization at the level of discourse production and reception. Genre thus pertains crucially to negotiations of identity and power – by invoking a particular genre, producers of discourse assert (tacitly or explicitly) that they possess the authority needed to decontextualize discourse that bears these historical and social connections and to recontextualize it in the current discursive setting. When great authority is invested in texts associated with elders or ancestors, traditionalizing discourse by creating links with traditional genres is often the most powerful strategy for creating textual authority (see Briggs 1988; Gossen 1974; Kuipers 1990). Building on Bourdieu (1977). We can say, thus, that generic intertextuality affords great power for naturalizing both texts and the cultural reality that they represent (see also Hanks 1987).

The variability that is evident in the way generic intertextual relationships are created points to an extremely important dimension of the diachronic dynamics of genre. We drew attention above to the fact that linguistic anthropologists, linguists, folklorists, and literary critics have largely followed Aristotle in viewing genre in empirical terms as involving a process through which rules or conventions impose structural and content-based constraints on textual production. Even writers who are particularly interested in the way speakers and hearers and writers and readers resist these rules and conventions generally see the nature of the entailed intertextual relations as relatively transparent and automatic. The fallacy of this assumption is evident when one realizes that genres are not road maps to particular texts. Invocations of genre rather entail the (re)construction of classes of texts. Specific features are then selected and abstracted, thus bringing into play a powerful process of decontextualization (see Bauman and Briggs 1990). As scholars in a number of fields have suggested, the power of genres emerges from the way they draw on a broad array of features – phonological, morphological, lexical, and syntactic, as well as contextual and interactive (see, for example, Ben-Amos 1976[1969]; Leitch 1991). By choosing to make certain features explicit (and particularly by foregrounding some elements through repetition and metapragmatic framing), producers of discourse actively (re)construct and reconfigure genres. Note the great similarity between the discourse practices associated with the use of genre in shaping extextualization, on the one hand, and the scholarly practices of linguistic anthropologists, literary critics, and the like, on the other: both entail creating classes of texts, selecting and abstracting features, and using this process in creating textual authority. (More later on the importance of this analogy.)

We have argued that the central role played by an active sociocultural and linguistic process of creating intertextual relations in genre renders it a powerful means of creating textual order, unity, and boundedness. The dynamic and constructed character of this relation is apparent in that the same text may be connected to the same genre to varying degrees, in highly contrastive ways, and for quite different reasons. We would now like to suggest that it becomes evident that these intertextual relations are not simply automatic effects of immanent properties of texts when the focus is shifted to the way that generic intertextuality simultaneously produces the *obverse* of these properties. Turning first to the synchronic dimensions of this problem, although generic intertextuality may help imbue texts with order, unit, and boundedness, it also draws attention to the *lack* of self-sufficiency and autonomy of the formal-functional configuration of the discourse at hand – recourse must be made to other discursive formations to interpret its patterning and significance. In Bakhtin's terms, genre points to the inherent dialogicality of the word. Just as genre can create order and sense in a text, it can render texts chaotic, fragmented, and nonsensical.

When viewed diachronically or vertically, the fit between a particular text and its generic model – as well as other tokens of the same genre – is never perfect; to paraphrase Sapir, we might say that all genres leak. Generic frameworks thus never provide sufficient means of producing and receiving discourse. Some elements of contextualization creep in, fashioning indexical connections to the ongoing discourse, social interaction, broader social relations, and the particular historical juncture(s) at which the discourse is produced and received. In short, other pragmatic and metapragmatic (cf. Silverstein 1976, 1992) frameworks must be brought into play in shaping production and reception.

The process of linking particular utterances to generic models thus necessarily produces an intertextual *gap*. Although the creation of this hiatus is unavoidable, its relative suppression or foregrounding has important effects. One the one hand, texts framed in some genres attempt to achieve generic transparency by *minimizing* the distance between texts and genres, thus rendering the discourse maximally interpretable through the use of generic precedents. This approach sustains highly conservative, traditionalizing modes of creating textual authority. On the other hand, *maximizing* and highlighting these intertextual gaps underlies strategies for building authority through claims of individual creativity and innovation (such as are common in twentieth-century Western literature), resistance to the hegemonic structures associated with established genres, and other motives for distancing oneself from textual precedents.

Examples of Strategies for Manipulating Generic Intertextuality

One of the most interesting facets of the way genre enters into discourse production and reception is the great variation that is evident in strategies for manipulating such gaps. Although we cannot present even a schematic inventory of the means by which intertextual distance is suppressed and foregrounded, some examples may serve to illustrate both the range of possibilities and the profound linguistic and social impact of these intertextual differences.

Kuipers's (1990) analysis of Weyewa ritual speech in Sumba, Indonesia, provides a striking example of the process of minimizing intertextual gaps. Ritual specialists attempt to decrease the distance between the "words of the ancestors" and their invocation in ritual performances. The three types of "ritual speech" with which Kuipers is primarily concerned – "divination," *zaizo* rites of placation, and "rites of fulfillment" – involve progressively greater suppression of demonstrative and personal pronouns, locutives (which frame discourse as reported speech), and discourse markers, features that contextualize the performance in its unique social and historical setting. The process goes hand in hand with building greater textual authority – and narrowing intertextual gaps – by affording more prominence to dyadic parallelism and proper names.

Such strategies for minimizing intertextual gaps bear directly on recent discussions of the complex social processes involved in the construction of history, tradition, authenticity, ethnicity, and identity (see, for example, Appadurai 1981; Clifford 1988; Dorst 1989; Handler and Linnekin 1984; Hobsbawm and Ranger 1983; Kirshenblatt-Gimblett 1991). Invocations of genre provide powerful strategies for building what Anderson (1991[1983]) terms "imagined communities." As in the Weyewa case, the speech genres that comprise the "talk of the elders of bygone days" among Spanish speakers in New Mexico play a key role in this process; unlike Weyewa "ritual speech," however, their use in constructing history, tradition, and ethnicity differs from genre to genre in both practice and ideology (see Briggs 1988).

The spiritual efficacy and experiential intensity of Lenten performances of hymns and prayers is contingent upon the progressive displacement of any perceived separation between the words uttered by Christ and the Virgin Mary in the course of the crucifixion, their inscription in sacred texts, and their utterance in performance. Worshippers assert that the written texts used in Lenten rituals have been handed down verbatim through the generations. Unison recitation suppresses intertextual variation within performances by regulating the volume, pitch, rate, breath, syntax, lexicon, and rhetorical structure of each worshipper's discourse production to such a point that differences between individual voices are nearly erased. The ritual process symbolically strips away elements that contextualize performances in terms of the social, temporal, spatial, and historical parameters of contemporary society and renders the here and now an icon of the crucifixion tableau. In attempting to achieve symbolic unification with Christ and the Virgin, participants deny the intertextual gap to such an extent that they seek to overcome the opposition between signifier and signified itself, merging the experience of the worshipper and that of Christ and the Virgin (as textually constructed). The control over ritual intertextuality that this process confers on the "Brothers," particularly elderly officers in the confraternity, affords them a great deal of religious authority and social power in general in their communities.

Mexicano speech genres are organized along a continuum, from genres that emphasize entextualization to those in which overt contextualization is crucial (Briggs 1988). Whereas hymns and prayers are highly extextualized, oral historical discourse is the most contextualized. In oral historical discourse, elders attempt to maximize the gap between "the talk of the elders of bygone days" and the contemporary discursive settings in which it emerges. One way in which this process is undertaken involves avoiding direct discourse, recasting this "talk" as the speaker's own utterances and personal experience; direct intertextual links to the words of "the elders of bygone days" are thus avoided. The maximization of intertextual distance plays a central role in both the rhetorical patterning of the discourse and its explicit framing by virtue of the way it motivates point-by-point contrasts between life *antes* "in bygone days" and the present. This is not to say that the discursive *effect* of such strategies is to achieve some sort of complete separation of text and genre – any invocation of generic features creates both intertextual relations and intertextual gaps. Such maximization is rather a rhetorical strategy that foregrounds the latter dimension of generic intertextuality.

Unlike the Weyewa case, this strategy does not render the discourse any less powerful in social terms than attempts to minimize the intertextual distance. For Weyewa, the ability to silence all dissenting voices and impose "unity" by linking monologic utterances as directly as possible to the "words of the ancestors" provides the central means of investing speech genres and individual performances with ritual and social power. In the *Mexicano* case, on the other hand, both minimizing and maximizing strategies, as differentially distributed according to genre, are used in appropriating – and (re)constructing – "the talk of the elders of bygone days," thereby legitimating courses of action and positions of social power.

Although genres tend to be linked to particular sets of strategies for manipulating intertextual gaps, it is clearly not the case that selection of a particular genre *dictates* the manner in which this process will be carried out. Transformation narratives ("myths") told by Warao storytellers in eastern Venezuela present narrators with a wide range of possible ways of manipulating intertextual gaps between the powerful speech of characters who lived "when our world was still being formed," the individual who told the particular narrative to the present narrator, and the narrating event. Authoritative, semantically monologic performances attempt to reduce the intertextual distance to zero, merging primordial and contemporary realms by suppressing explicit contextualization and centering the discourse deictically in the narrated (rather than the narrating) events (see Briggs 1992a). Like *Mexicano* oral historical discourse, Warao dialogic performances point precisely to differences between the two textual planes, playfully recontextualizing quoted utterances in both primordial and contemporary realms. Pedagogically oriented performances create maximal intertextual distance by focusing on the storytelling process itself, thus rendering the time when "our world was still being formed" experientially inaccessible. Not only can tokens of the same genre be performed in these intertextually contrastive fashions, but the same individual also can tell the same narrative in these three ways (see also Hymes 1985).

A shift in key (see Hymes 1972a) can similarly produce highly contrastive types of intertextual relations for the same genre. Recall Sherzer's (1983, 1991) analysis of the way that Kuna *ikarkana* can be used for practice, display, and as entertainment at drunken gatherings as well as incuring rituals; each type of performance would seemingly be related to quite different strategies for treating intertextual gaps.

Another example of the use of highly contrastive intertextual strategies in different performances of the same genre is apparent in Duranti's (1984) Samoan data, as discussed above. When fully performed in ceremonial contexts, *lauga* foreground intertextual relations with generic precedents. In political meetings (*fono*), on the other hand, elaborating stylistic features in displaying one's competence, vis-à-vis the textual authority invoked by the genre, is far less important than using *lauga* in shaping the ensuing discussions. Thus, both the nature of the intertextual links to prior and subsequent discourse and the strategies that guide the reception of *lauga*, and evaluations of the manner in which it is performed, contrast radically between settings. As was the case in the Warao and Kuna examples, these differences in strategies for creating intertextuality lie at the heart of both formal and functional patterning as well as the social power of the discourse.

Strategies for maximizing and minimizing intertextual gaps can coexist even more intimately as they enter dialogically into constituting the same text or performance. In nightlong performances of nativity plays (termed *coloquios*) in the Mexican state of Guanajuato, intertextual gaps are necessarily created as the script is subjected to a series of transformations; this process of recentering the text in performance takes place as the script is copied out, learned, rehearsed, and performed (see Bauman 1992b). In a production in Tierra Blanca de Abajo studied by Richard Bauman and Pamela Ritch, all the actors save one accepted the authority of the written script, as mediated by the *primer encargado*, the individual who has overall control of the production, and the prompter; they accordingly attempted to memorize their lines and reproduce them *por pura frase* 'by exact phrases' (i.e., word-for-word). Although they acknowledged that such factors as limited literacy, imperfections in the script, difficulties in hearing the prompter, lapses in memory, and the like prevent exact reproduction of the script, they sought to reduce the intertextual gap to zero. Fidelity to genre and text entailed adhering to a number of formal constraints, particularly the production of octasyllabic lines with assonant endings on alternating lines; assonance alternated with other patterns, such as rhymed couplets. Similarly, the script was rendered in a highly conventionalized style of delivery that featured three or four regular stresses per line and a fixed intonational pattern that was repeated (by some actors) for each line.

The actor who plays the Hermitaño (Hermit) adopted a mode of creating intertextuality that was diametrically opposed to that taken by the other actors. Although the fact that he is illiterate augmented the "technical" limitations to intertextual transparency, his departure from the script was more squarely motivated by a carnivalesque and subversive stance. As the Hermitaño offered few of his lines directly from memory, the prompter fed him his lines one-by-one, in a manner audible to the audience. Unlike the other actors who required prompting for each line, however, the Hermitaño decided whether to remain faithful to the stylistic and content-based features of the text and genre – the dominant intertextual ideology – or to transform it. He linked his utterances to text and genre by creating three types of intertextual relations. First, he often repeated at least some of the lexical items in the line as spoken by the prompter, and the syntactic structure remained largely identical across the two renditions; he repeated some lines verbatim. Second, the Hermitaño matched the phonological features of the line-final words in his utterances to those of their counterparts in the script. Third, the Hermitaño retained the characteristic intonational style of the *coloquio*. This retention of octasyllabic lines, rhyming schemes, and intonational patterns thus created strong generic intertextuality both with the essential characteristics of the *coloquio* and with the lines as read by the prompter.

With the exception of the lines he repeated verbatim, however, the Hermitaño's discourse departed subversively from the types of generic constraints observed by the other actors. Although the language of the *coloquio* and of the prompter's recitation was archaic, elevated, pious, and often magniloquent, the Hermitaño's recasting of them was colloquial, debased, richly sexual, and coarse. He similarly displaced much of the semantic content of his lines; although the sexual and other allusions he substituted can be parsed individually through familiarity with community social relations and the actor's own biography, they were so poorly linked to each other semantically that the Hermitaño's speeches essentially added up to rich nonsense. Interestingly, the Hermitaño created his parody by transforming features of the phonological patterning associated with the genre – alliteration, assonance, and rhyme – through punning. The strategies he adopted go beyond the creation of comic effect to objectify and foreground the pragmatics of recentering the text in the production process, as undertaken by the other actors, the *primer encargado,* and the prompter. By subversively recasting the lines that were recited for him by the prompter (and are heard by much of the audience as well), the Hermitaño revealed the central role played by the suppression of intertextual gaps in the genre. The Hermitaño's dramatic anti-language (Halliday 1978: 164–82) called attention to the possibility of creatively exploiting intertextual gaps rather than attempting to render them invisible. Yet the Hermitaño's burlesque creation and proliferation of such gaps is itself a generic convention of the *coloquio*; the Hermitaño is traditionally expected to take liberties with the scripted text. As performed, the *coloquio* genre exploits two strongly contrasting intertextual strategies.

The *coloquio* example points to the way that different strategies can be invested in different roles in the same performance. The tall tale provides a case in which different ways of approaching intertextual gaps are undertaken by the same participant and serve as constitutive features of the genre. Tall tales generally begin as personal-experience narratives; this framing entails a commitment to recounting episodes of the speaker's own life in a truthful manner. This told-as-true quality is signaled by metanarrative devices that assert the text's faithfulness, both to the events themselves and (through reported speech) to previous renditions of part or all of the narrative. A strategy used by a master Texas storyteller, the late Ed Bell, additionally involves directly addressing the audience's state of belief or disbelief and the credibility of the story itself: "And I don't blame y'all if you don't believe me about this tree, because I wouldn't believe it either if I hadn'ta seen it with my own eyes, I don't know whether I can tell ya how you could believe it or not, but that was a big tree" (Bauman 1986: 99).

As the story progresses, however, it increasingly transcends the limits of credibility. Hyperbolic details and metanarrative indications of the decreasing believability of the events create a sort of generic static, as it were, that interferes with interpreting the discourse as the relation of personal experience. The unreal qualities eventually become sufficiently prominent to lead most audience members to reinterpret the story as a tall tale. The genre thus involves a transformational process in discourse reception that moves from accepting strategies that seek to minimize intertextual gaps to perceiving a growing gap between the discourse and its purported generic framing to embracing a different form of generic intertextuality, one that celebrates intertextual gaps as powerful creative tools (see Bauman 1986: 78–111, 1987).

The movement evident in tall tales from one type of generic intertextuality to another points to the status of what Bakhtin (1986[1979]) refers to as *secondary* or *complex* genres as powerful means of creatively exploiting intertextual gaps. Here, possibilities for manipulating the gap between discourse and genre are multiplied as a text is linked to more than one set of generic features, to a genre that is itself mixed, or to both. Beyond opening up a range of possible interpretive relationships between generic precedents and the discourse being produced and received, mixing genres foregrounds the possibility of using intertextual gaps as points of departure for working the power of generic intertextuality backwards, as it were, in exploring and reshaping the formal, interpretive, and ideological power of the constituent genres and their relationship.

Let us turn to another type of Warao discourse in illustrating the role of intertextuality in mixed genres. When someone dies, female relatives compose and sing *sana* 'laments' until after the return from the graveyard (see Briggs 1992b). Beyond expressing the anger and sadness of the mourner, *sana* offer sharp criticism of actions seen as having contributed to the death or threatening the well-being of members of the community. One woman generally composes verses containing new material while the remaining wailers sing refrains – and listen. The other participants then either repeat the verses, changing both deictic elements and semantic content to reflect their own experience, or present their own verses.

Sana performances regulate intertextuality in three significant ways. First, wailers use reported speech in extracting discourse from a wide range of genres, including gossip, conversations, political rhetoric, arguments, and dispute mediation events. The intertextual reach of *sana* is thus quite impressive in that performers both create links with other lament performances and assimilate a broad range of other genres to the lament. Wailers exploit intertextual gaps to great effect by constantly reinterpreting this prior discourse in terms of the way its recontextualization is affected by the death and by juxtapositions with other reported utterances. Deictics and tense/aspect forms further manipulate the distance between reported and reporting speech. A second dimension of this intertextual regulation pertains to the carefully orchestrated polyphony that dominates performances. Extremely subtle features of the tempo, pitch, volume, and timbre of the women's voices, as well as the poetic interrelations between the verses they sing, foreground the emergence of both individual voices and a collective discourse (see Briggs 1989); the latter dimension shields individual wailers from retribution. Recall Urban's (1988) analysis of the way the iconic relations between the acoustic features of individual voices, other tokens of the genre, and the "natural icons" of crying constitute "meta-signals" regarding social solidarity and "adherence to a collective norm" in examples of ritual wailing recorded in other areas of South America. Warao women use the form, content, and performance dynamics of their laments in calling such social norms – and claims by others to adhere to them – into question. Third, these same features of *sana* regulate the intertextual relations between their laments and future discourse. *Sana* are seldom criticized or reinterpreted; although their content is subsequently recontextualized in narrative accounts of "what the women are crying," women sometimes specify in their *sana* how these stories should be told and to whom.

The interaction between gender and genre is crucial here. Outside of laments, Warao women have very little role in the production and reception of "mythic" narratives, political rhetoric, and shamanistic discourse. The ability of *sana* to incorporate other genres and, exploiting intertextual gaps, to question their authority provides women with frequently recurring opportunities to have a more powerful role in discourse production and reception. Research by Feld (1990a[1982], 1990b) and Seremetakis (1991) on the role of polyphony and intertextuality in, respectively, Kaluli (New Guinea) and Inner Maniat (Greek) laments points to the powerful role that generic intertextuality plays in constituting – and transgressing – gender roles. (We will have more to say about the relationship between gender, emotion, and genre below.)

Axes of Comparison

These examples point to the broad range of strategies that are used in minimizing and maximizing intertextual gaps. While we are still far from being able to present an exhaustive inventory of the forms of intertextuality associated with genre, we would like to adumbrate some of the principal loci in which variation is evident with respect to the nature of generic intertextuality and the means by which intertextual gaps are manipulated.

1. One axis of comparison is provided by the dimensions of the entextualization process that are exploited in creating and manipulating intertextual relations. Just as phonology, lexicon, morphosyntax, rhetorical structure, turn-taking, thematic content, prosody, gesture, participation roles, and other features can be used in linking discourse to generic precedents, strategies for minimizing and maximizing intertextual gaps can draw on an equally broad range of features. Dell Hymes (1981), Virginia Hymes (1987), and others have documented the recurrent use of rhetorical progressions of narrative action and patterns of versification in creating intertextual continuity and variation in Native American narratives. Bauman (1986: 54–77) argues that West Texas oral anecdotes, which use reported speech in building a punch line, are more stable over time than those in which reported speech is not the point of the story. As evident in the *coloquio* example, one of the most common strategies is to use formal features in creating generic intertextuality, while disjunctions in semantic content, participant structures, metapragmatic frames, and the like are used in challenging generic precedents; clearly, these relations can also be reversed.

2. Another source of variability with respect to the degree to which generic relations create order, unity, and boundedness lies in the fact that all genres are not created equal – or, more accurately, equally empowered – in terms of their ability to structure discourse. While "ordinary conversation" affords much greater room for disorder, heterogeneity, and open-endedness, some genres of ritual discourse provide almost no room for these characteristics or for structural flexibility in general. The Weyewa and *Mexicano* examples illustrate the differential distribution of this ordering capability by genre within particular discursive economies.

3. The power of genre to create textual structure also varies in keeping with the degree to which the generic patterning is imposed on a particular body of discourse. Although connections between a particular text and its generic precedent(s) sometimes crucially shape the formal structure and social force of the discourse, in other cases generic intertextuality is simply one of the available interpretive options. The use of *lauga* in ceremonial and political contexts provides an example in which these two options are evident in the case of a single genre. Generic features may not be overtly marked, and features that do appear may be foregrounded to various degrees (through repetition, metapragmatic signaling, et cetera) (see Briggs 1988). As we will argue below, the fact that the capacity of genre to create textual order, unity, and boundedness can be invoked to varying degrees is of profound interactive, ideological, and political-economic significance.

4. One of the most interesting loci of variation involves the extent to which intertextual strategies become, in Silverstein's (1992) terms, denotatively explicit, in the sense that the metapragmatic framing of intertextual relations is marked overtly through the denotative content of the entailed expressions. With regard to the preceding examples, Warao ritual

wailing and Texan tall tales make extensive use of explicit framings, whereas the Hermitaño's subversive transformations are not explicitly signaled. The latter example will serve as a warning against jumping to the ready (and ethnocentric) conclusion that denotationally explicit signals will be more salient in every case; when semantic interpretability is greatly limited by auditory interference, the use of unintelligible lexicons or languages, and the like, implicit signals expressed through prosodic or visual features may be more accessible. Basso's (1984) analysis of Apache moral narratives similarly provides a telling example of the social power of implicit framings. These parsimonious narratives contain little explicit information on intertextual relations; the framing seems to be limited to a statement regarding the place in which the reported event took place ("it happened at") and its temporal locus ("long ago"). The point of the performance is to induce an individual who is present to link her or his recent behavior – and what community members are saying about it – to the moral transgression committed in the story. Interestingly, these narratives contain explicit statements of intertextual relations (provided by the opening spatial and temporal frames) as well as entirely implicit relations (the link to talk about a member of the audience). This case also points to the fallacy in assuming that intertextual relations are established by performers or authors alone: a crucial part of the process of constructing intertextual relations may be undertaken by the audience.

5. A similar note of caution should be sounded with respect to the use of oral versus written resources in creating intertextuality. The work of Goody (1977), Ong (1967, 1982), and other writers, who sharply distinguish between "orality" and "literacy" as distinct modes of discourse production and reception and cognitive orientations, would lead us to expect that intertextual gaps will be minimized when written texts are used. The written text is indeed regarded as authoritative – and intertextual gaps are highly constrained – in the case of the scripts used in Mexican *coloquios* and New Mexican notebooks containing hymns and prayers. Nonetheless, the (re)production of written texts, along with their reception and recontextualization (in either oral or written form), necessarily creates intertextual gaps. The Hermitaño example shows how these gaps can be creatively expanded in establishing intertextual relations. Heath's (1982) research on class differences in literacy practices suggests that learning to exploit intertextual gaps by linking "ways of taking information from books" to other types of discourse production and reception (such as providing descriptions of everyday objects and events) is a crucial prerequisite to success in school. (We will have more to say later about the connection between intertextuality, language socialization, and social class.) Hanks (1987) and Lockhart (1991) similarly demonstrate the way that the production of written documents by, respectively, the Maya and Nahua of colonial Mexico drew on generic innovation as a key response for negotiating rapidly changing social and political relations.

6. A number of writers have argued for the need to examine how genre shapes the expression of emotions as well as the related question of the relationship between genre and gender. In an early extension of the ethnography of speaking to issues of gender and emotion, Keenan (1974) describes Malagasy men's control over speech styles and genres that minimize expressions of anger, criticism, and disagreement; women, on the other hand, use "unsophisticated" speech that expresses emotion in a direct and often confrontational manner. Feld (1990a[1982]) demonstrates the differing potential of contrastive genres for constructing emotions; in particular, women's ritual weeping provides a powerful means of expressing shared sentiments, whereas men's *gisalo* songs produce particular affective states in listeners. Schieffelin (1990) shows how Kaluli mothers develop teasing routines with sons yet discourage the same type of interactions – and the emotional expressions they occasion – with daughters. In a number of papers, Brenneis (1987, 1988, 1990) has pointed to the contrastive social values, patterns of social interaction, and emotional states that are evoked by different genres; he goes on to suggest that excluding women from participation in particular types of performances enacted by Hindi-speaking Fiji Indians largely

prevents them from obtaining access to a number of culturally valued emotional experiences.

Naturalizing the connection between genre, gender, and emotional experience can in turn rationalize the subordinate status of particular social groups or categories of persons; Lutz's (1990) discussion of the association between "emotionality" and the female in Western society provides a case in point. On the other hand, individuals who enjoy less social power due to gender, age, race, or other characteristics may draw on particular genres in expressing the injustice of their situation or in attempting to gain a more active role in social and political processes; women's performances of ritual wailing provide a striking example (see Briggs 1992b; Seremetakis 1991; Tolbert 1990).[5]

7. The role of music in creating intertextuality is also fascinating. By virtue of its capacity for closely regulating pitch, timbre, tempo, volume, and other features, and its frequent use in regulating movement (through dance), music can provide a powerful resource in attempting to suppress intertextual gaps. The use of music in parody and satire (as in Brecht's plays) points contrastively to its potential for foregrounding intertextual gaps. Feld (1990a[1982]) shows how musical features can simultaneously create intertextual links to generic precedents and to quite different types of discourse; the tonal characteristics of Kaluli "melodicsung-texted weeping" stimulate powerful emotional responses by connecting a woman's performance with the weeping of other women and with the tremendously evocative call of the *muni* bird. The fascinating problem of sonic or acoustic icons, including onomatopoeias, sound symbols, vocables, and the like, can be fruitfully analyzed with respect to their functions as powerful means of naturalizing intertextual relations. The relationship between musical and verbal modalities, along with dance, costume, and the like, in creating and challenging generic intextuality constitutes an area in which further research is needed.

8. A final axis of comparison pertains to the nature of generic intertextuality, The framing of some texts aligns them closely with a single genre; as we noted above, the link in other cases may be either to a number of different genres, to a mixed ("secondary") genre, or to both. Relations may be relatively fixed or emergent and open-ended. Warao ritual wailing, for example, affords a great deal of flexibility as to which genres are incorporated and how they enter into the performance. The routines performed by stand-up comics exhibit similar flexibility. In other examples, intertextual relations are established with two or more particular genres in relatively consistent ways.

Icelandic legends regarding magical poets, for example, embed recitations of verses imbued with magical efficacy into narratives (see Bauman 1992a). A number of types of intertextual relations play a central role in constituting these texts. First, narrators traditionalize texts, asserting their authenticity by recounting intertextual histories of the transmission of a particular example from narrator to narrator. This metanarrative framing both minimizes intertextual distance by constructing narrative continuity and maximizes the gap by questioning the authority of other interpretations of the story. Second, the intertextual gap between the reported recitation of the magical verse and its presentation in the narrative is minimized through the poetic distinctiveness of the verse. A gap remains, however, in that the narrator is not composing but re-presenting the magical verse; its performative potency for realizing supernatural violence is thus absent. Third, the narrative relates to the verse through content alone, describing the circumstances of its initial performance and reporting on its effects (e.g., a man cursed in a verse died in the brutal manner that it specified). Finally, the verse affects the narrative formally, magical verses extend beyond their textual confines to shape the lexical, grammatical, and rhetorical patterning of the narrative. Here the types of intertextual strategies that accrue to each genre as well as their dialogic interrelations are relatively conventional.

Broader Implications for Linguistic Anthropology

These examples suggest that generic intertextuality cannot be adequately understood in terms of formal and functional patterning alone – questions of ideology, political economy, and power must be addressed as well if we are to grasp the nature of intertextual relations. This discussion thus opens up a much larger theoretical and methodological issue that has emerged in linguistic anthropology and the study of discourse in general. At first glance, it seems as if the number of scholars who have aligned their work with the concept of discourse would have produced a fruitful integration or at least an articulation of a wide range of approaches and concerns. A closer look suggests that the highly divergent conceptualizations of the nature and significance of "discourse" have often *widened* the gap between research agendas. A great deal of recent work in linguistic anthropology resonates with Sherzer's call for a "discourse-centered" approach to the study of culture, one that focuses on detailed analyses of "actual instances of language in use," carefully documenting the relationship between formal and functional patterning and dimensions of social interaction, social structure, and cultural processes (1987: 296). The concept of "discourse" used by other scholars draws on Foucault, Bourdieu, and other post-structuralists; here, discourse is located more in the general processes by which social groups and institutions create, sustain, and question social power than in particular "speech events." Such practitioners are generally more interested in the rhetorical and political parameters of scholarly writing, mediated communication, and institutional discourse than in the situated speech of ethnographic "Others."

Unfortunately, this hiatus has further divided linguistic from social-cultural anthropology. The rift emerges in competing strategies for establishing textual authority, with linguistic anthropologists often claiming the low ground of methodological and analytic precision, and social-cultural types staking out the higher ground of sensitivity to the theoretical and political issues that prevail in the postmodern world. This situation frequently gives rise to ignorance of complementary perspectives and a hardening of intradisciplinary and epistemological lines. We believe that the perspective we have outlined in this article suggests ways that linguistic anthropologists can draw on the theoretical and methodological strengths of their training in challenging this unproductive opposition.

The preceding section focused mainly on formal and functional dimensions of strategies for creating intertextual relations. As we believe the examples clearly show, however, the roots of intertextual practices run just as deeply into social, cultural, ideological, and political-economic facets of social life as they do into the minutiae of linguistic structure and use. We would like to suggest that relations between intertextuality and ideology can be read in both directions – in terms of the way that broader social, cultural, ideological, and political-economic formations shape and empower intertextual strategies and the manner in which ideologies of intertextuality and their associated practices shape society and history.

The long-standing association between genre and order in Western discourse provides a strong sense of the impact of changing ideologies and social relations on intertextuality. The existence of a purportedly clearly defined and elaborate system of genres has often been associated with the social, political, and communicative value of national languages and literatures. For example, one of the central foci in many areas of Europe during the Renaissance was the legitimation of national languages (particularly vis-à-vis Latin and Greek) through the development and inculcation of an extensive set of rules for the generic structuring of texts (see Dubrow 1982: 58; Lewalski 1986). Like the establishment of a standard language, the production of a presumably fixed set of generic conventions played a role in the creation of "imagined communities" (see Anderson 1991 [1983]). The potential utility of an orderly system of literary genres for the establishment of an orderly social system was made explicit by such figures as Hobbes and Pope. A highly rigid characterization of genres formed a central concern during the neoclassic era in view of the prevalent fear of disorder in individuals and in society as a whole (see Dubrow 1982).

The association of genre with order has similarly often prompted those interested in countering established social and literary orders to challenge established genres or even the role of genres in general. The Romantics' search for a "natural" order led them, accordingly, to read the association between conventional order and genre as a basis for distrusting genre. Feminist scholars have argued that women often appropriate and manipulate generic conventions as a means of gaining entrance into male-dominated discourses (see Miller 1986). The scholarly production of such "folk" genres as the epic, proverb, fable, fairy tale, and ballad assisted in the nostalgic creation of a "folk" culture, which could be used in advancing nationalist agendas by appropriating the past as well as establishing the cultural autonomy and superiority of literary genres (see Hall 1981; Handler and Linnekin 1984; Herzfeld 1982; Kirshenblatt-Gimblett 1991; Stewart 1991).

A number of writers have argued that individual genres are hierarchically ordered (see, for example, Bourdieu 1991: 67; Kuipers 1990; Leitch 1992: 87). By virtue of the profound social and ideological associations of genres, hierarchies of genres are tied to social hierarchies. Given the connection between genres and conventional order, as well as their hierarchical organization, it is far from surprising that developing competence in different generic frameworks is a major focus of educational systems. Following Bourdieu's (1977, 1991; Bourdieu and Passeron 1977) analysis of the cultural politics of education, it is evident that the hierarchical organization of discursive competences according to genre provides efficient means for both controlling access to symbolic capital and evaluating the discursive competence of individuals.

Recall Heath's (1982) analysis of the connection between "ways of taking information from books" and educational success. The middle-class white, working-class white, and working-class African-American communities she studied were characterized by distinctive "ways of taking." Although books were accorded great authority and reading was highly encouraged in both of the predominantly white communities, the working-class parents "do not, upon seeing an item or event in the real world, remind children of a similar event in a book and launch a running commentary on similarities and differences" (Heath 1982: 61). Heath reports that although bedtime routines were not common in the working-class African-American community, participation in oral storytelling and other forms of verbal art afforded children great acuity in creating intertextual relations, particularly as based on metaphorical and fictionalized links.[6] Heath suggests, however, that classroom discourse discouraged these types of intertextuality "because they enable children to see parallels teachers did not intend, and indeed, may not recognize until the children point them out" (Heath 1982: 70). She goes on to argue that the compatibility between the "ways of taking" inculcated by middle-class white parents – even before the children were reading – and those rewarded in the classroom fostered much greater success in school. Rejecting the genres that predominated in the African-American community and the narrow constraints on recontextualization that prevailed among white members of the working class constituted crucial means of controlling access to symbolic capital.

Bauman's (1977a, 1982) account of children's "solicitational routines" – speech acts (such as riddles and knock-knock jokes) in which a response is solicited – presents analogous data drawn from genres in which literacy practices are not central. He suggests that solicitational routines provide contexts in which such educationally crucial intertextual skills as asking and answering questions can be learned and strategies for using them in gaining interactional power can be mastered. In an interesting parallel to Heath's data, the Anglo children in Bauman's Austin, Texas, sample were interested in a broader range of solicitational routines than either Chicano or African-American children; similarly, much more extensive intertextual relations between solicitational routines and television shows, comic books, and other forms of popular culture were evident in the repertoire of the Anglo children. Both sets of data suggest that both race and class regulate access to socialization into the types of intertextual strategies that are rewarded by the dominant society; the studies we cited earlier on genre and gender suggest that gender plays a crucial role in shaping the relevant socialization practices as well. We would go on to suggest that such differential distribution of competence in intertextual strategies provides an important means of naturalizing social inequalities based on race and ethnicity, gender, and social class.

One of the thorniest issues that divides social-cultural anthropologists from their linguistically oriented colleagues is the keen interest that many members of the former subdiscipline take in the "poetics and politics" of ethnography (see Clifford 1988; Clifford and Marcus 1986). Linguistic anthropologists – and more than a few social-cultural types as well – often regard their preoccupation with the writing of ethnography, both in "the field" and in the office, as a means of diverting scholarly energy away from the task of discovering the similarities and differences in the ways that people talk and act. Investigating intertextual strategies would seem to offer important possibilities for transcending this epistemological standoff. Fieldwork, analysis, and publication are just as dependent on intertextual strategies as are *coloquio* performances, ritual wailing, and the other forms we have discussed. Such techniques as interviewing draw on complex intertextual relations in creating discourse that is preconfigured for scholarly recontextualizations. As Paredes (1977) has so skillfully shown, ethnographers can be easily misled as to the types of generic intertextuality that their "informants" are using in framing their discourse. As in other types of discourse production and reception, what is negotiated is not just what types of intertextual links are being established, but who gets to control this process; race, class, gender, status, institutional position, and postcolonial social structures in general affect the production and reception of intertextual relations in fieldwork (see Briggs 1986; Mishler 1986).

A number of anthropologists have recently focused on literary intertextuality in ethnographic writing, illuminating the way that both fieldwork and its representation are shaped by intertextual relations; the generic parameters of ethnographies are shaped through intertextual links not simply with the discourse of Others, but with such literary genres as travel literature, autobiography, and colonial accounts (Clifford 1988; Clifford and Marcus 1986; Marcus and Fischer 1986; Taussig 1987, 1992). Although anthropological writing generally claims to derive its authority from knowledge gained "in the field," intertextual relations established through allegorical narratives and rhetorical tropes play a crucial role in creating authenticity and scientific authority. Examined from the perspective of the creation of generic intertextuality, these literary features are fascinating, both for the way they attempt to naturalize the ethnographer's control over intertextual processes and for the manner in which they seek to erase the monumental gap between the discourses they represent and their own textual representations. The extensive use of tape recorders in the field and side-by-side transcriptions/translations by linguistic anthropologists (present company included) clearly play a role in this process.

This is not to say that anthropological research, linguistic or otherwise, is untenable and should be abandoned. It is to say that fieldwork and its representation provide no less interesting examples of generic intertextuality than other types of discourse and that they are no less in need of scholarly attention. Attempts to dismiss analysis of the intertextual relations that we construct in the course of research and writing would seem to deny us vital information regarding the scientific status of these materials. Such proscriptions simply add up to another set of strategies for minimizing intertextual gaps; as in all such cases, we must inquire into the ideologies that sustain them and the power relations that render them effective or ineffective.

Conclusion

In this article we have critiqued views of genre that draw on purportedly immanent, invariant features in attempting to provide internally consistent systems of mutually exclusive genres. We presented an alternative view of genre, one that places generic distinctions not within texts but in the practices used in creating intertextual relations with other bodies of discourse. Since the establishment of such relations necessarily selects and abstracts generic features, we argued that generic intertextuality is not an inherent property of the relation between a text and a genre but the construction of such a relationship. A text can be linked to generic precedents in multiple ways; generic framings of texts are thus often mixed, blurred, ambiguous, contradictory. We accordingly suggested that generic links necessarily produce an intertextual gap; the strategies used for constructing intertextual relations can seek to minimize this gap, maximize it, or both. Choices between intertextual strategies are ideologically motivated, and they are closely related to social, cultural, political-economic, and historical factors.

Scholars have generally regarded systems of literary and speech genres as means of classifying or ordering discourse. Since intertextual relations produce disorder, heterogeneity, and textual open-endedness, as well as order, unity, and boundedness, scholarly strategies for creating generic links similarly involve arbitrary selections between competing intertextual relations and are affected by ideological, social, cultural, political-economic, and historical factors. Therefore, no system of genres as defined by scholars can provide a wholly systematic, empirically based, objective set of consistently applied, mutually exclusive categories.

One of the most interesting lines of inquiry in linguistic anthropology and folklore (see Ben-Amos 1976[1969], 1992) has located the study of speech genres in the ethnographic study of locally constructed classification systems rather than in a priori analytic categories. This shift has has a positive impact on research by drawing attention to the processes of discursive ordering undertaken by a broader range of producers and receivers of texts than those associated with scholarly practices alone. Unfortunately, it has also helped displace the reification of generic intertextuality from scholarly discourse to representations of ethnographic Others. Ethnographically based studies often portray the situated use of ethnic genres as a process of applying relatively stable, internally consistent, mutually exclusive, and well-defined categories in the production and reception of texts. In representing such an orderly process, scholars run the risk of doubly mystifying the problem by failing to discern the ideologies and power arrangements that underlie local impositions of generic order as well as by covering up their own rhetorical use of genres in ordering ethnographic data. In so doing, scholars collude with the members of the community in question who are deemed to have control over the production and reception of intertextual relations; they similarly often overlook the existence of marginalized and dissenting intertextual strategies (but see Appadurai et al. 1991). While the research on speech genres conducted by the two of us over the years has attempted to analyze the social, political, and linguistic processes that shape the production and reception of verbal art, our work is hardly immune from this sort of reification.

Our goal in this article is thus not to "rescue" the category of genre from these difficulties or to assert its centrality to research in linguistic anthropology. Any attempt to champion – or to dismiss – the concept of genre would have strong ideological underpinnings. We have rather tried to use our discussion of genre as a means of raising some basic issues regarding discourse production and reception. In an earlier article (Bauman and Briggs 1990) we argued that discourse analysis cannot best proceed either by (1) studying (socio)linguistic elements and processes apart from the process of discourse production and reception or by (2) studying social interactions as analytic microcosms. We rather pointed to the fruitfulness of studying discourse vis-à-vis the way it is transformed in the course of successive decontextualizations and recontextualizations and of exploring the process of entextualization that provides the formal and functional basis for such transformations.

We have attempted to advance this line of inquiry here by drawing attention to some of the ways that linguistic anthropologists have used the concept of genre in elucidating discourse processes; we have pointed to a number of problems in the theoretical underpinnings of these discussions that pose obstacles to progress along these lines. We went on to use the notion of generic intertextuality in analyzing particular strategies for decontextualizing and recontextualizing discourse, along with the ways that this process both reflects and produces social power. We hope that this discussion has demonstrated the value of integrating detailed formal and functional analysis, the sine qua non of linguistic anthropology, with attention to ideology, power, and scholarly practices. We also hope to have suggested some of the ways that such a critical synthetic approach can illuminate contrastive – and often competing – approaches to the study of discourse.

NOTES

1 The way that a number of anthropologists approached ethnographically situated genres converged with work in folkloristics; the distinction drawn by BenAmos (1976[1969]) between "analytical types," the etic categories used by scholars in comparative research, and "ethnic genres," the emic categories used by members of particular speech communities, was highly influential.

2 See studies by Bauman (1986), Briggs (1990, 1992b), Goodwin (1990), Hymes (1981), Philips (1986), Silverstein (1985), Tannen (1989), Urban (1984b), and a volume edited by Lucy entitled *Reflexive Language: Reported Speech and Metapragmatics* (1992).

3 The qualifier here suggests the fact that there are important exceptions. Some types of reported utterances, such as proverbs, may be attributed not to a particular individual or speech event but to a category of speakers or simply to "tradition" (see Briggs 1988: 101–35).

4 In developing his notion of the spatialization of the word in dialogue, Bakhtin discussed an opposition between the *horizontal* characterization of a word's status, a relationship between a writing subject and an addressee, and a *vertical* one, in which the word is viewed in its relationship to a preceding utterance.

5 Investigations of the relationship between genre and gender are currently providing a rich cross-disciplinary convergence of interests between linguistic and sociocultural anthropologists (see Appadurai et al. 1991; Gal 1991; Philips et al. 1987) and practitioners in such fields as ethnomusicology (see Herndon and Ziegler 1990; Koskoff 1989), folkloristics (Farrer 1975; Jordan and Kalčik 1985), and literary criticism (Miller 1986; Showalter 1985).

6 See also Labov (1972) on the sociolinguistic skills of inner-city African-American children; he similarly argues that the hegemony of sociolinguistic patterns associated with middle-class whites in schools thwarts the ability of African-American children to draw on their verbal abilities and sets them up for educational failure. Interestingly, Gates (1988) argues that intertextuality lies at the heart of African-American aesthetics.

REFERENCES

Abrahams, Roger D., and Richard Bauman (1971) Sense and Nonsense in St. Vincent: Speech Behavior and Decorum in a Caribbean Community. *American Anthropologist* 73(3): 262–72.

Abu-Lughod, Lila (1986) *Veiled Sentiments: Honor and Poetry in a Bedouin Society*. Berkeley: University of California Press.

Abu-Lughod, Lila (1990) Shifting Politics of Bedouin Love Poetry. In *Language and the Politics of Emotion*. Catherine A. Lutz and Lila Abu-Lughod, eds., pp. 24–45. Cambridge: Cambridge University Press.

Anderson, Benedict (1991[1983]) *Imagined Communities: Reflections on the Origin and Spread of Nationalism*. London: Verso.

Appadurai, Arjun (1981) The Past as a Scarce Resource. *Man* 16(2): 201–19.

Appadurai, Arjun, Frank J. Korom, and Margaret A. Mills, eds. (1991) *Gender, Genre, and Power in South Asian Expressive Traditions*. Philadelphia: University of Pennsylania Press.

Bakhtin, M. M. (1986[1979]) The Problem of Speech Genres. In *Speech Genres and Other Late Essays*. Caryl Emerson and Michael Holquist, eds., pp. 60–102. Austin: University of Texas Press.

Bakhtin, M. M., and P. M. Medvedev (1985 [1928]) *The Formal Method in Literary Scholarship: A Critical Introduction to Sociological Poetics*. Albert J. Wehrle, trans. Cambridge, Mass.: Harvard University Press.

Basso, Keith H. (1984) "Stalking with Stories": Names, Places, and Moral Narratives among the Western Apache. *In Text, Play, and Story*. Edward Bruner, ed., pp. 19–55. Washington, DC: American Ethnological Society.

Bauman, Richard (1977a) Linguistics, Anthropology, and Verbal Art: Toward a Unified Perspective, With a Special Discussion of Children's Folklore. In *Linguistics and Anthropology.* Muriel Saville-Troike, ed., pp. 13–36. Washington, DC: Georgetown University Press.

Bauman, Richard (1977b) *Verbal Art as Performance.* Prospect Heights, III.: Waveland Press.

Bauman, Richard (1982) The Ethnography of Children's Folklore. In *Children In and Out of School: Ethnographic Perspectives in Education.* Perry Gilmore and Alan Glatthorn, eds., pp. 172–86. Washington, DC: Center for Applied Linguistics.

Bauman, Richard (1986) *Story, Performance, and Event: Contextual Studies of Oral Narrative.* Cambridge: Cambridge University Press.

Bauman, Richard (1987) Ed Bell, Texas Storyteller: The Framing and Reframing of Life Experience. *Journal of Folklore Research* 24 (3): 197–221.

Bauman, Richard (1992a) Contextualization, Tradition, and the Dialogue of Genres: Icelandic Legends of the Kraftaskáld. In *Rethinking Context: Language as an Interactive Phenomenon.* Alessandro Duranti and Charles Goodwin, eds., pp. 77–99. Cambridge: Cambridge University Press.

Bauman, Richard (1992b) Transformations of the Word in the Production of Mexican Festival Drama. In *The Decentering of Discourse.* Michael Silverstein and Greg Urban, eds.

Bauman, Richard, and Charles L. Briggs (1990) Poetics and Performance as Critical Perspectives on Language and Social Life. *Annual Review of Anthropology* 19: 59–88.

Ben-Amos, Dan (1976[1969]) Analytical Categories and Ethnic Genres. In *Folklore Genres.* Dan Ben-Amos, ed., pp. 215–42. Austin: University of Texas Press.

Ben-Amos, Dan (1992) *Do We Need Ideal Types (in Folklore)? An Address to Lauri Honko.* Turku, Finland: Nordic Institute of Folklore.

Boas, Franz (1940a[1914]) Mythology and Folk-Tales of the North American Indians. In *Race, Language and Culture*, pp. 451–90. New York: Free Press.

Boas, Franz (1940b[1916]) The Development of Folk-Tales and Myths. In *Race, Language and Culture*, pp. 397–406. New York: Free Press.

Boas, Franz (1940c[1917]) Introduction to International Journal of American Linguistics. In *Race, Language and Culture*, pp. 199–210. New York: Free Press.

Bourdieu, Pierre (1977) *Outline of a Theory of Practice.* Richard Nice, trans. Cambridge: Cambridge University Press.

Bourdieu, Pierre (1991) *Language and Symbolic Power.* Gino Raymond and Matthew Adamson, trans. Cambridge, Mass.: Harvard University Press.

Bourdieu, Pierre, and Jean-Claude Passeron (1977) *Reproduction: In Education, Society and Culture.* Richard Nice, trans. Beverly Hills, Calif.: Sage.

Brenneis, Donald (1987) Performing Passions: Aesthetics and Politics in an Occasionally Egalitarian Community. *American Ethnologist* 14(2): 236–50.

Brenneis, Donald (1988) Telling Troubles: Narrative, Conflict and Experience. *Anthropological Linguistics* 30(3/4): 279–91.

Brenneis, Donald (1990) Shared and Solitary Sentiments: The Discourse of Friendship, Play, and Anger in Bhatgaon. In *Language and the Politics of Emotion.* Catherine A. Lutz and Lila Abu-Lughod, eds., pp. 113–25. Cambridge: Cambridge University Press.

Briggs, Charles L. (1986) *Learning How to Ask: A Sociolinguistic Appraisal of the Role of the Interview in Social Science Research.* Cambridge: Cambridge University Press.

Briggs, Charles L. (1988) *Competence in Performance: The Creativity of Tradition in* Mexicano *Verbal Art.* Philadelphia: University of Pennsylvania Press.

Briggs, Charles L. (1989) *"Please Pass the Poison": The Poetics of Dialogicality in Warao Ritual Wailing.* Paper presented at the Conference on Lament, Austin, Tex.

Briggs, Charles L. (1990) History, Poetics, and Interpretation in the Tale. In *The Lost Gold Mine of Juan Mondragón: A Legend from New Mexico* Performed by Melaquías Romero. Charles L. Briggs and Julián Josué Vigil, eds., pp. 165–240. Tucson: University of Arizona Press.

Briggs, Charles L. (1992a) Generic versus Metapragmatic Dimensions of Warao Narratives: Who Regiments Performance? In *Reflexive Language: Reported Speech and Metapragmatics*. John A. Lucy, ed., pp. 179–212. Cambridge: Cambridge University Press.

Briggs, Charles L. (1992b) "Since I Am a Woman, I Will Chastise My Relatives": Gender, Reported Speech, and the (Re)production of Social Relations in Warao Ritual Wailing. *American Ethnologist* 19(2): 337–61.

Clifford, James (1988) *The Predicament of Culture: Twentieth-Century Ethnography, Literature, and Art*. Cambridge, Mass.: Harvard University Press.

Clifford, James, and George E. Marcus, eds. (1986) *Writing Culture: The Poetics and Politics of Ethnography*. Berkeley: University of California Press.

Dorst, John D. (1989) *The Written Suburb: An American Site, an Ethnographic Dilemma*. Philadelphia: University of Pennsylvania Press.

Dubrow, Heather (1982) *Genre*. London: Methuen.

Dundes, Alan (1964) The Morphology of North American Indian Folktales. *Folklore Fellows Communications*, 195. Helsinki: Suomalainen Tiedeakatemia.

Dundes, Alan, ed. (1965) *The Study of Folklore*. Englewood Cliffs, NJ: Prentice-Hall.

Duranti, Alessandro (1984) *Lauga* and *Talanoaga:* Two Speech Genres in a Samoan Political Event. In *Dangerous Words: Language and Politics in the Pacific*. Donald L. Brenneis and Fred R. Myers, eds., pp. 217–42. New York: New York University Press.

Ervin-Tripp, Susan (1972) On Sociolinguistic Rules: Alternation and Co-Occurrence. In *Directions in Sociolinguistics: The Ethnography of Communication*. John J. Gumperz and Dell H. Hymes, eds., pp. 213–50. New York: Holt, Rinehart & Winston.

Farrer, Claire R., ed. (1975) Women and Folklore: Images and Genres. Special issue of *Journal of American Folklore* 88(347).

Feld, Steven (1990a[1982]) *Sound and Sentiment: Birds, Weeping, Poetics, and Song in Kaluli Expression*. 2d edn. Philadelphia: University of Pennsylvania Press.

Feld, Steven (1990b) Wept Thoughts: The Voicing of Kaluli Memories. *Oral Tradition* 5(2/3): 241–66.

Gal, Susan (1991) Between Speech and Silence: The Problematics of Research on Language and Gender. In *Gender at the Crossroads of Knowledge: Feminist Anthropology in the Postmodern Era*. Micaela di Leonardo, ed., pp. 175–203. Berkeley: University of California Press.

Gates, Henry Louis, Jr. (1988) *The Signifying Monkey: A Theory of African-American Literary Criticism*. New York: Oxford University Press.

Georges, Robert, and Alan Dundes (1963) Toward a Structural Definition of the Riddle. *Journal of American Folklore* 76(300): 111–18.

Goodwin, Marjorie Harness (1990) *He-Said-She-Said: Talk as Social Organization Among Black Children*. Bloomington: Indiana University Press.

Goody, John Rankin (1977) *The Domestication of the Savage Mind*. Cambridge: Cambridge University Press.

Gossen, Gary H. (1972) Chamula Genres of Verbal Behavior. In *Toward New Perspectives in Folklore*. Américo Paredes and Richard Bauman, eds., pp. 145–67. Austin: University of Texas Press.

Gossen, Gary H, (1974) *Chamulas in the World of the Sun: Time and Space in a Maya Oral Tradition*. Cambridge, Mass.: Harvard University Press.

Hall, Stuart (1981) Notes on Deconstructing "the Popular." In *People's History and Socialist Theory*. Raphael Samuel, ed., pp. 227–40. London: Routledge.

Halliday, M. A. K. (1978) *Language as Social Semiotic*. London: Arnold.

Handler, Richard, and Jocelyn Linnekin (1984) Tradition, Genuine or Spurious. *Journal of American Folklore* 97(385): 273–90.

Hanks, William F. (1987) Discourse Genres in a Theory of Practice. *American Ethnologist* 14(4): 668–92.

Heath, Shirley Brice (1982) What No Bedtime Story Means: Narrative Skills at Home and School. *Language in Society* 11 (1): 49–76; reproduced in Chapter 14 of this Reader.

Herndon, Marcia, and Susanne Ziegler, eds. (1990) *Music, Gender, and Culture.* Wilhelmshaven, Germany: Florian Noetzel Verlag.

Herzfeld, Michael (1982) *Ours Once More: Folklore, Ideology, and the Making of Modern Greece.* Austin: University of Texas Press.

Hobsbawm, Eric, and Terence Ranger, eds. (1983) *The Invention of Tradition.* Cambridge: Cambridge University Press.

Hymes, Dell H. (1962) The Ethnography of Speaking. In *Anthropology and Human Beahvior.* Thomas Gladwin and William C. Sturtevant, eds., pp. 13–53. Washington, DC: Anthropological Society of Washington.

Hynes, Dell H. (1964) Introduction: Toward Ethnographies of Communication. In *The Ethnography of Communication. American Anthropologist,* Special Publication 66, Number 6, Part 2. John J. Gumperz and Dell H. Hymes, eds., pp. 1–34. Washington, DC: American Anthropological Association.

Hynes, Dell H. (1967) Models of the Interaction of Language and Social Setting. *Journal of Social Issues* 23(2): 8–28.

Hynes, Dell H. (1972a) Models of the Interaction of Language and Social Life. In *Directions in Sociolinguistics: The Ethnography of Communication.* John J. Gumperz and Dell H. Hymes, eds., pp. 35–71. New York: Holt, Rinehart & Winston.

Hynes, Dell H. (1972b) The Contribution of Folklore to Sociolinguistic Research. In *Toward New Perspectives in Folklore.* Américo Paredes and Richard Bauman, eds., pp. 42–50. Austin: University of Texas Press.

Hynes, Dell H. (1974) Ways of Speaking. In *Explorations in the Ethnography of Speaking.* Richard Bauman and Joel Sherzer, eds., pp. 433–51. Cambridge: Cambridge University Press; reproduced in Chapter 6 of this Reader.

Hynes, Dell H. (1975a) Breakthrough Into Performance. In *Folklore: Performance and Communication.* Dan Ben-Amos and Kenneth S. Goldstein, eds., pp. 11–74. The Hague: Mouton.

Hynes, Dell H. (1975b) Folklore's Nature and the Sun's Myth. *Journal of American Folklore* 88(350): 346–69.

Hynes, Dell H. (1981) *"In Vain I Tried to Tell You": Essays in Native American Ethnopoetics.* Philadelphia: University of Pennsylvania Press.

Hynes, Dell H. (1985) Language, Memory, and Selective Performance: Cultee's "Salmon's Myth" as Twice Told to Boas. *Journal of American Folklore* 98(390): 391–434.

Hymes, Virginia (1987) Tonkawa Poetics: John Rush Buffalo's "Coyote and Eagle's Daughter." In *Native American Discourse: Poetics and Rhetoric.* Joel Sherzer and Anthony C. Woodbury, eds., pp. 62–102. Cambridge: Cambridge University Press.

Jacobs, Melville (1959) *Clackamas Chinook Texts.* Part 2. Bloomington: Indiana University Research Center in Anthropology, Folklore, and Linguistics.

Jakobson, Roman (1960) Closing Statement: Linguistics and Poetics. In *Style in Language.* Thomas A. Sebeok, ed., pp. 350–77. Cambridge, Mass.: MIT Press.

Jordan, Rosan A., and Susan Kalčik, eds. (1985) *Women's Folklore, Women's Culture.* Philadelphia: University of Pennsylvania Press.

Keenan, Elinor (1974) Norm-Makers, Norm-Breakers: Uses of Speech by Men and Women in a Malagasy Community. In *Explorations in the Ethnography of Speaking.* Richard Bauman and Joel Sherzer, eds., pp. 125–43. Cambridge: Cambridge University Press.

Kirshenblatt-Gimblett, Barbara (1991) Objects of Ethnography. In *Exhibiting Cultures: The Poetics and Politics of Museum Display.* Ivan Karp and Steven D. Lavine, eds., pp. 386–443. Washington, DC: Smithsonian Institution Press.

Koskoff, Ellen, ed. (1989) *Women and Music in Cross-Cultural Perspective.* Westport, Conn.: Greenwood Press.

Kristeva, Julia (1980) *Desire in Language.* Leon S. Roudiez, trans. New York: Columbia University Press.

Kuipers, Joel C. (1990) *Power in Performance: The Creation of Textual Authority in Weyewa Ritual Speech.* Philadelphia: University of Pennsylvania Press.

Labov, William (1972) *Language in the Inner City.* Philadelphia: University of Pennsylvania Press.

Leitch, Vincent B. (1991) (De)Coding (Generic) Discourse. *Genre* 24(1): 83–98.

Lewalski, Barbara Kiefer, ed. (1986) *Renaissance Genres: Essays on Theory, History, and Interpretation*. Cambridge, Mass.: Harvard University Press.

Lockhart, James (1991) *Nahuas and Spaniards: Postconquest Central Mexican History and Philology*. Stanford, Calif.: Stanford University Press.

Lucy, John, ed. (1992) *Reflexive Language: Reported Speech and Metapragmatics*. Cambridge: Cambridge University Press.

Lutz, Catherine (1990) Engendered Emotion: Gender, Power, and the Rhetoric of Emotional Control in American Discourse. In *Language and the Politics of Emotion*. Catherine A. Lutz and Lila Abu-Lughod, eds., pp. 69–91. Cambridge: Cambridge University Press.

Marcus, George E, and Michael M. J. Fischer (1986) *Anthropology as Cultural Critique: An Experimental Moment in the Human Sciences*. Chicago, IL: University of Chicago Press.

Miller, Nancy K., ed. (1986) *The Poetics of Gender*. New York: Columbia University Press.

Mishler, Elliot G. (1986) *Research Interviewing: Context and Narrative*. Cambridge, Mass.: Harvard University Press.

Ong, Walter J. (1967) *The Presence of the Word: Some Prolegomena for Cultural and Religious History*. Minneapolis: University of Minnesota Press.

Ong, Walter (1982) *Orality and Literacy: The Technologizing of the Word*. London: Methuen.

Paredes, Américo (1977) On Ethnographic Work among Minority Groups. *New Scholar* 6(1): 1–32.

Philips, Susan U. (1986) Reported Speech as Evidence in an American Trial. In *Languages and Linguistics: The Interdependency of Theory, Data, and Application*. Deborah Tannen, ed. Washington, DC: Georgetown University Press.

Philips, Susan U. (1987) The Concept of Speech Genre in the Study of Language and Culture. In *Working Papers and Proceedings of the Center for Psychosocial Studies*, 11, pp. 25–34. Chicago, IL: Center for Psychosocial Studies.

Philips, Susan U., Susan Steele, and Christine Tanz, eds. (1987) *Language, Gender and Sex in Comparative Perspective*. Cambridge: Cambridge University Press.

Propp, Vladímir (1968[1928]) *The Morphology of the Folktale*. Laurence Scott, trans. Austin: University of Texas Press.

Radin, Paul (1926) Literary Aspects of Winnebago Mythology. *Journal of American Folklore* 39(151): 18–52.

Reichard, Gladys (1925) Wiyot Grammar and Texts. *University of California Publications in American Archaeology and Ethnology*, 22 (1). Berkeley: University of California Press.

Reichard, Gladys (1947) *An Analysis of Coeur D'Alene Indian Myths. Memoirs of the American Folklore Society*, vol. 41. Philadelphia, Penn.: American Folklore Society.

Sapir, Edward (1909) *Wishram Texts. Publications of the American Ethnological Society*, vol. 2. Leiden: E. J. Brill.

Sapir, Edward, and Harry Hoijer (1942) *Navaho Texts*. Iowa City: Linguistic Society of America and University of Iowa.

Schieffelin, Bambi B. (1990) *The Give and Take of Everyday Life: Language Socialization of Kaluli Children*. Cambridge: Cambridge University Press.

Scott, Charles T. (1965) *Persian and Arabic Riddles: A Language-Centered Approach to Genre Definition*. Bloomington: Indiana University Research Center in Anthropology, Folklore, and Linguistics.

Sebeok, Thomas A. (1964[1953]) The Structure and Content of Cheremis Charms. In *Language in Culture and Society*. Dell H. Hymes, ed., pp. 356–71. New York: Harper & Row.

Seremetakis, C. Nadia (1991) *The Last Word: Women, Death, and Divination in Inner Mani*. Chicago, IL: University of Chicago Press.

Sherzer, Joel (1983) *Kuna Ways of Speaking*. Austin: University of Texas Press.

Sherzer, Joel (1987) A Discourse-Centered Approach to Language and Culture. *American Anthropologist* 89(2): 295–309.

Sherzer, Joel (1991) *Verbal Art in San Blas*. Cambridge: Cambridge University Press.

Shimkin, Demitri (1964[1947]) Wind River Shoshone Literary Forms: An Introduction.

In *Language in Culture and Society*. Dell H. Hymes, ed., pp. 344–55. New York: Harper & Row.

Showalter, Elaine, ed. (1985) *The New Feminist Criticism: Essays on Women, Literature, and Theory*. New York: Pantheon.

Silverstein, Michael (1976) Shifters, Linguistic Categories, and Cultural Description. In *Meaning in Anthropology*. Keith Basso and Henry A. Selby, eds., pp. 11–55. Albuquerque: University of New Mexico Press.

Silverstein, Michael (1985) The Culture of Language in Chinookan Narrative Texts; or, on Saying that ... in Chinook. In *Grammar Inside and Outside the Clause*. Johanna Nichols and Anthony Woodbury, eds., pp. 132–71. Cambridge: Cambridge University Press.

Silverstein, Michael (1992) Metapragmatic Discourse and Metapragmatic Function. In *Reflexive Language: Reported Speech and Metapragmatics*. John A. Lucy, ed., pp. 33–58. Cambridge: Cambridge University Press.

Stewart, Susan (1991) Notes on Distressed Genres. *Journal of American Folklore* 104 (411): 5–31.

Stross, Brian (1974) Speaking of Speaking: Tenejapa Tzeltal Metalinguistics. In *Explorations in the Ethnography of Speaking*. Richard Bauman and Joel Sherzer, eds., pp. 213–39. Cambridge: Cambridge University Press.

Tannen, Deborah (1989) *Talking Voices: Repetition, Dialogue, and Imagery in Conversational Discourse*. Cambridge: Cambridge University Press.

Taussig, Michael (1987) *Shamanism, Colonialism and the Wild Man: A Study in Terror and Healing*. Chicago, IL: University of Chicago Press.

Taussig, Michael (1992) *The Nervous System*. New York: Routledge.

Telford, Kenneth A. (1961) *Aristotle's Poetics: Translation and Analysis*. South Bend, Ind.: Gateway.

Tolbert, Elizabeth (1990) Magico-Religious Power and Gender in the Karelian Lament. In *Music, Gender, and Culture*. Marica Herndon and Suzanne Ziegler, eds., pp. 41–56. Berlin: Institute for Comparative Music Studies.

Urban, Greg (1984a) The Semiotics of Two Speech Styles in Shokleng. In *Semiotic Mediation*. Elizabeth Mertz and Richard J. Parmentier, eds., pp. 311–29. Orlando, Fla.: Academic Press.

Urban, Greg (1984b) Speech about Speech in Speech about Action. *Journal of American Folklore* 97(385): 310–28.

Urban, Greg (1988) Ritual Wailing in Amerindian Brazil. *American Anthropologist* 90 (2):385–400.

STUDY QUESTIONS

1 What are some of the problems and inconsistencies that Briggs and Bauman identify in previous studies of speech genres?
2 How does the notion of genre relate to Hymes's notion of "style" discussed by Hymes in Chapter 6?
3 Why do the authors say that genre has been under-theorized in linguistic anthropology?
4 How does the notion of "intertextuality" help us to rethink about the notion of genre in an anthropological perspective?
5 What is an "intertextual gap"? How are these gaps *minimized* or *maximized* through generic discourse?
6 Use the analysis and examples provided in this chapter to identify speech genres in your own speech community.

10

Narrating the Political Self in a Campaign for US Congress

Alessandro Duranti

Introduction

At least since Aristotle and continuing through the Roman tradition represented by Cicero all the way to contemporary authors, the language of politics has been presented and studied in terms of its ability to persuade an audience (of peers, subjects, or superiors) to go along with the speaker's view of the world and his or her proposals (Pernot 2000). In much of this literature, the successful political speaker is seen as a skillful manipulator who controls a variety of linguistic resources – from elaborate metaphors to paralinguistic features like volume, intonation, and rhythm – through which listeners can be convinced to accept a given decision or take a given course of action (including the action of voting for the speaker). A recent extension of this tradition is George Lakoff's bestselling book *Don't think of an elephant: Know your values and frame the debate* (2004), in which he provides a practical guide for progressives and liberals in the United States to counter the linguistic manipulations of conservatives. Lakoff uses his theory of metaphors as triggers for particular cognitive frames (Lakoff & Johnson 1980, Lakoff and Turner 1989, Lakoff 1996) to illuminate the ways in which what we call something makes a difference in our attitude toward it. One of his most recurring and by now famous examples is the Republicans' reframing of "tax cut" as "tax relief," a transformation that is said to trigger a conceptual frame in which taxes are an affliction of which people must be relieved and the person who can accomplish such relief is, by definition, a hero.

Within linguistic anthropology, the focus of research has been on the relations between political events and particular speech genres rather than on persuasion. Ethnographers of communication, among others, have documented how ambiguity, reported speech, and disclaimers of various kinds are used in stratified as well as in egalitarian societies to control the recognized power of words (e.g. Bloch 1975, Brenneis and Myers 1984, Duranti 1994, Hill and Irvine 1993, Keating 1998, Kuipers 1990).

The work presented in this article builds on these traditions and, at the same time, moves in new directions. It maintains the assumption, common among linguistic anthropologists, that the power of words must be understood vis-à-vis particular genres and situations. For

For permission to publish copyright material in this book, grateful acknowledgment is made to: A. Duranti (2006), "Narrating the Political Self in a Campaign for US Congress," *Language in Society* 35: 467–97.

this reason, for the purposes of this article I have decided to concentrate on one type of event: public debates during a political campaign for a seat in the US Congress. At the same time, my interest in such events and the analysis presented here originated from a research method that privileged not events but persons. From the very beginning of my project, I decided to follow ONE candidate throughout the entire campaign. In addition to giving me useful insights on the decision-making process of political campaigns, the focus on one candidate made me more aware of the demands placed on individuals running for political office and the kinds of existential dilemmas that candidates are faced with. From the beginning of the campaign, I was struck by the pervasive use of personal narratives in public speeches. Later on, by analyzing the transcripts of the video recordings made, it became apparent that personal narratives played an important role in the construction of the particular type of social persona that I call here the "political self." Once I made this discovery, I saw the need to go beyond my earlier interest in the grammatical framing of events in political arenas (e.g., Duranti 1994) to include the role of narrative accounts in the construction of a political identity.

Discourse analysts have shown that speakers use narrative accounts to make sense of their own experiences and to evaluate them in moral terms (e.g. Linde 1993: 81; Ochs and Capps 1996, 2001; Schiffrin 1996). In telling stories of personal experience, speakers must deal with two opposite constraints: the desire to provide an account that has an acceptable logic, and the desire to be authentic – that is, to stay as close as possible to one's own understanding of what it was like to be in a given event (Ochs 2004: 278). In this article, I argue that this potential contrast is particularly acute in politics, where candidates must tell stories of their own actions that are solid enough to stand the scrutiny of others in terms of their logic and at the same time must project a type of commitment to voters that can sound authentic. As we shall see, some candidates go so far as to interpret this challenge as a need to provide reasons for their own decision to run for office.

Discursive Consciousness

The present study is based on an assumption that is common among contemporary discourse analysts: that individuals' perspectives on their own experiences – including their emotional stance and the awareness of this stance – are often articulated and worked out through talk. If politicians are no exception to this kind of DISCURSIVE CONSCIOUSNESS, we can hypothesize that what a candidate says throughout a political campaign might offer valuable insights into the dilemmas that characterize any effort to gain the support and approval of a large number of people, an endeavor that is at the core of political campaigns. Understanding a candidate's dilemmas should, in turn, help us understand a number of important cultural assumptions, including the expectations that candidates and voters have about the "ideal" candidate and what is needed to achieve such ideal status.

Studies in a variety of fields, including anthropology, philosophy, sociology, and psychology, have taught us that human beings are constantly engaged in the construction of self and in the evaluation and monitoring of that construction. We know that language, or rather discourse – the temporal unfolding of linguistic communication – plays a major role in this existential-pragmatic enterprise, enabling individual speakers to articulate their self-understanding through a shared medium and in contexts where others are able to concur, correct, object, or redirect the meaning of what is being said. Candidates worry about how to project and maintain an image of themselves as beings whose past, present, and future actions, beliefs, and evaluations follow some clear basic principles, none of which contradicts another. This type of EXISTENTIAL COHERENCE is often dependent upon, but on a different level from, the textual coherence (or cohesion) associated with the ways in which different parts of a text can be said to form a whole (e.g., Conte 1988, Halliday and Hasan 1976, Stubbs 1983, van Dijk 1977).[1] Existential coherence is, however, closely related to the coherence that speakers-as-narrators search for and construct (e.g., Linde 1993, Garro and

Mattingly 2000, Ochs and Capps 2001, Polkinghorne 1991, Schiffrin 1996). As they narrate past experiences and accomplishments and project their future (as leaders, representatives, advocates, etc.) to their potential voters, political candidates closely monitor whether what they (and their opponents) say on one occasion may contradict what they (or their opponents) already said (or are likely to say) on another. They know that their statements are being evaluated by voters, opponents, and representatives of the media in terms of the kind of PERSON – in the anthropological sense first introduced by Mauss 1938 – that they may reveal. It is that reconstructed person that is then examined to establish whether a candidate is fit to adequately represent the interest of the voters.

As such, the construction of existential coherence seems to be both externally and internally motivated. On one hand, candidates are concerned with how to save face in front of an audience that evaluates their actions and words and might catch them in a contradiction. Candidates are thus constantly engaged in what Taylor 1991 called "radical reflexivity." They ask themselves the pragmatic question: "Am I (through my words, the positions I take and the decisions that I make) the person I PROMISED to be?" On the other hand, they must also deal with their own sense of coherence. That is, they face the question: "Am I (through my words, the positions I take and the decisions that I make) the person I WANT to be?" It is precisely through their search for ways of presenting themselves as politically coherent beings that they display in public their own theory of what an ideal candidate should be.

The process of constructing coherence intersects with morality to the extent to which being coherent is presented as evidence for the truth of what a candidate says, and therefore of his or her value as a moral being.

Data Collection

From 13 November 1995 through 6 November 1996, I documented a political campaign for the US House of Representatives in a portion of the Central Coast of California known (at the time) as the 22nd District (a territory that included the cities of Santa Barbara, Santa Maria, San Luis Obispo, and Paso Robles). The candidate whose campaign I documented was Walter Holden Capps, a professor of religious studies at the University of California, Santa Barbara (UCSB), whose only previous experience in politics was a brief campaign (in 1993–1994) for the same seat, which he had lost by less than 1 percent of the votes to former California Assemblywoman Andrea Seastrand (Republican). Capps was considered by many to be an unusual candidate. He was well known at UCSB for his unorthodox and highly successful courses, including the one on the Vietnam War,[2] where he invited people with vastly different views of the war (e.g., war veterans, antiwar activists, politicians) to discuss their war or antiwar experience and think publicly about the roots of war, its implications, and what could be done to avoid it. A Lutheran, Capps was interested professionally and personally in a wide range of religious beliefs and practices, including Buddhism, monasticism, and Native American religion (Capps 1983, 1989; Hultkrantz and Capps 1976). He often spoke about the "human spirit" as a positive force that should be protected and respected.

From November 1995 to November 1996, I was with Walter Capps on the campaign trail for a total of 21 days. In addition to being with him in his hometown, Santa Barbara, I also traveled with him (and usually with his wife, Lois) to Paso Robles, Santa Maria, Guadalupe, Lompoc, San Luis Obispo, and Oceano. I always brought my video camera and used it to record as much as possible of Capps's interactions at his home, in the car, and before, during, and after rallies and public debates. Although after a certain point in the campaign I was denied access to the Capps-For-Congress headquarters, Walter and Lois Capps never asked me to turn the camcorder off or to erase any portion of what I had recorded. In addition to fieldnotes and printed material (from the headquarters or from the press), I recorded about 40 hours of videotape that document Capps interacting with a wide range of people, including his opponents. I also had a number of occasions to talk

Table 10.1 *Final results of November 6, 1996 election, California 22nd District (San Luis Obispo-Santa Barbara)* (Los Angeles Times, *Nov. 7, 1996, Section A, p. 24)*.

Candidate	*Party affiliation*	*Number of votes*	*Percentage*
Walter H. Capps	Democratic	102,915	49%
Andrea Seastrand	Republican	90,374	43%
Steven Wheeler	Independent	8,308	4%
Richard D. Porter	Reform Party	3,429	2%
David L. Bersohn	Libertarian	1,948	1%
Dawn Tomastick	Natural Law Party	1,569	1%

informally with many of the people involved in the campaign, including family members.

The campaign was a very close and dramatic political race. In March 1996, Walter Capps fainted and had to be hospitalized (the word "heart attack" was avoided by campaign staff and by the doctors). In May of the same year, while Walter and Lois Capps were driving home on Highway 154, they were injured in a head-on collision with a drunk driver. As a result of his injuries, Walter Capps was confined to a wheelchair and kept away from the campaign trail for several weeks. The sharp differences between Capps and incumbent Seastrand drew national attention. There were articles in the *New York Times* and the *Los Angeles Times*, and the race was featured on National Public Radio programs and on ABC's *Nightline*. Capps's campaign received the backing of important political figures in the then Democratic administration, including a visit and rally in Santa Barbara with Hillary Clinton on 12 September 1996, an even bigger rally with President Clinton on 1 November, and two visits by George Stephanopolous, whose personal assistant was Laura Capps, Walter's younger daughter. At the end, Capps won the congressional seat – the first Democrat in 50 years to win this position in his district (see Table 10.1).

It was a happy ending for him and for my project, given that I had ended up with a rare documentation of a successful campaign. But sadly, less than a year later, as I was starting to analyze my transcripts and videotapes, Walter Capps died of a heart attack while trying to catch a cab at Dulles Airport in Washington, DC.

Since then I have been trying to find a way to analyze my collection of videotapes and fieldnotes in a way that could do justice to two ambitious and potentially contradictory goals: (i) a narrative of the extraordinary efforts and success of an unlikely candidate catapulted from a university campus to the world of national politics, and (ii) an analysis of such a story that could qualify as an account for members of my discipline, linguistic anthropology, and other students of political discourse. My first effort was an article (Duranti 2003) in which I document how Walter Capps's words and message during the first day of the campaign were designed for and, at the same time, affected by his interaction with the audience. In this article, I continue with a related issue: the public articulation of the inner and outer struggle for coherence in narrating the self. Listening to Capps on the campaign trail and later, while reviewing my fieldnotes and videotapes, I was often struck by the continuous efforts by Capps-the-candidate to reach out to his audience without having to compromise his sense of authenticity with respect to his other identities (e.g., Capps-the-scholar, Capps-the-family-person, Capps-the-teacher). Over time, I came to the realization that such efforts were part of a more general struggle, which all candidates for public office must face.

Existential Coherence as a Recurrent Issue for Candidates

One of the recurring features of the talk recorded during the campaign was the mention of existential issues in Capps's speeches. This was particularly striking during the first day of the campaign, when Capps voiced his own doubts about leaving a profession he loved – being a professor at the University of California, Santa Barbara – and entering the world of politics, where, instead of getting the job on the basis of professional qualifications, as he said, "you have to beat your opponent" (San Luis Obispo, 14 Nov. 1995). At first, I thought that this was a type of public self-reflection that only an academic would engage in. But as the campaign progressed, I learned that Capps's publicly articulated existential dilemmas were part of a larger discourse domain: the management of what I call here "existential coherence," by which I mean a coherence of actions, thoughts, and words aimed as supporting a PERSON in the anthropological sense of a culturally identifiable type of social being (Geertz 1983, Mauss 1985). As I will show in the rest of this article, all candidates are accountable for this type of coherence, but the extent to which and the manner in which they attend to it varies considerably across individuals.

Accusations of Lack of Coherence

Candidates' words are constantly inspected to see whether their accounts of past actions are accurate. Their ideas, plans, and promises are also scrutinized in search of potential contradictions or inconsistencies. Something a candidate said or did on one occasion can be framed as being at odds with what the same person – or, in some cases, his or her associates or staff – said (or did) on another. Examples abound in contemporary politics. In some cases, the charge of lacking coherence can be extended to include accusations that a candidate or politician in office "lied" (Wilson 2001) or failed to keep a promise (Hill 2000). In the data collected, candidates made accusations of inconsistencies or contradictions by quoting from a variety of sources, including political campaign ads and statements made by their opponents during the ongoing debate or in the past. Here I will briefly analyze two such cases. The first involves the meaning of the term "independent." The second centers on the meaning of "having been TO WASHINGTON." As I will show, in both cases a careful analysis of the contexts in which the two expressions were used demonstrates that despite their potential ambiguity, the accused (in this case, Capps) had used them in ways that were not inconsistent with his actions. Capps, however, did not spend time countering the accusations. This suggests that candidates may avoid spending too much time on semantics even when they might be able to show that the accusations are misplaced or that the accusers are disingenuous. There are possible explanations for such a choice; for instance, candidates may wish to avoid sounding defensive or giving credit to opponents by taking their criticism too seriously. At the same time, such accusations build up the pressure that all candidates feel to maintain coherence in what they say and do.

Case 1: "Independent"

In the following excerpt from a public debate sponsored by the League of Women Voters in Santa Barbara, 7 October 1996, Independent candidate Steven Wheeler accuses Walter Capps of claiming to be "an independent" despite the fact that he is running as a Democrat.[3] This accusation gives Wheeler a chance to remind the audience that he instead is running "without party affiliation," and that this was made possible thanks to the support of 13,000 people who signed a petition to put his name on the ballot.[4] (For transcription conventions, see Appendix A.)

(1) 7 October 1996; Santa Barbara; public debate sponsored by the League of Women Voters.

WHEELER: ... I'm running as **an independent** that means that I am running **without party affiliation**. now the last time uh- I checked it took thirteen thousand signatures to get on the ballot as an Independent that's what I went out and did=I got thirteen thousand signatures. it took me up and down. the Central Coast. I went to every city here and I had a chance to- talk to a lot of people and find out what their concerns about the issues were. (but) I just found out a couple of weeks ago, that I am not the only one who is running as an independent=my opponent here Walter Capps is taking out ads billing himself as a **non-partisan** kind of guy and he refers to himself twice as **an independent,** ... but- Walter, you know, I would suggest you check with your campaign the last time I hear you were running as a Democrat. uhm.

AUDIENCE: ((sparse chuckles, laughter))

Here the coherence issue centers on the meaning of "independent" and the pragmatic conditions for claiming that status. The term "independent" had indeed been used by Capps and his campaign office. For example, it is found in five ads produced in September of the same year (the month just before the debate from which excerpt 1 is taken). All five ads concluded with the voiceover slogan "Walter Capps, independent, in touch and in the mainstream."[5] One of the five ads also stated: "Walter Capps represents the independent nonpartisan spirit of our community."

In the debate from which the previous excerpt is taken, Capps did not respond to Wheeler's criticism.[6] But when we examine his speeches, his interviews with representatives of the media, and his conversations with members of his staff or family, we find evidence that his use of the term "independent" could be interpreted differently from Wheeler's notion of "having no party affiliation." In Capps's usage, "independent" implies "not easily influenced by special interest groups or partisan politics." For example, in response to a question by a Channel 12 reporter after his announcement speech in San Luis Obispo, on 14 November 1995, Capps describes himself as "an independent voice" in order to contrast himself with his characterization of the incumbent, Andrea Seastrand, whom he accuses of "taking orders" from the Republican Speaker of the House, Newt Gingrich.

(2) 14 November 1995; San Luis Obispo.

REPORTER: So what's going to make uh this time different from last time?

CAPPS: Oh. All kinds of things. First of all- (first of all), I'm a much better candidate. Last time was the first time I had run for office. [...] Second thing is that, this time we're running against a person who has a (background/record of service) [...] What I have discovered, is that she is not responding, to the needs and interests of the people of the 22nd district. She is taking her orders [...] from the uh- Republican uhm Speaker of the House. [...] I think that what the people want is **an independent voice.** Somebody, who knows the people so well that that person can speak on behalf of them. [...]

This example, together with the television spots, shows that there was an important semantic difference between Wheeler's and Capps's (and his campaign office's) use of the term "independent." The difference is semantic and syntactically marked. Wheeler uses "independent" as a noun, as in "AN independent," whereas Capps and the people who participated in the preparation of his ads use it as an adjective, as in "independent, in touch and in the mainstream" (in the above-mentioned ad) or "an independent voice," in Capps's own words.[7] To be "an independent" (noun) in Wheeler's terms, one needs to be NOT AFFILIATED with any of the existing certified political parties (e.g., Democratic Party, Republican Party, Green Party).[8] To be "independent" (adjective), in Capps's meaning of the term, candidates need to demonstrate that they are not just following whatever their party does or tells them to do. In this respect, one could argue that this particular accusation of lack of coherence (for pretending to be "[an] independent") is based on a semantic difference similar to the one hypothesized by Wilson 2001 and mentioned earlier. This type of analysis, however, should be considered only the first step in the attempt to understand the logic as well as the occurrence of such attacks on coherence. I will discuss what else we should consider after introducing the next round of attacks on coherence, a round that involves Walter Capps and Andrea Seastrand.

Case 2: Who has been to Washington?

The second case of other-generated coherence struggles centers on the meaning of the phrase "having been TO Washington." In the context of the campaign, and more generally in American political discourse, "Washington" is a metonym for "the (federal) government," which includes elected and nonelected officials. As illustrated in the following statement by a Democratic pollster, political candidates and their staff assumed in 1995–6 that a considerable percentage of the voters held negative opinions of the federal government and more generally of politicians.

(3) 28 December 1995; staff meeting of the Capps-for-Congress campaign.

POLLSTER: [...] There is a: ... a strong disconnect ... between the average person and their elected official (in Washington). <u>th</u>ey um ... uhm think what happens in Washington is that ... you get elected ... you go there with their ideals ... and three months later you're corrupted by the process. Because um you are no longer isolated you don't talk with (your) average (people) on the street. The only people you see in Washington are the lobbyists ... who give you gifts ... and who write legislation for you and wh- who talk to you before you go on the floor to put your card in to vote. [...]

Some candidates exploited this negative attitude in creating a contrast between "the government" and "the people." In the following excerpt, incumbent Seastrand speaks in support of tax cuts as an initiative that would benefit voters by allowing them greater control over a larger portion of their earnings. In this case, "Washington, DC" explicitly includes the Clinton administration as well as any other government "bureaucrats" who would have access to tax revenues for their salaries or programs.

(4) 15 August 1996; San Luis Obispo; public debate.

SEASTRAND: What we're trying to do is cut uh- uh- those government dollars from Washington D.C. and leave it in the pockets of those of us at home. And they're not gonna put it in their mattress. They're gonna do something with that money. Put it in the bank for a savings account. Save it for their children's college fund and maybe make some interest and let someone else from the local bank be able to borrow it for a home. Do all those things that we do with our dollars and uh- grow that economy. I'm a believer in the American spirit and I think we here at home know how best to use those dollars than **the bureaucrats and the Clinton administration in Washington D.C.**

A few minutes later, Capps uses his chance to answer a question from the audience to ridicule the inconsistency of those elected officials who criticize the very system of which they are part. Although this is expressed in generic terms – "the people who now serve in Washington" – the audience knows that Seastrand is the likely target of this criticism. In this classic example of what linguistic anthropologists call "veiled speech" (Brenneis 1978), Capps can be interpreted as blaming Seastrand for lacking coherence: She criticizes politicians and bureaucrats without admitting that she is one of them.

(5) 15 August 1996; San Luis Obispo; public debate.

WALTER: [...] uhm and you know it's- it's always kind of amazing to me that **the people who now serve in Washington** are the one's who are leading the anti-Washington charge.
AUDIENCE: ((sparse laughter))
WALTER: I mean, the ones who- who are <u>most</u> against politicians and bureaucrats are **the politicians and the bureaucrats.** // I'm not-
AUDIENCE: ((more sparse laughter))
WALTER: I'm not quite sure ... what that's saying about- about our society. [...]

Later in the same debate, Seastrand, in turn, criticizes Capps for misrepresenting himself as someone who has never been to Washington. If we take Seastrand's remarks to be motivated by the interpretation of Capps's earlier criticism of

Figure 10.1 Debate in San Luis Obispo, California, August 15, 1996. *At the table, from left:* Dick Porter, Rep. Andrea Seastrand, the moderator, Steven Wheeler, and (*holding the mike*) Walter Capps.

"the people who now serve in Washington" as a criticism aimed at her, we have here a case of what Morgan 1991 called "baited indirectness"[9]: Seastrand appears to "bite the bait" that is only IMPLICIT in Capps's generalized criticism. In (6), without referring to Capps's previous criticism of her statements – and yet using a discourse framing, *I'm amazed*, which echoes Capps's *it's always kind of amazing* in (5) – Seastrand focuses on his claim that he has never been to Washington and cites evidence that, on the contrary, he has been to Washington. I will first quote, in (6), Seastrand's criticism and then show, in (7), the passage of Capps's earlier talk where he appears to have made the claim in question.

(6) 15 August 1996; San Luis Obispo; public debate.

SEASTRAND: and, as far as my friend (uh-p-) Professor Walter Capps -hh uh- I'm amazed that you've stated on several occasions in this meeting that **you've never been to Washington.** I'm gonna have to go into my files and look at the *Santa Barbara News-Press,* because I think that they. reported that **you even went into the Oval Office of the President himself.** Your- uh one of your family members has or works there with (such Ste-) George Stephanopolous' office. and so uh I was given the impression on reading that article that **when you go to Washington, you meet the President.** So anyway it's interesting but it's an election time. [...]

Seastrand is here pointing out that Capps cannot claim that he has not been to Washington because, according to a newspaper, the *Santa Barbara News-Press,* he visited the President in the White House. This remark seems at first to rest on a literal interpretation of *having been to Washington*: the act of having physically been in the city of Washington, DC (implicit in the assertion that he went inside the White House to meet Clinton). But there is a subtler and potentially more damaging implication of her accusations: that Capps is only pretending to be an unknowing outsider. In fact, he can be shown to have strong connections to the White

House and, by implication, to politicians in the Democratic Party, through his daughter Laura's position as George Stephanopolous's personal assistant.

When we look at Capps's earlier statement, shown in (7) below, however, we see that an alternative reading is possible, in which he is claiming that he has *never been a bureaucrat in Washington*.

(7) 15 August 1996; San Luis Obispo; public debate.

WALTER: What- what I'm trying to establish here is that the way we make these decisions in Washington ... reflect our values, not just our views about economy but our values about what we- what we prioritize in our society, ... see I really pain. Every time we talk about **bureaucrats in Washington** uh people tend to- to applaud. But it-it-it pains me deeply. **I've never been there. I don't know what it's like.** ((13:49)) I'm not sure it's going to work at all. I don't know what it's like. but I wish we had- confidence in our government. I wish we could- talk about government in positive terms uh and- and- and not simply blame every problem in this country. on the government. [...]

Capps is here trying to force the audience to rethink the connotation of *bureaucrats in Washington* and the implications of the pervasive negative stereotype commonly held about such people. It is in this context that he claims that he has *never been there* and that he does not *know what it's like*. It is only with this more restricted interpretation in mind – that he has never been *in that position* – that we can make sense of his subsequent remark, *I'm not sure it's going to work at all*. He seems to be referring to the possibility of being elected and having then to go to Washington as a bureaucrat.

In this case as well, we could argue that there are two different semantic interpretations of the same expression – *having been to Washington* – and it is only on the basis of such different interpretations that we can simultaneously make sense of the accuser's criticism and of the claims made by the accused. But, as I mentioned earlier, the semantic analysis should not exhaust our search for the conditions that make competing interpretations of this kind not unusual in political discourse. We must ask: Why are WE able to see such semantic differences when the participants themselves do not? And why aren't these misunderstandings resolved by the participants themselves, or by others for them? I can think of two main reasons. The first has to do with aspects of the social organization of the events in which these kinds of attacks and criticisms appear. The second has to do with the adversarial nature of the political process and, perhaps more deeply, with interactional mechanisms and cultural expectations of the kind described by Tannen 1998 as "the argument culture."[10]

By "aspects of the social organization" of political debates I mean the organization of turn-taking and the roles that different speakers are given and assume in using the floor. The debates from which I drew my examples are typically structured by an EXCHANGE SYSTEM that differs radically from conversation (e.g., as defined in Sacks, Schegloff and Jefferson 1974), especially in terms of turn allocation and turn duration. In public debates, a speaker is given the floor for an extended period, sometimes for one or two minutes, without having to worry about other speakers intervening as they routinely do in the course of ordinary conversation. Moderators, who are in charge of managing the floor by allocating turns, monitoring their duration, and guiding the audience into proper behavior, rarely comment or encourage candidates to further clarify a point or provide specific evidence for their claims. This means that the type of exchange system typical of public debates is not conducive to the kind of fine tuning that is found in conversation. One consequence of this system is that it allows participants to attack without having to define their accusations further, or, in turn, to ignore an accusation or criticism made by a previous speaker. If necessary, those under attack can justify their lack of response on a variety of grounds, including the limited time at their disposal and the need to use it to get across their "message" rather than using it to respond to criticism.

The second reason for the recurrence of the type of accusation illustrated above is that candidates are under considerable pressure to attack any opponent who might be seen as a serious threat to them. Subtle semantic differences can be ignored because the premium is on making the opponent look bad and unreasonable rather than good and reasonable. Even a criticism based on misinterpreting a semantic distinction that should be obvious to most people can be useful if it can raise doubts about the integrity of a dangerous opponent. Candidates are particularly vulnerable in those areas that might make them appealing to a group of voters that their opponents are trying to reach. These are SACRED AREAS that must be guarded at all costs. In Wheeler's case, the sacred area is his identity as "an Independent." Since this is what distinguishes him from the candidates of the two main parties, he cannot let someone else take it over, especially when that person is the candidate of one of the two major parties. Capps, on the other hand, adopts the term "independent" as a way of suggesting that he is not a Democratic Party ideologue. This was particularly important in a district that for 50 years had sent Republicans to Congress.

In the case of the cycle of exchanges between Capps and Seastrand, the stakes are equally high. The conflict expressed in excerpts (4)–(7) starts from an implicit paradox: that both candidates recognize that the identity of "politician" has negative connotations, and yet they are competing for that identity (I will return to this paradox later in the article). Capps indirectly accuses Seastrand of being a hypocrite for criticizing politicians while being one of them. Seastrand, in turn indirectly accuses Capps of being disingenuous by wanting to sound like an outsider whereas in fact he is already well acquainted with major figures in the Democratic Party. The reference to Capps going to visit President Clinton is particularly important for Seastrand because it constitutes a potential counterattack to Capps's frequent accusation that she takes her orders from Newt Gingrich.[11]

The Narrative Construction of Existential Coherence

Exchanges like the previous ones make candidates keenly aware of their vulnerability in the public arena. Candidates are, however, also concerned with displaying or articulating their own individual sense of coherence. They problematize their actions, comparing past, present, and future decisions or experiences in search of an overarching logic, a principle or series of principles that justifies their choice to run for office or to take a particular stand on an issue. When candidates engage in such discursive construction of their life choices, coherence is represented as CONTINUITY of actions, thoughts, and feelings. As Eric Erikson (1980:190) pointed out, a person's identity involves "an unconscious striving for a CONTINUITY OF PERSONAL CHARACTER" (emphasis in original). As we shall see, for these candidates existential coherence is indeed built on continuity of personal character, as defined through specific actions or routine activities (e.g., the ones associated with one's profession outside the political arena). Coherence is typically created in two ways: (i) by showing that things stay the same – one's beliefs have not really changed over time; or (ii) by showing that things change in ways that reconfirm the continuity of some other feature – one's beliefs have changed because there is a higher-order logic that justifies the change. Recognition of a temporal dimension in the construction of existential coherence is crucial for capturing the process through which the political self is formed. This includes the verbal acts that reveal, sometimes in more public contexts, sometimes in more private ones, the logic of a candidate's reasons for presenting a particular type of self. In my data, three discursive strategies emerged in the construction of existential coherence: (i) narratives of belonging, (ii) the present as a "natural extension" of the past, and (iii) exposing potential contradictions, which are then shown to be only apparent.

Discourse strategy 1: Narrative of belonging

The narrative of belonging is a subset of narratives of personal experience. In the narrative of belonging, a sequence of life events is presented in a linear fashion, implying "a single, closed, temporal, and causal path" (Ochs and Capps 2001: 41), in order to show that a candidate has experienced events or has gone through states of mind that connect him or her emotionally and morally to the place and the people of the district. This strategy accomplishes this goal in a number of ways. First, it supports the view that, by having lived like others in the audience, the speaker-candidate is an "ordinary citizen," which is a positive value in contemporary American politics. Second, this type of narrative is also (at times explicitly) introduced to establish the likelihood that the candidate will be an ideal representative precisely because his or her potentially shared experiences recounted in the narrative define him or her as knowledgeable about what people in the district think and feel. In addition to the emphasis on shared "place" (e.g., "I have lived in the district for 20 years"), narratives of belonging introduce putatively universal or quasi-universal life experiences (e.g., being married, having children, sending children to school, seeing them grow, being exposed to traumatic events, taking care of one's parents or grandparents). These experiences help candidates connect to a large part of the audience. In particular, narratives of belonging work as coherence builders because they help candidates formulate a life history in which temporally and spatially separate events and experiences can be shown to have led toward the realization of a kind of person who values being part of a particular community (*Gemeinschaft*) as opposed to society at large.

I first became aware of narratives of belonging for political purposes while recording and then analyzing Walter Capps's speeches over the course of the first official day of his 1995–6 campaign, 14 November 1995. The most striking and complete narrative of belonging is found in the first speech of that day, in Paso Robles. Capps delivered his speech to a small group of supporters and activists, most of them elderly or retired. He addressed them while standing in front of the entrance to the Paso Robles Public Library, without notes, podium, or microphone. Most of what he said, however, was based on a written text that he had finished preparing the night before.

The passage from his speech reproduced in (8) below took place after Capps made the announcement that he was running for office again, and that this time he would win. The narrative of belonging is meant to provide

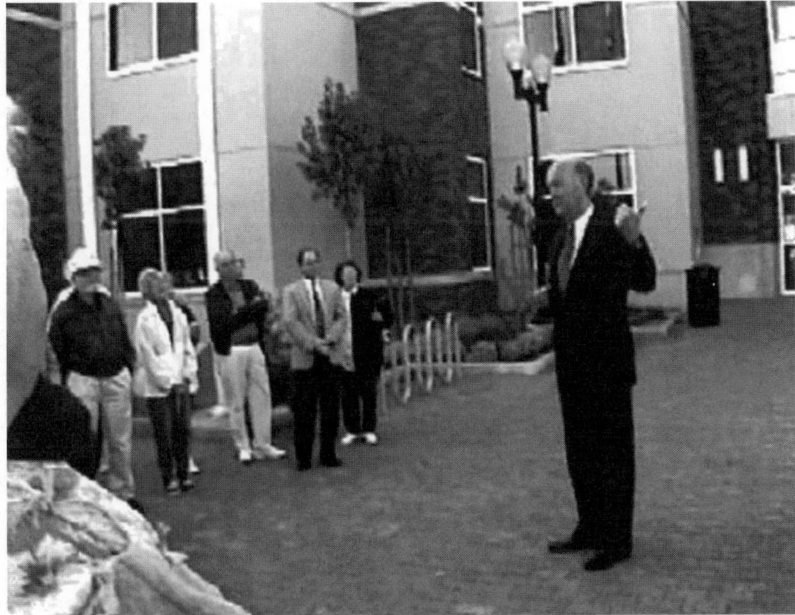

Figure 10.2 ("We stayed across the street") Walter Capps speaking to his supporters in Paso Robles, California, on November 14, 1995

evidence of the fact that he and his wife Lois have been in the district for a long time and therefore know its people:[12]

(8) 14 Nov. 1995; Paso Robles; announcement speech to supporters.

CAPPS: [. . .] because uh, Lois and I . . . have lived here, in fact the first time we came in here in- August of 1964, we stayed across the street. we- we came out from- from uh, Yale University, uh to teach uh at U.C. Santa Barbara. and we came down from Oregon. we stopped across the street, had a- . . . had a-.. we were carrying a- trailer with uh, our belongings. we didn't have any children then=that was in nineteen-sixty-four. . . . we've been here a:ll this time . . . we've lived here a:ll these years, we know the people . . . of the twenty-second district. . . . you know- . . . our. children were born. in the twenty-second district. they've all gone to school here. . . . uh so what I'm suggesting is, . . . not only suggesting I know this to be the case: that I represent . . . majority. opinion. in the twenty-second district. I mean=I know what people in the twenty-second district believe in because- these are our people. . . . **you are- . . . the people with whom we've lived our lives.**

This particular narrative of belonging was introduced in the context of an "origin" narrative, which included the description of a trip from Oregon with a trailer full of belongings, perhaps an implicit reference to the famous "Oregon Trail" story that American children learn in elementary school. The narrative is also spatio-temporally grounded to the specific location where Capps is speaking through the reference to a place *across the street* and to the date of his arrival, 1964. He provides further evidence of belonging by mentioning that his children were born and went to school in the 22nd District. In addition to being proof of his confidence in public institutions (indicated by the fact that he sent his children to public schools), this part of the narrative could also be interpreted as defining Capps as an ordinary citizen (reinforced by his standing on the sidewalk, with no podium or microphone). He shares the experience of having lived in the same district while raising children with most of the people in the audience, who are about his age or older. This was an important component of Capps's broader narrative of his candidacy. Quoting Thomas Jefferson, Capps often presented himself as the typical citizen-politician, who goes to Congress for a limited period of time to fulfill a sense of civic duty and then returns to his community to live the rest of his life among the people he had represented in Washington. Despite a ten-month separation between the two speeches, the last line of the passage in (9) is almost identical to the last line of the passage in (8):

(9) 15 August 1996; San Luis Obispo; public debate.

CAPPS: There's lot's of Thomas Jefferson in me. . . . Thomas Jefferson believed . . . that the person who represents the community in Congress . . . should come from that community. Should be somebody from any walk of life. Could be a teacher. . . . Could be a painter. Uh- a woman or a man. uh plumber or an attorney. Anyone. Would- would come. out of that community and serve for a- probably a brief period of time in Washington D.C.

MODERATOR: Thirty seconds Walter.

CAPPS: Okay. And then go back and live among **the people with whom you've lived your lives.**

An abbreviated version of the same narrative given in (8) was used by Capps on 14 November 1995, at two other stops on the same day, in San Luis Obispo and at Hancock College in Santa Maria, but not at the fourth stop, the Santa Barbara campus of the University of California. At UCSB, he began to talk about how long he and Lois had been married but then switched to an elaborate series of (only partly successful) jokes, all of which were meant to stress his personal connection to the university rather than to the district. Nine months later, a more abbreviated narrative of belonging appeared in Capps's opening statement at a public debate in Santa Maria and, one week later, he used a slightly more elaborate version in a San Luis Obispo debate. The two versions are reproduced below in (10) and (11) respectively:

(10) 9 August 1996; Santa Maria; public debate.

CAPPS: **we have lived in this district for thirty two years. uh-we've raised ... our children here. I've- I've been a member of the faculty at University of California at Santa Barbara** ... uh- during that period of time. uh- I was also the director for the center for the study of democratic institutions. ... There's been some question about whether I've ever ... had to deal with the payroll. I was director of that. I've been department chair, ... [...]

(11) 15 August 1996; debate in San Luis Obispo.

CAPPS: [...] **I've been on the faculty at the University of California at Santa Barbara for- about thirty years.** ... uh went to public schools. ... uh got my Ph.D. from Yale University = came out with my wife Lois who is here today. ... uhm ... **our children were born and raised in ... Santa Barbara ... in the 22nd district. They've gone on- they all went through uhm ... college in uh- in California**=the oldest one went to Stanford. ... Just got her PhD from UCLA. ... the middle one went to- to UCSB and went to ... uh the University of Sydney. In Australia. The youngest one was an honor student at UC Berkeley and now works in the White House. [...]

What remains of the original formulation given in (8) is that in both (10) and (11) Capps stresses his connection with the district through a reference to his children and his teaching at the University of California, Santa Barbara. In the first case (8 August 1996), the narrative concluded with information about having being the chair of the Department of Religious Studies at UCSB, which was cited as evidence of his administrative experience. In the second case (15 August 1996), Capps elaborated on information about where his three children went to college. This time his generalization that they all went to public school in the 22nd District could not be extended to say that they all went to public (state-funded) colleges. This might explain why Capps changed the generalization. In (11), he states that they went to college *in California* (with the partial exception of the middle one, Todd, who went to UCSB first and then to Australia). Although in (10) and (11) his connection to the district has been modified, a certain affective tone of the original narrative is preserved. This is achieved through bringing into the public domain such dimensions of personal experience as his children's upbringing and achievements. As he tells the audience where his children went to college, Capps's identity undergoes a momentary and yet dramatic shift: from political candidate to proud father boasting about his children's achievements, including the position that his younger daughter Laura had at the White House as Stephanopolous's personal assistant.

At first, I thought that the narrative of belonging was one of the rhetorical strategies that distinguished Capps from the other candidates. On further inspection, however, that hypothesis turned out to be wrong. During the public debate in Santa Maria organized by the Area Agency on Aging, on 8 August 1996, Independent Steven Wheeler produced an elaborate narrative of belonging.[13] When the time came to introduce himself, Wheeler stood up (the only candidate to do so) and delivered the speech that, as he later confided to me, he had been working on in the isolation of his study at home and without the benefit of political consultants or advisors.[14] As shown in excerpt (12) below, he linked sequentially different personal attributes and events to provide the audience with a glimpse of what would likely be interpreted by the audience as Wheeler's list of qualities that should qualify him as a serious candidate. Among them, the first two are (a) being a native Californian and (b) having lived in the district for an extended period (17 years). He indirectly reinforced his claim to be a "native" by informing the audience that he was a surfer and he was athletic (one can imagine other contexts or States of the Union where "being athletic" or being a surfer might not be judged to important qualities for someone running for a Congressional seat). Wheeler also mentions events and situations in which he came in contact with people in the district and showed compassion toward them (e.g., by assisting them at the gas station or outside grocery stores, or by helping people retrieve lost spouses at large gatherings). In turn, he presented the act of 13,000 registered voters signing petitions to put him on the ballot not as the condition but as the reason (*because [they] signed a petition*) for his presence in the race for Congress.

(12) 8 August 1996; Santa Maria; public debate. Independent candidate Steven Wheeler delivers the entire speech standing, alternating between quickly glancing down at his notes and looking up at the audience.

WHEELER: [...] Since most of you don't know me I'm gonna start by ... telling you about my personal and professional background. **I'm a native Californian and I've lived in this district for seventeen years.** I'm a certified public accountant. I owned and operated my own practice in Santa Barbara for the past fourteen years. ... **I've served on the board to** the National Council on Alcoholism and Drug Abuse, ... **the Santa Barbara J.C.'s, the Santa Barbara County Food Bank,** and the Environmental Defense Center. ... I'm married, my wife's name is Laura, and I have three children, Stephanie, Jared and Brian. ... **I've also been surfing since I was eleven. I've uh been up and down the Central Coast lately** and uh- fortunately **the waves have been flat** so I've uh- been able to spend more time campaigning.

AUDIENCE: ((chuckles))

WHEELER: uhm I have a black belt in martial arts. ... I keep a journal. And **I've coached my son's s- soccer team over the last three years.**
I'm <u>here</u> because over thirteen thousand people signed a petition to put my name on the ballot. This was truly a rewarding experience and it brought me ... to every city in the 22nd district.
It provided me an opportunity to meet people from all walks of life, ... and it gave me an opportunity to engage in discussions with people, and to learn about what their concerns about the issues are in this country today. ...
During this process, ... I helped people put gas in their cars, ... I held their-groceries, I held their shopping carts. I watched their children and their pets, and I even helped locate lost spouses ... in large crowds in special events. ... It w (a)s truly a rewarding experience. [...]

Like Capps in excerpts (7), (9) and (10), Wheeler is here justifying his candidacy by claiming his life connections to the geographical area and to its inhabitants. He does so by invoking public and private aspects of his life that present him as an "ordinary" person – he talks about his own practice, his wife and his children – who also cares about people outside his family. He has, in other words, a sense of civic duty.

Grammar plays an important role in the ways narratives of belonging unfold. The sense of connection to the place and its people is constructed in part through verb forms and with adverbial phrases that give a sense of continuity by building a bridge from the past into the present. To accomplish this, both Capps and Wheeler used simple present perfective (and more rarely present perfective progressive), usually in conjunction with temporal and spatial adverbial phrases. Following are some examples extracted from Capps's and Wheeler's narratives cited above:

(13) Simple present perfective (+ time/space adverbial).

a. <u>we have lived</u> in this district *for thirty years*
b. <u>we've raised</u> our children *here*.
c. <u>I've been</u> a member of the University of California *at Santa Barbara*.[15]
d. <u>I've been</u> on the faculty at the University of California at Santa Barbara *for about thirty years*

e. I've lived in this district *for seventeen years*
f. I've served on the board to the National Council on Alcoholism and Drug Abuse, ... the Santa Barbara J.C.'s, the Santa Barbara County Food Bank, and the Environmental Defense Center.
g. I've been up and down the Central Coast lately
h. the waves have been flat
i. I've coached my son's s- soccer team *over the last three years.*

(14) Present perfective progressive (+ space/time adverbial).

a. I've also been surfing *since I was eleven.*

On close inspection, in the other candidates' speeches we do not find narratives of belonging of the type illustrated in (8), (10) and (11) for Capps and in (12) for Wheeler. For two of the other candidates we do not find any narratives of personal experience throughout an entire debate.

In the three debates I recorded and in one organized and hosted by TV station KEYT in the last month of the campaign, the incumbent, Andrea Seastrand, mentioned some aspects of her personal life that were linked to the discursive context and had potential emotional appeal (e.g., her husband's struggle with cancer, her feelings toward her two adopted children). She also mentioned being the granddaughter of Polish immigrants and briefly recounted getting together with "wonderful citizens" in the district to discuss Medicare, but she did not construct temporally ordered personal narratives that directly or indirectly proved her connections to the district over an extended period. Having won the support of the majority of the voters in the last election, she might have felt that she already had a relationship of belonging with the voters. But familiarity versus lack of familiarity with the voters cannot explain why Dick Porter, from the Reform Party, during his first appearance in San Luis Obispo, on 15 August 1996, did not give any information about his origins or connections with the district. Instead, he spent most of his introduction time talking about his party. When he did provide a brief biographical sketch, during his second debate, at the League of Women Voters on 7 October 1996, Porter presented the information in a grammatical form quite different from what I illustrated above for Capps's and Wheeler's narratives. One of the most striking features of his biographical narrative is the repeated use of verb-elliptical utterances for seven consecutive utterances. Whereas Capps and Wheeler repeatedly employed finite verb forms, including the perfective forms summarized in (13) and (14) above, Porter chose to recount those aspects of his biography that he judged relevant to his presentation of self in a "timeless" fashion. This type of grammatical framing was accompanied by a matter-of-fact tone that, rather than conveying pride or pleasure in the potential connections with the experience of audience members, suggested different goals, such as an attempt to compress as much information as possible into the shortest possible time. The list-like quality of his narrative made it appear that he was reading from a form. His mention of military service suggests a possible experiential source for the unusual grammar of his biographical information. Following is Porter's narrative (I have used separate lines to approximate graphically the list-like character of his delivery):

(15) 7 October 1996; Santa Barbara, League of Women Voters; public debate.

PORTER: Thank you.
uh I am Dick Porter,
uh native Californian, from San Simeon, North of here ((looks down as if reading))
u:h military service in the. U.S. Army West of here in the Pacific
uh education South of here Bachelor and Masters from. USC
and doctorate from. UCLA.
profession educator.
uh=over twenty years service in California public schools
currently self employed as an education consultant.

now I am mostly: ... student. of political systems and government. I'm running
for Congress. now as a candidate, ...
uh my primary concerns and concerns.
uh of the Reform Party.
[...]

Another candidate, the Libertarian David Bersohn, used personal narratives with biographical information in both debates he attended. For example, he told the audience that he had lived in the area since 1987, but he spent more time telling them that he grew up elsewhere (in New York City) and went to school in other states than in elaborating on his connections with people in the district. His explicit connection between his background and the campaign was that his law degree should come in handy if he were to be elected.

(16) 9 August 1996; Santa Maria; public debate.

BERSOHN: [...] So I really appreciate being included today. uhm- my name is David Bersohn and you can repeat that to get the name recognition out there. I don't have a multi-million dollar campaign chest so I have to plug for myself here. uhm- (.) I'm uh libertarian. **I'm 43 years old. I've lived in the area here since 1987. I currently live in Arroyo Grande.** ... I'm a homeowner. um- single. uh- I grew up at (? ?) upstate New York. Grew up in New York City. uhm- I went to college in Ohio, uh- a major in economics and uh- **I also have a law degree from Columbia University so I hope I'll be able to make my way through the thick of the thousand page bills that seem to have went through congress these days.**

Two months later, in the debate at the League of Women Voters in Santa Barbara, Bersohn mentions his arrival in California and the fact that he was living in a rural town in the district after an even more elaborate description of growing up in New York and going to Oberlin College and Columbia University.

(17) 7 October 1996; Santa Barbara; League of Women Voters; public debate.

BERSOHN: Hi. My name is David Bersohn. I am the Libertarian Party candidate. I'll give you a short introduction to myself. uhm I grew up in New York City, first upstate New York. and downstate in the Bronx and Brooklyn. uhm ... I went to:- ... Oberlin College where I got a BA uh majored in economics ... after that I got a: doctorate in jurisprudence from Columbia University School of Law which I hope will- uh allow me to read my way through some of those thousands of page bills that emanate from Congress these days. uhm. **moved to California in 1987. I've lived in (rural) Arroyo Grande since 1991,** uh my primary occupation uh is- (that) as an artist.
[...]

The data presented so far suggest that candidates varied considerably as to whether they used personal narrative in their public speeches and whether they used it to build what I call "narratives of belonging." If, as I have been suggesting, the latter are part of a set of strategies to build existential coherence, differences across candidates could be at least in part related to their awareness of the coherence struggle – in this case, their need to show that they have come to the decision to run for political office as part of a series of experiences, which includes life events shared with people in the district. Do these narratives of belonging help establish a positive relationship with the audience? Have voters come to expect them in candidates' public presentations? These are difficult questions to answer under any circumstances, and even more difficult in my case, given the small sample of candidates and events. But there is some evidence that voters responded more positively to Wheeler's message than to Porter's and Bersohn's. In addition to the fact that, of the three, Wheeler received more votes on Election Day (as shown in Table 1), he was also more successful in terms of immediate feedback from the audience. His introductory speeches, despite the presence of large contingents of supporters for Seastrand

and Capps, received generous applause at all three of the debates I recorded, whereas Porter's and Bersohn's introductory speeches did not fare so well. Porter's introductory speeches on 15 August and 7 October 1996 were not followed by applause at all. Bersohn's introductory speech was followed by applause in only one of the two debates in which he participated. All other candidates' introductory speeches, including those of the Independent Wheeler and the one speech by the representative of the Natural Law Party, were followed by applause (see Appendix B).[16]

Strategy 2: The present as a natural extension of the past

Another strategy for constructing existential coherence through continuity is to make any present decision, including the decision to run for office, a "natural extension" of some past experience. An example of this strategy has been documented by the political scientist Richard Fenno, who, in describing Senator John Glenn's view of his own political career, writes:

> Glenn sees politics as a public service. For him, the decision to enter politics was **a natural extension** of what he had been doing all of his adult life – serving his country. Running for the Senate was the political equivalent of signing up for one more hitch in the marines. (Fenno 1996: 23; emphasis added)

Fenno captures here the gist of a perspective on one's political career choice that is also found in the data I collected, but only in Capps's and Wheeler's speeches. As shown in (18) below, Capps presented his decision to run for Congress as an extension of his teaching at UCSB, especially teaching his very large and popular course on the Vietnam War.

(18) 15 August 1996; San Luis Obispo; public debate.

CAPPS: [...] I got into the politics **as a kind of extension** of the ... teaching that I'd been doing. ... uh the- the courses that I teach. [...] I got into politics **as an extension** ... of the work that I've done on the- ... impact of the Vietnam War, the class that I teach ... that's been featured three times on [the television program] Sixty Minutes, ... I have- testified before congressional committees on three occasions.

As apparent from the last sentence in this excerpt, teaching experience was conceived and presented as ONE of the past experiences that better qualified Capps for the position he hoped to be elected to. Having testified before Congressional committees was another item in Capps's list to build his case.

In the case of Steven Wheeler, we find an example in his speeches where his "natural extension" narrative was pushed further back in time to include his ancestors. In (19), he frames his choice to run for the US Congress as part of a "family destiny" of altruistic public service.

(19) 15 August 1996; San Luis Obispo; public debate.

WHEELER: [...] most of you don't know me uhm- ... and I believe that I am here ... as a part of a family destiny. And I'd like to tell you a little bit about my family. My grandfather ... formed a chapter of the United Mine Workers in the 1930s in Kentucky. He was thrown in jail ... several times in that process. uhm- he was uh written about in songs by George Davis the singing miner whose works are in the Smithsonian. ... My father served in three wars. He started out in World War Two ... as an enlisted man. He ended up as a chief warrant officer (for/four)- he had two tours of duty at Vietnam. and ... **I'm here because I feel it's time to do my public service ... to this community and to this country ... and this is how I've chosen to do it.**

Consistent with the notion of the struggle for existential coherence, in (19) we see Wheeler building himself up as someone whose personal characteristics include, but are not limited to, being a descendant of a line of (male) ancestors who do things not in their own interest but in the interest of their community (from the community of co-workers to that of the entire nation).

Strategy 3: Exposing and reconciling potential contradictions

A third strategy in constructing existential coherence is to bring out and make explicit a potential contradiction in order to show that it is not a contradiction. By so doing, candidates may respond to a direct, indirect, or potential criticism by others. I will briefly discuss two such cases.

Sometimes candidates seemed satisfied simply to point out a potential contradiction and state that it was not a contradiction, offering no rationale for such a move. This was the case, for example, in the passage in excerpt (20) below, where Independent Steven Wheeler asserts that he sees no contradiction between being simultaneously pro-business and pro-environment. He then proceeds to list a series of other positions that voters might see as canceling each other out: (i) balancing the budget, (ii) maintaining a strong military, and (iii) not cutting social services (here represented by students, seniors, and *working people* making *large sacrifices*).

(20) 9 August 1996; Santa Maria; public debate.

WHEELER: [...] As a certified public accountant, what I bring to the table is a platform of fiscally conservative, yet socially moderate. and responsible positions on issues. ... **I believe that the terms pro business and pro environment do not need to be mutually exclusive terms not only in this district but in this country.** ((looks down)) ... ((looks up)) I believe that we can balance the budget, ... maintain a strong military, ... without requiring our seniors. our students. and our working people to make large sacrifices. We can do this simply by eliminating, wasteful. pork barrel.

A candidate may also choose to bring out a potential contradiction in order to offer a solution. This was the case when Capps addressed what he perceived as a potential paradox of his candidacy: reconciling his positive view of academic life with many voters' negative views of politics. By asking voters for their support, Capps felt that he might have been seen as implying that he was looking for a change of career. He wanted to be a congressman instead of a university professor. Capps, however, knew that such a goal could be seen as problematic because in contemporary American public discourse being a "politician" has a negative connotation (see ex. 21 below). But Capps was also aware that being a professor, in turn, could be seen in a negative light in the political context because it came with the connotation of being detached from mainstream America and the life of ordinary citizens – as captured in the phrase "being ivory tower." His solution was to operate on several discursive and argumentative levels at the same time. While praising the academic profession and himself as a member – partly in order to boost his record and partly to prove that he was not ashamed or tired of it – he presented himself as a "reluctant candidate," a nonprofessional politician (and also, as we saw before, an "independent" thinker), who would go to Washington to do his civic duty as part of a vocation. The first time this integrated model of the self is found in the data collected is on 14 November 1995, in Capps's speech at the third stop of the first day of campaigning, at Hancock College near Santa Maria, in front of a mixed audience which included the instructor and the students in a political science class, political supporters, and representatives of the local media.

(21) 14 November 1995; Santa Maria; inside a classroom at Hancock College.

CAPPS: Why would somebody who is enjoying a career- you know- I still write books. I still do research. I still teach. Why would somebody who's doing that, ... want to run for public office? The reason is very very simple. ... In that I think it isn't simply enough to study, ... the process. There comes a time in a person's life, when, by opportunity, by privilege, by vocation, by request from others, ... it's time ... to ... assume the responsibility of- of representative leadership. Because this is exactly the way that Thomas Jefferson talked about it.. [...]. So rather than saying, ... and rather than talking about **politicians- which is a negative thing**. And I guess if I'm now a politician I'll have to admit to that. I'd like to say **elected citizen**. An elected citizen ... responding ... to a kind of vocational call. **And I can also tell you that I- I wasn't thrilled to be doing this in the beginning because I so much enjoy what I am doing.**

The same attempt to recognize the contrast between academic life and politics without putting down either one of them is found ten months later in the campaign. This excerpt reproduces the part of a speech that is immediately prior to the segment in excerpt (18):

(22) 15 August 1996; San Luis Obispo; public debate.

CAPPS: [...] I've been accused of being ... ivory tower. ... uhm which I think is insulting to:: the entire teaching profession but- ... I- I don't think I'm very ivory tower. ... Although in some ways I wish I were. ... Because there's a- that's a great tradition as well- to be able to take a look at- at what's going on in society and make sense of it. ... But I got into politics as an extension ... of the work that I've done on the ... impact of the Vietnam War, [...]

As illustrated in (9), for Capps, the potential conflict between academia and politics could be reconciled by adopting what he characterized as Jefferson's conceptualization of the politician-citizen. In fact, the image of the ordinary citizen who goes to serve in Congress as a civic duty and then returns to the community from which he came was useful for Capps precisely because it allowed him to reconcile his multiple identities, providing a script that would help him construct the existential coherence that he was aiming at. But Jefferson was not his only model, in part because Capps was concerned with the spiritual side of his persona, the same side that attracted him to religious studies. This search for other models is made explicit in an exchange with a local reporter on 5 May 1996, while George Stephanopolous was in town to support Capps at a fund-raising event. In response to the reporter's question about what Stephanopolous brought to his campaign, Capps mentioned their common background in the study of theology and the fact that Stephanopolous's father and uncle were Orthodox priests. To honor that connection, Capps proudly announced that he decided to do something unusual in politics and quote in his speech a Greek theologian, John Chrysostom, *who talked about the compatibility of our beliefs and our politics*.

(23) 5 May 1996; Santa Barbara; outside a private home where a fund-raising event hosting George Stephanopolous is taking place.

REPORTER: alright. and what does someone like-uh-George bring to your campaign?
CAPPS: mhm. uhm-
REPORTER: you have him here and-
CAPPS: Well uhm you know these-I didn't even know him. I didn't know him until two years ago. but ... George- uh George is a student of theology. I don't know if you knew.
REPORTER: no, I didn't.
CAPPS: But his father was an Orthodox priest. A Greek Orthodox priest. his uncle is an Orthodox priest. he studied theology at Oxford. And he knew me-I don't know how-before he got into this politics thing. and I knew that he had this interest in religion so tonight when I get to talk, I'm gonna do a thing that no politician has ever done. I'm gonna start off by quoting John Chrysostom
[...]
CAPPS: A fifth century Greek Orthodox theologian who talked about **the compatibility of our beliefs and our politics**. And that's where George and I- we bond.
[...]

In his concern for this particular type of existential coherence – what he calls, in (23), *the compatibility of our beliefs and our politics* – Capps was probably unique; we might even speculate that it was such a concern that made him appealing to at least some of the voters. At the same time, his articulation of his doubts and possible solutions, just like his articulation of the reasons he gave to explain why people should vote for him, provide a glimpse into what other candidates may think and feel but not express in ways that are accessible in the public record.

Conclusion

Through an examination of the talk produced during a campaign for the US Congress, I have argued that some of the candidates' rhetorical strategies can be understood in terms of their common concern for creating and sustaining a sense of what I call "existential coherence." Because of the concern with issues of truth and consistency in political campaigns, the construction of existential coherence becomes an important aspect of the discursive construction of a candidate as a moral person in the Kantian sense of someone who should be the "object of respect" (Kant 1785).

I have here proposed that we think of existential coherence as something that can be questioned by others (e.g., one's opponents) and that can also explain candidates' presentation and framing of particular moments of their life history as manifesting a particular logic. In resorting to discourse strategies like the "narrative of belonging" and "the present as a natural extension of the past," candidates seemed to respond to a perceived need to justify a number of decisions, including (i) the decision to run for office, (ii) the decision to run in a particular district, and (iii) the decision to take stances that might appear contradictory. The data collected also show that candidates modified their discursive strategies over time and across types of situations. Democratic candidate Walter Capps, for example, used more elaborate narratives of personal experience when addressing his supporters at the beginning of his campaign than later on, when he began to participate in public debates with his opponents and in front of a mixed audience. In contrast, Reform Party candidate Dick Porter did not include any information about his biography or life experience in the first debate he participated in or in the two-minute statement he delivered on KEYT (see Appendix B). During his second debate, however, he introduced the telegraphic bio-sketch I reproduce in (15).

Repeatedly, throughout this article, the data I presented demonstrate a similarity in discursive strategies between two candidates: the Democrat Capps and the Independent Wheeler. They were the only candidates who produced what I called "narratives of belonging," and they were also the only ones who engaged in the other two discursive strategies – the "present as a natural extension of the past" and "exposing and reconciling potential contradictions" in their positions or choices. This common cluster of features begins to make sense if we return to the earlier discussion of the term "independent." Both Wheeler and Capps claimed to be "independent," even though, as we saw, each emphasized a slightly different meaning of the term. Wheeler wanted to be seen as an alternative to the two major parties, and Capps wanted to be seen as a Democrat who could think on his own and was not taking orders from anyone else in the Democratic Party. All of the other candidates, albeit in different ways and to different extents, were more concerned with presenting their politics in terms of the general goals and ideologies of their respective parties.

Whereas the stress on personal history and independence made sense in the case of Wheeler, who was running as a previously unknown candidate and in opposition to the Democrats and Republicans, who represented in his view "politics as usual" (as he said at the end of his introduction during the debate on 8 August 1996), the same stance was less obvious in the case of Capps, who was running as a Democrat and was backed by the Democratic leadership, including Bill and Hillary Clinton.

On closer analysis, however, it becomes apparent that in order to win, Capps had to reach out to people who in previous years voted for the Republican candidate (Michael Huffington), given that no Democrat had won an election in the district in 50 years. In addition, the campaign was taking place only a year after the Republicans, under the banner of Newt Gingrich's "Contract with America," had gained control of the US House of Representatives. This meant that during the fall of 1995 all the way through the summer of 1996, Democrats continued to doubt whether President Clinton was going to be reelected. The advice of Democratic strategists to Capps was then to avoid close association with Clinton. This advice resonated with Capps's own convictions and personal history. He did not want to lose his academic identity, which included a successful career in the pursuit of original pedagogical ideas (as in his famous and highly successful course on the Vietnam War) and a number of complex research topics. He was proud to be the author or editor of 13 books on a range of subjects, including the Vietnam War (Capps 1982, 1990), Native American religion, the "new religious right" (Capps 1990), and Thomas Merton and the monastic impulse (Capps 1976, 1983, 1989).

It could be argued that Capps was self-reflective in his speeches at least in part because of his academic background. This assumption would make it difficult to use his rhetorical strategies as a representative example of what other, nonacademic candidates do. There are, however, two reasons to reject the academic background as the sole or principal explanation of Capps's rhetorical strategies. First, as I demonstrated in this article, Capps was not alone in some of his rhetorical choices: the Independent candidate Steven Wheeler used some of the very same discursive strategies used by Capps. Second, in examining my data, I found variation in rhetorical strategies across individuals and across situations. Even Capps modified his strategies over time and to accommodate different audiences. Both sets of findings suggest that, in addition to being confronted with unique individuals under unique circumstances, there are TYPES of candidates, which are in part defined by TYPES of rhetorical strategies. I did not expect to find the rhetorical strategies that I described and, as far as I know, they have not been described before. They are, therefore, a potentially important addition to the documentation of how human actors involved in competitive tasks such as political races use particular linguistic resources to construct the kind of person that they want the voters to know and believe in.

Appendix A

Transcription Conventions

The excerpts presented in this article are transcribed according to a modified version of the conventions originally established by Gail Jefferson for the analysis of conversation (Sacks, Schegloff and Jefferson 1974: 731–4).

Capps:	name of speaker is separated from the rest by a colon (:) and one or more spaces.
anybody	underlining represents emphasis or contrastive stress.
NO!!	capital letters indicate high volume.
job=I mean	equal sign (=) stands for "latching," i.e. no hearable interval between two turns or between two utterances by the same speakers.
independent	boldface is used to highlight portions of the talk that are being discussed in the surrounding part of the article.
becau::se	colon (:) stands for lengthening of sound.
last time,	a comma indicates that the phrase ends with a rising intonation, e.g. the intonation found when speakers are projecting further talk or more items in a list.
I do.	a period stands for a falling intonation that suggests the possible end of a turn.

go //next	point in a party's turn where overlap by next speaker(s) starts.
(first of all)	talk between parentheses indicates an uncertain but reasonable guess at what might have been said.
(??)	question marks between parentheses indicate that a portion of talk could not be heard accurately and no guess was possible.
...	untimed pause.
((laughter))	double parentheses frame contextual information about the talk that follows.
[...]	a portion of the transcript was left out.

APPENDIX B

Political Debates Mentioned in the Article, with List of Candidates and Their Political Affiliation

Date, Place and Host	*Candidates who participated*
August 8, 1996, Santa Maria, organized by the Area Agency on Aging (as video recorded by A. Duranti)	1) David L. Bersohn (Libertarian) 2) Walter H. Capps (Democrat) 3) Andrea Seastrand (Republican) 4) Steven Wheeler (Independent)
August 15, 1996, San Luis Obispo, organized by the AARP (as video recorded by A. Duranti)	1) Walter H. Capps (Democrat) 2) Richard D. Porter (Reform Party) 3) Andrea Seastrand (Republican) 4) Steven Wheeler (Independent)
October 7, 1996, Santa Barbara, organized by the League of Women Voters (as video recorded by A. Duranti)	1) David L. Bersohn (Libertarian) 2) Walter H. Capps (Democrat) 3) Mr. Hospidar (Natural Law Party, standing in for candidate Dawn Tomastick) 4) Richard D. Porter (Reform Party) 5) Andrea Seastrand (Republican) 6) Steven Wheeler (Independent)
October 21, 1996, KEYT (broadcast version)	1) Walter H. Capps (Democrat) 2) Andrea Seastrand (Republican) Following the one hour debate between Capps and Seastrand, there were 2 minute statements by three other candidates: 3) Steven Wheeler (Independent) 4) David L. Bersohn (Libertarian Party) 5) Richard D. Porter (Reform Party)

NOTES

The research on which this article is based was in part supported by two small grants from the University of California at Los Angeles (UCLA) in 1996–7 and 1997–8 and by a John Simon Guggenheim Foundation Fellowship supplemented by funds from UCLA during the 1999–2000 academic year. An earlier version of this article was presented at the Discourse Lab in the Department of Anthropology at UCLA on June 2, 2004. I thank my colleagues and students for their generous feedback and comments. I am also indebted to Anjali Browning for her careful reading of my first draft and her useful editorial suggestions.

Some of the data and ideas presented in this article were first introduced in a number of seminars, workshops and conferences at the University of Rome "La Sapienza," the University of Florence, and the University of California at Santa Barbara. I would like to thank the participants in those events for their engagement with this material and their comments. I am also grateful to Jane Hill, former editor of *Language in Society*, and three anonymous reviewers for specific suggestions on how to improve the organization and content of the article.

A number of people made the project on which this article is based possible and a rewarding experience. First and foremost, I am deeply indebted to the late Walter Capps and to his wife Lois Capps – now Rep. Lois Capps (D-California) – and to their extended family for letting me enter their home and giving me access to their lives as they experienced an extraordinary series of events. I am also very thankful to Walter's brother, Doug Capps, who was Walter's campaign manager in 1996 and has continued over the years to be my liaison with the rest of the Capps family as I go through the challenging process of writing what I learned from this project while trying not to violate family members' privacy or their precious memories of Walter. Other members of the Capps-for-Congress campaign staff I could rely on for information include Bryant Wieneke, always the most generous with his time, Steve Boyd, Thu Fong, and Lindsey Capps. After Walter Capps's death, I gained a better understanding of his academic background and further insights into his persona from conversations with his colleague and friend Richard Hecht, Professor and former Chair of the Department of Religious Studies at the University of California, Santa Barbara. I am also thankful to the 1995–6 Independent candidate Steven Wheeler, who, in June 1998, consented to meeting with me and to being interviewed. Among my research assistants over the years, special thanks go to Jeff Storey who completed a first, rough transcription of the talk in most of my video tapes of the campaign and to Jennifer F. Reynolds and Sarah Meacham, who did some additional transcription and helped out with the recording on a day when I could not attend an important series of events. Sarah also helped me organize press releases and other written material collected during the 1995–6 political campaign. This project was born out of conversations with Walter Capps's daughter Lisa while she was a graduate student at UCLA. She remained a strong supporter of my efforts to capture her father's adventure in politics after she accepted a position in Psychology at the University of California, Berkeley, and even during the last year of her life, as she struggled with an incurable type of cancer. This article is dedicated to her memory.

1 Several discourse analysts have made distinctions within what I am here generically calling "textual coherence." For example, Widdowson 1979 distinguishes between textual cohesion (between sentences) and textual coherence (between speech acts); in a related but distinct fashion, Conte (1988: 29) distinguishes between what she calls "consistency," that is, the absence of contradictions, and coherence as the property of a series of utterances that are recognized as forming a whole. Bakhtin discusses the crucial role of the genre as a unit that provides guidance for performance and for interpretation of particular utterances through the process he calls "finalization" (*zavershenie*) – a concept related to the notion of semantic and pragmatic coherence (Medvedev and Bakhtin 1985). See also Hanks 1987.

2 Capps's course was called "The Impact of the Vietnam War" and regularly enrolled 750 to 900 students. Capps also taught another very popular undergraduate course, "The Voice of the Stranger," which at times enrolled more than 900 students (Richard Hecht, personal communication). The Vietnam course was also featured on the television program *60 Minutes*.

3 In the United States, candidates for political office who do not want to run in a list of one of the existing parties (Democratic Party, Republican Party, Reform Party, Green Party, etc.) have the option of signing up with the "Independent Party," which allows them to run on their own personal platform.

4 US federal rules require a small number of signatures by registered voters to allow someone to be on the ballot. However, a number of signatures in the thousands helps candidates pay off part or all of the fee that they need to pay when they register to run for election.

5 In writing about these particular TV spots, Bryant Wieneke, who worked on the 1995–6 Capps campaign from the very start, suggested that the phrase "independent, in touch, and in the mainstream" had been written by Democratic strategist Bill Carrick and was not something that Capps himself would have used: "The scripts [for the TV spots] came in from a highly competent, highly experienced professional by the name of Bill Carrick, and Doug [Capps], Cathy [Duvall] and Travis [Green] digested them. In my opinion, they were very well done. They were completely positive and would stay that way for the duration of the campaign. Walter did not even mention Seastrand which was definitely a positive. The only part that made me cringe was the sound-bite at the end, when the announcer characterized Walter as 'independent, in touch, and in the mainstream.' That part could have been in any candidate's spot around the country; it just did not sound like something Walter would say about himself" (Wieneke 2000: 133). Although the entire phrase does not seem like something that Capps would have said or something that I recorded, Capps did use the term "independent" in talking about the candidate he wanted to be, as shown in ex. (2). More generally, the quote above raises the issue of the grounds on which to attribute authorship for what is said by and about a candidate for political office. It is difficult at times to distinguish between situations in which a speech (or script) writer inserted a term or phrase that he or she heard the candidate use, and situations in which a candidate might adopt a term or phrase originally written for him or about him by someone else.

6 This avoidance of direct confrontation with Wheeler was quite consistent throughout the campaign. I came to see it as part of a conscious decision made by Capps to minimize the potential impact of Wheeler's candidacy by avoiding making him into an interlocutor, someone whose opinions mattered.

7 In the first case, *independent* is a predicate adjective, and in the second case it is a modifier of a noun. I thank Keith Murphy for first pointing this out to me after a talk I gave at UCLA based on this material.

8 This means that in Wheeler's definition, "an independent" cannot be affiliated with the American Independent Party, which is a certified political party. This was confusing to some people, as shown by the fact that in the debate in Santa Barbara at the League of Women Voters on 7 October 1996, the moderator erroneously introduced Wheeler as "of the Independent Party."

9 Morgan (1991: 429) defines "baited indirectness" as any case in which "a speaker says something general which is taken by the audience to be specific or addressed to someone in particular because of contextual evidence."

10 "With politics as with law, our system is inherently adversarial in its structure, but in recent years a kind of antagonistic inflation has set in whereby opposition has become more extreme, and the adversarial nature of the system is being routinely abused" (Tannen 1998: 96).

11 Both cases point toward an "anti-politics" attitude in contemporary American politics that has similarities with what in British politics has been called "the Third Way," that is, the avoidance of explicit affiliation with the "Old Left" and the "New Right" (see Weltman and Billig 2001).

12 Here is the segment immediately preceding the excerpt in (8):

CAPPS:	((smiles, look away)) and I'm- how do- how do I know that? How do I know we're gonna win?
???:	((laughter)) hehehe!
CAPPS:	well, you know, I can see it in your faces. (I mean)

AUDIENCE: ((laughter))
CAPPS: that I- and I- and I mean that totally because- because uh, Lois and I ... have lived here, [...]

13 An almost verbatim version of the same narrative also occupies a large portion of Wheeler's two-minute statement at the end of the televised debate between Walter Capps and Andrea Seastrand done at the KEYT headquarters on 21 October 1996.

14 From interview with Steven Wheeler, on June 25, 1998:

DURANTI: [...] how did you prepare for that speech, how did you- ...
WHEELER: I:- uhm I: did it uh here. at the house. I believe. uh. and. ... I just (uh) ... uhm you know got on the computer and- an:: uh thought about what I wanted to say and- and uh what seemed to be ... relevant in terms of- ... of my campaign and what I thought that I had to offer, // you know to:
DURANTI: right
WHEELER: uhm to the voters of the district // uhm
DURANTI: hu-hu
WHEELER: a:nd it seems like it was important to:: uhm talk uh about my background a little bit.
DURANTI: mh-mh.
WHEELER: and-uh ... [...] I didn't really have anyone advising me in terms of what to say or what not to say.

15 Although the spatial adverbial phrase *at Santa Barbara* is part of the standard way of distinguishing among different campus of the University of California, I believe that in this case it also works as a spatial qualifier, given that Santa Barbara is the main urban center in the 22nd District.

16 In the context of the present discussion, the applause received by the representative of the Natural Law Party needs explanation, given that he read a statement about the general philosophy and program of the Natural Law Party without any personal narrative or any obvious attempt to connect to the people of the district through narratives of personal experience. It is perhaps relevant however, that his statement ended with a general concern for the value of "coherence throughou society."

Debate at the League of Women Voters, Santa Barbara, 7 October 1996.

HOSPIDAR: [...] We stand. for government. in accordance with natural law. which is the infinite organizing power of nature. ... we should solve problems at their basis by bringing individual lives in our national policy into greater harmony with the natural law through proven educational programs. ... through- natural preventive health care renewable energy. sustainable agriculture and other forward looking prevention oriented programs. and we wish to reverse the current epidemics of individual and social stress by establishing groups professionally engaged in creating coherence throughout society. Scientific research has demonstrated the effects of these programs.

REFERENCES

Bloch, M. (1975). *Political Language and Oratory in Traditional Society.* London: Academic Press.

Brenneis, Donald (1978). The matter of talk: Political performance in Bhatgaon. *Language in Society* 7: 159–70.

—— , and Myers, Fred (1984) (eds.). *Dangerous words: Language and politics in the Pacific*. New York: New York University Press.

Capps, Walter H. (1976). *Hope against Hope: Molton [i.e. Moltmann] to Merton in One Decade*. Philadelphia: Fortress Press.

—— (1982). *The Unfinished War: Vietnam and the American Conscience*. Boston: Beacon. 2nd edn., 1990.

—— (1983). *The Monastic Impulse*. New York: Crossroad.

—— (1989) (ed.). *Thomas Merton: Preview of the Asian Journey.* New York: Crossroad.

—— (1990). *The New Religious Right: Piety, Patriotism, and Politics*. Columbia, SC: University of South Carolina Press.

Conte, Maria-Elizabeth (1988). *Condizioni di coerenza: Ricerche di linguistica testuale.* Florence: Nuova Italia.

Duranti, Alessandro (1994). *From Grammar to Politics: Linguistic Anthropology in a Western Samoan Village*. Berkeley and Los Angeles: University of California Press.

—— (2003). The voice of the audience in contemporary American political discourse. In J. E. Alatis and D. Tannen (eds.), *Georgetown University Round Table on Languages and Linguistics: Linguistics, Language, and the Real World – Discourse and Beyond*, pp. 114–36. Washington, DC: Georgetown University Press.

Erikson, Erik H. (1980). *Identity and the Life Cycle: A Reissue*. New York: Norton.

Fenno, Richard F. Jr. (1996). *Senators on the Campaign Trail: The Politics of Representation.* Norman and London: University of Oklahoma Press.

Garro, Linda C., and Mattingly, Cheryl (2000). Narrative as construct and construction. In Garro and Mattingly (eds.), *Narrative and the Cultural Construction of Illness and Healing*, pp. 1–49. Berkeley: University of California Press.

Geertz, Clifford (1983). "From the native's point of view": On the nature of anthropological understanding. In his *Local Knowledge: Further Essays in Interpretive Anthropology*, pp. 55–70. New York: Basic Books.

Halliday, M. A. K., and Hasan, Ruqaiya (1976). *Cohesion in English*. London: Longman.

Hanks, William F. (1987). Discourse genres in a theory of practice. *American Ethnologist* 14: 668–92.

Hill, Jane H. (2000). "Read my article": Ideological complexity and the overdetermination of promising in American presidential politics. In Paul V. Kroskrity (ed.), *Regimes of Language: Ideologies, Polities and Identities*, pp. 259–91. Santa Fe, NM: School of American Research.

——, & Irvine, Judith T. (1993) (eds.). *Responsibility and Evidence in Oral Discourse.* Cambridge: Cambridge University Press.

Hultkrantz, Åke, and Capps, Walter H. (1976). *Seeing with a Native Eye: Essays on Native American Religion*. New York: Harper & Row.

Kant, Immanuel (1785). *Grundlegung zur Metaphysik der Sitten*. Leipzig: Hartknoch.

Kuipers, Joel C. (1990). *Power in Performance: The Creation of Textual Authority in Weyewa Ritual Speech*. Philadelphia: University of Pennsylvania Press.

Keating, Elizabeth (1998). *Power Sharing: Language, Rank, Gender and Social Space in Pohnpei, Micronesia*. Oxford: Oxford University Press.

Lakoff, George (1996). *Moral Politics: What Conservatives Know that Liberals Don't*. Chicago, IL: University of Chicago Press.

—— (2004). *Don't Think of an Elephant! Know Your Values and Frame the Debate.* White River Junction, VT: Chelsea Green.

——, and Johnson, Mark (1980). *Metaphors We Live By*. Chicago, IL: Chicago University Press.

——, and Turner, Mark (1989). *More than Cool Reason: A Field Guide to Poetic Metaphor.* Chicago, IL: University of Chicago Press.

Linde, Charlotte (1993). *Life Stories: The Creation of Coherence*. New York: Oxford University Press.

Mauss, Marcel (1938). La Notion de personne, celle de "moi". *Journal of the Royal Anthropological Institute* 68: 263–81. English translation in Mauss (1985).

—— (1985). A category of the human mind: The notion of person; the notion of self. In M. Carrithers et al. (eds.), *The Category of Person: Anthropology, Philosophy, History*, pp. 1–25. Cambridge: Cambridge University Press.

Medvedev, P. N., and Bakhtin, M. M. (1985). *The Formal Method in Literary Scholarship*. Baltimore: Johns Hopkins University Press.

Morgan, Marcyliena (1991). Indirectness and interpretation in African American women's discourse. *Pragmatics* 1: 421–51.

Ochs, Elinor (2004). Narrative lessons. In Alessandro Duranti (ed.), *A Companion to Linguistic Anthropology*, pp. 269–89. Malden, MA: Blackwell.

—— , and Capps, Lisa (1996). Narrating the self. *Annual Review of Anthropology* 25:19–43.

—— ,—— (2001). *Living Narrative: Creating Lives in Everyday Storytelling*. Cambridge, MA: Harvard University Press.

Pernot, Laurent (2000). *La Rhétorique dans l'antiquité*. Paris: Librairie Générale Française.

Polkinghorne, Donald (1991). Narrative and self-concept. *Journal of Narrative and Life History* 1: 135–53.

Sacks, Harvey; Schegloff, Emanuel A.; and Jefferson, Gail (1974). A simplest systematics for the organization of turn-taking for conversation. *Language* 50: 696–735.

Schiffrin, Deborah (1996). Narrative as self-portrait: Sociolinguistic constructions of identity. *Language in Society* 25:167–203.

Stubbs, Michael (1983). *Discourse Analysis*. Oxford: Blackwell.

Tannen, Deborah (1998). *The Argument Culture: Stopping America's War of Words*. New York: Ballantine.

Taylor, Charles (1991). The dialogical self. In David Hiley et al. (eds.), *The Interpretive Turn: Philosophy, Science, Culture*, 304–14. Ithaca, NY: Cornell University Press.

van Dijk, Teun A. (1977). *Text and Context: Explorations in the Semantics and Pragmatics of Discourse*. London: Longman.

Weltman, David, and Billig, Michael (2001). The political psychology of contemporary anti-politics: A discursive approach to the end-of-ideology era. *Political Psychology* 22: 367–82.

Widdowson, H. G. (1979). *Explorations in Applied Linguistics*. London: Oxford University Press.

Wieneke, Bryant (2000). *Winning without the Spin: A True Hero in American Politics*. Huntington, NY: Kroshka.

Wilson, John (2001). Political discourse. In D. Schiffrin et al. (eds.), *The Handbook of Discourse Analysis*, pp. 398–415. Malden, MA: Blackwell.

STUDY QUESTIONS

1 Define the notions of "discursive consciousness" and "existential coherence" as discussed in the chapter.
2 Describe and explain the three discursive strategies that candidates used to construct existential coherence: (1) narratives of belonging; (2) the present as a 'natural extension' of the past; and (3) exposing and resolving potential contradictions. How did candidates differ in their use (or lack of use) of these strategies?
3 What do the term "independent" and the predicate "having been to Washington" illustrate about political discourse and political debates?
4 Identify ways in which political candidates in the study differed in their rhetorical strategies.
5 Apply any aspect of the analysis presented in this chapter to more recent political debates.

11

Hip Hop Nation Language

H. Samy Alim

Hip Hop Culture and its Investigation in the Street

The Black Language is constructed of – alright let me take it all the way back to the slave days and use something that's physical. All the slavemasters gave our people straight chittlins and greens, you feel me, stuff that they wasn't eating. But we made it into a delicacy. Same thing with the language. It's the exact *same formula. How our people can take the* worst, *or take our bad condition, and be able to turn it into something that we can benefit off of. Just like the drums. They didn't want the slaves playing drums because we was talkin through the drums. "What the hell did my slaves do? Oh, no, cut that! Take them drums!" you feel me? So through the music, that's kinda like going on now with the rap thang. It's* ghetto *music. People talkin about they issues and crime and, you feel me? "Don't push me cuz I'm close to the eeedge!" [Rappin Grandmaster Flash and the Furious Five's "The Message"] You feel me? He talkin about, "Man, I'm so fed up with you people in this society, man." So this is the voice of the ghetto. The rap come from the voice of the ghetto...Hip hop and the streets damn near is one, you might as well say that ... Straight from the streets.* [Interview with rapper JT the Bigga Figga, cited partially in Alim 2000]

Hip hop culture is sometimes defined as having four major elements: MCing (rappin), DJing (spinnin), breakdancing (streetdancing), and graffiti art (writing). To these, KRS-One adds knowledge as a fifth element, and Afrika Bambaata, a founder of the Hip Hop Cultural Movement, adds overstanding. Even with six elements, this definition of a culture is quite limited in scope, and it is useful to distinguish between the terms hip hop and rap. Rappin, one aspect of hip hop culture, consists of the aesthetic placement of verbal rhymes over musical beats, and it is this element that has predominated in hip hop cultural activity in recent years. Thus, language is perhaps the most useful means with which to read the various cultural activities of the Hip Hop Nation (HHN). This chapter provides a sociolinguistic profile of language use within the HHN in the sociocultural context of the streets. The chapter also examines the varied and rich hip hop cultural modes of discourse.

For permission to publish copyright material in this book, grateful acknowledgment is made to: H. S. Alim (2004), "Hip Hop Nation Language," in E. Finegan and J. R. Rickford (eds.), *Language in the USA: Themes for the Twenty-first Century.* New York: Cambridge University Press, pp. 387–409.

Sociolinguists have always been interested in analyzing language and language use within varying contexts. Given a healthy respect for vernacular languages among sociolinguists, and given the richly varied and diverse speech acts and communicative practices of the HHN, it is surprising that until the late 1990s no American sociolinguist had written about hip hop culture in any major academic journal. It was a Belgian student of African history and linguistics at the University of Ghent who first collected data about hip hop culture in the Lower East Side of New York City in 1986–7. In his quest to learn about the social and cultural context of rap performances, Remes (1991) produced one of the earliest sociolinguistic studies of rappin in a hip hop community (the borderless HHN comprises numerous hip hop communities around the world). His pioneering study provided a brief account of the origin of rap, identified several "Black English" linguistic features found in rap, and highlighted the communicative practices of call-and-response and verbal battling. Only in 1997 did sociolinguist Geneva Smitherman publish her pioneering analysis of the communicative practices of the HHN (Smitherman 1997, presented before an audience in South Africa in 1995).

Since then sociolinguists have presented papers at professional conferences and published in academic journals. In 2001 at the thirtieth anniversary meeting of New Ways of Analyzing Variation (or NWAV) Conference, the major gathering of sociolinguists, several scholars participated in a panel called "The Sociolinguistics of Hip Hop: New Ways of Analyzing Hip Hop Nation Language." To paraphrase the poet-dramatist Amiri Baraka, a leading figure of the Black Arts Movement of the 1960s and 1970s, African American linguists are now celebrating hip hop culture and beginning to see that the "Hip Hop Nation is Like Ourselves."

To be fair, at least since 1964, there has been considerable scholarship on language use within what are now called hip hop communities. It started with investigations "deep down in the jungle" in the streets of South Philly ("it's like a jungle sometimes it makes me wonder how I keep from goin under"[1]) that recorded "black talkin in the streets" of America (Abrahams 1964, 1970, 1976) and the analysis of "language behavior" of Blacks in Oakland (Mitchell-Kernan 1971) to the analysis of the narrative syntax and ritual insults of Harlem teenagers "in the inner city" (Labov 1972) to the critical examination of "the power of the rap" in the "Black Idiom" of the Black Arts Movement rappers and poets (Smitherman 1973, 1977) and an elucidation of the "language and culture of black teenagers" who skillfully "ran down some lines" in South Central Los Angeles (Folb 1980). In myriad ways, then, scholars had prepared the field for the extraordinary linguistic phenomenon that was about to leave an indelible mark on the language of parts of the English-speaking world. This linguistic phenomenon is, of course, hip hop culture. Most of the works cited above were published before the advent of the first hip hop recording in 1979, the Sugar Hill Gang's "Rapper's Delight." By describing the linguistic patterns and practices of African Americans in the "inner cities," these scholars were studying the linguistic forebears of the HHN. Some of the remaining sections of this chapter will show that language use within the HHN is intricately linked to language use within other African American institutions, such as churches and mosques, as well as to the everyday linguistic practices of Black folk in their communities from the hood to the amen corner.

The work of these pioneering scholars and others demonstrated the creativity, ingenuity, and verbal virtuosity of Africans in America by examining language use at the very loci of linguistic-cultural activity. What is the locus of the linguistic-cultural activity known as hip hop? "The street is hardcore and it is the rhythmic locus of the Hip Hop world" (Spady 1991: 406, 407). Foregrounding the streets as the site, sound, and soul of hiphopological activity allows one to gain a more thorough understanding of the origins and sociocultural context of hip hop culture, which is critical to understanding language use within this Nation. Rapper Busta Rhymes, often introduced on stage as being "straight from the muthafuckin street," defends the introduction with his characteristic tenacity:

> What do you mean what it mean?! It's straight and plain, plain and simple. Hip hop is street music! It ain't come from nobody's house! You know what I'm saying? It's something that we all gathered in the street to do. As far as the founders of the hip hop thing, you know what I'm saying, the hip hop way of life, it was established in the street. It wasn't established in people's houses, in people's homes, you know what I'm saying? People came from their homes to celebrate the culture of hip hop in the parks, in the streets, on the street corners, you know what I'm saying? (Spady, Lee, and Alim 1999: 183)

"Rap artists affirm that one has to come from the streets, or understand the urban black street tradition, in order to properly interpret and perform rap music," according to one ethnomusicologist (Keyes 1991). In the new millennium, the streets continue to be a driving force in hip hop culture. On "Streets Done Raised Us" (2001), rappers Drag-On and Baby Madison extend the notion that the streets are the center of hip hop cultural activity because for many young Black hip hop artists the streets are the locus of life itself. And as if to make certain of no misunderstanding, the LOX proudly proclaim *We Are the Streets* – equating self and street (2000).

Answering calls for Black linguists to set the standards for linguistic research on the language of Black Americans (Labov 1972, Hymes 1981), Baugh (1983: 36) went straight "to the people" in a variety of social contexts where "black street speech breathes." He writes: "It is one thing to recognize the need to gather data from representative consultants, but it is another matter altogether to get the job done." The "code of the streets" (Anderson 1999) does not look fondly upon someone carrying a tape recorder and asking too many questions, particularly in a cultural environment where people avoid "puttin their business out in the street" at all costs.

The hip hop saturated streets of America today are quite different from the streets of yesteryear. The changing nature of the city streets in the last decade of the twentieth century has been captured by Spady (1991: 407): "Changing. Those streets of yesteryear are no more. Now it is crack-filled and gang-banged. Loose and cracked. Yet most of our people walk straight through these streets night and day. Risking lives. But this is a risqué world...The street is hardcore and it is the locus of the Hip Hop world." What do we mean by hip hop saturated streets? In urban areas across the nation, it is clear that young hip hop heads exist in a state of hiphopness – their experience is saturated with the sights, sounds, smells, and stares of what it means to be a hip hop being. It is the "dynamic and constant sense of being alive in a hip hop, rap conscious, reality based world," Spady (1993: 95–6) explains. He writes:

> Hip hop is preeminently a cultural free space. Its transformatory and emancipatory powers are evident each time you see a young blood locked to the music being transmitted through the earphone. They exist in a community of expressive rebellion, in states of **always always**, altering what has traditionally been the culture of the ruling class.

The streets are saturated on multiple levels. An illuminating study of the "New Black Poetry" of the 1960s and 1970s uses the term "saturation" to mean both "the communication of Blackness in a given situation" and "a sense of fidelity to the observed and intuited truth of the Black Experience" (Henderson 1973: 62). In the hip hop saturated streets of America, we are speaking of the communication of the hip hop mode of being (Spady and Alim 1999) and the sense of fidelity to the absolute truth of existing in a state of hiphopness. A close examination of the hip hop saturated streets of America reveals that the street is not just a physical space – it is a site of creativity, culture, cognition, and consciousness. When Jigga (Jay-Z) said "the streets is watchin," and Beans (Beanie Sigel) turned it into "the streets is not only watchin, but they talkin now," they extended the notion of the streets into a living, breathing organism, with ears to hear, eyes to see, and a mouth to speak. Examination of hip hop culture and language must begin in the streets.

Hip Hop Nation Language [HHNL]

My own research on Hip Hop Nation Language and hip hop culture in general has led to the streets, homes, cars, jeeps, clubs, stadiums, backstage, performances, hotels, religious centers, conferences and ciphers (highly competitive lyrical circles of rhymers) where hip hop lives – up inside the "actual lived experiences in the corrugated spaces that one finds reflected in the lyrical content of rap songs" (Spady, Dupres, and Lee 1995). The centrality of language to the HHN is evident in such song and album titles as the "New Rap Language" (Treacherous Three 1980), "Wordplay" (Bahamadia 1996), "Gangsta Vocabulary" (DJ Pooh 1997), "Project Talk" (Bobby Digital 1998), "Slang Editorial" (Cappadonna 1998), *Real Talk 2000* (Three-X-Krazy 2000), "Ebonics" (Big L 2000), *Country Grammar* (Nelly 2000), and *Project English* (Juvenile 2001). In numerous ethnographic interviews, I have found that language is a favorite topic of discussion in the HHN, and its members are willing to discuss it with great fervor – and to defend its use.

What do we mean by "Nation Language"? In exploring the development of nation language in Anglophone Caribbean poetry, Caribbean historian, poet, and literary and music critic Kamau Brathwaite (1984: 13) writes: "Nation language is the language which is influenced very strongly by the African model, the African aspect of our New World/Caribbean heritage. English it may be in terms of some of its lexical features. But in its contours, its rhythm and timbre, its sound explosions, it is not English."

Concerned with the literature of the Caribbean and the sociopolitical matrix within which it is created, Brathwaite used the term "nation language" in contrast to "dialect." Familiar with the pejorative meanings of the term "dialect" in the folk linguistics of the people, he writes that while nation language can be considered both English and African at the same time, it is an English which is like a "howl, or a shout, or a machine-gun or the wind or a wave." Then he likened it to the blues. Surely, nation language is like hip hop (as rapper Raekwon spits his "machine-gun-rap" (1999)). HHNL is, like Brathwaite's description, new in one sense and ancient in another. It comprises elements of orality, total expression, and conversational modes (Brathwaite 1984).

Rapper Mystikal, known for having a unique, highly energetic rhyming style highlighted with lyrical sound explosions, provides a perfect example of Nation Language when he raps: "You know what time it is, nigga, and you know who the fuck this is/DAANNN-JAH!!! [Danger] DAANNN-JAH!!! [Danger]/ Get on the FLO' [floor]!/ The nigga right, yeaaahhHHH!"[2] (2000). Mystikal starts out speaking to his listener in a low, threatening growl, asserting his individuality ("you know who the fuck this is"), and then explodes as if sounding an alarm, letting everyone know that they have entered a dangerous verbal zone! "Get on the FLO'!" has a dual function – simultaneously warning listeners to lie down before the upcoming lyrical "DAANNN-JAH!" and directing them to get on the dance floor. When rapper Ludacris (2001) commands his listeners to "ROOOLLLL OUT!" and raps: "Oink, Oink, PIG! PIG! Do away with the POORRK-uh/ Only silverwuurrr [silverware] I need's a steak knife and FOORRK-uh!" he stresses his words emphatically, compelling one to do as he says. In that brief example, he is in conversation with African American Muslim and Christian communities currently dialoguing about the eating of swine flesh (which Muslims consider unholy).

When we speak of "language," we are defining the term in a sense that is congruent with the HHN's "linguistic culture" (Schiffman 1996), and HHNL can be situated in the broader context of African American speech:

> There is no single register of African American speech. And it's not words and intonations, it's a whole attitude about speech that has historical rooting. It's not a phenomenon that you can isolate and reduce to linguistic characteristics. It has to do with the way a culture conceives of the people inside of that culture. It has to do with a whole complicated protocol of silences and speech, and how you use speech in ways other than directly to

> communicate information. And it has to do with, certainly, the experiences that the people in the speech situation bring into the encounter. What's fascinating to me about African American speech is its spontaneity, the requirement that you not only have a repertoire of vocabulary or syntactical devices/constructions, but you come prepared to do something in an attempt to meet the person on a level that both uses the language, mocks the language, and recreates the language. (Wideman 1976: 34)

On her single recording "Spontaneity" (1996), Philadelphia rapper Bahamadia validates Wideman's assertion. She raps about her "verbal expansion" in a stream of consciousness style: "Rip here be dizz like everybody's on it cause eternal verbal expansion keeps enhancin brain child's ability to like surpass a swarm of booty-ass-no-grass-roots-havin-ass MC's." The verbal architect constructs her rhymes by consciously stretching the limitations of the "standard" language. In describing her lyrical influences, she cites rappers Kool Keith of the Ultramagnetic MCs, De La Soul, and Organized Konfusion as "masters at what they do in that they explore the English language and they try to push the boundaries and go against the grains of it, you know what I mean?" (Spady and Alim 1999: xviii).

"It's a very active exchange," says Wideman (1976: 34). "But at the same time as I say that, the silences and the refusal to speak is just as much a part, in another way, of African American speech." Rapper Fearless of the group Nemesis exemplifies the point: envisioning rappers, including himself, among the great orators and leaders in the Black community, he says:

> I always looked up to great orators like Martin Luther King, Malcolm X. Anybody who could ever stand up and persuade a group of young men or a nation . . . Just the way they were able to articulate. The way they emphasized their words. And the way they would use pauses. They would actually use *silence* powerfully . . . Just the way they made words cause feelings in you, you know what I'm saying? Just perpetuate thought within people, you know. (Spady and Alim 1999: xviii)

So "language" in HHNL obviously refers not only to the syntactic constructions of the language but also to the many discursive and communicative practices, the attitudes toward language, understanding the role of language in both binding/bonding community and seizing/smothering linguistic opponents, and language as concept (meaning clothes, facial expressions, body movements, and overall communication).

In addition to the above, HHNL can be characterized by ten tenets.

(1) HHNL is rooted in African American Language (AAL) and communicative practices (Spady 1991, Smitherman 1997, Yasin 1999). Linguistically, it is "the newest chapter in the African American book of folklore" (Rickford and Rickford 2000). It is a vehicle driven by the culture creators of hip hop, themselves organic members of the broader African American community. Thus HHNL both reflects and expands the African American Oral Tradition.

(2) HHNL is just one of the many language varieties used by African Americans.

(3) HHNL is widely spoken across the country, and used/borrowed and adapted/transformed by various ethnic groups inside and outside of the United States.

(4) HHNL is a language with its own grammar, lexicon, and phonology as well as unique communicative style and discursive modes. When an early hip hop group, The Treacherous Three, rhymed about a "New Rap Language" in 1980, they were well aware of the uniqueness of the language they were rappin in.

(5) HHNL is best viewed as the synergistic combination of speech, music, and literature. Yancy (1991) speaks of rap as "*musical literature* (or rhythmic-praxis discourse)." Henderson (1973) asserts that the Black poetry of the 1960s and 1970s is most distinctly Black when it derives its form from Black speech and Black music. HHNL is simultaneously the spoken, poetic, lyrical, and musical expression of the HHN.

(6) HHNL includes attitudes about language and language use (see Pharcyde dialogue below).
(7) HHNL is central to the identity and the act of envisioning an entity known as the HHN.
(8) HHNL exhibits regional variation (Morgan 2001a). For example, most members of the HHN recognize Master P's signature phrase, *Ya heeeaaard may?* ('You heard me?') as characteristic of a southern variety of HHNL. Even within regions, HHNL exhibits individual variation based on life experiences. For example, because California rapper Xzibit grew up in the hip hop saturated streets of Detroit, New Mexico and California, his HHNL is a syncretization of all these Hip Hop Nation Language varieties.
(9) The fundamental aspect of HHNL – and, to some, perhaps the most astonishing aspect – is that it is central to the lifeworlds of the members of the HHN and suitable and functional for all of their communicative needs.
(10) HHNL is inextricably linked with the sociopolitical circumstances that engulf the HHN. How does excessive police presence and brutality shift the discourse of the HHN? How do disproportionate incarceration rates and urban gentrification impact this community's language? As Spady (1993) writes: "Hip Hop culture [and language] mediates the corrosive discourse of the dominating society while at the same time it functions as a subterranean subversion... Volume is turned up to tune out the decadence of the dominant culture."

Rappers are insightful examiners of the sociopolitical matrix within which HHNL operates. Discussing the role of HHNL in hip hop lyrics, Houston's Scarface concludes that HHNL functions as a communal "code of communication" for the HHN:

> It's a code of communication, too... Because we can understand each other when we're rapping. You know, if I'm saying, [in a nasal, mocking voice] "Well, my friend, I saw this guy who shot this other guy and ..." I break that shit down for you and you say, "Goddamn, man! Them muthafuckas is going crazy out where this dude's from." You know what I'm saying? It's just totally different. It's just a code of communication to me. I'm letting my partner know what's going on. And anything White America can't control they call "gangsters." *Shit!* I get real. Politicians is gangsters, goddamn. The presidents is the gangsters because they have the power to change everything. That's a gangster to me. That's my definition of gangster. (Spady, Lee, and Alim 1999: 301)

Members of Tha Pharcyde actively debated the concept of HHNL:

BOOTY BROWN: There's more than just one definition for words! We talk in slang. We always talk basically in slang. We don't use the English dictionary for every sentence and every phrase that we talk!

PHARCYDE: No, there's a lot of words out of the words that you just said which all ...

BOOTY BROWN: Yeah, but the way I'm talking is not the English language... We're not using that definition... We're making our own... Just like they use any other word as a slang, *my brotha*! Anything. I'm not really your brother. Me and your blood aren't the same, but I'm your brother because we're brothas. That's slang... We make up our *own* words. I mean, it depends whose definition you glorify, okay? That's what I'm saying. Whose definition are you glorifying? Because if you go by my definition of "Black," then I can say "a Black person." But if you go by the *Webster Dictionary's*... You have your own definition. It's your definition.

(Spady, Lee, and Alim 1999: xix)

Sociolinguistically, so much is happening in the first exchange above. The HHN continues to "flip the script" (reverse the power of the dominant culture). Scarface is reacting to the media's labeling of reality-based rap lyrics as "gangster." By redefining gangster, he effectively turns the tables on what he believes is an oppressive state. If the presidents have the power to change everything, why ain't a damn thing changed?

In Tha Pharcyde conversation, when the *brotha* says the way he is talking is not the English language, he is talking about much more than slang. He asks pointedly, "Whose definition are you glorifying?" By making up your own words, he attests, you are freeing yourself from linguistic colonization (Wa Thiongo 1992). In an effort to combat the capitalistic comodification of hip hop culture, and to "unite and establish the common identity of the HHN," KRS-One refined the definition of hip hop terms and produced a document known as "The Refinitions" (2000) – putting the power of redefinition to action. KRS defines the language of hip hop culture as "street language" and proposes that "Hiphoppas" speak an Advanced Street Language, which includes "the correct pronunciation of one's native and national language as it pertains to life in the inner-city." KRS is reversing "standard" notions of correctness and appropriateness, realizing that the HHN has distinct values and aesthetics that differ from the majority culture. Clearly, members of the HHN would agree that the use of AAL stems "from a somewhat disseminated rejection of the lifestyles, social patterns, and thinking in general of the Euro-American sensibility," as the writer of the first AAL dictionary outside of the Gullah area put it (Major 1970: 10).

The Relationship between HHNL and AAL: Lexicon, Syntax, and Phonology

"Dangerous dialect/Dangerous dialect/I elect... to impress America." That's it, that's what it was about... Dangerous dialect, dangerous wording, you know what I mean? "I elect," that I pick, you know. "To impress America." That's what I pick to impress America, that dangerous dialect, you know. (San Quinn, 2000, Alim and Spady, unpublished interview)

The relationship between HHNL and AAL is a familial one. Since hip hop's culture creators are members of the broader African American community, the language that they use most often when communicating with each other is AAL. HHNL can be seen as the *submerged area* (Brathwaite 1984: 13) of AAL that is used within the HHN, particularly during hip hop centered cultural activities, but also during other playful, creative, artistic, and intimate settings. This conception of HHNL is broad enough to include the language of rap lyrics, album interludes, hip hop stage performances, and hip hop conversational discourse. African Americans are on the cutting edge of the sociolinguistic situation in the USA (as evidenced by abundant recent sociolinguistic research on the topic). HHNL, thus, is the cutting edge of the cutting edge.

A revised edition of the lexicon of "Black Talk" (Smitherman 1994, 2000) begins with a chapter entitled, "From Dead Presidents to the Benjamins." The term *dead presidents* (meaning 'money' and referring to American notes with images of dead presidents) has been in use in the African American community since the 1930s. In the late 1990s, hip hop group dead prez both shortened the term and made explicit its multivariate meanings (within the revolutionary context of their rhymes and philosophy, they are surely hinting at assassination – a form of verbal subversion). The *benjamins* is a term from the late 1990s popularized by rapper Sean "Puffy" Combs (P. Diddy).

While several scholars and writers have produced work on the lexicon of AAL (Turner 1949, Major 1970, 1994, Anderson 1994, Smitherman 1994, 2000, Stavsky, Mozeson and Mozeson 1995, Dillard 1977, Holloway and Vass 1997), it is important to note that hip hop artists, as street linguists and lexicographers, have published several dictionaries of their own. Old school legend Fab Five Freddy (Braithwaite 1992, 1995) documented the "fresh fly flavor" of the words and phrases of the hip hop generation (in English and German). Atlanta's Goodie Mob and several other artists have published glossaries on the inside flaps of their album covers. Of course, as lexicographers hip hop artists are only continuing the tradition of Black musicians, for many jazz and bebop artists compiled their own glossaries, most notable among them Cab Calloway (1944), Babs Gonzales, and Dan Burley.

Vallejo rapper E-40 discusses the genesis of *E-40's Dictionary Book of Slang, vol. 1* (2003):

> I feel that I *am* the ghetto. The majority of street slang... "It's all good." "Feel me." "Fo' shiiiiziiie," all that shit come from 40. "What's up, folks?" As a matter of fact, I'm writing my own dictionary book of slang right now... It's a street demand [for it]. Everywhere I go people be like, "Dude, you need to put out a dictionary. Let them know where all that shit come from," you know what I mean? (Spady, Lee, and Alim 1999: 290)

E-40 is credited with developing a highly individualized repertoire of slang words and phrases. If he were to say something like, "What's crackulatin, pimpin? I was choppin it up wit my playa-potna last night on my communicator – then we got to marinatin, you underdig – and I come to find out that the homie had so much fedi that he was tycoonin, I mean, pimpin on some real boss-status, you smell me?" not very many people would understand him. ("crackulatin" = happening, an extended form of "crackin"; "pimpin" is sometimes used as a noun to refer to a person, like, "homie"; "choppin it up" = making conversation; "playa-potna" = partner, friend; "communicator" = cell phone; "marinatin" = a conversation where participants are reasoning on a subject; "underdig" = understand; "fedi" = money; "tycoonin" = being a successful entrepreneur; "pimpin" = being financially wealthy; "boss-status" = managing things like a CEO; "you smell me?" = you feel me? or, you understand me?)

In HHNL, *pimp* refers not only to someone who solicits clients for a prostitute; it has several other meanings. One could be *pimpin a Lex* ("driving a Lexus while looking flashy"), suffering from *record company pimpin* ("the means by which record companies take advantage of young Black artists lacking knowledge of the music industry") or engaging in *parking lot pimpin* ("hanging around the parking lot after large gatherings"). As we also saw above, *pimpin* can also refer generally to an individual, or specifically to one who sports a flashy lifestyle. The word *politickin* can refer to the act of speaking about political subjects relevant to the Black community, simply holding a conversation, or trying to develop a relationship with a female. One might catch *frostbite* or get *goosebumps* from all of the *ice* they got on [*ice* = "diamonds"]. In the HHN, *rocks* can be a girl's best friend ("diamonds") or a community's silent killer ("crack cocaine"), while *to rock* can mean "to liven up a party," "to wear a fashionable article of clothing," or "to have sexual intercourse."

Given the fluidity of HHNL, speakers take a lot of pride in being the originators and innovators of terms that are consumed by large numbers of speakers. Rappers, as members of distinct communities, also take pride in regional lexicon. For instance, the term *jawn* emerged in the Philadelphia hip hop community. *Jawn* is what can be called a context-dependent substitute noun – a noun that substitutes for any other noun, with its definition so fluid that its meaning depends entirely upon context. For instance, you can say, *Oh, that's da jawn!* for *da bomb!* if you think something is superb; "Did you see that *jawn*?" for "female" when an attractive female walks by; "I like that new Beanie *jawn*" for "song," when the song is played on the radio, and so on. Recently, Philadelphia's Roots have handed out T-shirts with "JAWN" written on the front, advocating the use of the distinctive Philly hip hop term. Placed in a broader context, the meaning of the distinct lexicon of HHNL can be nicely summed up: "Slick lexicon is hip-hop's Magna Carta, establishing the rights of its disciples to speak loudly but privately, to tell America about herself in a language that leaves her puzzled" (Rickford and Rickford 2000: 86).

Several scholars have written that the syntax of HHNL is essentially the same as that of AAL (Remes 1991, Smitherman 1997, 2000, Morgan 1999, Spady and Alim 1999, Yasin 1999, Rickford and Rickford 2000, Morgan 2001b). This is true. We must also examine the syntax of HHNL closely enough to elucidate how the language users are behaving both within and beyond the boundaries of AAL syntax. What is happening syntactically when Method Man gets on the air and proclaims, "Broadcasting live from the Apocalypse, it be I, John Blazzzazzzziiinnnyyyyy!" (KMEL 2001b)? What is happening when Jubwa of Soul Plantation writes in his autobiography: "Jubwa be the dope mc, freestylin' to the beat deep cover" (cited in Alim 2001). An important question is, How does HHNL confirm our knowledge of AAL syntax – and how does it challenge that knowledge?

Probably the most oft-studied feature of AAL is *habitual* or *invariant be* (see chapter 5, this volume). Early studies of AAL syntax (Labov 1968, Wolfram 1969, Fasold 1972) noted the uniqueness of this feature and were in agreement that it was used for recurring actions (*We be clubbin on Saturdays*) and could not be used in finite contexts (*She be the teacher*). Building upon this research, we see that HHNL provides numerous examples of what I call *be*3 or the "equative copula" in AAL (Alim 2001b). Some examples of this construction (Noun Phrase *be* Noun Phrase) follow:

I be the truth. – Philadelphia's Beanie Sigel
Dr. Dre be the name. – Compton's Dr. Dre
This beat be the beat for the street. – New York's Busta Rhymes
Brooklyn be the place where I served them thangs. – New York's Jay-Z
I be that insane nigga from the psycho ward. – Staten Island's Method Man

These are but a few of countless examples in the corpus of hip hop lyrics, but this equative copula construction can also be found in everyday conversation, as in these examples:

We be them Bay boys. – Bay Area's Mac Mall in a conversation with James G. Spady
It [marijuana] be that good stuff. – Caller on the local Bay Area radio station
You know we be some baaad brothas. – Philadelphia speaker in conversation

It is possible that speakers of AAL have begun using this form only recently and that AAL has thus changed. Alternatively, the form may always have been present in the language but escaped the notice of investigators. Certainly it is present in the writings of Black Arts Movement poets of the 1960s and 1970s, most notably in Sonia Sanchez's *We Be Word Sorcerers*. We also find the form being cited in one linguistic study of Black street speech (*They be the real troublemakers; Leo be the one to tell it like it is*) (Baugh 1983). It is possible that members of the HHN, with their extraordinary linguistic consciousness and their emphasis on stretching the limits of language, have made this form much more acceptable by using it frequently (Alim, in press).

The HHN's linguistic consciousness refers to HHNL speakers' conscious use of language to construct identity. Addressing the divergence of AAL from standard English, Smitherman and Baugh (2002: 20) write:

> Graffiti writers of Hip Hop Culture were probably the coiners of the term "phat" (meaning excellent, great, superb)... although "phat" is spelled in obvious contrast to "fat," the former confirms that those who use it know that "ph" is pronounced like "f." In other words, those who first wrote "phat" diverged from standard English as a direct result of their awareness of standard English: the divergence was not by chance linguistic error. There is no singular explanation to account for linguistic divergence, but Hip Hop Culture suggests that matters of personal identity play a significant role.

This conscious linguistic behavior deals with matters of spelling and phonemic awareness. (See Morgan 2001a and Olivo 2001 on "spelling ideology.") One case – one of the more controversial uses of language in hip hop culture – is the term *nigga*. The HHN realized that this word had various positive in-group meanings and pejorative out-group meanings, and thus felt the need to reflect the culturally specific meanings with a new spelling (*nigger* becomes "nigga"). A *nigga* is your 'main man,' or 'one of your close companions,' your 'homie.' Recently the term has been generalized to refer to any male (one may even hear something like, "No, I was talkin about Johnny, you know, the white nigga with the hair") although it usually refers to a Black male. Demonstrating hip hop's affinity for acronyms, Tupac Shakur transformed the racial slur into the ultimate positive ideal for young Black males – never ignorant getting goals accomplished.

As with the highlighting of regional vocabulary, HHNL speakers intentionally highlight regional differences in pronunciation by processes such as vowel lengthening and syllabic stress (Morgan 2001b). When Bay Area rappers JT the Bigga Figga and Mac Mall announced the resurgence of the Bay Area to the national hip hop scene with "Game Recognize Game" (1993), they did so using a distinctive feature of Bay Area pronunciation. The Bay Area anthem's chorus repeated this line three times: "Game recognize game in the Bay, man (mane)." *Man* was pronounced "mane" to accentuate this Bay Area pronunciation feature. Also, as fellow Bay Area rapper B-Legit rhymes about slang, he does so using the same feature to stress his Bay Area linguistic origins: "You can tell from my slang I'm from the Bay, mane" (2000).

When Nelly and the St. Lunatics "busted" onto the hip hop scene, they were among the first rappers to represent St. Louis, Missouri on a national scale. Language was an essential part of establishing their identity in a fiercely competitive world of hip hop culture. For example, in a single by the St. Lunatics featuring Nelly they emphasize every word that rhymes with "urrrr" to highlight a well-known (and sometimes stigmatized) aspect of southern/midwest pronunciation (here → *hurrrr*; care → *currrr*; there → *thurrrr*; air → *hurrrr* and so on). By intentionally highlighting linguistic features associated with their city (and other southern cities), they established their tenacity through language as if to say, "We have arrived."

Nelly and the St. Lunatics are conscious not only of their pronunciation, but also of their syntax. On his platinum single "Country Grammar" (2000), Nelly proclaims, "My gramma bees Ebonics." Clearly, HHNL speakers vary their grammar consciously. An analysis of copula variation in the speech and the lyrics of hip hop artists concluded that higher levels of copula absence in the artists' lyrics represented the construction of a street conscious identity – where the speaker makes a linguistic-cultural connection to the streets, the locus of the hip hop world (Alim 2002). John Rickford has suggested (in a conference comment made in 2001) that the use of creole syntactic and phonological features by many rappers supports the ability of HHNL speakers to manipulate their grammar consciously. Like San Quinn (see opening quote in this section) HHNL speakers elect dialects to demonstrate their high degree of linguistic consciousness and in order to construct a street-conscious identity.

Hip Hop Cultural Modes of Discourse and Discursive Practices

Keyes (1984: 145) applied Smitherman's (1977) Black modes of discourse to HHNL. Working in hip hop's gestation period, she wrote that "Smitherman schematized four broad categories of black discourse: narrative sequencing, call-response, signification/dozens, and tonal semantics. All of these categories are strategically used in rap music." We know that rappin in and of itself is not entirely new – rather, it is the most modern/postmodern instantiation of the linguistic-cultural practices of Africans in America. Rappers are, after all, "postmodern African griots" (a class of musicians–entertainers who preserved African history through oral narratives) (Smitherman 1997). This section will demonstrate how the strategic use of the Black modes of discourse is manifested in HHNL and how the new ways in which these modes are practiced generate correspondingly new modes of discourse. This section is based on various forms of HHNL data – rap lyrics, hip hop performances and hip hop conversational discourse.

Call and response

Here is perhaps the most lucid definition of call and response:

> As a communicative strategy this call and response is the manifestation of the cultural dynamic which finds audience and listener or leader and background to be a unified whole. Shot through with action and interaction, Black communicative performance is concentric in quality – the "audience" becoming both observers and participants in the speech event. As Black American culture stresses commonality and group experientiality, the audience's linguistic

> and paralinguistic responses are necessary to co-sign the power of the speaker's rap or call. (Daniel and Smitherman 1976, cited in Spady 2000: 59)

The quintessential example of the HHN's use of call and response grows out of the funk performances and is still heard at nearly every hip hop performance today. "[Rapper] Say 'Hoooo!' [Audience] 'Hoooooooo!' [Rapper] Say 'Ho! Ho!' [Audience] 'Ho! Ho!' [Rapper] 'Somebody screeeaaaaammm!' [Audience] 'AAAHHHHHHHHHHHHHH!!!' " Anyone who has ever attended a hip hop performance can bear witness to this foundational call and response mechanism.

A description of a hip hop performance by Philadelphia's Roots paints a picture of a scene where lead MC Black Thought senses that there is a communicative schism developing between him and his Swiss audience (Jackson et al. 2001: 25). The rapper says, "Hold it, hold it, hold it!" and stops the music abruptly. What follows is an "impromptu instruction" in the call and response mode of Black discourse: "Y'all can't get the second part no matter what the fuck I say, right...I wonder if it's what I'm saying...A-yo! We gonna try this shit one more time because I like this part of the show." Providing more explicit instruction, Thought slows it down a bit: "Aight, Aight this is how I'm gonna break it down. I'm gonna be like "ahh," then everybody gonna be like "ahhh." Then – I don't know what I'm gonna say second but y'all gotta listen close cause then y'all gotta repeat that shit – that's the fun of the game!" Thought is not only providing instruction but he is also administering a challenge to his European audience: either *git sicwiddit* [get sick with it] *or git hitwiddit* [get hit with it]*!* (in this context meaning, "Become active participants in this activity or get caught off guard looking culturally ignorant!")

Call and response mechanisms are so pervasive in HHNL that talented MCs (rappers, Masters of Ceremonies) have taken this mode to new heights. Mos Def describes one of the elements that made Slick Rick a legendary rapper:

> Slick Rick is one of the greatest MC's ever born because he has so many different facilities that he would use. Style. Vocal texture. The way he would even record. Like, he was doing call and response with himself! He would leave four bars open, and then do another character, you understand what I'm saying? (Alim 2000, unpublished interview)

The individualized uses of call and response in the hip hop cultural mode of discourse deserve more attention. Also, as is evident from Mos Def's comments, HHNL speakers can be cognizant of the fact that they are operating within and expanding upon the African American Oral Tradition. The linguistic and communicative consciousness of the HHN also needs to be explored.

Multilayered totalizing expression

Beyond the explicit instruction, one can witness the multilayered nature of the call and response mode at hip hop performances where both performer and audience are fully conversant with hip hop cultural modes of discourse. At the first Spitkicker Tour (2000) in San Francisco's Maritime Hall, I observed this multilayered, multitextual mode. Here's an excerpt from my fieldnotes:

> Maaan, all performers are on stage at once – [DJ] Hi-Tek, Talib [Kweli], Common, Biz [Markie], De La [Soul], Pharoahe [Monch] – and they just kickin it in a fun-loving communal-type hip hop atmosphere! Common and Biz are exchanging lines from his classic hit...The DJ from De La starts cuttin up the music and before you know it, Common is center stage freestylin. The DJ switches the pace of the music, forcing Common to switch up the pace of his freestyle [improvisational rap], and the crowd's lovin it! 'Ooooooohhhhh!'...Hi-Tek and Maseo are circling each other on stage giving a series of hi-fives timed to the beat, smilin and laughin all along, as the crowd laughs on with them. Common, seizing the energy of the moment, says, "This is hip hop music, y'all!" Then he shouts, "It ain't nuthin like hip hop music!" and holds the microphone out to the crowd. "It ain't

nuthin like hip hop music!" they roar back, and the hall is transformed into a old school house party frenzy... Gotta love this hip hop music.

What is striking about this description is that there are multiple levels of call and multiple levels of response, occurring simultaneously and synergistically, to create something even beyond "total expression" (Brathwaite 1984: 18). This is a *multilayered totalizing expression* that completes the cipher (the process of constantly making things whole). We witness a call and response on the oral/aural, physical (body), and spiritual/metaphysical level. My final note ("Gotta love this hip hop music") captures a moment of realization that meaning resides in what I've just witnessed – in the creation of a continuum beyond audience and performer. We hear varied calls made by the DJ and responded to by a freestylin MC; by the two MC's exchanging lines and by their impromptu leading of the audience in celebration of hip hop; by the physical reaction of performers to each other and the audience (who were also slappin hands with the performers); and by the spirited and spiritual response created during the climax of the performance. Like Common says, "Find heaven in this music and God / Find heaven in this music and God / Find heaven in this music and God" (cited in Jackson et al. 2001).

Signifyin and bustin (bussin)

Scholars have studied signification or signifyin – or, in more contemporary, semantically similar Black terms, *bustin, crackin*, and *dissin* (Abrahams 1964, Kochman 1969, Mitchell-Kernan 1971, 1972, Smitherman 1973, 1977). Signifyin has been described as a means to encode messages or meanings in natural conversations, usually involving an element of indirection (Mitchell-Kernan 1972). Ironically noting the difficulty in pin-pointing a dictionary definition for the speech act, Rickford and Rickford (2000: 82) cite Mitchell-Kernan's (1972: 82) attempt:

> The black concept of *signifying* incorporates essentially a folk notion that dictionary entries for words are not always sufficient for interpreting meanings or messages, or that meaning goes beyond such interpretations. Complimentary remarks may be delivered in a left-handed fashion. A particular utterance may be an insult in one context and not in another. What pretends to be informative may intend to be persuasive. Superficially, self-abasing remarks are frequently self-praise.

In Scarface's comments and Tha Pharcyde dialogue given earlier, we see evidence of this folk notion that "standard" dictionaries are insufficient to interpret Black language and life. But looking more closely at Tha Pharcyde dialogue, we witness an extremely sly (skillful and indirect) signification in hip hop conversational discourse. In the dialogue, Booty Brown is advocating the Black folk notion described by Kernan above. He implies that his partner is glorifying a Eurocentric meaning-making system over a meaning-making system that is African derived. This does not become clear until Brown chooses his examples – carefully and cleverly. "Just like they use any other word as a slang, *my brotha!*" He emphasizes the "slang phrase" *my brotha*, as it is usually used as a sign of cultural unity and familial bond between African American males (females will use *my sista* in a similar way).

Then he proceeds to ask the direct question, "Whose definition are you glorifying?" which is, in fact, a statement. Finally, as if to *really* lay it on thick (add insult to injury), he chooses to use the word *Black* to show that *Webster's Dictionary* is inadequate. The heat is diffused when "P" says, "I'm sayin, that's what I'M sayin!" and they – and others around them – break into laughter. This dialogue is an example of how language is used to remind, scold, shame, or otherwise bring the other into a commonly shared ethic through signification.

We see an example of signifyin in Rapper Bushwick Bill's (of Houston's Geto Boys) description of the ever-changing, fluid and flexible nature of "street slang" and the dangers of not "keepin your ear to the street" (being aware of what's happening around you at all times). In this case, Bushwick is referring to the rapidly evolving street terminology for law enforcement officials. Bushwick takes us deep into the locus of hip hop linguistic-cultural activity:

> You lose flavor. You lose the slang. You lose the basic everyday kickin it, you know, knowing what's going on at all times, you know what I'm saying? Knowing the new names for "5–0s". They ain't even 5–0s no more. They call them "po-pos". That means everything changes. And they call them "one-time", you know what I'm saying? But you got to be in there to know that the police might know these words already. So they got to change up their dialect so that way it sounds like Pig Latin to the police. (Spady, Lee, and Alim 1999: 308)

Bushwick's comment refers us directly to tenet (10) above. He is describing the changing nature of the various terms for *police* in the streets – from *5–0s* to *po-pos* to *one-time*. At one time, bloods referred to the *one-time* as *black and whites* (Folb 1980). The socio-political contexts of many depressed and oppressed Black neighborhoods necessitate these speedy lexical transformations.

Even though the police are not present in the dialogue above, Bushwick signifies on them with a clever one-liner that also serves to buttress his point. After runnin down all of the various terms (which have gone out of vogue as quickly as the police comprehended them), he concludes, "So they got to change up their dialect so that way it sounds like Pig Latin to the police." *Pig Latin* is chosen here, rather than Greek, Chinese, Swahili, or other unfamiliar languages, to echo the fact that at one time police officers were called *pigs*. Bushwick is not only signifyin on the police, but he is also demonstrating yet another term for 'police' that has gone out of fashion! In addition, he is referencing an old form of Afroamericanized Pig Latin that employs innuendo, wordplay, letter and syllabic shifting, rhyming and coded language designed to communicate with those in the know.

Like call and response, signifyin is ubiquitous in hip hop lyrics. In an example of male–female urban verbal play, in "Minute Man" (2001) with Missy Elliot and Ludacris, Jay-Z signifies on female R&B group Destiny's Child. Some insider knowledge is required to fully understand this speech act. Earlier that year, Destiny's Child had released "Independent Women," in which they asked a series of questions of men who dogged ('treated poorly') females. For example, they introduced each question with the word *question* and then proceeded, "How you like them diamonds that I bought?" (to demonstrate to such men that they had their own income). Given that one of Jay-Z's many personas is the *playa-pimp*-type ('one who uses women for sex and money'), he rhymes to the listeners (including Destiny's Child): "I'm not tryin to give you love and affection / I'm tryin to give you 60 seconds of affection / I'm tryin to give you cash, fare and directions / Get your independent-ass outta here, Question!" The signification doesn't become clear until the last line or, really, the last word, when Jay-Z borrows the word *question* from their song (saying it in such a way as to match their rate of speech, tone and pronunciation). The only thing left to do is say, "Oooohhhhhh!"

We also witnessed signification in the call and response section of the Black Thought performance described above. As Jackson (2001) notes, Thought appears to be signifyin on the audience by highlighting their lack of familiarity with Black cultural modes of discourse: "I wonder if it's what I'm saying . . . A-yo!" The Roots have been known to signify on audiences that are not as culturally responsive as they would like them to be. During a 1999 concert at Stanford University, they stopped the music and began singing theme songs from 1980s television shows like "Diff'rent Strokes" and "Facts of Life," snapping their fingers and singing in a corny (not cool) way. The largely white, middle-class audience of college students sang along and snapped their fingers – apparently oblivious to the insult. After the show, the band's drummer and official spokesman, Ahmir, said: "Like if the crowd ain't responding, we've done shows where we've stopped the show, turned the equipment around, and played for the wall, you know" (Alim 1999). In this sense, the Roots remove any hint of indirection and blatantly *bust on* the unresponsive audience.

The examples above make clear that HHNL speakers readily incorporate *signifyin* and *bustin* into their repertoire. Whether hip hop heads are performing, writing rhymes, or just "conversatin," these strategies are skillfully employed. Other hip hop cultural modes of discourse and discursive practices, which fall out of the purview of this chapter, are tonal semantics and poetics, narrative sequencing and flow, battling and entering the cipher. Linguistic scholars of the hip hop generations (we are now more than one) are needed to uncover the complexity and creativity of HHNL speakers. In order to *represent* – reflect any semblance of hip hop cultural reality – these scholars will need to be in direct conversation with the culture creators of a very widely misunderstood Nation.

NOTES

It is my pleasure to acknowledge the assistance and encouragement of John Baugh, Mary Bucholtz, Austin Jackson, Marcyliena Morgan, Geneva Smitherman, James G. Spady, and Arthur Spears in the preparation of this chapter. I would also like to thank Ed Finegan for his scrupulous reading of the manuscript and for his insight and many helpful suggestions, and John Rickford for his support and careful review of an early draft of the manuscript. The chapter has been greatly improved by their efforts as editors. Lastly, much props to my students in Linguistics 74: "The Language of Hip Hop Culture"; they have challenged me to represent to the fullest.

1 Grandmaster Flash and the Furious Five released "The Message" in 1982 and it became one of the first major hip hop records to document street life and street consciousness. The line, "It's like a jungle sometimes it makes me wonder how I keep from goin under" is perhaps one of the most frequently quoted hip hop choruses to this day. In the epigraph to this chapter, we see JT the Bigga Figga rappin another part of the chorus, "Don't push me cuz I'm close to the eeedge!"
2 The transcription of HHNL into print often leaves a lot to be desired. I have attempted to reconstruct the verbal agility of these hip hop artists on the printed page, but, as Brathwaite (1984) admits, it is best for the reader to listen along to the music whenever possible (see discography).

SUGGESTIONS FOR FURTHER READING AND EXPLORATION

For a thorough understanding of the philosophies and aesthetic values of hip hop's culture creators, the Umum Hip Hop Trilogy is an excellent source. Its three volumes (Spady and Eure 1991, Spady et al. 1995, Spady et al. 1999) offer extensive hip hop conversational discourse with such members of the HHN as Ice Cube, Busta Rhymes, Chuck D, Kurupt, Common, Eve, Bahamadia, Grandmaster Flash, and others. These volumes also provide primary source material for scholars of language use within the HHN. For early works on hip hop culture, see Hager (1984), Toop (1984, 1994, 1999), Nelson and Gonzales (1991), Rose (1994), and Potter (1995).

For updates on what's happening in the HHN, the most informative website is Davey D's Hip Hop Corner (www.daveyd.com). Useful hip hop periodicals include *Murder Dog*, *The Source*, *XXL*, *Vibe* and *Blaze*. One might gain the most insight by "reading" the hip hop saturated streets of America.

REFERENCES

Abrahams, Roger (1964). *Deep Down in the Jungle: Negro Narrative Folklore from the Streets of Philadelphia*. Chicago, IL: Aldine Publishing Co.

Abrahams, Roger (1970). "Rapping and Capping: Black Talk as Art." In *In Black

America, ed. John Szwed. New York: Basic Books.

Abrahams, Roger (1976). *Talking Black*. Rowley, MA: Newbury House.

Alim, H. Samy (1999). "The Roots Rock Memorial Auditorium." "Intermission" section of *The Stanford Daily*, Stanford University.

Alim, H. Samy (2000). "360 Degreez of Black Art Comin at You: Sista Sonia Sanchez and the Dimensions of a Black Arts Continuum." In *360 Degreez of Sonia Sanchez: Hip Hop, Narrativity, Iqhawe and Public Spaces of Being*, ed. James G. Spady. Special issue of *BMa: The Sonia Sanchez Literary Review*, 6.1, Fall.

Alim, H. Samy ed. (2001a). *Hip Hop Culture: Language, Literature, Literacy and the Lives of Black Youth*. Special issue of *The Black Arts Quarterly*. Committee on Black Performing Arts: Stanford University.

Alim, H. Samy (2001b). "I Be the Truth: Divergence, Recreolization, and the 'New' Equative Copula in African American Language." Paper presented at NWAV 30, Raleigh, North Carolina, October.

Alim, H. Samy (2002). "Street Conscious Copula Variation in the Hip Hop Nation," *American Speech* 77: 288–304.

Alim, H. Samy (2003a). "On some serious next millenium rap ishhh: Pharoahe Monch, Hip Hop poetics, and the internal rhymes of Internal Affairs," *Journal of English Linguistics* 31(1): 60–84.

Alim, H. Samy (2003b). "'We are the streets': African American Language and the strategic construction of a street conscious identity." In Makoni, S., G. Smitherman, A. Ball, and A. Spears (eds.). *Black Linguistics: Language, Society, and Politics in Africa and the Americas*. New York: Routledge.

Alim, H. Samy (2005). *'You know my Steez': An Ethnographic and Sociolinguistic Study of Styleshifting in a Black American Speech Community*. Durham: Duke University Press.

Anderson, Elijah (1999). *Code of the Street: Decency, Violence, and the Moral Life of the Inner City*. New York: W. W. Norton.

Anderson, Monica (1994). *Black English Vernacular (From "Ain't" to "Yo Mama": The Words Politically Correct Americans Should Know)*. Highland City FL: Rainbow Books.

Baugh, John (1983). *Black Street Speech: Its History, Structure, and Survival*. Austin TX: University of Texas Press.

Baugh, John (1991). "The Politicization of Changing Terms of Self-Reference Among American Slave Descendants," *American Speech* 66: 133–46.

Braithwaite, Fred. (Fab Five Freddy) (1992). *Fresh Fly Flavor: Words and Phrases of the Hip-Hop Generation*. Stamford CT: Longmeadow Press.

Braithwaite, Fred (1995). *Hip Hop Slang: English–Deutsch*. Frankfurt am Main, Eichborn.

Brathwaite, Kamau (1984). *History of the Voice: The Development of Nation Language in Anglo-phone Caribbean Poetry*. London: New Beacon Books.

Calloway, Cab (1944). *Hepster's Dictionary: Language of Jive*. Republished as an appendix to Calloway's autobiography, *Of Minnie the Moocher and Me*. 1976. New York: Thomas Y. Crowell.

Daniel, Jack and Geneva Smitherman (1976). "How I Got Over: Communication Dynamics in the Black Community," *Quarterly Journal of Speech* 62 (February): 26–39.

Dillard, J. L (1977). *Lexicon of Black English*. New York: Seabury.

Fasold, Ralph (1972). *Tense Marking in Black English: A Linguistic and Social Analysis*. Washington DC: Center for Applied Linguistics.

Folb, Edith (1980). *Runnin' Down Some Lines: The Language and Culture of Black Teenagers*. Cambridge, MA: Harvard University Press.

Hager, Steven (1984). *Hip Hop: The Illustrated History of Breakdancing, Rap Music, and Graffiti*. New York: St Martin's Press.

Henderson, Stephen (1973). *Understanding the New Black Poetry: Black Speech and Black Music as Poetic References*. New York: William Morrow.

Holloway, Joseph E. and Winifred K. Vass (1997). *The African Heritage of American English*. Bloomington: University of Indiana Press.

Hymes, Dell (1981). "Foreword." In *Language in the U.S.A.*, eds. Charles A. Ferguson and Shirley B. Heath. New York: Cambridge University Press.

Jackson, Austin, Tony Michel, David Sheridan, and Bryan Stumpf (2001). "Making Connections in the Contact Zones: Towards a Critical Praxis of Rap Music and Hip Hop Culture." In *Hip Hop Culture: Language, Literature, Literacy and the Lives of Black Youth*, ed. H. Samy Alim. Special issue of *The Black Arts Quarterly*. Committee on Black Performing Arts: Stanford University.

JT the Bigga Figga, Personal interview with H. Samy Alim, November, 2000.

Keyes, Cheryl (1984). "Verbal Art Performance in Rap Music: the Conversation of the 80s," *Folklore Forum* 17(2): 143–52.

(1991). "Rappin' to the Beat: Rap Music as Street Culture Among African Americans." Unpublished PhD diss., Indiana University.

Kochman, Thomas (1969). " 'Rapping' in the Black Ghetto," *Trans-Action* (February): 26–34.

KRS-One (2000). "The First Overstanding: Refinitions." The Temple of Hip Hop Kulture.

Labov, William (1972). *Language in the Inner City: Studies in the Black English Vernacular.* Philadelphia: University of Pennsylvania Press.

Labov, William, Paul Cohen, Clarence Robins, and John Lewis (1968). *A Study of the Nonstandard English of Negro and Puerto Rican Speakers in New York City.* Report on Cooperative Research Project 3288. New York: Columbia University.

Major, Clarence (1970). [1994]. *Juba to Jive: A Dictionary of African American Slang.* New York and London: Penguin.

Mitchell-Kernan, Claudia (1971). *Language Behavior in a Black Urban Community.* University of California, Berkeley: Language Behavior Research Laboratory.

Mitchell-Kernan, Claudia (1972). "Signifying and Marking: Two Afro-American Speech Acts." In *Directions in Sociolinguistics*, eds. John J. Gumperz and Dell Hymes. New York: Holt, Rinehart and Winston, pp. 161–79.

Morgan, Aswan (1999). "Why They Say What Dey Be Sayin': An Examination of Hip-Hop Content and Language." Paper submitted for LING 073, *Introduction to African American Vernacular English*. Stanford University.

Morgan, Marcyliena (2001a). "Reading Dialect and Grammatical Shout-Outs in Hip Hop." Paper presented at the Linguistic Society of America Convention. Washington, DC, January.

Morgan, Marcyliena (2001b). "'Nuthin' But a G. Thang': Grammar and Language Ideology in Hip Hop Identity." In *Sociocultural and Historical Contexts of African American Vernacular English*, ed. Sonja L. Lanehard. Amsterdam: John Benjamins, pp. 187–210.

Mos Def, Personal interview with H. Samy Alim. October 2000.

Nelson, Havelock and Michael Gonzales (1991). *Bring the Noise: A Guide to Rap Music and Hip Hop Culture.* New York: Harmony Books.

Olivo, Warren (2001). "Phat Lines: Spelling Conventions in Rap Music," *Written Language and Literacy* 4(1): 67–85.

Potter, Russell (1995). *Spectacular Vernaculars: Hip-Hop and the Politics of Postmodernism.* Albany: State University of New York Press.

Remes, Pieter (1991). "Rapping: a Sociolinguistic Study of Oral Tradition in Black Urban Communities in the United States," *Journal of the Anthropological Society of Oxford*, 22(2): 129–49.

Rickford, John and Russell Rickford (2000). *Spoken Soul: The Story of Black English.* New York: John Wiley.

Rose, Tricia (1994). *Black Noise: Rap Music and Black Culture in Contemporary America.* Middletown CT: Wesleyan University Press.

San Quinn, Personal interview with H. Samy Alim and James G. Spady, November 2000.

Schiffman, Harold (1996). *Linguistic Culture and Language Policy.* London and New York: Routledge.

Smitherman, Geneva (1973). "The Power of the Rap: the Black Idiom and the New Black Poetry," *Twentieth Century Literature: A Scholarly and Critical Journal* 19: 259–74.

Smitherman, Geneva (1977 [1986]):. *Talkin and Testifyin: The Language of Black America*, Houghton Mifflin; reissued, with revisions, Detroit: Wayne State University Press.

Smitherman, Geneva (1991). " 'What is African to Me?': Language, Ideology and *African American*," *American Speech* 66(2): 115–32.

Smitherman, Geneva (1994 [2000]). *Black Talk: Words and Phrases from the Hood to the Amen Corner.* Boston and New York: Houghton Mifflin.

Smitherman, Geneva (1997). " 'The Chain Remain the Same': Communicative Practices in the Hip-Hop Nation," *Journal of Black Studies*, September.

Smitherman, Geneva (2000). *Talkin That Talk: Language, Culture and Education in African America.* London and New York: Routledge.

Smitherman, Geneva and John Baugh (2002). "The Shot Heard from Ann Arbor: Language Research and Public Policy in African America." *Howard Journal of Communication* 13: 5–24.

Spady, James G (1993). " 'IMA PUT MY THING DOWN': Afro-American Expressive Culture and the Hip Hop Community," *TYANABA: Revue de la Société d'Anthropologie*, December.

Spady, James G (2000). "The Centrality of Black Language in the Discourse Strategies and Poetic Force of Sonia Sanchez and Rap Artists." In *360 Degreez of Sonia Sanchez: Hip Hop, Narrativity, Iqhawe and Public Spaces of Being*, ed. James Spady. Special issue of *BMa: the Sonia Sanchez Literary Review*, 6.1, Fall.

Spady, James G., and H. Samy Alim (1999). "Street Conscious Rap: Modes of Being." In *Street Conscious Rap*. Philadelphia: Black History Museum/Umum Loh Publishers.

Spady, James G., and Joseph D. Eure, eds. (1991). *Nation Conscious Rap: The Hip Hop Vision.* New York/Philadelphia: PC International Press/Black History Museum.

Spady, James G., Stefan Dupres, and Charles G. Lee (1995). *Twisted Tales in the Hip Hop Streets of Philly.* Philadelphia: Black History Museum/Umum Loh Publishers.

Spady, James G., Charles G. Lee, and H. Samy Alim (1999). *Street Conscious Rap.* Philadelphia: Black History Museum/Umum Loh Publishers.

Stavsky, Lois, Isaac Mozeson, and Dani Reyes Mozeson (1995). *A 2 Z: The Book of Rap and Hip-Hop Slang.* New York: Boulevard Books.

Toop, David (1984 [1994, 1999]):. *Rap Attack: From African Jive to New York Hip Hop.* London: Pluto Press.

Turner, Lorenzo (1949). *Africanisms in the Gullah Dialect.* Chicago, IL: University of Chicago Press.

Wa Thiongo, Ngugi (1992). *Moving the Center: The Struggle for Cultural Freedom.* London: Heinemann.

Wideman, John (1976). "Frame and Dialect: The Evolution of the Black Voice in American Literature," *American Poetry Review* 5 (5): 34–7.

Wolfram, Walter (1969). *A Sociolinguistic Description of Detroit Negro Speech.* Washington, DC: Center for Applied Linguistics.

Yancy, George (1991). "Rapese." Cited in Spady and Eure, eds.

Yasin, Jon (1999). "Rap in the African-American Music Tradition: Cultural Assertion and Continuity." In *Race and Ideology: Language, Symbolism, and Popular Culture*, ed. Arthur Spears. Detroit: Wayne State University Press.

Discography

B-Legit (2000). *Hempin Ain't Easy.* Koch International.

Bahamadia (1996). *Kollage.* EMI Records.

Big L. (2000). *The Big Picture.* Priority Records.

Cappadonna (1998). *The Pillage.* Sony Records.

DJ Pooh (1997). *Bad Newz Travels Fast.* Da Bomb/Big Beat/Atlantic Records.

Drag-On and Baby Madison (2001). *Live from Lenox Ave.* Vacant Lot/Priority Records.

Grandmaster Flash and the Furious Five (1982). *The Message.* Sugarhill Records.

JT the Bigga Figga (1993). *Playaz N the Game.* Get Low Recordz.

Juvenile (2001). *Project English.* Universal Records.

LOX (2000). *We Are the Streets.* Ruff Ryders Records.

Ludacris (2001). *Word of Mouf.* Universal Records.

Missy Elliot f/ Jay-Z and Ludacris (2001). *Miss E... So Addictive*. Elektra/Asylum.
Mystikal (2000). *Let's Get Ready*. Jive Records.
Nelly (2000). *Country Grammar*. Universal Records.
Raekwon (1999). *Immobilarity*. Sony.
Rza (1998). *Rza as Bobby Digital in Stereo*. V2/BMG Records.
Three X Krazy (2000). *Real Talk 2000*. DU BA Records.
Treacherous Three (Kool Moe Dee, LA Sunshine, Special K and DJ Easy Lee) (1980). "New Rap Language." Enjoy Records.

STUDY QUESTIONS

1 Reflect upon and discuss the fact that the language of the African American/Black community in the US has been labeled in many ways including: Negro dialect, Black English, Black English Vernacular, African American English, African American Vernacular English, and African American Language. Why does Alim feel the need to add HHNL to this already long list?
2 What are some of the phonological, syntactic, or lexical features of HHNL described by Alim? Do you recognize any of these features in the language that you use or in the language that you hear on a daily basis? Extend his list to include other features of HHNL that you use or have heard.
3 How are the discursive practices of "Call and Response" and "Signifying" used in HHNL? Provide examples from this chapter and from your own experience.
4 What does Alim mean by the expression "language ideology" and how does it connect to the ways in which it is used by other authors in this collection (for example, see Chapters 16 and 17)?
5 What are the social and political implications of speaking HHNL according to the language users quoted by Alim?

Part III

Language Socialization and Literacy Practices

Introduction

Language acquisition does not happen in a social and cultural vacuum. Children are exposed to language in the midst of a lifeworld filled with chores, requests, moral and aesthetic evaluations, displays of feelings, expectations, and political stances. While they are learning the words and the grammar of the language (or languages) around them, children also learn what to say to whom, when, and how. Language is not just *part of* social life; language *is* social life: it helps organize activities and the roles that different people are expected to play in them. For these reasons, the process through which children acquire language must be a fundamental part of the process whereby children become competent members of their society. Elinor Ochs and Bambi Schieffelin conceptualized language socialization as a field that would provide the theoretical and methodological foundations for the study of how children are socialized *through* language use and are socialized *to* language use. Their programmatic article on language socialization is reproduced in Chapter 12. As shown by the rest of the chapters in this Part, language socialization does not stop after the child has learned to talk (primary language socialization). It continues throughout the life span as individuals participate in different activities and institutional settings that require them to use language in new ways (secondary socialization). An important and by now almost universal site for secondary language socialization is participation in literacy activities, that is, activities where individuals are introduced and must learn to engage with written (e.g., printed) material. Three of the chapters of this Part of the Reader deal with this important experience in children's lives. In Chapter 13, Susan Philips looks at the social organization of classroom interaction and shows that different "participation structures" favor or disfavor children's participation depending on their primary language socialization. In Chapter 14, Shirley Brice Heath compares the type of relationship established with texts within families from different social classes and ethnic groups, suggesting a strong link between school performance and earlier socialization to print. Finally, in Chapter 15, Patricia Baquedano-López examines the use of the same story in the construction of ethnic identity in two religious classes, one held in Spanish and the other in English.

SUGGESTIONS FOR FURTHER READING

Good collections of essays on language socialization in different speech communities are: B. B. Schieffelin and E. Ochs (1986), *Language Socialization across Cultures*, Cambridge: Cambridge University Press; and P. A. Duff and N. H. Hornberger (eds.) (2008), *Encyclopedia of Language and Education, Vol. 8: Language Socialization*, New York: Springer.

A broad review of the literature on children's acquisition of grammar and communicative competence is S. Romaine (1984), *The Language of Children and Adolescents: The Acquisition of Communicative Competence*, New York: Basil Blackwell.

A wide range of perspectives on child language is found in P. Fletcher and B. MacWhinney (eds.) (1995), *The Handbook of Child Language*, Oxford: Blackwell.

Model case studies of language socialization are: P. Miller (1982), *Amy, Wendy, and Beth: Learning Language in South Baltimore*, Austin: University of Texas Press; E. Ochs (1988), *Culture and Language Development: Language Acquisition and Language Socialization in a Samoan Village*, Cambridge: Cambridge University Press; and B. B. Schieffelin (1990), *The Give and Take of Everyday Life: Language Socialization of Kaluli Children*, Cambridge: Cambridge University Press; D. Kulick (1992), *Language Shift and Cultural Reproduction: Socialization, Self, and Syncretism in a Papua New Guinean Village*, Cambridge: Cambridge University Press; A. C. Zentella (1997), *Growing Up Bilingual: Puerto Rican Children in New York*, Oxford: Blackwell.

The broader cultural context of early childhood is investigated in R. A. LeVine, S. Dixon, S. LeVine, A. Richman, H. P. Leiderman, C. H. Keefer, and T. B. Brazelton (1996), *Childcare and Culture: Lessons from Africa*, Cambridge: Cambridge University Press; S. Stephens (ed.) (1995), *Children and the Politics of Culture*, Princeton, NJ: Princeton University Press; M. Woodhead, D. Faulkner, and K. Littleton (eds.) (1998), *Cultural Worlds of Early Childhood*, London: Routledge and The Open University.

The literature on literacy is vast. Earlier influential essays are found in J. Goody (ed.) (1968), *Literacy in Traditional Societies*, Cambridge: Cambridge University Press; see also J. Goody (1977), *The Domestication of the Savage Mind*, Cambridge: Cambridge University Press; and J. Goody (1986), *The Logic of Writing and the Organization of Society*, Cambridge: Cambridge University Press. For critical discussions of Goody's work and alternative models: S. Scribner and M. Cole (1981), *Psychology of Literacy*, Cambridge, MA: Harvard University Press; B. V. Street (1984), *Literacy in Theory and Practice*, Cambridge: Cambridge University Press; J. Collins and R. K. Blot (2003), *Literacy and Literacies*, Cambridge: Cambridge University Press.

Ethnographically oriented studies of literacy abound, among them see: R. Scollon and S. B. K. Scollon (1981), *Narrative, Literacy, and Face in Interethnic Communication*, Norwood, NJ: Ablex; S. B. Heath (1983), *Ways with Words: Language, Life and Work in Communities and Classrooms*, Cambridge: Cambridge University Press; N. Besnier (1995), *Literacy, Emotion, and Authority: Reading and Writing on a Polynesian Atoll*, Cambridge: Cambridge University Press; and the essays in J. Cook-Gumperz (ed.) (1986), *The Social Construction of Literacy*, Cambridge: Cambridge University Press; B. B. Schieffelin and P. Gilmore (1986), *The Acquisition of Literacy: Ethnographic Perspectives*, Norwood, NJ: Ablex; and J. A. Langer (ed.) (1987), *Language, Literacy, and Culture: Issues of Society and Schooling*, Norwood, NJ: Ablex; L. M. Ahearn (2001), *Invitations to Love: Literacy, Love Letters, and Social Change in Nepal*, Ann Arbor: The University of Michigan Press. For an extension of ethnographic approaches to literacy in early modern literature, see V. Barletta (2005), *Covert Gestures: Crypto-Islamic Literature as Cultural Practice in Early Modern Spain*, Minneapolis: University of Minnesota Press.

An ethnographic perspective on the use of language in the classroom is provided in C. B. Cazden, V. P. John, and D. Hymes (1972), *Functions of Language in the Classroom*, New York: Teachers College Press; S. Philips (1983), *The Invisible Culture: Communication in Classroom and Community on the Warm Springs Indian Reservation*, New York: Longman.

12

Language Acquisition and Socialization: Three Developmental Stories and Their Implications

Elinor Ochs and Bambi B. Schieffelin

This chapter addresses the relationship between communication and culture from the perspective of the *acquisition of* language and socialization *through language*. Heretofore the processes of language acquisition and socialization have been considered as two separate domains. Processes of language acquisition are usually seen as relatively unaffected by cultural factors such as social organization and local belief systems. These factors have been largely treated as "context," something that is *separable* from language and its acquisition. A similar attitude has prevailed in anthropological studies of socialization. The language used both *by* children and *to* children in social interactions has rarely been a source of information on socialization. As a consequence, we know little about the role that language plays in the acquisition and transmission of sociocultural knowledge. Neither the forms, the functions, nor the message content of language have been documented and examined for the ways in which they *organize* and *are organized by* culture.

Our own backgrounds in cultural anthropology and language development have led us to a more integrated perspective. Having carried out research on language in several societies (Malagasy, Bolivian, white middle-class American, Kaluli [Papua New Guinea], and Western Samoan), focusing on the language of children and their caregivers in three of them (white middle-class American, Kaluli, Western Samoan), we have seen that the primary concern of caregivers is to ensure that their children are able to display and understand behaviors appropriate to social situations. A major means by which this is accomplished is through language. Therefore, we must examine the language of caregivers primarily for its socializing functions, rather than for only its strict grammatical input function. Further, we must examine the prelinguistic and linguistic behaviors of children to determine the ways they are continually and selectively affected by values and beliefs held by those members of society who interact with them. What a child says, and how he or she

For permission to publish copyright material in this book, grateful acknowledgment is made to: E. Ochs and B. B. Schieffelin (1984), "Language Acquisition and Socialization: Three Developmental Stories," in R. A. Shweder and R. A. LeVine (eds.), *Culture Theory: Essays on Mind, Self, and Emotion*. Cambridge: Cambridge University Press, pp. 276–320.

says it, will be influenced by local cultural processes in addition to biological and social processes that have universal scope. The perspective we adopt is expressed in the following two claims:

1 The process of acquiring language is deeply affected by the process of becoming a competent member of a society.
2 The process of becoming a competent member of society is realized to a large extent through language, by acquiring knowledge of its functions, social distribution, and interpretations in and across socially defined situations, i.e., through exchanges of language in particular social situations.

In this chapter, we will support these claims through a comparison of social development as it relates to the communicative development of children in three societies: Anglo-American white middle class, Kaluli, and Samoan. We will present specific theoretical arguments and methodological procedures for an ethnographic approach to the development of language. Our focus at this point cannot be comprehensive, and therefore we will address developmental research that has its interests and roots in language development rather than anthropological studies of socialization.[1]

Approaches to Communicative Development

Whereas interest in language structure and use has been a timeless concern, the child as a language user is a relatively recent focus of scholarly interest. This interest has been located primarily in the fields of linguistics and psychology, with the wedding of the two in the establishment of developmental psycholinguistics as a legitimate academic specialization. The concern here has been the relation of language to thought, both in terms of conceptual categories and in terms of cognitive processes (such as perception, memory, recall). The child has become one source for establishing just what that relation is. More specifically, the language of the child has been examined in terms of the following issues:

1 The relation between the relative complexity of conceptual categories and the linguistic structures produced and understood by young language-learning children at different developmental stages.[2]
2 Processes and strategies underlying the child's construction of grammar.[3]
3 The extent to which these processes and strategies are language universal or particular.[4]
4 The extent to which these processes and strategies support the existence of a language faculty.[5]
5 The nature of the prerequisites for language development.[6]
6 Perceptual and conceptual factors that inhibit or facilitate language development.[7]

Underlying all these issues is the question of the *source* of language, in terms of not only what capacities reside within the child but the relative contributions of biology (nature) and the *social* world (nurture) to the development of language. The relation between nature and nurture has been a central theme around which theoretical positions have been oriented. B. F. Skinner's (1957) contention that the child brings relatively little to the task of learning language and that it is through responses to specific adult stimuli that language competence is attained provided a formulation that was subsequently challenged and countered by Chomsky's (1959) alternative position. This position, which has been termed nativist, innatist, rationalist (see Piattelli-Palmarini 1980), postulates that the adult verbal environment is an inadequate source for the child to inductively learn language. Rather, the rules and principles for constructing grammar have as their major source a genetically determined language faculty:

> Linguistics, then, may be regarded as that part of human psychology that is concerned with the nature, function, and origin of a particular "mental organ." We may take UG (Universal Grammar) to be a theory of the language faculty, a common human attribute, genetically determined, one component of the human mind. Through interaction with the environment,

> this faculty of mind becomes articulated and refined, emerging in the mature person as a system of knowledge of language. (Chomsky 1977: 164)

It needs to be emphasized that an innatist approach does not eliminate the adult world as a source of linguistic knowledge; rather, it assigns a different role (vis-à-vis the behaviorist approach) to that world in the child's attainment of linguistic competence: The adult language presents the relevant information that allows the child to select from the Universal Grammar those grammatical principles specific to the particular language that the child will acquire.

One of the principal objections that could be raised is that although "the linguist's grammar is a theory of this [the child's] attained competence" (Chomsky 1977: 163), there is no account of *how* this linguistic competence is attained. The theory does not relate the linguist's grammar(s) to processes of acquiring grammatical knowledge. Several psycholinguists, who have examined children's developing grammars in terms of their underlying organizing principles, have argued for similarities between these principles and those exhibited by other cognitive achievements (Bates et al. 1979; Bever 1970).

A second objection to the innatist approach has concerned its characterization of adult speech as "degenerate," fragmented, and often ill formed (McNeill 1966; Miller and Chomsky 1963). This characterization, for which there was no empirical basis, provoked a series of observational studies (including tape-recorded documentation) of the ways in which caregivers speak to their young language-acquiring children (Drach 1969; Phillips 1973; Sachs, Brown, and Salerno 1976; Snow 1972). Briefly, these studies indicated not only that adults use well-formed speech with high frequency but that they modify their speech to children in systematic ways as well. These systematic modifications, categorized as a particular speech register called baby-talk register (Ferguson 1977), include the increased (relative to other registers) use of high pitch, exaggerated and slowed intonation, a baby-talk lexicon (Garnica 1977; Sachs 1977; Snow 1972, 1977b), diminutives, reduplicated words, simple sentences (Newport 1976), shorter sentences, interrogatives (Corsaro 1979), vocatives, talk about the "here-and-now," play and politeness routines – peek-a-boo, hi–good-bye, say "thank you" (Andersen 1977; Gleason and Weintraub 1978), cooperative expression of propositions, repetition, and expansion of one's own and the child's utterances. Many of these features are associated with the expression of positive affect, such as high pitch and diminutives. However, the greatest emphasis in the literature has been placed on these features as evidence that caregivers *simplify* their speech in addressing young children (e.g., slowing down, exaggerating intonation, simplifying sentence structure and length of utterance). The scope of the effects on grammatical development has been debated in a number of studies. Several studies have supported Chomsky's position by demonstrating that caregiver speech facilitates the acquisition of only language-specific features but not those features widely (universally) shared across languages (Feldman, Goldin-Meadow, and Gleitman 1978; Newport, Gleitman, and Gleitman 1977). Other studies, which do not restrict the role of caregiver speech to facilitating only language-specific grammatical features (Snow 1977b, 1979), report that caregivers appear to adjust their speech to a child's cognitive and linguistic capacity (Cross 1977). And as children become more competent, caregivers use fewer features of the baby-talk register. Whereas certain researchers have emphasized the direct facilitating role of caregiver speech in the acquisition of language (van der Geest 1977), others have linked the speech behavior of caregivers to the caregiver's desire to communicate with the child (Brown 1977; Snow 1977a, 1977b, 1979). In this perspective, caregivers simplify their own speech in order to make themselves understood when speaking to young children. Similarly, caregivers employ several verbal and nonverbal strategies to understand what the child is trying to communicate. For example, the caregiver attends to what the child is doing, where the child is looking, and the child's behavior to determine the child's communicative intentions (Foster 1981; Golinkoff 1983; Keenan, Ochs, and

Schieffelin 1976). Further, caregivers often request clarification by repeating or paraphrasing the child's utterance with a questioning intonation, as in Example 1 (Bloom 1973: 170):

Example 1*

Mother	*Allison* (16 mos 3 wks)
(*A picks up a jar, trying to open it)*	more wídə/ə wídə/ ə wídə/ ə wídə/
(*A* holding jar out to *M*)	up/ Mama/ Mama/
	Mama ma ə wídə/ Mama Mama ə wídə/
What, darling?	
	Mama wídə/ Mama/ Mama wídə/ Mama/ Mama wídə/
What do you want Mommy to do?	
	—/ə wídə/ ə wídə/ —/here/
(*A* gives jar to *M*) (*A* tries to turn top on jar in *M*'s hand)	
	Mama/ Mama/ ə wídə/
Open it up?	
	up/
Open it? OK. (*M* opens it)	

* Examples 1–5 follow transcription conventions in Bloom and Lahey 1978.

In other cases, the caregiver facilitates communication by jointly expressing with the child a proposition. Typically, a caregiver asks a question to which the child supplies the missing information (often already known to the caregiver), as in Example 2 (Bloom 1973: 153):

Example 2

Mother	*Allison*
What's Mommy have (*M* holding cookies)	
(*A* reaching for cookie)	cookie/
Cookie! OK. Here's a cookie for you	
(*A* takes cookie; reaching with other hand toward others in bag)	more/
There's more in here. We'll have it in a little while.	
(*A* picking up bag of cookies)	bag/

These studies indicate that caregivers make extensive accommodations to the child, assuming the perspective of the child in the course of engaging him or her in conversational dialogue. Concurrent research on interaction between caregivers and prelinguistic infants supports this conclusion (Bruner 1977; Bullowa 1979; Lock 1978; Newson 1977, 1978; Schaffer 1977; Shotter 1978). Detailed observation of white middle-class mother–infant dyads (English, Scottish, American, Australian, Dutch) indicates that these mothers attempt to engage their very young infants (starting at birth) in "conversational exchanges." These so-called protoconversations (Bullowa 1979) are constructed in several ways. A protoconversation may take place when one party responds to some facial expression, action, and/or vocalization of the other. This response may be nonverbal, as when a gesture of the infant is "echoed" by his or her mother.

> As a rule, prespeech with gesture is watched and replied to by exclamations of pleasure or surprise like "Oh, my my!", "Good heavens!", "Oh, what a big smile!", "Ha! That's a big one!" (meaning a story), questioning replies like, "Are you telling me a story?", "Oh really?", or even agreement by nodding "Yes" or saying "I'm sure you're right". … A mother evidently perceives her baby to be a person like herself. Mothers interpret baby behavior as not only intended to be communicative, but as verbal and meaningful. (Trevarthen 1979a: 339)

On the other hand, mother and infant may respond to one another through verbal means, as, for example, when a mother expresses agreement, disagreement, or surprise following an infant behavior. Social interactions may be sustained over several exchanges by the mother assuming both speaker roles. She may construct an exchange by responding on behalf of the infant to her own utterance, or she may verbally interpret the infant's interpretation. A combination of several strategies is illustrated in Example 3 (Snow 1977a: 12).

Example 3

Mother	*Ann* (3 mos)
	(smiles)
Oh what a nice little smile!	
Yes, isn't that nice?	
There.	
There's a nice little smile.	(burps)
What a nice wind as well!	
Yes, that's better, isn't it?	
Yes.	
Yes.	(vocalizes)
Yes!	
There's a nice noise.	

These descriptions capture the behavior of white middle-class caregivers and, in turn, can be read for what caregivers believe to be the capabilities and predispositions of the infant. Caregivers evidently see their infants as sociable and as capable of intentionality, particularly with respect to the intentional expression of emotional and physical states. Some researchers have concluded that the mother, in interpreting an infant's behaviors, provides meanings for those behaviors that the infant will ultimately adopt (Lock 1981; Ryan 1974; Shotter 1978) and thus emphasize the active role of the mother in socializing the infant to her set of interpretations. Other approaches emphasize the effect of the infant on the caregiver (Lewis & Rosenblum 1974), particularly with respect to the innate mechanisms for organized, purposeful action that the infant brings to interaction (Trevarthen 1979b).

These studies of caregivers' speech to young children have all attended to what the child is learning from these interactions with the mother (or caregiver). There has been a general movement away from the search for *direct* causal links between the ways in which caregivers speak to their children and the emergence of grammar. Instead, caregivers' speech has been examined for its more general communicative functions, that is, how meanings are negotiated, how activities are organized and accomplished, and how routines and games become established. Placed within this broader communicative perspective, language development is viewed as one of several achievements accomplished through verbal exchanges between the caregiver and the child.

The Ethnographic Approach

Ethnographic orientation

To most middle-class Western readers, the descriptions of verbal and nonverbal behaviors of middle-class caregivers with their children seem very familiar, desirable, and even natural. These descriptions capture in rich detail what goes on, to a greater or lesser extent, in many middle-class households. The characteristics of caregiver speech (baby-talk register) and comportment that have been specified are highly valued by members of white middle-class society, including researchers, readers, and subjects of study. They are associated with good mothering and can be spontaneously produced with little effort or reflections. As demonstrated by Shatz and Gelman (1973), Sachs and Devin (1976), and Andersen and Johnson (1973), children as young as 4 years of age often speak and act in these ways when addressing small children.

From our research experience in other societies as well as our acquaintance with some of the cross-cultural studies of language socialization[8] the general patterns of white middle-class caregiving that have been described in the psychological literature are characteristic neither of all societies nor of all social groups (e.g., all social classes within one society). We would like the reader, therefore, to reconsider the descriptions of caregiving in the psychological literature as ethnographic descriptions.

By ethnographic, we mean descriptions that take into account the perspective of members of a social group, including beliefs and values that underlie and organize their activities and utterances. Ethnographers rely heavily on observations and on formal and informal elicitation of members' reflections and interpretations as a basis for analysis (Geertz 1973). Typically, the ethnographer is not a member of the group under study. Further, in presenting an ethnographic account, the researcher faces the problem of communicating world views or sets of values that may be unfamiliar and strange to the reader. Ideally, such statements provide for the reader a set of organizing principles that give coherence and an analytic focus to the behaviors described.

Psychologists who have carried out research on the verbal and nonverbal behavior of caregivers and their children draw on both methods. However, unlike most ethnographers, the psychological researcher *is* a member of the social group under observation. (In some cases, the researcher's own children are the subjects of study.) Further, unlike the ethnographer, the psychologist addresses a readership familiar with the social scenes portrayed.

That the researcher, reader, and subjects of study tend to have in common a white middle-class literate background has had several consequences. For example, by and large, the psychologist has not been faced with the problem of cultural translation, as has the anthropologist. There has been a tacit assumption that readers can provide the larger cultural framework for making sense out of the behaviors documented, and, consequently, the cultural nature of the behaviors and principles presented have not been explicit. From our perspective, language and culture as bodies of knowledge, structures of understanding, conceptions of the world, and collective representations are extrinsic to any individual and contain more information than any individual could know or learn. Culture encompasses variations in knowledge between individuals, but such variation, although crucial to what an individual may know and to the social dynamic between individuals, does not have its locus within the individual. Our position is that culture is not something that can be considered separately from the accounts of caregiver–child interaction; rather, it is what organizes and gives meaning to that interaction. This is an important point, as it affects the definition and interpretation of the behaviors of caregivers and children. How caregivers and children speak and act toward one another is linked to cultural patterns that extend and have consequences beyond the specific interactions observed. For example, how caregivers speak to their children may be linked to other institutional adaptations to young children. These adaptations, in turn, may be linked to how members of a given society view children more generally (their "nature," their social status and expected comportment) and to how members think children develop.

We are suggesting here that the sharing of assumptions between researcher, reader, and subjects of study is a mixed blessing. In fact, this sharing represents a paradox of familiarity. We are able to apply without effort the cultural framework for interpreting the behavior of caregivers and young children in our own social group; indeed, as members of a white middle-class society, we are socialized to do this very work, that is, interpret behaviors, attribute motives, and so on. Paradoxically, however, in spite of this ease of effort, we can not easily isolate and make explicit these cultural principles. As Goffman's work on American society has illustrated, the articulation of norms, beliefs, and values is often possible only when faced with violations, that is, with gaffes, breaches, misfirings, and the like (Goffman 1963, 1967; Much and Shweder 1978).

Another way to see the cultural principles at work in our own society is to examine the ways in which *other* societies are organized in terms of social interaction and of the society at large. In carrying out such research, the ethnographer offers a point of contrast and comparison with our own everyday activities. Such comparative material can lead us to reinterpret behaviors as cultural that we have assumed to be natural. From the anthropological perspective, every society will have its own cultural constructs of what is natural and what is not. For example, every society has its own theory of procreation. Certain Australian Aboriginal societies believe that a number of different factors contribute to conception. Von Sturmer (1980) writes that among the Kugu-Nganychara (West Cape York Peninsula, Australia) the spirit of the child may first enter the man through an animal that he has killed and consumed. The spirit passes from the man to the woman through sexual intercourse, but several sexual acts are necessary to build the child (see also Hamilton 1981; Montagu 1937). Even within a single society there may be different beliefs concerning when life begins and ends, as the recent debates in the United States and Europe concerning abortion and mercy killing indicate. The issue of what is nature and what is nurtured (cultural) extends to patterns of caregiving and child development. Every society has (implicitly or explicitly) given notions concerning the capacities and temperament of children at different points in their development (see, e.g., Dentan 1978; Ninio 1979; Snow, de Blauw, and van Roosmalen 1979), and the expectations and responses of caregivers are directly related to these notions.

Three developmental stories

At this point, using an ethnographic perspective, we will recast selected behaviors of white middle-class caregivers and young children as pieces of one "developmental story." The white middle-class developmental story that we are constructing is based on various descriptions available and focuses on those patterns of interaction (both verbal and nonverbal) that have been emphasized in the literature. This story will be compared with two other developmental stories from societies that are strikingly different: Kaluli (Papua New Guinea) and Western Samoan.

A major goal in presenting and comparing these developmental stories is to demonstrate that communicative interactions between caregivers and young children are culturally constructed. In our comparisons, we will focus on three facets of communicative interaction: (1) the social organization of the verbal environment of very young children, (2) the extent to which children are expected to adapt to situations or that situations are adapted to the child, (3) the negotiation of meaning by caregiver and child. We first present a general sketch of each social group and then discuss in more detail the consequences of the differences and similarities in communicative patterns in these social groups.

These developmental stories are not timeless but rather are linked in complex ways to particular historical contexts. Both the ways in which caregivers behave toward young children and the popular and scientific accounts of these ways may differ at different moments in time. The stories that we present represent ideas currently held in the three social groups.

The three stories show that there is more than one way of becoming social and using language in early childhood. All normal children will become members of their own social group, but the process of becoming social, including becoming a language user, is culturally constructed. In relation to this process of construction, every society has its own developmental stories that are rooted in social organization, beliefs, and values. These stories may be explicitly codified and/or tacitly assumed by members.

An Anglo-American white middle-class developmental story

The middle class in Britain and the United States includes a broad range of lower middle-, middle middle-, and upper middle-class white-collar and professional workers and their families.[9] The literature on communicative development has been largely based on middle middle- and upper middle-class households. These households tend to consist of a single nuclear family with one, two, or three children. The primary caregiver almost without exception is the child's natural or adopted mother. Researchers have focused on communicative situations in which one child interacts with his or her mother. The generalizations proposed by these researchers concerning mother–child communication could be an artifact of this methodological focus. However, it could be argued that the attention to two-party encounters between a mother and her child reflects the most frequent type of communicative interaction to which most young middle-class children are exposed. Participation in two-party as opposed to multiparty interactions is a product of many considerations, including the physical setting of households, where interior and exterior walls bound and limit access to social interaction.

Soon after an infant is born, many mothers hold their infants in such a way that they are face-to-face and gaze at them. Mothers have been observed to address their infants, vocalize to them, ask questions, and greet them. In other words, from birth on, the infant is treated as a *social being* and as an *addressee* in social interaction. The infant's vocalizations and physical movements and states are often interpreted as meaningful and are responded to verbally by the mother or other caregiver. In this way, protoconversations are established and sustained along a dyadic, turn-taking model. Throughout this period and the subsequent language-acquiring years, caregivers treat very young children as communicative partners. One very important procedure in facilitating these social exchanges is the mother's (or other caregiver's) taking the perspective of the child. This perspective is evidenced in her own speech through the many simplifying and affective features of the baby-talk register that have been described and through the various strategies employed to identify what the young child may be expressing.

Such perspective taking is part of a much wider set of accommodations by adults to young children. These accommodations are manifested in several domains. For example, there are widespread material accommodations to infancy and childhood in the form of cultural artifacts designed for this stage of life, for example, baby clothes, baby food, miniaturization of furniture, and toys. Special behavioral accommodations are coordinated with the infant's perceived needs and capacities, for example, putting the baby in a quiet place to facilitate and ensure proper sleep; "baby-proofing" a house as a child becomes increasingly mobile, yet not aware of, or able to control, the consequences of his or her own behavior. In general, the pattern appears to be one of prevention and intervention, in which situations are adapted or modified to the child rather than the reverse. Further, the child is a focus of attention, in that the child's actions and verbalizations are often the starting point of social interaction with more mature persons.

Although such developmental achievements as crawling, walking, and first words are awaited by caregivers, the accommodations have the effect of keeping the child dependent on, and separate from, the adult community for a considerable period of time. The child, protected from those experiences considered harmful (e.g., playing with knives, climbing stairs), is thus denied knowledge, and his or her competence in such contexts is delayed.

The accommodations of white middle-class caregivers to young children can be examined for other values and tendencies. Particularly among the American middle class, these accommodations reflect a discomfort with the competence differential between adult and child. The competence gap is reduced by two strategies. One is for the adult to simplify her/his speech to match more closely what the adult considers to be the verbal competence of the young child. Let us call this strategy the self-lowering strategy, following Irvine's (1974) analysis of inter-caste demeanor. A second strategy is for the caregiver to richly interpret (Brown 1973) what the young child is expressing. Here the adult acts *as if* the child were more competent than his behavior more strictly would indicate. Let us call this strategy the child-raising (no pun intended!) strategy. Other behaviors conform to this strategy, such as when an adult cooperates in a task with a child but treats that task as an accomplishment of the child.

For example, in eliciting a story from a child, a caregiver often cooperates with the child in the telling of the story. This cooperation typically takes the form of posing questions to the child, such as "Where did you go?" "What did you see?" and so on, to which the adult knows the answer. The child is seen as telling the story even though she or he is simply supplying the information the adult has preselected and organized (Greenfield & Smith 1976; Ochs, Schieffelin and Platt 1979; Schieffelin and Eisenberg 1984). Bruner's (1978) description of scaffolding, in which a caregiver constructs a tower or other play object, allowing the young child to place the last block, is also a good example of this tendency. Here the tower may be seen by the caregiver and others as the child's own work. Similarly, in later life, caregivers playing games with their children let them win, acting as if the child can match or more than match the competence of the adult.

The masking of incompetence applies not only in white middle-class relations with young children but also in relations with mentally, and to some extent to physically, handicapped persons as well. As the work of Edgerton (1967) and the film *Best Boy* indicate, mentally retarded persons are often restricted to protected environments (family households, sheltered workshops or special homes) in which trained staff or family members make vast accommodations to their special needs and capacities.

A final aspect of this white middle-class developmental story concerns the willingness of many caregivers to interpret unintelligible or partially intelligible utterances of young children (cf. Ochs 1982c), for example, the caregiver offers a paraphrase (or "expansion"; Brown and Bellugi 1964; Cazden 1965), using a question intonation. This behavior of caregivers has continuity with their earlier attributions of intentionality to the ambiguous utterances of the infant. For both the prelinguistic and language-using child, the caregiver provides an explicitly verbal interpretation. This interpretation or paraphrase is potentially available to the young child to affirm, disconfirm, or modify.

Through exposure to, and participation in, these clarification exchanges, the young child is socialized into several cultural patterns. The first of these recognizes and defines an utterance or vocalization that may not be immediately understood. Second, the child is presented with the procedures for dealing with ambiguity. Through the successive offerings of possible interpretations, the child learns that more than one understanding of a given utterance or vocalization may be possible. The child is also learning who can make these interpretations and the extent to which they may be open to modification. Finally, the child is learning how to settle upon a possible interpretation and how to show disagreement or agreement. This entire process socializes the child into culturally specific modes of organizing knowledge, thought, and language.[10]

A Kaluli developmental story

A small (population approximately 1,200), non-literate egalitarian society (E. Schieffelin 1976), the Kaluli people live in the tropical rain forest on the Great Papuan Plateau in the southern highlands of Papua New Guinea.[11] Most Kaluli are monolingual, speaking a non-Austronesian verb final ergative language. They maintain large gardens and hunt and fish. Traditionally, the sixty to ninety individuals that comprise a village lived in one large longhouse without internal walls. Currently, although the longhouse is maintained, many families live in smaller dwellings that provide accommodations for two or more extended families. It is not unusual for at least a dozen individuals of different ages to be living together in one house consisting essentially of one semipartitioned room.

Men and women use extensive networks of obligation and reciprocity in the organization of work and sociable interaction. Everyday life is overtly focused around verbal interaction. Kaluli think of, and use, talk as a means of control, manipulation, expression, assertion, and appeal. Talk gets you what you want, need, or feel you are owed. Talk is a primary indicator of social competence and a primary means of socializing. Learning how to talk and become independent is a major goal of socialization.

For the purpose of comparison and for understanding something of the cultural basis for the ways in which Kaluli act and speak to their children, it is important first to describe selected aspects of a Kaluli developmental story constructed from various ethnographic data. Kaluli describe their babies as helpless, "soft" (*taiyo*), and "having no understanding" (*asugo andoma*). They take care of them, they say, because they "feel sorry for them." Mothers, the primary caregivers, are attentive to their infants and physically responsive to them. Whenever an infant cries, it is offered the breast. However, while nursing her infant, a mother may also be involved in other activities, such as food preparation, or she may be engaged in conversation with individuals in the household. Mothers never leave their infants alone and only rarely with other caregivers. When not holding their infants, mothers carry them in netted bags suspended from their heads. When the mother is gardening, gathering wood, or just sitting with others, the baby sleeps in the netted bag next to the mother's body.

Kaluli mothers, given their belief that infants "have no understanding," never treat their infants as partners (speaker/addressee) in dyadic communicative interactions. Although they greet their infants by name and use expressive vocalizations, they rarely address other utterances to them. Furthermore, a mother and infant do not gaze into each other's eyes, an interactional pattern that is consistent with adult patterns of not gazing when vocalizing in interaction with one another. Rather than facing their babies and speaking to them, Kaluli mothers tend to face their babies outward so that they can see, and be seen by, other members of the social group. Older children greet and address the infant, and the mother responds in a high-pitched nasalized voice "for" the baby while moving the baby up and down. Triadic exchanges such as that in Example 4 are typical (Golinkoff 1983).

Example 4
Mother is holding her infant son Bage (3 mo). Abi (35 mo) is holding a stick on his shoulder in a manner similar to that in which one would carry a heavy patrol box (the box would be hung on a pole placed across the shoulders of the two men).

Mother	*Abi*
	(to baby) *Bage/ do you see my box here?/* Bage/ ni bokisi we badaya?/ *Do you see it?/* olibadaya?/
(high nasal voice talking as if she is the baby, moving the baby who is facing Abi): *My brother, I'll take half, my brother.* nao, hɛbɔ ni diɛni, nao.	
	(holding stick out) *mother give him half/* nɔ hɛbɔ emɔ dimina/ *mother, my brother here/ here take half/* nao we/we hɛbɔ dima/
(in a high nasal voice as baby): *My brother, what half do I take?* nao, hɛbɔ diɛni hɛh? *What about it? my brother, put it on the shoulder!* Wangaya? nao, kɛlɛnɔ wɛla diɛfoma! (to Abi in her usual voice): *Put it on the shoulder.* kɛlɛnɔ wɛla diɛfɔndo.	
	(rests stick on baby's shoulder)
There, carefully put it on. ko dinafa diɛfoma. (stick accidentally pokes baby) *Feel sorry, stop.* Heyɔ, kadɛfoma.	

When a mother takes the speaking role of an infant she uses language that is well formed and appropriate for an older child. Only the nasalization and high-pitch mark it as "the infant's." When speaking as the infant to older children, mothers speak assertively, that is, they never whine or beg on behalf of the infant. Thus, in taking this role the mother does for the infant what the infant cannot do for itself, that is, appear to act in a controlled and competent manner, using language. These kinds of interactions continue until a baby is between 4 and 6 months of age.

Several points are important here. First, these triadic exchanges are carried out primarily for the benefit of the older child and help create a relationship between the two children. Second, the mother's utterances in these exchanges are not based on, nor do they originate with, anything that the infant has initiated – either vocally or gesturally. Recall the Kaluli claim that infants have no understanding. How could someone with "no understanding" initiate appropriate interactional sequences?

However, there is an even more important and enduring cultural construct that helps make sense out of the mother's behaviors in this situation and in many others as well. Kaluli say that "one cannot know what another thinks or feels." Although Kaluli obviously interpret and assess one another's available behaviors and internal states, these interpretations are not culturally acceptable as topics of talk. Individuals often talk about their own feelings (I'm afraid, I'm happy, etc.). However, there is a cultural dispreference for talking about or making claims about what another might think, what another might feel, or what another is about to do, especially if there is no external evidence. As we shall see, these culturally constructed behaviors have several important consequences for the ways in which Kaluli caregivers verbally interact with their children and are related to other pervasive patterns of language use, which will be discussed later.

As infants become older (6–12 months), they are usually held in the arms or carried on the shoulders of the mother or an older sibling. They are present in all ongoing household activities, as well as subsistence activities that take place outside the village in the bush. During this time period, babies are addressed by adults to a limited extent. They are greeted by a variety of names (proper names, kin terms, affective and relationship terms) and receive a limited set of both negative and positive imperatives. In addition, when they do something they are told not to do, such as reach for something that is not theirs to take, they will often receive such rhetorical questions such as "who are you?!" (meaning "not someone to do that") or "is it yours?!" (meaning "it is not yours") to control their actions by shaming them (*sasidiab*). It should be stressed that the language addressed to the preverbal child consists largely of "one-liners" that call for no verbal response but for either an action or termination of an action. Other than these utterances, very little talk is directed to the young child by the adult caregiver.

This pattern of adults treating infants as noncommunicative partners continues even when babies begin babbling. Although Kaluli recognize babbling (*dabedan*), they call it noncommunicative and do not relate it to the speech that eventually emerges. Adults and older children occasionally repeat vocalizations back to the young child (age 12–16 months), reshaping them into the names of persons in the household or into kin terms, but they do not say that the baby is saying the name nor do they wait for, or expect, the child to repeat those vocalizations in an altered form. In addition, vocalizations are not generally treated as communicative and given verbal expression except in the following situation. When a toddler shrieks in protest of the assaults of an older child, mothers say "I'm unwilling" (using a quotative particle), referring to the toddler's shriek. These are the only circumstances in which mothers treat vocalizations as communicative and provide verbal expression for them. In no other circumstances did the adults in the four families in the study provide a verbally expressed interpretation of a vocalization of a preverbal child. Thus, throughout the preverbal period very little language is directed to the child, except for imperatives, rhetorical questions, and greetings. A child who by Kaluli terms has not yet begun to speak is not expected to respond either verbally or vocally. As a result, during the first 18 months or so very little sustained dyadic verbal exchange takes place between adult and infant. The infant is only minimally treated as an addressee and is not treated as a communicative partner in dyadic exchanges. Thus, the conversational model that has been described for many white middle-class caregivers and their preverbal children has no application in this case. Furthermore, if one defines language input as language directed to the child then it is reasonable to say that for Kaluli children who have not yet begun to speak there is very little. However, this does not mean that Kaluli children grow up in an impoverished verbal environment and do not learn how to speak. Quite the opposite is true. The verbal environment of the infant is rich and varied, and from the very beginning the infant is surrounded by adults and older children who spend a great deal of time talking to one another. Furthermore, as the infant develops and begins to crawl and engage in play activities and other independent actions, these actions are frequently referred to, described, and commented upon by members of the household, especially older children, to each other. Thus the ongoing activities of the preverbal child are an important topic of talk among members of the household, and this talk about the here-and-now of the infant is available to the infant, though it is not talk addressed to the infant. For example, in referring to the infant's actions, siblings and adults use the infant's name or kin term. They say, "Look at Seligiwo! He's walking." Thus the child may learn from these contexts to attend the verbal environment in which he or she lives.

Every society has its own ideology about language, including when it begins and how children acquire it. The Kaluli are no exception. Kaluli claim that language begins at the time when the child uses two critical words, "mother" (*nɔ*) and "breast" (*bo*). The child may be using other single words, but until these two words are used, the beginning of language is not recognized. Once a child has used these words, a whole set of interrelated behaviors is set into motion. Once a child has begun to use language, he or she then must be "shown how to speak" (Schieffelin 1979). Kaluli show their children language in the form of a teaching strategy, which involves providing a model for what the child is to say followed by the word *ɛlɛma*, an imperative meaning "say like that." Mothers use this method of direct instruction to teach the social uses of assertive language (teasing, shaming, requesting, challenging, reporting). However, object labeling is never part of an *ɛlɛma* sequence, nor does the mother ever use *ɛlɛma* to instruct the child to beg or appeal for food or objects. Begging, the Kaluli say, is natural for children. They know how to do it. In contrast, a child must be taught to be assertive through the use of particular linguistic expressions and verbal sequences.

A typical sequence using *ɛlɛma* is triadic, involving the mother, child (20–36 months), and other participants, as in Example 5 (Schieffelin 1979).

Example 5
Mother(M), daughter Binalia(B) (5 yrs), cousin Mama ($3\frac{1}{2}$ yrs), and son Wanu(W) (27 mos) are at home, dividing up some cooked vegetables. Binalia has been begging for some, but her mother thinks that she has had her share.

M → W →> B:*
Whose is it?! say like that.
Abɛnowo?! ɛlɛma.

  whose is it?!/
  abɛnowo?!/

Is it yours?! say like that.
Gɛnowo?! ɛlɛma.

  Is it yours?!/
  gɛnowo?!/

Who are you?! say like that.
ge oba?! ɛlɛma.

  who are you?!/
  ge oba?!/

Mama → W → > B:
Did you pick?! say like that.
gi suwo?! ɛlɛma.

  did you pick?!/
  gi suwo?!/

M → W → > B:
My grandmother picked! say like that.
ni nuwɛ suke! ɛlɛma.

  My grandmother picked!/
  ni nuwɛ suke!/

Mama → W → > B:
This my g'mother picked! say like that
we ni nuwɛ suke! ɛlɛma.

  This my g'mother picked!/
  we ni nuwɛ suke!/

*→ = speaker to addressee
→ > = addressee to intended addressee

In this situation, as in many others, the mother does not modify her language to fit the linguistic ability of the young child. Instead, her language is shaped so as to be appropriate (in terms of form and content) for the child's intended addressee. Consistent with the way she interacts with her infant, what a mother instructs her young child to say usually does not have its origins in any verbal or nonverbal behaviors of the child but in what the mother thinks should be said. The mother pushes the child into ongoing interactions that the child may or may not be interested in and will at times spend a good deal of energy in trying to get the child verbally involved. This is part of the Kaluli pattern of fitting (or pushing) the child into the situation rather than changing the situation to meet the interests or abilities of the child. Thus mothers take a directive role with their young children, teaching them what to say so that they may become participants in the social group.

In addition to instructing their children by telling them what to say in often extensive interactional sequences, Kaluli mothers pay attention to the form of their children's utterances. Kaluli correct the phonological, morphological, or lexical form of an utterance or its pragmatic or semantic meaning. Because the goals of language acquisition include the development of a competent and independent child who uses mature language, Kaluli use no baby-talk lexicon, for they said (when I asked about it) that to do so would result in a child sounding babyish, which was clearly undesirable and counterproductive. The entire process of a child's development, in which language acquisition plays a very important role, is thought of as a hardening process and culminates in the child's use of "hard words" (Feld and Schieffelin 1982).

The cultural dispreference for saying what another might be thinking or feeling has important consequences for the organization of dyadic exchanges between caregiver and child. For one, it affects the ways in which meaning is negotiated during an exchange. For the Kaluli, the responsibility for clear expression is with the speaker, and child speakers are not exempt from this. Rather than offering possible interpretations or guessing at the meaning of what a child is saying, caregivers make extensive use of clarification requests such as "huh?" and "what?" in an attempt to elicit clearer expression from the child. Children are held to what they say and mothers will remind them that they in fact have asked for food or an object if they don't act appropriately on receiving it. Because the responsibility of expression lies with the speaker, children are also instructed with *ɛlɛma* to request clarification (using similar forms) from others when they do not understand what someone is saying to them.

Another important consequence of not saying what another thinks is the absence of adult expansions of child utterances. Kaluli caregivers put words into the mouths of their children, but these words originate from the caregiver. However, caregivers do not elaborate or expand utterances initiated by the child. Nor do they jointly build propositions across utterances and speakers except in the context of sequences with *ɛlɛma* in which they are constructing the talk for the child.

All these patterns of early language use, such as the lack of expansions and the verbal attribution of an internal state to an individual are consistent with important cultural conventions of adult language usage. The Kaluli avoid gossip and often indicate the source of information they report. They make extensive use of direct quoted speech in a language that does not allow indirect quotation. They use a range of evidential markers in their speech to indicate the source of speakers' information, for example, whether something was said, seen, heard or gathered from other kinds of evidence. These patterns are also found in a child's early speech and, as such, affect the organization and acquisition of conversational exchanges in this face-to-face egalitarian society.

A Samoan developmental story

In American and Western Samoa, an archipelago in the southwest Pacific, Samoan, a verb-initial Polynesian language, is spoken.[12] The following developmental story draws primarily on direct observations of life in a large, traditional village on the island of Upolu in Western Samoa; however, it incorporates as well analyses by Mead (1927), Kernan (1969), and Shore (1982) of social life, language use, and childhood on other islands (the Manu'a islands and Savai'i).

As has been described by numerous scholars, Samoan society is highly stratified. Individuals are ranked in terms of whether or not they have a title, and if so, whether it is an orator or a chiefly title – bestowed on persons by an extended family unit (*'āiga potopoto*) – and within each status, particular titles are reckoned with respect to one another.

Social stratification characterizes relationships between untitled persons as well, with the assessment of relative rank in terms of generation and age. Most relevant to the Samoan developmental story to be told here is that caregiving is also socially stratified. The young child is cared for by a range of untitled persons, typically the child's older siblings, the mother, and unmarried siblings of the child's mother. Where more than one of these are present, the older is considered to be the higher ranking caregiver and the younger the lower ranking caregiver (Ochs 1982c). As will be discussed in the course of this story, ranking affects how caregiving tasks are carried out and how verbal interactions are organized.

From birth until the age of 5 or 6 months, an infant is referred to as *pepemeamea* (baby thing thing). During this time, the infant stays close to his or her mother, who is assisted by other women and children in child-care tasks. During this period, the infant spends the periods of rest and sleep near, but somewhat separated from, others, on a large pillow enclosed by a mosquito net suspended from a beam or rope. Waking moments are spent in the arms of the mother, occasionally the father, but most often on the hips or laps of other children, who deliver the infant to his or her mother for feeding and in general are responsible for satisfying and comforting the child.

In these early months, the infant is talked *about* by others, particularly in regard to his or her physiological states and needs. Language addressed *to* the young infant tends to be in the form of songs or rhythmic vocalizations in a soft, high pitch. Infants at this stage are not treated as conversational partners. Their gestures and vocalizations are interpreted for what they indicate about the physiological state of the child. If verbally expressed, however, these interpretations are directed in general not to the infant but to some other more mature member of the household (older child), typically in the form of a directive.

As an infant becomes more mature and mobile, he or she is referred to as simply *pepe* (baby). When the infant begins to crawl, his or her immediate social and verbal environment changes. Although the infant continues to be carried by an older sibling, he or she is also expected to come to the mother or other mature family members on his or her own. Spontaneous language is directed to the infant to a much greater extent. The child, for example, is told to "come" to the caregiver.

To understand the verbal environment of the infant at this stage, it is necessary to consider Samoan concepts of childhood and children. Once a child is able to locomote himself or herself and even somewhat before, he or she is frequently described as cheeky, mischievous, and willful. Very frequently, the infant is negatively sanctioned for his actions. An infant who sucks eagerly, vigorously, or frequently at the breast may be teasingly shamed by other family members. Approaching a guest or touching objects of value provokes negative directives first and mock threats second. The tone of voice shifts dramatically from that used with younger infants. The pitch drops to the level used in causal interactions with adult addressees and voice quality becomes loud and sharp. It is to be noted here that caregiver speech is largely talk directed *at* the infant and typically caregivers do not engage in "conversations" *with* infants over several exchanges. Further, the language used by caregivers is not lexically or syntactically simplified.

The image of the small child as highly assertive continues for several years and is reflected in what is reported to be the first word of Samoan children: *tae* (shit), a curse word used to reject, retaliate, or show displeasure at the action of another. The child's earliest use of language, then, is seen as explicitly defiant and angry. Although caregivers admonish the verbal and nonverbal expression of these qualities, the qualities are in fact deeply valued and considered necessary and desirable in particular social circumstances.

As noted earlier, Samoan children are exposed to, and participate in, a highly stratified society. Children usually grow up in a family compound composed of several households and headed by one or more titled persons. Titled persons conduct themselves in a particular manner in public, namely, moving slowly or being stationary, and they tend to disassociate themselves from the activities of lower status persons in their immediate environment. In a less dramatic fashion, this demeanor characterizes high ranking caregivers in a household as well, who tend to leave the more active tasks, such as bathing, changing, and carrying an infant to younger persons (Ochs 1982c).

The social stratification of caregiving has its reflexes in the verbal environment of the young child. Throughout the day, higher ranking caregivers (e.g., the mother) direct lower ranking persons to carry, put to sleep, soothe, feed, bathe, and clothe a child. Typically, a lower ranking caregiver waits for such a-directive rather than initiate such activities spontaneously. When a small child begins to speak, he or she learns to make his or her needs known to the higher ranking caregiver. The child learns not to necessarily expect a direct response. Rather, the child's appeal usually generates a conversational sequence such as the following:

Child appeals to high ranking caregiver	(A → B)
High ranking caregiver directs lower ranking caregiver	(B → C)
Lower ranking caregiver responds to child	(C → A)

These verbal interactions differ from the ABAB dyadic interactions described for white middle-class caregivers and children. Whereas a white middle-class child is often alone with a caregiver, a Samoan child is not. Traditional Samoan houses have no internal or external walls, and typically conversations involve several persons inside and outside the house. For the Samoan child, then, multiparty conversations are the norm, and participation is organized along hierarchical lines.

The importance of status and rank is expressed in other uses of language as well. Very small children are encouraged to produce certain speech acts that they will be expected to produce later as younger (i.e., low ranking) members of the household. One of these speech acts is reporting of news to older family members. The reporting of news by lower status persons complements the detachment associated with relatively high status. High status persons ideally (or officially) receive information through reports rather than through their own direct involvement in the affairs of others. Of course, this ideal is not always realized. Nonetheless, children from the one-word stage on will be explicitly instructed to notice others and to provide information to others as Example 6 illustrates.

Example 6
Pesio, her peer group including Maselino 3 yrs 4 mos, and Maselino's mother, Iuliana, are in the house. They see Alesana (member of research project) in front of the trade store across the street. Iuliana directs the children to notice Alesana.

Pesio (2 yrs 3 mos)	*Others*	
	Iuliana:	Va'ai Alesana. *Look (at) Alesana!*
ā?/ *Huh?*		
	Iuliana:	Alesana
	Maselino:	Alesaga/
ai Alesaga/ *Look (at) Alesana*		
	Iuliana:	Vala'au Alesana *Call (to) Alesana.*
((very high, loud)) SAGA?/ *Alesana!*	Iuliana:	((high, soft)) Mālō. (*Congratulations/hello*)
((loud)) ALŌ! (*Congratulations/hello*)		
	Iuliana:	(Fai) o Elegoa lea. (Say) prt. Elenoa here. (*say*) *"Elenoa [is] here."*
Sego lea/ *Elenoa here* Elenoa [is] here.		

The character of these instructions is similar to that of the triadic exchanges described in the Kaluli developmental story. A young child is to repeat an utterance offered by a caregiver to a third party. As in the Kaluli triadic exchanges, the utterance is designed primarily for the third party. For example, the high, soft voice quality used by Iuliana expresses deference in greeting Alesana, the third party. Caregivers use such exchanges to teach children a wide range of skills and knowedge. In fact, the task of repeating what the caregiver has said is *itself* an object of knowledge, preparing the child for his or her eventual role as messenger. Children at the age of 3 are expected to deliver *verbatim* messages on behalf of more mature members of the family.

The cumulative orientation is one in which even very young children are oriented toward others. In contrast to the white middle-class tendencies to accommodate situations to the child, the Samoans encourage the child to meet the needs of the situation, that is, to notice others, listen to them, and adapt one's own speech to their particular status and needs.

The pervasiveness of social stratification is felt in another, quite fundamental aspect of language, that of ascertaining the meaning of an utterance. Procedures for clarification are sensitive to the relative rank of conversational participants in the following manner. If a high status person produces a partially or wholly unintelligible utterance, the burden of clarification tends to rest with the hearer. It is not inappropriate for high status persons to produce such utterances from time to time. In the case of orators in particular, there is an expectation that certain terms and expressions will be obscure to certain members of their audiences. On the other hand, if a low status person's speech is unclear, the burden of clarification tends to be placed more on the speaker.

The latter situation applies to most situations in which young children produce ambiguous or unclear utterances. Both adult and child caregivers tend not to try to determine the message content of such utterances by, for example, repeating or expanding such an utterance with a query intonation. In fact, unintelligible utterances of young children will sometimes be considered as not Samoan but another language, usually Chinese, or not language at all but the sounds of an animal. A caregiver may choose to initiate clarification by asking "What?" or "Huh?" but it is up to the child to make his or her speech intelligible to the addressee.

Whereas the Samoans place the burden of clarification on the child, white middle-class caregivers assist the child in clarifying and expressing ideas. As noted in the white middle-class developmental story, such assistance is associated with good mothering. The good mother is one who responds to her child's incompetence by making greater efforts than normal to clarify his or her intentions. To this end, a mother tries to put herself in the child's place (take the perspective of the child). In Samoa good mothering or good caregiving is almost the reverse: A young child is encouraged to develop an ability to take the perspective of higher ranking persons in order to assist them and facilitate their well-being. The ability to do so is part of showing *fa'aaloalo* (respect), a most necessary demeanor in social life.

We can not leave our Samoan story without touching on another dimension of intelligibility and understanding in caregiver–child interactions. In particular, we need to turn our attention to Samoan attitudes toward motivation and intentionality (cf. Ochs 1982c). In philosophy, social science, and literary criticism, a great deal of ink has been spilled over the relation between act and intention behind an act. The pursuit and ascertaining of intentions is highly valued in many societies, where acts are objects of interpretation and motives are treated as explanations. In traditional Samoan society, with exceptions such as teasing and bluffing, actions are not treated as open to interpretation. They are treated for the most part as having one assignable meaning. An individual may not always know what that meaning is, as in the case of an oratorical passage; in these cases, one accepts that there is one meaning that he may or may not eventually come to know. For the most part as well, there is not a concern with levels of intentions and motives underlying the performance of some particular act.

Responses of Samoan caregivers to unintelligible utterances and acts of young children need to be understood in this light. Caregivers tend not to guess, hypothesize, or otherwise interpret such utterances and acts, in part because these procedures are not generally engaged in, at least explicitly, in daily social interactions within a village. As in encounters with others, a caregiver generally treats a small child's utterances as either clear or not clear, and in the latter case prefers to wait until the meaning becomes known to the caregiver rather than initiate an interpretation.

When young Samoan children participate in such interactions, they come to know how "meaning" is treated in their society. They learn what to consider as meaningful (e.g., clear utterances and actions), procedures for assigning meaning to utterances and actions, and procedures for handling unintelligible and partially intelligible utterances and actions. In this way, through language use, Samoan children are socialized into culturally preferred ways of processing information. Such contexts of experience reveal the interface of language, culture, and thought.

Implications of developmental stories: Three proposals

Interactional design reexamined. We propose that infants and caregivers do not interact with one another according to one particular "biologically designed choreography" (Stern 1977). There are many choreographies within and across societies, and cultural as well as biological systems contribute to their design, frequency, and significance. The biological predispositions constraining and shaping the social behavior of infants and caregivers must be broader than thus far conceived in that the use of eye gaze, vocalization, and body alignment are orchestrated differently in the social groups we have observed. As noted earlier, for example, Kaluli mothers do not engage in sustained gazing at, or elicit and maintain direct eye contact with, their infants as such behavior is dispreferred and associated with witchcraft.

Another argument in support of a broader notion of a biological predisposition to be social concerns the variation observed in the participant structure of social interactions. The literature on white middle-class child development has been oriented, quite legitimately, toward the two-party relationship between infant and caregiver, typically infant and mother. The legitimacy of this focus rests on the fact that this relationship is primary for infants within this social group. Further, most communicative interactions are dyadic in the adult community. Although the mother is an important figure in both Kaluli and Samoan developmental stories, the interactions in which infants are participants are typically triadic or multiparty. As noted, Kaluli mothers organize triadic interactions in which infants and young children are oriented away from their mothers and toward a third party. For Samoans, the absence of internal and external walls, coupled with the expectation that others will attend to, and eventually participate in, conversation, makes multiparty interaction far more common. Infants are socialized to participate in such interactions in ways appropriate to the status and rank of the participants.

This is not to say that Kaluli and Samoan caregivers and children do not engage in dyadic exchanges. Rather, the point is that such exchanges are not accorded the same significance as in white middle-class society. In white middle-class households that have been studied, the process of becoming social takes place predominantly through dyadic interactions, and social competence itself is measured in terms of the young child's capacity to participate in such interactions. In Kaluli and Samoan households, the process of becoming social takes place through participation in dyadic, triadic, and multiparty social interactions, with the latter two more common than the dyad.

From an early age, Samoan and Kaluli children must learn how to participate in interactions involving a number of individuals. To do this minimally requires attending to more than one individual's words and actions and knowing the norms for when and how to enter interactions, taking into account the social identities of at least three participants. Further, the sequencing of turns in triadic and multiparty interactions has a far wider range of possibilities vis-à-vis dyadic exchanges and thus requires considerable knowledge and skill. Whereas dyadic exchanges can only be ABABA..., triadic or multiparty exchanges can be sequenced in a variety of ways, subject to such social constraints as speech content and the status of speaker (as discussed in the Samoan developmental story). For both the Kaluli and the Samoan child, triadic and multiparty interactions constitute their earliest social experiences and reflect the ways in which members of these societies routinely communicate with one another.

Caregiver register reexamined

A second major proposal based on these three developmental stories is that the simplifying features of white middle-class speech are not necessary input for the acquisition of language by young children. The word "input" itself implies a directionality toward the child as information processor. The data base for the child's construction of language is assumed to be language directed *to* the child. It is tied to a model of communication that is dyadic, with participation limited to the roles of speaker and addressee. If we were to apply this strict notion of input (language addressed to the child) to the Kaluli and Samoan experiences, we would be left with a highly restricted corpus from which the child is expected to construct language. As we have emphasized in these developmental stories, the very young child is less often spoken to than spoken about. Nonetheless, both Kaluli and Samoan children become fluent speakers within the range of normal developmental variation.

Given that the features of caregivers' speech cannot be accounted for primarily in terms of their language-facilitating function, that is, as input, we might ask what can account for the special ways in which caregivers speak to their children. We suggest that the particular features of the caregiver register are best understood as an expression of a basic sociological phenomenon. Every social relationship is associated with a set of behaviors, verbal and nonverbal, that set off that relationship from other relationships. Additionally, these behaviors indicate to others that a particular social relationship is being actualized. From this point of view, the "special" features of caregiver speech are not special at all, in the sense that verbal modifications do occur wherever social relationships are called into play. This phenomenon has been overlooked in part because in describing the language of caregivers to children it is usually contrasted with a generalized notion of the ways in which adults talk to everyone else. The most extreme example of this is found in interviews with adults in which they are asked to describe special ways of talking to babies (Ferguson 1977). A less extreme example is found in the procedure of comparing caregiver speech to children with caregiver speech to the researcher/outsider (Newport, Gleitman, and Gleitman 1977). In the latter case, only one adult–adult relationship is used as a basis of comparison, and this relationship is typically formal and socially distant.

The social nature of caregiver speech has been discussed with respect to its status as a type of speech register. Nonetheless, the language-simplifying features have been emphasized more than any other aspect of the register. The dimension of simplification is significant with respect to the white middle-class caregiver registers documented; however, the notion of simplification has been taken as synonymous with the caregiver register itself. More to the point of this discussion is the apparent tendency to see simplification as a universal, if not natural, process. Ferguson's insightful parallel between caregiver speech and foreigner talk (1977) has been taken to mean that more competent speakers everywhere spontaneously accommodate their speech to less competent interactional partners, directly influencing language change in contact situations (pidgins in particular) as well as in acquisition of a foreign language. Ferguson's own discussion of "simplified registers" does not carry with it this conclusion, however. Further, the stories told here of Kaluli and Samoan caregiver speech and comportment indicate that simplification is culturally organized in terms of when, how, and extent. In both stories, caregivers do not speak in a dramatically more simplified manner to very young children. They do not do so for different cultural reasons: The Kaluli do not simplify because such speech is felt to inhibit the development of competent speech, the Samoans because such accommodations are dispreferred when the addressee is of lower rank than the speaker.

The cultural nature of simplification is evidenced very clearly when we compare Samoan speech to young children with Samoan speech to foreigners (*pālangi*). As discussed by Duranti (1981), "foreigner talk" *is* simplified in many ways, in contrast to "baby talk." To understand this, we need only return to the social principle of relative rank. Foreigners typically (and historically) are persons to whom respect is appropriate – strangers or guests of relatively high status. The appropriate comportment toward such persons is one of accommodation to their needs, communicative needs being basic. The Samoan example is an important one, because we can use it to understand social groups for whom speaking to foreigners is like speaking to children. That is, we can at least know where to *start* the process of understanding this speech phenomenon; to see the phenomenon as expressive of cultural beliefs and values. Just as there are cultural explanations for why and how Samoans speak differently to young children and foreigners, so there are cultural explanations for why and how white middle-class adults modify their speech in similar ways to these two types of addressees. These explanations go far beyond the attitudes discussed in the white middle-class story. Our task here is not to provide an adequate cultural account but rather to encourage more detailed research along these lines. An understanding of caregiver or baby-talk register in a particular society will never be achieved without a more serious consideration of the sociological nature of register.

What caregivers do with words

In this section we build on the prior two proposals and suggest that:

1 A functional account of the speech of both caregiver and child must incorporate information concerning cultural knowledge and expectations;
2 Generalizations concerning the relations between the behavior and the goals of caregivers and young children should not presuppose the presence or equivalent significance of particular goals across social groups.

In each of these developmental stories we saw that caregivers and children interacted with one another in culturally patterned ways. Our overriding theme has been that caregiver speech behavior must be seen as part of caregiving and socialization more generally. What caregivers say and how they interact with young children are motivated in part by concerns and beliefs held by many members of the local community. As noted earlier, these concerns and beliefs may not be conscious in all cases. Certain beliefs, such as the Kaluli notions of the child as "soft" and socialization as "hardening" the child, are explicit. Others, such as the white middle-class notions of the infant and small child as social and capable of acting intentionally (expressing intentions), are not explicitly formulated.

To understand what any particular verbal behavior is accomplishing, we need to adopt ethnographic procedures, namely, to relate particular behaviors to those performed in other situations. What a caregiver is doing in speaking to a child is obviously related to what she or he does and/or others do in other recurrent situations. We have suggested, for example, that the accommodations that middle-class (particularly American) caregivers make in speaking to young children are linked to patterned ways of responding to incompetence in general (e.g., handicapped persons, retardates). Members of this social group appear to adapt situations to meet the special demands of less competent persons to a far greater extent than in other societies, for example, Samoan society. We have also suggested that the heavy use of expansions by middle-class caregivers to query or confirm what a child is expressing is linked to culturally preferred procedures for achieving understanding, for example, the recognition of ambiguity, the formulation and verification of hypotheses (interpretations, guesses). In participating in interactions in which expansions are used in this way, the child learns the concepts of ambiguity, interpretation, and verification, and the procedures associated with them.

A common method in child language research has been to infer function or goal from behavior. The pitfalls of this procedure are numerous, and social scientists are acutely aware of how difficult it is to establish structure–function relations. One aspect of this dilemma is that one cannot infer function on the basis of a structure in isolation. Structures get their functional meaning through their relation to contexts in which they appear. The "same" structure may have different functions in different circumstances. This is true within a society, but our reason for mentioning it here is that it is true also across societies and languages. Although caregivers in two different societies may expand their children's utterances, it would not necessarily follow that the caregivers shared the same beliefs and values. It is possible that their behavior is motivated by quite different cultural processes. Similarly, the absence of a particular behavior, such as the absence of expansions among caregivers, may be motivated quite differently across societies. Both the Kaluli and the Samoan caregivers do not appear to rely on expansions, but the reasons expansions are dispreferred differ. The Samoans do not do so in part because of their dispreference for guessing and in part because of their expectation that the burden of intelligibility rests with the child (as lower status party) rather than with more mature members of the society. Kaluli do not use expansions to resay or guess what a child may be expressing because they say that "one cannot know what someone else thinks," regardless of age or social status.

Our final point concerning the structure–function relation is that the syntax of our claims about language acquisition must be altered to recognize variation across societies. The bulk of research on communicative development has presupposed or asserted the universality of one or another function, for example, the input function, the communicative function, and the illustrated verbal and nonverbal behaviors that follow from, or reflect, that function. Our three stories suggest that generalizations must be context-restricted. Thus, for example, rather than assuming or asserting that caregivers desire to communicate with an infant, the generalization should be expressed: "Where caregivers desire communication with an infant, then ..." or "If it is the case that caregivers desire communication with an infant then..."

A Typology of Socialization and Caregiver Speech Patterns

At this point, with the discussion nearing its conclusion, we have decided to stick our necks out a bit further and suggest that the two orientations to children discussed in the developmental stories – adapting situations to the child and adapting the child to situations – distinguish more than the three societies discussed in this chapter. We believe that these two orientations of mature members toward children can be used to create a typology of socialization patterns. For example, societies in which children are expected to adapt to situations may include not only Kaluli and Samoan but also white and black working-class Americans (Heath 1983; Miller 1982; Ward 1971).

The typology of course requires a more refined application of these orienting features. We would expect these orientations to shift as children develop; for example, a society may adapt situations to meet the needs of a very small infant, but as the infant matures, the expectation may shift to one in which the child should adapt to situations. Indeed, we could predict such a pattern for most, if not all, societies. The distinction between societies would be in terms of *when* this shift takes place and in terms of the *intensity* of the orientation at any point in developmental time.

Having stuck our necks out this far, we will go a little further and propose that these two orientations will have systematic reflexes in the organization of communication between caregivers and young children across societies: We predict, for example, that a society that adapts or fits situations to the needs (perceived needs) of young children will use a register to the

Table 12.1 Two orientations toward children and their corresponding caregiver speech patterns

Adapt situation to child	*Adapt child to situation*
Simplified register features baby-talk lexicon	Modeling of (unsimplified) utterances for child to repeat to third party (wide range of speech act, not simplified)
Negotiation of meaning via expansion and paraphrase	
Cooperative proposition building between caregiver and child	Child directed to notice others
Utterances that respond to child-initiated verbal or nonverbal act	Topics arise from range of situational circumstances to which caregiver wishes child to respond
Typical communicative situation: two-party	Typical communicative situation: multiparty

children that includes a number of simplifying features, for example, shorter utterances, with a restricted lexicon, that refer to here-and-now. Such an orientation is also compatible with a tendency for caregivers to assist the child's expression of intentions through expansions, clarification requests, cooperative proposition building and the like. These often involve the caregiver's taking the perspective of a small child and correlate highly with allowing a small child to initiate new topics (evidencing child-centered orientation).

On the other hand, societies in which children are expected to meet the needs of the situation at hand will communicate differently with infants and small children. In these societies, children usually participate in multiparty situations. Caregivers will socialize children through language to notice others and perform appropriate (not necessarily polite) speech acts toward others. This socialization will often take the form of modeling, where the caregiver says what the child should say and directs the child to repeat. Typically, the child is directed to say something to someone other than the caregiver who has modeled the original utterance. From the Kaluli and Samoan cases, we would predict that the utterances to be repeated would cover a wide range of speech acts (teasing, insulting, greeting, information requesting, begging, reporting of news, shaming, accusations, and the like). In these interactions, as in other communicative contexts with children, the caregivers do not simplify their speech but rather shape their speech to meet situational contingencies (table 12.1).

A Model of Language Acquisition through Socialization (the Ethnographic Approach)

Cultural organization of intentionality

Like many scholars of child language, we believe that the acquisition of language is keyed to accomplishing particular goals (Bates et al. 1979; Greenfield and Smith 1976; Halliday 1975; Lock 1978; Shotter 1978; Vygotsky 1962). As Bates and her colleagues (1979) as well as Carter (1978) and Lock (1981) have pointed out, small children perform communicative acts such as drawing attention to an object and requesting and offering before conventional morphemes are produced. They have acquired knowledge of particular social acts before they have acquired language in even the most rudimentary form. When language emerges, it is put to use in these and other social contexts. As Bates and her colleagues suggest, the use of language here is analogous to other behaviors of the child at this point of development; the child is using a new means to achieve old goals.

Although not taking a stand as to whether or not language is like other behaviors, we support the notion that language is acquired in a social world and that many aspects of the social world have been absorbed by the child by the time language emerges. This is not to say that functional considerations determine grammatical structure but rather that ends motivate means and provide an orienting principle for producing and understanding language over developmental time. Norman (1975), as well as Hood, McDermott, and Cole (1978), suggests that purpose/function is a mnemonic device for learning generally.

Much of the literature on early development has carefully documented the child's capacity to react and act intentionally (Harding and Golinkoff 1979). The nature and organization of communicative interaction is seen as integrally bound to this capacity. Our contribution to this literature is to spell out the social and cultural systems in which intentions participate. The capacity to express intentions is human but which intentions can be expressed by whom, when, and how is subject to local expectations concerning the social behavior of members. With respect to the acquisition of competence in language use, this means that societies may very well differ in their expectations of what children can and should communicate (Hymes 1967). They may also differ in their expectations concerning the capacity of young children to understand intentions (or particular intentions). With respect to the particular relationship between a child and his or her caregivers, these generalizations can be represented as follows:

Social expectations and language acquisition

Expectations	*Influence*	Participation in social situations	How & which intentions are expressed by child *Influences* How & which intentions are expressed by caregiver	Structure of child language *Influence* Structure of caregiver language

Let us consider examples that illustrate these statements. As noted in the Samoan development story, Samoans have a commonly shared expectation that a child's first word will be *tae* (shit) and that its communicative intention will be to curse and confront (corresponding to the adult for *'ai tae* (eat shit)). Whereas a range of early consonant-vowel combinations of the child are treated as expressing *tae* and communicative, other phonetic strings are not treated as language. The Kaluli consider that the child has begun to use language when he or she says "mother" and "breast." Like the Samoans, the Kaluli do not treat other words produced before these two words appear as part of "language," that is, as having a purpose.

Another example of how social expectations influence language acquisition comes from the recent work by Platt (1980) on Samoan children's acquisition of the deictic verbs "come," "go," "give," "take." The use of these verbs over developmental time is constrained by social norms concerning the movement of persons and objects. As noted in the Samoan story, higher ranking persons are expected to be relatively inactive in the company of lower ranking (e.g., younger) persons. As a consequence, younger children who are directed to "come" and who evidence comprehension of this act, tend not to perform the same act themselves. Children are socially constrained not to direct the more mature persons around them to move in their direction. On the other hand, small children are encouraged to demand and give out goods (particularly food). At the same developmental point at which the children are *not* using "come," they *are* using "give" quite frequently. This case is interesting because it indicates that a semantically more complex form ("give" – movement of object and person toward deictic center) may appear in the speech of a child earlier than a less complex form ("come" – movement of person toward deictic center) because of the social norms surrounding its use (Platt 1980).

Although these examples have focused on children's speech, we also consider caregiver speech to be constrained by local expectations and the values and beliefs that underlie them. The reader is invited to draw on the body of this chapter for examples of these relationships, for example, the relation between caregivers who adapt to young children and use of a simplified register. Indeed, the major focus of our developmental stories has been to indicate precisely the role of sociocultural processes in constructing communication between caregiver and child.

Sociocultural knowledge and code knowledge

In this section we will build on our argument that children's language is constructed in socially appropriate and culturally meaningful ways. Our point will be that the process of acquiring language must be understood as the process of integrating code knowledge with sociocultural knowledge.

Sociocultural knowledge is generative in much the same way that knowledge about grammar is generative. Just as children are able to produce and understand utterances that they have never heard before, so they are able to participate in social situations that don't exactly match their previous experiences. In the case of social situations in which language is used, children are able to apply both grammatical and sociocultural principles in producing and comprehending novel behavior. Both sets of principles can be acquired out of conscious awareness.

Developmental time ↑

Sociocultural knowledge	⟶ ⟵	code knowledge

In the case of infants and young children acquiring their first language(s), socio-cultural knowledge is acquired hand-in-hand with the knowledge of code properties of a language. Acquisition of a foreign or second language by older children and adults may not necessarily follow this model. In classroom foreign-language learning, for example, a knowledge of code properties typically precedes knowledge of the cultural norms of code use. Even where the second language is acquired in the context of living in a foreign culture, the cultural knowledge necessary for appropriate social interaction may lag behind or never develop, as illustrated by Gumperz (1977) for Indian speakers in Great Britain.

Another point to be mentioned at this time is that the sociocultural principles being acquired are not necessarily shared by all native speakers of a language. As noted in the introduction, there are variations in knowledge between individuals and between groups of individuals. In certain cases, for example, children who are members of a nondominant group, growing up may necessitate acquiring different cultural frameworks for participating in situations. American Indian and Australian Aboriginal children find themselves participating in interactions in which the language is familiar but the interactional procedures and participant structures differ from earlier experiences (Philips 1983). These cases of growing up monolingually but biculturally are similar to the circumstances of second-language learners who enter a cultural milieu that differs from that of first socialization experiences.

On the unevenness of language development

The picture we have built up suggests that there is quite a complex system of norms and expectations that the young language acquirer must attend to, and does attend to, in the process of growing up to be a competent speaker-hearer. We have talked about this system as affecting structure and content of children's utterances at different points in developmental time. One product of all this is that children come to use and hear particular structures in certain contexts but not in others. In other words, children acquire forms in a subset of contexts that has been given "priority" by members.

Priority contexts are those in which children are encouraged to participate. For example, Kaluli and Samoan children use affect pronouns, for example, "poor-me," initially in begging, an activity they are encouraged to engage in. The use of affect pronouns in other speech acts is a later development. Similarly, many white middle-class children use their first nominal forms in the act of labeling, an activity much encouraged by caregivers in this social group. Labeling is not an activity which Kaluli and Samoan caregivers and children engage in. Each social group will have its preferences, and these, in turn, will guide the child's acquisition of language.

On lack of match between child and caregiver speech

Those who pursue the argument concerning how children acquire language often turn to correlational comparisons between children's and caregivers' speech strategies. Lack of match is taken as support for some input-independent strategy of the child and as evidence that some natural process is at work. We suggest that this line of reasoning has flaws.

If the reader has accepted the argument that societies have ideas about how children can and should participate in social situations and that these ideas differ in many respects from those concerning how more mature persons can and should behave, then the reader might further accept the conclusion that children may speak and act differently from others because they have learned to do so. Why should we equate input exclusively with imitation, that is, with a match in behavior? Of course there are commonalities between child and adult behavior, but that does not imply that difference is not learned. In examining the speech of young children, we should not necessarily expect their speech and the functions to which it is put to match exactly those of caregivers. Children are neither expected nor encouraged to do many of the things that older persons do, and, conversely, older persons are neither expected nor encouraged to do many of the things that small children do. Indeed, unless they are framed as "play," attempts to cross these social boundaries meet with laughter, ridicule, or other forms of negative sanctioning.

A note on the role of biology

Lest the reader think we advocate a model in which language and cognition are the exclusive product of culture, we note here that sociocultural systems are to be considered as *one* force influencing language acquisition. Biological predispositions, of course, have a hand in this process as well. The model we have presented should be considered as a subset of a more general acquisition model that includes both influences.

Social expectations	Influence	Language over developmental time
Biological predispositions		

Conclusions

This is a chapter with a number of points but one message: That the process of acquiring language and the process of acquiring sociocultural knowledge are intimately tied. In pursuing this generalization, we have formulated the following proposals:

1 The specific features of caregiver speech behavior that have been described as simplified register are neither universal nor necessary for language to be acquired. White middle-class children, Kaluli children, and Samoan children all become speakers of their languages within the normal range of development and yet their caregivers use language quite differently in their presence.
2 Caregivers' speech behavior expresses and reflects values and beliefs held by members of a social group. In this sense, caregivers' speech is part of a larger set of behaviors that are culturally organized.
3 The use of simplified registers by caregivers in certain societies may be part of a more general orientation in which situations are adapted to young children's perceived needs. In other societies, the orientation may be the reverse, that is, children at a very early age are expected to adapt to requirements of situations. In such societies, caregivers direct children to notice and respond to other's actions. They tend not to simplify their speech and frequently model appropriate utterances for the child to repeat to a third party in a situation.
4 Not only caregivers' but children's language as well is influenced by social expectations. Children's strategies for encoding and decoding information, for negotiating meaning, and for handling errors are socially organized in terms of who does the work, when, and how. Further, every society orchestrates the ways in which children participate in particular situations, and this, in turn, affects the form, the function, and the content of children's utterances. Certain features of the grammar may be acquired quite early, in part because their use is encouraged and given high priority. In this sense, the process of language acquisition is part of the larger process of socialization, that is, acquiring social competence.

Although biological factors play a role in language acquisition, sociocultural factors have a hand in this process as well. It is not a trivial fact that small children develop in the context of organized societies. Cultural conditions for communication organize even the earliest interactions between infants and others. Through participation as audience, addressee, and/or "speaker," the infant develops a range of skills, intuitions, and knowledge enabling him or her to communicate in culturally preferred ways. The development of these faculties is an integral part of becoming a competent speaker.

Coda

This chapter should be in no way interpreted as proposing a view in which socialization determines a fixed pattern of behavior. We advocate a view that considers human beings to be flexible and able to adapt to change, both social and linguistic, for example, through contact and social mobility. The ways in which individuals change is a product of complex interactions between established cultural procedures and intuitions and those the individual is currently acquiring. From our perspective, socialization is a continuous and open-ended process that spans the entire life of an individual.

NOTES

This chapter was written while the authors were research fellows at the Research School of Pacific Studies, the Australian National University. We would like to thank Roger Keesing and the Working Group in Language and Its Cultural Context. Ochs's research was supported by the National Science Foundation and the Australian National University. Schieffelin's research was supported by the National Science Foundation and the Wenner-Gren Foundation for Anthropological Research. We thank these institutions for their support.

1 For current socialization literature, the reader is recommended to see Briggs 1970; Gallimore, Boggs, and Jordon 1974; Geertz 1959; Hamilton 1981; Harkeness and Super 1980; Korbin 1978; Leiderman, Tulkin, and Rosenfeld 1977; LeVine 1980; Levy 1973; Mead and MacGregor 1951; Mead and Wolfenstein 1955; Montagu 1978; Munroe and Munroe 1975; Richards 1974; Wagner and Stevenson 1982; Weisner and Gallimore 1977; Whiting 1963; Whiting and Whiting 1975; Williams 1969; and Wills 1977.

2 Bloom 1970, 1973; Bowerman 1977, 1981; Brown 1973; Clark 1974; Clark and Clark 1977; Greenfield and Smith 1976; Karmiloff-Smith 1979; MacNamara 1972; Nelson 1974; Schlesinger 1974; Sinclair 1971; Slobin 1979.

3 Bates 1976; Berko 1958; Bloom, Hood, and Lightbown 1974; Bloom, Lightbown, and Hood 1975; Bowerman 1977; Brown and Bellugi 1964; Brown, Cazden, and Bellugi 1969; Dore 1975; Ervin-Tripp 1964; Lieven 1980; MacWhinney 1975; Miller 1982; Scollon 1976; Shatz 1978; Slobin 1973.

4 Berman 1985; Bowerman 1973; Brown 1973; Clancy 1985; Clark 1985; Johnston and Slobin 1979; MacWhinney and Bates 1978; Ochs 1982b, 1985; Slobin 1981, 1985; Aksu-Koç and Slobin 1985.

5 Chomsky 1959, 1968, 1977; Fodor, Bever, and Garrett 1974; Goldin-Meadow 1977; McNeill 1970; Newport 1981; Newport, Gleitman, and Gleitman 1977; Piattelli-Palmarini 1980; Shatz 1981; Wanner and Gleitman 1982.

6 Bates et al. in press; Bloom 1973; Bruner 1975, 1977; Bullowa 1979; Carter 1978; de Lemos 1981; Gleason and Weintraub 1978; Golinkoff 1983; Greenfield and Smith 1976; Harding and Golinkoff 1979; Lock 1978, 1981; Sachs 1977; Shatz 1983; Slobin 1983; Snow 1979; Snow and Ferguson 1977; Vygotsky 1962; Werner and Kaplan 1963.

7 Andersen, Dunlea, and Kekelis 1982; Bever 1970; Greenfield and Smith 1976; Huttenlocher 1974; Menyuk and Menn 1979; Piaget 1955/1926; Slobin 1981; Sugarman 1984; Wanner and Gleitman 1982.

8 Blount 1972; Bowerman 1981; Clancy 1985; Eisenberg 1982; Fischer 1970; Hamilton 1981; Harkness 1975; Harkness and Super 1977; Heath 1983; Miller 1982; Philips 1983; Schieffelin and Eisenberg 1984; Scollon and Scollon 1981; Stross 1972; Ward 1971; Watson-Gegeo and Gegeo 1982; Wills 1977.

9 This story is based on the numerous accounts of caregiver–child communication and interaction that have appeared in both popular and scientific journals. Our generalizations regarding language use are based on detailed reports in the developmental psycholinguistic literature, which are cited throughout. In addition,

we have drawn on our own experiences and intuitions as mothers and members of this social group. We invite those with differing perceptions to comment on our interpretations.

10 We would like to thank Courtney Cazden for bringing the following quotation to our attention: "It seems to us that a mother in expanding speech may be teaching more than grammar; she may be teaching something like a world-view" (Brown and Bellugi 1964).

11 This analysis is based on the data collected in the course of ethnographic and linguistic fieldwork among the Kaluli in the Southern Highlands Province between 1975 and 1977. During this time, E. L. Schieffelin, a cultural anthropologist, and S. Feld, an ethnomusicologist, were also conducting ethnographic research. This study of the development of communicative competence among the Kaluli focused on four children who were approximately 24 months old at the start of the study. However, an additional twelve children were included in the study (siblings and cousins in residence), ranging in age from birth to 10 years. The spontaneous conversations of these children and their families were tape-recorded for one year at monthly intervals with each monthly sample lasting from 3 to 4 hours. Detailed contextual notes accompanied the taping, and these annotated transcripts, along with interviews and observations, form the data base. A total of 83 hours of audio-tape were collected and transcribed in the village. Analyses of Kaluli child acquisition data are reported in Schieffelin 1981, 1985, and 1990.

12 The data on which this analysis is based were collected from July 1978 to July 1979 in a traditional village in Western Samoa (now Samoa). The village, Falefa, is located on the island of Upolu, approximately 18 miles from the capital, Apia. The fieldwork was conducted by Alessandro Duranti, Martha Platt, and Elinor Ochs. Our data collection consisted of two major projects. The language development project, carried out by Ochs and Platt, was a longitudinal documentation, through audio- and videotape, of young children's acquisition of Samoan. This was accomplished by focusing on six children from six different households, from 19 to 35 months of age at the onset of the study. These children were observed and taped every five weeks, approximately three hours each period. Samoan children live in compounds composed of several households. Typically, numerous siblings and peers are present and interact with a young child. We were able to record the speech of seventeen other children under the age of 6, who were part of the children's early social environment. A total of 128 hours of audio and 20 hours of video recording were collected. The audio material is supplemented by handwritten notes detailing contextual features of the interactions recorded. All the audio material has been transcribed in the village by a family member or family acquaintance and checked by a researcher. Approximately 18,000 pages of transcript form the child language data base. Analyses of Samoan child language are reported in Ochs 1982a, 1982b, and 1985.

REFERENCES

Aksu-Koç, A., and Slobin, D. I. (1985). Acquisition of Turkish. In D. I. Slobin (ed.), *The Cross-linguistic Study of Language Acquisition*. Hillsdale, N.J.: Erlbaum.

Andersen, E. (1977). Learning to Speak with Style. Unpublished doctoral dissertation, Stanford University.

Andersen, E. S., Dunlea, A., and Kekelis, L. (1982). Blind Children's Language: Resolving Some Differences. Paper presented at the Stanford Child Language Research Forum, Stanford, Calif.

Andersen, E. S., and Johnson, C. E. (1973). Modifications in the Speech of an Eight-year-old to Younger Children. *Stanford Occasional Papers in Linguistics*, No. 3: 149–60.

Bates, E. (1976). *Language and Context: The Acquisition of Pragmatics*. New York: Academic Press.

Bates, E., Beeghly-Smith, M., Bretherton, I., and McNew, S. (1982). Social bases of language development: A reassessment. In H. W. Reese & L. P. Lipsitt (eds.), *Advances in Child Development and Behavior*, vol. 16. New York: Academic Press.

Bates, E., Benigni, L., Bretherton, I., Camaioni, L., and Volterra, V. (1979). *The Emergence of Symbols*. New York: Academic Press.

Berko, J. (1958). The Child's Learning of English Morphology. *Word* 14: 150–77.

Berman, R. (1985) Acquisition of Hebrew. In D. I. Slobin (ed.), *The Crosslinguistic Study of Language Acquisition*. Hillsdale, N.J.: Erlbaum.

Bever, T. (1970). The Cognitive Basis for Linguistic Structure. In J. R. Hayes (ed.), *Cognition and the Development of Language*. New York: Wiley.

Bloom, L. (1970). *Language Development: Form and Function in Emerging Grammars*. Cambridge, Mass.: MIT Press.

Bloom, L. (1973). *One Word at a Time*. The Hague: Mouton.

Bloom, L., Hood, L., and Lightbown, P. (1974). Imitation in Language Development: If, when, and why? *Cognitive Psychology* 6: 380–420.

Bloom, L., and Lahey, M. (1978). *Language Development and Language Disorders*. New York: Wiley.

Bloom, L., Lightbown, P., and Hood, L. (1975). Structure and Variation in Child Language. *Monographs of the Society for Research in Child Development* 40(2, serial no. 160).

Blount, B. (1972). Aspects of Socialization among the Luo of Kenya. *Language in Society* 1: 235–48.

Bowerman, M. (1973). *Early Syntactic Development: A Cross-linguistic Study with Special Reference to Finnish*. Cambridge: Cambridge University Press.

Bowerman, M. (1977). Semantic and Syntactic Development: A Review of What, When and How in Language Acquisition. In R. Schiefelbusch (ed.), *Bases of Language Intervention*. Baltimore: University Park Press.

Bowerman, M. (1981). Language Development. In H. Triandis and A. Heron (eds.), *Handbook of Cross-cultural Psychology*, vol. 4. Boston: Allyn & Bacon.

Briggs, J. L. (1970). *Never in Anger: Portrait of an Eskimo Family*. Cambridge, Mass.: Harvard University Press.

Brown, R. (1973). *A First Language: The Early Stages*. Cambridge, Mass.: Harvard University Press.

Brown, R. (1977). Introduction. In C. Snow and C. Ferguson (eds.), *Talking to Children: Language Input and Acquisition*. Cambridge: Cambridge University Press.

Brown, R., and Bellugi, U. (1964). Three Processes in the Child's Acquisition of Syntax. *Harvard Educational Review* 34: 133–51.

Brown, R., Cazden, C., and Bellugi, U. (1969). The Child's Grammar from I to III. In J. P. Hill (ed.), *Minnesota Symposium on Child Psychology*, vol. 2. Minneapolis: University of Minnesota Press.

Bruner, J. S. (1975). The Ontogenesis of Speech Acts. *Journal of Child Language* 2: 1–19.

Bruner, J. S. (1977). Early Social Interaction and Language Acquisition. In H. R. Schaffer (ed.), *Studies in Mother–Infant Interaction*. London: Academic Press.

Bruner, J. S. (1978). The Role of Dialogue in Language Acquisition. In A. Sinclair, R. J. Jarvella, and W. J. M. Levelt (eds.), *The Child's Conception of Language*. New York: Springer-Verlag.

Bullowa, M. (1979). Introduction: Prelinguistic Communication: A Field for Scientific Research. In M. Bullowa (ed.), *Before Speech: The Beginnings of Interpersonal Communication*. Cambridge: Cambridge University Press.

Carter, A. L. (1978). From Sensori-motor Vocalizations to Words. In A. Lock (ed.), *Action, Gesture and Symbol: The Emergence of Language*. London: Academic Press.

Cazden, C. (1965). Environmental Assistance to the Child's Acquisition of Grammar. Unpublished doctoral dissertation, Harvard University.

Chomsky, N. (1959). Review of *Verbal Behavior* by B. F. Skinner. *Language* 35: 26–58.

Chomsky, N. (1965). *Aspects of the Theory of Syntax*. Cambridge, Mass.: MIT Press.

Chomsky, N. (1968). *Language and Mind.* New York: Harcourt Brace Jovanovich.

Chomsky, N. (1975). *Reflections on Language.* Glasgow: Fontana/Collins.

Chomsky, N. (1977). *Essays on Form and Interpretation.* New York: North Holland.

Clancy, P. (1985). Acquisition of Japanese. In D. I. Slobin (ed.), *The Cross-linguistic Study of Language Acquisition.* Hillsdale, N.J.: Erlbaum.

Clark, E. V. (1974). Some Aspects of the Conceptual Basis for First Language Acquisition. In R. L. Schiefelbusch and L. Lloyd (eds.), *Language Perspectives: Acquisition, Retardation and Intervention.* Baltimore: University Park Press.

Clark, E. V. (1985). Acquisition of Romance, with special reference to French. In D. I. Slobin (ed.), *The Crosslinguistic Study of Language Acquisition.* Hillsdale, N.J.: Erlbaum.

Clark, H. H., and Clark, E. V. (1977). *Psychology and Language.* New York: Harcourt Brace Jovanovich.

Corsaro, W. (1979). Sociolinguistic Patterns in Adult–child Inter-action. In E. Ochs and B. B. Schieffelin (eds.), *Developmental Pragmatics.* New York: Academic Press.

Cross, T. (1977). Mothers' Speech Adjustments: The Contributions of Selected Child Listener Variables. In C. Snow and C. Ferguson (eds.), *Talking to Children: Language Input and Acquisition.* Cambridge: Cambridge University Press.

de Lemos, C. (1981). Interactional Processes in the Child's Construction of Language. In W. Deutsch (ed.), *The Child's Construction of Language.* London: Academic Press.

Dentan, R. K. (1978). Notes on Childhood in a Nonviolent Context: The Semai Case. In A. Montagu (ed.), *Learning Non-aggression: The Experience of Nonliterate Societies.* Oxford: Oxford University Press.

Dore, J. (1975). Holophrases, Speech Acts and Language Universals. *Journal of Child Language* 2: 21–40.

Drach, K. (1969). *The Language of the Parent.* Working paper 14, Language Behavior Research Laboratory, University of California, Berkeley.

Duranti, A. (1981). *The Samoan Fono: A Sociolinguistic Study.* Pacific Linguistic Series B, vol. 80. Canberra: Australian National University.

Edgerton, R. (1967). *The Cloak of Competence: Stigma in the Lives of the Mentally Retarded.* Berkeley: University of California Press.

Eisenberg, A. (1982). Language Acquisition in Cultural Perspective: Talk in Three Mexicano Homes. Unpublished doctoral dissertation, University of California, Berkeley.

Ervin-Tripp, S. (1964). Imitation and Structural Change in Children's Language. In E. Lenneberg (ed.), *New Directions in the Study of Language.* Cambridge, Mass.: MIT Press.

Feld, S., and Schieffelin, B. B. (1982). Hard Words: A Functional Basis for Kaluli Discourse. In D. Tannen (ed.), *Analyzing Discourse: Talk and Text.* Washington, DC: Georgetown University Press.

Feldman, H., Goldin-Meadow, S., and Gleitman, L. (1978). Beyond Herodotus: The Creation of Language by Linguistically Deprived Deaf Children. In A. Lock (ed.), *Action, Gesture and Symbol.* London: Academic Press.

Ferguson, C. (1977). Baby Talk as a Simplified Register. In C. Snow and C. Ferguson (eds.), *Talking to Children: Language Input and Acquisition.* Cambridge: Cambridge University Press.

Fischer, J. (1970). Linguistic Socialization: Japan and the United States. In R. Hill and R. Konig (eds.), *Families in East and West.* The Hague: Mouton.

Fodor, J., Bever, T., and Garrett, M. (1974). *The Psychology of Language.* New York: McGraw-Hill.

Foster, S. (1981). The Emergence of Topic Type in Children under 2,6: A Chicken and Egg Problem. *Papers and Reports in Child Language Development*, No. 20. Stanford, Calif.: Stanford University Press.

Gallimore, R., Boggs, J., and Jordan, C. (1974). *Culture, Behavior and Education: A Study of Hawaiian Americans.* Beverly Hills, Calif.: Sage.

Garnica, O. (1977). Some Prosodic and Paralinguistic Features of Speech to Young Children. In C. Snow and C. Ferguson (eds.), *Talking to Children: Language Input and*

Acquisition. Cambridge: Cambridge University Press.

Geertz, C. (1973). *The Interpretation of Cultures*. New York: Basic Books.

Geertz, H. (1959). The Vocabulary of Emotion: A Study of Javanese Socialization Processes. *Psychiatry* 22: 225–37.

Gleason, J. B., and Weintraub, S. (1978). Input Language and the Acquisition of Communicative Competence. In K. Nelson (ed.), *Children's Language*, vol. 1. New York: Gardner Press.

Goffman, E. (1963). *Behavior in Public Places*. New York: Free Press.

Goffman, E. (1967). *Interaction Ritual: Essays on Face to Face Behavior*. Garden City, N.Y.: Doubleday (Anchor Books).

Goldin-Meadow, S. (1977). Structure in a Manual Language System Developed without a Language Model: Language without a Helping Hand. In H. Whitaker and H. A. Whitaker (eds.), *Studies in Neurolinguistics*, vol. 4. New York: Academic Press.

Golinkoff, R. (ed.) (1983). *The Transition from Prelinguistic to Linguistic Communication*. Hillsdale, N.J.: Erlbaum.

Goody, E. (1978). Towards a Theory of Questions. In E. Goody (ed.), *Questions and Politeness*. Cambridge: Cambridge University Press.

Greenfield, P. (1979). Informativeness, Presupposition and Semantic Choice in Single-word Utterances. In E. Ochs and B. B. Schieffelin (eds.), *Developmental Pragmatics*. New York: Academic Press.

Greenfield, P. M., and Smith, J. H. (1976). *The Structure of Communication in Early Language Development*. New York: Academic Press.

Gumperz, J. (1977). The Conversational Analysis of Interethnic Communication. In E. L. Ross (ed.), *Interethnic Communication. Proceedings of the Southern Anthropological Society*. Athens: University of Georgia Press.

Halliday, M. A. K. (1975). *Learning How to Mean: Explorations in the Development of Language*. London: Arnold.

Hamilton, A. (1981). *Nature and Nurture: Aboriginal Childrearing in North-Central Arnhem Land*. Canberra, Australia: Institute of Aboriginal Studies.

Harding, C., and Golinkoff, R. M. (1979). The Origins of Intentional Vocalizations in Prelinguistic Infants. *Child Development* 50: 33–40.

Harkness, S. (1975). Cultural Variation in Mother's Language. In W. von Raffler-Engel (ed.), *Child Language – 1975, Word* 27: 495–8.

Harkness, S., and Super, C. (1977). Why African Children are so Hard to Test. In L. L. Adler (ed.), *Issues in Cross Cultural Research: Annals of the New York Academy of Scences* 285: 326–31.

Harkness, S., and Super, C. (eds.) (1980). *Anthropological Perspectives on Child Development*. New Directions for Child Development, no. 8. San Francisco: Jossey-Bass.

Heath, S. B. (1983). *Ways with Words: Language, Life and Work in Communities and Classroom*. Cambridge: Cambridge University Press.

Hood, L., McDermott, R., and Cole, M. (1978). Ecological Niche-picking (Working Paper 14). Unpublished manuscript, Rockefeller University, Laboratory of Comparative Human Cognition, New York.

Huttenlocher, J. (1974). The Origins of Language Comprehension. In R. L. Solso (ed.), *Theories of Cognitive Psychology*. Hillsdale, N.J.: Erlbaum.

Hymes, D. (1967). Models of the Interaction of Language and Social Setting. *Journal of Social Issues* 23(2): 8–28.

Hymes, D. (1974). *Foundations in Sociolinguistics: An Ethnographic Approach*. Philadelphia: University of Pennsylvania Press.

Irvine, J. (1974). Strategies of Status Manipulation in the Wolof Greeting. In R. Bauman and J. Sherzer (eds.), *Explorations in the Ethnography of Speaking*. Cambridge: Cambridge University Press.

Johnston, J. R., and Slobin, D. I. (1979). The Development of Locative Expressions in English, Italian, Serbo-Croatian and Turkish. *Journal of Child Language* 6: 529–45.

Karmiloff-Smith, A. (1979). *A Functional Approach to Child Language*. Cambridge: Cambridge University Press.

Keenan, E., Ochs, E., and Schieffelin, B. B. (1976). Topic as a Discourse Notion: A Study of Topic in the Conversations of

Children and Adults. In C. Li (ed.), *Subject and Topic*. New York: Academic Press.

Kernan, K. T. (1969). The Acquisition of Language by Samoan Children. Unpublished doctoral dissertation, University of California, Berkeley.

Korbin, J. 1978. Caretaking Patterns in a Rural Hawaiian Community. Unpublished doctoral dissertation, University of California, Los Angeles.

Leiderman, P. H., Tulkin, S. R., and Rosenfeld, A. (eds.) (1977). *Culture and Infancy*. New York: Academic Press.

LeVine, R. (1980). Anthropology and Child Development. *Anthropological Perspectives on Child Development*. New Directions for Child Development, no. 8. San Francisco: Jossey-Bass.

Levy, R. (1973). *The Tahitians*. Chicago, IL: University of Chicago Press.

Lewis, M., and Rosenblum, L. A. (eds.) (1974). *The Effect of the Infant on its Caregiver*. New York: Wiley.

Lieven, E. (1980). Different Routes to Multiple-word Combinations? *Papers and Reports in Child Language Development*, no. 19, Standford University, Stanford, Calif.

Lock, A. (ed.) (1978). *Action, Gesture and Symbol*. London: Academic Press.

Lock, A. (1981). *The Guided Reinvention of Language*. London: Academic Press.

MacNamara, J. (1972). The Cognitive Basis of Language Learning in Infants. *Psychological Review* 79: 1–13.

McNeill, D. (1966). The Creation of Language by Children. In J. Lyons and R. J. Wales (eds.), *Psycholinguistic Papers*. Edinburgh: Edinburgh University Press.

McNeill, D. (1970). *The Acquisition of Language*. Harper & Row.

MacWhinney, B. (1975). Rules, Rote and Analogy in Morphological Formation by Hungarian Children. *Journal of Child Language* 2: 65–77.

MacWhinney, B., and Bates, E. (1978). Sentential Devices for Conveying Givenness and Newness: A Cross-cultural Developmental Study. *Journal of Verbal Learning and Verbal Behavior* 17: 539–58.

Mead, M. (1927). *Coming of Age in Samoa*. New York: Blue Ribbon Books.

Mead, M. (1975). *Growing Up in New Guinea*. New York: Morrow. (Originally published 1935.)

Mead, M., and MacGregor, F. (1951). *Growth and Culture*. New York: Putnam.

Mead, M., and Wolfenstein, M. (1955). *Childhood in Contemporary Cultures*. Chicago: University of Chicago Press.

Menyuk, P. and Menn, L. (1979). Early Strategies for the Perception and Production or Words and Sounds. In P. Fletcher and M. Garman (eds.), *Language Acquisition*. Cambridge: Cambridge University Press.

Miller, G., & Chomsky, N. (1963). Finitary Models of Language Users. In R. Bush, E. Galanter, and R. Luce (eds.), *Handbook of Mathematical Psychology*, vol. 2. New York: Wiley.

Miller, P. (1982). *Amy, Wendy and Beth: Learning Language in South Baltimore*. Austin: University of Texas Press.

Montagu, A. (1937). *Coming into Being Among the Australian Aborigines: A Study of the Procreation Beliefs of the Native Tribes of Australia*. London: Routledge.

Montagu, A. (ed.) (1978). *Learning Non-aggression: The Experience of Nonliterate Societies*. Oxford: Oxford University Press.

Much, N., and Shweder, R. (1978). Speaking of Rules: The Analysis of Culture in Breach. In W. Damon (ed.), *Moral Development*. New Directions for Child Development, no. 2. San Francisco: Jossey-Bass.

Munroe, R. L., and Munroe, R. N. (1975). *Cross Cultural Human Development*. Monterey, Calif.: Brooks/Cole.

Nelson, K. (1974). Concept, Word and Sentence: Interrelations in Acquisition and Development. *Psychological Review* 81: 267–85.

Newport, E. L. (1976). Motherese: The Speech of Mothers to Young Children. In N. J. Castellan, D. B. Pisoni, and G. R. Potts (eds.), *Cognitive Theory*, vol. 2. Hillsdale, N.J.: Erlbaum.

Newport, E. L. (1981). Constraints on Structure: Evidence from American Sign Language and Language Learning. In W. A. Collins (ed.), *Minnesota Symposium on Child Psychology*, vol. 14. Hillsdale, N.J.: Erlbaum.

Newport, E. L., Gleitman, H., and Gleitman, L. R. (1977). Mother, I'd Rather Do it Myself: Some Effects and Non-effects of Maternal Speech Style. In C. Snow and C. Ferguson (eds.), *Talking to Children: Language Input and Acquisition*. Cambridge: Cambridge University Press.

Newson, J. (1977). An Intersubjective Approach to the Systematic Description of Mother–Infant Interaction. In H. R. Schaffer (ed.), *Studies in Mother–Infant Interaction*. London: Academic Press.

Newson, J. (1978). Dialogue and Development. In A. Lock (ed.), *Action, Gesture and Symbol*. London: Academic Press.

Ninio, A. (1979). The Naive Theory of the Infant and Other Maternal Attitudes in Two Subgroups in Israel. *Child Development* 50: 976–80.

Norman, D. A. (1975). Cognitive Organization and Learning. In P. M. A. Rabbitt and S. Dornic (eds.), *Attention and Performance V*. New York: Academic Press.

Ochs, E. (1982a). Affect in Samoan Child Language. Paper presented to the Stanford Child Language Research Forum, Stanford, Calif.

Ochs, E. (1982b). Ergativity and Word Order in Samoan Child Language: A Sociolinguistic Study. *Language* 58: 646–71.

Ochs, E. (1982c). Talking to Children in Western Samoa. *Language in Society* 11: 77–104.

Ochs, E. (1985). Variation and Error: A Sociolinguistic Study of Language Acquisition in Samoa. In D. I. Slobin (ed.), *The Crosslinguistic Study of Language Acquisition*. Hillsdale, N.J.: Erlbaum.

Ochs, E., Schieffelin, B. B., and Platt, M. (1979). Propositions across Utterances and Speaker. In E. Ochs and B. B. Schieffelin (eds.), *Developmental Pragmatics*. New York: Academic Press.

Philips, S. (1983). *The Invisible Culture*. New York: Longman.

Phillips, J. (1973). Syntax and Vocabulary of Mothers' Speech to Young Children: Age and Sex Comparisons. *Child Development* 44: 182–5.

Piaget, J. (1955). *The Language and Thought of the Child*. London: Routledge & Kegan Paul. (Originally published 1926.)

Piattelli-Palmarini, M. (ed.) (1980). *Language and Learning: The Debate Between Jean Piaget and Noam Chomsky*, Cambridge, Mass.: Harvard University Press.

Platt, M. (1980). The Acquisition of "Come," "Give," and "Bring" by Samoan Children. *Papers and Reports in Child Language Development*, no. 19. Stanford, Calif.: Stanford University.

Richards, M. P. M. (ed.) (1974). *The Integration of a Child into a Social World*. Cambridge: Cambridge University Press.

Ryan, J. (1974). Early Language Development: Towards a Communicational Analysis. In M. P. M. Richards (ed.), *The Integration of a Child into a Social World*. Cambridge: Cambridge University Press.

Sachs, J. (1977). Adaptive Significance of Input to Infants. In C. Snow and C. Ferguson (eds.), *Talking to Children: Language Input and Acquisition*. Cambridge: Cambridge University Press.

Sachs, J., Brown, R., and Salerno, R. (1976). Adults' Speech to Children. In W. von Raffler-Engel and Y. Lebrun (eds.), *Baby Talk and Infant Speech*. Lisse: Riddler Press.

Sachs, J., and Devin, J. (1976). Young Children's Use of Age-appropriate Speech Styles. *Journal of Child Language* 3: 81–98.

Schaffer, H. R. (ed.) (1977). *Studies in Mother–Infant Interaction*. London: Academic Press.

Schieffelin, B. B. (1979). Getting it Together: An Ethnographic Approach to the Study of the Development of Communicative Competence. In E. Ochs and B. B. Schieffelin (eds.), *Developmental Pragmatics*. New York: Academic Press.

Schieffelin, B. B. (1981). A Developmental Study of Pragmatic Appropriateness of Word Order and Case Marking in Kaluli. In W. Deutsch (ed.), *The Child's Construction of Language*. London: Academic Press.

Schieffelin, B. B. (1985). Acquisition of Kaluli. In D. I. Slobin (ed.), *The Crosslinguistic Study of Language Acquisition*. Hillsdale, N.J.: Erlbaum.

Schieffelin, B. B. (1990). *The Give and Take of Everyday Life: Language Socialization of Kaluli Children*. Cambridge: Cambridge University Press.

Schieffelin, B. B., and Eisenberg, A. (1984). Cultural Variation in Children's Conversations. In R. L. Schiefelbusch and J. Pickar (eds.), *Communicative Competence: Acquisition and Intervention.* Baltimore: University Park Press.

Schieffelin, E. L. (1976). *The Sorrow of the Lonely and the Burning of the Dancers.* New York: St Martin's Press.

Schlesinger, I. M. (1974). Relational Concepts Underlying Language. In R. Schiefelbusch and L. Lloyd (eds.), *Language Perspectives–Acquisition, Retardation and Intervention.* Baltimore: University Park Press.

Scollon, R. (1976). *Conversations with a One Year Old.* Honolulu: University Press of Hawaii.

Scollon, R. and Scollon, S. (1981). The Literate Two-year old: The Fictionalization of Self. Abstracting Themes: A Chipewyan Two-year-old. *Narrative, Literacy and Face in Interethnic Communication.* Vol. 7 of R. O. Freedle (ed.), *Advances in Discourse Processes.* Norwood, N.J.: Ablex.

Shatz, M. (1978). The Relationship between Cognitive Processes and the Development of Communication Skills. In C. B. Keasey (ed.), *Nebraska Symposium on Motivation,* vol. 25. Lincoln: University of Nebraska Press.

Shatz, M. (1981). Learning the Rules of the Game: Four Views of the Relation between Social Interaction and Syntax Acquisition. In W. Deutsch (ed.), *The Child's Construction of Language.* London: Academic Press.

Shatz, M. (1983). Communication. In P. Mussen, J. H. Flavell, and E. M. Markman (eds.), *Handbook of Child Psychology* (4th edn.), Volume III: *Cognitive Development.* New York: John Wiley & Sons.

Shatz, M., and Gelman, R. (1973). The Development of Communication Skills: Modifications in the Speech of Young Children as a Function of Listener. *Monographs of the Society for Research in Child Development,* 152 (38, serial no. 5).

Shore, B. (1982). *Sala' ilua: A Samoan Mystery.* New York: Columbia University Press.

Shotter, J. (1978). The Cultural Context of Communication Studies: Theoretical and methodological issues. In A. Lock (ed.), *Action, Gesture and Symbol.* London: Academic Press.

Sinclair, H. (1971). Sensorimotor Action Patterns as a Condition for the Acquisition of Syntax. In R. Huxley and E. Ingram (eds.), *Language Acquisition: Models and Methods.* New York: Academic Press.

Skinner, B. F. (1957). *Verbal Behavior.* New York: Appleton-Century-Crofts.

Slobin, D. I. (1973). Cognitive Prerequisites for Grammar. In C. Ferguson and D. I. Slobin (eds.), *Studies in Child Language Development.* New York: Holt, Rinehart, and Winston.

Slobin, D. I. (1979). *Psycholinguistics,* 2nd edn. Glenview, Ill.: Scott Foresman.

Slobin, D. I. (1981). The Origin of Grammatical Encoding of Events. In W. Deutsch (ed.), *The Child's Construction of Language.* London: Academic Press.

Slobin, D. I. (1982). Universal and Particular in the Acquisition of Language. In E. Wanner and L. R. Gleitman (eds.), *Language Acquisition: The State of the Art.* Cambridge: Cambridge University Press.

Slobin, D. I. (ed.) (1967). *A Field Manual for Cross-cultural Study of the Acquisition of Communicative Competence.* Language Behavior Research Laboratory, University of California, Berkeley.

Slobin, D. I. (ed.) (1985). *The Crosslinguistic Study of Language Acquisition.* Hillsdale, NJ: Erlbaum.

Snow, C. (1972). Mothers' Speech to Children Learning Language. *Child Development* 43: 549–65.

Snow, C. (1977a). The Development of Conversation between Mothers and Babies. *Journal of Child Language* 4: 1–22.

Snow, C. (1977b). Mothers' Speech Research: From Input to Inter-action. In C. Snow and C. Ferguson (eds.), *Talking to Children: Language Input and Acquisition.* Cambridge: Cambridge University Press.

Snow, C. (1979). Conversations with Children. In P. Fletcher and M. Garman (eds.), *Language Acquisition.* Cambridge: Cambridge University Press.

Snow, C., de Blauw, A., and van Roosmalen, G. (1979). Talking and Playing with Babies: The Role of Ideologies of Child-rearing. In M. Bullowa (ed.), *Before Speech: The Beginnings of Interpersonal Communication.* Cambridge: Cambridge University Press.

Snow, C., and Ferguson, C. (eds.) (1977). *Talking to Children: Language Input and*

Acquisition. Cambridge: Cambridge University Press.

Stern, D. (1977). *The First Relationship: Infant and Mother.* Cambridge, Mass.: Harvard University Press.

Stross, B. (1972). Verbal Processes in Tzeltal Speech Socialization. *Anthropological Linguistics* 14:1.

Sugarman, S. (1984). The Development of Preverbal Communication: Its Contribution and Limits in Promoting the Development of Language. In R. L. Schiefelbusch and J. Pickar (eds.), *Communicative Competence: Acquisition and Intervention*. Baltimore: University Park Press.

Trevarthen, C. (1979a). Communication and Cooperation in Early Infancy: A Description of Primary Intersubjectivity. In M. Bullowa (ed.), *Before Speech: The Beginnings of Interpersonal Communication*. Cambridge: Cambridge University Press.

Trevarthen, C. (1979b). Instincts for Human Understanding and for Cultural Cooperation: Their Development in Infancy. In M. von Cranach, K. Foppa, W. Lepenies, and D. Ploog (eds.), *Human Ethology: Claims and Limits of a New Discipline*. Cambridge: Cambridge University Press.

van der Geest, T. (1977). Some Interactional Aspects of Language Acquisition. In C. Snow and C. Ferguson (eds.), *Talking to Children: Language Input and Acquisition*. Cambridge: Cambridge University Press.

von Sturmer, D. E. (1980). Rights in Nurturing. Unpublished master's thesis, Australian National University, Canberra.

Vygotsky, L. S. (1962). *Thought and Language*. Cambridge, Mass.: MIT Press.

Wagner, D., and Stevenson, H. W. (eds.) (1982). *Cultural Perspectives on Child Development*. San Francisco: Freeman.

Wanner E., and Gleitman, L. R. (eds.) (1982) *Language Acquisition: The State of the Art*. Cambridge: Cambridge University Press.

Ward, M. (1971). *Them Children: A Study in Language Learning*. New York: Holt, Rinehart, and Winston.

Watson-Gegeo, K., and Gegeo, D. (1982). Calling Out and Repeating: Two Key Routines in Kwara'ae Children's Language Acquisition. Paper presented at the American Anthropological Association meetings, Washington, DC.

Weisner, T. S., and Gallimore, R. (1977). My Brother's Keeper: Child and Sibling Caretaking. *Current Anthropology* 18(2): 169–90.

Werner, H., and Kaplan, B. (1963). *Symbol Formation*. New York: Wiley.

Whiting, B. (ed.) (1963). *Six Cultures: Studies of Child Rearing*. New York: Wiley.

Whiting, B., and Whiting, J. (1975). *Children of Six Cultures*. Cambridge, Mass.: Harvard University Press.

Williams, T. R. (1969). *A Borneo Childhood: Enculturation in Dusun Society.* New York: Holt, Rinehart, and Winston.

Wills, D. (1977). Culture's Cradle: Social Structural and Interactional Aspects of Senegalese Socialization. Unpublished doctoral dissertation, University of Texas, Austin.

STUDY QUESTIONS

1 Using examples from the chapter by Ochs and Schieffelin, illustrate the difference between socialization *to* language and socialization *through* language.

2 What are the three "developmental stories" told by Ochs and Schieffelin and how do they help build a model of different styles of socialization?

3 What is *ethnographic* about the ways in which Ochs and Schieffelin (a) conducted their own research on children's language and (b) wrote about it?

4 What are the features of the two orientations that adults display when they communicate with children (i.e., "adapt situation to child" and "adapt child to situation")?

5 Using two examples from this chapter, discuss how language is considered to be a carrier of culture.

6 Using the features discussed by Ochs and Schieffelin, provide a brief description of language socialization practices in the communities you are familiar with.

13

Participant Structures and Communicative Competence: Warm Springs Children in Community and Classroom

Susan U. Philips

Introduction

Recent studies of North American Indian education problems have indicated that in many ways Indian children are not culturally oriented to the ways in which classroom learning is conducted. The Wax–Dumont study (Wax et al., 1964) of the Pine Ridge Sioux discusses the lack of interest children show in what goes on in school and Wolcott's (1967) description of a Kwakiutl school tells of the Indian children's organized resistance to his ways of structuring classroom learning. Cazden and John (1968) suggest that the "styles of learning" through which Indian children are enculturated at home differ markedly from those to which they are introduced in the classroom. And Hymes (1967) has pointed out that this may lead to sociolinguistic interference when teacher and student do not recognize these differences in their efforts to communicate with one another.

On the Warm Springs Indian Reservation in central Oregon, where I have been carrying out research in patterns of speech usage, teachers have pointed to similar phenomena, particularly in their repeated statements that Indian children show a great deal of reluctance to talk in class, and that they participate less and less in verbal interaction as they go through school. To help account for the reluctance of the Indian children of Warm Springs (and elsewhere as well) to participate in classroom verbal interactions, I am going to demonstrate how some of the social conditions governing or determining when it is appropriate for a student to speak in the classroom differ from those that govern verbal participation and other types of communicative performances in the Warm Springs Indian community's social interactions.

The data on which discussion of these differences will be based are drawn, first of all, from comparative observations in all-Indian classes in the reservation grammar school and non-Indian or white classes in another grammar school at the first- and sixth-grade levels. The purpose here is to define the communicative contexts in which Indian and non-Indian

For permission to publish copyright material in this book, grateful acknowledgment is made to: S. U. Philips (1972), "Participant Structures and Communicative Competence: Warm Springs Children in Community and Classroom," in C. B. Cazden, V. P. John, and D. Hymes (eds.), *Functions of Language in the Classroom*. New York: Columbia Teachers Press, pp. 370–94.

behavior and participation differ, and to describe the ways in which they differ.

After defining the situations or social contexts in which Indian students' verbal participation is minimal, discussion will shift to consideration of the social conditions in Indian cultural contexts that define when speaking is appropriate, attending to children's learning experiences both at home and in the community-wide social activities in which they participate.

The end goal of this discussion will be to demonstrate that the social conditions that define when a person uses speech in Indian social situations are present in classroom situations in which Indian students use speech a great deal, and absent in the more prevalent classroom situations in which they fail to participate verbally.

There are several aspects of verbal participation in classroom contexts that should be kept in mind during the discussion of why Indians are reluctant to talk. First of all, a student's use of speech in the classroom during structured lesson sessions is a communicative performance in more than one sense of "performance." It involves demonstration of sociolinguistic competency, itself a complex combination of linguistic competency and social competency involving knowledge of when and in what style one must present one's utterances, among other things. This type of competency, however, is involved in every speech act. But in the classroom there is a second sense in which speaking is a performance that is more special although not unique to classroom interactions. In class, speaking is the first and primary mode for communicating competency in all of the areas of skill and knowledge that schools purport to teach. Children communicate what they have learned to the teacher and their fellow students through speaking; only rarely do they demonstrate what they know through physical activity or creation of material objects. While writing eventually becomes a second important channel or mode for communicating knowledge or demonstrating skills, writing, as a skill, is to a great extent developed through verbal interaction between student and teacher, as is reading.

Consequently, if talk fails to occur, then the channel through which learning sessions are conducted is cut off, and the structure of classroom interaction that depends on dialogue between teacher and student breaks down and no longer functions as it is supposed to. Thus, while the question "Why don't Indian kids talk more in class?" is in a sense a very simple one, it is also a very basic one, and the lack of talk a problem that needs to be dealt with if Indian children are to learn what is taught in American schools.

Cultural and Educational Background of the Warm Springs Indians

Before embarking on the main task of the discussion outlined above, some background information on the setting of the research, the Warm Springs Indian Reservation, is necessary to provide some sense of the extent to which the cultural, linguistic, and educational situation there may be similar to or different from that of North American Indians in other parts of the country.

Today the reservation of 564,209 acres is populated by some 1,500 descendants of the "bands" of Warm Springs Sahaptin, Wasco Chinook, and Paiute Indians who gradually settled there after the reservation was established in 1855. The Warm Springs Indians have always been the largest group numerically, followed by the Wasco, with the Paiutes so small in number that their influence in the culture of the reservation has been of relatively small significance. Although they spoke different languages, the Warm Springs and Wasco groups were geographically quite close to one another before the reservation was established and were culturally similar in many respects. Thus, after over a hundred years together on the reservation, they presently share approximately the same cultural background.

The "tribe," as the Indians of Warm Springs now refer to themselves collectively, today comprises a single closely integrated community with strong tribal leadership, which receives the full backing of the people. Until after World War II the Indians here experienced considerable poverty and hardship. Since that time, however, tribal income from the sale of reservation timber has considerably improved the economic situation, as has tribal purchase of a sawmill and a small resort, which provide jobs for tribal members.

With the income from these enterprises, and drawing as well on various forms of federal aid available to them, the tribe has developed social programs to help members of the tribe in a number of ways. Chief among their concerns is the improvement of the education of their children, whom they recognize to be less successful in school than their fellow non-Indian students. Tribal leaders have taken numerous important steps to increase the educational opportunities of their young people, including the establishment of a scholarship program for college students and a tribal education office with half a dozen full-time employees supervising the tribally sponsored kindergarten, study halls, and community center courses as well as the federally sponsored programs such as VISTA, Head Start, and Neighborhood Youth Corps. The education office employees also act as liaisons between parents of children with problems in school and the administrators and teachers of the public schools the children attend. In sum, the tribe is doing a great deal to provide the Warm Springs children with the best education possible.

Despite their efforts, and those of the public school officials, who are under considerable pressure from tribal leaders to bring about changes in the schools that will result in the improvement of the academic performance of Indian students, the Indians continue to do poorly in school when compared to the non-Indian students in the same school system.

One of the most important things to know about the schools the Indian children attend is the "ethnic" composition of their classes. For the first six grades, Warm Springs children attend a public school that is located on the reservation. Here their classmates are almost all Indians and their teachers are all non-Indians or whites. After the first six grades, they are bused into the town of Madras, a distance of fifteen to thirty miles, depending on where they live on the reservation. Here, encountering their fellow white students for the first time, the Indian students are outnumbered by a ratio of five to one. From the point of view of tribal leaders, it is only when they reach the high school, or ninth grade, that the Indian students' "problems" really become serious, for it is at this point that hostility between Indian and non-Indian is expressed openly, and the Indian students' failure to participate in classroom discussions and school activities is recognized by everyone.

There is, however, abundant evidence that Indian students' learning difficulties begin long before they reach the high school. The statistics that are available on their educational achievements and problems are very similar to those which have been reported for Indians in other parts of the country (Berry, 1969). On national achievement tests the Warm Springs Indian children consistently score lower than the national average in skills tested. Their lowest scores are in areas involving verbal competencies, and the gap between their level of performance on such tests and the national averages widens as they continue into the higher grade levels (Zentner, 1960).

Although many people on the reservation still speak an Indian language, today all of the Warm Springs children in school are monolingual speakers of English. The dialect of English they speak, however, is not the Standard English of their teachers, but one that is distinctive to the local Indian community, and that in some aspects of grammar and phonology shows influence from the Indian languages spoken on the reservation.

In addition, there is some evidence that many children are exposed to talk in the Indian languages that may affect their acquisition of English. Because older people on the reservation are very concerned about the Indian languages' dying out, many of them make a concerted effort to teach young children an Indian language, particularly the Warm Springs Sahaptin. Thus some infants and young children are spoken to consistently in both Warm Springs and English. Every Indian child still knows some Indian words, and many informants report that while their children refuse to speak the Warm Springs Sahaptin – particularly after they start school – they understand much of what is said to them in it.

The effects of the acquisition of a very local dialect of English and the exposure to the Warm Springs language on classroom learning are difficult for local educators to assess because children say so little in the presence of the teachers. Observations of Indian children's verbal interactions outside the classroom indicate a control and productive use of linguistic rules that is manifested infrequently in classroom utterances, indicating that the appropriate social conditions for speech use, from the Indians' point of view, are lacking. It is this problem with appropriate social contexts for speaking that will now be considered in greater detail.

Conditions for Speech Use in School Classrooms

When the children first enter school, the most immediate concern of the teachers is to teach them the basic rules for classroom behavior upon which the maintenance of continuous and ordered activity depends. One of the most important of these is the distinction between the roles of teacher and student. In this there is the explicit and implicit assumption that the teacher controls all of the activity taking place in the classroom and the students accept and are obedient to her authority. She determines the sociospatial arrangements of all interactions; she decrees when and where movement takes place within the classroom. And most important for our present concern with communication, she determines who will talk and when they will talk.

While some class activities are designed to create the sense of a class of students as an organized group with class officers, or student monitors carrying out various responsibilities contributing to the group, actual spontaneous organization within the student group that has not been officially designated by the teacher is not encouraged. It interferes with the scheduling of activities as the teacher has organized them. The classroom situation is one in which the teacher relates to the students as an undifferentiated mass, much as a performer in front of an audience. Or she relates to each student on a one-to-one basis, often with the rest of the class as the still undifferentiated audience for the performance of the individual child.

In comparing the Indian and non-Indian learning of these basic classroom distinctions which define the conditions in which communication will take place, differences are immediately apparent. Indian first-graders are consistently slower to begin acting in accordance with these basic arrangements. They do not remember to raise their hands and wait to be called on before speaking, they wander to parts of the room other than the one in which the teacher is conducting a session, and they talk to other students while the teacher is talking, much further into the school year than do students in non-Indian classes. And the Indian children continue to fail to conform to classroom procedure much more frequently *through* the school year.

In contrast to the non-Indian students, the Indian students consistently show a great deal more interest in what their fellow students are doing than in what the teacher is doing. While non-Indian students constantly make bids for the attention of their teachers, through initiating dialogue with them as well as through other acts, Indian students do very little of this. Instead they make bids for the attention of their fellow students through talk. At the first-grade level, and more noticeably (with new teachers only) at the sixth-grade level, Indian students often act in deliberate organized opposition to the teacher's directions. Thus, at the first-grade level, if one student is told not to put his feet on his chair, another will immediately put his feet on his chair, and he will be imitated by other students who see him do this. In non-Indian classrooms, such behavior was observed only at the sixth-grade level in interaction with a substitute teacher.

In other words, there is, on the part of Indian students, relatively less interest, desire, and/or ability to internalize and act in accordance with some of the basic rules underlying classroom maintenance of orderly interaction. Most notably, Indian students are less willing than non-Indian students to accept the teacher as director and controller of all classroom activities. They are less interested in developing the one-to-one communicative relationship between teacher and student, and more interested in maintaining and developing relationships with their peers, regardless of what is going on in the classroom.

Within the basic framework of teacher-controlled interaction, there are several possible variations in structural arrangements of interaction, which will be referred to from here on as "participant structures." Teachers use different participant structures, or ways of arranging verbal interaction with students, for communicating different types of educational material, and for providing variation in the presentation of the same material to hold children's interest. Often the notion that different kinds of materials are taught better and more efficiently through one sort of participant structuring rather than another is also involved.

In the first type of participant structure the teacher interacts with all of the students. She may address all of them, or a single student in the presence of the rest of the students. The students may respond as a group or chorus in unison, or individually in the presence of their peers. And finally, student verbal participation may be either voluntary, as when the teacher asks who knows the answer to her question, or compulsory, as when the teacher asks a particular student to answer, whether his hand is raised or not. And always it is the teacher who determines whether she talks to one or to all, receives responses individually or in chorus, and voluntarily or without choice.

In a second type of participant structure, the teacher interacts with only some of the students in the class at once, as in reading groups. In such contexts participation is usually mandatory rather than voluntary, individual rather than chorus, and each student is expected to participate or perform verbally, for the main purpose of such smaller groups is to provide the teacher with the opportunity to assess the knowledge acquired by each individual student. During such sessions, the remaining students who are not interacting with the teacher are usually working alone or independently at their desks on reading or writing assignments.

A third participant structure consists of all students working independently at their desks, but with the teacher explicitly available for student-initiated verbal interaction, in which the child indicates he wants to communicate with the teacher by raising his hand, or by approaching the teacher at her desk. In either case, the interaction between student and teacher is not witnessed by the other students in that they do not hear what is said.

A fourth participant structure, and one that occurs infrequently in the upper primary grades, and rarely, if ever, in the lower grades, consists of the students' being divided into small groups that they run themselves, though always with the more distant supervision of the teacher, and usually for the purpose of so-called "group projects." As a rule such groups have official "chairmen," who assume what is in other contexts the teacher's authority in regulating who will talk when.

In observing and comparing Indian and non-Indian participation or communicative performances in these four different structural variations of contexts in which communication takes place, differences between the two groups again emerge very clearly.

In the first two participant structures where students must speak out individually in front of the other students, Indian children show considerable reluctance to participate, particularly when compared to non-Indian students. When the teacher is in front of the whole class, they volunteer to speak relatively rarely, and teachers at the Warm Springs grammar school generally hold that this reluctance to volunteer to speak out in front of other students increases as the children get older.

When the teacher is with a small group, and each individual must give some kind of communicative verbal performance in turn, Indian children much more frequently refuse, or fail to utter a word when called upon, and much less frequently, if ever, urge the teacher to call on them than the non-Indians do. When the Indian children do speak, they speak very softly, often in tones inaudible to a person more than a few feet away, and in utterances typically shorter or briefer than those of their non-Indian counterparts.

In situations where the teacher makes herself available for student-initiated communication during sessions in which students are working independently on assignments that do not involve verbal communication, students at the first-grade level in the Indian classes at first rarely initiate contact with the teachers. After a few weeks in a classroom they do so as frequently as the non-Indian students. And at the sixth-grade level Indian students initiate such relatively private encounters with teachers much more frequently than non-Indian students do.

When students control and direct the interaction in small group projects, as described for the fourth type of participant structure, there is again a marked contrast between the behavior of Indian and non-Indian students. It is in such contexts that Indian students become most fully involved in what they are doing, concentrating completely on their work until it is completed, talking a great deal to one another within the group, and competing, with explicit remarks to that effect, with the other groups. Non-Indian students take more time in "getting organized," disagree and argue more regarding how to go about a task, rely more heavily on appointed chairmen for arbitration and decision-making, and show less interest, at least explicitly, in competing with other groups from their class.

Observations of the behavior of both Indian and non-Indian children outside the classroom during recess periods and teacher-organized physical education periods provide further evidence that the differences in readiness to participate in interaction are related to the way in which the interaction is organized and controlled.

When such outside-class activity is organized by the teachers, it is for the purpose of teaching children games through which they develop certain physical and social skills. If the games involve a role distinction between leader and followers in which the leader must tell the others what to do – as in Simon Says, Follow the Leader, Green Light Red Light, and even Farmer in the Dell – Indian children show a great deal of reluctance to assume the leadership role. This is particularly true when the child is appointed leader by the teacher and must be repeatedly urged to act in telling the others what to do before doing so. Non-Indian children, in contrast, vie eagerly for such positions, calling upon the teacher and/or other students to select them.

If such playground activity is unsupervised, and the children are left to their own devices, Indian children become involved in games of team competition much more frequently than non-Indian children. And they sustain such game activities for longer periods of time and at younger ages than non-Indian children. While non-Indian children tend more to play in groups of two and three, and in the upper primary grades to form "friendships" with one or two persons from their own class in school, Indian children interact with a greater number of children consistently, and maintain friendships and teams with children from classes in school other than their own.

In reviewing the comparison of Indian and non-Indian students' verbal participation under different social conditions, two features of the Warm Springs children's behavior stand out. First of all, they show relatively less willingness to perform or participate verbally when they must speak alone in front of other students. Second, they are relatively less eager to speak when the point at which speech occurs is dictated by the teacher, as it is during sessions when the teacher is working with the whole class or a small group. They also show considerable reluctance to be placed in the "leadership" play roles that require them to assume the same type of dictation of the acts of their peers.

Parallel to these negative responses are the positive ones of a relatively greater willingness to participate in group activities that do not create a distinction between individual performer and audience, and a relatively greater use of opportunities in which the point at which the student speaks or acts is determined by himself, rather than by the teacher or a "leader."

It is apparent that there are situations arising in the classroom that do allow for the Indian students to verbalize or communicate under or within the participant structures their behavior indicates they prefer; otherwise it would not have been possible to make the distinctions between their behavior and that of non-Indians in the areas just discussed. However, the frequency of occurrence of such situations in the classroom is very low when compared to the frequency of occurrence of the type of participant structuring in which Indian students fail to participate verbally, particularly in the lower grades.

In other words, most verbal communication that is considered part of students' learning experience does take the structure of individual students' speaking in front of other students. About half of this speaking is voluntary insofar as students are invited to volunteer to answer, and half is compulsory in that a specific student is called on and expected to answer. In either case, it is the teacher who establishes when talk will occur and within what kind of participant structure.

There are many reasons why most of the verbal communication takes place under such conditions. Within our particular education system, a teacher needs to know how much her students have learned or absorbed from the material she has presented. Students' verbal responses provide one means – and the primary means, particularly before students learn to write – of measuring their progress, and are thus the teacher's feedback. And, again within our particular educational system, it is not group but individual progress with which our teachers are expected to be concerned.

In addition, it is assumed that students will learn from each others' performances both what is false or wrong, and what is true or correct. Another aspect of this type of public performance that may increase educators' belief in its efficacy is the students' awareness that these communicative acts *are* performances, in the sense of being demonstrations of competency. The concomitant awareness that success or failure in such acts is a measure of their worth in the eyes of those present increases their motivation to do well. Thus they will remember when they made a mistake and try harder to do well to avoid public failure, in a way they would not were their performances in front of a smaller number of people. As I will try to demonstrate further on, however, the educators' assumption of the validity or success of this type of enculturation process, which can briefly be referred to as "learning through public mistakes," is not one the Indians share, and this has important implications for our understanding of Indian behavior in the classroom.

The consequences of the Indians' reluctance to participate in these speech situations are several. First of all, the teacher loses the primary means she has of receiving feedback on the children's acquisition of knowledge, and is thus less able to establish at what point she must begin again to instruct them, particularly in skills requiring a developmental sequencing, as in reading.

A second consequence of this reluctance to participate in speech situations requiring mandatory individual performances is that the teachers in the Warm Springs grammar school modify their teaching approach whenever possible to accommodate, in a somewhat ad hoc fashion, what they refer to as the Indian students' "shyness." In the first grade it is not easy to make very many modifications because of what teachers perceive as a close relationship between the material being taught and the methods used to teach it. There is some feeling, also, that the teaching methods that can be effective with children at age six are somewhat limited in range. However, as students go up through the grades, there is an increasing tendency for teachers to work with the notion, not always a correct one, that given the same body of material there are a number of different ways of "presenting" it, or in the terms being used here, a range of different participant structures and modes of communication (e.g., talking versus reading and writing) that can be used.

Even so, at the first-grade level there are already some changes made to accommodate the Indian children that are notable. When comparing the Indian first-grade classes with the non-Indian first-grade classes, one finds very few word games being used that involve students' giving directions to one another. And even more conspicuous in Indian classes is the absence of the ubiquitous "show and tell" or "sharing," through which students learn to get up in front of the class, standing where the teacher stands, and presenting, as the teacher might, a monologue relating an experience or describing a treasured object that is supposed to be of interest to the rest of the class. When asked whether this activity was used in the classroom, one teacher explained that she had previously used it, but so few children ever volunteered to "share" that she finally discontinued it.

By the time the students reach the sixth grade, the range of modes and settings for communication has increased a great deal, and the opportunity for elimination of some participant structures in preference to others is used by the teachers. As one sixth-grade teacher put it, "I spend as little time in front of the class as possible." In comparison with non-Indian classes, Indian classes have a relatively greater number of group "projects." Thus, while non-Indian students are learning about South American history through reading texts and answering the teacher's questions, Indian students are doing group-planned and -executed murals depicting a particular stage in Latin American history; while non-Indian students are reading science texts and answering questions about how electricity is generated, Indian students are doing group-run experiments with batteries and motors.

Similarly, in the Indian classes "reports" given by individual students are almost nonexistent, but are a typical means in non-Indian classes for demonstrating knowledge through verbal performance. And finally, while in non-Indian classes students are given opportunities to ask the teacher questions in front of the class, and do so, Indian students are given fewer opportunities for this because when they do have the opportunity, they don't use it. Rather, the teacher of Indians allows more periods in which she is available for individual students to approach her alone and ask their questions where no one else can hear them.

The teachers who make these adjustments, and not all do, are sensitive to the inclinations of their students and want to teach them through means to which they most readily adapt. However, by doing so they are avoiding teaching the Indian children how to communicate in precisely the contexts in which they are least able but most need to learn if they are to "do well in school." The teachers handicap themselves by setting up performance situations for the students in which they are least able to arrive at the evaluations of individual competence upon which they rely for feedback to establish at what level they must begin to teach. And it is not at all clear that students do acquire the same information through one form of communication as they do through another. Thus these manipulations of communication settings and participant structures, which are intended to transmit knowledge to the students creatively through the means to which they are most adjusted, may actually be causing the students to miss completely types of information their later high school teachers will assume they picked up in grammar school.

The consequences of this partial adaptation to Indian modes of communication become apparent when the Indian students join the non-Indian students at the junior and senior high school levels. Here, where the Indian students are outnumbered five to one, there is no manipulation and selection of communication settings to suit the inclinations of the Indians. Here the teachers complain that the Indian students never talk in class, and never ask questions, and everyone wonders why.

It does not necessarily follow from this that these most creative teachers at the grade school level should stop what they are doing. Perhaps it should be the teachers at the junior and senior high school levels who make similar adaptations. Which of these occurs (or possibly there are *other* alternatives) depends on the goals the Indian community has for its youngsters, an issue that will be briefly considered in the conclusion of the paper.

Conditions for Speech Use in the Warm Springs Indian Community

To understand why the Warm Springs Indian children speak out readily under some social conditions but fail to do so under others, it is necessary to examine the sociolinguistic assumptions determining the conditions for communicative performances, particularly those involving explicit demonstrations of knowledge or skill, in the Indian community. It will be possible here to deal with only some of the many aspects of communication involved. Attention will focus first on the social structuring of learning situations or contexts in which knowledge and skills are communicated to children in Indian homes. Then some consideration will be given to the underlying rules or conditions for participation in the community-wide social events that preschool children, as well as older children, learn through attending such events with their families.

The Indian child's preschool and outside-school enculturation at home differs from that of many non-Indian or white middle-class children's in that a good deal of the responsibility for the care and training of children is assumed by persons other than the parents of the children. In many homes the oldest children, particularly if they are girls, assume these responsibilities when the parents are at home, as well as when they are not. Frequently, also, grandparents, uncles, and aunts assume the full-time responsibility for care and instruction of children. Children thus become accustomed to interacting with and following the instructions and orders of a greater number of people than is the case with non-Indian children. Equally important is the fact that all of the people with whom Indian children form such reciprocal nurturing and learning relationships are kinsmen. Indian children are rarely, if ever, taken care of by "baby-sitters" from outside the family. Most of their playmates before beginning school are their siblings and cousins, and these peer relationships typically continue to be the strongest bonds of friendship through school and adult life, later providing a basis for reciprocal aid in times of need, and companionship in many social activities.

Indian children are deliberately taught skills around the home (for girls) and in the outdoors (for boys) at an earlier age than many middle-class non-Indian children. Girls, for example, learn to cook some foods before they are eight, and by this age may be fully competent in cleaning a house without any aid or supervision from adults.

There are other areas of competence in which Indian children are expected to be proficient at earlier ages than non-Indian children, for which the means of enculturation or socialization are less visible and clear-cut. While still in grammar school, at the age of ten or eleven, some children are considered capable of spending afternoons and evenings in the company of only other children, without the necessity of accounting for their whereabouts or asking permission to do whatever specific activity is involved. At this same age many are also considered capable of deciding where they want to live, and for what reasons one residence is preferable to another. They may spend weeks or months at a time living with one relative or another, until it is no longer possible to say that they live in any particular household.

In general, then, Warm Springs Indian children become accustomed to self-determination of action, accompanied by very little disciplinary control from older relatives, at much younger ages than middle-class white children do.

In the context of the household, learning takes place through several sorts of somewhat different processes. First of all, children are present at many adult interactions as silent but attentive observers. While it is not yet clear how adult activities in which children are not full participants are distinguished from those in which children may participate fully, and from those for which they are not allowed to be present at all, there are clearly marked differences. What is most remarkable, however, is that there are many adult conversations to which children pay a great deal of silent, patient attention. This contrasts sharply with the behavior of non-Indian children, who show little patience in similar circumstances, desiring either to become a full participant through verbal interaction, or to become completely involved in some other activity.

There is some evidence that this silent listening and watching was, in the Warm Springs culture, traditionally the first step in learning skills of a fairly complex nature. For example, older women reminisce about being required to watch their elder relatives tan hides when they were very young, rather than being allowed to play. And certainly the winter evening events of myth-telling, which provided Indian children with their first explicitly taught moral lessons, involved them as listening participants rather than as speakers.

A second type of learning involves the segmentation of a task by an older relative, and the partial carrying out of the task or one of its segments by the child. In household tasks, for example, a child is given a very simple portion of a job (e.g., in cleaning a room the child may begin by helping move the furniture) and works in cooperation with and under the supervision of an older relative. Such activities involve a small amount of verbal instruction or direction from the older relative, and allow for questions on the part of the child. Gradually the child comes to learn all of the skills involved in a particular process, consistently under the supervision of an older relative who works along with him.

This mode of instruction is not unique to the Warm Springs Indians, of course; many non-Indian parents use similar methods. However, there are aspects of this type of instruction that differ from its use among non-Indians. First of all, when it occurs among the Indians it is likely to be preceded by the long periods of observation just described. The absence of such observation among non-Indian children is perhaps replaced by elaborate verbal instructions outlining the full scope of a task before the child attempts any part of it.

A second way in which this type of instruction among the Warm Springs Indians differs from that of non-Indians is the absence of "testing" of the child's skill by the instructing kinsman before the child exercises the skill unsupervised. Although it is not yet clear how this works in a diversity of situations, it appears that in many areas of skill, the child takes it upon himself to test the skill unsupervised and alone, without other people around. In this way, if he is unsuccessful his failure is not seen by others. If he is successful, he can show the results of his success to those by whom he has been taught, whether it be in the form of a deer that has been shot, a hide tanned, a piece of beadwork completed, or a dinner on the table when the adults come home from work.

Again there is some evidence that this type of private individual's testing of competency, followed by public demonstration only when competency is fully developed and certain, has been traditional in the Warm Springs Indian culture. The most dramatic examples of this come from the processes of acquisition of religious and ritual knowledge. In the vision quests through which adolescents, or children of even younger ages, acquired spirit power, individuals spent long periods in isolated mountain areas from which they were expected to emerge with skills they had not previously demonstrated. While some of these abilities were not fully revealed until later in life, the child was expected to be able to relate some experience of a supernatural nature that would prove that he had, in fact, been visited by a spirit. Along the same lines, individuals until very recently received and learned, through dreams and visions, ritual songs that they would sing for the first time in full and completed form in the presence of others.

The contexts described here in which learning takes place can be perceived as an idealized sequence of three steps: (1) observation, which of course includes listening; (2) supervised participation; and (3) private, self-initiated self-testing. It is not the case that all acquisition of skills proceed through such phases, however, but rather only some of these skills that Indian adults consciously and deliberately teach their children, and which the children consciously try to learn. Those which are learned through less deliberate means must to some extent invoke similar structuring, but it is difficult to determine to what extent.

The use of speech in the process is notably minimal. Verbal directions or instructions are few, being confined to corrections and question-answering. Nor does the final demonstration of skill particularly involve verbal performance, since the validation of skill so often involves display of some material evidence or non-verbal physical expression.

This process of Indian acquisition of competence may help to explain, in part, Indian children's reluctance to speak in front of their classmates. In the classroom, the processes of *acquisition* of knowledge and *demonstration* of knowledge are collapsed into the single act of answering questions or reciting when called upon to do so by the teacher, particularly in the lower grades. Here the assumption is that one will learn, and learn more effectively, through making mistakes in front of others. The Indian children have no opportunity to observe others performing successfully before they attempt it, except for their fellow classmates who precede them and are themselves uninitiated. They have no opportunity to "practice," and to decide for themselves when they know enough to demonstrate their knowledge; rather, their performances are determined by the teacher. And finally, their only channel for communicating competency is verbal, rather than non-verbal.

Turning now from learning processes in the home to learning experiences outside the home, in social and ritual activities involving community members other than kinsmen, there is again considerable evidence that Indian children's understanding of when and how one participates and performs individually, and thus demonstrates or communicates competence, differs considerably from what is expected of them in the classroom.

Children of all ages are brought to every sort of community-wide social event sponsored by Indians (as distinct from those sponsored by non-Indians). There is rarely, if ever, such a thing as an Indian community event that is attended by adults only. At many events children participate in only certain roles, but this is true of everyone. Sociospatially and behaviorally, children must always participate minimally, as do all others, in sitting quietly and attentively alongside their elders.

One of the social features that characterizes social events that are not explicitly kin group affairs, including activities like political general councils, social dinners, and worship dances, is that they are open to participation by all members of the Warm Springs Indian community. While different types of activities are more heavily attended by certain Indians rather than others, and fairly consistently sponsored and arranged by certain individuals, it is always clear that everyone is invited, both by community knowledge of this fact and by explicit announcements on posters placed in areas where most people pass through at one time or another in their day-to-day activities.

A second feature of such activities is that there is usually no one person directing the activity verbally, or signaling changes from one phase to another. Instead the structure is determined either by a set procedure or ritual, or there is a group of people who in various complementary ways provide such cuing and direction. Nor are there any participant roles that can be filled or are filled by only one person. In dancing, singing, and drumming there are no soloists, and where there are performers who begin a sequence, and are then joined by others, more than one performer takes a turn at such initiations. The speaking roles are handled similarly. In contexts where speeches are appropriate, it is made clear that anyone who wants to may "say a few words." The same holds true for political meetings, where the answerer to a question is not necessarily one who is on a panel or council, but rather the person who feels he is qualified, by his knowledge of a subject, to answer. In all situations thus allowing for anyone who wants to to speak, no time limit is set, so that the talking continues until everyone who wants to has had the opportunity to do so.

This does not mean that there are never any "leaders" in Indian social activities, but rather that leadership takes quite a different form from that in many non-Indian cultural contexts. Among the people of Warm Springs, a person is not a leader by virtue of holding a particular position, even in the case of members of the tribal council and administration. Rather, he is a leader because he has demonstrated ability in some sphere and activity, and many individuals choose to follow his suggestions because they have independently each decided they are good ones. If, for example, an individual plans and announces an activity, but few people offer to help him carry it out or attend it, then that is an indication that the organizer is not a respected leader in the community at the present time. And the likelihood that he will repeat his efforts in the near future is reduced considerably.

This type of "leadership," present today among the people of Warm Springs, is reminiscent of that which was described by Hoebel for the Comanche chiefs:

> In matters of daily routine, such as camp moving, he merely made the decisions himself, announcing them through a camp crier. Anyone who did not like his decision simply ignored it. If in time a good many people ignored his announcements and preferred to stay behind with some other man of influence, or perhaps to move in another direction with that man, the chief

> had then lost his following. He was no longer chief, and another had quietly superseded him. (Hoebel 1954: 132)

A final feature of Indian social activities, which should be recognized from what has already been said, is that all who do attend an activity may participate in at least some of the various forms participation takes for the given activity, rather than there being a distinction made between participants or performers and audience. At many Indian gatherings, particularly those attended by older people, this aspect of the situation is reflected in its sociospatial arrangement: People are seated in such a way that all present are facing one another, usually in an approximation of a square, and the focus of activity is either along one side of the square, or in its center, or a combination of the two.

And each individual chooses the degree of his participation. No one, other than, perhaps, those who set up the event, is committed to being present beforehand, and all participating roles beyond those of sitting and observing are determined by the individual at the point at which he decides to participate, rather than being prescheduled.

In summary, the Indian social activities to which children are early exposed outside the home generally have the following properties: (1) they are community-wide, in the sense that they are open to all Warm Springs Indians; (2) there is no single individual directing and controlling all activity, and, to the extent that there are "leaders," their leadership is based on the choice to follow made by each person; (3) participation in some form is accessible to everyone who attends. No one need be exclusively an observer or audience, and there is consequently no sharp distinction between audience and performer. And each individual chooses for himself the degree of his participation during the activity.

If one now compares the social conditions for verbal participation in the classroom with the conditions underlying many Indian events in which children participate, a number of differences emerge.

First of all, classroom activities are not community-wide, and, more importantly, the participants in the activity are not drawn just from the Indian community. The teacher, as a non-Indian, is an outsider and a stranger to these events. In addition, by virtue of her role as teacher, she structurally separates herself from the rest of the participants, her students. She places herself outside the interaction and activity of the students. This encourages their cultural perceptions of themselves as the relevant community, in opposition to the teacher, perhaps much as they see themselves in opposition to other communities, and on a smaller scale, as one team is in opposition to another. In other words, on the basis of the Indians' social experiences, one is either a part of a group or outside it. The notion of a single individual being structurally set apart from all others, in anything other than an observer role, and yet still a part of the group organization, is one that children probably encounter for the first time in school, and continue to experience only in non-Indian-derived activities (e.g., in bureaucratic, hierarchically structured occupations). This helps to explain why Indian students show so little interest in initiating interaction with the teacher in activities involving other students.

Second, in contrast to Indian activities where many people are involved in determining the development and structure of an event, there is only one single authority directing everything in the classroom, namely the teacher. And the teacher is not the controller or leader by virtue of the individual students' choices to follow her, as in the case in Indian social activities, but rather by virtue of her occupation of the role of teacher. This difference helps to account for the Indian children's frequent indifference to the directions, orders, and requests for compliance with classroom social rules that the teacher issues.

Third, it is not the case in the classroom that all students may participate in any given activity, as in Indian community activities. Nor are they given the opportunity to choose the degree of their participation, which, on the basis of evidence discussed earlier, would in Indian contexts be based on the individual's having already ascertained in private that he was capable of successful verbal communication of competence. Again these choices belong to the teacher.

Conclusion

In summary, Indian children fail to participate verbally in classroom interaction because the social conditions for participation to which they have become accustomed in the Indian community are lacking. The absence of these appropriate social conditions for communicative performances affects the most common and everyday speech acts that occur in the classroom. If the Indian child fails to follow an order or answer a question, it may not be because he doesn't understand the linguistic structure of the imperative and the interrogative, but rather because he does not share the non-Indian's assumption in such contexts that use of these syntactic forms by definition implies an automatic and immediate response from the person to whom they were addressed. For these assumptions are sociolinguistic assumptions that are not shared by the Indians.

Educators cannot assume that because Indian children (or any children from cultural backgrounds other than those that are implicit in American classrooms) speak English, or are taught it in the schools, that they have also assimilated all of the sociolinguistic rules underlying interaction in classrooms and other non-Indian social situations where English is spoken. To the extent that existing cultural variation in sociolinguistic patterning that is not recognized by the schools results in learning difficulties and feelings of inferiority for some children, changes in the structuring of classroom learning situations are needed. Ultimately the nature of the changes to be made should be determined by the educational goals of the particular communities where this type of problem exists.

If, as may be the case on the Warm Springs Indian Reservation, the people's main concern is to enable Indian children to compete successfully with non-Indians, and to have the *choice* of access to the modes of interaction and life styles of non-Indians, then there should be a conscious effort made in the schools to teach the children the modes for appropriate verbal participation that prevail in non-Indian classrooms. Thus, rather than shifting away from situations in which children perform individually in front of their peers only with great reluctance, conscious emphasis on and encouragement of participation in such situations should be carried out in the early grades.

If, on the other hand, as also may be the case in Warm Springs (there are strong differences of opinion here on this issue that complicate the teachers' actions), there is strong feeling in the community that is culturally distinctive modes of communication should be maintained and encouraged to flourish rather than be eliminated through our educational system's apparent pursuit of cultural uniformity throughout the country, then quite a different shift in the orientation of classroom modes of instruction would be called for. Here an effort to adapt the community's conditions for appropriate speech usage to the classroom should be made, not in an ad hoc and partial fashion as at Warm Springs, but consistently and systematically. And where the classroom situation is one in which children of more than one cultural background come together, efforts should be made to allow for a complementary diversity in the modes of communication through which learning and measurement of "success" take place.

REFERENCES

Berry, Brewton (1969). *The Education of American Indians: A Survey of the Literature*. Prepared for the Special Subcommittee on Indian Education of the Committee on Labor and Public Welfare, United States Senate. Washington, DC: Government Printing Office.

Cazden, Courtney B., and John, Vera P. (1968). Learning in American Indian Children. In *Styles of Learning among American Indians: An Outline for Research*. Washington, DC: Center for Applied Linguistics.

Hoebel, E. Adamson (1954). *The Law of Primitive Man*. Cambridge, Mass.: Harvard University Press.

Hymes, Dell 2001 On Communicative Competence. In A. Duranti (ed.), *Linguistic Anthropology: A Reader.* Malden, MA: Blackwell, pp. 53–73; First published in Renira Huxley and Elizabeth Ingram (eds.), *Mechanisms of Language Development.* London: Centre for Advanced Study in the Developmental Science and CIBA Foundation. (Article first appeared 1967.)

Wax, Murray, Wax, Rosalie, and Dumont, Robert V., Jr. (1964). *Formal Education in an American Indian Community.* Social Problems Monograph No. 1. Kalamazoo, Mich.: Society for the Study of Social Problems.

Wolcott, Harry (1967). *A Kwakiutl Village and School.* New York: Holt, Rinehart, and Winston.

Zentner, Henry (1960). *Oregon State College Warm Springs Research Project.* Vol. II: *Education.* Corvallis: Oregon State College.

STUDY QUESTIONS

1 What is the process of Warm Springs children's acquisition of communicative competence as described by Philips? How does it differ from the modes of interaction experienced by the same children in the classroom?
2 What does Philips mean by "participant structure"? How does this concept help make sense of the ways in which children are expected to be involved in literacy tasks?
3 Why did Warm Springs Indian children speak out more readily under some circumstances than under others?
4 How is silence used and interpreted in the situations described in this chapter? Identify situations that you have experienced in which silence was or could have been explained in culturally different ways?
5 How do the themes and issues discussed in this chapter relate to the themes and issues discussed in Chapter 4 (how respect is communicated in different speech communities), Chapter 7 (formality), and Chapter 12 (language socialization)?

14

What No Bedtime Story Means: Narrative Skills at Home and School

Shirley Brice Heath

In the preface to *Introduction to S/Z*, Roland Barthes's work on ways in which readers read, Richard Howard writes: "We require an education in literature … in order to discover that *what we have assumed* – with the complicity of our teachers – *was nature is in fact culture, that what was given is no more than a way of taking*" (emphasis not in the original; Howard 1974: ix).[1] This statement reminds us that the *culture* children learn as they grow up is, in fact, "ways of taking" meaning from the environment around them. The means of making sense from books and relating their contents to knowledge about the real world is but one "way of taking" that is often interpreted as "natural" rather than learned. The quote also reminds us that teachers (and researchers alike) have not recognized that ways of taking from books are as much a part of learned behavior as are ways of eating, sitting, playing games, and building houses.

As school-oriented parents and their children interact in the preschool years, adults give their children, through modeling and specific instruction, ways of taking from books that seem natural in school and in numerous institutional settings such as banks, post offices, businesses, and government offices. These *mainstream* ways exist in societies around the world that rely on formal educational systems to prepare children for participation in settings involving literacy. In some communities these ways of schools and institutions are very similar to the ways learned at home; in other communities the ways of school are merely an overlay on the home-taught ways and may be in conflict with them.[2]

Yet little is actually known about what goes on in storyreading and other literacy-related interactions between adults and preschoolers in communities around the world. Specifically, though there are numerous diary accounts and experimental studies of the preschool reading experiences of mainstream middle-class children, we know little about the specific literacy features of the environment upon which the school expects to draw. Just how does what is frequently termed "the literate tradition" envelop the child in knowledge about interrelationships between oral and written language,

For permission to publish copyright material in this book, grateful acknowledgment is made to: S. B. Heath (1982), "What No Bedtime Story Means: Narrative Skills at Home and School," *Language in Society* 11(1): 49–76.

between knowing something and knowing ways of labeling and displaying it? We have even less information about the variety of ways children from *nonmainstream* homes learn about reading, writing, and using oral language to display knowledge in their preschool environment. The general view has been that whatever it is that mainstream school-oriented homes have, these other homes do not have it; thus these children are not from the literate tradition and are not likely to succeed in school.

A key concept for the empirical study of ways of taking meaning from written sources across communities is that of *literacy events*: occasions in which written language is integral to the nature of participants' interactions and their interpretive processes and strategies. Familiar literacy events for mainstream preschoolers are bedtime stories; reading cereal boxes, stop signs, and television ads; and interpreting instructions for commercial games and toys. In such literacy events, participants follow socially established rules for verbalizing what they know from and about the written material. Each community has rules for socially interacting and sharing knowledge in literacy events.

This paper briefly summarizes the ways of taking from printed stories families teach their preschoolers in a cluster of mainstream school-oriented neighborhoods of a city in the southeastern region of the United States. I then describe two quite different ways of taking used in the homes of two English-speaking communities in the same region that do not follow the school-expected patterns of bookreading and reinforcement of these patterns in oral storytelling. Two assumptions underlie this paper and are treated in detail in the ethnography of these communities (Heath 1983): (1) Each community's ways of taking from the printed word and using this knowledge are interdependent with the ways children learn to talk in their social interactions with caregivers; (2) there is little or no validity to the time-honored dichotomy of "the literate tradition" and "the oral tradition." This paper suggests a frame of reference for both the community patterns and the paths of development children in different communities follow in their literacy orientations.

Mainstream School-oriented Bookreading

Children growing up in mainstream communities are expected to develop habits and values that attest to their membership in a "literate society." Children learn certain customs, beliefs, and skills in early enculturation experiences with written materials: The bedtime story is a major literacy event that helps set patterns of behavior that reoccur repeatedly through the life of mainstream children and adults.

In both popular and scholarly literature, the bedtime story is widely accepted as a given – a natural way for parents to interact with their child at bedtime. Commercial publishing houses, television advertising, and children's magazines make much of this familiar ritual, and many of their sales pitches are based on the assumption that in spite of the intrusion of television into many patterns of interaction between parents and children, this ritual remains. Few parents are fully conscious of what bedtime storyreading means as preparation for the kinds of learning and displays of knowledge expected in school. Ninio and Bruner (1978), in their longitudinal study of one mainstream middle-class mother–infant dyad in joint picturebook reading, strongly suggest a universal role of bookreading in the achievement of labeling by children.

In a series of "reading cycles," mother and child alternate turns in a dialogue: The mother directs the child's attention to the book and/or asks what-questions and/or labels items on the page. The items to which the what-questions are directed and labels given are two-dimensional representations of three-dimensional objects, so that the child has to resolve the conflict between perceiving these as two-dimensional objects and as representations of a three-dimensional visual setting. The child does so "by assigning a privileged, autonomous status to pictures as visual objects" (1978: 5). The arbitrariness of the picture, its decontextualization, and its existence as something that cannot be grasped and manipulated like its "real" counterparts are learned through the routines of structured interactional dialogue in which mother and child take turns playing a labeling game. In a "scaffolding" dialogue (cf. Cazden 1979), the mother points and asks "What is *x*?" and the child vocalizes and/or gives a nonverbal signal of attention. The mother then provides verbal feedback and a label. Before the age of 2, the child is socialized into the initiation–reply–evaluation sequences repeatedly described as the central structural feature of classroom lessons (e.g., Sinclair and Coulthard 1975; Griffin and Humphry 1978; Mehan 1979). Teachers ask their students questions to which the answers are prespecified in the mind of the teacher. Students respond, and teachers provide feedback, usually in the form of an evaluation. Training in ways of responding to this pattern begins very early in the labeling activities of mainstream parents and children.

Maintown ways

This patterning of "incipient literacy" (Scollon and Scollon 1979) is similar in many ways to that of the families of fifteen primary-level schoolteachers in Maintown, a cluster of middle-class neighborhoods in a city of the Piedmont Carolinas. These families (all of whom identify themselves as "typical," "middle-class," or "mainstream") had preschool children, and the mother in each family was either teaching in local public schools at the time of the study (early 1970s) or had taught in the academic year preceding participation in the study. Through a research dyad approach, using teacher-mothers as researchers with the ethnographer, the teacher-mothers audiorecorded their children's interactions in their primary network – mothers, fathers, grandparents, maids, siblings, and frequent visitors to the home. Children were expected to learn the following rules in literacy events in these nuclear households:

1 As early as 6 months of age, children *give attention to books and information derived from books*. Their rooms contain bookcases and are decorated with murals, bedspreads, mobiles, and stuffed animals that represent characters found in books. Even when these characters have their origin in television programs, adults also provide books that either repeat or extend the characters' activities on television.
2 Children, from the age of 6 months, *acknowledge questions about books*. Adults expand nonverbal responses and vocalizations from infants into fully formed grammatical sentences. When children begin to verbalize about the contents of books, adults extend their questions from simple requests for labels ("What's that?" "Who's that?") to ask about the attributes of these items ("What does the doggie say?" "What color is the ball?")
3 From the time they start to talk, children *respond to conversational allusions to the content of books; they act as question-answerers who have a knowledge of books*. For example, a fuzzy black dog on the street is likened by an adult to Blackie in a child's book: "Look, there's a Blackie. Do you think *he's* looking for a boy?" Adults strive to maintain with children a running commentary on any event or object that can be book-related, thus modeling for them the extension of familiar items and events from books to new situational contexts.
4 Beyond 2 years of age, children *use their knowledge of what books do to legitimate their departures from "truth."* Adults encourage and reward "book talk," even when it is not directly relevant to an ongoing conversation. Children are allowed to suspend reality, to tell stories that are not true, to ascribe fiction-like features to everyday objects.
5 Preschool children *accept book and book-related activities as entertainment*. When preschoolers are "captive audiences" (e.g., waiting in a doctor's office, putting a toy together, or preparing for bed), adults reach for books. If there are no books present, they talk about other objects as though they were pictures in books. For example, adults point to items and ask children to name, describe, and compare them to familiar objects in their environment. Adults often ask children to state their likes or dislikes, their view of events, etc., at the end of the captive-audience period. These

affective questions often take place while the next activity is already under way (e.g., moving toward the doctor's office, putting the new toy away, or being tucked into bed), and adults do not insist on answers.

6 Preschoolers *announce their own factual and fictive narratives* unless they are given in response to direct adult elicitation. Adults judge as most acceptable those narratives that open by orienting the listener to setting and main character. Narratives that are fictional are usually marked by formulaic openings, a particular prosody, or the borrowing of episodes in storybooks.

7 When children are about 3 years old, adults discourage the highly interactive participative role in bookreading children have hitherto played and children *listen and wait as an audience*. No longer does either adult or child repeatedly break into the story with questions and comments. Instead, children must listen, store what they hear, and, on cue from the adult, answer a question. Thus children begin to formulate "practice" questions as they wait for the break and the expected formulaic questions from the adult. It is at this stage that children often choose to "read" to adults rather than be read to.

A pervasive pattern of all these features is the authority that books and book-related activities have in the lives of both the preschoolers and members of their primary network. Any initiation of a literacy event by a preschooler makes an interruption, an untruth, a diverting of attention from the matter at hand (whether it be an uneaten plate of food, a messy room, or an avoidance of going to bed) acceptable. Adults jump at openings their children give them for pursuing talk about books and reading.

In this study, writing was found to be somewhat less acceptable as an "anytime activity," since adults have rigid rules about times, places, and materials for writing. The only restrictions on bookreading concern taking good care of books: They should not be wet, torn, drawn on, or lost. In their talk to children about books and in their explanations of why they buy children's books, adults link school success to "learning to love books," "learning what books can do for you," and "learning to entertain yourself and to work independently." Many of the adults also openly expressed a fascination with children's books "nowadays." They generally judged them as more diverse, wide-ranging, challenging, and exciting than books they had as children.

The mainstream pattern

A close look at the way bedtime-story routines in Maintown taught children how to take meaning from books raises a heavy sense of the familiar in all of us who have acquired mainstream habits and values. Throughout a lifetime, any school-successful individual moves through the same processes described above thousands of times. Reading for comprehension involves an internal replaying of the same types of questions adults ask children about bedtime stories. We seek *what-explanations*, asking what the topic is, establishing it as predictable and recognizing it in new situational contexts by classifying and categorizing it in our minds with other phenomena. The what-explanation is replayed in learning to pick out topic sentences, write outlines, and answer standardized tests that ask for the correct titles to stories, and so on. In learning to read in school, children move through a sequence of skills designed to teach what-explanations. There is a tight linear order of instruction that recapitulates the bedtime-story pattern of breaking down the story into small bits of information and teaching children to handle sets of related skills in isolated sequential hierarchies.

In each individual reading episode in the primary years of schooling, children must move through what-explanations before they can provide *reason-explanations* or *affective commentaries*. Questions about why a particular event occurred or why a specific action was right or wrong come at the end of primary-level reading lessons, just as they come at the end of bedtime stories. Throughout the primary-grade levels, what-explanations predominate, reason-explanations come with increasing frequency in the upper grades, and affective comments most often come in the extra-credit portions of the reading workbook or at the end of the list of suggested activities in textbooks across grade levels. This sequence characterizes the total school career. Highschool freshmen who are judged poor in compositional and reading skills spend most of their time on what-explanations and practice in advanced versions of bedtime-story questions and answers. They are given little or no chance to use reason-giving explanations or assessments of the actions of stories. Reason-explanations result in configurational rather than hierarchical skills, are not predictable, and thus do not present content with a high degree of redundancy. Reason-giving explanations tend to rely on detailed knowledge of a specific domain. This detail is often unpredictable to teachers, and is not as highly valued as is knowledge that covers a particular area of knowledge with less detail but offers opportunity for extending the knowledge to larger and related concerns. For example, a primary-level student whose father owns a turkey farm may respond with reason-explanations to a story about a turkey. His knowledge is intensive and covers details perhaps not known to the teacher and not judged as relevant to the story. The knowledge is unpredictable and questions about it do not continue to repeat the common core of content knowledge of the story. Thus such configured knowledge is encouraged only for the "extras" of reading – an extra-credit oral report or a creative picture and story about turkeys. This kind of knowledge is allowed to be used once the hierarchical what-explanations have been mastered and displayed in a particular situation and, in the course of one's academic career, only when one has shown full mastery of the hierarchical skills and subsets of related skills that underlie what-explanations. Thus reliable and successful participation in the ways of taking from books that teachers view as natural must, in the usual school way of doing things, precede other ways of taking from books.

These various ways of taking are sometimes referred to as "cognitive styles" or "learning styles." It is generally accepted in the research literature that they are influenced by early socialization experiences and correlated with such features of the society in which the child is reared as social organization, reliance on authority, male-female roles, and so on. These styles are often seen as two contrasting types, most frequently termed "field independent–field dependent" (Witkin et al. 1966) or "analytic-relational" (Kagan, Sigel, and Moss 1963; Cohen 1968, 1969, 1971). The analytic/field-independent style is generally presented as that which correlates positively with high achievement and general academic and social success in school. Several studies discuss ways in which this style is played out in school – in preferred ways of responding to pictures and written text and selecting from among a choice of answers to test items.

Yet we know little about how behaviors associated with either of the dichotomized cognitive styles (field-dependent/relational and field-independent/analytic) were learned in early patterns of socialization. To be sure, there are vast individual differences that may cause an individual to behave so as to be categorized as having one or the other of these learning styles. But much of the literature on learning styles suggests that a preference for one or the other is learned in the social group in which the child is reared and in connection with other ways of behaving found in that culture. But how is a child socialized into an analytic/field-independent style? What kinds of interactions does he enter into with his parents and the stimuli of his environment that contribute to the development of such a style of learning? How do these interactions mold selective attention practices such as "sensitivity to parts of objects," "awareness of obscure, abstract, nonobvious features," and identification of "abstractions based on the features of items" (Cohen 1969: 844–5)? Since the predominant stimuli used in school to judge the presence and extent of these selective attention practices are written materials, it is clear that the literacy orientation of preschool children is central to these questions.

The foregoing descriptions of how Maintown parents socialize their children into a literacy orientation fit closely those provided by Scollon and Scollon for their own child, Rachel. Through similar practices, Rachel was "literate before she learned to read" (1979: 6). She knew, before the age of 2, how to focus on a book and not on herself. Even when she told a story about herself, she moved herself out of the text and saw herself as author, as someone different from the central character of her story. She learned to pay close attention to the parts of objects, to name them, and to provide a running commentary on features of her environment. She learned to manipulate the contexts of items, her own activities, and language to achieve book-like, decontextualized, repeatable effects (such as puns). Many references in her talk were from written sources; others were modeled on stories and questions about these stories. The substance of her knowledge, as well as her ways of framing knowledge orally, derived from her familiarity with books and bookreading. No doubt this development began by labeling in the dialogue cycles of reading (Ninio and Bruner 1978), and it will continue for Rachel in her preschool years along many of the same patterns described by Cochran Smith (1984) for a mainstream nursery school. There teacher and students negotiated storyreading through the scaffolding of teachers' questions and running commentaries that replayed the structure and sequence of storyreading learned in their mainstream homes.

Close analyses of how mainstream school-oriented children come to learn to take from books at home suggest that such children learn not only how to take meaning from books, but also how to talk about it. In doing the latter, they repeatedly practice routines that parallel those of classroom interaction. By the time they enter school, they have had continuous experience as information givers; they have learned how to perform in those interactions that surround literate sources throughout school. They have had years of practice in interaction situations that are the heart of reading – both learning to read and reading to learn in school. They have developed habits of performing that enable them to run through the hierarchy of preferred knowledge about a literate source and the appropriate sequence of skills to be displayed in showing knowledge of a subject. They have developed ways of decontextualizing and surrounding with explanatory prose the knowledge gained from selective attention to objects.

They have learned to listen, waiting for the appropriate cue that signals it is their turn to show off this knowledge. They have learned the rules for getting certain services from parents (or teachers) in the reading interaction (Merritt 1979). In nursery school, they continue to practice these interaction patterns in a group rather than in a dyadic situation. There they learn additional signals and behaviors necessary for getting a turn in a group and for responding to a central reader and to a set of centrally defined reading tasks. In short, most of their waking hours during the preschool years have enculturated them into: (1) all those habits associated with what-explanations, (2) selective attention to items of the written text, *and* (3) appropriate interactional styles for orally displaying all the know-how of their literate orientation to the environment. This learning has been finely tuned and its habits are highly interdependent. Patterns of behaviors learned in one setting or at one stage reappear again and again as these children learn to use oral and written language in literacy events and to bring their knowledge to bear in school-acceptable ways.

Alternative Patterns of Literacy Events

But what corresponds to the mainstream pattern of learning in communities that do not have this finely tuned, consistent, repetitive, and continuous pattern of training? Are there ways of behaving that achieve other social and cognitive aims in other sociocultural groups?

The data below are summarized from an ethnography of two communities – Roadville and Trackton – located only a few miles from Maintown's neighborhoods in the Piedmont Carolinas. Roadville is a white working-class community of families steeped for four generations in the life of the textile mill. Trackton is a working-class black community whose older generations have been brought up on the land, either farming their own land or working for other landowners. However, in the past decade, they have found work in the textile mills. Children of both communities are unsuccessful in school; yet both communities place a high value on success in school, believing earnestly in the personal and vocational rewards school can bring and urging their children "to get ahead" by doing well in school. Both Roadville and Trackton are literate communities in the sense that the residents of each are able to read printed and written materials in their daily lives, and on occasion they produce written messages as part of the total pattern of communication in the community. In both communities, children go to school with certain expectancies of print and, in Trackton especially, children have a keen sense that reading is something one does to learn something one needs to know (Heath 1980). In both groups, residents turn from spoken to written uses of language and vice versa as the occasion demands, and the two modes of expression seem to supplement and reinforce each other. Nonetheless there are radical differences between the two communities in the ways in which children and adults interact in the preschool years; each of the two communities also differs from Maintown. Roadville and Trackton view children's learning of language from two radically different perspectives: In Trackton, children "learn to talk"; in Roadville, adults "teach them how to talk."

Roadville

In Roadville, babies are brought home from the hospital to rooms decorated with colorful, mechanical, musical, and literacy-based stimuli. The walls are decorated with pictures based on nursery rhymes, and from an early age children are held and prompted to "see" the wall decorations. Adults recite nursery rhymes as they twirl the mobile made of nursery-rhyme characters. The items of the child's environment promote exploration of colors, shapes, and textures: a stuffed ball with sections of fabrics of different colors and textures is in the crib; stuffed animals vary in texture, size, and shape. Neighbors, friends from church, and relatives come to visit and talk to the baby and about him to those who will listen. The baby is fictionalized in the talk to him: "But this baby wants to go to sleep, doesn't he? Yes, see those little eyes gettin' heavy." As the child grows older, adults pounce on wordlike sounds and turn them into "words," repeating the "words," and expanding them into well-formed sentences. Before they can talk, children are introduced to visitors and prompted to provide all the expected politeness formulas, such as "Bye, bye," "Thank you," and so forth. As soon as they can talk, children are reminded about these formulas, and book or television characters known to be "polite" are involved as reinforcement.

In each Roadville home, preschoolers first have cloth books, featuring a single object on each page. They later acquire books that provide sounds, smells, and different textures or opportunities for practicing small motor skills (closing zippers, buttoning buttons, etc.). A typical collection for a 2-year-old consisted of a dozen or so books – eight featured either the alphabet or numbers; others were books of nursery rhymes, simplified Bible stories, or "real-life" stories about boys and girls (usually taking care of their pets or exploring a particular feature of their environment). Books based on Sesame Street characters were favorite gifts for 3- and 4-year-olds.

Reading and reading-related activities occur most frequently before naps or at bedtime in the evening. Occasionally an adult or older child will read to a fussy child while the mother prepares dinner or changes a bed. On weekends, fathers sometimes read with their children for brief periods of time, but they generally prefer to play games or play with the children's toys in their interactions. The following episode illustrates the language and social interactional aspects of these bedtime events; the episode takes place between Wendy (2;3 at the time of this episode) and Aunt Sue, who is putting her to bed.

> [Aunt Sue (AS) picks up book, while Wendy crawls about the floor, ostensibly looking for something]
>
> W: Uh uh
>
> AS: Wendy, we're gonna read, uh, read this story, come on, hop up here on this bed. [Wendy climbs up on the bed, sits on top of the pillow, and picks up her teddy bear. Aunt Sue opens book, points to puppy]

AS: Do you remember what this book is about? See the puppy? What does the puppy do? [Wendy plays with the bear, glancing occasionally at pages of the book, as Aunt Sue turns. Wendy seems to be waiting for something in the book]

AS: See the puppy?
[Aunt Sue points to the puppy in the book and looks at Wendy to see if she is watching]

W: Uh huh, yea, yes ma'am

AS: Puppy sees the ant, he's a li'l [Wendy drops the bear and turns to book] fellow. Can you see that ant? Puppy has a little ball.

W: Ant bite puppy [Wendy points to ant, pushing hard on the book]

AS: No, the ant won't bite the puppy, the [turns page] puppy wants to play with the ant, see? [Wendy tries to turn the page back; AS won't let her, and Wendy starts to squirm and fuss]

AS: Look here, here's someone else, the puppy [Wendy climbs down off the bed and gets another book]

W: Read this one

AS: Okay, you get back up here now. [Wendy gets back on bed]

AS: This book is your ABC book. See the A, look, here, on your spread, there's an A. You find the A. [The second book is a cloth book, old and tattered, and long a favorite of Wendy's. It features an apple on the cover, and its front page has an ABC block and ball. Through the book, there is a single item on each page, with a large representation of the first letter of the word commonly used to name the item. As AS turns the page, Wendy begins to crawl about on her quilt, which shows ABC blocks interspersed with balls and apples. Wendy points to each of the A's on the blanket and begins talking to herself. As reads the book, looks up, and sees Wendy pointing to the A's in her quilt]

AS: That's an A, can you find the A on your blanket?

W: There it is, this one, there's the hole too. [Pokes her finger through a place where the threads have broken in the quilting]

AS: [Points to ball in book] Stop that, find the ball, see, here's another ball.

This episode characterizes the early orientation of Roadville children to the written word. Bookreading time focuses on letters of the alphabet, numbers, names of basic items pictured in books, and simplified retellings of stories in the words of the adult. If the content or story plot seems too complicated for the child, the adult tells the story in short, simple sentences, frequently laced with requests that the child give what-explanations.

Wendy's favorite books are those with which she can participate; that is, those to which she can answer, provide labels, point to items, give animal sounds, and "read" the material back to anyone who will listen to her. She memorizes the passages and often knows when to turn the pages to show that she is "reading." She holds the book in her lap, starts at the beginning, and often reads the title – "Puppy."

Adults and children use either the title of the book (or phrases such as "the book about a puppy") to refer to reading material. When Wendy acquires a new book, adults introduce the book with phrases such as "This is a book about a duck, a little yellow duck. See the duck. Duck goes quack quack." On introducing a book, adults sometimes ask the child to recall when they have seen a real specimen of the one treated in the book: "Remember the duck on the College lake?" The child often shows no sign of linking the yellow fluffy duck in the book with the large brown and gray mallards on the lake, and the adult makes no effort to explain that two such disparate-looking objects go by the same name.

As Wendy grows older, she wants to "talk" during the stories and Bible stories, and carry out the participation she so enjoyed with the alphabet books. However, by the time she reaches $3\frac{1}{2}$, Wendy is restrained from such wide-ranging participation. When she interrupts, she is told: "Wendy, stop that, you be quiet when someone is reading to you" or "You listen; now sit still and be quiet." Often Wendy will immediately get down and run away into the next room, saying "No, no." When this happens, her father goes to get her, pats her bottom, and puts her down hard on the sofa beside him. "Now you're gonna learn to listen." During the third and fourth years, this pattern occurs more and more frequently; only when Wendy can capture an aunt who does not visit often does she bring out the old books and participate with them. Otherwise, parents, Aunt Sue, and other adults insist that she be read a story and that she "listen" quietly.

When Wendy and her parents watch television, eat cereal, visit the grocery store, or go to church, adults point out and talk about many types of written material. On the way to the grocery, Wendy (3;8) sits in the back seat, and when her mother stops at a corner, Wendy says, "Stop." Her mother says, "Yes, that's a stop sign." Wendy has, however, misread a yield sign as a stop. Her mother offers no explanation of what the actual message on the sign is, yet when she comes to the sign she stops to yield to an oncoming car. Her mother, when asked why she had not given Wendy the word "yield," said it was too hard, Wendy would not understand, and "It's not a word we use like *stop*."

Wendy recognized animal-cracker boxes as early as 10 months, and later, as her mother began buying other varieties, Wendy would see the box in the grocery store and yell, "Cook cook." Her mother would say, "Yes, those are cookies. Does Wendy want a cookie?" One day Wendy saw a new type of cracker box, and screeched, "Cook cook." Her father opened the box and gave Wendy a cracker and waited for her reaction. She started the "cookie," then took it to her mother, saying, "You eat." The mother joined in the game and said, "Don't you want your *cookie*?" Wendy said, "No cookie. You eat." "But Wendy, it's a cookie box, see?" and her mother pointed to the C of "crackers" on the box. Wendy paid no attention and ran off into another room.

In Roadville's literacy events, the rules for cooperative discourse around print are repeatedly practiced, coached, and rewarded in the preschool years. Adults in Roadville believe that instilling in children the proper use of words and understanding of the meaning of the written word are important for both their educational and religious success. Adults repeat aspects of the learning of literacy events they have known as children. In the words of one Roadville parent, "It was then that I began to learn ... when my daddy kept insisting I *read* it, *say* it right. It was then that I *did* right, in his view."

The path of development for such performance can be described in three overlapping stages. In the first, children are introduced to discrete bits and pieces of books – separate items, letters of the alphabet, shapes, colors, and commonly represented items in books for children (apple, baby, ball, etc.). The latter are usually decontextualized, and they are represented in two-dimensional, falt line drawings. During this stage, children must participate as predictable information givers and respond to questions that ask for specific and discrete bits of information about the written matter. In these literacy events, specific features of the two-dimensional items in books that are different from their real counterparts are not pointed out. A ball in a book is flat; a duck in a book is yellow and fluffy; trucks, cars, dogs, and trees talk in books. No mention is made of the fact that such features do not fit these objects in reality. Children are not encouraged to move their understanding of books into other situational contexts or to apply it in their general knowledge of the world about them.

In the second stage, adults demand an acceptance of the power of print to entertain, inform, and instruct. When Wendy could no longer participate by contributing her knowledge at any point in the literacy event, she learned to recognize bookreading as a performance. The adult exhibited the book to Wendy: she was to be entertained, to learn from the information conveyed in the material, and to remember the book's content for the sequential follow-up questioning, as opposed to ongoing cooperative, participatory questions.

In the third stage, Wendy was introduced to preschool workbooks that provided story information and was asked questions or provided exercises and games based on the content of the stories or pictures. Follow-the-number coloring books and preschool push-out-and-paste workbooks on shapes, colors, and letters of the alphabet reinforced repeatedly that the written word could be taken apart into small pieces and one item linked to another by following rules. She had practice in the linear, sequential nature of books: Begin at the beginning, stay in the lines for coloring, draw straight lines to link one item to another, write your answers on lines, keep your letters straight, match the cutout letter to diagrams of letter shapes.

The differences between Roadville and Maintown are substantial. Roadville adults do not extend either the content or the habits of literacy events beyond bookreading. They do not, upon seeing an item or event in the real world, remind children of a similar event in a book and launch a running commentary on similarities and differences. When a game is played or a chore done, adults do not use literate sources. Mothers cook without written recipes most of the time; if they use a recipe from a written source, they do so usually only after confirmation and alteration by friends who have tried the recipe. Directions to games are read, but not carefully followed, and they are not talked about in a series of questions and answers that try to establish their meaning. Instead, in the putting together of toys or the playing of games, the abilities or preferences of one party prevail. For example, if an adult knows how to put a toy together, he does so; he does not talk about the process, refer to the written material and "translate" for the child, or try to sequence steps so the child can do it.[3] Adults do not talk about the steps and procedures of how to do things; if a father wants his preschooler to learn to hold a miniature bat or throw a ball, he says, "Do it this way." He does not break up "this way" into such steps as "Put your fingers around here," "Keep your thumb in this position," "Never hold it above this line." Over and over again, adults do a task and children observe and try it, being reinforced only by commands such as "Do it like this" and "Watch that thumb."

Adults at tasks do not provide a running verbal commentary on what they are doing. They do not draw the attention of the child to specific features of the sequences of skills or the attributes of items. They do not ask questions of the child, except questions which are directive or scolding in nature ("Did you bring the ball?" "Didn't you hear what I said?"). Many of their commands contain idioms that are not explained: "Put it up" or "Put that away now" (meaning "Put it in the place where it usually belongs") or "Loosen up," said to a 4-year-old boy trying to learn to bat a ball. Explanations that move beyond the listing of names of items and their features are rarely offered by adults. Children do not ask questions of the type "But I don't understand? What is that?" They appear willing to keep trying, and if there is ambiguity in a set of commands, they ask a question such as "You want me to do this?" (demonstrating their current efforts), or they try to find a way of diverting attention from the task at hand.

Both boys and girls during their preschool years are included in many adult activities, ranging from going to church to fishing and camping. They spend a lot of time observing and asking for turns to try specific tasks, such as putting a worm on the hook or cutting cookies. Sometimes adults say, "No, you're not old enough." But if they agree to the child's attempt at the task, they watch and give directives and evaluations: "That's right, don't twist the cutter." "Turn like this." "Don't try to scrape it up now, let me do that." Talk about the task does not segment its skills and identify them, nor does it link the particular task or item at hand to other tasks. Reason-explanations such as "If you twist the cutter, the cookies will be rough on the edge" are rarely given – or asked for.

Neither Roadville adults nor children shift the context of items in their talk. They do not tell stories that fictionalize themselves or familiar events. They reject Sunday school materials that attempt to translate Biblical events into a modern-day setting. In Roadville, a story must be invited or announced by someone other than the storyteller, and only certain community members are designated good storytellers. A story is recognized by the group as a story about one and all. It is a true story, an actual event that happened to either the storyteller or someone else present. The marked behavior of the storyteller and audience alike is seen as exemplifying the weaknesses of all and the need for persistence in overcoming such weaknesses. The sources of stories are personal experience. They are tales of transgressions that make the point of reiterating the expected norms of behavior of man, woman, fisherman, worker, and Christian. They are true to the facts of the event.

Roadville parents provide their children with books; they read to them and ask questions about the books' contents. They choose books that emphasize nursery rhymes, alphabet learning, animals, and simplified Bible stories, and they require their children to repeat from these books and to answer formulaic questions about their contents. Roadville adults also ask questions about oral stories that have a point relevant to some marked behavior of a child. They use proverbs and summary statements to remind their children of stories and to call on them for simple comparisons of the stories' contents to their own situations. Roadville parents coach children in their telling of a story, forcing them to tell about an incident as it has been precomposed or pre-scripted in the head of the adult. Thus in Roadville children come to know a story as either an accounting from a book or a factual account of a real event in which some type of marked behavior occurred and there is a lesson to be learned. Any fictionalized account of a real event is viewed as a *lie*; reality is better than fiction. Roadville's church and community life admit no story other than that which meets the definition internal to the group. Thus children cannot decontextualize their knowledge or fictionalize events known to them and shift them about into other frames.

When these children go to school they perform well in the initial stages of each of the three early grades. They often know portions of the alphabet, some colors and numbers, and can recognize their names and tell someone their address and their parents' names. They will sit still and listen to a story, and they know how to answer questions asking for what-explanations. They do well in reading workbook exercises that ask for identification of specific portions of words, items from the story, or the linking of two items, letters, or parts of words on the same page. When the teacher reaches the end of storyreading or the reading circle and asks questions such as "What did you like about the story?" relatively few Roadville children answer. If asked questions such as "What would you have done if you had been Billy [a story's main character]?" Roadville children most frequently say, "I don't know" or shrug their shoulders.

Near the end of each year, and increasingly as they move through the early primary grades, Roadville children can handle successfully the initial stages of lessons. But when they move ahead to extra-credit items or to activities considered more advanced and requiring more independence, they are stumped. They turn frequently to teachers, asking, "Do you want me to do this? What do I do here?" If asked to write a creative story or tell it into a tape recorder, they retell stories from books; they do not create their own. They rarely provide emotional or personal commentary on their accounting of real events or book stories. They are rarely able to take knowledge learned in one context and shift it to another; they do not compare two items or events and point out similarities and differences. They find it difficult either to hold one feature of an event constant and shift all others or to hold all features constant but one. For example, they are puzzled by questions such as "What would have happened if Billy had not told the policemen what happened?" They do not know how to move events or items out of a given frame. To a question such as "What habits of the Hopi Indians might they be able to take with them when they move to a city?" they provide lists of features of life of the Hopi on the reservation. They do not take these items, consider their appropriateness in an urban setting, and evaluate the hypothesized outcome. In general, they find this type of question impossible to answer, and they do not know how to ask teachers to help them take apart the questions to figure out the answers. Thus their initial successes in reading, being good students, following orders, and adhering to school norms of participating in lessons begin to fall away rapidly about the time they enter the fourth grade. As the importance and frequency of questions and reading habits with which they are familiar decline in the higher grades, they have no way of keeping up or of seeking help in learning what it is they do not even know they don't know.

Trackton

Babies in Trackton come home from the hospital to an environment that is almost entirely human. There are no cribs, car beds, or carseats, and only an occasional highchair or infant seat. Infants are held during their waking hours, occasionally while they sleep, and they usually sleep in the bed with parents until they are about 2 years of age. They are held, their faces fondled, their cheeks pinched, and they eat and sleep in the midst of human talk and noise from the television, stereo, and radio. Encapsulated in an almost totally human world, they are in the midst of constant human communication, verbal and nonverbal. They literally feel the body signals of shifts in emotion of those who hold them almost continuously; they are talked about and kept in the midst of talk about topics that range over any subject. As children make cooing or babbling sounds, adults refer to this as "noise," and no attempt is made to interpret these sounds as words or communicative attempts on the part of the baby. Adults believe they should not have to depend on their babies to tell them what they need or when they are uncomfortable; adults know, children only "come to know."

When a child can crawl and move about on his or her own, he or she plays with the household objects deemed safe for him or her – pot lids, spoons, plastic food containers. Only at Christmastime are there special toys for very young children; these are usually trucks, balls, doll babies, or plastic cars, but rarely blocks, puzzles, or books. As children become completely mobile, they demand ride toys or electronic and mechanical toys they see on television. They never request nor do they receive manipulative toys, such as puzzles, blocks, take-apart toys or literacy-based items, such as books or letter games.

Adults read newspapers, mail, calendars, circulars (political and civic-events-related), school materials sent home to parents, brochures advertising new cars, television sets, or other products, and the Bible and other church-related materials. There are no reading materials especially for children (with the exception of children's Sunday school materials), and adults do not sit and read to children. Since children are usually left to sleep whenever and wherever they fall asleep, there is no bedtime or naptime as such. At night, they are put to bed when adults go to bed or whenever the person holding them gets tired. Thus going to bed is not framed in any special routine. Sometimes in a play activity during the day an older sibling will read to a younger child, but the latter soon loses interest and squirms away to play. Older children often try to "play school" with younger children, reading to them from books and trying to ask questions about what they have read. Adults look on these efforts with amusement and do not try to persuade the small child to sit still and listen.

Signs from very young children of attention to the nonverbal behaviors of others are rewarded by extra fondling, laughter, and cuddling from adults. For example, when an infant shows signs of recognizing a family member's voice on the phone by bouncing up and down in the arms of the adult who is talking on the phone, adults comment on this to others present and kiss and nudge the child. Yet when children utter sounds or combinations of sounds that could be interpreted as words, adults pay no attention. Often by the time they are 12 months old, children approximate words or phrases of adults' speech; adults respond by laughing or giving special attention to the child and crediting him with "sounding like" the person being imitated. When children learn to walk and imitate the walk of members of the community, they are rewarded by comments on their activities: "He walks just like Toby when he's tuckered out."

Children between the ages of 12 and 24 months often imitate the tune or "general Gestalt" (Peters 1977) of complete utterances they hear around them. They pick up and repeat chunks (usually the ends) or phrasal and clausal utterances of speakers around them. They seem to remember fragments of speech and repeat these without active production. In this first stage of language learning, the *repetition* stage, they imitate the intonation contours and general shaping of the utterances they repeat. Lem (1;2) in the following example illustrates this pattern.

Mother [talking to neighbor on porch while Lem plays with a truck on the porch nearby]: But they won't call back, won't happen=

LEM: =call back
NEIGHBOR: Sam's going over there Saturday, he'll pick up a form=
LEM: =pick up on, pick up on [Lem here appears to have heard "form" as "on"]

The adults pay no attention to Lem's "talk," and their talk, in fact, often overlaps his repetitions.

In the second stage, *repetition with variation*, Trackton children manipulate pieces of conversation they pick up. They incorporate chunks of language from others into their own ongoing dialogue, applying productive rules, inserting new nouns and verbs for those used in the adults' chunks. They also play with rhyming patterns and varying intonation contours.

MOTHER: She went to the doctor again.
LEM (2;2): Went to de doctor, doctor, tractor, dis my tractor, [in a singsong fashion] doctor on a tractor, went to de doctor.

Lem creates a monologue, incorporating the conversation about him into his own talk as he plays. Adults pay no attention to his chatter unless it gets so noisy as to interfere with their talk.

In the third stage, *participation*, children begin to enter the ongoing conversations about them. They do so by attracting the adult's attention with a tug on the arm or pant leg, and they help make themselves understood by providing nonverbal reinforcements to help recreate a scene they want the listener to remember. For example, if adults are talking, and a child interrupts with seemingly unintelligible utterances, the child will make gestures or extra sounds, or act out some outstanding features of the scene he is trying to get the adult to remember. Children try to create a context, a scene, for the understanding of their utterance.

This third stage illustrates a pattern in the children's response to their environment and their ways of letting others know their knowledge of the environment. Once they are in the third stage, their communicative efforts are accepted by community members, and adults respond directly to the child instead of talking to others about the child's activities as they have done in the past. Children continue to practice for conversational participation by playing, when alone, both parts of dialogues, imitating gestures as well as intonation patterns of adults. By 2;6 all children in the community can imitate the walk and talk of others in the community or of frequent visitors such as the man who comes around to read the gas meters. They can feign anger, sadness, fussing, remorse, silliness, or any of a wide range of expressive behaviors. They often use the same chunks of language for varying effects, depending on nonverbal support to give the language different meanings or cast it in a different key (Hymes 1972). Girls between 3 and 4 years of age take part in extraordinarily complex stepping and clapping patterns and simple repetitions of handclap games played by older girls. From the time they are old enough to stand alone, they are encouraged in their participation by siblings and older children in the community. These games require anticipation and recognition of cues for upcoming behaviors, and the young girls learn to watch for these cues and to come in with the appropriate words and movements at the right time.

Preschool children are not asked for what-explanations of their environment. Instead, they are asked a preponderance of analogical questions that call for non-specific comparisons of one item, event, or person with another: "What's that like?" Other types of questions ask for specific information known to the child but not the adults: "Where'd you get that from?" "What do you want?" "How come you did that?" (Heath 1982b). Adults explain their use of these types of questions by expressing their sense of children: They are "comers," coming into their learning by experiencing what knowing about things means. As one parent of a 2-year-old boy put it: "Ain't no use me tellin' 'im, 'Learn this, learn that, what's this, what's that?' He just gotta learn, gotta know; he see one thing one place one time, he know how it go, see sump'n like it again, maybe it be the same, maybe it won't."

Children are expected to learn how to know when the form belies the meaning, and to know contexts of items and to use their understanding of these contexts to draw parallels between items and events. Parents do not believe they have a tutoring role in this learning; they provide the experiences on which the child draws and reward signs of their successfully coming to know.

Trackton children's early stories illustrate how they respond to adult views of them as "comers." The children learn to tell stories by drawing heavily on their abilities to render a context, to set a stage, and to call on the audience's power to join in the imaginative creation of story. Between the ages of 2 and 4 years, the children, in a monologue-like fashion, tell stories about things in their lives, events they see and hear, and situations in which they have been involved. They produce these spontaneously during play with other children or in the presence of adults. Sometimes they make an effort to attract the attention of listeners before they begin the story, but often they do not. Lem, playing off the edge of the porch, when he was about $2\frac{1}{2}$ years of age, heard a bell in the distance.

> He stopped, looked at Nellie and Benjy, his older siblings, who were nearby, and said:
>
> Way
> Far
> Now
> It a churchbell
> Ringin'
> Dey singin'
> Ringin'
> You hear it?
> I hear it
> Far
> Now.

Lem had been taken to church the previous Sunday and had been much impressed by the churchbell. He had sat on his mother's lap and joined in the singing, rocking to and fro on her lap, and clapping his hands. His story, which is like a poem in its imagery and linelike prosody, is in response to the current stimulus of a distant bell. As he tells the story, he sways back and forth.

This story, somewhat longer than those usually reported from other social groups for children as young as Lem,[4] has some features that have come to characterize fully developed narratives or stories. It recapitulates in its verbal outline the sequence of events being recalled by the storyteller. At church, the bell rang while the people sang. In the line "It a churchbell," Lem provides his story's topic and a brief summary of what is to come. This line serves a function similar to the formulas often used by older children to open a story: "This is a story about (a church bell)." Lem gives only the slightest hint of story setting or orientation to the listener; where and when the story took place are capsuled in "Way / Far." Preschoolers in Trackton almost never hear "Once upon a time there was a – – " stories, and they rarely provide definitive orientations for their stories. They seem to assume listeners "know" the situation in which the narrative takes place. Similarly, preschoolers in Trackton do not close off their stories with formulaic endings. Lem poetically balances his opening and closing in an *inclusio*, beginning "Way / Far / Now" and ending "Far / Now." The effect is one of closure, but there is no clearcut announcement of closure. Throughout the presentation of action and result of action in their stories, Trackton preschoolers invite the audience to respond or evaluate the story's actions. Lem asks, "You hear it?" which may refer either to the current stimulus or to yesterday's bell, since Lem does not productively use past tense endings for any verbs at this stage in his language development.

Preschool storytellers have several ways of inviting audience evaluation and interest. They may themselves express an emotional response to the story's actions; they may have another character or narrator in the story do so, often using alliterative language play; or they may detail actions and results through direct discourse or sound effects and gestures. All these methods of calling attention to the story and its telling distinguish the speech event as a story, an occasion for audience and story teller to interact pleasantly and not simply to hear an ordinary recounting of events or actions.

Trackton children must be aggressive in inserting their stories into an ongoing stream of discourse. Storytelling is highly competitive.

Everyone in a conversation may want to tell a story, so only the most aggressive wins out. The content ranges widely, and there is "truth" only in the universals of human experience. Fact is often hard to find, though it is usually the seed of the story. Trackton stories often have no point – no obvious beginning or ending; they go on as long as the audience enjoys and tolerates the storyteller's entertainment.

Trackton adults do not separate out the elements of the environment around their children to tune their attentions selectively. They do not simplify their language, focus on single-word utterances by young children, label items or features of objects in either books or the environment at large. Instead, children are continuously contextualized, presented with almost continuous communication. From this ongoing, multiple-channeled stream of stimuli, they must themselves select, practice, and determine rules of production and structuring. For language, they do so by first repeating, catching chunks of sounds and intonation contours, and practicing these without specific reinforcement or evaluation. But practice material and models are continuously available. Next, the children seem to begin to sort out the productive rules for the speech and practice what they hear about them with variation. Finally, they work their way into conversations, hooking their meanings for listeners into a familiar context by recreating scenes through gestures, special sound effects, and so on. These characteristics continue in their story-poems and their participation in jump-rope rhymes. Because adults do not select out, name, and describe features of the environment for the young, children must perceive situations, determine how units of the situations are related to each other, recognize these relations in other situations, and reason through what it will take to show their correlation of one situation with another. The children can answer questions such as "What's that like?" ("It's like Doug's car"), but they can rarely name the specific feature or features that make two items or events alike. For example, in saying a car seen on the street is "like Doug's car," a child may be basing the analogy on the fact that this car has a flat tire and Doug's also had one last week. But the child does not name (and is not asked to name) what is alike between the two cars.

Children seem to develop connections between situations or items not by specification of labels and features in the situations but by configuration links. Recognition of similar general shapes or patterns of links seen in one situation and connected to another seems to be the means by which children set scenes in their nonverbal representations of individuals, and later of their verbal chunking, and then their segmentation and production of rules for putting together isolated units. They do not decontextualize; instead they heavily contextualize nonverbal and verbal language. They fictionalize their "true stories," but they do so by asking the audience to identify with the story through making parallels from their own experiences. When adults read, they often do so in a group. One person, reading aloud, for example, from a brochure on a new car decodes the text and displays illustrations and photographs, and listeners relate the text's meaning to their experiences, asking questions and expressing opinions. Finally, the group as a whole synthesizes the written text and the negotiated oral discourse to construct a meaning for the brochure (Heath 1982a).

When Trackton children go to school, they face unfamiliar types of questions that ask for what-explanations. They are asked as individuals to identify items by name and to label features such as shape, color, size, number. The stimuli to which they are to give these responses are two-dimensional flat representations that are often highly stylized and bear little resemblance to the real items. Trackton children generally score in the lowest percentile range on the Metropolitan Reading Readiness tests. They do not sit at their desks and complete reading workbook pages; neither do they tolerate questions about reading materials that are structured in the usual lesson format. Their contributions are in the form of "I had a duck at my house one time"; "Why'd he do that?" or they imitate the sound effects teachers may produce in stories they read to the children. By the end of the first three primary grades, their general language-arts scores have been consistently low, except for those few who have begun to adapt to and adopt some of the behaviors they have had to learn in school. But the majority not only fail to learn the content of lessons, but also do not adopt the social-interactional rules for school literacy events. Print in isolation bears little authority in their world. The kinds of questions asked about reading books are unfamiliar. The children's abilities to link metaphorically two events or situations and to recreate scenes are not tapped in the school; in fact, *these abilities often cause difficulties*, because they enable children to see parallels teachers did not intend and, indeed, may not recognize until the children point them out (Heath 1978).

By the end of the lessons or by the time in their total school career when reason-explanations and affective statements call for the creative comparison of two or more situations, it is too late for many Trackton children. They have not picked up along the way the composition and comprehension skills they need to translate their analogical skills into a channel teachers can accept. They seem not to know how to take meaning from reading; they do not observe the rules of linearity in writing, and their expression of themselves on paper is very limited. Taped oral stories are often much better, but these rarely count as much as written compositions. Thus Trackton children continue to collect very low or failing grades, and many decide by the end of the sixth grade to stop trying and turn their attention to the heavy peer socialization that usually begins in these years.

From Community to Classroom

A recent review of trends in research on learning pointed out that "learning to read through using and learning from language has been less systematically studied than the decoding process" (Glaser 1979: 7). Put another way, how children learn to use language to read to learn has been less systematically studied than decoding skills. Learning how to take meaning from writing before one learns to read involves repeated practice in using and learning from language through appropriate participation in literacy events such as exhibitor/questioner and spectator/respondent dyads (Scollon and Scollon 1979) or group negotiation of the meaning of a written text. Children have to learn to select, hold, and retrieve content from books and other written or printed texts in accordance with their community's rules or "ways of taking," and the children's learning follows community paths of language socialization. In each society, certain kinds of childhood participation in literacy events may precede others, as the developmental sequence builds toward the whole complex of home and community behaviors characteristic of the society. The ways of taking employed in the school may in turn build directly on the preschool development, may require substantial adaptation on the part of the children, or may even run directly counter to aspects of the community's pattern.

At home

In *Maintown* homes, the construction of knowledge in the earliest preschool years depends in large part on labeling procedures and what-explanations. Maintown families, like other mainstream families, continue this kind of classification and knowledge construction throughout the child's environment and into the school years, calling it into play in response to new items in the environment and in running commentaries on old items as they compare to new ones. This pattern of linking old and new knowledge is reinforced in narrative tales that fictionalize the teller's events or recapitulate a story from a book. Thus for these children the bedtime story is simply an early link in a long chain of interrelated patterns of taking meaning from the environment. Moreover, along this chain the focus is on the individual as respondent and cooperative negotiator of meaning from books. In particular, children learn that written language may represent not only descriptions of real events, but decontextualized logical propositions, and the occurrence of this kind of information in print or in writing legitimates a response in which one brings to the interpretation of written text selected knowledge from the real world. Moreover, readers must recognize how certain types of questions assert the priority of meanings in the written word over reality. The "real" comes into play only after prescribed decontextualized meanings; affective responses and reason-explanations follow conventional presuppositions that stand behind what-explanations.

Roadville also provides labels, features, and what-explanations, and prescribes listening and performing behaviors for preschoolers. However, Roadville adults do not carry on or sustain in continually overlapping and interdependent fashion the linking of ways of taking meaning from books to ways of relating that knowledge to other aspects of the environment. They do not encourage decontextualization; in fact, they proscribe it in their own stories about themselves and their requirements of stories from children. They do not themselves make analytic statements or assert universal truths, except those related to their religious faith. They lace their stories with synthetic (non-analytic) statements that express, describe, and synthesize real-life materials. Things do not have to follow logically so long as they fit the past experience of individuals in the community. Thus children learn to look for a specific moral in stories and to expect that story to fit their facts of reality explicitly. When they themselves recount an event, they do the same, constructing the story of a real event according to coaching by adults who want to construct the story as they saw it.

Trackton is like neither Maintown nor Roadville. There are no bedtime stories; in fact, there are few occasions for reading to or with children specifically. Instead, during the time these activities would take place in mainstream and Roadville homes, Trackton children are enveloped in different kinds of social interactions. They are held, fed, talked about, and rewarded for nonverbal, and later verbal, renderings of events they witness. Trackton adults value and respond favorably when children show they have come to know how to use language to show correspondence in function, style, configuration, and positioning between two different things or situations. Analogical questions are asked of Trackton children, although the implicit questions of structure and function these embody are never made explicit. Children do not have labels or names of attributes of items and events pointed out for them, and they are asked for reason-explanations, not what-explanations. Individuals express their personal responses and recreate corresponding situations with often only a minimal adherence to the germ of truth of a story. Children come to recognize similarities of patterning, though they do not name lines, points, or items that are similar between two items or situations. They are familiar with group literacy events in which several community members orally negotiate the meaning of a written text.

At school

In the early reading stages, and in later requirements for reading to learn at more advanced stages, children from the three communities respond differently, because they have learned different methods and degrees of taking from books. In contrast to Maintown children, Roadville children's habits learned in bookreading and toy-related episodes have not continued for them through other activities and types of reinforcement in their environment. They have had less exposure to both the content of books and ways of learning from books than have mainstream children. Thus their need in schools is not necessarily for an intensification of presentation of labels, a slowing down of the sequence of introducing what-explanations in connection with bookreading. Instead they need *extension of these habits to other domains* and to opportunities for practicing habits such as producing running commentaries, creating exhibitor/questioner and spectator/respondent roles, etc. Perhaps, most important, Roadville children need to have articulated for them *distinctions in discourse strategies and structures*. Narratives of real events have certain strategies and structures; imaginary tales, flights of fancy, and affective expressions have others. Their community's view of narrative discourse style is very narrow and demands a passive role in both creation of and response to the account of events. Moreover, these children have *to be reintroduced to a participant frame of reference to a book*. Though initially they were participants in bookreading, they have been trained into passive roles since the age of 3 years, and they must learn once again to be active information givers, taking from books and linking that knowledge to other aspects of their environment.

Trackton students present an additional set of alternatives for procedures in the early primary grades. Since they usually have few of the expected "natural" skills of taking meaning from books, they must not only learn these but also *retain their analogical reasoning practices* for use in some of the later stages of learning to read. They must *learn to adapt the creativity in language, metaphor, fictionalization, recreation of scenes, and exploration of functions and settings of items they bring to school.* These children already use narrative skills highly rewarded in the upper primary grades. They distinguish a fictionalized story from a real-life narrative. They know that telling a story can be in many ways related to play; it suspends reality and frames an old event in a new context; it calls on audience participation to recognize the setting and participants. They must now *learn as individuals to recount factual events in a straightforward way* and *recognize appropriate occasions for reason-explanations and affective expressions.* Trackton children seem to have skipped learning to label, list features, and give what-explanations. Thus they need to *have the mainstream or school habits presented in familiar activities with explanations related to their own habits of taking meaning* from the environment. Such "simple," "natural" things as distinctions between two-dimensional and three-dimensional objects may need to be explained to help Trackton children learn the stylization and decontextualization that characterize books.

To lay out in more specific detail how Roadville's and Trackton's ways of knowing can be used along with those of mainstreamers goes beyond the scope of this paper. However, it must be admitted that a range of alternatives to ways of learning and displaying knowledge characterizes all highly school-successful adults in the advanced stages of their careers. Knowing more about how these alternatives are learned at early ages in different sociocultural conditions can help the schools to provide opportunities for all students to avail themselves of these alternatives early in their school careers. For example, mainstream children can benefit from early exposure to Trackton's creative, highly analogical styles of telling stories and giving explanations, and they can add the Roadville true story with strict chronicity and explicit moral to their repertoire of narrative types.

In conclusion, if we want to understand the place of literacy in human societies and ways children acquire the literacy orientations of their communities, we must recognize two postulates of literacy and language development:

1 Strict dichotomization between oral and literate traditions is a construct of researchers, not an accurate portrayal of reality across cultures.
2 A unilinear model of development in the acquisition of language structures and uses cannot adequately account for culturally diverse ways of acquiring knowledge or developing cognitive styles.

Roadville and Trackton tell us that the mainstream type of literacy orientation is not the only type even among Western societies. They also tell us that the mainstream ways of acquiring communicative competence do not offer a universally applicable model of development. They offer proof of Hymes's assertion a decade ago that "it is impossible to generalize validly about 'oral' vs. 'literate' cultures as uniform types" (1974: 54).

Yet in spite of such warnings and analyses of the uses and functions of writing in the specific proposals for comparative development and organization of cultural systems (cf. Basso 1974: 432), the majority of research on literacy has focused on differences in class, amount of education, and level of civilization among groups having different literacy characteristics.

"We need, in short, a great deal of ethnography" (Hymes 1973) to provide descriptions of the ways different social groups "take" knowledge from the environment. For written sources, these ways of taking may be analyzed in terms of *types of literacy events*, such as group negotiation of meaning from written texts, individual "looking things up" in reference books, writing family records in Bibles, and the dozens of other types of occasions when books or other written materials are integral to interpretation in an interaction. These must in turn be analyzed in terms of the specific *features of literacy events*, such as labeling, what-explanation, affective comments, reason-explanations, and many other possibilities. Literacy events must also be interpreted in relation to the *larger sociocultural patterns* that they may exemplify or reflect. For example, ethnography must describe literacy events in their sociocultural contexts, so we may come to understand how such patterns as time and space usage, caregiving roles, and age and sex segregation are interdependent with the types and features of literacy events a community develops. It is only on the basis of such thoroughgoing ethnography that further progress is possible toward understanding cross-cultural patterns of oral and written language uses and paths of development of communicative competence.

NOTES

1 First presented at the Terman Conference on Teaching at Stanford University, 1980, this paper has benefited from cooperation with M. Cochran Smith of the University of Pennsylvania. She shares an appreciation of the relevance of Roland Barthes's work for studies of the socialization of young children into literacy; her research (1984) on the storyreading practices of a mainstream school-oriented nursery school provides a much-needed detailed account of early school orientation to literacy.

2 Terms such as *mainstream* and *middle-class* are frequently used in both popular and scholarly writings without careful definition. Moreover, numerous studies of behavioral phenomena (for example, mother–child interactions in language learning) either do not specify that the subjects being described are drawn from mainstream groups or do not recognize the importance of this limitation. As a result, findings from this group are often regarded as universal. For a discussion of this problem, see Chanan and Gilchrist 1974; Payne and Bennett 1977. In general, the literature characterizes this group as school-oriented, aspiring toward upward mobility through formal institutions, and providing enculturation that positively values routines of promptness, linearity (in habits ranging from furniture arrangement to entrance into a movie theatre), and evaluative and judgmental responses to behaviors that deviate from their norms. In the United States, mainstream families tend to locate in neighborhoods and suburbs around cities. Their social interactions center not in their immediate neighborhoods but in voluntary associations across the city. Thus a cluster of mainstream families (and not a community – which usually implies a specific geographic territory as the locus of a majority of social interactions) is the unit of comparison used here with the Trackton and Roadville communities.

3 Behind this discussion are findings from cross-cultural psychologists who have studied the links between verbalization of task and demonstration of skills in a hierarchical sequence, e.g., Childs and Greenfield 1980. See Goody 1979 on the use of questions in learning tasks unrelated to a familiarity with books.

4 Cf. Umiker-Sebeok's (1979) descriptions of stories of mainstream middle-class children, ages 3–5, and Sutton-Smith 1981.

REFERENCES

Basso, K. (1974). The Ethnography of Writing. In R. Bauman and J. Sherzer (eds.), *Explorations in the Ethnography of Speaking*. Cambridge: Cambridge University Press, pp. 425–32.

Cazden, C. B. (1979). Peekaboo as an Instructional Model: Discourse Development at Home and at School. *Stanford Papers and Reports in Child Language Development* 17: 1–29.

Chanan, G. and Gilchrist, L. (1974). *What School Is For*. New York: Praeger.

Childs, C. P. and Greenfield, P. M. (1980). Informal Modes of Learning and Teaching. In N. Warren (ed.), *Advances in Cross-Cultural Psychology*, vol. 2. London: Academic Press, pp. 269–316.

Cochran Smith, M. (1984). *The Making of a Reader*. Norwood, N.J.: Ablex.

Cohen, R. (1968). The Relation between Socio-conceptual Styles and Orientation to School Requirements. *Sociology of Education* 41: 201–20.

Cohen, R. (1969). Conceptual Styles, Culture Conflict, and Nonverbal Tests of Intelligence. *American Anthropologist* 71, 5: 828–56.

Cohen, R. (1971). The Influence of Conceptual Rule-sets on Measures of Learning Ability. In C. L. Brace, G. Gamble, and J. Bond (eds.), *Race and Intelligence*. Anthropological Studies, no. 8. Washington, DC: American Anthropological Association, pp. 41–57.

Glaser, R. (1979). Trends and Research Questions in Psychological Research on Learning and Schooling. *Educational Researcher* 8, 10: 6–13.

Goody, E. (1979). Towards a Theory of Questions. In E. N. Goody (ed.), *Questions and Politeness: Strategies in Social Interaction*. Cambridge: Cambridge University Press, pp. 17–43.

Griffin, P. and Humphry, F. (1978). Task and Talk. In *The Study of Children's Functional Language and Education in the Early Years*. Final Report to the Carnegie Corporation of New York. Arlington, Va.: Center for Applied Linguistics.

Heath, S. (1978). *Teacher Talk: Language in the Classroom*. Language in Education 9. Arlington, Va.: Center for Applied Linguistics.

Heath, S. (1980). The Functions and Uses of Literacy. *Journal of Communication* 30, 1: 123–33.

Heath, S. (1982a). Protean Shapes: Ever-shifting Oral and Literate Traditions. In Deborah Tannen (ed.), *Spoken and Written Language: Exploring Orality and Literacy*. Norwood, NJ: Ablex, pp. 91–118.

Heath, S. (1982b). Questioning at Home and at School: A Comparative Study. In George Spindler (ed.), *Doing Ethnography: Educational Anthropology in Action*. New York: Holt, Rinehart, & Winston, pp. 102–31.

Heath, S. (1983). *Ways with Words: Language, Life and Work in Communities and Classrooms*. Cambridge: Cambridge University Press.

Howard, R. (1974). A Note on S/Z. In R. Barthes, *Introduction to S/Z*, trans. Richard Miller. New York: Hill & Wang, pp. ix–xi.

Hymes, D. H. (1972). Models of the Interaction of Language and Social Life. In J. J. Gumperz and D. Hymes (eds.), *Directions in Sociolinguistics*. New York: Holt, Rinehart, & Winston, pp. 35–71.

Hymes, D. H. (1973). Speech and Language: On the Origins and Foundations of Inequality among Speakers. *Daedalus* 102: 59–85.

Hymes, D. H. (1974). Speech and Language: On the Origins and Foundations of Inequality among Speakers. In E. Haugen and M. Bloomfield (eds.), *Language as a Human Problem*. New York: Norton, pp. 45–71.

Kagan, J., Sigel, I., and Moss, H. (1963). Psychological Significance of Styles of Conceptualization. In J. Wright and J. Kagan (eds.), *Basic Cognitive Processes in Children*. Monographs of the Society for Research in Child Development 28, 2: 73–112.

Mehan, H. (1979). *Learning Lessons*. Cambridge, Mass.: Harvard University Press.

Merritt, M. (1979). Service-like Events during Individual Work Time and Their Contribution to the Nature of the Rules for Communication. NIE Report EP 78-0436.

Ninio, A. and Bruner, J. (1978). The Achievement and Antecedents of Labelling. *Journal of Child Language* 5: 1–15.

Payne, C. and Bennett, C. (1977). "Middle Class Aura" in Public Schools. *Teacher Educator* 13, 1: 16–26.

Peters, A. (1977). Language learning strategies. *Language* 53: 560–73.

Scollon, R. and Scollon, S. (1979). *The Literate Two-Year-Old: The Fictionalization of Self*. Working Papers in Sociolinguistics. Austin: Southwest Regional Laboratory.

Sinclair, J. M. and Coulthard, R. M. (1975). *Toward an Analysis of Discourse*. New York: Oxford University Press.

Sutton-Smith, B. (1981). *The Folkstories of Children*. Philadelphia: University of Pennsylvania Press.

Umiker-Sebeok, J. D. (1979). Preschool Children's Intraconversational Narratives. *Journal of Child Language* 6, 1: 91–110.

Witkin, H., Faterson, F., Goodenough, R., ar Birnbaum, J. (1966). Cognitive Patterning in Mildly Retarded Boys. *Child Development* 37, 2: 301–16.

STUDY QUESTIONS

1 Explain the notion of "ways of taking" introduced by Heath at the beginning of her chapter. How is this notion used throughout the chapter to describe the differences among three communities where she studied literacy events?
2 How does the concept of "literacy event" help us understand the differences in literacy skills across the three communities?
3 What kind of book reading did Heath identify as "mainstream school-oriented" and why? What makes this type of book reading similar to classroom literacy practices?
4 Use the notion of "developmental story" that is introduced by Ochs and Schieffelin in Chapter 12 to give an account of the three socialization styles to literacy that are described by Heath.
5 According to Heath, what is problematic about the literacy/orality dichotomy?
6 How could you use the approach exemplified in this chapter to provide a narrative of your own "ways of taking" from books and other written sources of information?

15

Creating Social Identities through *Doctrina* Narratives

Patricia Baquedano-López

This study describes how teachers and students in *doctrina* class (a religious education class in Spanish) composed of Mexican immigrants at a Catholic parish in Los Angeles construct social identities in the course of telling the narrative of the apparition of *Nuestra Señora de Guadalupe* (Our Lady of Guadalupe). During the telling of this narrative, *doctrina* teachers at the parish of St Paul[1] employ several discursive and interactional resources to represent a multiplicity of identities within a coherent collective narrative, establishing in this way links to traditional Mexican world views. Like narratives of personal experience, this traditional narrative organizes collective experience in a temporal continuum, extending past experience into the present (Heidegger 1962; Ricoeur 1985/1988; Polkinghorne 1988; Bruner 1990; Brockelman 1992; Ochs 1994; Ochs and Capps 1996).

Narrating the Collectivity

Through narrative we relate not only events, but also stances and dispositions towards those events (Labov and Waletzky 1968). While they emerge from experience, narratives also shape experience (Ochs and Capps 1996); thus, we tell our stories for their potency to explain, rationalize, and delineate past, present, and possible experience. As collaborative undertakings, narratives are co-told and designed with the audience's input, addressing an audience's present and even future concerns (Duranti and Brenneis 1986; Ochs 1994). Stories of personal experience are told from present perspectives, from the here and now, evoking present emotions and creating present experiences for both narrator and audience (Capps and Ochs 1995; Ochs and Capps 1996; Heidegger 1962; Ricoeur 1985/1988). Collective narratives, which tell the experiences of a group, organize diversity in the collectivity. And while they tend to normalize the existing status quo, Chatterjee (1993) reminds us that they can also be expressions of resistances in the face of master story lines. Morgan (1995) has noted that certain narratives of African-American experience, in particular those alluding to the times of slavery, contest and resist both past and present experience. Through indirection and linguistic "camouflage," story-tellers describe and explain a

For permission to publish copyright material in this book, grateful acknowledgment is made to: P. Baquedano-López (1997), "Creating Social Identities through *Doctrina* Narratives," *Issues in Applied Linguistics* 8(1): 27–45.

collective history of African Americans as an economically exploited and socially marginalized minority group. Like these stories of African-American collective experience, *doctrina* narratives of *Nuestra Señora de Guadalupe* also create explanations for the social worlds of *doctrina* teachers and students as a community with past experiences of oppression. This is achieved in part by *doctrina* classroom narrative activity in which narrated events are brought to bear upon ongoing class discussion, illustrating how past experience might continue to influence and shape the present. Indeed, at *doctrina*, a traditional religious narrative becomes not only a story to live by, it affirms and contests the community's past, present, and possible stories.

The narrative

In Los Angeles, a city with a large Mexican population, one does not need to journey far before noticing the ubiquity of popular written and pictorial versions of the narrative of *Nuestra Señora de Guadalupe* on bookmarks, greeting cards, candle vases in supermarket stores, and on city street wall murals. This narrative tells the story of a Mexican peasant, Juan Diego, who had a vision of the Virgin Mary at Mount Tepeyac, near Mexico City in the year 1531. The following excerpt, taken from the legend of a greeting card, represents one of many popular versions:

> Ten years after the bloody Spanish conquest of Mexico, the Mother of God appeared to an Aztec craftsman named Juan Diego. She appeared as an Aztec herself and addressed him in Nahuatl, the Aztec tongue, in a manner one would address a prince. She appeared several miles outside of Mexico City, which had become the center of Spanish power; she insisted, however, that a shrine in her honor be built on that spot among the conquered people. She sent Juan Diego back to the Spanish clergy to "evangelize" them – [the] ones who felt they already had all the truth. In each of these ways she restored dignity and hope to native people who had been dehumanized by foreign oppression. A shrine was built where Mary appeared, and Juan Diego spent the remaining 17 years of his life there, repeating her message of hope and liberation to all who would come. About eight million Native Americans became Christians in response to this message. (Lentz 1987)

While the master story line remains constant across versions, there is, inevitably, elaboration of details. Indeed, in *doctrina* classes, teachers craft particular renditions of the narrative emphasizing certain events. The message, however, is perennial; a Mexican Indian (and therefore, Mexico, the place of the apparition) was chosen as the recipient of an important message. Versions of the narrative are based on two relatively unknown written sources, one in Nahuatl and the other in Spanish, which date back to the sixteenth century (Rodriguez 1994 and sources therein). Poole (1995) has most vigorously challenged the historical origins of the narrative concluding that manipulations of the narrative have served at various points in time to politically define and redefine Mexican identity. Indeed, *doctrina* narrative practices support his conclusion. Neither the Nahuatl nor the Spanish written text versions are mentioned during *doctrina* instruction; instead, a particular local version emerges from collaborative narrative activity.

Language Socialization in Religious Institutions

In its broadest sense, socialization is the process of becoming a competent member of society, of internalizing the norms, role expectations, and values of the community; in sum, of becoming culturally competent (Bernstein 1970; Schieffelin and Ochs 1986). Within this paradigm, language socialization constitutes socialization through language and socialization to use language (Schieffelin and Ochs 1986). In this paper I concentrate on the discourse and interaction of teachers and students during religious instruction, and on the process of socialization in *doctrina* classes.

As some anthropologists have noted, a child's first exposure to literacy and other formal uses of his or her language can take place in churches. Heath (1983) described church literacy practices in the Piedmont Carolinas where interactions at church mirrored those of the home, reinforcing socialization practices learned in the home. Ethnographic research in Western Samoa has shown how Bible lessons socialize children not only to formal registers of Samoan, but also to the English language and American cultural norms (Duranti 1994; Ochs 1986; Duranti and Ochs 1986). In turn, immigrant Samoan groups in the United States find the institution of the church to be an important link to their culture. Indeed, the teaching of the Samoan alphabet and numbers in a Samoan-American Sunday school in Southern California constitutes a nexus of cultural networks beyond the home and the church (Duranti, Ochs, and Ta'ase 1995). The church in these immigrant situations is a powerful agent in the maintenance of the community's world views and language. As in the Samoan case, *doctrina* is a culturally significant space where both language and religious instruction take place. Through narrative activity enacted around the telling of the narrative of *Nuestra Señora de Guadalupe*, teachers link their students' present experiences to the experiences evoked in the narrative.

Language socialization at doctrina

Early records of *doctrina* instruction date back to the Spanish conquest. In colonial Mexico, *doctrina* classes were offered daily and were conducted in the native languages. Indeed, students were so numerous that the term "*doctrina*" was also used to describe entire towns of newly converted indigenous groups.[2] An ethnography of the town of Mexquitic in Central Mexico notes that in the year 1680, the number of converts was so large that a visiting bishop felt the need to declare Castillian Spanish the language of *doctrina* instruction to enforce the use of the colonizers' language. This decision, however, extended the use of Spanish to other aspects of public life in the town, concatenating linguistic and religious conversion (Frye, 1996). This move towards religious and linguistic uniformity was soon politically reinforced, and by the year 1770, a Spanish royal decree instituted the teaching of Castillian in Mexico, with the eventual goal of eliminating the native languages (Suárez 1983). As this bit of historical background suggests, religious instruction is part of an institution which has socialized children not only to religious tenets but to dominant languages as well.

Religious instruction at St. Paul's

In Southern California, Catholic parishes with a large Spanish-speaking Latino membership often hold *doctrina* and religious services in Spanish. At St Paul's Catholic church, *doctrina* classes were first offered in 1979 as a parallel to religious instruction classes offered in English, called catechism. The use of Spanish by the Latino membership of the St Paul's parish is best explained in the words of a bilingual Latina parishioner, who, upon being asked her choice of language for religious practice categorically stated: "I talk to God in the language of the heart." For her and others in this parish, that language is Spanish. And while these Latinos reside in a state where English is the official language of the public sphere[3] children in *doctrina* are being socialized to use Spanish for what is close to the heart: for them, religious practice. Ironically, this situation illustrates the achieved goal of colonial Spanish friars, as today in this Los Angeles parish, in what constitutes a former Spanish colony, Spanish is the local indigenous language that now needs to be eradicated.

In April 1996, amid much local debate, the parish council at St Paul's voted to eliminate *doctrina*. The major concern expressed by the leaders of this predominantly English-speaking parish was that *doctrina* and other Spanish-speaking activities fostered an image of separate parishes within what should be perceived as a single religious unit. Yet, when interviewed regarding this proposed change, both English- and Spanish-speaking parishioners often cited poor race relations as the main reason behind the decision to eliminate *doctrina*. During these interviews, parishioners expressed varying degrees of intolerance towards the religious practices of the Spanish-speaking group. A catechism teacher, whose class will be discussed in a later section of this paper, stated that Latinos were "too superstitious." Given the current race relations and conflicting perceptions of religious practice at St Paul's, which reflect a generalized movement against multilingualism in the state of California, it comes as no surprise that English is being instituted as the language of instruction. The 1680 *doctrina* mandate of the Mexquitic town, which replaced Nahuatl with Spanish, is echoed 316 years later in the parish of St Paul's decision to eliminate Spanish as the language of instruction in *doctrina* in favor of English.

Religious instruction classes at St Paul's take place on Saturday mornings during the academic year in the classrooms of the St Paul's Elementary School, the parish's private school located across the street from the main church building. Approximately 150 children participate in these religious education classes. Perhaps the most salient difference between *doctrina* and catechism can be summarized in the following terms: Whereas *doctrina* instructional policies seem to be more locally managed and community-oriented, often blending religious and cultural practice, the catechism curriculum follows a uniform format adhered to by parishes throughout the United States which concentrates on the teaching of Catholic precepts.

Doctrina

Student ages at *doctrina* range from 6–15. Most students come from working-class families and attend public schools, as few can afford the costly monthly fees of the St Paul's Elementary School.[4] *Doctrina* children are bilingual speakers of Spanish and English, and only a few seem to be more competent in English. Most are recent immigrants from Mexico, with only a few of them being US-born Latinos. The *doctrina* teachers, all of Mexican descent, tend to be monolingual Spanish speakers and long-time residents of Los Angeles. At *doctrina*, all interaction is carried out in Spanish, including the religious services associated with religious instructional activities.[5]

Catechism

English catechism classes meet an hour before *doctrina* classes begin, so that by the time *doctrina* students arrive, the catechism children have left, making the interaction between these two groups of children very limited. The children enrolled in catechism represent a variety of different ethnic backgrounds, including Latino, Asian-American, and European American. While it might seem surprising to find Latinos in the English catechism classes, these children are often second- and third-generation immigrants from Mexico and South America who are more proficient in English than Spanish.

The children's ages in catechism range from 6–9, constituting a considerably younger student population than that of *doctrina*. Because Catholic children who are enrolled in parochial schools must also receive religious instruction at their local parishes, many children who attend other parish schools attend St Paul's Saturday instruction. In general, children in catechism come from a slightly higher socioeconomic level. The two catechism teachers at the time of the study were European American and conducted their classes entirely in English.

Data Base

Data for this paper are drawn from a corpus of video and audio recordings of *doctrina* and catechism classes, interviews, field notes, and on-going conversations with teachers, parents, and children collected over the span of 20 months of participant-observation, from September 1994 to May 1996. The *doctrina* class described here is composed of 42 students. Teresa, the teacher of the class, is a monolingual, Spanish-speaking woman who immigrated in her early twenties to the United States, and has lived in Los Angeles for over 30 years. The study also draws on one catechism class composed of 15 students. The catechism teacher, Nancy, is a monolingual, English-speaking woman in her late forties. She is a native of Los Angeles. The *doctrina* segments discussed in the next few paragraphs include transcribed[6] excerpts from the telling of the narrative of *Nuestra Señora de Guadalupe* in

Teresa's *doctrina* class and illustrate how her class collaboratively constructs the identities of dark-skinned Mexicans with a history of oppression. In contrast, the catechism excerpt presented here is part of a lesson on the multiple apparitions of the Virgin Mary and illustrates a different ideology about Our Lady of Guadalupe[7] and ethnicity in general.

Constructing Social Identities through *Doctrina* Narratives

As previously noted, narratives are collaboratively told and socially organized. As such, in the course of telling a narrative version, participants take socially relevant roles as teller and listener. At *doctrina*, this activity is also highly affiliative. But the most significant characteristic of the telling of the narrative of *Nuestra Señora de Guadalupe* is that it serves as a locus of identity construction. Classroom interaction draws children into crafting narrative renditions of the apparition of *Nuestra Señora de Guadalupe* which encourage identification with the place of the apparition and the Virgin Mary. These classroom narratives describe the socio-historical setting of colonial Mexico as a setting of past oppressive experience, which might reflect *doctrina* children's lives as ethnic minorities in the United States. The narration of events often spawns a great deal of questions about the students' lives. Similar to "whole language" approaches to literacy which are used in other formal classrooms, Teresa's teaching style contextualizes the narrative being presented, breaking it down into more manageable parts. She stops frequently in the course of telling the narrative to directly relate the experiences being described to those of the students in the class. This link is created both at the interactional level (through pauses, questions, and repetitions) and at the grammatical level (through predication and the temporal dynamics of tense and aspect).

The narrative construction of Mexican identity

Example (1) below illustrates how Teresa and her *doctrina* class collaboratively construct a Mexican identity. As Teresa begins to recount the events of the story, she first situates these events as taking place in colonial Mexico. She does this by stopping the narration, and through questions, determining how many of her students are from Mexico, the setting of the ongoing narrative. In this way, she includes her students from Mexico as part of the narrative in progress, making the telling relevant to the students' present lives. This also constitutes a highly affiliative activity, and as we will see, students who were not born in Mexico can claim participation in this collective identity through their parents' heritage:

Example (1)

Teresa:	↑ **Hace (.) muchos**	**años**	**que**	**se**	**apareció**
	has been many	years	that	REFX	appear-PAST-3Sg
	Many years ago appeared				
	(0.8)				
	la Santísima Virgen de Guadalupe				
	the Blessed Virgin of Guadalupe				
	en el <u>cerro</u> **(0.2) del**	**Tepeyac,**			
	in the mount of	Tepeyac			
	at mount Tepeyac				
	(0.2)				
	en la capital	**de México.**			
	in the capital	*of Mexico*			
	(0.8)				
	>**Quiénes son**	**de México.**			
	how many be-PRES-Pl	from Mexico			
	who is from Mexico				

Class: ((raises hands))
Teresa: **Los demás son de a ↑ quí**
the rest be-PRES-Pl from here
the rest are from here
(1.0)
Class: Sí:[:
yes
Teresa: **[Quiénes somos de México**
how many be-1Pl from Mexico
how many of us are from Mexico
Carlos: **Mis pa- mi madres son de México,**
my pa- my mothers be-3Pl from Mexico
my fa- my mothers are from Mexico
Teresa: **A-Oh ↑ sí**
oh yes
(0.8)
Bueno. bajen la manita
good low-CMD the hand-DIM
good lower your little hand

As Teresa begins to tell the events of the narrative, she establishes a link from the place where the Virgin Mary appeared, *la capital de México* ("the capital of Mexico"), to present times by relating the setting to the students' place of birth. In her question *Quiénes son de México* ("who is from Mexico") she asks her Mexican students to publicly identify as Mexicans couching this affiliative interaction in present tense, in the here and now. The first time a collectivity is invoked in this class, it describes two contrasting groups: those *de México* ("from Mexico") and those who are not – those *de aquí* ("from here") understood as from the United States.

Teresa's second invocation of a collective identity as Mexican is found in the utterance *Quiénes somos de México*, which now includes her, aligning with those students who first identified as *de México* ("from Mexico"). In her question *Quiénes somos de México* ("how many of us are from Mexico") Teresa uses a form of the verb to be, *somos* ("we are" the first person plural form), which in its inclusive form indexes a collective identity as Mexican. Such is the affiliative force of Teresa's question that Carlos, a student presumably *de aquí* ("from here"), states that his parents *son de México* ("are from Mexico"). Students like Carlos, whose parents come from Mexico (though we assume that he himself does not), are included in the evolving "we" as illustrated by Teresa's affirmative response *A-Oh ↑ sí* ("Oh yes").

Narrative activity at *doctrina*, thus socializes children to identify as Mexican. Through questions about the students' place of birth, a group of Mexicans and a group *de aquí* ("from here") are identified. Though Teresa begins a classroom rendition by narrating the past, the *then* of the story, locating the place where the Virgin Mary appeared in Mexico, she then switches to the moment of the telling to collaboratively redefine the setting of the story in relation to the present participants. Thus the narrative is not only about the apparition of the Virgin Mary in the Mexico of many years ago; it is also a narrative about the Mexican students in this *doctrina* class as they have been made an integral part of the story.

The narrative construction of oppression

As Teresa continues to orchestrate a particular classroom narrative rendition, a history of oppression in colonial times is discursively constructed. Having identified as Mexicans, this class now collectively recounts its own colonial history. In Example (2), through temporal dynamics available in Spanish, in particular, through the use of the imperfective (IMPF) aspect, Teresa guides her class through an historical revisitation of the social landscape of colonial Mexico as she describes in more detail the setting at the time of the apparition of the Virgin Mary.

As a language that encodes tense and aspect morphologically, the imperfect in Spanish is realized in suffixation in the forms *-ía-*, *-aba*. The imperfective portrays actions as viewed from within and in progress, and stands in contrast to the perfective usually encoded in past tense, which denotes actions as completed, viewing a situation from the outside (Comrie 1976). The choice of imperfective is thus a particularly effective resource which allows for a more vivid[8] and highly affiliative use of language to describe the setting of the story, a setting depicting a series of oppressive acts carried out by Spanish conquistadores which warranted intervention (as is often the case in postcolonial histories; see Chatterjee 1993). The following example illustrates the imperfective as the vehicle through which the class travels the oppressive landscape of sixteenth-century Mexico; a journey that stops abruptly with a contrasting switch to past tense to explain that the entire situation, the panorama of oppression which the class has now "witnessed," was untenable:

Example (2)

Teresa: **Entonces este[9] (1.2)**
then

fíjense bien lo que les voy a decir
Attend-CMD well it that to you go-FUT to say-INF
pay attention to what I'm going to say to you
(1.2)

cuando (0.5) en México había mucha opresión, (.)
when in Mexico be-IMPF-Sg much oppression
when in Mexico there was a lot of oppression

por los españoles
by the Spaniards
by the Spaniards
(1.5)

que a-oprimían mucho al indígena.
who oppress-IMPF-Pl much to + the indian
who oppressed the Indians a lot
(1.5)

Y entonces e:ran (.) muy católicos
and then be-IMPF-P*l* very catholic
and they were very catholic

> **porque bueno porque nos dejaban muchas iglesias** <
because well because to us leave-IMPF-Pl many churches
because well because they left us many churches

en todo el país de México
in all the country of Mexico
(0.5)

es que también este (0.5)
is that too
it's that too

querían. tener. sometidos, (.8) a (.) a la gente más pobre
want-IMPF-Pl have-INF subjugated to the people more poor
they [Spaniards] wanted to have subjugated the poorest people

o l-la trabajaban mu:cho verdad,
or work-IMPF-Pl much right
or they worked them hard, right

> pues	**ellos**	**que**	**querían**	**más**[10]
well	they	that	want-IMPF-Pl	more

well they wanted more

que (.)	**los**	**indígenas**
than	the	indians

than the Indians

(0.8)

ésto **<u>no</u>** (.)	**le pareció**	**a**	**la**	**Virgen**
that no	seem-PAST-Sg	to	the	virgin

that didn't seem [right] to the Virgin

First note that the orientation to the story, the detailed description of the setting, is conveyed exclusively using the imperfective:

• en México **había** opresión	• in Mexico there was (IMPF) oppression
• los españoles **oprimían**	• the Spaniards oppressed(IMPF)
• eran católicos	• (they) were(IMPF) Catholic
• nos **dejaban** muchas iglesias	• they left(IMPF) us many churches
• **querían** tener sometidos	• They wanted(IMPF) to have subjugated
• la **trabajaban** mucho	• (they) worked(IMPF) (the people) hard
• ellos **querían** más	• they wanted(IMPF) more

Precisely at the end of this description, a switch to past tense, in *ésto no le pareció a la Virgen* ("this didn't seem [right] to the Virgin") summarizes the previous description (indicated in *ésto* "this") indicating a switch in action, the Virgin Mary's intervention. The grammatical resources in this narrative telling, including the use of the imperfective to access knowledge about the past, makes the description of Mexico's colonial setting not only more vivid but more affiliative. The unfolding of the oppressive events which describe the indigenous Mexicans as oppressed, subjugated, and overworked, immediately after this class has publicly identified as Mexican, is a powerful means for affiliating with that past.

The oppressive acts embedded in the setting of the story are so consequential in the making of this story of redemption that the teacher quizzes her students at the end of the class period precisely on those acts which motivated the Virgin Mary's appearance in Mexico. In Example (3) below, the socio-economic inequality of colonial Mexico is emphasized again, this time co-narrated by the teacher and a student named Enrique:

In response to Teresa's question about the reason for the Virgin Mary's apparition in

Example (3)

Teresa:	**Y**	**por qué se**	**quiso**	**aparecer**	**la Virgen**	**en México**
	and	why REFX	want-PAST-3Sg	appear-INF	the virgin	in Mexico
	and why did the Virgin want to appear in Mexico					
Enrique:	**Para**	**cuidar**	**a México** ↑			
	To	take care-INF	of Mexico			
	to take care of Mexico					
	(0.5)					
Teresa:	**Claro.**	**para**	**rescatar a:::-a**	**los** (0.5)	**indígenas**	
	of course	to	rescue-INF DO	the	indians	
	Of course, to rescue the Indians					
	de	**la**	**<u>o</u>presión**	**de**	**los**	**españoles.**
	from	the	oppression	of	the	Spaniards
	from Spanish oppression.					

Mexico, Enrique answers that she appeared in Mexico to take care of the country; a response which Teresa accepts with *claro* ("of course") reformulating it from *para cuidar a México* ("to take care of Mexico") into *para rescatar a los indígenas* ("to take care of the Indians"). She further elaborates on Enrique's response, indicating that the Indians needed to be rescued from Spanish oppression. Recall that Teresa's class's journey to Mexico's past is a journey to a past that is now shared by the Mexicans in her class; one which has described two groups of people, the Spaniards and the Indians as actors from an unequal past. This interaction between Teresa and Enrique emphasizes one distinguishing aspect of this class's narrative: that the Virgin Mary chose to appear in Mexico not only to take care of Mexico, but also because the Indians needed to be liberated from Spanish oppression. But what is also interesting to note, is that these *doctrina* members have thus far identified as Mexican in the present (recall that Teresa asks students to publicly identify as Mexican) and as Indian in terms of a collaboratively constructed reference to an oppressive past. This blurred distinction between a Mexican present and an Indian past is emphasized again in the course of the narrative, as the class creates an identity as dark-skinned people.

The narrative construction of skin color

As Teresa continues to narrate the story of *Nuestra Señora de Guadalupe*, she describes the color of the Virgin Mary's skin establishing two skin colors representative of two groups of people. Example (4) below illustrates how a switch from the narrated past to the moment of the telling creates yet another collective identity for this class, this time making reference to skin color. Since current discussion in the social sciences has been problematizing the boundaries between ethnic and racial identity (Hollinger 1995; Omi and Winant 1993; Waters 1990), it is particularly revealing to see how at *doctrina*, ethnic identity is based on skin color. In the example below, Teresa explains to her class the physical features of *Nuestra Señora de Guadalupe* as similar to their own:

In this example, a particular shade of skin color, *morenita* ("a little dark"), is identified as the defining feature of the Virgin of Guadalupe, and the predicate construction *como nosotros*

Example (4)

Teresa: **la Santísima Virgen quiso ser (.) se**
the blessed virgin want-PAST-3Sg be-INF REFX
The Blessed Virgin wanted to be
parecerse morenita como nosotros.
look-INF-REFX dark-DIM like Pro-1Pl
to look a little dark like us
(1.0)
porque la Virgen, (.) de Guadalupe
because the Virgin of Guadalupe
because the Virgin of Guadalupe
no es blanca como (.) la Virgen del Carmen
no is white like the Virgin of Carmen
is not white like the Virgin of Carmen
que se apareció (.)
who REFX appear-PAST-3Sg
who appeared
y es la patrona de España,
and is the patroness of Spain
and is the patroness of Spain
la Virgen del Carmen es blanca.
the Virgin of Carmen is white
the Virgin of Carmen is white

(0.5)
y la Virgen de Guadalupe
and the Virgin of Guadalupe
and the Virgin of Guadalupe
es morenita como nosotros
is dark-DIM like Pro-1Pl
is a little dark like us

("like us") embraces the *doctrina* class in a collectivity of dark-skinned peoples. By switching to the moment of the telling, the narration of past events and the description of the narrative's characters includes the dark-skinned *doctrina* people of the present. As the example illustrates, the Virgin of Guadalupe was/is (yesterday/today) dark like the people at *doctrina*.

It is also interesting to note that in this display of ethnic awareness with skin color as the most salient element of contrast, the Virgin of Guadalupe and the Virgin of Carmen co-exist in the present, that is, at the moment of the telling. Notice too that Teresa emphasizes that the Virgin of Guadalupe is not white like the Virgin of Carmen, implying that the Mexican children who look like the Virgin of Guadalupe are not white either. The description and emphasis through repetition, that the Virgin of Guadalupe is *morenita como nosotros* ("a little dark like us"), is indexical of the class of dark Mexicans, and, by extension, the oppressed dark Indians of the past. By disaffiliating her class from the white Virgin of Carmen, Teresa disaffiliates her class from the oppressor Spaniards of colonial Mexico who share the white Virgin's skin color, while at the same time, recognizing and claiming a dark skin color for her class.

This particular *doctrina* narrative telling is an example of how variation in narrative details respond to the recipient organization and the goals of the narrative activity. Clearly, Teresa keeps the main story line, compared, for example, to the plot depicted in the greeting card example I presented before, yet she elaborates on the setting and the skin color of the Virgin Mary. As Poole (1995) has noted, the narrative has served as a means for creating a Mexican identity. Through the continuous unfolding of the narrative, Teresa and her students represent their multiple identities in temporal blends: In the past, they were dark-skinned oppressed Indians in Mexico; they are now dark-skinned Mexicans; and they can also be people *de aquí* ("from here"). This tracing of identities along a temporal and spatial continuum illustrates the diasporic potential of narrative as it creates and explains life in the "borderlands" (Anzaldúa 1987). *Doctrina* members are linked to Mexico through place, as the birth-place of the majority of the students; they are also linked to Mexico in time, as Indians of the past; and they are also people from here (be it the United States, Los Angeles, or the parish) *both* in time and place. The narrative renditions of the apparition of *Nuestra Señora de Guadalupe* are thus sites where *doctrina* children are socialized to Mexican identity.

Multi-ethnic Mary

As the parish of St Paul's moves towards its own "English Only" policy, Latino children will probably join children in other religious instruction classes in which English is the medium of instruction. The effect this multiracial environment will have on *doctrina* students' experiences and on the collaborative telling of particular versions of the narrative of *Nuestra Señora de Guadalupe* remains to be assessed. As I have indicated before, English catechism classes at St Paul's are racially diverse. On the day the classroom interaction described here was recorded, there were Latino, Asian, and Caucasian students present. A segment of classroom interaction depicted in Example (5) below, illustrates two distinct phenomena. First, the dynamics of tense and aspect are used differently, especially distinct from the *doctrina* class examples presented above. Second, Mexican ethnicity is positioned as one of many ethnicities representative of a generic model of American society. In Example (5), Nancy, the teacher, explains to her catechism class the many apparitions of the Virgin Mary:

Example (5)

Nancy: Now. (0.2) remember that Mary has appeared (0.2)
in many many countries (.) to many many people,
(0.5)
differently.
(0.2)
Our Lady of Guadalupe she appeared to the Indian.
she looked like an Indian.
°hh when she appeared over [he:re
[((walking towards cast statue on desk))
(1.5)
uh (0.5) Our Lady of Grace
(0.8) [this is Our Lady of Grace
[((touching statue))
(0.5)
she's crushing the snake, (0.5) with her ↑ feet
(0.5)
cause the snake represents the ↑ Devil
(0.5)
and she's standing on top of the world,
this is (.) Our Lady of Grace.
(0.5)
We have (0.5) uh (0.2) Our Lady of Mount Carmel.
We saw[11] the Pilgrim Virgin, (0.2) Our Lady of Fatima:,
(0.5)
She has appeared (.) to many many many many places.
(0.2)
She's appeared in Lourdes.
(.)
and when she was in ↑ Lourdes,
she wore the costume of the
French ladies, (.) she looked like a French lady.
(0.2)
when she appears in Japa:n, (.) she appears (0.2) Japa ↑ nese
(0.5)
When she appears in Hawaii: (0.2)
if she does. she'd appears Hawaiian,
(0.5)
So Our Lady can (.) can change her (0.5) features,
(.) to look like (.) the country that she is appearing in.

Let's consider first the temporal organization of this list. Present perfect is initially used to state that the Virgin Mary has appeared to several people in the past, in Nancy's words: *Mary has appeared in many many countries to many many people*. Nancy's first example of the Virgin Mary's apparition is Our Lady of Guadalupe who appear*ed* (past tense) to the Indian. In all cases in which the place (and manner) of apparition is mentioned, the past tense is used (*looked like an Indian; she wore the costume; she looked like a French lady*). Present tense variants are used to describe the different apparitions of the Virgin Mary, portraying what seem to be generic manifestations. This stands in contrast to the particularization observed in the *doctrina* narrative rendition, where the telling of the apparition of Our Lady of Guadalupe is embedded in a unique historical moment. Moreover, the emphasis in this catechism class seems to be on describing a generic, multiethnic Mary, which contrasts with the emphasis of the *doctrina* narrative discussed before to create a Mexican identity and describe Spanish oppression in colonial Mexico. While Nancy notes Mary's apparitions without making reference to specific historical contexts, in fact, this generic portrayal leaves the possibility open for a future apparition in Hawaii, she does make sure that the list recognizes many ethnicities, including Mexican, French, and Japanese. This teacher's teaching style[12] is certainly inclusive, yet it denies a particular historicity and the opportunity to organize and explain past and present experience of particular ethnic groups in the class. Moreover, Nancy's recitational style does not encourage participation from the students in her class.

Even though the two classes described in this paper cannot be compared in terms of the actual telling of the narrative, there is one important difference in the way in which both teachers make reference and assign meaning to Our Lady of Guadalupe. Whereas the narrative of *Nuestra Señora de Guadalupe* promotes affiliative activities and creates a unique Latino identity, a collective self and history, in Nancy's catechism class, Our Lady of Guadalupe is mentioned ahistorically as part of a list that becomes a representative sample of the multiethnic composition of the class and of society at large. Given the changes in language policy at St Paul's, the *doctrina* children of the parish will be joining catechism classes, like Nancy's, where the opportunities to create a collective identity as Mexican are limited and where homogenizing and generic discourses pervade.

Implications

Doctrina teachers design collaborative narrative activities that socialize children to acquire and display knowledge of a collective class version of the narrative of *Nuestra Señora de Guadalupe*. That is, creating a collective version of the narrative not only promotes recall of information, it legitimizes the experiences of the *then* and *now* – both the experiences narrated in the story and those which include the teacher's and students' present lives. The study of the language socialization practices of this church community sheds explanatory light on the ways in which language is a potent way to either constitute or minimize identities. We have seen how a *doctrina* teacher orchestrates an oral collaborative rendition of the narrative of the apparition of *Nuestra Señora de Guadalupe* to socialize children to a range of social identities. We have also seen how a catechism teacher positions ethnic identities as part of a representative list.

The analysis of the practices of the *doctrina* community described in this article has implications for understanding the complexity of the social worlds in which the children of this community live, especially as school-aged minority children. Meaning-making in this Latino learning context is carried out differently. At *doctrina* children acquire and learn to verbally display socio-historical knowledge that is affiliative and which they share with their classmates and teachers. The language socialization practices of *doctrina* linguistically and interactionally reaffirm membership in a particular Latino community, linking children to the world views of their community. Yet these practices will become difficult to enact given the parish's mandate to use English as the medium of instruction. The practices at *doctrina* are examples of the ways in which a community not only retells its past, it affirms and claims social identities while gradually being relegated to the linguistic and cultural margins of a local parish in Los Angeles.

NOTES

I am indebted to Elinor Ochs for her insight and guidance. Many thanks to Betsy Rymes, Adrienne Lo, and the members of the UCLA Discourse, Identity, and Representation Collective (D.I.R.E) for their helpful commentary and suggestions. Special thanks to Marcyliena Morgan. The research presented here was made possible by a grant from the UCLA Institute of American Cultures and the Chicano Studies Research Center. Any errors remaining are my own.

1 All names have been changed.
2 *VOX Diccionario Manual Ilustrado de la Lengua Española*, 8th edition. Calabria, Barcelona: Biblograf. See also Frye, 1996 for a brief description of early colonial religious practices and life in Mexico.
3 Certain states, including California, have legally adopted "English Only" policies that restrict the use of languages other than English in public places such as the workplace and government offices.
4 For the academic year of 1995–6, tuition was $200.00 per month, not including books and other school supplies.
5 Most notably, First Communion preparation culminates with a celebratory religious service at the main church building.
6 Transcription symbols used in this paper: ↑ Indicates sharp rising intonation; a period at the end of words marks falling intonation; > indicates speech faster than normal cadence; underlining represents sounds pronounced with emphasis; colons indicate elongated sounds; ".hh" indicates inhalations; numbers in parentheses indicate time elapsed in tenths of seconds, with periods indicating micropauses or noticeable pauses that are less than two tenths of a second; brackets indicate overlapping speech; information contained in ((double parentheses)) indicates nonverbal behavior; CMD is command verbal form; DIM is diminutive suffix, often encoding affect; REFX is a reflexive pronoun; Sg denotes singular; Pl denotes plural; INF is the infinitive tense; IMPF is the imperfective (in Spanish both tense and aspect); DO is direct object.
7 I will be using the English name of Our Lady of Guadalupe when describing the catechism class.
8 Silva-Corvalán (1983) has noted that certain Spanish tenses, in particular the historical present (HP), provide "vividness" and act as an evaluative device. This same argument has been made for the HP in English by Schiffrin (1981). Here I extend Silva-Corvalán's claim to include the Spanish imperfective as functioning both as an evaluative and affiliative device.
9 Similar to American English "uhm."
10 From context it is understood that the Spaniards wanted more material goods than did the Indians.
11 On an earlier trip to the temple that morning, the class met a woman carrying the statue of the Pilgrim Virgin.
12 It remains unknown whether Nancy's choice of examples and descriptive attributes of the different Virgin Marys reflect more than instructional ideology; that is, whether the examples reflect personal and community attitudes towards different cultural groups.

REFERENCES

Anzaldúa, G. (1987). *Borderlands/La Frontera: The New Mestiza*. San Francisco: Aunt Lute Books.

Bernstein, B. (1970/1972). Social Class, Language, and Socialization. In P. Gigioli (ed.), *Language and Social Context*. London: Penguin.

Brockelman, P. (1992). *The Inside Story: A Narrative Approach to Religious Understanding and Truth*. Albany: State University of New York Press.

Bruner, J. (1990). *Acts of Meaning*. Cambridge, MA: Harvard University Press.

Capps, L., and Ochs, E. (1995). *Constructing Panic: The Discourse of Agoraphobia*. Cambridge, MA: Harvard University Press.

Chatterjee, P. (1993). *The Nation and its Fragments: Colonial and Postcolonial Histories*. Princeton, NJ: Princeton University Press.

Comrie, B. (1976). *Aspect: An Introduction to the Study of Verbal Aspect and Related Problems*. Cambridge: Cambridge University Press.

Duranti, A. (1994). *From Grammar to Politics: Linguistic Anthropology in a Western Samoan Village*. Berkeley: University of California Press.

Duranti, A., and Brenneis, D. (eds.) (1986). The Audience as Co-author. Special Issue of *Text* (6.3). New York: Mouton de Gruyter.

Duranti, A., and Ochs, E. (1986). Literacy Instruction in a Samoan Village. In B. Schieffelin and P. Gilmore (eds.), *The Acquisition of Literacy: Ethnographic Perspectives* (pp. 213–32). Norwood, NJ: Ablex.

Duranti, A., Ochs, E., and Ta'ase, E. (1995). Change and Tradition in Literacy Instruction in a Samoan American Community. Paper presented at the Annual Meeting of the American Educational Research Association (AERA), San Francisco, California, April 18.

Frye, D. (1996). *Indians into Mexicans: History and Identity in a Mexican Town*. Austin: University of Texas Press.

Heath, S.B. (1983). *Ways with Words: Language, Life, and Work in Communities and Classrooms*. Cambridge: Cambridge University Press.

Heidegger, M. (1962). *Being and Time*. Trans. J. Macquarrie. and E. Robinson. New York: Harper & Row.

Hollinger, D. (1995). *Postethnic America: Beyond Multiculturalism. New York: Basic Books.*

Labov, W., and Waletzky, J. (1968). Narrative analysis. In W. Labov (ed.), *A Study of the Non-standard English of Negro and Puerto Rican Speakers in New York City* (pp. 286–338). New York: Columbia University.

Lentz, R. (1987). *Nuestra Señora de Guadalupe/Our Lady of Guadalupe*. Burlington, VT: Bridge Building Images.

Morgan, M. (1995). Just to Have Something: Camouflaged Narratives of African American Life. Unpublished manuscript. University of California, Los Angeles.

Ochs, E. (1986). *Culture and Language Development: Language Acquisition and Language Socialization in a Samoan Village*. Cambridge: Cambridge University Press.

Ochs, E. (1994). Stories that Step into the Future. In D. Biber and E. Finegan (eds.), *Perspectives on Register: Situating Register* Variation within Sociolinguistics *(pp. 106–35). Oxford: Oxford University Press.*

Ochs, E., and Capps, L. (1996). Narrating the Self. *Annual Review of Anthropology* 25: 19–43. Palo Alto, CA: Annual Reviews.

Omi, M., and Winant, H. (1993). On the Theoretical Concept of Race. In C. McCarthy and W. Crichlow (eds.), *Race, Identity, and Representation in Education* (pp. 3–10). New York: Routledge.

Polkinghorne, D. (1988). *Narrative Knowing in the Human Sciences*. Albany: State University of New York Press.

Poole, S. (1995). *Our Lady of Guadalupe: The Origins and Sources of a Mexican National Symbol, 1531–1797*. Tucson: University of Arizona Press.

Ricoeur, P. (1985/1988). *Time and Narrative*. Chicago, IL: University of Chicago Press.

Rodriguez, J. (1994). *Our Lady of Guadalupe: Faith and Empowerment among Mexican-American Women*. Austin: University of Texas Press.

Schiffrin, D. (1981). Tense Variation in Narrative, *Language* 57: 45–62.

Schieffelin, B., and Ochs, E. (eds.) (1986). *Language Socialization across Cultures*. Cambridge: Cambridge University Press.

Silva-Corvalán, C. (1983). Tense and Aspect in Oral Spanish Narrative: Context and Meaning. *Language* 59(4): 760–80.

Suárez, J. (1983). *The Mesoamerican Indian Languages*. New York: Cambridge University Press.

Waters, M. (1990). *Ethnic Options: Choosing Identities in America*. Berkeley: University of California Press.

STUDY QUESTIONS

1 What does Baquedano-López mean when she says that social identities (and even "skin color") are "constructed"? When you reflect about your own experience in different kinds of classroom contexts, can you identify and describe situations in which you felt that your teacher was "constructing" an identity for you or for some other students?

2 How were the narratives about Nuestra Señora de Guadalupe different in the two classes observed by Baquedano-López? How were those differences involved in the construction of the children's social identity?

3 What discursive strategies did the teacher of the doctrina class use to connect the story of "Nuestra Señora de Guadalupe" with students' experiences?

4 In what sense is this a study of language socialization?

5 Apply Baquedano-López's analysis of narrative strategies to similar situations that you are familiar with.

Part IV

The Power of Language

Introduction

There is a long tradition of study on the power of words, including ancient Greek and Roman treatises on political rhetoric, the Romantics' discussions of language as the "spirit" of a nation, and the so-called "Sapir-Whorf Hypothesis" on the alleged impact of language on our ways of perceiving reality. The chapters presented in this fourth and last part of the Reader represent some of the more recent contributions to this old and established concern with what language "does" for and to its speakers. They all share the assumption that language is never a completely neutral medium nor is it an innocent participant in the interactions where it is used. Language carries with it a heavy load of assumptions about its users, the kinds of stances that are expected from them, and the contexts in which they live. All of the chapters in Part IV show that it is practically impossible to speak without somehow implicitly subscribing to preconceived ideas about who is supposed to use which kind of language with whom and to do what. Language is thus shown again and again not only to mediate speakers' social relations but also to organize them in ways that might go against some of their own interests or goals in life. Although they are aware of the fact that to resist or reject such assumptions embedded in language use is no small task, the authors of the chapters that follow are united in their desire to make their readers aware of what language does to us. In sharing such a goal, they demonstrate a commitment to reach a wider audience than usual.

The first two chapters explicitly use the notion of language ideology to discuss how language matters are affected by sociopolitical processes and, in turn, affect people's perception of themselves and others. In Chapter 16, combining the study of everyday code switching with the discussion of how ritual speech becomes an ideal model for language use, Paul Kroskrity discusses the strategies that speakers of Arizona Tewa use to stop innovation and shows the limits of what speakers can consciously control. He also argues that their language ideology allows the Arizona

Tewa to resist assimilation. In Chapter 17, drawing from their work on African and East European speech communities, Judith Irvine and Susan Gal argue that speakers interpret certain linguistic features as indications of particular qualities of persons or groups. They project these differences at one level (for example, between two different groups) into differences at another level (for example, between language varieties of the same language), and ignore or reduce existing complexities.

Moving from the level of the nation to the level of everyday interaction, in Chapter 18, Elinor Ochs and Carolyn Taylor look at the production of narratives at the dinner table and uncover how gender asymmetries are reproduced through the division of linguistic labor among family members locked in often predictable roles (for example, introducer, initial teller, primary recipient, problematizer, and judge). Another detailed analysis of narrative accounts is provided in Chapter 19 by Charles Goodwin who brings together two very different contexts – a summer school for archaeologists and a highly publicized court case – to show the techniques whereby experts provide ways of seeing. In so doing, they convince others of seeing what at first could not be seen and thus organize the perception of nature (among archaeologists) or of behavior (among members of the jury and the public) to fit into a particular interpretive scheme instead of other equally possible ones.

In Chapter 20, Jane Hill revisits an apparently innocuous phenomenon, "Mock Spanish" (also known as "Spanglish"), to unveil what she sees as the racist discourse that informs it and determines its use and interpretation. In the concluding chapter, Don Kulick uses the concept of performativity to show how speakers are not in control of their own intentions in using the word "no" when engaged in interactions that involve requests for sex. In both of these last two chapters, language is shown to have a force that simultaneously builds on cultural stereotypes and reproduces them by offering a culturally loaded and highly restricted range of choices to speakers.

SUGGESTIONS FOR FURTHER READING

For a philosophical perspective on language as action, here are some classics: J. L. Austin (1975), *How to Do Things with Words*, 2nd edn., ed. J. O. Urmson and Marina Sbisà, Cambridge, MA: Harvard University Press; L. Wittgenstein (1958), *Philosophical Investigations*, 2nd edn., ed. G. E. M. Anscombe and R. Rhees, trans. G. E. M. Anscombe, Oxford: Blackwell; J. R. Searle (1969), *Speech Acts: An Essay in the Philosophy of Language*, Cambridge: Cambridge University Press. A related but distinct approach is provided by H. P. Grice (1989), *Study in the Way of Words*, Cambridge, MA: Harvard University Press, a collection of very influential articles on how we understand what is not explicitly said. Grice's work had an impact on linguistic and philosophical pragmatics but less so on linguistic anthropology, with the notable exception of P. Brown and S. C. Levinson (1987), *Politeness: Some Universals in Language Usage*, Cambridge: Cambridge University Press.

A good introduction to linguistic and philosophical approaches to pragmatics, covering speech acts, conversational maxims, and conversation analysis is S. C. Levinson (1983), *Pragmatics*, Cambridge: Cambridge University Press. For a more recent and theoretically challenging reformulation of a pragmatic approach based on Grice's maxims, see S. C. Levinson (2000), *Presumptive Meanings: The Theory of*

Generalized Conventional Implicature, Cambridge, MA: MIT Press. See also Jacob L. Mey (2001), *Pragmatics: an Introduction*. Malden, MA: Blackwell.

The acquisition of the pragmatic force of language is discussed in the contributions to E. Ochs and B. B. Schieffelin (1979), *Developmental Pragmatics*, New York: Academic Press.

The power of language is often discussed in the context of linguistic relativity, that is, the impact that the linguistic encoding of experience and speaking habits have on speakers' thinking and acting. The literature on linguistic relativity is vast, especially in the form of articles. Useful collections of articles by two pioneer linguistic anthropologists, Edward Sapir and Benjamin Lee Whorf, include: D. G. Mandelbaum (ed.) (1949), *Selected Writings of Edward Sapir in Language, Culture, and Personality*, Berkeley and Los Angeles: University of California Press; and J. B. Carroll (ed.) (1956), *Language, Thought, and Reality: Selected Writings of Benjamin Lee Whorf*, Cambridge, MA: MIT Press; for an excellent intellectual biography of Sapir, see R. Darnell (1990), *Edward Sapir: Linguist, Anthropologist, Humanist*, Berkeley: University of California.

An in-depth review of a wide range of articles and books on linguistic relativity can be found in: J. A. Lucy (1992), *Language Diversity and Cognitive Development: A Reformulation of the Linguistic Relativity Hypothesis*, Cambridge: Cambridge University Press; and P. Lee (1996), *The Whorf Theory Complex: A Critical Reconstruction*, Amsterdam: John Benjamins. The power of language to reflect on itself is the focus of J. A. Lucy (ed.) (1993), *Reflexive Language: Reported Speech and Metapragmatics*, New York: Cambridge University Press. For new perspectives on linguistic relativity: John A. Lucy (1992), *Grammatical Categories and Cognition: A Case Study of the Linguistic Relativity Hypothesis*, Cambridge: Cambridge University Press; and the articles in J. J. Gumperz and S. C. Levinson (eds.) (1996), *Rethinking Linguistic Relativity*, Cambridge: Cambridge University Press.

The analysis of nonverbal communication is a vast field that has seen the contributions of researchers from a variety of disciplines. In addition to Erving Goffman's books on everyday encounters (mentioned in Part II), other works that have been considered relevant to linguistic anthropology include: R. L. Birdwhistell (1970), *Kinesics and Context: Essays on Body Motion Communication*, Philadelphia: University of Philadelphia Press; R. A. Hinde (ed.) (1972), *Non-Verbal Communication*, Cambridge: Cambridge University Press; A. Kendon, R. Harris, and M. R. Key (eds.) (1975), *Organization of Behavior in Face-to-Face Interaction*, The Hague and Paris: Mouton; T. Polhemus (ed.) (1978), *Social Aspects of the Human Body*, Harmondsworth: Penguin Books; A. Kendon (2004), *Gesture: Visible Action as Utterance*, Cambridge: Cambridge University Press; D. McNeill (2000), *Language and Gesture: Language, Culture, and Cognition, 2*, Cambridge: Cambridge University Press; D. McNeill (2005), *Gesture and Thought*, Chicago, IL: The University of Chicago Press.

On the interaction between talk, eye-gaze, and other gestures, see C. Goodwin (1981), *Conversational Organization: Interaction Between Speakers and Hearers*, New York: Academic Press; A. Kendon (1990), *Conducting Interaction: Patterns of Behavior in Focused Encounters*, Cambridge: Cambridge University Press. On the interaction between language, gesture, and the material world, see C. Goodwin (ed.) (2003), *Conversation and Brain Damage*, Oxford: Oxford University Press. For an evolutionary perspective, see K. R. Gibson and T. Ingold (eds.) (1993), *Tools, Language and Cognition in Human Evolution*, Cambridge: Cambridge University Press.

The relationship between language and ideology is the focus of a number of books and collections by linguistic anthropologists, including B. B. Schieffelin, K. Woolard, and P. Kroskrity (1998), *Language Ideologies: Practice and Theory*, New York: Oxford University Press; S. U. Philips (1998), *Ideology in the Language of Judges: How Judges Practice Law, Politics, and Courtroom Control*, New York: Oxford University Press; J. Blommaert (ed.) (1999), *Language Ideological Debates*, Berlin and New York: Mouton de Gruyter; A. Jaffe (1999), *Ideologies in Action: Language Politics on Corsica*, Berlin and New York: Mouton de Gruyter; P. V. Kroskrity (ed.) (2000), *Regimes of Language: Ideologies, Politics and Identities*, Santa Fe, NM: School of American Research Press; M. Makihara and B. B. Schieffelin (eds.) (2007), *Consequences of Contact: Language Ideologies and Sociocultural Transformations in Pacific Societies*, Oxford: Oxford University Press.

For the original formulation of the notion of "hegemony," which is often mentioned in the language ideology literature, see A. Gramsci (1971), *Selections from the Prison Notebooks of Antonio Gramsci*, New York: International Publishers.

Some useful collections of essays on the language of politics and conflict across cultural contexts include: M. Bloch (1975), *Political Language and Oratory in Traditional Society*, London: Academic Press; R. Paine (ed.) (1981), *Politically Speaking: Cross-Cultural Studies of Rhetoric*, Philadelphia: Institute for the Study of Human Issues; D. L. Brenneis and F. Myers (eds.) (1984), *Dangerous Words: Language and Politics in the Pacific*, New York: New York University; K. Watson-Gegeo and G. White (eds.) (1990), *Disentangling: Conflict Discourse in Pacific Societies*, Stanford, CA: Stanford University Press; B. R. O'G. Anderson (1990), *Language and Power: Exploring Political Cultures in Indonesia*, Ithaca, NY: Cornell University Press. (For more references on language and politics, see Suggestions for Further Reading for Part II).

An impressive comparative study of the use of language for mediating differences in power is P. Brown and S. C. Levinson (1987), *Politeness: Some Universals in Language Usage*, Cambridge: Cambridge University Press.

The literature on language and gender is quite vast. Here are some good collections of articles to start with: S. Philips, S. Steele, and C. Tanz (eds.) (1987), *Language, Gender, and Sex in Comparative Perspective*, Cambridge: Cambridge University Press; D. Tannen (ed.) (1993), *Gender and Conversational Interaction*, New York: Oxford University Press (a set of good articles that critically review past literature and define new research agendas); K. Hall and M. Bucholtz (eds.) (1995), *Gender Articulated: Language and the Socially Constructed Self*, New York: Routledge; M. Bucholtz, A. C. Liang, and L. A. Sutton (eds.) (1999), *Reinventing Identities: The Gendered Self in Discourse*, New York: Oxford University Press. Ethnographic case studies with far-reaching theoretical implications include M. H. Goodwin (1990), *He-Said-She-Said: Talk as Social Organization among Black Children*, Bloomington, IN: Indiana University Press; E. Keating (1998), *Power Sharing: Language, Rank, Gender and Social Space in Pohnpei, Micronesia*, Oxford: Oxford University Press; J. Holmes and M. Meyerhoff (eds.) (2003), *The Handbook of Language and*

Gender, Malden, MA: Blackwell; M. Inoue (2006), *Vicarious Language: Gender and Linguistic Modernity in Japan*, Berkeley: University of California Press.

The literature on language and sexuality from an anthropological perspective is rapidly growing. Here are some suggestions to start: W. Leap (1995), *Beyond the Lavender Lexicon: Authenticity, Imagination and Appropriation in Gay and Lesbian Languages*, New York: Gordon and Breach; W. Leap (1996), *Word's Out: Gay Men's English*, Minneapolis and London: University of Minnesota Press; P. Baker (2002), *Polari: The Lost Language of Gay Men*, London: Routledge; A. Livia and K. Hall (eds.) (1997), *Queerly Phrased: Language, Gender, and Sexuality*, New York and Oxford: Oxford University Press; K. Harvey and C. Shalom (eds.) (1997), *Language and Desire: Encoding Sex, Romance and Intimacy*, London: Routledge; S. Ehrlich (2001), *Representing Rape: Language and Sexual Consent*, London and New York: Routledge; K. Campbell, R. Pdesva, S. J. Roberts, and A. Wong (eds.) (2002), *Language and Sexuality: Contesting Meaning in Theory and Practice*, Stanford, CA: CSLI Publications; P. McIlvenny (ed.) (2002), *Talking Gender and Sexuality*, Amsterdam: John Benjamins; D. Cameron and D. Kulick (2003), *Language and Sexuality*, Cambridge: Cambridge University Press; D. Cameron and D. Kulick (eds.) (2006), *The Language and Sexuality Reader*, London: Routledge.

16

Arizona Tewa Kiva Speech as a Manifestation of a Dominant Language Ideology

Paul V. Kroskrity

"What have you learned about the ceremonies?" Back in the summer of 1973, when I first began research on Arizona Tewa, I was often asked this and similar questions by a variety of villagers. I found this strange, even disconcerting, since the questions persisted after I explained my research interest as residing in the language "itself," or in "just the language, not the culture." But my response was very much a managed production. For though my originally formulated object of study was the Arizona Tewa language, even early on in what was to become long-term field research I had become very interested in the tangled relationship of Arizona Tewa language, culture, and society. But despite this interest, I had been coached by my academic advisers and informed by a scholarly tradition of research on Pueblo Indians to recognize the cultural sensitivity of research on religion and the suspicion directed at those who would nevertheless attempt to study it, even in its more esoteric forms. My professional training thus encouraged me to attribute these periodic inquiries to a combination of secrecy and suspicion regarding such culturally sensitive topics as ceremonial language. Yet despite my careful attempts to disclaim any research interest in kiva speech (*te'e hi:li*) and to carefully distinguish between it and the more mundane speech of everyday Arizona Tewa life, I still experienced these occasional interrogations. Did these questions betray a native confusion of the language of the kiva with that of the home and plaza? Was there a connection between these domains of discourse that was apparent to most Tewa villagers, yet hidden from me? In the past few years, after more than two decades of undertaking various studies of Arizona Tewa grammar, sociolinguistic variation, language contact, traditional narratives, codeswitching, and chanted announcements, an underlying pattern of language use has gradually emerged that, via the documentary method of interpretation, has allowed me to attribute a new meaning to these early inquiries.[1] The disparate

For permission to publish copyright material in this book, grateful acknowledgment is made to: P. V. Kroskrity (1998), "Arizona Tewa Kiva Speech as a Manifestation of a Dominant Language," in B. B. Schieffelin, K. Woolard, and P. Kroskrity (eds.), *Language Ideologies*. New York: Oxford University Press, pp. 103–22.

linguistic and discourse practices of everyday speech, I contend, display a common pattern of influence from *te'e hi:li* "kiva speech." The more explicit rules for language use in ritual performance provide local models for the generation and evaluation of more mundane speech forms and verbal practices.

"LINGUISTIC IDEOLOGIES," taken in Michael Silverstein's (1979) sense as "sets of beliefs about language articulated by users as a rationalization or justification of perceived language structure and use," provide a useful frame for understanding the Arizona Tewa pattern. By viewing members' reflectivity, or what Giddens (1984) calls "reflexive monitoring," as an irreducible force in language behavior, the notion of linguistic ideology directs attention to cultural actors' rationalization of their own language activity. "The total linguistic fact, the datum for a science of language, is irreducibly dialectic in nature. It is an unstable mutual interaction of meaningful sign forms contextualized to situations of interested human use mediated by the fact of cultural ideology" (Silverstein 1985: 220).

Examining the Arizona Tewa culture of language as a site for the investigation of language ideologies is multiply warranted. As a Pueblo Indian group that removed itself from Spanish influence in 1700 by migrating to the easternmost of the Hopi mesas and, since then, has maintained its indigenous Kiowa-Tanoan language, the Arizona Tewa are "twice blessed" with a cultural self-consciousness about language use. First, as Pueblo Indians, they are paragons of what Joel Sherzer (1976) and others have termed "linguistic conservatism" – that celebrated penchant for resistance to linguistic borrowing. But whatever analytical value this concept may have to students of language contact, it has at best only the most tentative footing in terms of its foundations in Arizona Tewa cultural experience. Examination of Arizona Tewa linguistic ideology, I contend, offers an alternative, socioculturally based interpretation – a deconstruction of "linguistic conservatism" into dimensions that are simultaneously more analytically precise and more rooted in Arizona Tewa local knowledge.

A second source of Arizona Tewa cultural emphasis on language is their own remarkable history of language contact and language maintenance. In the diaspora of the Pueblo Revolts of 1680 and 1696, the Arizona Tewa are the only outmigrating group that has retained its language into the present.[2] Maintenance of the Tewa language has served not only to perpetuate an ethnic boundary and to embody a "contrapuntal" linguistic consciousness (Said 1984: 171–2) but also to mask a pattern of dramatic cultural change in adapting to the Hopi, the group to whom the ancestors of the Arizona Tewa migrated almost three hundred years ago. This adaptation was quite necessary for physical survival in the harsh western Pueblo environment. The Arizona Tewa saying *Na:-bí hi:li na:-bí wowa:ci na-mu* "My language is my life (history)" reveals the intimate relationships among language, history, and identity that this migration has fostered, as well as the cultural salience of the connection. Thus, the culture-specific history of the Arizona Tewa has enhanced a Pan-Puebloan attention to language that may account for its magnified local significance.

Local Knowledge and Linguistic Ideology

Though the role of native language maintenance in response to their Hopi hosts is somewhat peculiar to the Arizona Tewa, the cultural prominence of kiva speech – the speech performed in religious chambers when sacred ceremonial altars are erected – is common to all Pueblo societies. As a key symbol of Tewa linguistic values, kiva talk embodies four closely related cultural preferences: regulation by convention, indigenous purism, strict compartmentalization, and linguistic indexing of identity. For each of these I briefly sketch: (1) their basis in kiva talk, (2) their cultural salience as manifested in members' awareness, and (3) the "scope" and "force" with which these preferences are manifested in nonritual speech. By "cultural salience" I mean approximate location on a scale of awareness that ranges from practical consciousness/tacit knowledge, on the one hand, to discursive consciousness/explicit knowledge on the other (Giddens 1984). In using "scope" and "force" I follow Geertz's (1968) study of Islamic belief, in which he used the former to refer to the range of contexts in which some value or belief would be manifested and the latter to characterize its intensity.

Regulation by convention

In the kiva, ritual performers rely on fixed prayer and song texts. Innovation is neither desired nor tolerated. Proper ritual performance should replicate past conventions, and, if such repetition is impossible, the ritual should not be performed at all. Thus, in instances where the ceremonial knowledge has not been effectively transmitted from one priest to his apprentice, the ceremony becomes defunct. This concern with regulation by convention is manifested in everyday speech preferences by adherence to greeting formulae, to the extended use of kinship terms in address forms, to rules of hospitality involving kinsmen and visitors, and to avoidance of direct confrontation in interaction with fellow villagers. Culturally valued native genres, involving either histories or traditional stories, must carefully conform to the traditional formal precedents associated with those genres.

In traditional stories, for example, from the Arizona Tewa genre *pé:yu'u*, audience members and performers alike honor a tradition that employs stylized, nonverbal accompaniment and uses familiar storytelling conventions. Foremost among these ways of "speaking the past" is the use of evidential *ba* as a genre marker (Kroskrity 1985a). By disclaiming any novelty on the part of the narrator, this particle and its repeated use provide a continuous and obligatory indexing of "the voice" of the traditional narrator. In example 1, the introductory sentence of the story "Coyote and Bullsnake" (Kroskrity and Healing 1978) exemplifies a pattern of multiple occurrence within each sentence uttered in the voice of the narrator (as opposed to story characters' voices or frame-breaking asides in a personal voice).

(1) owę́heyam-ba	long:ago ba	Long ago, so they say
bayɛna-senó ba	Old Man Coyote ba	Old Man Coyote so
na-tha.[3]	he lived.	he lived.

Thus a particle that denotes the secondhand nature and traditional character of what is said – similar to our "so they say" – aptly functions as a discourse marker of a genre of traditional stories.

Even when narrators chose to "speak the present" – to contextualize their stories for specific audiences – such innovations should ideally occur in the voice of the narrator (e.g., through episode editing and elaboration, nonverbal audience specification, or the addition of identifying details that might be tied to specific audience members). Narrators who chose such frame-breaking strategies as codeswitching and the introduction of a personal voice (unmarked by *ba*) or who merely forgot to clearly delineate the "voice of the traditional narrator" by excluding *ba* were negatively evaluated for their efforts by audience members, who criticized them for not telling it "right," not telling it the "old way."

If innovation, even in the form of contextualization, is to be culturally sanctioned, it must be cloaked in traditional garb. I encountered an interesting and creative use of traditional linguistic form one summer when I heard what sounded like a traditional Tewa public announcement (*tų́-khé*). The chanter was clearly using the dramatic rising and falling intonations associated with the "public address" style reserved for crier chiefs to announce upcoming ceremonies or call for volunteers for village projects like cleaning out a spring, replastering the kiva, or for individuals to offer birth announcements or stylized grievance chants (Black 1967). But, while the form was traditional, its content and presenter were not. The chanter was issuing a call for a yard sale and inviting all within earshot to examine items of used clothing and some small appliances that she hoped to sell! An example of this is provided in example 2.

Though the "commercial" message was hardly traditional, the chanter won general village approval by conforming to the expected

(2) (a) kwiyó: he:wɛ khe: 'i-kw'ón wí-t'olo-kánt'ó
women some clothes they-lie I/you-tell-will
Women: I'm telling you there are some clothes lying.

(b) n ɛ́' ɛ́ phíní-bí-k'ege 'i:-k ų̨́-kwín - ɛ́' ɛ́-mí
here Phini-s-house you:all-buy-look-come-should
You all should come and shop at Phini's house.

(c) kinán dí-t ų̨́-'án-dán wí-t'olo-'án
this I/other-say-since I/you-tell-past
This is what I was told to tell you.

intonational and other prosodic patterns, as well as the verbal formulae associated with the genre. Despite the brevity of this "short notice" announcement, its obedience to such generic norms as initial addressee specification and its explicit acknowledgment of the announcer role, as well as its prosodic fidelity to traditional models, prompted all but the most ultra-conservative villagers to overlook the fact that the chanter was a woman (Kroskrity 1992: 110–12).[4] Importantly, both the gender of the chanter and the chant's commercial content – both violations in a genre normally performed by men announcing communal activities – were subordinated in public opinion to an approval of its traditional form.

Members' awareness of the value of conventionality is often, as the preceding examples show, quite explicit. While many individuals praise traditionality for its own sake and accept it as a guiding principle, relatively few (with the exception of older members of the ceremonial elite) related this value to the emphasis on replicating past performances or the importance of precedent in calculating ceremonial privilege. One ceremonially well-placed man compared everyday speech to prayers:

> You know when we talk to each other it is like when we pray. We look for a way of saying things that has been handed down to us by our grandfathers and grandmothers. We like something old that has lived into the present. It must be strong and powerful to do that. Only difference between prayers and [everyday] talk is that we don't send our prayers to people.

This analogy suggests that ceremonial practitioners' greater experiential familiarity with the realm of kiva speech may provide them with a greater awareness of the intertextuality of kiva and mundane speech than is accessible to those less experienced.

Indigenous purism

Indigenous purism and strict compartmentalization are two dimensions of Arizona Tewa linguistic ideology that, though analytically distinguishable, are intimately joined in most linguistic practices. During ritual performance there is an explicit and enforced proscription against the use of foreign words and/or native vocabulary clearly identified with an equally alien social dialect (such as slang, recently manufactured words lacking any association to prestigious individuals or activities [Newman 1955]). As for enforcement, Frank Hamilton Cushing's experience is exemplary. For uttering a Spanish word in a Zuni kiva he was struck forcefully across the arms by a whipper kachina. After being so purified, he was instructed to say the Zuni equivalent of "Thank you." In his discussion of vocabulary levels of the Zuni, Stanley Newman appears to dismiss purism in passages such as the following:

> Likewise obviously borrowed words, such as *melika* "Anglo-American" cannot be used in the kiva. This prohibition against loanwords is obviously not to be equated with traditions of linguistic purism, whereby organizations in many modern national states legislate against foreignisms that threaten to adulterate the native language. It stems rather from the general Zuni injunction against bringing unregulated innovation into ceremonial situations. Using a word like *melika*, as one

informant expressed it, would be like bringing a radio into the kiva. (1955: 349)

Though Newman has discouraged the interpretation of such kiva practices as strictly analogous to enforced policies of language purism in contemporary nation-states, the kind of purism that Newman is dismissing amounts to an official proscription of linguistic diffusion (e.g., loanwords, grammatical interference) not only in ceremonial speech but in everyday speech as well. But Tewa ceremonial leaders, like those of other pueblos, are not waging a campaign to dictate everyday speech norms. Any purging of foreignisms in everyday speech represents a popular extrapolation, a symbolic "trickle-down" influence of the salient and prestigious model of kiva speech. The primary concern of ceremonial leaders is with maintaining and delimiting a distinctive and appropriate linguistic variety, or vocabulary level, for religious expression, not with minimizing foreign linguistic influence. The strong sanctions against foreign expressions in ceremonial speech, sanctions that involve physical punishment, are motivated not by the linguistic expression of xenophobia or extreme ethnocentrism but by the need for stylistic consistency in a highly conventionalized liturgical speech level. Similarly, the negative evaluation of instances of codemixing in everyday speech by members of the Arizona Tewa speech community reflects not the prevalence of negative attitudes about these other languages but rather the functioning of ceremonial speech as a local model of linguistic prestige. This role should not be too surprising when we observe that the prestige that accrues to "standard languages" in modern nation-states emanates, in part, from the support of and their use by national governments and in part from their association with formal education. Since Pueblo societies are traditionally theocratic, fusing political power and religious authority, and since ceremonial leaders must acquire appropriate knowledge through rigorous verbal instruction, the functional role and cultural associations of ceremonial speech are actually quite analogous to standard languages that derive their prestige from the institutional support of both government and formal education.

Further supporting this claim that the negative evaluation of codemixing, especially prevalent in older speakers (Kroskrity 1978), is attributable more to local models than to xenophobia are two types of telling observations. First, speakers regulate language mixing from languages that they highly value and use proficiently. Certainly, the Arizona Tewa, as I have argued elsewhere (Kroskrity 1993: 46–7, 206–10), have many social identities that are performed in the nonethnic languages of their linguistic repertoire: Hopi and English. Hopi is an essential medium of intervillage communication and the appropriate language for relating to Hopi kinsmen. Command of English has permitted the Arizona Tewa to gain significant economic and political advantages over the Hopi in their role as cultural brokers, mediating between Euro-Americans and the more conservative Hopi. Fluency in these languages is necessary for full participation in Arizona Tewa society. Though fluency in these languages is never criticized by the Tewa, language mixing between these languages is routinely and consistently devalued. Second, there is a well-established tradition of "song renewal" from other linguistic traditions (Humphreys 1982). Entire songs, solely encoded in foreign languages, are often performed in Tewa Village and throughout the Pueblos. It is difficult to explain the popularity of this tradition if one wants to argue for a xenophobic interpretation of ideal speech norms against codeswitching.

Though the Arizona Tewa clearly lack the deliberation and institutional enforcement often associated with "purist" movements, Arizona Tewa indigenous purism may not lack other attributes that language planning theorists associate with linguistic purism. Scholars such as Jernudd (1989:4), for example, view such movements in modern nation-states as consisting of a bidirectional process that involves the simultaneous opening of native resources and the closing off of nonnative ones for linguistic change. Manfred Henningsen (1989: 31–2) expands on the latter aspect when he says, "the politics of purity ... originates in a quest for identity and authenticity of a cultural Self that feels threatened by the hegemonic pressure of another culture." Annamalai (1989: 225), too, observes that purism is "manifest when there is social change affecting the structure of social control." But while resistance to hegemony and rapid sociocultural change may be the prerequisite of linguistic purism in modern nation-states, these conditions have also prevailed for the Arizona Tewa and their Southern Tewa ancestors since the time of Spanish contact in the sixteenth century. From the repressive colonial program of the Spanish, to post-migration Hopi stigmatization and segregation, to "domestic" colonization by the United States, it is certainly possible to find a consistent pattern of Tewa resistance to hegemonic pressure. But it would be wrong to assume that purism is coincident with such hegemony, that it is largely a component of a "counterlinguistic" response by the Arizona Tewa and their ancestors to a series of oppressions.[5] Data from contact with Apachean languages traceable to the late pre-Spanish contact period shows the same pattern of loanword suppression (Kroskrity 1982, 1985b) and strongly suggests that the practice of indigenous purism was already in place. What has been even more continuous than hegemonic pressure from outside is the prestigious position of the traditional religious leaders – an "internal" hegemonic force – and the speech norms associated with them.

But if Arizona Tewa indigenous purism lacks a social organization dedicated to its systematic enforcement, the Arizona Tewa people themselves are usually quite explicit about its value. In Albert Yava's approximation of a life history known as *Big Falling Snow*, he proudly compares the Arizona Tewa to the Rio Grande Tewa: "We still speak the Tewa language and we speak it in a more pure form than the Rio Grande Tewas do. Over there in New Mexico the Tewa language has been corrupted by other Pueblo languages and Spanish. We also speak Hopi fluently though there are very few Hopi who can converse in Tewa" (1978: 1).

Strict compartmentalization

The third value, strict compartmentalization, is also of great importance to the understanding of Arizona Tewa linguistic ideology. Essential to kiva talk is the maintenance of a distinctive linguistic variety that is dedicated to a well-demarcated arena of use. Kiva talk would lose its integrity if it admitted expressions from other languages or from other linguistic levels. Likewise, if kiva talk were to be spoken outside of ceremonial contexts, it would profane this liturgical variety and constitute a flagrant violation. This strict compartmentalization of language forms and use has often been recognized as a conspicuous aspect of the language attitudes of Pueblo cultures (Dozier 1956; Sherzer 1976: 244). What is novel here is the recognition that this value, like regulation by convention and indigenous purism, is traceable to the adoption of kiva talk as the local model of linguistic prestige. Just as ceremonial practitioners can neither mix linguistic codes nor use them outside their circumscribed contexts of use, so – ideally – Tewa people should observe comparable compartmentalization of their various languages and linguistic levels in their everyday speech. The mixing of Tewa with either English or Hopi is explicitly devalued by members of the Tewa speech community, though in unguarded speech some mixing does occur. It is interesting that in the Tewa folk account of speech variation, social categories are ranked in respect to the perceived avoidance of language mixing. Older speakers, for example, are said to approximate this ideal more than younger. Men do so more than women. It should be emphasized that this folk perception can be readily interpreted as a reflection of the different participation of these groups in ceremonial activities, of their differential proximity to the realm of kiva talk.

Examination of both historical linguistic data and more contemporary sociolinguistic studies of the Arizona Tewa confirms the selective influence of indigenous purism and strict compartmentalization. Since I have already extensively reviewed this trend elsewhere (Kroskrity 1993: 55–108), it is appropriate to summarize and highlight a pattern of linguistic ideology that shapes the form of linguistic diffusion in three periods of language contact. The pattern features the suppression of linguistic borrowing, especially in the lexicon. In multilingual episodes with Apacheans, the Spanish, and the Hopi lasting 100, 150, and 191 years, respectively, the Arizona Tewa language has admitted two Apachean, seventeen Spanish, and one Hopi loanword (Kroskrity

1982, 1993). Clearly, Arizona Tewa folk linguists have put into practice the indigenous purist and the strict compartmentalization planks of Arizona Tewa linguistic ideology. But there is also clear evidence that folk attention is selective. The approximation of these ideals in actual practice presupposes a folk perception of "alien" linguistic structures, and yet Arizona Tewa linguists, unlike our own, are primarily if not exclusively lexicographers. Abundant evidence suggests that several grammatical structures in Arizona Tewa are the result of linguistic convergence. Thus, as illustrated in example 3, the innovation of a possessive or relational suffix in Tewa appears to be the result of contact with Apachean languages.

(3)

TEWA	NAVAJO
sen-bí 'é:nu	hastiin bi-ye'
man-'s son	man 's[6]-song
(a) man's son	(a) man's song
'é:nu -bí nų̧'ų̧	hastiin bi-ch'ą̧ą̧h
boy -'s under	man 's-front
under the boy	in front of the man

These two phrases, in both Arizona Tewa and Navajo, demonstrate both the phonological and the grammatical similarity of the affixes. In both languages, these constituents are used in possessive constructions and with locative postpositions. Significantly, no other Kiowa-Tanoan language has this constituent (Kroskrity 1985b). This strongly suggests grammatical diffusion from Apachean languages as the source for Arizona Tewa *-bí*.

Similarly, Arizona Tewa has innovated a new passive suffix, which now alternates with an inherited one shared by Rio Grande Tewa. Example 4 illustrates the parallel Arizona Tewa and Hopi constructions.

(4)

TEWA	HOPI
p'o na-kulu-tí	taawi yuk-ilti
water it-pour-PASSIVE	song finish-PASSIVE
The water was poured.	The song was finished.

(Kalectaca 1978:132)

Though Arizona Tewa has a passive suffix, *-n*, which it shares with Rio Grande Tewa, the *-tí* suffix represents a grammatical borrowing from analogous Hopi structures. Again, in an instance of ongoing linguistic change emerging from sociolinguistic variation, younger Arizona Tewa speakers now produce only one of the three structural alternatives for realizing phrasal conjunction that are available for the oldest generation of speakers (Kroskrity 1982). Significantly, it is the one that converges with English structures of the type N and N (i.e., N-ádí N), as represented in example 5:

(5) sen-ná-dí kwiyó-wá-dí
sen-ná-dí kwiyó
sen kwiyó-wá-dí
the man and the woman

There is also evidence that some discourse phenomena join grammar in their location outside the awareness of speakers. In comparative studies of Hopi, Arizona Tewa, and Rio Grande Tewa narratives, I found that, though the Arizona Tewa evidential particle *ba*, as discussed in relation to example 1, was clearly related to a homologous one in Rio Grande Tewa, its pattern of usage more clearly resembled that of the Hopi quotative particle *yaw*, as in Arizona Tewa (example 6) and Hopi (example 7):

In its frequent and multiple occurrence within sentences, as well as its general service as a genre marker, the Arizona Tewa pattern of use appears to have converged with the Hopi and departed from the norms of other Tewa narrative traditions.

(6) 'i-wɛ ba, di-powa-di ba, 'ó:bé-khwo:li-mak'a-kánt'ó-di
there-at ba, they-arrive-SUB[7] they:INV-fly-teach-SUB
From there so, having arrived so, they were being taught to fly.

(7) noq yaw 'ora:yvi 'atka ki:tava yaw piw 'tłpcvo ki'yta
and yaw Oraibi below:south from:village yaw also wren she-live
And wren also lived below Oraibi, south of the village.
(from Seumptewa, Voegelin, and Voegelin 1980)

As an ideological preference, "strict compartmentalization" is tangible not only in the practical consciousness of Arizona Tewa speech behavior but also in the "discursive consciousness" of some members. One older man who had recently had primary responsibility for the performance of an important village ceremony offered the following agricultural imagery in his explication of the practice of strict compartmentalization and its ceremonial connections.

> This way we keep kiva speech separate from everyday speech reminds me of the way we plant corn. You know those different colors [of corn] just don't happen. If you want blue corn, if you want red corn, you must plant your whole field only in that color. If you plant two together you get only mixed corn. But we need to keep our colors different for the ceremonies. That's why we have so many fields far from one another. Same way our languages. If you mix them they are no longer as good and useful. The corn is a lot like our languages – we work to keep them separate.

This example of native explication demonstrates that strict compartmentalization is not always an unconscious activity but, on occasions and by some individuals, also a discursive strategy that can be both rationalized and naturalized as obedience to ceremonial dictates.

Linguistic indexing of identity

The final dimension of Tewa linguistic idelogy concerns itself with the Tewa preference for locating the speaking self in a linguistically well-defined, possibly positional, sociocultural identity and the belief that speech behavior in general expresses important information about the speaker's identity. Related to this is a comment once made to me by Albert Yava regarding the way attention to the speech of others is used to locate them in sociocultural space: "I only have to hear someone talk for a short while before I know who they are and where they have been." In addition to this cultural idea that one's speech is a linguistic biography, the model of ritual speech foregrounds the importance of positional, rather than personal, identities and the use of appropriate role-specific speech.

Outside of kiva talk, we find similar emphases in the more mundane genres of traditional stories and public announcements. In stories, as mentioned earlier, the narrator establishes and maintains his status through adoption of the full range of narrative conventions, including the use of evidential *ba*. These practices permit narrators to adopt the voice of the traditional storyteller in order to "speak the past." Similarly, a conventional component of public announcements is the explicit acknowledgement by the chanter of his mediating status as spokesperson. The scope of this penchant for conveying identity through use of an associated code extends to casual conversation. Among trilingual Tewa men conversing in domestic settings it was not unusual to hear codeswitching deployed for just such expressive purposes. Example 8, extracted from a more detailed study of codeswitching (Kroskrity 1993: 193–210) is a brief strip of talk in which a codeswitch signals a reformulation of identity for the speaking selves.

(8) F: [HOPI] Tutuqayki-t qa-naanawakna.
"Schools were not wanted."

G: [TEWA] Wé-dí-t'ókán-k'ege-na'a-di im-bí akhon-i-di.
"They didn't want a school on their land."

H: [TEWA] Nɛmbie:yɛ nɛ̨lɛ̨ɛ̨-mo díbí-t'o-'am-mí ką:
yį́'i we-di-mu:di.
"It's better our children go to school right here rather than far away."

Three senior Tewa men have been discussing then recent news about the selection of an on-reservation site for the building of a high school. This topic follows from prior discussion of other building projects on the reservation. As is customary in discussing extravillage reservation matters, the conversation, to which all three men have contributed, has been conducted in Hopi. Speaker F merely notes the opposition to previous efforts to create an on-reservation high school. But speakers G and H switch to Tewa to reformulate their speaking selves as Tewa – members of a group that historically has opposed Hopi obstruction of building plans. G's use of Tewa further distances him from the Hopi "they" who opposed use of "their" tribal lands as school sites. H states what has historically been the Arizona Tewa argument for a reservation high school. Since, in retrospect, most Hopi and Tewa individuals now recognize the disruptive impact on their children over the past few decades of attending boarding schools, H's remark also evaluates the essential correctness of the position promoted by their ethnic group. In both G's and H's remarks, the selection of the "marked" code given the topic reformulates their relevant interactional identity as Arizona Tewa. Thus, the practice of maintaining maximally distinctive codes through strict compartmentalization provides the Tewa with appropriate linguistic resources in order to invoke a variety of corresponding sociocultural identities in interaction. Awareness (Silverstein 1981) of this aspect of language use on the part of Arizona Tewa speakers is, predictably, selective. Many speakers recognize the resources that their linguistic repertoires provide in permitting them to perform multiple social identities. These speakers often liken their languages and linguistic levels to masks and costumes worn for a specific ceremony.

But it is useful to note that, although the Arizona Tewa openly acknowledge a close association between language and identity, as mentioned earlier, they do not recognize conversational codeswitching as a locus for the expression of identity. This is, no doubt, tied to the fact that most Arizona Tewa trilinguals deny that they codeswitch, even though they routinely engage in this practice. This denial may reflect not only the fact that these behaviors are largely taken for granted but also a popular confusion between culturally devalued "codemixing" and codeswitching. Of much greater cultural salience are members' discourses on language and identity, which either invoke the Tewa practice of multiple names or compare the activity of speaking different languages to wearing different ceremonial masks (Kroskrity 1993: 46–7).

Some members view the cultural practice of having many names and acquiring new names as one progresses through the ceremonial system as the most salient connection between language and identity. The discourse involving analogies to impersonation of kachinas is, of course, limited to those men who have "impersonated" kachinas in public ceremonies. The comparisons to such ceremonial performances requires some further commentary, since the dramaturgical imagery of a western view – involving personae, masks, and impersonation – invites a very nonlocal interpretation. For the Arizona Tewa, as for other Pueblo groups, so-called masks are viewed as living "friends" (*k'ema*), and masking is not a means of hiding one's "real" identity or donning a false one but rather an act of transformation in which the performer becomes the being that is iconically represented by his clan's "friend." When such local meanings are taken into account, it is clear that the imagery of ceremonial performance, even if available only to a restricted group, provides a discourse that recognizes the constitutive role of language in iconically signaling a member's relevant identity.

Conclusions

In this chapter I have explored the potentially fruitful application of the notion of language ideology to the Arizona Tewa speech community. In this section, I attempt to highlight some of the uses of a language ideological approach to the Arizona Tewa data by examining its applicability to two general accounts of Pueblo languages and cultures: the "linguistic conservatism" of the Pueblo Southwest and the relationship of Arizona Tewa language ideology to the political economies of Western Pueblo societies. After this, I return to the issue of members' awareness, or consciousness, as a criterial attribute of language ideologies and suggest that successfully "naturalized" and "contending" language ideologies are routinely associated with different levels of members' awareness.

I start by agreeing with Friedrich (1989: 309), who distinguishes several especially valuable senses of "ideology." I employ two of these distinctions in my concluding remarks as a means of assessing both what has been accomplished and what remains to be done. Attending to the "notional" sense of ideology as the basic notions or ideas that members have about a well-demarcated area of a culture, an attention to culturally dominant linguistic ideology greatly improves on the limited "etic" understanding provided by the notion of "linguistic conservatism." Though Pueblo Indian communities are often said to exhibit this trait, scholars have also prematurely reified the notion of linguistic conservatism, treating it as if it were both a self-explanatory and an irreducible analytical account (Kroskrity 1993: 213–21). Representative of this approach is Joel Sherzer when he attempts to account for why the indigenous Southwest lacks evidence of linguistic sharing despite its relatively high population density and long-term coresidence of neighboring groups:

> The explanation for this situation may be found in a sociolinguistic factor about which we rarely have data – attitude toward language. The Southwest is one area for which many observers have reported attitudes toward one's own language and that of others, perhaps because these attitudes are often very explicit. Southwest Indians are very conservative with respect to language ... taking pride in their own language and sometimes refusing to learn that of others. (1976: 244)

But language ideology, in this notional sense, permits an account that better captures the cultural unity of otherwise disparate linguistic norms and discourse practices and the guided agency of Tewa speakers in exercising their necessarily selective control over their linguistic resources. In the "pragmatic" (Friedrich 1989: 297) or "critical" sense (see Woolard 1998) elaborated here, language ideology provides analytical access to the social processes that construct those practices and attitudes labeled "linguistically conservative" by outside experts. The Arizona Tewa were and continue to be an instructive example of how folk consciousness and rationalization of language structure and use can have a powerful effect on language contact outcomes.

The "pragmatic" sense of ideology – the strategies, practical symbols, and systems of ideas used for promoting, perpetuating, or changing a social or cultural order – directs attention to the role of such local models of language as instruments of power and social control. It is important to remember that Pueblo ceremonial language, like ceremonial behavior in general, is not only the expression of religious belief through the sacred manipulation of cosmic forces but also the implicit justification of rule by a largely hereditary ceremonial elite. Thus, linguistic ideology provides a socially motivated explanation for the sociocultural processes that inform the local beliefs about language and the linguistic products that are labeled merely by the expression "linguistic conservatism." Moreover, linguistic ideology offers an ethno-linguistic account that provides an insightful microcultural complement to recent ethnographic and ethnohistorical efforts to rethink the sociocultural order of "egalitarian" Pueblo societies. Peter Whiteley's (1988) *Deliberate Acts* and Jerrold Levy's *Orayvi Revisited* (1992) have signaled an important turn in a scholarly tradition that had represented the Hopi and other Pueblo groups as if each were an "apolitical, egalitarian society" (Whiteley 1988: 64). In Whiteley's analysis of how the Orayvi – the oldest continuously inhabited Hopi village – split as a resolution of factional disputes, he recognizes the importance of local distinctions between *pavansinom* "ruling people" and *sukavuungsinom* "common people." In this ceremonically based system of stratification, ritual privilege – such as ownership and control of group ceremony – symbolizes and rationalizes an indigenous hierarchy that is critical to understanding the accomplishment of order, as well as the occasional disorders that characterize Hopi village societies. Levy's reanalysis of early field research in Orayvi by the anthropologist Mischa Titiev further establishes the stratified nature of Hopi society and also offers an account of why Hopi social inequality was routinely reconfigured in representations by such scholars as Mischa Titiev (1944) and Fred Eggan (1950) as basically egalitarian. Levy reveals a patterned relationship between ceremonial standing and the control of land that indicates that those clans that "owned" the most important ceremonies also had the most and the best land for farming. As Levy (1992: 156) observes, "The system of stratification worked to manage scarcity, not abundance." In a subsistence economy in a high desert environment notorious for meager and inconsistent resources, the Hopi religious hierarchy created a stratification, not only of clans but of lineages within clans, that prioritized those most essential to the performance of required village ceremonies. In times of famine, the hierarchy served as a built-in mechanism for instructing lowstatus clans and lineages to leave the village so as to create the least disruption to the ceremonial order. While Levy's discussion about the management of scarcity is more true of Western Pueblos and their necessary reliance on "dry farming," the notion of an indigenous hierarchy is clearly extendable to Rio Grande Tewa pueblos like San Juan, where Ortiz (1969: 16–18) recognizes an opposition between "made people" and "dry food people" that parallels that between "ruling" and "commoner" classes. The Arizona Tewa also recognize a similar opposition between *pa: t'owa* (made people) and *wɛ t'owa* (weed people).[8]

But it is important to emphasize that in Levy's analysis the ceremonial system not only rationalizes a hierarchy but also serves to mask it by offering an alternative ideology of equality and mutual dependence. For village ritual to be successful, it must enjoy the participation not only of sponsoring clans and lineages but also of many others who participate in a variety of ways – from actual ritual performance to the provision of food for performers. In participating in a ritual sponsored by another clan, villagers expected that their efforts would be reciprocated by others when a ceremony sponsored by their own clan was to be performed. The net effect of what Levy calls the "ceremonial ideology" is the erasure of clan ownership and the transformation of a clan-specific ritual into "shared" village ceremony:

> Although an ideology emphasizing the importance of all Hopis and all ceremonial activities was probably an essential counterbalance to the divisiveness of social stratification, it is important to recognize that the integrative structual mechanisms were also an important ingredient. Opportunity for participation in the ceremonial life was sufficient to prevent the alienation of the common people under the normal conditions of life. (1992: 78)

Thus, in Levy's analysis, the ceremonial system served to integrate Hopi society by providing crosscutting relationships of responsibility across clans and lineages, making Hopi society more than the sum of its otherwise divisively strong kin groups. Coupled with such structural mechanisms as marriage regulation (the requirement that one marry outside both of one's parents' clans) and the extension of kinship relations along ceremonial lines (e.g., ceremonial "mothers" and "fathers"), the importance of the ceremonial system as a means of both erasing clan and class divisions and fostering village and ethnic identities becomes clear (Kroskrity 1994). Thus, the ceremonial system can be viewed as a source of the "ideal" egalitarian society, as well as the "ideal" person (Geertz 1990), often felt and expressed by members who have, in turn, communicated this vision to anthropologists who have, in turn, represented it as an essential feature of Hopi society.[9] Given the importance and power of ritual performance as a rite of unification, it is no wonder that the kiva serves as the "site" of the Arizona Tewa dominant language ideology (Silverstein 1992, 1998). Associated both with the theocratic "authority" of a ruling elite and the promise of a ceremonially based social mobility to commoners, kiva speech provides a model that crosses the boundaries of class and clan. For as Bourdieu (1991: 113) observes, "the language of authority never governs without the collaboration of those it governs, without the help of the social mechanisms capable of producing this complicity."

Although kiva speech is associated with the cultural salience of group ritual, these highly "naturalized" (Bourdieu 1977: 164) ritual privileges and events, including kiva speech itself, promote a "taken for grantedness" (Schutz 1967: 74) of this language ideological site and a "practical consciousness" (Giddens 1984) of the role of kiva speech as a model for everyday speech. As discussed earlier in this chapter, members have a partial awareness of this system, which occasionally surfaces in members' "discursive consciousness" of selected aspects of their language structure and use. The consistency of Arizona Tewa beliefs about language, their partial awareness of how these beliefs can affect language practices, their selective success in activating this awareness in actual practice, and the capacity of individuals to alter their consciousness of the system depending on their interests and "zones of relevance" (Heeren 1974) all argue for a treatment as "language ideological," despite the general lack of "discursive consciousness."[10] It is perhaps a further commentary on the internal diversity of the language ideology literature noted by Woolard (1998) that as I argue for the expansion and recentering of "language ideology" to be more inclusive, partly by the inclusion of ideologies of practice and practical consciousness, others have called for its elimination. Charles Briggs (1992: 400), for example, argues that "ideology" tends to suggest either a "fixed, abstracted, and circumscribed set of beliefs" divorced from their constitution in action or "erroneous and derivative notions that can only provide insight into the means by which Others celebrate their own mystification."

Noting that "beliefs about language are multiple, competing, contradictory and contested," Briggs proposes a Foucault-inspired conceptual shift to "metadiscursive strategies" (Briggs 1992: 398–400). But while such a perspective might better capture the more self-conscious reflections of Warao shamans, or of American feminists in their rejection of generic "he" (Silverstein 1985), it is important to observe that ideological contention and discursive consciousness are in a relationship of mutual dependence. Debates and other displays of contention necessarily problematize formerly taken-for-granted language practices, and this self-consciousness of language is the very condition for rationalizing or challenging conventional practices.

Of course, such an emphasis on strategy and contestation suggests that these are omnipresent in social life and consciousness. But I have already argued that successfully "naturalized" beliefs and practices, such as the role of Arizona Tewa kiva speech as a "prestige model" for everyday verbal conduct, are not publicly challenged and seldom enter members' discursive consciousness. Any rethinking of language ideology that would exclude naturalized, dominant ideologies and thus analytically segregate beliefs about language according to a criterion of consciousness seems to me to be unwise. Since dominant ideologies can become contended ideologies over time and since members vary, both interindividually and intraindividually, in their degree of consciousness, the creation of a categorical boundary between such language beliefs would falsify their dynamic relationship. But while I can hardly second Briggs's proposed shift to "metadiscursive strategies," I do share his concern to avoid associating language ideology with either the pejorative vision of others' "false consciousness" of their linguistic resources or the valorization of the sociolinguist who can truly and exhaustively comprehend the total system. [...]

Given the connections between ceremonial and more mundane speech delineated here, as well as the partial awareness of it reflected in the rejection of my early claims to diplomatic immunity through appeal to an "autonomous" language, it is no wonder that my early Tewa interrogators found their language so valuable and my linguistic research so controversial.

NOTES

1 By "documentary method of interpretation" I mean the ethnomethodological process that provides that retrospective clarity and revised interpretation in the construction of both commonsense and expert knowledge (Garfinkel 1967: 77 ff.).

2 For a more complete discussion of the Pueblo diaspora, interested readers should consult Sando 1992: 63–78, Simmons 1979, and Schroeder 1979. In using the

term "diaspora" to describe the impact of the Spanish colonial program and the resulting Pueblo Revolts, I am following the more "descriptive" model suggested by Clifford 1994, rather than the prescriptive model endorsed by Safran 1991 and others. Insofar as the Arizona Tewa are concerned, they certainly qualify as an expatriate minority community, and their history on First Mesa has been characterized by what Said 1984 has described as the "contrapuntal" self-consciousness, the imposed awareness of exile. The Arizona Tewa do not fit models that require that a diasporic group maintain an ongoing memory of the displaced homeland or a desire to return to such an ancestral site. Though this is not the place for an extended discussion on this topic, it is useful to indicate that the Arizona Tewas' lack of nostalgia for their ancestral homeland is importantly connected to their successful multiethnic integration into First Mesa Hopi society and to the fact that their former villages are not ongoing communities but rather defunct pueblos long since abandoned.

3 For ease of presentation to a diverse audience, I have opted to use an orthography that departs from conventional Americanist practices in at least two respects. I have eliminated superscript indications of secondary articulation (e.g., aspiration, palatalization) and have instead represented these with digraphs.

4 Announcements display varying degrees of elaboration, depending on whether they are seen as "advance" or "short" notice. The latter are often viewed as reminders and do not contain the full details.

5 I am using "counterlinguistic" here as an adjectival form of what Marcyliena Morgan 1993 calls "counterlanguage." In this and other works, she successfully demonstrates how indigenous discourse preferences, especially those involving indirection, inform African American counterlanguage by creating messages that are simultaneously transparent to members yet opaque to outside oppressors. My point here is that purism appears to predate the Spanish colonial program and therefore is not explainable as a response to Spanish hegemony. It is interesting to speculate that kiva speech may have acquired a connotation of counterlanguage during the early colonial program, when native religion was actively suppressed by the Spanish. It is doubtful, however, that such a connotation would have extended to the Hopi mesas, where the Spanish were never a formidable military presence, or last into the period of "cultural adjustment" after the second Pueblo Revolt, when the Spanish terminated the policy of religious persecution (Schroeder 1972: 59–67). It is also important to observe that African-American "counterlanguage" utilizes African speech values that are embodied in everyday mundane speech behavior.

6 Though Apachean *bi-* is the source for Tewa *-bí*, Tewa has overgeneralized it as a general possessive morpheme, whereas in the Apachean languages it is limited to the third person.

7 SUB is an abbreviated gloss for subordinator, a grammatical marker for dependent clauses.

8 Ortiz 1969 also recognizes a third class that mediates this opposition between made people and "dry food people" – the *t'owa 'e*, a level of secular government officials that dates at least to the time of Spanish occupation.

9 Levy 1992 also suggests that once prevailing social science notions such as Redfield's "folk society" contributed to an intellectual climate in which ethnographers like Titiev and Eggan would deemphasize Hopi social stratification.

10 Here I follow a phenomenological approach (Schutz 1966; Heeren 1974) in which "zones of relevance" reflect the degree of relevance to an actor's project of a given interaction. Thus, awareness of interactional or symbolic detail may be heightened or altered, depending on the immediacy of that actor's imposed or intrinsic interests. For example, a young Tewa man might become acutely aware

of kinship and the practicalities of the rules of clan exogamy when he begins to "date" women from his own village. Yet this same awareness might have been previously regarded as "relatively irrelevant" before that point.

REFERENCES

Annamalai, E. (1989). The Linguistic and Social Dimensions of Purism. In *The Politics of Language Purism*, ed. Björn H. Jernudd and Michael J. Shapiro, pp. 225–31. Berlin: Mouton de Gruyter.

Black, Robert (1967). Hopi Grievance Chants: A Mechanism of Social Control. In *Studies in Southwestern Ethnolinguistics*, ed. Dell H. Hymes and William E. Bittle, pp. 54–67. The Hague: Mouton.

Briggs, Charles L. (1992). Linguistic Ideologies and the Naturalization of Power in Warao Discourse. *Pragmatics* 2: 387–404.

Bourdieu, Pierre (1977). *Outline of a Theory of Practice*. Cambridge: Cambridge University Press.

Bourdieu, Pierre (1991). *Language and Symbolic Power.* Cambridge, Mass.: Harvard University Press.

Clifford, James (1986). Introduction: Partial Truths. In *Writing Culture*, ed. James Clifford and George E. Marcus, pp. 1–26. Berkeley: University of California Press.

Clifford, James (1994). Diasporas. *Cultural Anthropology* 9: 302–38.

Collins, James (1992). Our Ideologies and Theirs. *Pragmatics* 2: 405–16.

Dozier, Edward P. (1956). Two Examples of Linguistic Acculturation: The Yaqui of Sonora and the Tewa of New Mexico. *Language* 32: 146–57.

Dozier, Edward P. (1966). Factionalism at Santa Clara Pueblo. *Ethnology* 5: 172–85.

Eggan, Fred (1950). *Social Organization of the Western Pueblos*. Chicago, Ill.: University of Chicago Press.

Friedrich, Paul (1989). Language, Ideology, and Political Economy. *American Anthropologist* 91: 295–312.

Garfinkel, Harold (1967). *Studies in Ethnomethodology.* Englewood Cliffs, N.J.: Prentice Hall.

Geertz, Armin W. (1990). Hopi Hermeneutics: Ritual Person Among the Hopi Indians of Arizona. In *Concepts of the Person in Religion and Thought*, ed. H. G. Kippenberg, Y. B. Kuiper, and A. F. Sanders, pp. 309–35. Berlin: Mouton.

Geertz, Clifford (1968). *Islam Observed: Religious Developments in Morocco and Indonesia.* Chicago, Ill.: University of Chicago Press.

Giddens, Anthony (1984). *The Constitution of Society.* Berkeley: University of California Press.

Heeren, John (1974). Alfred Schutz and the Sociology of Common-sense Knowledge. In *Understanding Everyday Life*, ed. Jack D. Douglas, pp. 45–56. London: Routledge and Kegan Paul.

Henningsen, Manfred (1989). The Politics of Purity and Exclusion. In *The Politics of Language Purism*, ed. Björn H. Jernudd and Michael J. Shapiro, pp. 31–52. Berlin: Mouton de Gruyter.

Hill, Jane H. (1992). "Today There Is No Respect": Nostalgia, "Respect," and Oppositional Discourse in Mexicano (Nahuatl) Language Ideology. *Pragmatics* 2: 263–80.

Humphreys, Paul (1982). The Tradition of Song Renewal among the Pueblo Indians of North America. *American Indian Culture and Research Journal* 6: 9–24.

Jernudd, Björn H. (1989). The Texture of Language Purism. In *The Politics of Language Purism*, ed. Björn H. Jernudd and Michael J. Shapiro, pp. 1–19. Berlin: Mouton de Gruyter.

Kalectaca, Milo (1978). *Lessons in Hopi.* Tucson: University of Arizona Press.

Kroskrity, Paul V. (1978). Aspects of Syntactic and Semantic Variation in the Arizona Tewa Speech Community. *Anthropological Linguistics* 20: 235–58.

Kroskrity, Paul V. (1982). Language Contact and Linguistic Diffusion: The Arizona Tewa Speech Community. In *Bilingualism and Language Contact*, ed. Florence Barkin, Elizabeth A. Brandt, and Jacob Ornstein-Galicia, pp. 51–72. New York: Columbia Teachers College Press.

Kroskrity, Paul V. (1985a). "Growing with Stories": Line, Verse, and Genre in an Arizona Tewa Text. *Journal of Anthropological Research* 41: 183–200.

Kroskrity, Paul V. (1985b). Areal Influences on Tewa Possession. *International Journal of American Linguistics* 51: 486–9.

Kroskrity, Paul V. (1992). Arizona Tewa Public Announcements: Form, Function, and Language Ideology. *Anthropological Linguistics* 34: 104–16.

Kroskrity, Paul V. (1993). *Language, History, and Identity: Ethnolinguistic Studies of the Arizona Tewa*. Tucson: University of Arizona Press.

Kroskrity, Paul V. (1994). Language Ideologies in the Expression and Representation of Arizona Tewa Ethnic Identity. Paper presented at School of American Research Advanced Seminar on Language Ideology. Santa Fe, N.M.

Kroskrity, Paul V., and Dewey Healing (1978). Coyote and Bullsnake. In *Coyote Stories*, ed. William Bright, pp. 162–70. IJAL Native American Texts Series, Monograph No. 1. Ann Arbor: University Microfilms.

Levy, Jerrold E. (1992). *Orayvi Revisited.* Santa Fe, N.M.: School of American Research.

Mertz, Elizabeth (1992). Linguistic Ideology and Praxis in U.S. Law School Classrooms. *Pragmatics* 2: 325–34.

Morgan, Marcyliena (1993). The Africanness of Counterlanguage among Afro-Americans. In *Afro-American Language Varieties*, ed. Salikoko Mufwene, pp. 423–35. Athens: University of Georgia Press.

Newman, Stanley (1955). Vocabulary Levels: Zuni Sacred and Slang Usage. *Southwestern Journal of Anthropology* 11: 345–54.

Ortiz, Alfonso (1969). *The Tewa World*. Chicago, Ill.: University of Chicago Press.

Safran, William (1991). Diasporas in Modern Societies: Myth of Homeland and Return. *Diaspora* 1: 83–99.

Said, Edward (1984). Reflections of Exile. *Granta* 13: 159–72.

Sando, Joe S. (1992). *Pueblo Nations: Eight Centuries of Pueblo Indian History.* Santa Fe, NM: Clear Light.

Schroeder, Albert H. (1972). Rio Grande Ethnohistory. In *New Perspectives on the Pueblos*, ed. Alfonso Ortiz, pp. 41–70. Albuquerque: University of New Mexico Press.

Schroeder, Albert H. (1979). Pueblos Abandoned in Historic Times. In *Southwest.* Vol. 9 of *Handbook of North American Indians*, ed. Alfonso Ortiz, pp. 236–54. Washington, DC: Smithsonian.

Schutz, Alfred (1966). *Collected Papers*. Vol. 3: *Studies in Phenomenological Philosophy.* The Hague: Martinus Nijhoff.

Schutz, A. ([1932]1967). *The Phenomenology of the Social World*, trans. G. Walsh and F. Lehnert. Evanston, Ill.: Northwestern University Press.

Seumptewa, Evelyn, C.F. Voegelin, and F. M. Voegelin (1980). Wren and Coyote (Hopi). In *Coyote Stories*, Vol. 2, ed. Martha B. Kendall, pp. 104–10. IJAL Native American Texts Series, Monograph No. 6. Ann Arbor: University Microfilms.

Sherzer, Joel (1976). *An Areal-Typological Study of American Indian Languages North of Mexico*. Amsterdam: North-Holland.

Silverstein, Michael (1979). Language Structure and Linguistic Ideology. In *The Elements: A Parasession on Linguistic Units and Levels*, ed. Paul R. Clyne, William F. Hanks, and Carol L. Hofbauer, pp. 193–247. Chicago, Ill.: Chicago Linguistics Society.

Silverstein, Michael (1981). The Limits of Awareness. Working Papers in Sociolinguistics 84. Austin, Tex.: Southwest Educational Development Library.

Silverstein, Michael (1985). Language and the Culture of Gender: At the Intersection of Structure, Usage, and Ideology. In *Semiotic Mediation*, ed. Elizabeth Mertz and Richard J. Parmentier, pp. 219–39. Orlando, Fla.: Academic Press.

Silverstein, Michael (1992). The Uses and Utility of Ideology: Some Reflections. *Pragmatics* 2: 311–24.

Silverstein, M. (1998). The Uses and Utility of Ideology. A Commentary. In *Language Ideologies: Practice and Theory*, ed. B. B. Schieffelin, K. Woolard, and P. Kroskrity, pp. 123–45. New York: Oxford University Press.

Simmons, Marc (1979). History of Pueblo–Spanish Relations to 1821. In *Southwest.* Vol. 9 of *Handbook of North American*

Indians, ed. Alfonso Ortiz, pp. 178–93. Washington, DC: Smithsonian.

Titiev, Mischa (1944). *Old Oraibi: A Study of the Hopi Indians of Third Mesa*. Papers of the Peabody Museum of American Archaeology and Ethnology, vol. 2, no. 1. Cambridge, Mass.: Harvard University Press.

Whiteley, Peter M. (1988). *Deliberate Acts: Changing Hopi Culture through the Oraibi Split*. Tucson: University of Arizona Press.

Woolard, Kathryn (1989). Sentences in the Language Prison: The Rhetorical Structuring of an American Language Policy Debate. *American Ethnologist* 16: 268–78.

Woolard, K. A. (1998). Introduction: Language Ideology as a Field of Inquiry. In *Language Ideologies: Practice and Theory*, ed. B. B. Schieffelin, K. Woolard, and P. Kroskrity, pp. 3–47. New York: Oxford University Press.

Woolard, Kathryn, and Bambi B. Schieffelin (1994). Language Ideology. *Annual Review of Anthropology* 23: 55–82.

Yava, Albert (1978). *Big Falling Snow*. New York: Crown.

STUDY QUESTIONS

1 What does the notion of "language ideology" refer to and how is it exemplified in Kroskrity's account of the Arizona Tewa speech community?
2 On the basis of Kroskrity's discussion of the Arizona Tewa linguistic ideology, define (1) regulation by convention; (2) indigenous purism; and (3) strict compartmentalization, using examples from languages and speech communities you are familiar with.
3 For the Tewa, the ideal models of person and language are taken from the ideal ritual person and ideal ritual language. Explain and illustrate this idea using examples from Kroskrity's article.
4 What are some examples of linguistic convergence provided in the chapter?
5 Illustrate the Arizona Tewa's idea that one's speech is a linguistic biography. Can you think of how this might apply to your own way of assessing the background and recent past history of people you are talking with?

17

Language Ideology and Linguistic Differentiation

Judith T. Irvine and Susan Gal

A language is simply a dialect that has an army and a navy – so goes a well-known saying in linguistics.[1] Although only semiserious, this dictum recognizes an important truth: The significance of linguistic differentiation is embedded in the politics of a region and its observers. Just as having an army presupposes some outside force, some real or putative opposition to be faced, so does identifying a language presuppose a boundary or opposition to other languages with which it contrasts in some larger sociolinguistic field. We focus on the ideological aspects of that linguistic differentiation – the ideas with which participants and observers frame their understanding of linguistic varieties and map those understandings onto people, events, and activities that are significant to them. With Silverstein (1979), Kroskrity, Schieffelin, and Woolard (1992), Woolard and Schieffelin (1994), and others, we call these conceptual schemes *ideologies* because they are suffused with the political and moral issues pervading the particular sociolinguistic field and are subject to the interests of their bearers' social position.

Linguistic ideologies are held not only by the immediate participants in a local sociolinguistic system. They are also held by other observers, such as the linguists and ethnographers who have mapped the boundaries of languages and peoples and provided descriptive accounts of them. Our attention here is therefore just as appropriately directed to those mappings and accounts as to their subject matter. There is no "view from nowhere," no gaze that is not positioned. Of course, it is always easier to detect positioning in the views of others, such as the linguists and ethnographers of an earlier era, than in one's own. Examining the activities of linguists a century or more ago reveals, via the wisdom of hindsight or at least via historical distance, the ideological dimensions of their work in drawing and interpreting linguistic boundaries. This historical inquiry also has a contemporary relevance, to the extent that early representations of sociolinguistic phenomena influenced later representations and even contributed to shaping the sociolinguistic scene itself.

Our discussion is less concerned with history per se, however, than with the dynamics of a sociolinguistic process. In exploring ideologies of linguistic differentiation, we are concerned not only with the ideologies' structure but also,

For permission to publish copyright material in this book, grateful acknowledgment is made to: J. T. Irvine and S. Gal (2000), "Language Ideology and Linguistic Differentiation," in P. Kroskrity (ed.), *Regimes of Language: Ideologies, Polities, and Identities*. Santa Fe, NM: School of American Research Press, pp. 35–83.

and especially, with their consequences. First, we explore how participants' ideologies concerning boundaries and differences may contribute to language change. Second, we ask how the describer's ideology has consequences for scholarship, how it shapes his or her description of language(s). Third, we consider the consequences for politics, how linguistic ideologies are taken to authorize actions on the basis of linguistic relationship or difference.

To address these questions we have examined ethnographic and linguistic cases from several parts of the world, involving different kinds of linguistic differentiation. Since Africa and Europe are the sites of our own research, we have looked most particularly to these regions for examples of relevant ethnography, linguistics, and historical investigation. But whether in these parts of the world or elsewhere, in all the cases we have examined – those described in this paper and many others as well – we find some similarities in the ways ideologies "recognize" (or misrecognize) linguistic differences: how they locate, interpret, and rationalize sociolinguistic complexity, identifying linguistic varieties with "typical" persons and activities and accounting for the differentiations among them. We have identified three important semiotic processes by which this works: iconization, fractal recursivity, and erasure.

Before we offer more specific discussions of what these three processes are, let us note that all of them concern the way people conceive of links between linguistic forms and social phenomena. Those conceptions can best be explicated by a semiotic approach that distinguishes several kinds of sign relationships, including (as Peirce long ago suggested) the iconic, the indexical, and the symbolic.[2] It has become a commonplace in sociolinguistics that linguistic forms, including whole languages, can index social groups. As part of everyday behavior, the use of a linguistic form can become a pointer to (index of) the social identities and the typical activities of speakers. But speakers (and hearers) often notice, rationalize, and justify such linguistic indices, thereby creating linguistic ideologies that purport to explain the source and meaning of the linguistic differences. To put this another way, linguistic features are seen as reflecting and expressing broader cultural images of people and activities. Participants' ideologies about language locate linguistic phenomena as part of, and evidence for, what they believe to be systematic behavioral, aesthetic, affective, and moral contrasts among the social groups indexed. That is, people have, and act in relation to, ideologically constructed representations of linguistic differences. In these ideological constructions, indexical relationships become the ground on which other sign relationships are built.

The three semiotic processes we have identified are thus the means by which people construct ideological representations of linguistic differences. Examples will follow, but first let us describe the processes more particularly:

Iconization involves a transformation of the sign relationship between linguistic features (or varieties) and the social images with which they are linked. Linguistic features that index social groups or activities appear to be iconic representations of them, as if a linguistic feature somehow depicted or displayed a social group's inherent nature or essence. This process entails the attribution of cause and immediate necessity to a connection (between linguistic features and social groups) that may be only historical, contingent, or conventional. The iconicity of the ideological representation reinforces the implication of necessity. By picking out qualities supposedly shared by the social image and the linguistic image, the ideological representation – itself a sign – binds them together in a linkage that appears to be inherent.[3]

Fractal recursivity involves the projection of an opposition, salient at some level of relationship, onto some other level. For example, intragroup oppositions might be projected outward onto intergroup relations, or vice versa. Thus the dichotomizing and partitioning process that was involved in some understood opposition (between groups or linguistic varieties, for example) recurs at other levels, creating either subcategories on each side of a contrast or supercategories that include both sides but oppose them to something else. Reminiscent of fractals in geometry and the structure of segmentary kinship systems – as well as other phenomena anthropologists have seen as involving segmentation or schismogenesis, such as nationalist ideologies and gender rituals[4] – the myriad oppositions that can create identity may be reproduced repeatedly, either within each side of a dichotomy or outside it. When such oppositions are reproduced within a single person, they do not concern contrasting *identities* so much as oppositions between *activities* or *roles* associated with prototypical social persons. In any case, the oppositions do not define fixed or stable social groups, and the mimesis they suggest cannot be more than partial. Rather, they provide actors with the discursive or cultural resources to claim and thus attempt to create shifting "communities," identities, selves, and roles, at different levels of contrast, within a cultural field.

Erasure is the process in which ideology, in simplifying the sociolinguistic field, renders some persons or activities (or sociolinguistic phenomena) invisible. Facts that are inconsistent with the ideological scheme either go unnoticed or get explained away. So, for example, a social group or a language may be imagined as homogeneous, its internal variation disregarded. Because a linguistic ideology is a totalizing vision, elements that do not fit its interpretive structure – that cannot be seen to fit – must be either ignored or transformed. Erasure in ideological representation does not, however, necessarily mean actual eradication of the awkward element, whose very existence may be unobserved or unattended to. It is probably only when the "problematic" element is seen as fitting some alternative, threatening picture that the semiotic process involved in erasure might translate into some kind of practical action to remove the threat, if circumstances permit.

By focusing on linguistic differences, we intend to draw attention to some semiotic properties of those processes of identity formation that depend on defining the self as against some imagined "Other." This is a familiar kind of process, one by now well known in the literature. Anthropologists, at least, are now well acquainted with the ways in which the Other, or simply the other side of a contrast, is often essentialized and imagined as homogeneous. The imagery involved in this essentializing process includes, we suggest, linguistic images – images in which the linguistic behaviors of others are simplified and seen as if deriving from those persons' essences rather than from historical accident. Such representations may serve to interpret linguistic differences that have arisen through drift or long-term separation. But they may also serve to influence or even generate linguistic differences in those cases where some sociological contrast (in presumed essential attributes of persons or activities) seems to require display.

In the hope that examples will illustrate and clarify these points, we have chosen three cases for discussion. One, from southern Africa, concerns the motivation of language change; the second, from West Africa, concerns linguistic description in grammars and dictionaries; and the third, from southeastern Europe, concerns political contestation.

The Motivation of Linguistic Change: The Nguni Languages' Acquisition of Clicks

Our first case concerns the Nguni languages of southern Africa (especially Zulu and Xhosa) and their acquisition of click consonants. Clicks were not originally part of the consonant repertoire of the Nguni languages – the southernmost branch of the Bantu language family – but were acquired from the Khoi languages, indigenous to southern Africa at the time the Bantu languages arrived there. The question is why this change happened. It is common enough for otherwise unrelated languages in a geographical area, given sufficient time, to come to have certain resemblances to one another, or "areal characteristics." In this case it is possible to see something of how the resemblance came about. (We draw on work by Herbert 1990 and others, including Irvine 1992.)

Because they are conspicuous sounds that are unusual in the phonological repertoires of the world's languages, clicks have drawn the attention of many visitors and newcomers to southern Africa over the centuries. Many early European observers compared them with animal noises: hens' clucking, ducks' quacking, owls' hooting, magpies' chattering, or "the noise of irritated turkey-cocks" (Kolben 1731: 32). Others thought clicks were more like the sounds of inanimate objects, such as stones hitting one another. To these observers and the European readers of their reports, such iconic comparisons suggested (before our more enlightened days, at least) that the speakers of languages with clicks were in some way subhuman or degraded, to a degree corresponding to the proportion of clicks in their consonant repertoires. Commenting on clicks, the linguist F. Max Müller wrote (1855: lxxix):

> I cannot leave this subject without expressing at least a strong hope that, by the influence of the Missionaries, these brutal sounds will be in time abolished, at least among the Kaffirs [Zulu and Xhosa], though it may be impossible to eradicate them in the degraded Hottentot dialects [i.e., Khoi, which had more of them].

Clicks must also have sounded very foreign to Bantu-language speakers when they first arrived in southern Africa. The very concept of speaking a foreign language seems, unsurprisingly, to have been focused on the Khoisan languages, which were observably full of clicks. Thus the Xhosa term *úkukhumsha* [Zulu *ukuhúmusha*] "speak a foreign language, interpret" borrows its stem from Khoi, as in Nama *khom* "speak" (see Louw 1977: 75, which also includes some other inferences, based on Nguni loans from Khoi, about early Nguni attitudes toward Khoisan-speakers).[5] Yet it was apparently for the very reason of their conspicuous foreignness that the clicks were first adopted into the Nguni languages, providing a means for Nguni-speakers themselves to express social difference and linguistic abnormality. The principal route by which clicks entered the Nguni languages seems to have been via an avoidance register, which required certain lexical items in everyday speech to be avoided or altered out of respect. By adopting clicks, Nguni-speakers could create lexical substitutions that were conspicuously different from their everyday equivalents.

The Nguni avoidance (or respect) register, called *hlonipha*, is reported for all the Nguni languages and is evidently of some antiquity among them. It also occurs in Southern Sotho, another Bantu language in the region and the only one outside the Nguni group to include a click consonant. In all these languages, however, *hlonipha* is tending to fall out of use today. It is still practiced among rural Xhosa women (see Finlayson 1978, 1982, 1984 for examples of recent usage), and perhaps also among some rural Zulu, but it seems to have become rare for Zulu in urban contexts. Published sources on Zulu *hlonipha*, while providing extensive lists of its vocabulary and some information on use, describe the practices of decades ago (see, for example, Bryant 1949; Doke 1961; Doke and Vilakazi 1958; Krige 1950), and Herbert (1990: 308) reports that "many urban Zulu postgraduate students have described their reading of the *hlonipha* literature as 'like reading about a foreign culture'."

The norms of *hlonipha* behavior prescribe modesty and a display of respect in the presence or neighborhood of certain senior affines and, in precolonial times at least, of royalty. The norms apply to gesture and clothing as well as words: to *hlonipha* is to avoid eye contact, cover one's body, and restrain one's affectivity. Talk about bodily functions, for example, is to be avoided or, if not avoidable, to be mentioned only in conventional euphemisms. What the descriptions of *hlonipha* focus on most, however, is the importance of covering over or avoiding the linguistic expression of sound-sequences that would enunciate respected persons' names. Included in the prohibition are not just the names themselves but any word containing one of the name's core syllables.

The *hlonipha* words are thus lexical alternants that enable speakers to avoid uttering respected persons' names and any other word containing sounds similar to the name's root or stem. So, for example, if the name of a woman's husband's father happens to sound like *imvuɓu* 'hippopotamus', that woman must call hippos *incuɓu* instead. Where names are composed of meaningful expressions, as was traditionally the case, many ordinary words might be affected by the need to avoid name-sounds. As Bryant (1949: 221) notes,

> Thus, if one of the [respected] persons were named *uMutí* (Mr. Tree), not only would this (the ordinary) word for 'a-tree' be disused, and the *Hlonipa* word, *umCakantshi*, substituted for it, but, further, every other word containing within its root the particle, *ti*, would be similarly avoided; thus, for *uku Tíba* would be used *ukuPúnga*; for *umTákatí, umKúnkuli*; for *ukuTí, ukuNki*, and so on.

The respectful substitute term could derive from a descriptive or metaphorical construction, or it could derive from patterned phonological shifts altering a name-word's syllable-initial consonants. Although there were several different patterns, the most common kinds of phonological shifts were for stem-initial consonants to become [+ Coronal], especially the coronal affricates *tš* and *dž* (*j*), or to become clicks.[6] Since – at least in the early phases of the process – the expressions from which names were constructed used ordinary Bantu roots, which did not include clicks and most probably did not include coronal affricates either (Herbert 1990: 305; Finlayson 1982: 49), a convenient way to construct a *hlonipha* word would have been to substitute one of these "foreign" sounds for the offending consonant. The result was a click-laden respect vocabulary, perhaps consisting partly of idiosyncratic, ad hoc formulations but also including words that were widely known as *hlonipha* alternants. The fact that the respect vocabulary shows such a high percentage of click consonants, compared with the everyday vocabulary, is one of the major pieces of evidence for supposing that it was the vehicle for these consonants' entry into Nguni phonological repertoires.[7]

Table 17.1 gives some examples of *hlonipha* words in Zulu. The first group of words illustrates consonant substitutions of various kinds, especially substitutions of a click for a nonclick consonant. These words are presumably name-avoidance forms; so, if a respected person's name sounded like *aluka* "graze, weave," the speaker must refer to grazing as *acuka* instead. The *hlonipha* word *injušo* (for *indaɓa*, "affair") is a lexical substitution occasioned by avoidance of the name Ndaba, a Zulu royal ancestor.

The second group of words in table 17.1 are forms referring to persons requiring respect because of their social positions. The creation of *hlonipha* alternants may therefore have been occasioned as a respectful way to refer to those positions, and not necessarily because of a need to avoid particular names that might be based upon these stems. Bryant (1949: 220) documents this process, which was not limited to words referring to persons: "For a Zulu woman to call a porcupine by its proper name, iNgungumbane, were but to provoke it to increased depredation in her fields; therefore it must be referred to 'politely' as 'the-little-woman', or umFazazana." The third group of words in table 17.1 illustrates the fact that the substitution of clicks for corresponding non-click consonants sometimes created homonyms in the *hlonipha* vocabulary.

That the *hlonipha* vocabulary was the vehicle for the entry of clicks into the Nguni consonant inventories is argued in greater detail in Herbert's (1990) paper. As he points out, however, some questions remain. Why would

Table 17.1 Zulu hlonipha (respect) vocabulary examples

	Ordinary	*Hlonipha*
(1)		
graze, weave	*aluka*	*acuka*
be dejected	*jaba*	*gxaba*
affair	*indaɓa*	*injušo*
hippopotamus	*imvuɓu*	*incuɓu*
lion	*imbuɓe*	*injuɓe*
house	*indlu*	*incumba*
our	-ithu	-itšu
thy	-kho	-to
(2)		
my father	*uɓaɓa*	*utšatša*
brother-in-law	*umlamu*	*umcamu*
chief	*inkosi*	*inqoɓo, inqotšana (dim.)*
(3)		
swing	*lenga*	*cenga*
annoy	*nenga*	*cenga*

Source: Doke & Vilakazi 1958
Note: c, q, x = clicks (gx = voiced click) ɓ = implosive bilabial stop

particular name-avoidance alternants be used, or even known, more widely than within the immediate circle of a respected person's dependents? And why are clicks now found in everyday words as well as in the respect vocabulary?

The first of these questions arises partly because the ethnographic literature tends to focus on a narrow portion of *hlonipha* behavior and so makes the practice appear more limited and idiosyncratic than it actually was. Drawing on participants' statements, observers emphasize the relationship between a married woman and her husband's father as the "explanation" of the *hlonipha* practice. That is, all *hlonipha* speech is supposedly based on the individual woman's respectful avoidance of a particular man's name. Were this the extent of the usage, of course, *hlonipha* alternants would be created idiosyncratically; each woman would have a different set (and men would use none); only a few vocabulary items would be affected for any particular speaker; and a respect alternant would disappear upon the daughter-in-law's death.

The focus on the daughter-in-law/father-in-law relationship seems, however, to be a folk rationalization – a piece of language ideology – that corresponds only in part to the distribution of actual usages. A wider distribution would be entailed even if *hlonipha* were practiced only by married women, since a married woman owes respect to all the senior members of her husband's lineage and household, and the respect terms deriving from these names would affect all women married into the same patrilineal, patrilocal community. But there is abundant documentation also of a much more widespread phenomenon involving male as well as female speakers, court as well as domestic contexts, and various kinds of respected beings. From Krige (1950: 31) we learn, for example, that Zulu *hlonipha* terms were also used by men to avoid uttering the name of the mother-in-law, though the custom was "not so strict" for men as it was for women. Furthermore, "the whole tribe" must *hlonipha* the name of the king or chief, while those resident at the royal court must *hlonipha* the names of the king's father and grandfather as well (Krige 1950: 31, 233). Bryant (1949: 220) adds, "The men, or indeed the whole clan, may Hlonipa the name of a renowned chief or ancestor, as, for instance, the Zulus, a few generations ago, Hlonipa'd the words, iMpande (root) and iNdlela (path), calling them, respectively, iNgxabo and iNyatuko, owing to certain then great personages being named uMpande and uNdlela." Recall, also, Bryant's statement about the porcupine, to which he adds similar comments about cats, red ants, snakes, and lightning.

Among Xhosa, too, *hlonipha* repertoires were relatively large and widespread, as Finlayson's research indicates. A brief transcript of a conversation between two rural women (Finlayson 1984: 139) shows that more than 25 percent of the words used are *hlonipha*. These women had some eight or nine affines in common, whose name-sounds were thus being avoided. But although the women's family members could point to particular persons who were being shown respect in this conversation,[8] it is not always obvious how the avoided words relate to their name-sounds. Indeed, some *hlonipha* words are or have become disconnected from specific name-avoidances, serving instead, as Finlayson (1984: 140) notes, as a "core" respect vocabulary consisting "of words which are generally known and accepted as *hlonipha* words," used as a display of respect regardless of the particulars of individual names.[9]

In short, the daughter-in-law who avoids uttering her father-in-law's name-sounds is the cultural image, in Nguni language ideology, to which the respect register is linked. She provides the Nguni prototype for the respectful, modest behavior required of dependents and outsiders (nonmembers of a patrilineage, in her case). *Hlonipha* practice is not confined, however, to that particular in-law relationship. Instead, that relationship merely provides the model for what is actually a more widespread phenomenon, both socially, as regards the range of speakers and settings, and linguistically, as regards the range of words affected by the practice.

If clicks entered these languages via the respect vocabulary, how did they come to be found also in ordinary vocabulary? There are probably two routes by which click-including words could have entered the everyday lexicon. As Herbert (1990: 308–9) notes, the adoption of clicks in *hlonipha* would have made them more familiar as sounds and therefore more likely to be retained in other lexical borrowings from the Khoi languages (i.e., words borrowed for quite other reasons, such as place names and terms for Khoi specialty activities and goods). The other source for click-bearing everyday words is the *hlonipha* vocabulary itself, because some *hlonipha* words may have gradually lost their "respectful" aura over time and passed over into everyday vocabulary. There, in turn, they would be subject to replacement by new avoidance forms.

This type of process, in which respect alternants behave like currency in inflationary conditions, is known to have occurred in other parts of the world (see Irvine 1992). The process seems to be hastened when speakers strive to mark their behavior as being extraordinarily respectful or conscientious. As Kunene (1958: 162) remarks for Southern Sotho *hlonepha*, some speakers go so far as to replace almost all stems in daily vocabulary "due to an exaggerated loyalty to the custom, or to a competitive spirit, in order to outdo So-and-So, or to a desire to make assurance doubly sure..." In such circumstances, respect vocabulary, overused, eventually becomes commonplace and everyday and must be replaced by terms more conspicuously special.

Thus, by means of the conspicuous click consonants, seen as *icons* of "foreignness" in the early years of the process, the contrast between Nguni and Khoi consonant repertoires was mobilized to express social distance and deference within Nguni. To put this another way, a cultural framework for understanding linguistic difference at one level (the difference between Bantu and Khoi languages) was the basis for constructing difference at another level (a difference in registers within a particular Bantu language). This is an example of what we mean by recursivity. It is a process that led to phonological change in the Nguni languages, introducing click consonants into a special register that eventually began to leak, as respect registers will.

Notice that this idea of clicks as emblematically "foreign" and of their utterance as signaling deference ideologically emphasizes the sharpness of a boundary between Nguni and Khoi, and the domination of Nguni-speakers over Khoi-speakers. What the ideology ignores, that is, erases, is the historically attested complexity of Nguni-Khoi relations. Many Khoi were multilingual, living on the margins of Nguni society, moving in and out of it as their fortunes fell or rose. Some Khoi, moreover, served Nguni as traders and ritual specialists; some Nguni men took Khoi wives, and some Khoi men took Nguni wives; and some Nguni entered Khoi society as leaderless refugees, outcast from Nguni chiefdoms as a result of political disputes (Denoon 1992; Giliomee 1989; Harinck 1969; Prins and Lewis 1992). Another kind of erasure occurred when some European observers, writing about *hlonipha* after the power of precolonial kingdoms and chiefdoms had declined, described it as "women's speech" – ignoring its political dimension and its use by men.

This case is interesting for many reasons, among them the fact that its main outlines are precolonial and involve language ideologies other than the European or European-derived. However, it is hardly the only instance of the ideological mediation of language change. More familiar to a sociolinguistic audience is Labov's (1963) classic study of vowel change on Martha's Vineyard. Contrasts among ethnic groups of islanders (Yankees, Portuguese, and Indians) in the 1930s were replaced by a contrast between islanders and mainlanders in the 1960s. Islander phonology diverged ever more sharply from mainland forms after the development of the tourist industry made that contrast more socially significant than local, intra-island differences. Although Labov did not explore the content of the language ideology giving rise to these changes, the case seems to beg for just this kind of analysis and illustrates language change as an ideologically fueled process of increasing divergence. We can call the divergence ideologically mediated because it depended on local images of salient social categories that shifted over time.

Linguistic Descriptions of Senegalese Languages

Our second case concerns the work of nineteenth-century European linguists and ethnographers who described the languages of Senegal, particularly Fula, Wolof, and Sereer. The question we explore is how representations of Senegalese languages and peoples were influenced by the ideologies of European observers interacting with Africans (who had ideologies of their own) in a complex sociolinguistic situation. The ways these languages were identified, delimited, and mapped, the ways their relationships were interpreted, and even the ways they were described in grammars and dictionaries were all heavily influenced by an ideology of racial and national essences. This essentializing move, when applied to Senegalese languages, involved the three semiotic processes we have discussed. Although our main concern is with nineteenth-century accounts, their representations of language have had some long-lasting effects, as we shall suggest.

Most linguists today agree that Fula, Wolof, and Sereer are three distinct but related languages forming a "Senegal group" within the Atlantic branch of the Niger-Congo language family. The languages in this group do not now constitute a dialect chain. Still, their geographical distributions overlap because of multilingualism and intermingling of speakers. Within the present-day country of Senegal, in the region north of the Gambia River (see Figure 17.1), Fula is most concentrated in the northeast and Sereer most concentrated in the south, but the three languages do not sort out into neatly discrete territories. Within this region, too, is a set of small linguistic islands – villages where still other languages are spoken. (These

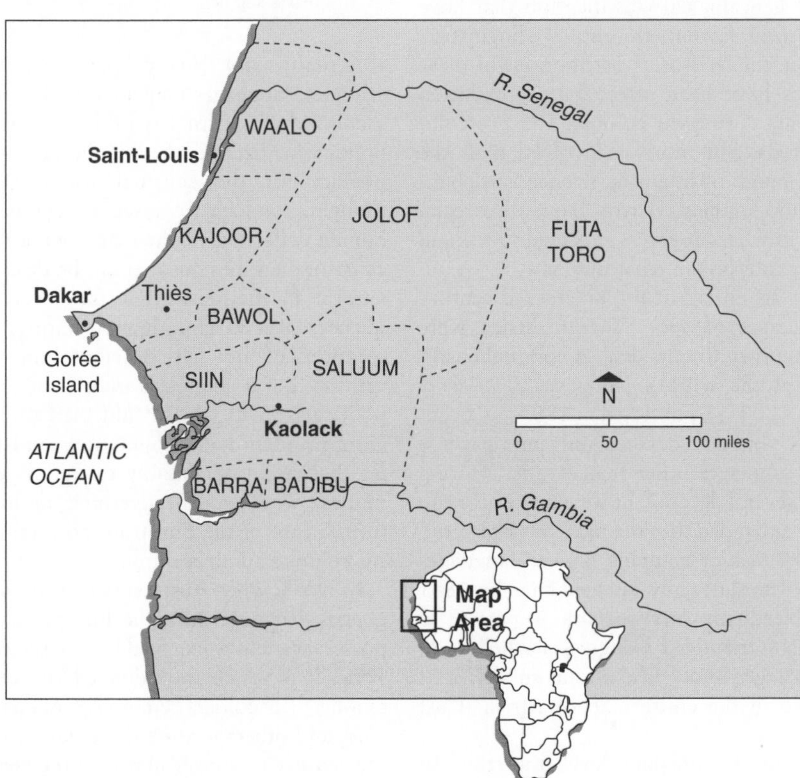

Figure 17.1 *Geographical region of present-day Senegal and The Gambia, showing precolonial Senegalese states circa 1785 (boundaries approximate) and some modern cities.*

villages are located near the city of Thiès. In precolonial times they were enclaves within the territory of the kingdom of Kajoor and subject to its rule. See figure 17.1 for the region's precolonial kingdoms and some major cities.) These other languages, now known to linguists as the Cangin languages, form a group belonging to the Atlantic family, which is very diverse, but not to the "Senegal group," from which most linguists consider them quite different (see Wilson 1989). A century ago, however, Fula, Wolof, and Sereer were mapped as occupying separate territories; most linguists considered Fula unrelated genealogically to Wolof and Sereer; and Sereer itself was thought to include the varieties now termed Cangin.

Why have these representations of the Senegalese linguistic scene changed? Part of the answer lies, of course, in the greater accumulation of linguistic observations, the greater care in their recording, and the more stringent principles of genealogical classification that have characterized twentieth-century linguistics. Moreover, the territorial distributions of these languages have been affected by population movements during the colonial and postcolonial periods. But more is involved than the onward march of linguistic science and changing demographics. There have also been changes in what observers expected to see and how they interpreted what they saw.

At the beginning of the nineteenth century the languages of sub- Saharan Africa were scarcely known to outsiders. A comprehensive survery of the world's languages (Hervas y Panduro 1800–5), published in 1805 and occupying six volumes, devoted only one page to African languages other than Arabic. During the next several decades, however, as European interests expanded into the interior of the continent, the task of mapping African languages was so enthusiastically pursued that by 1881 Robert Needham Cust was able to present to that year's Orientalist Congress a schedule of 438 languages and 153 dialectal subdivisions that filled in the entire map of Africa (Cust 1883).

At the most immediate level, the study of African languages involved control over communication with local populations, communication that would otherwise have to rely on African interpreters. Also important, however, were the ethnological, political, and cultural implications that were presumed to follow from the discovery of language boundaries and relationships. If languages were "the pedigree of nations," as Samuel Johnson had said, then identifying languages was the same thing as identifying "nations" and a logical first step in comparing, understanding, and ordering their relations to each other and to Europeans. As Lepsius (1863: 24) wrote (in the introduction to his proposal for a universal orthography),

> From the relations of separate languages, or groups of languages, to one another, we may discover the original and more or less intimate affinity of the nations themselves ... [Thus] will the chaos of the nations in [Africa], Asia, America, and Polynesia, be gradually resolved into order, by the aid of linguistic science.[10]

Actually, for many post-Enlightenment scholars, languages coincided with nations in a cultural or spiritual sense but preceded any political realization of nationhood. As the expression of the spiritual (or even, some thought, biological) essences of particular human collectivities, languages were regarded as natural entities out there to be discovered – natural in the sense that they were consequences of a variable human nature, not the creations of any self-conscious human intervention. But if languages were prior to human political activity, they could then serve as its warrant, identifying populations and territories that could be suitably treated as political unities, whether self-governing nation-states (in the case of the European powers) or units for colonial administration.

By 1883, when Cust's survey of African languages was published, the European imperial powers were fully engaged in the "scramble for Africa" in which they divided the continent among their colonial empires. Concomitantly, Cust and others writing in the last decades of the century no longer normally referred to the speakers of African languages as "nations" but instead as "tribes" or "races," a change that reflects, among other things, Africans' loss of political autonomy – or at least their right to political autonomy in European eyes. Although some of those "tribes" are best understood as the population subject to a particular precolonial polity, to describe them in terms of language and customs made it possible to imply that indigenous political structures were epiphenomenal and dispensable.

Cust, a retired administrator from British India, likened his task to other imperial administrative projects (1883: 6–7):

> With such a wealth of Materials pouring in upon me from every quarter, and a deepening conviction of the importance of the task, as well as the difficulty, I could only go on, and . . . lay down clear and distinct principles upon which this work should be constructed. Possessed of a trained capacity for order and method, a strong will and love for steady work, which is the characteristic of old Indians, I had to grapple with this entangled subject, just as twenty-five years ago I should have grappled with the affairs of a District in India which had got into disorder, or with the Accounts of a Treasury which had fallen into arrears.

Cust acknowledged that his task was difficult, but he never doubted the possibility that languages *could* be definitively identified and mapped, or that they corresponded to separate tribes inhabiting discrete territories. What was needed was to clear away the confusion of alternative and "unnecessary" names (pp. 10–11), to "avoid a lax phraseology," and to "place one foot firmly down upon Geographical facts, and the other upon such a statement of Linguistic facts as seem to my judgment sufficient" (p. 7). These principles being rigorously followed, any linguistic information that could not be made to fit the map was simply to be excluded because (Cust concluded) it did not exist: It was an error or fantasy. "Unless he [Cust's cartographer] can find a place in his Map for the tribe, the Language can find no place in my Schedule" (p. 8). Functional or superposed varieties, multilingualism, polysemous language labels, and contested boundaries were incompatible with this approach.

These assumptions were by no means limited to Cust or to British investigators, who, in any case, relied heavily on an international cadre of missionaries to conduct the basic fieldwork. By the late nineteenth century, European scholars of language, whatever their nationality, their particular opinions about grammatical forms and comparative methods, or their connection with specific colonial policies, generally concurred on many basic points. They had acquired a firm belief in linguistics' scientific basis, the naturalness and distinctness of its objects of study, and the relevance of linguistic classifications for models of evolutionary progress. Assuming, too, that ethnic groups were normally monolingual and that there was some primordial relationship between language and the particular "spirit" of a nation, they thought it obvious that the study of language could serve as a tool for identifying ethnic units, classifying relationships among peoples, and reconstructing their history. Ideas like these, then, informed the efforts of mid- to late-nineteenth-century scholars, administrators, military men, and missionaries who set about describing the languages of Senegal.[11]

The linguistic situation they encountered, insofar as we can reconstruct it today, involved a complex regional system in which linguistic repertoires were – as they still are – bound up with political and religious relationships. Fula had the strongest connection with Islamic orthodoxy because it was associated with the region's first converts to Islam in the eleventh century and with the strongest proponents of the late-eighteenth-century Muslim revival. Sereer, in contrast, was associated with resistance to Islam and with the preservation of pre-Islamic ritual practices. As a French missionary remarked (Lamoise 1873: vii), "The *marabouts* [Muslim clerics] have invented this false adage: whoever speaks Sereer cannot enter heaven." Wolof, meanwhile, was the dominant language in the coastal kingdoms where the French first established outposts, and it served as a language of politics and trade in other parts of the region as well.

Wolof's role in the political life of Senegal apparently dates back to the fifteenth-century heyday of the Jolof Empire, a state then dominating most of the region. In Jolof, whose very name is connected with the Wolof language, Wolof was the language of a political administration sufficiently centralized to keep the language fairly uniform geographically. (Arabic, not Wolof, was the official language of religion, however, although many of the Muslim clerics in the days of the Jolof Empire were probably of Fula-speaking origin.) This sociolinguistic pattern extended beyond the territories Jolof governed directly and persisted for centuries after the empire's breakup in the mid-sixteenth century. So even in the nineteenth century, in the kingdoms of Siin and Saluum (see fig. 17.1) – client states to Jolof's south which may never have been administered by it directly but were within its international sphere – Wolof lexicon was used for political offices and Wolof language for the conduct of high-level political relations, even though much of the population probably spoke Sereer as a language of the home.[12] In consequence many Sereer-speakers in the south were (and are) bilingual in Wolof, while Wolof-speakers further north resist acquiring Sereer, which many of them associate with low-ranking, heathen peasants.

European observers in the mid- to late nineteenth century interpreted this regional situation in terms of a supposed history of race relations, migrations, and conquests. Assuming that a language ought to have a distinct territory and nation (or ethnic group or race) associated with it, scholars interpreted other kinds of language distributions as "mixtures," departures from some original linguistic and territorial purity. Assuming further that black Africans were essentially primitive and simple-minded people who knew no social organization more complex than the family group, these scholars explained African social hierarchy, multilingualism, and conversions to Islam in terms of conquering races from the north who supposedly brought Islam, the state, and some admixture of Caucasian blood and language to the region by force of arms and intellectual superiority. Fula-speakers, some of whom are lighter-skinned than their Wolof neighbors, were deemed "higher" in race and intelligence. Accorded an origin in Upper Egypt, they were thought to have brought their "superior" religion, hierarchical social organization, and language to bear upon the Wolof, who in turn (perhaps along with the Manding, a people to the southeast) influenced the "simple" Sereer.[13]

Informed by these notions, the language-mapping project was thus an effort not only to discover what languages were spoken where but also to disentangle the supposed history of conquests and represent legitimate territorial claims. In regions where the language of state or of an aristocracy differed from the domestic speech of the state's subjects, as was the case in some areas of Senegal, only one of these languages could be put on the map. In many such cases (Siin and Saluum, for example) it was the political language that was omitted from the map – removed just as the African state apparatus was to be.

Of particular interest with regard to language mapping are the military expeditions led in 1861 and 1864–5 by Colonel Pinet-Laprade, the French commander at Gorée Island, and General Faidherbe, military governor of the French colony at Saint-Louis. Part of the effort to extend French military domination to the east and south, these expeditions carried out research and cartography along with their military objectives. Expedition reports, published in the official journal *Annuaire du Sénégal*, were accompanied by linguistic analyses, ethnographic notices, and a detailed map. The map (Faidherbe 1865), which shows towns and villages, lakes and rivers, and the frontiers between the French colony and the existing African states, also shows neatly drawn "lines of separation" between supposedly distinct Wolof and Sereer populations. Similar lines were drawn between each of these and the Manding, further south and east. The map does not extend as far as the main areas where Fula might be spoken in a village context, but it does show an area of "Peuls" – Fula-speakers – set off in a similar manner. These populations, identified by language, are thus accorded distinct territories in the map's representation of the supposed relationship between language, population, and territory.

To produce this representation, the cartographers had to ignore the multilingualism that characterized indigenous political life in the southern regions. But doing away with indigenous political institutions was the ultimate purpose anyway. Since the French colonizers' conception of regional history was that the Sereer had been enslaved and tyrannized by Wolof and/ or Manding aristocrats and Muslim clerics, France would be justified in overthrowing these oppressors and substituting French rule. Until this was accomplished, and the French *mission civilisatrice* could get properly underway, wrote Pinet-Laprade (1865: 147), the populations of "countries like Siin and Saluum ... could not attempt any progress, because of the state of stupefaction *[abrutissement]* in which they were held under the regime of the Gelwaar [aristocratic lineages]." As for "Sereer" further north (i.e., Cangin), who, Pinet-Laprade suggested, were less thoroughly dominated by the Wolof state of Kajoor in which they formed an enclave, they were a simple, childlike people who would be easily led (by France) once the threat of Kajoor was removed:

> [The enclave populations] are, like all peoples in infancy, very little advanced along the way of social organization [*association*]: they are generally grouped by families, in the vicinity of their fields. This state of affairs will facilitate the action we are called upon to take on them, because we will not have to overturn established authorities, sever close ties, or combat blind fanaticism. (Pinet-Laprade 1865: 155)

Notice that the mapping project involves our three semiotic processes. The language map depicted the relationship ideologically supposed to obtain between language, population, and territory (*iconization*), but it could only do so by tidying up the linguistic situation, removing multilingualism and variation from the picture (*erasure*). The multilingualism was supposed to have been introduced, along with religious and political complexity, through a history of conquest and conversion that paralleled the European conquest and the hierarchical relationships thought to obtain between Europeans and Africans – relationships of white to black, complex to simple, and dominant to subordinate. That is, relationships between Europeans and Africans were the implicit model for a history of relationships within Africa itself (*recursivity*).

This putative hierarchy of racial essences and conquests supposedly explained not only multilingualism but also the specific characteristics and relationships of the three African languages. Most linguists of the time, and indeed for generations afterward, refused to see Fula as genetically related to Wolof and Sereer at all, seeking its kin among Semitic languages instead. And Fula's linguistic characteristics, such as its syllable structure and its noun classification system, were taken by scholars such as Guiraudon (1894) and Tautain (1885), as well as Faidherbe (1882), as emblems of its speakers' "delicacy" and "intelligence" as compared to speakers of Wolof. The Wolof language, these scholars claimed, was "less supple, less handy" than Fula and signaled less intelligent minds.[14] Meanwhile, Sereer was considered the language of primitive simplicity.

To represent Sereer, with its complex morphology, as "simple" compared to Wolof – as Father Lamoise, the author of the first substantial grammar of Sereer (Lamoise 1873), claimed it was – seems to us something of an uphill battle. It required paying selective attention, regularizing grammatical structures, and interpreting complexities and variations as "interference." Accordingly, Lamoise suggested that if Sereer now deviated from its original purity and simplicity – the language God had placed among these simple people – the deviations were due to "errors and vices" (1873: 329): either the errors of fetishism into which Sereers had fallen, or the vicious influence of Islam and its Wolof perpetrators. The missionary's task in describing Sereer was to retrieve as much of the pure language as possible and, Lamoise implied, to purge it of error. The task was difficult, for, as he commented darkly (in a section of his grammar discussing figures of speech), "everywhere, as one can see, the infernal serpent is to be found" (1873: 284).

One way to retrieve Sereer's original purity was to select the variety that seemed to have the fewest traces of interference from Wolof or Islam. Lamoise selected the regional variety of Sereer spoken in Siin as the most "pure," yet it was still flawed and inadequate. Apparently rejecting or downplaying words and expressions he thought came from Wolof, he also seems to have avoided registers or texts that might incorporate a relatively large number of Wolof loans, such as aristocrats' political discourse relating to the state.[15] Since linguistic purity was, in his view, primarily a matter of returning to a divinely inspired condition, the purest Sereer of all was exemplified in the religious discourse he and his assistants could produce when translating Catholic prayers and religious writings. Actual prayers by Sereers themselves would not do, "since the rare aspirations that emerge from the mouths of the Sereers ... are far too incomplete and inadequate" (1873: 333).

Even while presenting Sereer as a language that contrasted with Wolof, however, Lamoise organized his description from a Wolof starting point, emphasizing Sereer's departures from a Wolof grammatical norm. His grammar of Sereer was modeled upon a grammar of Wolof recently published by his religious superior, the Bishop of Dakar (Kobès 1869). These descriptions of the two languages, though organized in parallel, highlight – perhaps even maximize – their differences by erasing variation and overlap. Just as Lamoise's description of Sereer and his text citations removed (among other things) most of the lexicon and discourse types associated with Wolof, so too the descriptions of Wolof tended to purge those registers connected with non-Islamic ritual (such as the language of non-Islamic portions of circumcision ceremonies) in which some vocabulary and expressions might be identified as "Sereer."

Each language, in short, was represented in an impoverished way to differentiate it from the other and to accord with an ideology about its essence. At the same time, regional varieties that seemed to overlap were ignored. An example would be the variety of Sereer spoken in Baol, which has been reported as a mix. Pinet-Laprade (1865: 135) called it a language "derived from Sérère-Sine ... and from Wolof"; a more recent linguist (de Tressan 1953) called it "Sinsin [i.e., the Siin variety of Sereer], penetrated lexically by Wolof." Unsurprisingly, this variety has never been studied in its own right.

The same notions of language purity that led nineteenth-century linguists to ignore "mixed" varieties, multilingualism, and expressions they could attribute to linguistic borrowing also discouraged research on African regional dialectology. Once a variety had been declared to belong to the "same" language as another, already-described variety, there was no reason to investigate it, unless its speakers stubbornly refused to speak anything else. So the languages today called Cangin – spoken by "Sereers" living northwest of Siin, in enclaves within the kingdom of Kajoor – were but little documented until the 1950s and 1960s. Since their speakers obligingly used Wolof in dealings with Europeans and other outsiders and had little contact with Sereer-speakers farther south, there was no pressing need for missionaries or administrators to worry about the fact that these ways of speaking failed to resemble the Sereer of Siin.

The real question is why these Cangin varieties were ever called Sereer at all. The difference was conspicuous enough to have been noticed early on by Faidherbe, whose 1865 report on Sereer includes some notes on one of the Cangin languages. But he and other European writers treated this diversity as dialect, rather than language, differentiation. A particularly important reason Faidherbe and others assigned the Cangin group to Sereer, despite linguistic differences, was that these people were called "Sereer" by their Wolof neighbors, who apply that label in a fairly sweeping way to non-Muslim peasant populations in the region regardless of linguistic niceties. Since French colonists had intensive contacts with Wolof well before penetrating any of the areas of "Sereer" occupation, Wolof identifications of other populations seem to have been accepted and imposed on language identifications even when the linguistic facts pointed in very different directions.[16]

Also supporting the "Sereer" label was the fact that the Cangin-speakers' social life fit relatively well with European notions of Sereer "primitive simplicity" – better, at least, than did the social arrangements of Siin. The Cangin-speakers' small egalitarian village communities, their resistance to Islam, their agricultural economy, and their relative lack of interest in military matters were characteristics thought to be typical of black Africans in general when uninfluenced by waves of conquest from outside, and of Sereers in particular. Since a language reflected the cultural or spiritual essence of a collectivity of speakers, the Cangin languages must be Sereer, for their speakers seemed to fit the ethnic label on other grounds. The reasoning was similar to that which rejected Fula's linguistic resemblance to Wolof or Sereer on grounds of supposed cultural and racial difference.

In sum, the Europeans who described these Senegalese languages in the nineteenth century saw their differentiation as reflecting differences in mentality, history, and social organization among their speakers. Working from an ideology that linked language with national and racial essences, European linguists represented the particular characteristics of Senegalese languages as emblematic of these supposed essential differences, which could be diagrammed in charts of genealogical relationship and located on a territorial map. Thus our first semiotic process, *iconization*, emerges in several aspects of these linguistic descriptions and analyses: in map drawing, in family trees and schedules of relationship, and in discourse describing the (emblematic) linguistic particulars, such as their "delicacy" or their "simplicity." The second process, *fractal recursivity*, is evidenced when, as we mentioned earlier, European representations of linguistic relationships within the Senegal group modeled these relationships upon contrasts supposed to obtain between Europeans and Africans. Recursivity is also involved when the differences among varieties of Sereer were ideologically interpreted as replicating the larger relationship between Sereer and Wolof; that is, less versus more thoroughly penetrated by Islam. Finally, those linguistic features and varieties that could not be made to fit an essentializing scheme were ignored or attributed to "outside" influence. They were assumed to be borrowings, forms that could be omitted from a grammar or dictionary. Those omissions are *erasures* whether they pertain only to representations, as when a linguistic description ignores some vocabulary or some registers, or whether they pertain also to some active policy of eradication, as when the French overthrew the "Wolofized" political administration of Siin and Saluum. As a result, descriptions of each language were impoverished, and, on a more practical level, the languages became indices primarily of ethnicity rather than rank, political status, or religious setting.

In sum, our discussion of this case has concerned the influence of language ideology on linguistic descriptions made during the period of initial colonization of Senegal. Nineteenth-century European ideologies of race relations, ethnic separateness, and African "simplicity" led to maps, schedules, grammars, and dictionaries that purged registers, ignored variation, and rewrote complex sociolinguistic relationships as ethnic relationships. Even though many linguists and anthropologists today no longer share our predecessors' essentializing assumptions – and so can see those assumptions as ideological more easily than our own – the influence of these earlier representations has been long-lasting. Not until the work of Greenberg in the 1950s and 1960s (if even then) were race-based arguments about Fula's linguistic relationships put to rest, and the Cangin languages were listed as "Sereer" until Pichl's study of them in the 1960s (Pichl 1966).[17] Meanwhile, many works by nonlinguists continue to assign Sereer ethnicity to Cangin-speakers without further discussion.

Indeed, the alignment of language with ethnicity – understood as subnationalism and reinforced by colonial policy – is a particularly important dimension of the representational process, though one that is hard to disentangle. Today it is difficult to reconstruct precisely what Africans a century and a half ago took labels such as "Wolof" and "Sereer" to mean – under exactly what conditions they applied such terms to linguistic phenomena, sociological phenomena, or connections they saw between these. Linguistically, for example, one cannot now be completely sure whether expressions that nineteenth-century linguists treated as borrowings were or were not considered so by Africans at the time. This is a hugely complicated matter. But despite uncertainties and complexities, what we would like to emphasize here is the role of ideological representations – European, African, or both – in "tidying up" a complex sociolinguistic situation through register stripping and boundary drawing. It is not just that language came to be taken as an index of ethnic group membership (thus delimiting an ethnic boundary), but also that the contents of a language – materials assigned to it, rather than to some other language from which it "borrowed" them – seem to have been rearranged to match.

Language Ideologies in Political Contestation: Conflicts over Macedonian

For our final case we turn to southeastern Europe and consider attempts to identify and standardize speech varieties in Macedonia. Macedonia was never the colony of any European state. Nevertheless, as in the Senegalese colonial situation discussed above, nineteenth-century descriptions of the languages and peoples of Macedonia were crucially affected by the ways in which the linguistic ideologies of Western European observers interacted with the ideologies and communicative practices of speakers in Macedonia.[18] However, although we start with a discussion of this clash of ideologies, our further aim here is to focus on the political contestation surrounding contrasting scholarly claims. In Macedonia, linguistic relationships came to be used as authorization for political and military action that changed sociolinguistic practices, thereby bringing into existence patterns of language use that more closely matched the ideology of Western Europe. This ideology (often linked with Herder; see Bauman and Briggs 2000) imagined inherent, natural links between a unitary mother tongue, a territory, and an ethnonational identity. It relied for its persuasiveness on the three semiotic processes we have proposed.

The Republic of Macedonia declared its independence from Yugoslavia in November 1991 and was accepted as a member of the United Nations in December 1993. The new country inherited over a century of acrimonious debate about its boundaries, its name, and its language, a debate that, in the rhetoric of nationhood, ultimately questions its right to exist. Each of Macedonia's current neighbors – Bulgaria, what remains of Yugoslavia (i.e., Serbia and Montenegro), Albania, and Greece – has made serious claims to parts of the same territory in the past century, always at least partly on linguistic grounds. Despite the official codification, recognition, and widespread use of the Macedonian literary language, Bulgarian and Greek scholars have continued to deny its existence and independent standing. By concentrating on the late-nineteenth- and early-twentieth-century antecedents to these conflicts, we aim to explore the semiotic processes through which they have worked. We consider first how popular Western European opinion viewed Macedonia at the turn of the century. Then we turn to the linguistic arguments and actions of the competing nationalisms within the region.

The political economy of nineteenth-century Europe is the crucial context for the clashes of ideology we examine below. Eastern and southeastern Europe had for four centuries been the site of violent competition in empire building among the Austria-based Habsburgs, the Russia-based Romanovs, and the Ottomans of Turkey. In the course of the nineteenth century, however, Turkey became increasingly weak, losing control of large parts of its European territories to nationalist movements in Greece, Serbia, Romania, and Bulgaria. During the same period, Serbian and Bulgarian Orthodox churches were successfully reestablished and gained considerable leverage in challenging the hegemony of the Greek Orthodox church within the Ottoman Empire. Finally, Greece, Bulgaria, Serbia, and Montenegro united to drive Turkey out of Europe in 1912, only to fight each other for control of the newly liberated territory of geographic Macedonia. The subsequent peace treaty divided geographic Macedonia between them, with borders that have since remained relatively stable though always contested (see figure 17.2).[19]

Throughout this period, distant European powers, most especially Britain, France, Russia, and Germany, were intent on establishing or maintaining their presence and influence in the region to defend substantial economic interests as well as supply routes and military commitments to their colonial outposts in

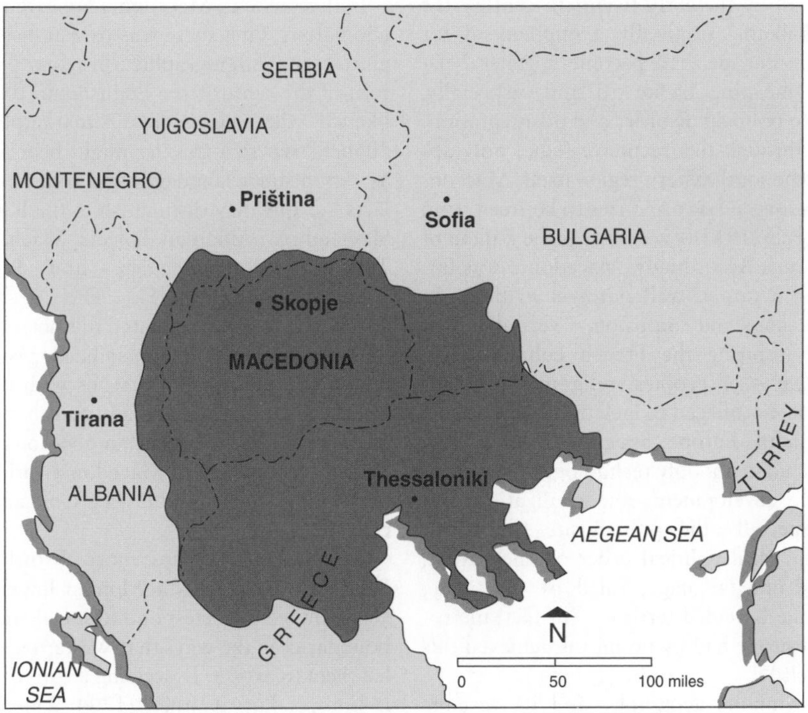

Figure 17.2 *Republic of Macedonia (1995). Approximate extent of regions that have variously been considered geographic Macedonia.*

Asia. The strategic involvement of the Great Powers produced among Western Europeans a widespread popular interest in the region. Instigated by news of revolutions, wars, and exotic customs, this interest was further fueled, in the second half of the century, by a burgeoning literature of journalism, ethnography, philology, and travel.

Representations of Europe in popular and scholarly writing had been considerably altered during the eighteenth century. Scientific cartography had earlier established the boundaries of the continent, while in more philosophical approaches there remained the Renaissance trope of a civilized South endangered by the depredations of Northern barbarians. But by the start of the nineteenth century this axis of contrast had shifted significantly. The earlier North/South imagery had been transformed into a spatial opposition between a newly invented, backward, barbaric "East" and a civilized "West" (see Wolff 1994). Western European observers came to see the southeast of the continent through the lens of a dichotomizing orientalism that, as we shall argue, was also recursive.

In some respects the Balkan region was considered quintessentially European, indeed home of the heroic Christian defenders of the continent against the incursions of Asia and Islam during Ottoman campaigns of earlier centuries.[20] But this distinction between Europe and Asia, between East and West, could be deployed again and projected onto Europe itself, thereby producing a backward orient within Europe. Throughout the nineteenth century, the southeast of the continent was known as the "Near East" or "*l'Orient européen*," or even part of the "Levant." Precisely because it was conquered for centuries by the Ottomans, this region came to be seen as itself oriental, thus distinguished from enlightened Western civilization by its primitive lack of order: it was the least European part of Europe. It is telling that by the early twentieth century the term "Balkan," originally a euphemism for Turkey-in-Europe, had become a general pejorative meaning backward and, especially, subject to political disorder and disintegration. Finally, through this recursive logic, now applied to the southeastern region itself, Macedonia – one of the last provinces to be freed from Turkish rule (1913) – was seen as the Balkan of the Balkans. Accordingly, Macedonia was imagined in fiction as well as travel writing as a place of chaos and confusion, a veritable fruit salad – inspiring the French culinary term *macédoine* – of peoples, religions, and languages. It was alleged to lack the positive traits metropolitan Europe assigned itself. These traits included not only technological progress, economic development, and civilization, but most especially the prerequisite for all of these: the ideal political order of one nation, speaking one language, ruled by one state, within one bounded territory. (In fact, metropolitan Europe had by no means achieved this ideal itself.)[21]

This symbolic geography and its variants have received considerable scholarly attention recently (e.g., Bakić-Hayden and Hayden 1992; Brown 1995; Todorova 1994). What has not been noticed, however, is the role of linguistic ideologies in its formation. For example, Max Müller (1855: 65) understood many of the characteristics of the "Slavonic" languages through their location "on the threshold between barbarism and civilization." More specifically, local Macedonian language practices and the metropolitan European linguistic ideology through which they were seen by travelers, scholars, and government officials were crucial to the construction of such images. Western European elites had come to think of language as the least socially malleable and therefore the most authentic indicator of a speaker's sociopolitical identity. As early as 1808 Fichte (1845–6: 453) had declared, "Wherever a separate language can be found, there is also a separate nation which has the right to manage its affairs and rule itself." And a hundred years later, the noted linguist Antoine Meillet was calling language the principal factor determining national sentiment in Europe (cited in Wilkinson 1951: 276).

In this context, Macedonia appeared doubly anomalous. First there was its astonishing linguistic and ethnographic diversity.[22] At the turn of the century, the Englishman Brailsford likened the Macedonian marketplace to "Babel," where a traveler might hear as many as "six distinct languages and four allied dialects ... one may distinguish in the Babel two Slav and two Albanian dialects, Vlach, Greek, Turkish, Hebrew-Spanish, and Romany" (Brailsford 1906: 85). The Frenchman Lamouche (1899: 1) equated this heterogeneity with disorder and an uncivilized past: "This region still presents itself to us with the variation and ethnographic confusion that reigned as the result of the barbarian invasions." Later British accounts called Macedonia "primitive," "barbaric," and "hybrid" (see Goff and Fawcett 1921).

Second, and perhaps more disturbing for Western observers, Macedonian linguistic diversity failed to correspond to social and ethnic boundaries in the ways that Western ideologies led them to expect. Describing a trip to Turkey-in-Europe, Lucy Garnett (1904: 234–5) registered a widespread exasperation. In Macedonia, she noted,

> A Greek-speaking community may prove to be Wallachian, Albanian or even Bulgarian, and the inhabitants of a Slav-speaking village may claim to be of Greek origin ... All these various ethnical elements are, in many country districts of Macedonia, as well as in the towns, so hopelessly fused and intermingled.

Garnett's comment was echoed in more scholarly – and more racialized – tones by a German geographer, Karl von Östreich (1905: 270): "Instead of racially pure Turks and Albanians we find people who are racially mixed ... and whose multilingualism misleads us about their real origins, so that they can be counted sometimes as Greeks, sometimes as Bulgarians, sometimes as Wallachians."

Other authors were "puzzled" at the "peculiar phenomenon" that members of "Bulgarian" families in Macedonia could be persuaded to become "Greek" or "Serbian" (Moore 1906: 147). Brailsford (1906: 102) reported with consternation that families often sent each son to a different school – Bulgarian, Greek, Rumanian, Serbian – whose language and nationality the child would then adopt. Western observers failed to perceive this practice as an attempt to extend social networks in uncertain times. Rather, the ethnic profusion and confusion predicated of the region as a whole, and implicitly contrasted with "European" order, were seen to be reproduced within families. In the recurrence and persistence of such anecdotes we note again the workings of *fractal recursivity.* A somewhat later observer, writing about his journey "across the new Balkans" and the "Levant" (which for him began in Prague), demonstrated that this dichotomy of East and West was even projected onto individuals: "The Levantine type in the areas between the Balkans and the Mediterranean is, psychologically and socially, truly a 'wavering form,' a composite of Easterner and Westerner, multilingual ... superficial, unreliable" (Ehrenpreis 1928: 12).

The importance of this "composite" image for our purposes lies not only in its evidence of further recursivity but also in the way it shows that ethnolinguistic heterogeneity had consequences for the moral reputation of Macedonians. Ehrenpreis's comment explicitly links supposedly labile allegiances to linguistic practice. Multiple languages were assumed to indicate multiple loyalties and thus a temperamental flaw, a lack of trustworthiness. It was because linguistic practices and character were seen by Westerners as *iconically* linked that shifting language use could be used as evidence for equally shiftable, hence dubious and shallow, allegiances. Indeed, a French consul in Macedonia is reported to have declared that with a fund of a million francs for bribes, he could make all Macedonians French (cited in Brailsford 1906: 103).

If recursivity and iconization are apparent in these turn-of-the-century accounts, the third semiotic process, *erasure*, is also evident. Because the relationship between linguistic practices and social categories in Macedonia diverged so fundamentally from the expectations of Western Europeans, the region appeared chaotic to them. These observers therefore missed – and their representations erased – the local logic by which the inhabitants of Macedonia understood categories of language and identity such as "Greek," "Turkish," "Bulgarian," and "Macedonian" during the long Ottoman period and before the rise of Balkan nationalisms.

One major constraint on local practices was the Ottoman *millet* system (often mistranslated as "nationality"), which categorized and administered populations according to religious affiliation irrespective of territorial location, ethnic provenance, or language. Moslems counted as "Turks," while Orthodox Christians, including people who spoke various forms of Slavic, Romance, Albanian, and Greek, were counted as "Greeks." During most of the nineteenth century, "Greeks" were officially ruled by the Greek Orthodox Church in European Turkey. But "Greek" and "Turk" were not merely imperial administrative categories; they affected local understandings as well. A Christian peasant in mid-nineteenth-century Macedonia would identify his "nationality" (*millet*) as Greek, regardless of the language he spoke. Similarly, Moslem peasants, even those speaking Albanian, identified themselves as Turkish well into the twentieth century (see, for example, Friedman 1975; Lunt 1984).

Yet Greek was not only a religious and administrative category but also a marker of stratification. As Stoianovich (1960: 311) notes, "The Hellenization of the upper social strata of the non-Greek Balkan Orthodox peoples made possible the emergence of a single, relatively united, inter-Balkan merchant class which was of Greek, Vlach, Macedo-Slav and Bulgarian ethnic origin, but called itself and was known to others as 'Greek.' " When contrasted with "Greek," the designation "Bulgarian" was also, in part, a category of social stratification, particularly in the early part of the century. In Macedonia it could be equivalent to *raya*, that is, a rural, usually Christian, lower-class subject of Ottoman rule. It was not necessarily linked to the use of the Bulgarian literary language that was being developed actively during the nineteenth century. Moreover, a rural-urban contrast was also salient. Greek-speaking merchants and intellectuals, whatever their ethnic origins, tended to live in cities and towns; Slavic- and Albanian-speakers, whatever their religion, were more likely to be rural.

Clearly, multilingualism was widespread. "Greek" merchants of various backgrounds continued to speak diverse home languages, while using Greek for trade and intellectual activity. Ottoman Turkish was employed for administration and often for market activities by many speakers of other languages; *katharevousa* Greek and Church Slavonic were languages of liturgy and church administration in Greek Orthodox and (later) in Bulgarian and Serbian Orthodox churches, respectively. But these languages were not always strictly compartmentalized by function. Many a mid-nineteenth-century merchant wrote his accounts not in Greek, as might be expected, but in Bulgarian with Greek letters and Turkish numbers (Todorova 1990: 439). The occurrence of codeswitching in mid-nineteenth-century folktales suggests that multilingualism was not limited to those persons directly involved in trade, administration, and religious institutions. Even many rural speakers or recent migrants to small cities could switch to Turkish and Greek or use other vernaculars – dialects of Slavic, Albanian, Rumanian, Greek, Romany – for everyday communication. Indeed, at least in urban areas, rates of multilingualism apparently increased as one moved down the socioeconomic ladder (Friedman 1995; see also Brailsford 1906: 85–6).

These patterns of usage suggest that while there were regularities that systematically and predictably linked a range of linguistic practices to social uses and to categories of identity, there were no "total" categories in mid-nineteenth-century Macedonia that encompassed and subordinated all other categories while being also indissolubly linked to linguistic forms understood as single languages. In short, in the understanding of identity, the criteria of religion, region, occupation, social stratum, and language group had not been aligned, hierarchized, or regimented on the model of the Western, nationalist imagination.[23]

By the end of the nineteenth century, however, the reign of just such national ideas was well under way in the Balkan states that had gained independence from Ottoman rule. Hence, the multilingual situation we have described proved fertile ground for nationalist movements originating outside geographic Macedonia. Each "imagined" the territory and inhabitants of Macedonia as part of its own emerging "community." Well before the final expulsion of Ottoman rule from geographic Macedonia, neighboring elites were funding political agitation there and establishing schools run in each of their national literary languages. Local elites within geographic Macedonia were inciting action for independence. Relying on the very equation of nation, language, and territory that outside observers had earlier found lacking in Macedonia, advocates of Serbian, Bulgarian, and Greek expansion, as well as those calling for Macedonian autonomy, appealed to linguistic descriptions to prove the existence of *social* boundaries that would authorize their claims to popular loyalty.

At the same time, competing elites were also producing census figures, ethnographic and linguistic maps, and historical treatises written in national terms familiar to the West. They were all designed to convince Great Power audiences that one set of claims to Macedonian territory was more justified than others. These works appeared both before and after partition. They were written in Western languages and published in Paris, London, Vienna, Berlin, Zürich, and New York. As Wilkinson's (1951) compilation of ethnographic and linguistic maps of the period illustrates, this body of scholarship was often politically partisan, contradictory, and sometimes simply mendacious. We examine it here for what it reveals about the broader ideological assumptions concerning language and identity. By analyzing the arguments of Greek, Serbian, Bulgarian, and distinctively Macedonian positions, along with some of the policies they inspired, we can trace once again how the three semiotic processes work, this time in the fierce contestation among local linguistic nationalisms.[24]

To understand these controversies, it is helpful to start with aspects of Slavic dialectology about which there is general scholarly agreement. A dialect continuum in South Slavic runs from Serbian to Bulgarian through Macedonia (see figure 17.2).[25] Dialects located in Macedonia share many lexical and phonological features with dialects in Serbia, but in morphology they bear a stronger resemblance to varieties in Bulgaria. For instance, West South Slavic dialects (Serbia) retain much of the complex declensional system of Common Slavic, but East South Slavic dialects, including those in what is now Bulgaria and the Republic of Macedonia, have lost inflections, replacing case marking with prepositions and syntactic features. Similarly, East South Slavic dialects share a postposed definite article as well as analytical rather than morphological forms of the infinitive and comparative (see Friedman 1975; Lunt 1984).[26]

In this context, we can see how the battles between Serbian, Bulgarian, and Greek claims to Macedonia provide examples of argument through *iconization.* "Deep" linguistic relationship was the key, identified by selecting some linguistic features and ignoring (or explaining away) others. Thus Bulgarian linguists emphasized the Macedonian dialects' relatively analytic morphology, which resembled literary Bulgarian, to argue for the languages' deep kinship; they explained phonological differences as superficial "new developments." Social relations of "closeness" and "distance" were projected iconically from presumed or claimed "closeness" of linguistic relations and were used to justify political unity. Indeed, the Bulgarian position simply asserts that Macedonian dialects are forms of Bulgarian, thereby erasing Macedonian altogether (see, for example, Brancoff 1905; Sís 1918).[27] Serbian linguists, on the other hand, picked only certain phonological features to emphasize, claiming they revealed the ancient kinship of dialects in Macedonia with those in Serbia (see, for example, Belić 1919; Cvijić 1907). Finally, Greek scholars argued that, because the Slavic forms spoken in Greek Macedonia were so heavily reliant on Greek lexicon, they were actually a dialect of Greek. A speculative history was iconically projected to explain this surprising hypothesis through historically "deep" social relations: it was argued that Greek-speakers in antiquity must have assimilated to later Slavic immigrants and, having gone through a period of bilingualism, retained the lexicon (though not the grammar) of their original language (see Andriotes 1957: 15–16).

Iconization operated in other ways as well. Between the two world wars, in the section of geographic Macedonia that had become part of Yugoslavia, Macedonian was treated as a dialect of Serbo-Croatian. In Macedonian-Serbian conversations a largely similar lexical stock assured that mutual intelligibility could be achieved, but at the price of a subjective impression "that the other was using an irritating kind of pidgin" (Lunt 1959: 21). It was the Serbs who, on hearing the relatively simpler nominal morphology of Macedonian, took this as an icon of simple thought and so assumed Macedonians to be uncultivated country bumpkins. Through such iconization, the perception that Macedonian "had no grammar" apparently contributed to legitimating far-reaching political tactics. Serbs, who dominated the interwar Yugoslav government, "quickly became annoyed at the linguistic ineptitude of the mass of Macedonians and found [in this] a righteous justification for accusing them of stupidity and ingratitude and hence for treating the region almost as a colony" (Lunt 1959: 22). Ironically, such characterizations of Macedonian as "simple" could only be sustained by focusing on the language's relatively few nominal inflections and ignoring, thus erasing, the complexities of its verbal system.

But processes of *erasure* in the arguments we are considering were often much more drastic than this. In linguistic maps of Macedonia from the turn of the century, evidence of the widespread multilingualism characteristic of the region disappeared altogether. The maps displayed neatly bounded regions, each in a different color to indicate the presence of speakers of a single, named language (see Wilkinson 1951). Maps drawn by Serbian and Bulgarian advocates each claimed all Slavic forms as dialects of their own standard languages. Furthermore, they showed virtually no one speaking Greek, despite the fact that some Slavic-speakers, especially in the south, continued to use it in commerce, writing, and intellectual life.

Greek maps, in contrast, showed great areas of Greek-speakers in Macedonia by counting only the use of "commercial language" rather than "mother tongue." Clearly driven by political motives, and vastly overstating the numbers, Greek arguments such as those of Nicolaïdes (1899) nevertheless allow us to see "mother tongue" itself as a deeply ideological construct that disallows claims of identity based on other linguistic considerations. After all, as we have seen, at least some urban, educated inhabitants of nineteenth-century Macedonia might well have agreed with Nicolaïdes's categorization of them as "Greek," despite the other languages they also spoke. Later Greek erasures were less benign, however. Between the world wars, the existence of Slavic-speakers and Slavic forms was denied altogether in Greek Macedonia. Official policy prohibited their mention, census questions asked only whether individuals spoke Greek, village and family names were forcibly changed, and Slavic speakers were jailed. In the 1950s Slavic-speaking villagers were coerced to take "language oaths" promising never to speak Slavic again (see Karakasidou 1993).

In the debates among competing nationalisms, processes of *recursivity* were also evident, operating in tandem with erasures and iconization. As we have noted, within the logic of linguistic nationalism, the equation of a language with a delimited territory and population required the elision of multilingualism in maps and other representations. This elision ultimately led as well to the attempted elimination, through schooling and legal means, of repertoires in which different languages were used for different social functions. But the new conceptual opposition of "our own national language" versus "foreign language" that motivated such erasure was also recursively applied within the literary languages of the region as these were successively codified. The choices of language planners were often made at least in part to avoid or downplay similarities with competing languages nearby that were conceptualized as foreign because they "belonged" to other nations. For example, in the official codification of Macedonian in 1944, the preference for the Western dialects as the basis of the literary language was supported by historical precedent, since they were already evident in literary productions dating from the mid-nineteenth century. Another major motivation for this choice, however, was that it produced maximal differentiation from both Bulgarian and Serbo-Croatian standards (Friedman 1989: 31).

Most significantly, heated debates about linguistic purity have involved the recursive application of this native/foreign distinction to the lexical stock of the region's languages. Ottoman rule had resulted in the heavy lexical influence of Greek and Turkish on all Balkan languages. As early as the 1840s Bulgarian language reformers engaged in what we have called "register-stripping": the attempt to purge Turkish elements from the literary Bulgarian then being created because such elements were now seen as "alien" despite their pervasiveness in colloquial speech. For familiar Turkish words the reformers provided unfamiliar Slavic glosses, often borrowed from Russian or revived from Church Slavonic (Pinto 1980: 46). These latter languages were analyzed as historically related to Bulgarian and doubtless perceived to be, by iconic logic, less "foreign."

Equally interesting is the case of Macedonian, in which Turkish influence has included productive derivational morphology as well as the usual individual lexical items and calques of idiomatic phrases. What is significant is not the actual source of such elements but speakers' continuing perception of many of them as Turkisms. In Macedonian debates some planners in the 1940s argued for the replacement of Turkisms with Slavic forms in the literary language. Turkisms perceived as such suffered a stylistic lowering after the Ottoman's defeat, so that they came to connote archaism, local color, pejoration, or irony. Planners feared that their retention in the Macedonian literary language (especially after they had been purged from neighboring languages) would threaten to make all of Macedonian sound "lower" and less refined (Koneski, quoted in Friedman 1996). Thus, by an application of recursive logic, Turkisms (as both alien and low) were systematically stripped from the literary language. Simultaneously, registers perceived as native were newly "stretched" through neologisms or revival of dialect and archaic forms to cover broader functions (see Friedman 1989; Koneski 1980).

In sum, the complex Macedonian linguistic scene, and nationalist arguments within it, reveal all three semiotic processes we have discussed and show them to operate in a number of different ways. The continuing intensity of contestation over the representation of Macedonian speech forms is hardly surprising, given the consequences envisaged and authorized by the reigning language ideology and occasionally enacted under its auspices. It is an ideology in which claims of linguistic affiliation are crucial and exclusivist because they are also claims to territory and sovereignty.

Implications

The analysis we have presented here has implications relating to at least three intellectual arenas in social science research. The first is the study of historical fields of contact among peoples. European colonialism provides a major set of examples. In particular, part of our analysis contributes to the study of "colonial discourses," illuminating some of their semiotic properties. The second group of problems and issues we seek to address concerns ethnicity and its relation to communicative practices. The concept of "speech community," prominent in linguistic anthropology and sociolinguistics since the 1960s, is among the ideas we seek to reconceptualize. Finally, the third arena is that concerned with conceptions of language itself. Although these intellectual arenas have obvious overlaps, we now take them up in turn, adumbrating some of the implications our analysis has for each.

The semiotic processes we have identified, though not limited to any particular historical period, nevertheless always occur in history and operate in relation to contingent facts. The study of colonialism offers an important opportunity to study ideologies – linguistic and otherwise – because of colonialism's obvious consequentiality, the clash of interests at stake, and the evident differences in points of view. As scholars are increasingly recognizing, however, the colonial period is more than just an interesting topic for historical research. Ideas that were forged in that context have remained deeply embedded in our analytical frameworks.

A considerable body of recent research by historians and anthropologists has focused on the dichotomizing discourses of orientalism through which, in the nineteenth century and earlier, Europe created itself in opposition to a broadly defined "East" that often included not only Asia but also Africa. That "East" also found parallels elsewhere in the world, even within Europe itself, where a similar axis of opposition distinguished metropolitan centers of "higher" civilization from their "lower," especially their eastern, peripheries. As Mudimbe (1988), Olender (1992), Said (1978), and others have pointed out, scholars of language and ideas about linguistic differences played a significant part in the development of such categories of identity (see also Bauman and Briggs, this volume). Arguments about language were central in producing and buttressing European claims to difference from the rest of the world, as well as claims to the superiority of the metropolitan bourgeoisie over "backward" or "primitive" Others, whether they were residents of other continents, other provinces, or other social classes.

Language could be central to these arguments because by the mid-nineteenth century it had become common in the scholarly world to see language as crucially unaffected by human will or individual intent (see Formigari 1985; Taylor 1990b). For many scholars of the time, linguistic differences appeared to be the "natural" consequences of spiritual or even biological differences between collectivities of speakers, rather than the consequence of social action. August Schleicher (1869: 20–1), for example, promoting a Darwinian model of linguistic evolution and differentiation, argued that "languages are organisms of nature; they have never been directed by the will of man ... The science of language is consequently a natural science." In a more religious vein but with a similar implication, F. Max Müller (1861) proposed that a "science of language" should be theistic and historical, yet it should employ the methods of geology, botany, and anatomy, for the very reason that such a science – comparative philology – would deal with the works of God, not of man. Although later approaches differed sharply in many ways, the argument for a "science of language" that would be divorced from the everyday speech and social life of its speakers remained, Saussure's formulation being today the most familiar.[28]

Despite increasing awareness in recent years of these European ideologies of language and their historical contexts, anthropologists and linguists have not sufficiently explored their implications. Our disciplines' conceptual tools for understanding linguistic differences and relationships still derive from this massive scholarly attempt to create the differentiation of Europe from the rest of the world. We have sought to redirect this intellectual project. In this paper we have argued that linguistic differentiation crucially involves ideologically embedded and socially constructed processes. Moreover, the scholarly enterprise of describing linguistic differentiation is itself ideologically and socially engaged (see also Gal and Irvine 1995).

For instance, the Senegal case discussed above provides an opportunity to show how the study of language participated in colonial discourses. Such discourses reveal the complex interaction of ideologies, both the colonizers' and those of the colonized. Since then there have been many changes in the methods of linguistic analysis and the genres of linguistic description; nevertheless, those early discourses of language form the beginnings of a "culture of linguistics" of the region, a tradition to which scholars today fall heir. Contemporary understandings of language differentiation in Senegal thus have a complex history, with European and African language ideologies contributing to interpretations of local sociolinguistic phenomena.

In a parallel way, the case of Macedonia demonstrates the specific ways in which linguistic analyses have contributed to shaping "orientalist discourses." The perception of linguistic chaos in Macedonia emerged from an interaction of local and Western European language ideologies. And metropolitan Europe constructed its own self-image in opposition to just such representations of the sociolinguistic scene in the "East." As soon as Balkan elites appealed to Western powers in Western terms, moreover, linguistic scholarship became the ground on which political economic contests were fought. In such contests today, too, current linguistic scholarship in the region remains significant.

Recent scholarly reflections on colonialism and orientalism have focused on nineteenth-century Europe's discursive construction of boundaries and the projection of ideas and images across them. Thinking about boundaries and their construction has an older genealogy in anthropology, however. It is now many years since the publication of Fredrik Barth's *Ethnic Groups and Boundaries* (1969), a work that transformed anthropological thinking about ethnicity. Barth argued that ethnic groups represent a way people organize themselves within a larger social field – a way people identify themselves in contrast with others. Relationships *across* a boundary, Barth suggested, are thus more crucial to the existence and persistence of the boundary than are any group-internal attributes an anthropological observer might identify.

Barth's essay coincided with the appearance of sociolinguistic works (such as Gumperz and Hymes 1964, 1972; Hymes 1968; Weinreich, Labov, and Herzog 1968) that similarly emphasized the social organization of diversity and attacked the idea that any particular type of community, ethnic or otherwise, is the necessary outcome of homogeneous language. From those intellectual antecedents we derive our emphasis on functional relationships among linguistic varieties, relationships that lend systematicity to regional patterns of diversity. We also derive from the ethnography of speaking our concern with participants' ideas about the meanings attaching to the deployment of codes in a repertoire. Thus some of the themes we emphasize in this paper have been present in sociolinguistics and the ethnography of speaking from the beginnings of those fields' existence.

We believe, however, that the full potential of these sociolinguistic insights has yet to be felt. In sociolinguistics and the ethnography of communication, a concept of "speech community," though useful for understanding the organization of local repertoires, nevertheless neglected larger boundary relationships, cultural oppositions, borders, and conflict (see Gal 1987, 1989; Irvine 1987). Classic sociolinguistic research sought first of all to demonstrate that linguistic diversity did not necessarily produce or imply social disorder. This endeavor was not inconsistent with the sociological theories dominant at the time, theories that assumed consensus as the basis of social formations. So, while recognizing the importance and organization of social and linguistic diversity, this foundational research only rarely examined the ways in which identity is produced by ideas of opposition between culturally defined groups, and by practices that promote exclusion, divergence, and differentiation.[29] Later, an attempted switch in analytic unit from speech communities to social networks – though valuable in many ways, including its exploration of the nature of communicative ties – still did not give much attention to problematizing the boundaries of networks but instead treated them, in this respect, much like communities. The analytical focus centered on the social control and peer pressures that produce linguistic uniformity "within" them (Gal 1979; Milroy 1980).

In many branches of anthropology and other social sciences, meanwhile, the assumption persists that the communities anthropologists study will normally be linguistically homogeneous. Even so influential a student of ethnicity and nationalism as Benedict Anderson (1983:38) laments what he assumes to be the "fatality" of monolingualism: "Then [in the sixteenth century] as now, the bulk of mankind is monoglot." For Anderson it is this (supposedly) inevitable monolingualism that provides the fertile ground for linguistic nationalism, the indispensable context in which "capitalism and print created monoglot mass reading publics" (p. 43). He thereby ignores the variety of culturally and often politically significant linguistic differentiation – the registers, dialects, and languages – present in the linguistic repertoires of speakers before print capitalism and within contemporary states that are only legally or nominally "monolingual." Missing from Anderson's perspective, we suggest, is the insight that homogeneous language is as much imagined as is community. That is, Anderson naturalizes the process of linguistic standardization, as if linguistic homogeneity were a real-world precondition rather than a construction concurrent with, or consequent to, print capitalism (for discussion, see Silverstein 2000). An assumption of normative monolingualism tends to persist, as well, in schools of linguistics where dominant models of language are cognitively and not socially based. These models often include the supposition that dialects arise automatically out of communicative isolation and for no other reason.

We propose that what is needed is to shift attention to linguistic differentiation rather than community. But it is crucial to recognize that the differentiation is ideologically mediated, both by its participants and by its observers. It has now often been noted (by, among others, Cameron 1990; Ferguson 1994; and Irvine 1985) that linguistic differentiation is not a simple reflection of social differentiation or vice versa, because linguistic and social oppositions are not separate orders of phenomena. As Ferguson (1994: 19) writes, "Language phenomena are themselves sociocultural phenomena and are in part constitutive of the very social groups recognized by the participants or identified by analysts." It is that mediating *recognition* and *identification*, together with ideological frameworks and pressures, whose relationship with processes of linguistic differentiation we seek to explore.[30]

A final implication of a shift of attention from linguistic communities to linguistic boundaries is to open the door to reflections on some fundamental questions about language itself. One set of such questions involves the mechanisms of linguistic change. In their study of language contact and language change, Thomason and Kaufman (1988) have shown that, contrary to what linguists have supposed for many decades, there are no strictly linguistic motivations of change that operate in lawlike fashion no matter what the social circumstances. Even such linguistic constraints as pattern pressure and markedness considerations are easily overridden by social factors. But Thomason and Kaufman's argument is primarily a negative one, showing that linguistic explanations alone are inadequate rather than supplying a substantial indication of what the social factors are or how they might operate. In this work we have tried to suggest how one might begin to supply that missing dimension. Our materials suggest that the direction and motivation of linguistic change can be illuminated if we attend to the ideologizing of a sociolinguistic field and the consequent reconfiguring of its varieties through processes of iconization, recursive projection, and erasure.

Another set of questions whose importance is signaled by our analysis concerns register phenomena. Our examples show various ways in which registers serve as sites for borrowing and for the negotiation of social relationships via recursive projections and/or claims about linguistic and social connectedness or distance. But we have also seen that an ideology of societal monolingualism and linguistic homogeneity renders functional varieties anomalous. That ideology, moreover, often imagines languages as corresponding with essentialized representations of social groups. Essentialized linguistic and social categories are made to seem isomorphic when ideologies omit inconvenient linguistic facts (such as "borrowed" lexicon, registers, or functionally specialized languages), or when they lead people to create linguistic facts (such as neologisms or new registers) to match the representation. We contend that scholarly analyses are improved when registers are systematically included in discussions of relationships among languages and dialects and in discussions of what competence in "a language" includes, rather than being omitted or inserted under those ideological pressures. To be sure, the concept of register is itself problematic and also subject to ideological pressures besides the ones we have discussed here (see Silverstein 1992).

Finally, we note that our analysis of semiotic processes in linguistic differentiation has implications for our understanding of sign relationships in language itself, such as the notion of the linguistic sign's quintessential arbitrariness. In our view, the notion of arbitrariness is more problematic than has generally been supposed. Saussure's assertion of the "arbitrariness of the sign" is often celebrated as the originary moment of modern linguistics. But publicly voiced claims about the inherent properties of particular languages, or of standards as opposed to dialects, have not abated in contemporary life. We suggest that a useful way to unpack this term and its dilemmas is to distinguish among the possible social positions from which the judgment of "arbitrariness" is made.

First, from the perspective of ordinary speakers, linguistic differences are understood through folk theories (ideologies) that often posit their inherent hierarchical, moral, aesthetic, or other properties within broader cultural systems that are themselves often contested and rarely univocal. The second perspective is that of contemporary linguistics. In constituting itself as an academic discipline, linguistics rejected precisely this culturally embedded speaker's perspective. It insisted instead on de-culturing linguistic phenomena and establishing the theoretical and thus disciplinary autonomy of language. Linguistics has its own set of relevances driven by changing theoretical considerations that differ from those of native speakers. Thus, from the perspective of many kinds of post-Saussurean linguistics, signs are indeed "arbitrary" because the cultural systems that make them iconic are stringently and systematically excluded from consideration, for the sake of science. This suggests a third, metatheoretical, perspective: as we recognize that ordinary speakers' theories about the non-arbitrariness of signs make a difference in the production, interpretation, and reporting of linguistic differentiation, we must add that the equally ideological theories of linguists do so as well.

The very real facts of linguistic variation constrain what linguists and native speakers can persuasively say and imagine about them. Linguistic facts have a certain recalcitrance in the face of ideological construction. But, as we remarked at the outset, there is no "view from nowhere" in representing linguistic differences. Moreover, acts of speaking and acts of describing both depend on and contribute to the "work of representation." Those representations, in turn, influence the phenomena they purport to represent.

In sum, we have identified three semiotic processes at work in language ideologies as these apply to the question of linguistic boundaries and differentiation. The three are *iconization*, *fractal recursivity*, and *erasure*. We have argued that these processes operate worldwide; that they are not dependent on the historical contexts of European colonialism (although they do appear conspicuously there, they also appear elsewhere); and that they are deeply involved in both the shaping of linguistic differentiation and the creating of linguistic description.

NOTES

1 The source for this saying, long a part of linguistics' oral tradition, is difficult to identify. Many linguists attribute it to Max Weinreich.

2 See, for example, the compendium of relevant statements by Peirce (1955) assembled by Justus Buchler under the title "Logic as semiotic: The theory of signs."

3 For further discussion and illustration in a contemporary ethnographic example, see Irvine (1989, 1990).

4 Well-known analyses of such processes from an earlier generation of anthropologists include Bateson (1936) and Evans-Pritchard (1940); more recent discussions include Abbott (1990), Gal (1991), Herzfeld (1987), and Wagner (1991), although the thrust of Wagner's argument about "fractals" is somewhat different from ours.

5 Notice, also, that entries in the Doke and Vilakazi (1958) Zulu dictionary seem to link click sounds, Khoisan languages, and chatter. Thus *nxapha*, a verb meaning "to utter click sounds" (especially in annoyance or vexation), is exemplified in *Ulimi lwaɓaThwa luyanxaphanxapha*, "The Bushman tongue is full of clicks"; the same verb also means "misfire (of a gun)." Another word, *qheɓeqheɓe*, refers to "clicking (as of latch or catch)", "liveliness", and a "lively, talkative person, a gossiper". These links are suggestive, although we do not consider dictionary entries of this kind to be actual evidence that speakers draw a conceptual link between a word's different senses.

6 We have identified these patterns mainly by examining the citations for *hlonipha* words given in Doke and Vilakazi's 1958 Zulu dictionary. Although there are some problems in the dictionary's treatment of these words (for instance, the seemingly haphazard collection of *hlonipha* lists from many regions, assembled for a pan-Zulu set of dictionary entries), the various phonological patterns observable in the dictionary are not contradicted by *hlonipha* data from other sources. See also Herbert (1990) for more discussion of *hlonipha* word formation.

7 See Herbert 1990 for discussion, and refutation, of some alternative views.

8 It is interesting that this conversation is a quarrel. Evidently, the speakers were showing respect not to one another but to third parties.

9 Herbert (1990: 307) attributes the existence of this core vocabulary to urbanization and the decline of *hlonipha*. That it does not conform to the normative pattern of name-avoidance does not necessarily mean, however, that it is very recent or only urban. Finlayson (1984: 140, 143) states, in fact, that she found the core vocabulary throughout the Xhosa-speaking area where *hlonipha* has been investigated. The change among some urban Xhosa is apparently not the emergence of a common *hlonipha* vocabulary but the loss of specific name-avoidances. The urban speakers display respect for tradition but do not orient their respect to the names of particular persons.

10 In the full text of this passage, Lepsius discussed the classification of African languages before continuing, "In like manner will the chaos of the nations in Asia ..."

11 For a related discussion, see Irvine 1993.

12 For a historical discussion of Sereer-speakers' participation in a largely Wolof international system, see Klein (1968, especially pp. 7–8) and Diagne (1967). There is good documentation that kings and officials in Siin and Saluum dealt with nineteenth-century European visitors in Wolof, just as they did other outsiders; see, for example, the visit of the Kobès and other missionaries to the court of Saluum (Abiven n.d.).

13 Although most authors agreed on the main outlines of this picture, details varied. There was some disagreement between French administrators and missionaries – and among missionaries themselves – as to whether Islam, compared with animism, was a sign of higher civilization or of greater corruption. Another complication arose because of the sociological diversity of Fula-speakers. Some scholars claimed that it was only the pastoralist populations who came close to a "pure" Fula racial type and that sedentary populations were the product of racial *métissage* (the supposed cause of social hierarchy in sedentary communities).

14 The role of supposed racial and cultural characteristics in analyses of Fula and, especially, in its placement in language families is relatively well known since Greenberg's critiques (see Greenberg 1963; note also Sapir 1913). For this reason we devote more of our discussion to Sereer, a less familiar case.

15 Space does not permit a detailed discussion supporting our characterization of Lamoise's work. We will just note that he does supply more examples of texts and discourse than is common in grammars of the period (or today), but some of them appear to have been composed by himself or his assistants, and none of them records aristocrats' political discourse. Other important evidence would come, for example, from his treatment of key pairs of words such as *Yalla/rôg* ("God"), each of which occurs in both Wolof and Sereer grammatical structures but in different situational contexts, which Lamoise and others seem to interpret as ethnic contexts.

16 Although Faidherbe accepted the identification of the Kajoor enclave populations (i.e., Cangin-speakers) as "Sereer," he did recognize its source (1865: 175): "The populations *which the Wolof designate by the name of Sereers* speak two distinct languages: one called Kéguem and the other None ... The populations who speak the None dialects do not understand Kéguem at all, and reciprocally" (emphasis added). So firmly was the label "Sereer" attached to these languages, however, that Faidherbe used it in all his later works, while other authors, including Cust and Lamoise, merely list "None" and other Cangin varieties along with other regional varieties of Sereer. (Note that Faidherbe's "Kéguem" was apparently a mistaken name for the same Siin variety of Sereer described by Lamoise [1873] and, more recently, Crétois [1972].)

17 Pichl's research was almost the first to be published on this language group since Faidherbe's brief notice in 1865. In a 1953 linguistic survey, however, de Tressan looked at these enclave languages and called them "faux-Sérère."

18 Many thanks to Victor Friedman for indispensable discussion and advice on Macedonian matters. There is considerably more agreement on the outlines of a geographic region called Macedonia than on the matter of which states have political rights to it. Historically, the following regions have been considered geographical Macedonia: the current Republic of Macedonia, the southwestern corner of Bulgaria, a northern province of Greece, and small parts of eastern Albania. Figure 17.2 illustrates this distinction. For parallel discussions of this by several generations of scholars, see Wilkinson (1951); Friedman (1985); and Poulton (1995).

19 McNeill (1964) provides the classic account of interimperial competition. Some important milestones in the gradual dissolution of Ottoman rule in Europe – through a series of revolts, wars, and treaties – include Serbia's relative autonomy, secured in 1817; the independence of Greece, proclaimed after 1830; the establishment of Bulgarian schools in 1835 and the Bulgarian Church (exarchate) in 1870; and the final independence of Serbia and Romania, and the autonomy of Bulgaria, gained at the Treaty of Berlin in 1878. The Balkan Wars of 1912–13 reduced Turkish rule in Europe to its present boundary and produced the partition

of Macedonia (for a useful summary, see Okey 1982).

20 The nationalist movements of nineteenth-century eastern Europe often claimed the distinction of having defended Europe, especially in literature targeted at Western audiences. Western views often recognized this claim, based on the earlier Christian/Moslem opposition, while also applying the contrast emphasizing civilization and barbarism (see Wolff 1994, chap. 1). For the Frenchman Lamouche, along with many other Westerners, the Greek struggle for independence was self-evidently a replay of "European civilization against Asiatic barbarism" (1899: 134); Longfellow's poem about Skenderbeg, the early Albanian hero defending Christendom from the Turks, enjoyed considerable popularity in the late-nineteenth-century US; and as late as 1918 Lloyd George, as British prime minister, declared the Serbs to be "Guardians of the Gate" of Europe (Laffan 1918).

21 See, for example, Eugen Weber's (1976) discussion of the lack of cultural, linguistic, and political unity in the most centralized of European powers, France.

22 The views discussed here were very widespread despite the fact that, as Brown (1995) and Todorova (1994), among others, have noted, Western European observers varied widely in their class backgrounds, political commitments (e.g., socialist vs. conservative), national loyalties, and visions of what would be the best political solution for the Balkans.

23 For further complex examples and discussion see Brown's (1995) persuasive work on the 1903 Ilinden rising in Macedonia, showing how these cross-cutting categories were transformed and regimented into the familiar images of Western European national ideology.

24 For further discussion of different kinds of contestation among linguistic ideologies, see Gal 1993.

25 The classic view of South Slavic dialectology adds a degree of regional organization to this picture. It maintains that in one part of this Balkan region, corresponding roughly to what is today the political border between Serbia and Bulgaria, a bundle of significant isoglosses permits Serbian and Bulgarian to emerge as linguistically distinct from one another. Farther south, however, isoglosses fan out. So while the dialectological transition from Serbian to Bulgarian in the north is relatively rapid, that from Serbian to Bulgarian through Macedonia (in the south) is very gradual. These claims about relative distinctness have recently been challenged, however (V. Friedman, personal communication 1998).

26 An early work describing these features is Lamouche (1899). Sandfeld's (1930) classic study on Balkan linguistics provides more detail. More recent and sophisticated descriptions include the cited works by Lunt and Friedman.

27 These arguments from the early years of the century continue unabated in attempts by Bulgarian linguists to deny the existence and historical depth of Macedonian. Macedonian linguists and historians, in turn, counter by producing evidence of early moves toward national autonomy in Macedonia, early literary production, and programmatic plans for a literary language; see Dimitrovski, Koneski, and Stamatoski (1978) and Lunt (1984) for summaries.

28 As Bauman and Briggs (2000) show, important aspects have earlier roots in the work of Locke.

29 Noteworthy exceptions include Labov's (1963) research on Martha's Vineyard, Gumperz's (1958) study of linguistic organization in a North Indian village, and Fischer's (1958) discussion of social factors that influence phonological variation. A later example of a work focusing on linguistic aspects of culturally imagined opposition between groups is Basso's (1979) *Portraits of "the Whiteman"*.

30 Note our debt here to Silverstein's (1979) argument that language ideologies, in their dialectical relationship with the distribution of linguistic forms, introduce dynamics of change into sociolinguistic systems.

REFERENCES

Abbott, Andrew (1990) Self-similar Social Structures. ms. Dept of Sociology, University of Chicago.

Abiven, O. (n.d.) *Annales réligieuses de St.-Joseph de Ngasobil, 1849–1929*. Archevêché de Dakar.

Anderson, Benedict (1983) *Imagined Communities*. London and New York: Verso.

Andriotes, Nic. P. (1957) *The Confederate State of Skopje and its Language*. Athens.

Bakić-Hayden, Milica, and Robert Hayden (1992) "Orientalist Variations on the Theme 'Balkans'," *Slavic Review* 51: 1–15.

Barth, Fredrik, ed. (1969) *Ethnic Groups and Boundaries*. Boston: Little, Brown.

Basso, Keith (1979) *Portraits of "The Whiteman": Linguistic Play and Cultural Symbols among the Western Apache*. Cambridge: Cambridge University Press.

Bateson, Gregory (1936) *Naven*. Cambridge: Cambridge University Press.

Bauman, R., and C. L. Briggs (2000) "Language Philosophy as Language Ideology: John Locke and Johann Gottfried Herder," in P. V. Kroskrity, ed., *Regimes of Language: Ideologies, Politics and Identities*. Santa Fe, NM: School of American Research Press, pp. 139–204.

Belić, Alexandr (1919) *La Macédoine: Études ethnographiques et politiques*. Paris and Barcelona: Bloud & Gay.

Brailsford, Henry (1906) *Macedonia: Its Races and its Future*. London: Methuen.

Brancoff, Dimitur M. (1905) *La Macédoine et sa population chrétienne*. Paris: Plon.

Brown, Keith (1995) Of Meanings and Memories: The National Imagination in Macedonia. PhD Dissertation, Department of Anthropology, University of Chicago.

Bryant, Alfred T. (1949) *The Zulu People*. Pietermaritzburg: Shuter and Shooter.

Cameron, Deborah (1990) "Demythologizing Sociolinguistics: Why Language Does Not Reflect Society," in John Joseph and Talbot J. Taylor, eds., *Ideologies of Language*. London: Routledge.

Crétois, Père Léonce (1972) *Dictionnaire Sereer-Français*. Dakar: Centre de Linguistique Appliquée de Dakar.

Cust, Robert Needham (1883) *A Sketch of the Modern Languages of Africa*. London: Trübner.

Cvijić, J. (1907) *Remarques sur l'ethnographie de la Macédoine*. Paris: Georges Roustan.

Denoon, D. (1992) "Dependence and Interdependence: Southern Africa from 1500 to 1800," in B. A. Ogot, ed., *General History of Africa V: Africa from the Sixteenth to the Eighteenth Century*. Berkeley, CA: University of California Press, for UNESCO, pp. 683–702.

de Tressan, M. de L. (1953) *Inventaire linguistique de l'Afrique Occidentale Française et du Togo*. Mémoires #30. Dakar: Institut Français d'Afrique Noire.

Diagne, Pathé (1967) *Pouvoir politique traditionnel en Afrique Occidentale*. Paris: Présence Africaine.

Dimitrovski, Todor, Blaze Koneski, Trajko Stamatoski, eds. (1978) *About the Macedonian Language*. Skopje: Macedonian Language Institute.

Doke, Clement (1961) *Textbook of Zulu Grammar* (6th edn.). Johannesburg: Longmans.

Doke, Clement, and B. W. Vilakazi (1958) *Zulu-English Dictionary* (2nd edn.). Johannesburg: Witwatersrand University Press.

Ehrenpreis, Marcus (1928) *The Soul of the East: Experiences and Reflections*. New York: Viking.

Evans-Pritchard, Edward E. (1940) *The Nuer*. Oxford: Clarendon Press.

Faidherbe, Louis Léon César (1865) "Etude sur la langue Kuégem ou Sérère-Sine," *Annuaire du Sénégal pour l'année 1865*. Saint-Louis: Imprimerie du Gouvernement, pp. 175–245.

Faidherbe, Louis Léon César (1882) *Grammaire et vocabulaire de la langue poul*. Paris: Maisonneuve.

Ferguson, Charles (1994) "Dialect, Register, and Genre: Working Assumptions about Conventionalization," in D. Biber and E. Finegan, eds., *Sociolinguistic Perspectives on Register*. New York and Oxford: Oxford University Press, pp. 15–30.

Finlayson, Rosalie (1978) "A Preliminary Survey of *Hlonipha* among the Xhosa," *Taalfasette* 24: 48–63.

Finlayson, Rosalie (1982) "*Hlonipha* – the Women's Language of Avoidance among the Xhosa. *South African Journal of African Languages* 1/1.

Finlayson, Rosalie (1984) "The Changing Nature of *isihlonipho sabafazi*," *African Studies* 43: 137–46.

Fischer, John L. (1958) "Social Influences on the Choice of a Linguistic Variant," *Word* 14: 47–56.

Formigari, Lia (1985) "Théories du langage et théories du pouvoir en France, 1800–1848," *Historiographia Linguistica* 12: 63–83.

Friedman, Victor (1985) "The Sociolinguistics of Literary Macedonian," *International Journal of the Sociology of Language* 52: 31–57.

Friedman, Victor (1989) "Macedonian: Codification and Lexicon," in I. Fodor and C. Hagège, eds., *Language Reform: History and Future*. Vol. IV. Hamburg: Helmut Buske, pp. 329–34.

Friedman, Victor (1995) "Persistence and Change in Ottoman Patterns of Codeswitching in the Republic of Macedonia: Nostalgia, Duress and Language Shift in Contemporary Southeastern Europe," *Summer School Code-Switching and Language Contact*. Ljouwert/Leeuwarden, The Netherlands: Fryske Academy, pp. 58–67.

Friedman, Victor (1996) "The Turkish Lexical Element in the Languages of the Republic of Macedonia from the Ottoman Period to Independence," *Zeitschrift für Balkonologie* 32.

Gal, Susan (1979) *Language Shift: Social Determinants of Language Change in Bilingual Austria*. New York: Academic Press.

Gal, Susan (1987) "Codeswitching and Consciousness in the European Periphery," *American Ethnologist* 14/4: 637–53.

Gal, Susan (1989) "Language and Political Economy," *Annual Review of Anthropology* 18: 345–67.

Gal, Susan (1991) "Bartók's Funeral: Representations of Europe in Hungarian Political Rhetoric," *American Ethnologist* 18: 440–58.

Gal, Susan (1993) "Diversity and Contestation in Linguistic Ideologies: German-speakers in Hungary," *Language in Society* 22: 337–59.

Gal, Susan, and Judith T. Irvine (1995) "The Boundaries of Languages and Disciplines: How Ideologies Construct Difference," *Social Research* 62/4.

Garnett, Lucy (1904) *Turkish Life in Town and Country*. New York: Putnam.

Geyer, Michael (1989) "Historical Fictions of Autonomy and the Europeanization of National History," *Central European History* 22: 316–42.

Giliomee, Hermann (1989) "The Eastern Frontier, 1770–1812," in *The Shaping of South African Society, 1652–1840*, Richard Elphick and Hermann Giliomee, eds. Middletown, CT: Wesleyan University Press, pp. 421–71.

Goff, A. and Hugh A. Fawcett (1921) *Macedonia: A Plea for the Primitive*. London: John Lane.

Greenberg, Joseph (1963) *The Languages of Africa. International Journal of American Linguistics* 29/1: Part II.

Guiraudon, T. G. de (1894) *Bolle Fulbe: Manuel de la langue foule, parlée dans la sénégambie et le soudan. Grammaire, textes, vocabulaire*. Paris and Leipzig: H. Welter.

Gumperz, John (1958) "Dialect Differences and Social Stratification in a North Indian Village," *American Anthropologist* 60: 668–82.

Gumperz, John, and Dell Hymes, eds. (1964) The Ethnography of Communication. *American Anthropologist* 66/6 Part 2 (Special Publication).

Gumperz, John, and Dell Hymes, eds. (1972) *Directions in Sociolinguistics: The Ethnography of Communication*. New York: Holt, Rinehart, & Winston.

Harinck, Gerrit (1969) "Interaction between Xhosa and Khoi: Emphasis on the Period 1620–1750," in *African Societies in Southern Africa*, Leonard Thompson, ed. London: Heinemann, pp. 145–70.

Herbert, Robert K. (1990) "The Sociohistory of Clicks in Southern Bantu," *Anthropological Linguistics* 32: 295–315.

Hervas y Panduro, Lorenzo (1800–05) *Catalogo de las lenguas de las naciones conocidas, y numeración, división, y clases de estas segun la diversidad de sus idiomas y dialectos*. Madrid: Renz.

Herzfeld, Michael (1987) *Anthropology Through the Looking Glass*. Cambridge: Cambridge University Press.

Hymes, Dell (1968) "Linguistic Problems in Defining the Concept of 'Tribe'," in June Helm, ed., *Essays on the Problem of Tribe: Proceedings of the 1967 Annual Spring Meeting of the American Ethnological Society.* Seattle: University of Washington Press (for the A.E.S.), pp. 23–48.

Irvine, Judith T. (1985) "Status and Style in Language," *Annual Review of Anthropology* 14: 557–81.

Irvine, Judith T. (1987) "Domains of Description in the Ethnography of Speaking: A Retrospective on the 'Speech Community'," in R. Bauman, J. T. Irvine, and S. U. Philips, *Performance, Speech Community and Genre. Working Papers and Proceedings of the Center for Psychosocial Studies*, #11. Chicago, IL: Center for Psychosocial Studies, pp. 13–24.

Irvine, Judith T. (1989) "When Talk isn't Cheap: Language and Political Economy," *American Ethnologist* 16/2: 248–67.

Irvine, Judith T. (1990) "Registering Affect: Heteroglossia in the Linguistic Expression of Emotion," in C. A. Lutz and L. Abu-Lughod, eds., *Language and the Politics of Emotion.* Cambridge: Cambridge University Press, pp. 126–61.

Irvine, Judith T. (1992) "Ideologies of Honorific Language," in Paul Kroskrity, Bambi Schieffelin, and Kathryn Woolard, eds., Special Issue on Language Ideologies. *Pragmatics* 2: 251–62.

Irvine, Judith T. (1993) "Mastering African Languages: The Politics of Linguistics in Nineteenth-century Senegal," in D. Segal and R. Handler, eds., *Nations, Colonies and Metropoles.* Special issue, *Social Analysis* No. 33, pp. 27–46.

Karakasidou, Anastasia (1993) "Policing Culture: Negating Ethnic Identity in Greek Macedonia," *Journal of Modern Greek Studies* 11: 1–28.

Klein, Martin (1968) *Islam and Imperialism in Senegal: Sine-Saloum 1847–1914.* Stanford, CA: Stanford University Press.

Kobès, Alois (1869) *Grammaire de la langue volofe.* Saint-Joseph de Ngasobil: Imprimerie de la mission.

Kolben, Peter (1731) *The Present State of the Cape of Good Hope; Or, a Particular Account of the Several Nations of the Hottentots, their Religion, Government, Laws, Customs, Ceremonies, and Opinions; their Art of War, Professions, Language, Genius, etc.; Together with a Short Account of the Dutch Settlement at the Cape.* London: W. Innys.

Koneski, Blaze (1980) "Macedonian," in Alexander Schenker and Edward Stankiewicz, eds., *The Slavic Literary Languages: Formation and Development.* New Haven: Yale Concilium on International and Area Studies, pp. 53–64.

Krige, Eileen (1950) [1936] *The Social System of the Zulus.* Pietermaritzburg: Shuter and Shooter.

Kroskrity, Paul, Bambi Schieffelin and Kathryn Woolard (eds.) (1992) Special issue on Language Ideologies. *Pragmatics* 2/3.

Kunene, Daniel P. (1958) "Notes on Hlonepha among the Southern Sotho," *African Studies* 17: 159–82.

Labov, William (1963) "The Social Motivation of a Sound Change," *Word* 19: 273–309.

Laffan, R. D. G. (1918) *The Guardians of the Gate: Historical Lectures on the Serbs.* Oxford: Clarendon Press.

Lamoise, Père (1873) *Grammaire de la langue sérère avec des exemples et des exercices renfermant des documents très-utiles.* Saint-Joseph de Ngasobil (Sénégambie): Imprimerie de la mission.

Lamouche, L. (1899) *La Péninsule balkanique: Esquisse historique ethnographique, philologique et littéraire.* Paris: Paul Ollendorff.

Lepsius, Karl Richard (1863) *Standard Alphabet for Reducing Unwritten Languages and Foreign Graphic Systems to a Uniform Orthography in European Letters*, 2nd ed. London: Williams and Norgate; Berlin: W. Hertz.

Louw, J. A. (1977) "The Adaptation of Non-click Khoi Consonants in Xhosa," *Khoisan Linguistic Studies* 3: 74–92.

Lunt, Horace (1959) "The Creation of Standard Macedonian: Some Facts and Attitudes," *Anthropological Linguistics* 16: 19–26.

Lunt, Horace (1984) "Some Sociolinguistic Aspects of Macedonian and Bulgarian," in Ben Stoltz, I.R. T. Hunik and Lubomire Dolezel, eds., *Language and Literary Theory.* Ann Arbor: University of Michigan Press, pp. 83–132.

McNeill, William (1964) *Europe's Steppe Frontier, 1500–1800*. Chicago, IL: University of Chicago Press.

Milroy, Lesley (1980) *Language and Social Networks*. Oxford: Blackwell.

Moore, Frederick (1906) *The Balkan Trail*. London: Smith, Elder and Co.

Mudimbe, V. Y. (1988) *The Invention of Africa*. Bloomington, IN: Indiana University Press.

Müller, F. Max (1855) *The Languages of the Seat of War in the East*, 2nd edn. London: Williams and Norgate.

Müller, F. Max (1861) *Lectures on the Science of Language*. London.

Nicolaïdes, Cleanthes (1899) *Macedonien: Die geschichtliche Entwicklung der macedonischen Frage im Altertum, in Mittelalter und in der neueren Zeit*. Berlin: Verlag von Johannes Räder.

Okey, Robin (1982) *Eastern Europe 1740–1985: Feudalism to Communism*. Minneapolis: University of Minnesota Press.

Olender, Maurice (1992) *The Languages of Paradise*. Cambridge, MA: Harvard University Press.

Östreich, Karl von (1905) "Die Bevölkerung von Makedonien," *Geographische Zeitschrift* XI: 268–92.

Peirce, Charles Sanders (1955) "Logic as Semiotic: The Theory of Signs," in *Philosophical Writings of Peirce*, ed. Justus Buchler. New York: Dover, pp. 98–119.

Pichl, W. J. (1966) *The Cangin Group: A Language Group in Northern Senegal*. Duquesne University, Institute of African Affairs. Pittsburgh: Duquesne University Press.

Pinet-Laprade, E. (1865) "Notice sur les Sérères," *Annuaire du Sénégal pour l'année 1865*. Saint-Louis: Imprimerie du Gouvernement, pp. 131–71.

Pinto, Vivian (1980) "Bulgarian," in Alexander Schenker and Edward Stankiewicz, eds., *The Slavic Literary Languages: Formation and Development*. New Haven, CT: Yale Concilium on International and Area Studies, pp. 37–52.

Poulton, Hugh (1995) *Who Are the Macedonians?* Bloomington, IN: Indiana University Press.

Prins, Frans E., and Hester Lewis (1992) "Bushmen as Mediators in Nguni Cosmology," *Ethnology* 31: 133–48.

Said, Edward (1978) *Orientalism*. New York: Pantheon.

Sandfeld, Karl (1930) *Linguistique balkanique: Problèmes et résultats*. Paris: C. Klincksieck.

Sapir, Edward (1913) Review of Carl Meinhof, *Die Sprachen der Hamiten. Current Anthropological Literature* 2: 21–27.

Schleicher, August (1869) *Darwinism Tested by the Science of Language*, tr. Alexander Bikkers. London: John Camden Hotten; first published 1863 as *Die Darwinsche Theorie und die Sprachwissenschaft*.

Silverstein, Michael (1979) "Language Structure and Linguistic Ideology," in R. Clyne, W. Hanks, and C. Hofbauer, eds., *The Elements: A Parasession on Linguistic Units and Levels*. Chicago, IL: Chicago Linguistic Society, pp. 193–247.

Silverstein, Michael (1992) "The Uses and Utility of Ideology: Some Reflections," in P. Kroskrity, B. Schieffelin, and K. Woolard, eds., Special Issue on Language Ideologies. *Pragmatics* 2/3: 311–24.

Silverstein, Michael (2000) "Whorfianism and the Linguistic Imagination of Nationality," in Paul V. Kroskrity ed, *Regimes of Language: Ideologies, Polities, and Identities*. Santa Fe: SAR Press, pp. 85–138.

Sís, Vladimír (1918) *Mazedonien: Eine Studie über Geographie, Geschichte, Volkskunde und die wirtschaftlichen und kulturellen Zustände des Landes mit statistischen Ergängzungen*. Zürich: Art. Institut Orell Füssli.

Stoianovich, Traian (1960) "The Conquering Balkan Orthodox Merchant," *Journal of Economic History* XX: 234–313.

Tautain, L. (1885) "Etudes critiques sur l'ethnologie et l'ethnographie des peoples du bassin du Sénégal," *Revue d'Ethnographie* 4: 61–80, 137–47, 254–68.

Taylor, Talbot J. (1990) "Which is To Be Master? The Institutionalization of Authority in the Science of Language," in Joseph, John E. and Talbot J. Taylor, eds., *Ideologies of Language*. London and New York: Routledge, pp. 9–26.

Thomason, Sarah G., and T. Kaufman (1988) *Language Contact, Creolization, and Genetic Linguistics*. Berkeley and Los Angeles, CA: University of California Press.

Todorova, Maria (1994) "The Balkans: From Discovery to Invention," *Slavic Review* 53/2: 453–82.

Wagner, Roy (1991) "Fractal Persons," in Maurice Godelier and Marilyn Strathern, eds., *Great Men and Big Men*. Cambridge and Paris: Cambridge University Press, pp. 159–73.

Weber, Eugen (1976) *Peasants into Frenchmen*. Stanford, CA: Stanford University Press.

Weinreich, Uriel, William Labov, and Marvin Herzog (1968) "Empirical foundations of linguistic theory," in W. Lehmann and Y. Malkiel, eds., *Directions for Historical Linguistics*. Austin: University of Texas Press, pp. 95–195.

Wilkinson, Henry R. (1951) *Maps and Politics: A Review of the Ethnographic Cartography of Macedonia*. Manchester: Manchester University Press.

Wilson, W. A. A. (1989) "Atlantic," in J. Bendor-Samuel, ed., *The Niger-Congo Languages*. Lanham, MD: University Press of America, pp. 81–104.

Wolff, Larry (1994) *Inventing Eastern Europe: The Map of Civilization in the Mind of the Enlightenment*. Stanford, CA: Stanford University Press.

Woolard, Kathryn A., and Bambi B. Schieffelin (1994) "Language ideology," *Annual Review of Anthropology* 23: 55–82.

STUDY QUESTIONS

1 What do Irvine and Gal mean when they write that "There is no 'view from nowhere,' no gaze that is not positioned" when we are examining the use of language by speakers and its representation by linguists?
2 What do the authors mean by "ideologies of language differentiation"? Can you use their discussion to enlighten your own understanding of linguistic differences as they appear to you in your daily life?
3 Describe and discuss the three semiotic processes of iconization, fractal recursivity, and erasure. How are all three processes illustrated by the study of the development of "clicks" in the Nguni languages of southern Africa, the classification of Senegalese languages by Europeans, and the debates over Macedonian?
4 Describe the practice of *hlonipha* (the use of respect terms) among Nguni speakers and illustrate why it is used as an example of ideological representations of linguistic differences.
5 How does this chapter build upon, expand, and in some respects revise the notion of speech community assumed by other authors in this book?

18

The "Father Knows Best" Dynamic in Dinnertime Narratives

Elinor Ochs and Carolyn Taylor

Historical and sociological studies of gender have pursued the plethora of ways in which cultural concepts of gender impact social life, especially institutions such as the family, the church, the workplace, and the state. Of critical importance to all gender research is the idea that gender ideologies are closely linked to the management of social asymmetries. As Marie Withers Osmond and Barrie Thorne (1993: 593) concisely put it, "Gender relations are basically power relations." Notions of patriarchy, male authority, male domination, and gender hierarchy have gained considerable intellectual vitality within feminist argumentation. The import of gender pervades all levels of analysis, from historical and ethnographic studies of gender ideologies, structures, and customs to interactional studies of gendered activities and actions. From a poststructuralist perspective, we need both macro- and micro-analyses to illuminate continuity and change in the rights, expectations, and obligations vis-à-vis the conduct, knowledge, understandings, and feelings that constitute the lived experience of being female or male in society.

The present chapter addresses gender asymmetry in middle-class European American families through an examination of a single social activity: narrating a story or a report over family dinner. While recognizing that family interaction is socially and historically enmeshed in the prevailing interests of economic and political institutions (e.g., Hartmann 1981; Stack 1974), we offer a window into how family hierarchies are constituted in day-to-day family life. Our position is that family exchanges do not simply exemplify gender relations otherwise shaped by forces outside the family but, rather, are the primordial means for negotiating, maintaining, transforming, and socializing gender identities. Certainly from the point of view of a child, routine moments of family communication are the earliest and perhaps the most profound medium for constructing gender understandings (Cole and Cole 1989; Dunn 1984; Freud [1921] 1949; Goodwin 1990; Kohlberg 1966; Maccoby and Jacklin 1974; Schieffelin 1990). Awakenings to gender asymmetry may occur from infancy on, for example, in two-parent families, through such

For permission to publish copyright material in this book, grateful acknowledgment is made to: E. Ochs and C. Taylor, C. (1995), "The 'Father Knows Best' Dynamic in Dinnertime Narratives," in K. Hall and M. Bucholtz (eds.), *Gender Articulated: Language in the Socially Constructed Self*. New York: Routledge, pp. 97–120.

everyday activity as watching how mothers and fathers interact with each other and with their daughters and sons.

Our particular attention has been captured by the pervasiveness and importance of collaborative narration, wherein children interact with others in co-narrating, as a locus of socialization (Ochs, Smith, and Taylor 1989; Ochs and Taylor 1992a, b; Ochs, Taylor, Rudolph, and Smith 1992). In the present study, we examine how such narrative practices may instantiate gender-relevant narrator and family-role identities of women and men as mother and father, wife and husband, in white middle-class families in the United States.[1] Indeed, our observations of these households suggest that children are overhearers, recipients, and active contributors to gender-implicative, asymmetrical storytelling exchanges dozens of times in the course of sharing a single meal together.

One of the important tenets of this research is that all social identities, including gender identities, are constituted through actions and demeanors. Individuals come to understand a range of social identities primarily by learning, first in childhood, to recognize and/or display certain behaviors and stances that are permitted or expected by particular community members in particular activity settings. We suggest that, among other routes, children (and adults, taking on new roles as spouses and parents) come to understand family and gender roles through differential modes of acting and expressing feelings in narrative activity.

Another important perspective we propose to be essential to a fuller understanding of gender instantiation concerns the attention we place on family interactions – that is, families as multiparty activity systems (Engeström 1987). In gender research on social interaction, the exchanges analyzed have tended to be dyadic ones, i.e., female–male, female–female, or male–male interactions. This design lends itself to dichotomous comparisons between female and male conduct in these communicative arrangements. While two people may wear many hats within one dyad, which we also recognize, dyadic identity construction seems inherently less complex, less hierarchical than multiparty, and also less representative of the contexts in which most people are socialized into gender notions and roles.

Our study of family narrative-activity interactions examines multiparty two-parent contexts in which participants construct themselves and one another simultaneously as spouse, parent, child, and sibling – as mother and wife, father and husband, daughter and sister, son and brother. Within the variety of dynamics and alignments available, on the one hand, women and men may often work together to inquire about and control their children – and women can be seen as part of a dominating force. On the other hand, these parental alignments may co-occur with sustained internal-dyad exchanges wherein one spouse dominates the other – and women may regularly be part of (and a model for) the dominated.

We argue that the narrative practices of all family members in this study instantiate a form of gender asymmetry that we call a "Father knows best" dynamic. Within this dynamic, the father is typically set up – through his own and others' recurrent narrative practices – to be primary audience, judge, and critic of family members' actions, conditions, thoughts, and feelings as narrative protagonists (actors in the past) or as co-narrators (actors in the present). In our corpus, we are particularly struck by the practices of the women as mothers and wives that contribute to this dynamic, instantiating and modeling in their conduct as narrators a pervasive orientation toward fathers as evaluators. In this chapter, we focus especially on those specific practices.

The "Father knows best" ideology is usually associated with a prefeminist, presumably passé 1950s conceptualization of idyllic domestic order that was popularized and concretized by the television program of the same name. In that situation comedy, the title was often ironic, given that its episodes regularly served to point out that Father did not, in fact, know best but often learned that Mother had been right all along. Yet lip service to a "Father knows best" ideology was often maintained on the surface in that Mother would modestly defer to or indulge Father's ego. In the 1980s, variations on this formula for domestic gender relations included its extension to Black middle-class families, most popularly in *The*

Bill Cosby Show. Our appropriation of this title is intended to suggest that the ideology may still be getting daily reinforcement in the everyday narrative practices of postfeminist 1990s American families – with considerable (perhaps unwitting) help from wives and mothers. Indeed, it seems to us that the ideology was instantiated even more strongly in the everyday dinnertime discourse in our study than it was or is in mass-media fictionalized versions of family life – that is, more implicitly and without the irony.

Database

For several years, we have been analyzing discourse practices in twenty middle-class, European American families, focusing especially on dinnertime communication patterns in narrative activity. The present study isolates a subcorpus of these families: seven two-parent families who earned more than $40,000 a year during the 1987–9 period in which the study was conducted. Each family had a five-year-old child who had at least one older sibling.[2] Two fieldworkers video- and audiotaped each family on two evenings from an hour or so before dinner until the five-year-old went to bed. During the dinner activity, fieldworkers left the camera on a tripod and absented themselves.

The specific database for this study consists of the exactly one hundred past-time narratives (stories and reports) that the seven families told during thirteen dinners where both parents were present. As we elaborate in Ochs and Taylor (1992a, b) and Ochs, Taylor, Rudolph, and Smith (1992), we define a *story* as a problem-centered past-time narrative (e.g., the narrative activity eventually orients toward solving some aspect of the narrated events seen as problematic), whereas a *report* does not entail such a problem-centered or problem-solving orientation.

Narrative Instantiation of Gender Roles in the Family

The narrative roles that we address here as relevant to the construction of gender identities within families are those of *protagonist, introducer* (either elicitor or initial teller), *primary recipient, problematizer,* and *problematizee* (or *target*). Below we define each of these roles and discuss the extent to which that role was assumed by particular family members in our study.[3]

Protagonist

A *protagonist* is here defined as a leading or principal character in a narrated event. Our examination is limited to those narratives where at least one protagonist in the narrative is present at the dinner table, such as in (1), where the chief protagonist is five-year-old Jodie:

(1) zJodie's TB Shots Report (introductory excerpt)[4]

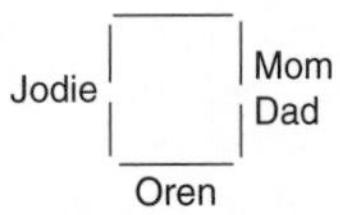

Participants:

Mom
Dad
Jodie (female, 5 years)
Oren (male, 7 years, 5 months)

The following excerpt introduces the first past-time narrative told at this dinner, when the family has just begun eating.

MOM: *((to Jodie))* = oh:: You know what? You wanna tell Daddy what happened to you today? =

DAD: *((looking up and off))* = Tell me everything that happened from the moment you went in—until:

[

JODIE: I got a sho::t?=

DAD: = <u>EH</u> *((gasping))* what? *((frowning))*
JODIE: I got a sho::t
[
DAD: <u>no</u>
JODIE: *((nods yes, facing Dad))*
DAD: *((shaking head no))* – Couldn't be
JODIE: (mhm?) *((with upward nod, toward Dad))*
[
OREN: a TV test? *((to Mom))*
(0.4)
OREN: TV test? Mommy?
MOM: *((nods yes))* – mhm
JODIE: and a sho:t
DAD: *((to Jodie))* (what) Did you go to the uh:: – *((to Mom))* Did you go to the ? animal hospital?
MOM: mhh – <u>no:?.</u>
DAD: (where)
JODIE: I just went to the doctor and I got a shot
DAD: *((shaking head no))* I don't believe it
JODIE: <u>ri:?lly::</u> ...

Protagonist is an important role with respect to the "Father knows best" dynamic in that the protagonist is presented as a topic for comment (e.g., in Jodie's case above, for belief or disbelief) by family members. While being a protagonist puts one's narrative actions, conditions, thoughts, and feelings on the table as a focus of attention, this attention is not always a plus, given that protagonists' actions, thoughts, and feelings are not only open to praise but also exposed to familial scrutiny, irony, challenge, and critique. Furthermore, if there is asymmetric distribution in the allocation of protagonist status, one family member may be more routinely exposed to such evaluation by others than the rest, impacting the degree to which some members' identities are constructed as protagonists more than others. In our corpus, such as asymmetry existed, whereby children were the preferred narrative protagonists, as exemplified in the report of Jodie's activities in (1). Children composed nearly 60 percent of all family-member protagonists; mothers figured as protagonists 23 percent of the time; fathers, 19 percent.[5] Father's being least often in the role of protagonist meant that their past actions, thoughts, and feelings were least often exposed to the scrutiny of others and, in this sense, they were the least vulnerable family members.

Introducer

In light of the vulnerability of protagonists to familial scrutiny, an important factor to consider is the extent to which family members assumed this role through their own initiative as opposed to having this role imposed on them through the elicitations and initiations of other family members. To address this issue, we consider next how narratives about family members were introduced.

The narrative role of *introducer* is here defined as the co-narrator who makes the first move to open a narrative, either by elicitation or by direct initiation. We define these two introducer roles as follows. An *elicitor* is a co-narrator who asks for a narrative to be told. In (1) above, Jodie's mother assumes this role and, in so doing, introduces the narrative. An *initial teller* is a co-narrator who expresses the first declarative proposition about a narrative event. In (1), Jodie assumed this role but, because her mother had elicited her involvement, Jodie was not the narrative introducer per se. In unelicited narratives such as (2), the initial teller (in this case, the mother) is also the narrative introducer.

(2) Broken Chair Story

Participants:

Josh
Ronnie | | Mom
Dad

Mom
Dad
Ronnie (male, 4 years, 11 months)
Josh (male, 7 years, 10 months)

During dinner preparation, as Mom brings Ronnie a spoon to open a can of Nestlé Quik, she scoots Ronnie's chair in to the table. Josh is at his place; Dad is in kitchen area to the right of the table, as shown above.

MOM: Oh This chair? broke – today
[
((microwave? buzzer goes off))
DAD: I? know =
((Mom heads back toward kitchen, stops by Josh's chair; Josh begins looking at Ronnie's chair and under table))
MOM: =I- no:: I mean it rea:?lly broke today
[
DAD: I? know (0.2) I know?
MOM: Oh You knew that it was split?
DAD: yeah?,
MOM: the whole wood('s) split?
DAD: yeah,
MOM: Oh Did you do it?
(0.4)
DAD: I don't know if I did? it but I saw that it wa:?s=
[
MOM: (oh)
((Josh goes under table to inspect chairs; Mom bends over to chair))
Ron?: (what? where?)
=[
MOM: yeah I sat down? in it and the whole thing split so I – I tie:d
[
DAD: *((with a somewhat taunting intonation))* (That's a)
rea:l si:gn? that you need to go on a di:?et.
Ron?: *((going under table too))* (where)
MOM: hh *grinning as she rises from stooped position next to Josh's chair))*
RON?: (where where where)=
JOSH: =Mi:ne? broke?
MOM: I fixed it – I tied (it to the-)
[
JOSH: mi:ne? I'm not gonna sit on that chair (if it's broken)
Josh pushes his chair away and takes Mom's; Mom pushes Josh's chair over to her place, tells the boys to sit down; the subject of the broken chair is dropped))

The role of introducer is one that we see as pivotal in controlling narrative activity. The introducer nominates narrative topics, thus proposing who is to be the focus of attention (i.e., the protagonist), what aspects of their lives are to be narrated, and when. In (1), Jodie's mother directs the family's attention to Jodie at a particular moment in the dinner, suggesting that there is a narrative to be told as well as the tone, focus, and implicit boundaries of that narrative. For that moment, the introducer proposes what is important (to know) about that family member, as a protagonist. In addition, the introducer controls who is to initiate the narrative account itself, either self-selecting, as in (2), or eliciting a co-narrator, as in (1). Finally, introducers also exert control in that they explicitly or implicitly select certain co-narrator(s) to be primary recipients of the narrative (see following section). In both examples above, mother as introducer selected father as primary recipient.

Although the majority of the protagonists in our corpus were the children, the majority of the narrative introducers were the parents (who introduced seventy-one of the one hundred stories and reports), mothers more often than fathers. (Mothers and fathers *elicited* narratives from others almost equally; their difference derives from mothers' greater tendency to introduce by *direct initiation* as well – and often about others rather than about themselves.) All family members were vulnerable to having narratives about themselves introduced by others. Moreover, for parents, there was relative parity in this regard: for mothers and fathers equally, fully half of all narratives in which they figured as protagonists were introduced by themselves – and almost half by someone else.

A striking asymmetry exists, however, between parents and children. Only one-third of the narratives about children were introduced by the child protagonists themselves (for five-year-olds and younger, the figure was only one-quarter).[6] Children became protagonists chiefly because mothers introduced them as such and often by mothers' direct initiation of the narrative account. Thus, mothers were largely responsible for determining which children and which aspects of children's lives were subject to dinnertime narrative examination – and when and how. In light of this finding, we suggest that, for mothers, the role of introducer may be appropriated (at least in some family cultures and contexts within the United States) as a locus of narrative control over children – and, among family members, children may be particularly vulnerable in this sense.

Primary recipient

The narrative role of *primary recipient* is here defined as the co-narrator(s) to whom a narrative is predominantly oriented. This role is a powerful one in that it implicitly entitles the family member who assumes it to evaluate the narrative actions, thoughts, and feelings of family members as protagonists and/or as narrators. Anyone who recurrently occupies this position is instantiated as "family judge." As noted earlier, the introducer is critical to the assignment of primary recipient. In some cases, as in (1) and (2), the introducer designated another family member to be primary recipient; in other cases, as in (3), an introducer may select herself or himself.

(3) Lucy's Swim Team Report (introductory excerpt)

Near the end of dinner, Lucy (9 years, 7 months) has been describing her swim class when Dad raises a new, related narrative.

DAD: (Your) mother said you were thinking of uh: – getting on the swim team?
LUCY: *((nods yes once emphatically))* (1.0) *((Mom, who has finished eating, takes plate to nearby counter and returns))*
DAD: *((nods yes))* – (good) ...

Not surprising but nevertheless striking was the privileging of parents as primary recipients of dinnertime narratives: parents assumed that role 82 percent of the time. Within this privileging of parents as preferred audience, fathers were favored over mothers. Whereas fathers often positioned themselves as primary recipients through their own elicitation of narratives (as in example 3, above), in some families mothers regularly nominated fathers as primary recipients through their narrative introductions, such as in (1): *You wanna tell Daddy what happened to you today?* When we overlay this finding on those discussed above, the overall pattern suggests a fundamental asymmetry in family narrative activity, whereby children's lives were told to parents but, by and large, parents did not narrate their lives to their children.

This preference for fathers as primary recipients is partly accounted for by the fact that the father is often the person at the dinner table who knows least about children's daily lives. Typically, even the women who work outside the home arrived home earlier than their husbands and had more opportunity to hear about the events in their children's days prior to dinner. However, there are several reasons to see that being "unknowing" is an inadequate account for fathers' prominence as primary recipients in these narratives. First, in two of the thirteen dinners studied here, mothers knew less about their children's day that day than did fathers, yet we did not observe fathers nominating mothers as primary recipients of narratives about children (i.e., in this corpus, we did not find fathers saying, "Tell Mommy what you did today"). Second, child initiators oriented more narratives to mothers than to fathers in spite of the mothers' generally greater prior knowledge of children's lives. Third, mothers and children were typically as unknowing about fathers' reportable experiences as fathers were about theirs, yet fathers seldom addressed their lives to mothers or children as preferred recipients. (We also did not find mothers – or fathers – saying to each other the equivalent of "Honey, tell the children what you did today.") These considerations suggest to us that it was not simply being unknowing (about family members' daily activities) that determined primary-recipient selection but, perhaps, a matter of *who* was unknowing.

By considering who the initial teller was for each narrative (i.e., the one who was typically the first to address the primary recipient directly), we determined that it was neither children nor fathers themselves who accounted for fathers' assuming the role of overall preferred recipient. Instead, it was mothers who – in addition to often directing children to orient to fathers through elicitations (e.g., *Tell Daddy about* ...) – also directly initiated many narratives to fathers as primary recipients. In fact, mothers' direct initiation to fathers was the single greatest factor in accounting for fathers' privileging as preferred recipient. Mothers initiated twice as many narratives oriented to fathers as fathers initiated toward mothers. In light of these findings, we suggest that a gender-socialization factor entered into the nonequation, prompting mothers' elevation of unknowing fathers into primary recipients – and judges – of other family members' lives, unmatched by fathers' similar elevation of unknowing mothers to such status.

We have noted above that narrative introducers exert control by designating primary recipients, but here we emphasize that, at the same time, such designation passes control to the co-narrator who is so designated: the primary recipient is in a position to evaluate, reframe, or otherwise pass judgment on both the tale and how it is told. In our view, the role of primary recipient affords a panopticon-like perspective and power (Bentham 1791; Foucault 1979). The term *panopticon* refers to an all-seeing eye or monitoring gaze that keeps subjects under its constant purview (e.g., a prison guard in a watchtower). Similarly, we suggest that narrative activity exposes protagonists to the surveillance of other co-narrators, especially to the scrutiny of the designated primary recipient (see Ochs and Taylor 1992b). Given that this role was played mainly by the fathers in our data, we further suggest that it is potentially critical to the narrative reconstruction of "Father knows best" because it sets up the father to be the ultimate purveyor and judge of other family members' actions, conditions, thoughts, and feelings.

The family-role preferences we have found with regard to these first three narrative roles – protagonist, introducer, and primary recipient – already present an overall picture of the way in which narrative activity may serve to put women, men, and children into a politics of asymmetry. As noted earlier, in the family context, issues of gender and power cannot be looked at as simply dyadic, i.e., *men* versus *women* as *haves* versus *have-nots*. Rather, in two-parent families, women and men manifest asymmetries of power both dyadically as spouses and triadically as mothers and fathers with children. Although there *are* interesting dyadic observations here regarding women versus men (e.g., women tend to raise narrative topics; men tend to be positioned – often by women – to evaluate them), these apparently genderbased distinctions are part of a *triadic* interaction, or larger picture, wherein children are often the subjects of these narrative moves. Neither women's nor men's control is merely a control over each other but particularly encompasses and impacts children. Furthermore, a narrative role such as that of introducer (seen here to be more aligned with women, at least as initial teller) may have a complex relationship to power, both empowering the holder in terms of agenda-setting, choice of protagonist, and topic, but also disempowering to the degree that the introducer sets up someone else (here more often the man) to be ultimate judge of the narrated actions and protagonists.

Problematizer/problematizee

The narrative role of *problematizer* is here defined as the co-narrator who renders an action, condition, thought, or feeling of a protagonist or a co-narrator problematic, or possibly so. The role of *problematizee* (or *target*) is defined as the co-narrator whose action, condition, thought, or feeling is rendered problematic, or a possible problem. As such, in this study, we consider only problematizing that targeted copresent family members.

An action, condition, thought, or feeling may be problematized on several grounds. For example, it may be treated as untrue, incredible, or doubtful, as when, in (1), the father problematized Jodie's TB shots narrative with mock disbelief (*no, couldn't be*, and *I don't believe it*). In other cases, it is problematized because it has or had negative ramifications (e.g., is deemed thoughtless or perilous), as when, in (2), the wife implicitly problematized her husband as thoughtless for not warning her about the broken chair (*Oh You knew that it was split?*).

We also see in (2) how an action, condition, thought, or feeling may be problematized on grounds of incompetence. When the husband indicted his wife for being overweight as the cause of the chair's breaking (*That's a rea:l si: gn? that you need to go on a di:?et.*), we suggest he was implicitly problematizing her for lack of self-control. In (4), the same father again problematizes his wife, this time as too lenient a boss and thus incompetent in her workplace as well:

(4) Mom's Job Story (excerpt)

Same family as in (2). At the end of dinner, Mom is at the sink doing dishes as Dad eats an ice cream sundae and seven-year-old Josh does homework at the table opposite Dad. This excerpt comes near the end of a story about Mom's hiring a new assistant at work, which Dad has elicited and already probed considerably.

DAD: *((eating dessert))* Well – I certainly think that – you're a- you know you're a fair bo?ss – You've been working there how long?
MOM: fifteen years in June *((as she scrapes dishes at kitchen sink))*
DAD: fifteen years – and you got a guy *((turns to look directly at Mom as he continues))* that's been workin there a few weeks? and you do (it what) the way he wants.
MOM: hh *((laughs))*
(0.6) *((Dad smiles slightly?, then turns back to eating his dessert))*
MOM: It's not a matter of my doin it the way he:wa:nt – It does help in that I'm getting more work? done It's just that I'm workin too hard? I don't wanta work so hard
DAD: *((rolls chair around to face Mom halfway))* Well – You're the bo:ss It's up to you to set the standards...

Further grounds for problematizing were on the basis that an action is out-of-bounds – e.g., unfair, rude, excessive. In (5), the father problematizes his wife for her wasteful consumption (e.g., *You had a dress right?; Doesn't that sound like a – total: – w:aste?)* and for her lack of consideration toward his mother (e.g., *Why did you let my Mom get you something (that you –); Oh she just got it for you?)*:

(5) Mom's Dress Story (Round 2 of two-round story)[7]

Same family as in (1). The children have finished eating and just gone outside to play; Dad is helping himself to more meat; Mom had begun a story about her new dress, interrupted by a phone call from his mother.

Round 2 *((begins after Mom hangs up phone and sits at table))*

DAD: So as you were saying?
MOM: (As I was) saying *((turning abruptly to face Dad))* What was I telling you
DAD: I ?don't? know
MOM: oh about the ?dress?
DAD: (the) dress
(1.2) *((Mom is drinking water; Dad looks to her, to his plate, then back to her))*
DAD: You had a dress right?
MOM: *((nodding yes once))* Your mother bought (me it) – My mother didn't (like) it.
(0.4) *((Mom tilts head, facing Dad, as if to say "What could I do?"))*
DAD: *((shaking head no once))* You're kidding
MOM: no
DAD: You gonna return it?
MOM: No you can't return it – It wasn't too expensive – It was from Loehmann's
(0.8)
MOM: So what I'll probably do? – is wear it to the dinner the night before – when we go to the (Marriott)?
(1.8) *((Dad turns head away from Mom with a grimace, as if he is debating whether he is being conned, then turns and looks off))*
DAD: (Doesn't that) sound like a – (total:) – w:aste?
MOM: no?:
DAD: no
MOM: *((with hands out, shaking head no))* It wasn't even that expen?sive
(1.2)
MOM: *((shaking head no, facing Dad))* even if it were a complete waste
(0.4) *((Dad looks down at plate, bobs head right and left as if not convinced))*
MOM: but it's not. *((looking away from Dad))*
(0.6) *((Mom looks outside, then back to Dad))*
MOM: (but the one) my mom got me is gr:ea::t –
[
((Dad eats from son Oren's plate next to him))
MOM: (Is the *((inaudible))* okay?)
DAD: *((gesturing with palm up, quizzical))* (Well why did) you have – Why did you let my mom get you something (that you –)
MOM: Your mo:ther bought it – I hh –
DAD: Oh she just got it for you?
MOM: *((turning away from Dad, nodding yes))* (yeah)
DAD: You weren't there?
MOM: I was there (and your mom) said "No no It's great Let me *buy* it for you" *((turning back to face Dad))* – I didn't ask her to buy it for me?
(5.0) *((Dad is eating more food from son's plate; Mom looking toward table))*

DAD: So they're fighting over who gets you things?
MOM: *((nods yes slightly))* – *((smiling to Dad))* tch – (cuz I'm) so won?derful (9.0) *((no visible reaction from Dad; Mom turns to look outside; the subject of the dress is dropped))*

In the narratives in our corpus, exactly half of them involved someone problematizing a family member at the dinner table. Those fifty narratives generated a total of 229 problematizations of oneself or, much more often, of another family member.[8] Problematizing displays the most significantly asymmetric narrator-role distribution found in this study and reveals a "Father knows best" dynamic in family interaction. Men took on the role of problematizer 45 percent more often than women did and 3.5 times as often as did children. Strikingly, this pattern was mirrored in female and male children's uptake of the problematizer role. Among children, boys did 50 percent more problematizing than girls (even though there were nine girls and eight boys in the corpus who were old enough to co-narrate). With regard to family members' role constitution vis-à-vis narrative problematizing, men were problematizers almost twice as often as they were problematizees; women were as often problematizees as problematizers; and children were predominantly positioned as problematizees.

Examining individual instances to assess who problematized whom (i.e., the preferred target for each family member), we found that the bulk of narrative problematizing occurred between spouses. In 80 percent of the eighty-four instances in which mothers were problematized, the problematizer was the husband. In 63 percent of sixty-seven instances in which fathers were targeted, the problematizer was the wife. Thus, although women also targeted their spouses, men did so 60 percent more often. The targeting of women by their husbands represents the largest allocation of problematizings in our corpus of narratives. The differential in both absolute numbers and percentages of cross-spousal problematizing suggests in more detail the across-the-board nature of men's domination.[9] That is, both women and men vastly outproblematized their children, but men also considerably outproblematized their wives. Examples (1), (2), (4), and (5) above illustrate how men problematized their spouse or their child.

In addition to this overall quantitative difference, there were differences as well in the qualitative nature of women's versus men's problematizations. Notably, there was a distinction in spouses' use of two domains of problematizing: the problematizing of someone's actions, thoughts, or feelings (in the past) as a protagonist versus the problematizing of someone's comments (in the present) as a co-narrator. The latter category includes counterproblematizing in self-defense, as a response to a previous problematizing (here, by the spouse). The distribution of cross-spousal use of these problematizing strategies indicates that husbands criticized their spouse as protagonist far more often than was the case for wives (thirty-six times versus fourteen times).

Many of the husbands' problematizings of wives as protagonists entailed targeting the wife on grounds of incompetence, as exemplified in (4), Mom's Job Story. In contrast, wives did not problematize husbands on the basis of incompetence as protagonists; as noted above, wives relatively infrequently problematized their spouses as protagonists at all. Rather, women most often problematized men as narrators and much of that was of the counterproblematizing type, either in self-defense or in defense of their children. In other words, fathers would target what mothers had done in the reported events and then mothers would refute the fathers' comments as co-narrators. Men's problematizing focused on "You shouldn't have done *x*"; women's problematizing was more a form of resistance – to being problematized. Women were more often saying in essence, "No, that's not the way it happened . . . "; "Your interpretation is wrong . . . "; "You don't see the context." Thus, women – to the degree that they are regularly targeted for problematization – may get the impression that they cannot *do* anything right (and wind up defending past actions, as seen in the Mom's Job and Mom's Dress Stories), whereas men – to the degree they are regularly targeted more for their comments as co-narrator – may get the impression that they can't *say* anything right.

Men's preeminence as problematizers is further seen in the fact that they problematized their spouses over a much wider range of narrative topics than did women. Wives' conduct and stance concerning child care, recreation, meal preparation, and even their professional lives were open to husbands' critiques. Narratives about men's workdays, however, were exceedingly rare and were virtually never problematized. This asymmetry, wherein men had or were given "problematizing rights" over a wider domain of their spouses' experiences than were women, further exemplifies how narrative activity at dinner may instantiate and socialize a "Father knows best" worldview, i.e., it is men as fathers and husbands who scrutinize and problematize everything.[10]

Given men's presumption to quantitative and qualitative dominance as problematizers *par excellence* in this corpus, an important issue to raise is the extent to which men's prominence as problematizers was related to their role as preferred primary recipients. There was clearly a strong link between the two roles for them: 86 of men's 116 problematizings occurred when they were primary recipients of the narrative. However, the status of primary recipient does not, in itself, completely account for who assumed the role of problematizer.

Three observations in particular dispute such an interpretation. First, men exploited the primary-recipient role to do problematizing to a far greater extent than other family members did. As primary recipient, fathers problematized a family member, on average, 1.6 times per narrative; women did so only 0.55 times per narrative, and children only 0.05 times per narrative. In both degree and range of problematizing, men used their recipient status distinctively. Second, the whole level of problematizing went up when the father/husband was primary recipient. Of the 229 problematizings in the corpus, 155 occurred when he was primary recipient, averaging 2.8 problematizings per narrative, considerably more than when either women or children were primary recipients (1.6 per narrative and 0.5 per narrative, respectively). As already suggested in the discussion of counterproblematizing, this heightened level of problematization overall occurred largely because men's problematizing of women (as protagonists) triggered women's own counterproblematizing of their husbands. As a result, women became problematizers much more often when men were primary recipients than when the women themselves were primary recipients (54 times versus 22 times). Third, we note that men problematized more than women did even in narratives where the woman was primary recipient (24 times versus 22 times).

For all these reasons, a primary recipient-becomes-problematizer explanation is too simplistic an account. Rather, our corpus suggests conceptualizations of recipientship that differentiate women, men, and children, i.e., differing dispositions and perhaps entitlements to problematize, with men in privileged critical positions. The role of problematizer seems to be a particular prerogative of the family role of father/ husband, manifesting the ideology that "Father knows best," socializing and (re)constituting paternal prerogative and point of view in and through narrative activity.

Because an important issue we are pursuing here is women's role in establishing a "Father knows best" dynamic at the family dinner table and because we have seen that women's most notable narrative role was that of introducer, we examined the introducer-problematizer relationship to discover in particular the extent to which men's problematizings occurred in narratives introduced by women. Our finding is that women's introductions may indeed have triggered men's problematizations. First, when women introduced narratives, problematizing in general was more prevalent than when men or children did the introducing.[11] In narratives introduced by women, family members were problematized, on average, 3.4 times per narrative, considerably more than for narratives introduced by men (2.0 times) or by children (1.1). Second, the majority of men's problematizings (72 out of 116) occurred in narratives introduced by women. Men problematized other family members 1.8 times per narrative in those introduced by women, i.e., an even higher rate than we noted above when the factor of men's status as primary recipients was considered. Furthermore, men problematized more often in narratives introduced by women than in narratives they introduced themselves.

This higher number of problematizations in narratives introduced by one's spouse might seem expectable but it was not matched by women, who wound up (counter) problematizing more often in the narratives they themselves introduced.[12] We see in these data an asymmetrical pattern wherein women's raising a topic seems to have promoted men's problematizing but not the reverse.

Women's assumption of the role of introducer co-occurred not only with increased problematization by men but also with increased targeting of women themselves. Women were problematized most often in the very narratives they introduced: 75 percent of all targetings of women occurred in those narratives, an average of 1.6 times per narrative. These figures contrast markedly with those for men: only 33 percent of the problematizings of men occurred in narratives they themselves introduced, an average of only 0.7 times per narrative.

These findings suggest that women were especially vulnerable to exposing themselves to criticism, particularly from their husbands, and thus may have been "shooting themselves in the foot" in bringing up narratives in the first place, as illustrated in (2), the Broken Chair Story, where a woman's designation (i.e., control) of narrative topic and primary recipient boomeranged in an explicit attack on her weight. In (1), Jodie's TB Shots Report, we see an example of how mother-introduced narratives also expose children to problematization by fathers. Reconsidering our earlier observation that women were problematized over a wider range of daily activities, including professional lives, than were men, we can posit that this may have resulted largely from women's introducing themselves as protagonists in a much wider range of contexts to begin with.

One final issue with regard to problematization concerns the extent to which family members self-problematized. In our corpus, women displayed the highest proportion of self-targetings and, in keeping with the findings just discussed, this was also associated with narratives that women themselves raised. Although such targetings account for a relatively small proportion (12 percent) of the targetings of women overall, and they came essentially from only two families, these female self-problematizings are noteworthy in their provoking of a "dumping-on" response. That is, when women did question their own past actions, it seemed to invite considerable additional problematizing by their husbands. As illustrated in (6), a wife problematizes herself as protagonist and her husband elaborates:

(6) Bev Story (excerpt)

This family consists of Mom (Marie), Dad (Jon), and four children (who at this point in the dinner have finished eating). Mom runs a day-care center in their home; she has been recounting to Dad how one of her day-care children's mothers, Bev, had given her more money than was owed for day-care services and that she had not accepted the extra money. She then recalled how Bev had not given a required two weeks' notice for withdrawing her daughter from day care, whereupon Dad problematized Mom's nonacceptance of the money as naive (i.e., incompetent).

MOM: *((head on hand, elbow on table, facing Dad opposite her))* You know – Jon <u>I</u> verbally <u>did</u> tell Bev two weeks' notice Do you think I should've stuck to that? or just done what I did? (0.8) *((The children are standing by their seats, apparently listening))*

DAD: When I say something I stick to it. unless <u>she:</u> -s-brings it up. If <u>I</u> set a policy – and a- – and – they accept that policy – unless <u>they</u> have reason to change it and and say something? <u>I</u> do not <u>change</u> it – I don't <u>au</u>tomatically assume .h "We:ll it's not the <u>right</u> thing to do" If I were to <u>do</u> that e-I would be saying in the first place I should never have mentioned it I should never have set the policy if I didn't believe in it If I thought it was – a <u>hard</u>ship on people I shouldn't a brought it up? – shoulda kept my mouth shut .h If <u>I:</u> say there's two weeks' notice required – .h I automatically charge em for two weeks' notice without thinking twice? about it I say and i- "If you-you need – Your pay will include till such and such a date because of the two neek-weeks' notice that's required." -I:f THE:Y feel hardship it's on thei:r part – it's – THEIRS to say .h "Marie I really? – you know – I didn't expect this to happen 'n I'm *((softly))* sorry I didn't give you two weeks' notice but it was really un – avoidable" – a:nd you can say "We:ll – okay I'll split the difference with you – it's har- – a one week's notice" – and then they s- then if they push it

[

MOM: See? you know in one way wi- in one (instance) *((pointing to Dad))* she owed me that money – but I just didn't feel right? taking it=

[

DAD: well you're – you

MOM: =on that pretense because she (wanted) -she thought she was paying it for something *((twirling her corncob))* that *(she didn't)*

[

DAD: You: give her the money and then you let it bother you then – you – get all ups-set You'll be upset for weeks

[

MOM: No no no – I'm not upset – it's just

(0.4) *((Mom plops corncob down, raps knuckles on table))*

MOM: I guess I just wish I would have s:aid – I'm not upset with what happened – I just wanted – I think I – would feel better if I had said (something). ...

In questioning her own actions as protagonist (*Do you think I should've stuck to that? or just done what I did?*), Marie invites her husband's evaluation and exposes herself to his critical uptake as he problematizes both her past actions (*You: give her the money*) and her present feelings (*... you let it bother you then – you – get all upsset You'll be upset for weeks*). She is left to backtrack in self-defense, countering his portrayal of her present state and (re)defining her self-problematization on her own terms (*... I just wish I would have ...*), no longer as a question inviting further dumping on.[13]

In our corpus, the uptake on self-problematizing further distinguished women's and men's narrative practices; in contrast to this dumping-on response, women did not further problematize men after the men problematized themselves. When women took the opposite tack and presented themselves as problem-solvers rather than self-problematizers, another asymmetric practice entailed the husband's dismissing his wife's solution and problematizing it until she conceded at least partially. An example of this is seen in (5), Mom's Dress Story, when Mom offers her own solution to the two-dress situation (*So what I'll probably do? – is wear it to the dinner the night before ...*), to which Dad responds, "(Doesn't) that sound like a – (total:) – w: aste?" Mom initially rebuts (*no?:*) but, in the face of Dad's skepticism, concedes "... even if it were a complete waste," thus implicitly problematizing herself by Dad's terms in acknowledging that she might have been wasteful.

Our data also suggest that women's self-problematizing may have socializing effects. This was vividly illustrated in a lengthy story focusing on a mother and her son in a restaurant (the same family as in Jodie's TB Shots Report and Mom's Dress Story). In this narrative, the son, Oren, recalls eating a chili pepper his mother thought was a green bean. Although Oren initially frames the experience as funny, his mother tells him it wasn't funny, that his mouth was burning and hurting. While problematizing his stance as narrator, she also implicates herself as a culprit, thereby self-problematizing as protagonist. In the course of the story, Oren eventually takes on his mother's more serious framing of events, to the point of shouting, "YOUR FAULT – YOUR FAULT." She agrees, nodding her head and saying, "It *was* my fault." While she is saying this, he leans over and pinches her cheeks hard. She gasps and pulls his hands away, saying, "OW

That really hurts honey?" As she holds a napkin to her mouth and cheeks, her son comments, "Your fault – I get to do whatever I want to do once – (That was my fee?)," laughs, and adds, "Just like it happened to me it happens to you." Just as husbands piled on to wives' self-targeting, Oren thus follows up on his mother's self-problematizing, extending condemnation and executing punishment for her self-problematized actions. In so doing, he seems to be assuming a dramatic version of what, in this corpus, was a male narrator role.

This discussion calls attention to an appropriate ending caveat to our findings throughout this chapter. Namely, there is family variation even within this sample of seven families of similar socioeconomic status and racial-cultural background. There were men who took up the role of monitor and judge with what seemed almost a vengeance; there were others who displayed much less assertion of the prerogatives of power as primary recipient. Furthermore, we do not wish to fix particular men's (or women's) narrator personae based on two evenings in the lives of these families. Our aim is not to polarize the genders, but, rather, to shed potential new light on some underexplored aspects of gender construction and socialization in everyday narrative activity.

Conclusion

Synthesizing these findings – with the caveats noted above – we construe a commonplace scenario of narrative activity at family dinners characterized by a sequence of the following order. First, mothers introduce narratives (about themselves and their children) that set up fathers as primary recipients and implicitly sanction them as evaluators of others' actions, conditions, thoughts, and feelings. Second, fathers turn such opportunities into forums for problematizing, with mothers themselves as their chief targets, very often on grounds of incompetence. And third, mothers respond in defense of themselves and their children via the counterproblematizing of fathers' evaluative, judgmental comments.

In the first stage, we see mothers' narrative locus of power; in the second, however, we see that such exercise of power is ephemeral and may even be self-destructive by giving fathers a platform for monitoring and judging wives and children. In the third stage, we see mothers striving to reclaim control over the narratives they originally put on the table. Given our impression of the recurrence of these preferences and practices, it seems that the struggle of the third stage is not ultimately successful in that the fathers reappear as primary recipients and the cycle of narrative reenactment characterized by this generalized scenario prevails. It may be that all parties obtain a particular type of satisfaction or stasis through this interplay such that it serves underlying needs, self-conceptions, and communicative goals. However, in this generalized scenario, mothers seem to play a pivotal role in enacting and socializing a hegemonic activity system (Engeström 1987; Gramsci 1971) in which fathers are regularly reinstantiated as arbiters of conduct narratively laid before them as in a panopticon.

In the family interactions we observed, when women directed their narratives to their husbands (or when children directed their narratives, voluntarily or not, to their fathers), they disadvantaged themselves by exposing their experiences to male scrutiny and standards of judgment. They performed actions as narrators that rendered them vulnerable to repeated spousal/paternal criticism of them, especially as protagonists. Through such means and with such effects, "Father knows best" – a gender ideology with a deeply rooted politics of asymmetry that has been contested in recent years – is still in reverberating evidence at the two-parent family dinner table, jointly constituted and re-created through everyday narrative practices. In this chapter, we hope to have raised awareness of the degree to which some women as wives and mothers may wittingly or unwittingly contribute to – and even set up – the daily reconstruction of a "Father knows best" ideological dynamic.

NOTES

This chapter is the result of the equal work of both authors. We are grateful for the support this research has received from the National Institute of Child Health Development (1986–90: "Discourse Processes in American Families," Principal Investigators Elinor Ochs and Thomas Weisner, Research Assistants Maurine Bernstein, Dina Rudolph, Ruth Smith, and Carolyn Taylor) and from the Spencer Foundation (1990–3: "Socialization of Scientific Discourse," Principal Investigator Elinor Ochs, Research Assistants Patrick Gonzales, Sally Jacoby, and Carolyn Taylor). We thank Marcelo Diversi for his assistance in editing the final version of this chapter. A preliminary version of this article appeared in the proceedings of the Second Berkeley Women and Language Conference (Ochs and Taylor 1992c).

1 Clearly, our findings are implicative for certain family cultures and are not inclusive of the range of linguistic, ethnic, economic, and other forms of group variation within the United States. This study is offered as a basis for possible future studies of family narrative activity as a medium for constituting gender relations in other socioeconomic and cultural settings for which we do not presume to speak here. At the same time, while we suggest a certain resonance in these findings, we recognize the limits of our corpus and do not wish to overgeneralize regarding narrative practices even for white middle-class families.

2 This choice of five-year-olds follows from our interest in the roles played by children of an age to be fully capable of collaboration in family talk but still in their earliest, most pivotal years of language socialization (prior to much formal schooling). We also wanted at least one older child in the families so as to capture sibling as well as parent–child interaction.

3 For simplicity, we will often refer to participants by only one family role, e.g., to women as *mothers*, men as *fathers*, and girls and boys as *children*, but we note again, in keeping with our introductory perspectives, that at any one moment each participant may be constructing more than one family identity, e.g., also as spouses, as siblings, as females, as males.

4 All family names are pseudonyms. Transcription procedures are essentially those established by Gail Jefferson (see Atkinson and Heritage 1984: ix–xvi):

[	a left-hand bracket indicates the onset of overlapping, simultaneous utterances
=	two equals signs (latches) link utterances either by two speakers where the second jumps in on the end of the first, without any interval, or by the same speaker when lengthy overlap by another speaker requires that a continuous utterance be interrupted on the transcript to show simultaneity with another
(0.4)	indicates length of pause within and between utterances, timed in tenths of a second
a – a	a hyphen with spaces before and after indicates a short pause, less than 0.2 seconds
sa-	a hyphen immediately following a letter indicates an abrupt cutoff in speaking
(())	double parentheses enclose nonverbal and other descriptive information
( )	single parentheses enclose words that are not clearly audible (i.e., best guesses)
you	underlining indicates stress on a syllable or word(s)
CAPS	upper case indicates louder or shouted talk
:	a colon indicates a lengthening of a sound, the more colons, the longer
.	a period indicates falling intonation
,	a comma indicates a continuing intonation
?	a question mark indicates a rising intonation as a syllable or word ends *Note*: bounding question marks (e.g., *Did you go to the ?animal hospital?*) are used (instead of rising arrows) to indicate a higher pitch for enclosed word(s).
h	an *h* indicates an exhalation, the more *h*'s, the longer the exhalation
.h	an *h* with a period before it indicates an inhalation, the more *h*'s, the longer.

5 For tables detailing the quantitative findings of this study, see Ochs and Taylor (1992c).

6 For more detail and elaborated consideration of the roles of children in the narrative activity of this corpus, see Ochs and Taylor (1992b).

7 When a narrative is interrupted or dropped and taken up again after an interval of at least two other turns, we consider the restart to constitute a new "round."

8 Only 10 percent of all problematizations were "self-inflicted," meaning that 90 percent of the problematizations targeted others. The percentage of problematizing directed toward oneself was highest for women, although still only 12 percent. In keeping with our present focus on exploring women's roles in particular, we will discuss and illustrate these self-problematizations in more detail following our examination of cross-spousal problematizing.

9 Accounting for the percentage differential in cross-spousal targeting, the children, albeit infrequent problematizers, did twice as much targeting of fathers as they did of mothers.

10 Perhaps contrary to general expectation, spouses in our corpus did not tend to elicit narratives from each other about their workdays (Mom's Job Story being an exception), so that parental "what-my-day-was-like" narratives, unlike the narratives of children, tended to be directly self-initiated to the spouse without elicitation.

11 Out of the 39 narratives introduced by women, 62 percent included at least one instance of someone's problematizing a family member at the dinner table. In contrast, only 44 percent of the narratives introduced by men and 41 percent of those introduced by children evidenced such problematizing.

12 On average, men problematized in narratives that they introduced themselves only 1.2 times per narrative, i.e., less often than they problematized in narratives introduced by women (1.8 times per narrative). In contrast, women problematized in narratives that they introduced themselves 1.4 times per narrative, i.e., much more often than they problematized in narratives introduced by men (only 0.5 times per narrative).

13 Regarding the roles and implications of problematization or challenges in co-narrators' theories of everyday events, and the potential here for Marie to incorporate her husband's challenge into something of a paradigm shift in her own stance, see Ochs, Smith, and Taylor (1989) and Ochs, Taylor, Rudolph, and Smith (1992).

REFERENCES

Atkinson, J. Maxwell, and John Heritage (eds.) (1984). *Structures of Social Action: Studies in Conversation Analysis*. Cambridge: Cambridge University Press.

Bentham, Jeremy (1791). *Panopticon*. London: T. Payne.

Cole, Michael, and Sheila Cole (1989). *The Development of Children*. New York: Scientific American Books.

Dunn, Judy (1984). *Sisters and Brothers*. Cambridge, MA: Harvard University Press.

Engeström, Yrjö (1987). *Learning by Expanding: An Activity-theoretical Approach to Developmental Research*. Helsinki: Orienta-Konsultit Oy.

Foucault, Michel (1979). *Discipline and Punish: The Birth of the Prison*. Translated by Alan Sheridan. New York: Random House.

Freud, Sigmund ([1921] 1949). *The Standard Edition of the Complete Psychological Works of Sigmund Freud*. London: Hogarth Press.

Goodwin, Marjorie Harness (1990). *He-Said-She-Said: Talk as Social Organization among Black Children*. Bloomington: Indiana University Press.

Gramsci, Antonio (1971). *Selections from the Prison Notebooks of Antonio Gramsci*. Translated and edited by Quintin Hoare and Geoffrey Nowell Smith. New York: International Publishers.

Hartmann, Heidi I. (1981). The family as the locus of gender, class, and political struggle: The example of housework. *Signs* 6(3): 366–94.

Kohlberg, Lawrence (1966). *The Development of Sex Differences.* Stanford: Stanford University Press.

Maccoby, Eleanor E., and Carol N. Jacklin (1974). *The Psychology of Sex Differences.* Stanford: Stanford University Press.

Ochs, Elinor, Ruth Smith, and Carolyn Taylor (1989). Detective stories at dinnertime: Problem- solving through co-narration. *Cultural Dynamics* 2(2): 238–57.

Ochs, Elinor, and Carolyn Taylor (1992a). Science at dinner. In Claire Kramsch and Sally McConnell -Ginet (eds.), *Text and Context: Cross-disciplinary Perspectives on Language Study.* Lexington, MA: Heath, pp. 29–45.

Ochs, Elinor, and Carolyn Taylor (1992b). Family narrative as political activity. *Discourse & Society* 3(3): 301–40.

Ochs, Elinor, and Carolyn Taylor (1992c). Mothers' role in the everyday reconstruction of "Father knows best." In Kira Hall, Mary Bucholtz, and Birch Moonwomon (eds.), *Locating Power: Proceedings of the Second Berkeley Women and Language Conference.* Berkeley: Berkeley Women and Language Group, pp. 447–62.

Ochs, Elinor, Carolyn Taylor, Dina Rudolph, and Ruth Smith (1992). Storytelling as a theory- building activity. *Discourse Processes* 15(1):37–72.

Osmond, Marie Withers, and Barrie Thorne (1993). Feminist theories: The social construction of gender in families and society. In Pauline G. Boss, William J. Doherty, Ralph LaRossa, Walter R. Schumm, and Suzanne K. Steinmetz (eds.), *Sourcebook of Family Theories and Methods: A Contextual Approach.* New York: Plenum Press, pp. 591–623.

Schieffelin, Bambi B. (1990). *The Give and Take of Everyday Life: Language Socialization of Kaluli Children.* Cambridge: Cambridge University Press.

Stack, Carol (1974). *All our Kin: Strategies for Survival in a Black Community.* New York: Harper & Row.

STUDY QUESTIONS

1 How does this article contribute to the study of family relations in terms of power relations? How does the phrase "Father knows best" illustrate these relations?
2 What is the definition of a *story* for Ochs and Taylor and how does their definition help them identify what they call *narrative activity*?
3 Define the following narrative roles: protagonist, introducer, primary recipient, problematizer, problematizee; and explain the significance of each role for the power relations within the family structure analyzed by Ochs and Taylor.
4 In what ways does gender emerge as an important variable in the asymmetries revealed by the linguistic analysis of dinnertime interactions?
5 How does this chapter relate to the chapters on language socialization? Who is being socialized, to what, and how?

19

Professional Vision

Charles Goodwin

Discursive practices are used by members of a profession to shape events in the domains subject to their professional scrutiny. The shaping process creates the objects of knowledge that become the insignia of a profession's craft: the theories, artifacts, and bodies of expertise that distinguish it from other professions. Analysis of the methods used by members of a community to build and contest the events that structure their lifeworld contributes to the development of a practice-based theory of knowledge and action.[1] In this article, I examine two contexts of professional activity: archaeological field excavation and legal argumentation. In each of these contexts, I investigate three practices: (1) *coding*, which transforms phenomena observed in a specific setting into the objects of knowledge that animate the discourse of a profession; (2) *highlighting*, which makes specific phenomena in a complex perceptual field salient by marking them in some fashion; and (3) *producing and articulating material representations*. By applying such practices to phenomena in the domain of scrutiny, participants build and contest *professional vision*, which consists of socially organized ways of seeing and understanding events that are answerable to the distinctive interests of a particular social group.

In the 1992 trial of four white police officers charged with beating Mr. Rodney King, an African-American motorist who had been stopped for speeding, a videotape of the beating (made without the knowledge of the officers by a man in an apartment across the street) became a politically charged theater for contested vision. Opposing sides in the case used the murky pixels of the same television image to display to the jury incommensurate events: a brutal, savage beating of a man lying helpless on the ground versus careful police response to a dangerous "PCP-crazed giant" who was argued to be in control of the situation. By deploying an array of systematic discursive practices, including talk, ethnography, category systems articulated by expert witnesses, and various ways of highlighting images provided by the videotape, lawyers for both sides were able to structure, in ways that suited their own distinctive agendas, the complex perceptual field visible on the TV screen.

The Rodney King trial provides a vivid example of how the ability to see a meaningful event is not a transparent, psychological process but instead a socially situated activity

For permission to publish copyright material in this book, grateful acknowledgment is made to: C. Goodwin (1994), "Professional Vision," *American Anthropologist* 96: 606–33.

accomplished through the deployment of a range of historically constituted discursive practices. It would, however, be quite wrong to treat the selective vision that is so salient in the King trial as a special, deviant case, merely a set of lawyers' tricks designed to distort what would otherwise be a clear, neutral vision of objective events unambiguously visible on the tape. All vision is perspectival and lodged within endogenous communities of practice. An archaeologist and a farmer see quite different phenomena in the same patch of dirt (for example, soil that will support particular kinds of crops versus stains, features, and artifacts that provide evidence for earlier human activity at this spot). An event being seen, a relevant *object of knowledge*, emerges through the interplay between a *domain of scrutiny* (a patch of dirt, the images made available by the King videotape, etc.) and a set of *discursive practices* (dividing the domain of scrutiny by highlighting a figure against a ground, applying specific coding schemes for the constitution and interpretation of relevant events, etc.) being deployed within a *specific activity* (arguing a legal case, mapping a site, planting crops, etc.). The object being investigated is thus analogous to what Wittgenstein (1958: 7) called a *language game*, a "whole, consisting of language and the actions into which it is woven."

My Own Practices for Seeing

It is not possible to work in some abstract world where the constitution of knowledge through a politics of representation has been magically overcome. The analysis in this article makes extensive use of the very same practices it is studying. Graphic representations, including transcripts of talk, diagrams, and frame grabs of scenes recorded on videotape, are annotated and highlighted in order to make salient specific events within them. Such highlighting guides the reader to see within a complex perceptual field just those events that I find relevant to the points I am developing. Applying a category such as *highlighting*, *graphic representation*, or *coding scheme* to diverse practices in different environments is itself an example of how coding schemes are used to organize disparate events into a common analytical framework. It is thus relevant to note briefly why I made the representational choices that I did.

To analyze how practice is organized as a temporally unfolding process encompassing both human interaction and situated tool use, I require as data records that preserve not only sequences of talk but also body movements of the participants and the phenomena to which they are attending as they use relevant representations. I use videotapes as my primary source of data, recognizing that, like transcription, any camera position constitutes a theory about what is relevant within a scene – one that will have enormous consequences for what can be seen in it later – and what forms of subsequent analysis are possible. A tremendous advantage of recorded data is that they permit repeated, detailed examination of actual sequences of talk and embodied work practices in the settings where practitioners actually perform these activities. Moreover, others can look at – and possibly challenge – my understanding of the events being examined.

As part of continuing fieldwork focusing ethnographically on how scientists actually do their work, activities at one archaeological field school in Argentina and two in the United States were videotaped. All the material analyzed in this article is drawn from one of the American field schools. Tapes of the first Rodney King trial were made from broadcasts of Court TV. I was unable to record the entire trial, so my own recordings were supplemented by an edited summary of the trial purchased from Court TV. The second trial was not broadcast on either radio or television. I was able to get into the courtroom only for the prosecution's closing arguments.

Practices of transcription constitute one local site within anthropology where the politics of representation emerge as a practical problem.[2] For a journal article, the rich record of complicated vocal and visual events moving through time provided by a videotape must be transformed into something that can silently inhabit the printed page.

Both linguistic anthropologists and conversation analysts have devoted considerable complementary and overlapping attention to questions of how talk should be transcribed, including the issue of how speakers themselves parse the stream of speech into relevant units. A major analytic focus of conversation analysis is the description of the procedures used by participants in the midst of talk-in-interaction to construct the events that constitute the lived lifeworld within ongoing processes of action.[3] This has required developing methods of transcription that permit detailed analysis of actors' changing orientations as events unfold though time. Linguistic anthropologists, concerned with maintaining the complex structure of oral performance, have argued that the division of talk into lines within a transcript should make visible to the reader how the speaker organized his or her talk into relevant units.[4] I have tried to do that in this article, breaking lines at intonational units and indenting the continuation of units too long to fit within the page margins. Given the rich interplay of different kinds of units in the stream of speech, the divisions I've made should not be treated as anything more than a provisional attempt to deal with a very complicated issue. In all other respects, my transcription uses the system developed by Gail Jefferson[5] for the analysis of conversation. The conventions most relevant to the analysis in this article include the use of *bold italics* to indicate talk spoken with special emphasis, a left bracket ([) to mark the onset of overlapping talk, and numbers in parentheses – for example, (1.2) – to note the length of silences in seconds and tenths of seconds. A dash marks the cut-off of the current sound. An equal sign indicates "latching," signifying that there is no interval between the end of one unit and the beginning of a next. Transcribers' comments are italicized in double parentheses; single parentheses around talk indicate a problematic hearing. Punctuation symbols are used to mark intonation changes rather than as grammatical symbols: a period indicates a falling contour; a question mark, a rising contour; and a comma, a falling-rising contour, as might be found in the midst of a list.

Coding Schemes

Central to the organization of human cognition are processes of classification. *Coding schemes* are one systematic practice used to transform the world into the categories and events that are relevant to the work of the profession (Cicourel 1964, 1968). For example, linguists classify sounds in terms of phonetic distinctions; sociologists classify people according to sex and class.

The pervasive power of coding schemes to organize apprehension of the world is demonstrated in particularly vivid fashion in scientific work. Ethnographic analysis of what is usually considered the epitome of abstract, objective, universal, disembodied cognition – Western science – has revealed it to be a patchwork of situated, disparate, locally organized cultures in which knowledge is constituted through a variety of social and political processes.[6] Central to the cognitive processes that constitute science are both material objects (tools and machines of many different types) and writing practices quite unlike those typically studied by anthropologists investigating literacy. In order to generate a data set, collections of observations that can be compared with each other, scientists use coding schemes to circumscribe and delineate the world they examine. When disparate events are viewed through a single coding scheme, equivalent observations become possible.

Let us briefly investigate this process using the example of a field school for young archaeologists. The medium in which archaeologists work is dirt. Students are given a form that contains an elaborate set of categories for describing the color, consistency, and texture of whatever dirt they encounter. They are even expected to taste a sample of the dirt to determine how sandy it is. Moreover, some of the categories are supported by additional tools of inscription, such as a Munsell color chart, used by archaeologists all over the world as a standard for color descriptions.

The process of filling in the form requires physical, cognitive, and perceptual work. Thus, in order to determine the color of a specimen of dirt, the students must obtain a sample with a trowel, highlight it by squirting it with water, and then hold the sample under the holes in the Munsell color chart (see figure 19.1). The Munsell book encapsulates in a material object the theory and solutions developed by earlier workers faced with this task of classification (Hutchins 1993). The pages juxtapose color patches and viewing holes that allow the dirt to be seen right next to the color sample, providing a historically constituted architecture for perception.

Though apparently distant from the abstract world of archaeological theory and from the debates that are currently animating the discipline, this encounter between a coding scheme and the world is a key locus for scientific practice, the place where the multifaceted complexity of "nature" is transformed into the phenomenal categories that make up the work environment of a scientific discipline. It is precisely here that nature is transformed into culture.

Despite the rigorous way in which a tool such as this one structures perception of the dirt being scrutinized, finding the correct category is not an automatic or even an easy task (Goodwin 1993). The very way in which the Munsell chart provides a context-free reference standard creates problems of its own. The color patches on the chart are glossy, while the dirt never is, so that the chart color and the sample color never look exactly the same. Moreover, the colors being evaluated frequently fall between the discrete categories provided by the Munsell chart. Two students at the field school looking at exactly the same dirt and reference colors can and do disagree as to how it should be classified. However, the definitiveness provided by a coding scheme typically erases from subsequent documentation the cognitive and perceptual uncertainties that these students are grappling with, as well as the work practices within which they are embedded.

The use of such coding schemes to organize the perception of nature, events, or people within the discourse of a profession carries with it an array of perceptual and cognitive operations that have far-reaching impact. First, by using such a system, a worker views the world from the perspective it establishes. Of all the possible ways that the earth could be looked at, the perceptual work of students using this form is focused on determining the exact color of a minute sample of dirt. They engage in active cognitive work, but the parameters of that work have been established by the system that is organizing their perception. Insofar as the coding scheme establishes an orientation toward the world, it constitutes a structure of intentionality whose proper locus is

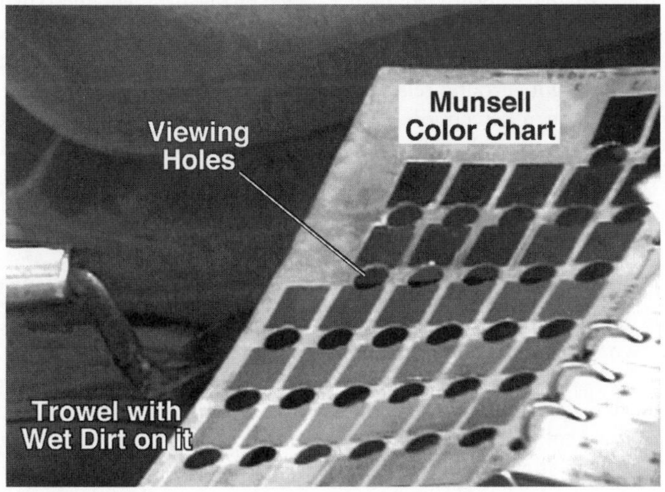

Figure 19.1 *Munsell color chart*

not an isolated, Cartesian mind but a much larger organizational system, one that is characteristically mediated through mundane bureaucratic documents such as forms. Forms, with their coding schemes, allow a senior investigator to inscribe his or her perceptual distinctions into the work practices of the technicians who code the data. Such systems provide an example of how distributed cognition is organized through the writing practices that coordinate action within an organization (Smith 1990: 121–2).

Highlighting

Human cognitive activity characteristically occurs in environments that provide a complicated perceptual field. A quite general class of cognitive practices consists of methods used to divide a domain of scrutiny into a figure and a ground, so that events relevant to the activity of the moment stand out. For example, forms and other documents packed with different kinds of information are a major textual component of many work environments. Faced with such a dense perceptual field, workers in many settings *highlight* their documents with colored markers, handwritten annotations, and stick-on notes. In so doing they tailor the document so that those parts of it which contain information relevant to their own work are made salient. Psychologists have long talked about figure/ground relations as a basic element of human perception. Situating such processes not only within the mind but as visible operations on external phenomena has a range of significant consequences. As we will see in subsequent examples, through these practices structures of relevance in the material environment can be made prominent, thus becoming ways of shaping not only one's own perception but also that of others.

Highlighting will be examined first in the work practices of archaeologists. In looking at the earth, archaeologists attend to an array of color distinctions in order to discern the traces of past human structures. For example, even though a post that supported a roof of an ancient house has long since decayed, the earth where it stood will have subtle color differences from the dirt around it. Archaeologists attempt to locate *features* such as these post molds[7] by scrutinizing the earth as they dig. Categories of relevance to the profession, such as post molds, are thus used to structure interpretation of the landscape. When a possible feature is found, the archaeological category and the traces in the dirt that possibly instantiate it are each used to elaborate the other in what has been called the *documentary method of interpretation.*[8] Thus the category "post mold" provides a texture of intelligibility that unifies disparate patches of color into a coherent object. These patches of color in turn provide evidence for the existence in this patch of dirt of an instance of the object proposed by the category.

Features can be difficult to see. In order to make them visible to others, the archaeologist outlines them by drawing a line in the dirt with a trowel. By doing this the archaeologist establishes a figure in what is quite literally a very amorphous ground. This line in the sand has very powerful persuasive consequences. As a visible annotation of the earth, it becomes a public event that can guide the perception of others while further reifying the object that the archaeologist proposes to be visible in the color patterning in the dirt. The perceptual field provided by the dirt is enhanced in a work-relevant way by human action on it. Through such highlighting and the subsequent digging that it will help to organize, the archaeologist discursively shapes from the materials provided by the earth the phenomenal objects – that is, the archaeological features – that are the concerns of his or her profession.

Graphic Representations as Embodied Practice

Most linguists analyzing literacy have focused on the writing of words, sentences, and other written versions of spoken language. However, graphic representations of many different types constitute central objects in the discourse of various professions. Scientific talks and papers

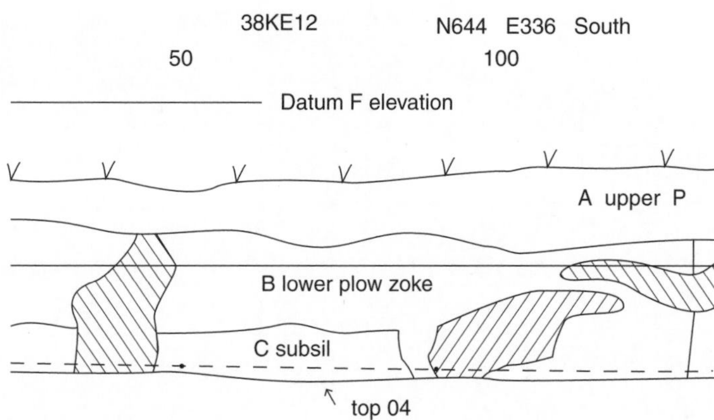

Figure 19.2 *Map scan*

are best seen not as a purely linguistic text but as a reflexive commentary on the diagrams, graphs, and photographs that constitute the heart of a presentation.[9] More generally, since the pioneering work of Latour and Woolgar (1979), the central importance of *inscriptions* in the organization of scientific knowledge has become a major focus of research. A theory of discourse that ignored graphic representations would be missing both a key element of the discourse that professionals engage in and a central locus for the analysis of professional practice. Instead of mirroring spoken language, these external representations complement it, using the distinctive characteristics of the material world to organize phenomena in ways that spoken language cannot – for example, by collecting records of a range of disparate events onto a single visible surface.

To explore such issues and prepare the ground for investigation of how lawyers articulated graphic representations in the Rodney King trial, the practices that archaeologists use to make maps will now be investigated. This will allow us to examine the interface between writing practices, talk, human interaction, and tool use as these professionals build representations central to the work of their discipline. A team of archaeologists is at work producing a map (see figure 19.2). This particular map is of a *profile*, the layers of dirt visible on the side of one of the square holes that are dug to excavate a site. Maps of this sort are one of the distinctive forms of professional literacy that constitute archaeology as a profession.

To demarcate what the archaeologist believes are two different layers of dirt, a line is drawn between them with a trowel. The line and the ground surface above it are then transferred to a piece of graph paper. This is a task that involves two people. One measures the length and depth coordinates of the points to be mapped, using a ruler and a tape measure. He or she reports the measurements as pairs of numbers, such as "At forty, plus eleven point five" (see figure 19.3). A second archaeologist transfers the numbers provided by the measurer to a piece of graph paper. After plotting a set of points, he or she makes the map by drawing lines between them. What we find here is a small activity system that encompasses talk, writing, tools, and distributed cognition as two parties collaborate to inscribe events they see in the earth onto paper.

The activity of inscription that we will now examine begins with a request from Ann, the writer, to Sue, the measurer (lines 1–2):

1 Ann: Give me the ground surface over here
2 to about *nine*ty.
3 (1.7)
4 Ann: No- No- Not *at* ninety.=
5 From you *to* about ninety.

However, before Sue has produced any numbers, indeed before she has said anything

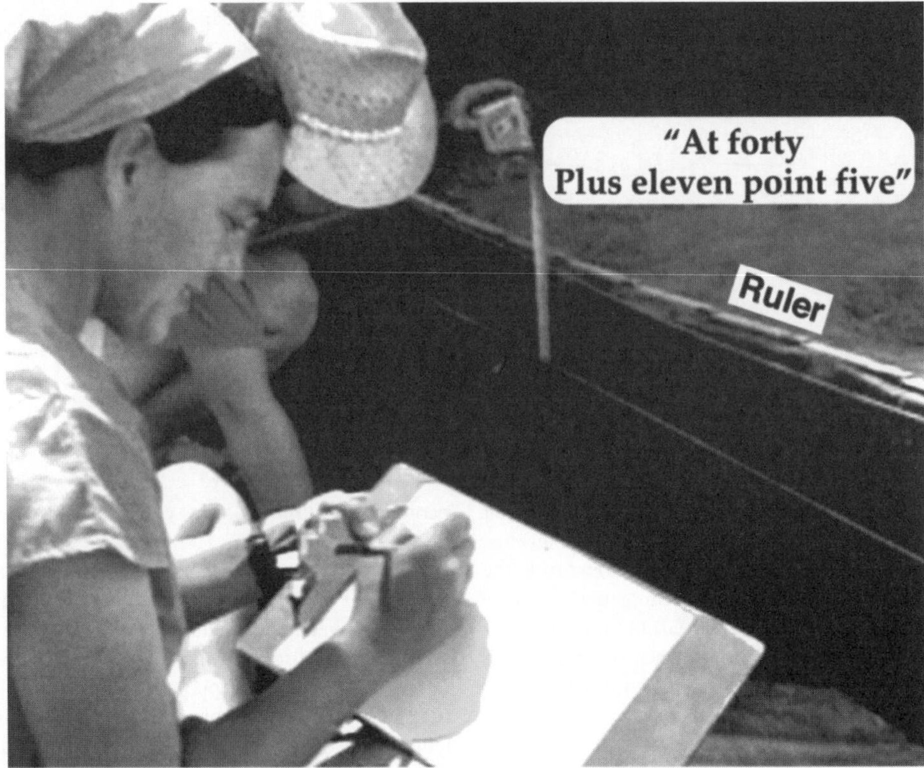

Figure 19.3 *Measuring and writing for an archaeological chart*

whatsoever, Ann, who is her professor, challenges her, telling her that what she is doing is wrong (lines 4–5). How can Ann see that there is something wrong with a response that has not even occurred yet? Crucial to this process is the phenomenon of *conditional relevance* (Schegloff 1968). A first utterance creates an interpretive environment that will be used by participants to analyze whatever occurs after it. Here no subsequent talk has yet been produced. However, providing an answer in this activity system encompasses more than talk: before speaking the set of numbers, Sue must first locate a relevant point in the dirt and measure its coordinates. Both her movement through space and her use of tools such as the tape measure are visible events.[10]

As Ann finishes her directive, Sue is holding the tape measure against the dirt at the left or zero end of the profile. However, just after hearing "ninety," Sue moves both her body and the tape measure to the right, stopping near the 90 mark on the upper ruler. By virtue of the field of interpretation opened up through conditional relevance, Sue's movement and tool use as elements of the activity she has been asked to perform can now be analyzed by Ann and found wanting. Immediately after this Ann produces her correction (lines 4–5).

Additional elements of cognitive operations that Ann expects Sue to perform in order to make her measurements are revealed as the sequence continues to unfold. Making the relevant measurements presupposes the ability to locate where in the dirt measurements should be made. Sue's response to the correction calls this presupposition into question and leads to Ann telling her explicitly, in several different ways, what she should look for in order to determine where to measure. The process begins after Ann tells Sue to measure points between 0 and 90 (line 5). Sue does not immediately move to this region but instead hesitates for a full second (line 6) before replying with a weak "Oh."

1	Ann:		Give me the ground surface over here
2			to about *nine*ty.
3			(1.7)
4	Ann:		No- No- Not *at* ninety.=
5			From you *to* about ninety.
6	Sue:		(1.0) Oh.
7	Ann:	→	Wherever there's a change in slope.
8	Sue:		(0.6) Mm kay.

In line 7 Ann moves from request to instruction by telling Sue what she should be looking for in the landscape: "Wherever there's a change in slope." Though most approaches to the study of meaning in language focus on the issue of how concepts can best be defined (for example, componential analysis and other approaches to semantics), Wittgenstein (1958: 242) notes that "If language is to be a means of communication there must be agreement not only in definitions but also (queer as this may sound) in judgments." In the present case, in order to use what Ann has just said to pursue the task they are collaboratively engaged in, Sue must be able to find in the dirt what will count as "a change in slope." As the party who has set her this task, Ann is in a position to evaluate her success. Sue again moves her tape measure far to the right (see Figure 19.4, image *A*). At this point, instead of relying on talk alone to make explicit the phenomena that she wants Sue to locate, Ann moves into the space that Sue is attending to (image *B*) and points to one place that should be measured while describing in more vernacular language what constitutes "a change in slope": "where it *stops* being flat" (line 11). She then points to additional places for measurement (lines 13–17).

Labeling what Ann does here either deictic gesture or ostensive definition does not do adequate justice to its complexity. Analysis of the gesture cannot focus on the gesture alone or on some possible mental state of the speaker it is externalizing (effectively drawing an analytic bubble at the skin of the actor); it requires simultaneous attention to the environment that the hand is highlighting, the talk that sets

9		(2.0)	
10	Ann:	So so if it's *fairly flat*	
11		I'll need one where it stops being fairly	flat.=
12	Sue:		Okay.
13	Ann:	=Like right there.	
14		Then I'll need one there.	
15		Then I'll need one the:re.	
16	Sue:	(0.3) °All right.	
17	Ann:	And then one at the-	

Figure 19.4 *Talk and gesture mutually elaborate on each other*

the coding problem for the addressee, and the activity that these participants are working to accomplish. Talk and gesture mutually elaborate on each other within a framework of action that includes at least three components: (1) a semantic description, such as "a change in slope"; (2) a complex perceptual field where an instantiation of that category is to be located; and (3) the hand of an actor moving within that perceptual field. The activity in progress, including the sequence of talk within which these ostensive demonstrations emerge, provides a relevant language game that can be used to make inferences about precisely which features of the complex perceptual field being pointed at should be attended to. What Sue is being taught is not something that falls within the scope of language as an isolated system – not a definition (she already knows what a "change in slope" is in the abstract) – but a mode of practice, how to code a relevant perceptual field in terms of categories that are consequential for her work. In turn this process is embedded within the larger activity of doing archaeological fieldwork, as well as a local interactive field that structures participants' mutual access to both each other and the domain of scrutiny where relevant work is being done. Within such an interactive field, the actions that Sue is expected to perform enable Ann to evaluate her comprehension and, where relevant, to take remedial action in subsequent moves. The cognitive activities occurring here are situated, distributed, and interactively organized. In this process coding tasks (Sue is set the problem of finding an example of a particular category in the materials she is looking at) and highlighting (the movement of Ann's hand that displays where a solution to Ann's problem is to be found) function together in the production of a relevant graphic representation (the map).

One of the things that is occurring within this sequence is a progressive expansion of Sue's understanding as the distinctions she must make to carry out the task assigned to her are explicated and elaborated. In this process of socialization through language,[11] growth in intersubjectivity occurs as domains of ignorance that prevent the successful accomplishment of collaborative action are revealed and transformed into practical knowledge – a way of seeing that is sufficient to complete the job at hand – in a way that allows Sue to understand what Ann is asking her to do and make an appropriate, competent response to her request.

It would, however, be quite wrong to see the unit within which this intersubjectivity is lodged as being simply two minds coming together to do the work at hand. Instead, the distinctions being explicated, the ability to see in the very complex perceptual field provided by the landscape to which they are attending those few events that count as points to be transferred to the map, are central to what it means to see the world as an archaeologist and to use that seeing to build the artifacts, such as this map, that are constitutive of archaeology as a profession. All competent archaeologists are expected to be able to do this; it is an essential part of what it means to *be* an archaeologist,[12] and it is to these professional perceptual standards that Sue is being held accountable. The relevant unit for the analysis of the intersubjectivity at issue here is thus not these individuals as isolated entities but archaeology as a profession, a community of competent practitioners, most of whom have never met each other but nonetheless expect each other to be able to see and categorize the world in ways that are relevant to the work, tools, and artifacts that constitute their profession.

This sequence brings together an important range of cognitive phenomena relevant to the organization of human action, including interaction with both other human beings and the world itself, talk as a form of social action, writing practices, and the construction of cognitive artifacts that provide relevant representations of the world. These inscription practices are accomplished through the appropriate use of artifacts such as graph paper, rulers, and tape measures. Supporting such tool use are sets of perceptual structures, the ability to see what and where to measure. Moreover, we are able to glimpse how these structures are passed on from one generation to the next through apprenticeship.

Contested Vision

The use of coding schemes, highlighting practices, and the articulation of graphic representations to organize perception will now be examined in another professional setting: the courtroom. On March 3, 1991, an amateur video photographer taped a group of Los Angeles police officers administering a very violent beating with metal clubs to an African-American motorist, Mr. Rodney King, who had been stopped for a traffic violation. When the tape was broadcast on television, there was public outrage, and four police officers involved in the beating were put on trial for excessive use of force. The principal piece of evidence against them was the tape of the beating. The violence it showed was so graphic that many people assumed that a conviction was almost automatic. However, the jury found the police officers innocent, a verdict that triggered the Los Angeles uprising. At a second federal trial a year later, two of the four officers were convicted of violating King's civil rights and two were acquitted.

Perhaps surprisingly, the main evidence used in the defense of the police officers was the tape showing them beating King. Indeed, one of the officers convicted in the second trial, Sergeant Stacy Koon, spent much of his time between the two trials watching and rewatching the tape, seeing how it looked when projected on different walls in his house. Rather than wanting to minimize the events on the tape, he told a reporter that

> if we had our way, we'd go down to Dodger Stadium and rip off that big-screen Mitsubishi and bring it into the courtroom and say, 'Hey, folks, you're in for the show of your life because when this tape gets blown up it's awesome.' (Mydans 1993d: A10)

For Rodney King the experience of looking at the tape was quite different: "It's sickening to see it. It makes me sick to my stomach to watch it" (Newton 1993a: A16).

At the first trial the prosecution presented the tape of the beating as a self-explicating, objective record. Thus the chief prosecutor said,

> What more could you ask for? You have the videotape that shows objectively, without bias, impartially, what happened that night. The videotape shows conclusively what happened that night. It can't be rebutted. (Mydans 1993b: A7)

But the lawyers defending the police officers did not treat the tape as a record that spoke for itself. Instead they argued that it could be understood only by embedding the events visible on it within the work life of a profession. The defense proposed that the beating constituted an example of careful police work, a form of professional discourse with the victim in which he was a very active coparticipant – indeed, the party who controlled the interaction.

To successfully make this claim, the defense provided the jury with ethnography about police practices and with a coding scheme to be used to analyze the events on the tape. The power of coding schemes to control perception in this fashion was central to the defense strategy. The defense contended that if the police officers could legitimately see King's actions as aggressive and a threat to them, then the police were entitled to use force to protect themselves and take him into custody. The central point debated within the trial was what the police officers who beat King perceived him to be doing. These perceptions were treated not as idiosyncratic phenomena lodged within the minds of individual police officers but as socially organized perceptual frameworks shared within the police profession.

These assumptions about the conventions maintained by the police had two consequences for the organization of discourse within the courtroom: (1) police perceptions, as a domain of professional competence, can be described and analyzed through use of highlighting, coding schemes, and graphic representations; (2) in that these perceptions are not idiosyncratic phenomena restricted to individuals but frameworks shared by a profession, *expert testimony* is possible. An expert who was not present at the scene can describe authoritatively what police officers could legitimately see as they looked at the man they were beating.

Expert testimony is given a very distinctive shape within the adversarial system of the American courtroom.[13] Each side hires its own experts and attacks the credibility of its opponents' experts. Moreover, the use of expert witnesses intersects with rules establishing what counts as adequate proof. Reasonable doubt can be created by muddying the water with a plausible alternative. In the words of the lawyer for Officer Theodore Briseno, one of the defendants:

> Your experts really don't have to be better than their [the prosecution's] experts. All you've got to have are experts on both sides. I think [jurors] wonder: 'How could we as lay people know beyond a reasonable doubt, when the experts can't decide?' (Lieberman 1993b: A32).

Such a strategy can be quite successful. One of the jurors who acquitted the police officers in the first King trial said, "Our instructions of how we could consider evidence stated ... if there are two reasonable explanations for an event, we had to pick the one that points to innocence, not the one that points to guilt" (Lieberman 1993b: A32).

Coding Aggression as Professional Practice

Allowing expert testimony on the use of force by the police had the effect of filtering the events visible on the tape through a police coding scheme, as articulated by an expert who instructed the jury how to see the body movements of the victim in terms of that system. What one finds in the trial is a dialogic framework encompassing the work of two different professions, as the discourse of the police with one of their suspects is embedded within the discourse of the courtroom.

In order to measure police perception, a coding scheme for the escalation of force was applied to the tape: (1) if a suspect is aggressive, the proper police response is escalation of force in order to subdue him; (2) when the suspect cooperates, then force is de-escalated. When an expert applies this coding scheme to the tape, a new set of finely differentiated events is produced, described through appropriate language drawn from the social sciences. In the words of one expert:

Expert: There were,
ten distinct (1.0) uses of force.
rather than one single use of force.
...
In each of those, uses of force
there was an escalation and a de
escalation, (0.8)
an assessment period, (1.5)
and then an escalation and a de-
escalation again. (0.7)
And another assessment period.

The massive beating is now transformed into ten separate events, each with its own sequence of stages.

The use of this category system radically transforms the images visible on the tape by placing them within an expert frame of reference. Thus when King is hit yet another blow, this is transformed from a moment of visible violence – what the prosecution in the second trial will instruct the jury to see as "beating a suspect into submission" – into a demonstration that the "period of de-escalation has ceased":

Defense: Four oh five, oh one.
[We see a blow being delivered. =]
=Is that correct.
Expert: That's correct.
[The- force has been again escalated (0.3) to the level it had been previously, (0.4) and the de-escalation has ceased.]
...
Defense: And at-
At this point which is,
for the record four thirteen
twenty nine, (0.4)
[We see a blow being struck
and thus the end of the period
of, de-escalation?]
Is that correct Captain.

Expert: That's correct.
Force has now been elevated to the previous level, (0.6) after this period of de-escalation.

A reader looking at this sequence might argue that what the expert is saying is a mere tautology: if someone is being hit again, then – almost by definition – any period of de-escalation of force (the moments when the suspect is not being hit) has ceased. However, much more than tautology is involved. By deploying the escalation/de-escalation framework, the expert has provided a coding scheme that transforms the actions being coded into displays of careful, systematic police work. One of the defense lawyers said that what he wanted to show the jury was that "what looks like uncontrolled uh brutality and random violence is indeed a very disciplined and controlled effort to take King into custody" (interview with Court TV, CRT 018:03:30). A major resource for affecting such a perceptual transformation is the use of coding schemes such as the one articulated above by the defense's expert witness. Such schemes provide the jury with far from neutral templates for viewing and understanding in a particular way the events visible on the tape.

These structures also define the instruments of violence visible on the tape. Earlier it was noted how the conditional relevance of an utterance creates a context that shapes interpretation of the events it points to. When the escalation framework was first introduced, the defense attorney showed the jury a chart of *tools* used by the police that included not only the batons with which they were beating him but also the kicks that they administered:

Defense: And this chart will show you the *tools*
that Sergeant Koon had available
to him on March third.
. . .
The next tool up, (1.9)
Is: (0.3) a side handle baton. (0.8)
a metal (0.3) baton. (1.0)
is: a tool (0.8)
to protect yourself (0.9)
and to take people into custody.
(1.0)
And in addition to that (0.3)
on the same level with this (0.5)
the experts will tell you as well
as Sergeant Koon, (0.4)
that there are *k*icks,

A coding scheme, classifying phenomena visible on the tape as tools required for the work of a particular occupation, is deployed to move what the prosecution described as brutal "cowardly stomps" inflicted on a prone, beaten man into a domain of professional police work.

The escalation/de-escalation framework was taught in the police academy as a guide for appropriate action when applying force. It generated a second coding scheme focused on the suspect's body. Central to the case made by the defense was the proposal that the police officers themselves were required to evaluate King's actions as either *aggressive* or *cooperative* in order to decide whether to escalate or de-escalate force – that is, whether they should hit him again. The key perceptual decision posed in the analysis of the tape thus becomes whether the police officers can legitimately see the suspect as aggressive, in which case, it is argued, they are justified in applying further force. The following is from the cross-examination of defendant Laurence Powell, the officer who landed the most blows on King:

Prosecutor: You can't look at that video and say
that every one of those blows
is reasonable can you.
(1.0)
Powell: Oh I *can* if I put my perceptions in.

Crucially, the defense argues that an interpretive framework focused on the suspect's actions vests control of the situation in the victim, since his actions control the response of the police:

Defense: Rodney **King**
and Rodney King alone
was in control of the situation.

The net effect of buying into this category system as a framework for the interpretation of the tape is a most consequential structuring of the dense and complicated perceptual field provided by the tape, with the suspect/victim King becoming the figure, the focus of minute scrutiny, while the officers performing the beating recede into the background.

Expert Testimony: An Ethnography of Seeing

To analyze the tape in these terms, the defense calls Sergeant Charles Duke from the Los Angeles Police Department as an expert on the use of force by the police (see figure 19.5). Commentators on the first trial considered Duke to be the most important and persuasive witness in the case.

At the point where we enter the following sequence, the prosecutor has noted that King appears to be moving into a position appropriate for handcuffing him and that one officer is in fact reaching for his handcuffs – the suspect is being cooperative.

1	Prosecutor:	So uh would you,
2		again consider this to be:
3		a nonagressive, movement by Mr. King?
4	Sgt. Duke:	At this time no I wouldn't. (1.1)
5	Prosecutor:	It is aggressive.
6	Sgt. Duke:	Yes. It's starting to be. (0.9)
7		This foot, is laying flat, (0.8)
8		There's starting to be a ***bend***, in uh (0.6)
9		this leg (0.4)
10		in his butt (0.4)
11		The buttocks area has started to rise. (0.7)
12		which would put us,
13		at the beginning of our ***spec***trum again.

Here the process of coding events within a relevant perceptual field becomes an open contest as prosecution and defense use a range of discursive practices to debate whether body movements of King visible on the videotape should be coded as cooperative or aggressive. By noting both the submissive elements in King's posture and the fact that one of the officers is reaching for his handcuffs, the prosecutor has tried to make the case that the tape demonstrates that at this point the officers perceive King as cooperative. If he can establish this point, hitting King again would be unjustified and the officers should be found guilty of the crimes they are charged with. The contested vision being debated here has very high stakes.

To rebut the vision proposed by the prosecutor, Duke uses the semantic resources provided by language to code as aggressive extremely subtle body movements of a man lying facedown beneath the officers (lines 7–11). Note, for example, not only his explicit placement of King at the very edge, the beginning, of the aggressive spectrum (line 13) but also how very small movements are made much larger by situating them within a prospective horizon through repeated use of "starting to" (lines 6, 18, 11), for example, "The buttocks area has started to rise." The events visible on the tape are enhanced and amplified by the language used to describe them.

This focusing of attention organizes the perceptual field provided by the videotape into a salient figure, the aggressive suspect, who is highlighted against an amorphous background containing nonfocal participants, the officers doing the beating. This structuring of the materials provided by the image is accomplished not only through talk but also through gesture. As Duke speaks, he brings his hand to the screen and points to the parts of King's body that, he is arguing, display aggression (see figure 19.6). In looking at how the senior archaeologist pointed to where examples of the categories her student was searching for could be found, it was noted how a category, a gesture, and the perceptual field that it was articulating mutually elaborated on each other. Here the touchable events on the television screen provide visible *evidence* for the description constructed through talk. What emerges from Duke's testimony is not just a *statement*, a static category, but a *demonstration* built through the active interplay between the coding scheme and the domain of scrutiny to which it is being applied. As talk and image mutually enhance each other, a demonstration that is greater than the sum of its parts emerges. Simultaneously, King, rather than the officers, becomes the focus of attention as the expert's

Figure 19.5 *Sergeant Duke analyzes the Rodney King video tape. Historical still of the Rodney King Beating courtesy of George Holliday © 1991 George Holliday. All rights reserved.* NO REPRODUCTION OF THIS STILL MAY BE MADE WITHOUT THE PRIOR WRITTEN CONSENT OF GEORGE HOLLIDAY

finger, articulating the image, delineates what is relevant within it.

By virtue of the category systems erected by the defense, the minute rise in King's buttocks noted on the tape unleashes a cascade of perceptual inferences that have the effect of exonerating the officers. A rise in King's body is interpreted as aggression, which in turn justifies an escalation of force. Like other parties faced with a coding task, the jury members were led to engage in intense, minute cognitive scrutiny as they looked at the tape of the beating to decide the issues at stake in the case. However, once the defense's coding scheme is accepted as a relevant framework for looking at the tape, the operative perspective for viewing it is no longer a layperson's reaction to a man lying on the ground being beaten but instead a microanalysis of the movements being made by that man's body to see if it is exhibiting aggression.

The expert witnesses for the defense simultaneously construct actions as both rational and without moral responsibility, in the case of the police, and as mindlessly mechanical and morally responsible, in the case of Rodney King.[14] Thus references to phenomena such as "an assessment period" imply rational deliberation on the part of the police without individual moral responsibility in terms other than the correctness of assessment – for example, the agentless passive voice of "We see a blow being delivered," "The force has again been escalated," and "kicks" as tools of the trade. On the other hand, King is characterized both as an almost mindless, moving force – for example, "The buttocks area has started to rise" – and as being "in control of the situation." This is accomplished in part by the disassembly of King's body from a responsible agent into a bunch of moving parts that become the triggering mechanism for a typified

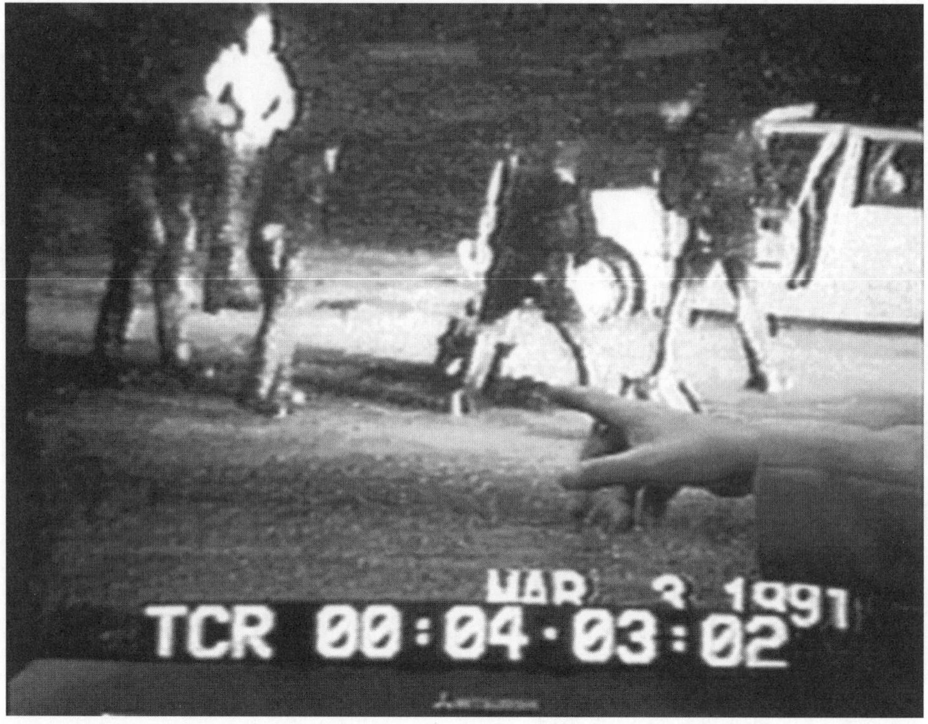

Figure 19.6 *Sergeant Duke shows display of aggression by Rodney King. Historical still of the Rodney King Beating courtesy of George Holliday © 1991 George Holliday. All rights reserved.* NO REPRODUCTION OF THIS STILL MAY BE MADE WITHOUT THE PRIOR WRITTEN CONSENT OF GEORGE HOLLIDAY

process to which, it is argued, the police are required to respond in a disciplined, dispassionate way. Discourses of rationality, of mechanism, and of moral responsibility are simultaneously, but strategically and selectively, deployed.

In the first trial, though the prosecution disputed the analysis of specific body movements as displays of aggression, the relevance of looking at the tape in terms of such a category system was not challenged. Observers considered this to be a very serious mistake (Lieberman 1993a: A26). A key difference in the second trial, which led to the conviction of two of the officers, was that there the prosecution gave the jury alternative frameworks for interpreting the events on the tape. These included both an alternative motive for the beating, namely that the police officers were teaching a lesson to a man who had been disrespectful to them (Mydans 1993c), and an alternative interpretation of the movements of King's body that Sergeant Duke highlighted, namely as normal reactions of a man to a beating rather than as displays of incipient aggression. In the prosecution's argument, King "cocks his leg" not in preparation for a charge but because his muscles naturally jerk after being hit with a metal club. The prosecution's alternative interpretive template also instructed the jury to look at the physical behavior of the police officers who were not hitting King, portraying them as nonchalantly watching a beating rather than poised to subdue a still dangerous suspect. Instead of restricting focus to the body of King, the prosecution drew the jury's attention to the slender stature of Officer Briseno, the officer sent in alone at the end of the beating to handcuff the man that the defense was portraying as a dangerous giant. The prosecutor in the second trial also emphasized to the jury inherent contradictions in the arguments being made by the defense. The defense had portrayed King as both a cunning martial arts expert, scanning the scene to plot his next move, and as a man crazed by drugs. Instead, the prosecution argued, he was simply a beaten man who fell helplessly to the ground.[15] Though most of the evidence used in the two trials was the same (most crucially the tape), the prosecutors in the second trial were able to build discursively their own interpretive frameworks to counter those that had been so effectively deployed by the defense, and thus provide their jury with ways of looking at the tape that had not been available to the first jury.

The perspectival framework provided by a professional coding scheme constitutes the objects in the domain of scrutiny that are the focus of attention. By using the coding scheme to animate the events being studied, the expert teaches the jury how to look at the tape and how to see relevant events within it (Shuy 1982: 125). He provides them with an ethnography of seeing that situates the events visible on the tape within the worklife and phenomenal world of a particular work community. Here this ethnographer is not an outside anthropologist but an actual member of the community whose work is being explicated. Expert testimony in court forces members of a discourse community to become metapragmatically aware of the communication practices that organize their work, including, in this case, violence as a systematic mode of discourse capable of being described scientifically as professional practice in minute detail.

Insofar as the courtroom provides a dialogic framework encompassing the discourse of two different professions, scrutiny is occurring on a number of distinct levels: first, police scrutiny of the suspect's body as a guide for whether to beat him; second, scrutiny by those in court, including the jury and expert witnesses, as they assess the scrutiny of the police;[16] and third, within the framework of this article, our scrutiny of how those in the courtroom scrutinize the police scrutinizing their victim.

Graphic Demonstrations and Material Artifacts: The Birth of Rodney King as a Visible Actor

The perceptual field provided by the tape was manipulated and enhanced in other ways as well. At the very beginning of the tape, while the camera was still slightly out of focus, King ran toward the officers. On the tape itself, this event is hard to see: it happens very quickly and is difficult to discern in the midst of a dark but very complex perceptual field filled with other events, including numerous police officers, a police car, and King's own car, which, because of its light color and lack of movement, is the most salient object in the frame – indeed, the only item that can be easily recognized. The images visible on the tape are made even more difficult to see by the movement of the zooming camera and its lack of focus.

One of the defense attorneys in the first trial had photographs made from individual tape frames. The photos were cropped, enlarged, and pasted in sequence to form a display over a meter long that was placed in front of the jury on an easel. The salience of King in these images was amplified through use of *highlighting*. As the defense attorney unveiled his display, he placed clear overlays with large white lines outlining King's body on top of the photos (see figure 19.7). Earlier we saw an archaeologist weave a post mold into existence by drawing a line through subtle patches of color differences in a bit of dirt. Here the defense attorney uses similar procedures for enhancing objects in the domain of scrutiny to call forth from the murky pixels on the video screen the discursive object that is the point of his argument, a large, violent, charging African-American man who was so dangerous that hitting him 47 times with metal clubs was reasonable and justified. By virtue of the figure/ground relationship established through such highlighting, the police officers, all situated beyond the boundaries of the lines drawn by the lawyer, recede into the background.

When videotape is used as the medium for displaying King's movements, a sense of what

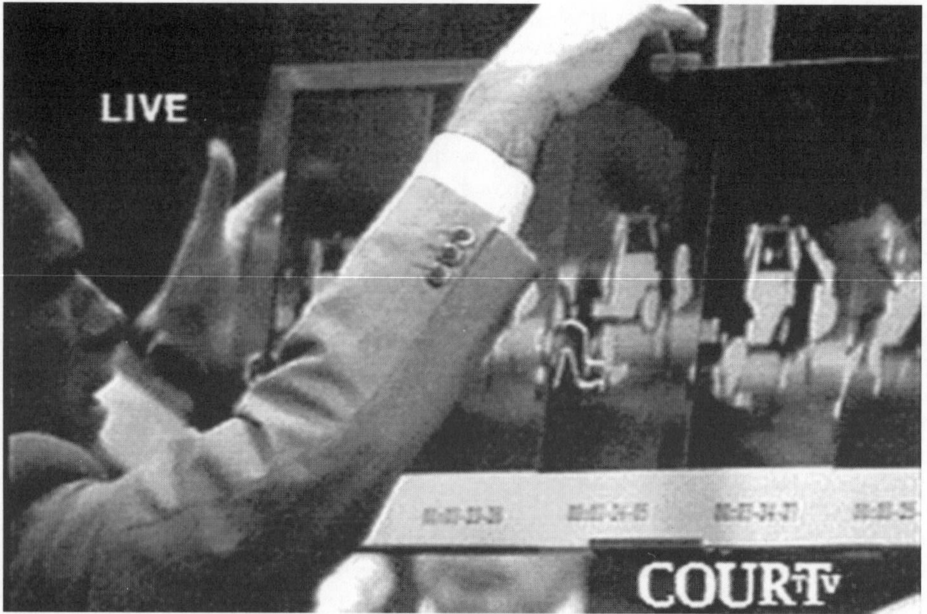

Figure 19.7 *Use of white lines to highlight King's body. Historical still of the Rodney King Beating courtesy of George Holliday © 1991 George Holliday. All rights reserved.* NO REPRODUCTION OF THIS STILL MAY BE MADE WITHOUT THE PRIOR WRITTEN CONSENT OF GEORGE HOLLIDAY

is happening as events unfold rapidly through time can be obtained only by replaying the tape repeatedly while trying to select from the confusing images on the screen that subset of visible events on which one is trying to concentrate. The work of the viewer is radically changed when these scenes are transformed into the photographic array. Movement through time becomes movement through space, that is, the left-to-right progression of the cropped frames. Each image remains available to the viewer instead of disappearing when its successor arrives, so that both the sequence as a whole and each event within it can be contemplated and rescanned at leisure. Much of the visual clutter[17] in the original images is eliminated by cropping the photos.

In his analysis of similar representational practices in scientific discourse, Lynch (1988) wrote about them providing an *externalized retina*. The defense lawyer makes precisely the same argument, stating that by enhancing the image in this way, he is able to structure the world being scrutinized so that it reveals what his client perceived (lines 5–8):

1 Defense: *R*odney *K*ing, (0.4) in the very beginning, (1.0)
2 in the first six frames, (2.2)
3 of this incident, (2.4)
4 *Went* (4.7) from the grou:nd, (0.4) to a charge. (1.2)
5 And what Sergeant Koon will tell you=
6 =*this* is his rendi:tion, (0.4) of *what* he sa:w. (0.7)
7 *((Laying White Line Overlays on Top of Photos))*
8 *This* is how he perceived it. (3.6)
9 But once he saw Rodney King.
10 *rise* to his feet, (1.2) and attack at Powell, (1.4)
11 That in *Koon*'s mind, (0.9) in charge of his officers (1.2)
12 that Rodney King has set the tone. (1.6)
13 *Rod*ney King, (1.1) was trying to get in that position.

Once again talk and visual representation mutually amplify each other. Descriptors such as "a charge" (line 4) provide instructions for how to see the highlighted sequence on the easel, while that very same sequence provides seeable proof for the argument being made in the defense attorney's talk. (At the second trial, King testified that he ran after one of the officers said, "We're going to kill you nigger. Run.") At line 13 the defense attorney points with his finger toward the last photo in the series, the one where King is actually making contact with Officer Powell. This deictic gesture establishes that image as the referent for "that position" at the end of line 13 – the attacking position that the defense is arguing Rodney King was repeatedly trying to gain. Traditional work on gesture in interaction (and deixis in linguistics) has drawn a bubble around the perimeters of the participants' bodies. The body of the actor has not been connected to the built world within which it is situated. In these data the graphic display that receives the point is as much a constructed discursive object as the pointing finger or the spoken words; all three mutually elaborate on each other. Theoretical frameworks that partition the components of this process into separate fields of study cannot do justice to the reflexive relationship that exists between the talk, the gesture, and the artifacts that have been built and put in place precisely to receive that pointing. It is necessary to view all these phenomena as integrated components of a common activity.

The Power to Speak as a Professional

I will now briefly investigate the phenomenal structure and social organization that provide the ground from which the power to speak as a professional emerges.

Expert witnesses, such as Sergeant Duke, are entitled to speak about events in the courtroom because of their membership in a relevant community of practitioners. Duke's voice can be heard because he is a police officer, an expert on police use of force, and thus someone who can speak about what the police officers on the tape are perceiving as they look at King writhing on the ground. The structure of Duke's expertise, which gives him his right to speak authoritatively, creates a situated perspective from which events on the tape are viewed.

	After demonstrating by playing the videotape that Mr. King appears to be moving his right hand behind his back with the palm up.
1 Prosecutor:	That would be the position you'd want him in.=
2	=Is that correct. (0.6)
3 Sgt. Duke:	Not, (0.2) Not with uh:, (0.2) the way he is. (0.6)
4	His uh:, (0.4) His leg is uh
5	Is bent in this area. (0.6)
6	Uh:, (0.2) Had he moved in this hand here being uh:
7	(0.4) straight up and down.
8	That causes me concern (0.7)
9 Prosecutor:	Uh does it also cause you concern that
10	someone's *step*ped on the back of his neck.
11 Sgt. Duke:	(0.6) No it does not.

Here, as in the data examined earlier, Duke displays intense concern about very small movements of King's leg and hand (lines 4–8). However, when asked about the fact that an officer has stepped on the back of King's neck (see figure 19.8), Duke states in effect that violent actions performed by police officers against their suspect cause him no concern at all (lines 9–11). The events on the tape are being viewed and articulated by Duke from a local, situated perspective – that of the police who are beating King – which is precisely his domain of expertise.

Insofar as the perceptual structures that organize interpretation of the tape are lodged within a profession and not an isolated individual, there is a tremendous asymmetry about who can speak as an expert about the events on the tape and thus structure interpretation of it. Here Duke states that his training makes it possible for him to "perceive the perceptions" of the police officers, but that he has no access to the perceptions of

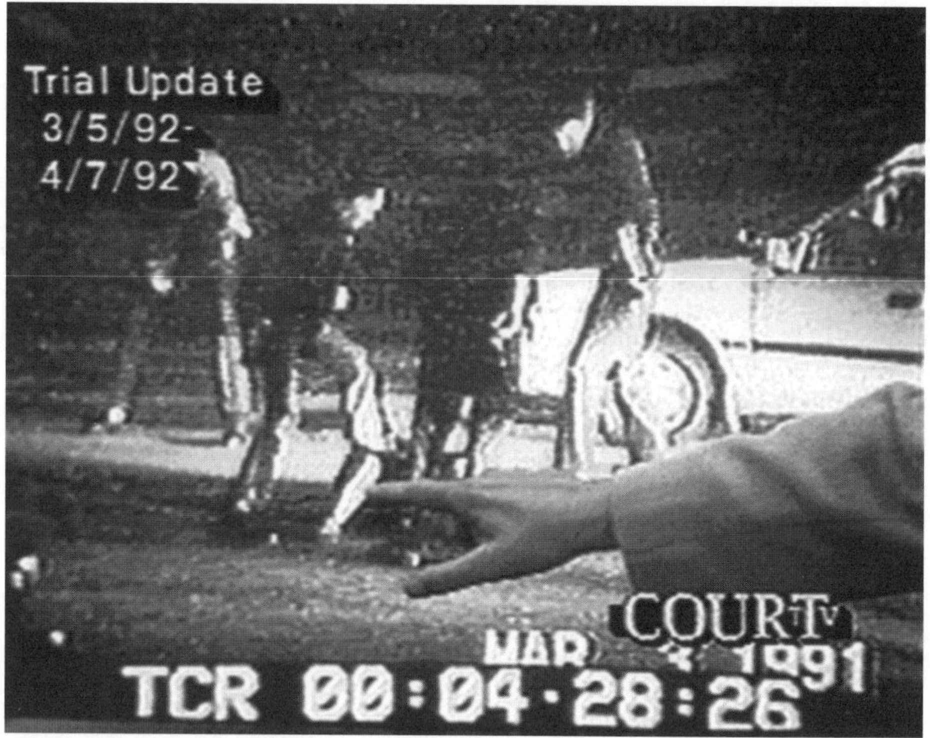

Figure 19.8 *Sergeant Duke discusses officer stepping on King's neck. Historical still of the Rodney King Beating courtesy of George Holliday © 1991 George Holliday. All rights reserved.*

the man they are beating, since Duke himself has "never been a suspect":

1 Sgt. Duke They're taught to evaluate.
2 And that's what they were doing
  in the last two
3 frames.
4 Or three frames.
5 Prosecutor: Can you read their mind uh,
  (1.4) Sergeant Duke.
6 (1.3)
7 Sgt. Duke: I can, (0.4) form an opinion
  based on my training.
8 and having trained people,
9 what I can perceive that their
  perceptions are.
10 (0.6)
11 Prosecutor: Well what's Mr. King's perceptions at this time.
12 (0.6)
13 Sgt. Duke: I've never been a suspect.
14 I don't know.

While administering a beating like this is recognized within the courtroom as part of the work of the police profession, no equivalent social group exists for the suspect. Victims do not constitute a profession. Thus no expert witnesses are available to interpret these events and animate the images on the tape from King's perspective. In the second trial, King was called as a witness, but he could not testify about whether the police officers beating him were using unreasonable force since he lacked "expertise on the constitution or the use of force" (Newton 1993a: A16).

The effect of all this is the production of a set of contradictory asymmetries. Within the domain of discourse recorded on the videotape, it is argued that King is in control of the interaction, and that is what the first jury found. But within the discourse of the courtroom, no one can speak for the suspect. His perception is not lodged within a profession and thus publicly available to others as a set of official discursive procedures. Within the discourse of the trial, he is an object to be scrutinized, not an actor with a voice of his own. However, within the discourse made visible on the tape, he is constituted as the controlling actor.

The way in which professional coding schemes for constituting control and asymmetry in interaction are used by the police to justify the way that they beat someone alerts us to ethical problems that can arise when we put our professional skills as social scientists at the service of another profession, thereby amplifying its voice and the power it can exert on those who become the objects of its scrutiny.

Conclusion

Central to the social and cognitive organization of a profession is its ability to shape events in the domain of its scrutiny into the phenomenal objects around which the discourse of the profession is organized: to find archaeologically relevant events such as post holes in the color stains visible in a patch of a dirt and map them or to locate legally consequential instances of aggression or cooperation in the visible movements of a man's body. This article has investigated three practices used to accomplish such professional vision – coding schemes, highlighting, and the production and articulation of graphic representations – in the work settings of two professions: an archaeological field excavation and a courtroom.

Such work contributes to efforts by linguistic anthropologists, practice theorists, and conversation analysts to develop anthropologically informed analyses of human action and cognition as socially situated phenomena, activities accomplished through ongoing, contingent work within the historically shaped settings of the lived social world. In this process some traditional dichotomies that have isolated subfields from each other, such as the assignment of language and the material world to separate domains of inquiry, disappear. The ability to build and interpret a material cognitive artifact, such as an archaeological map, is embedded within a web of socially articulated discourse. Talk between coworkers, the lines they are drawing, measurement tools, and the ability to see relevant events in the dirt all mutually inform each other within a single coherent activity. Simultaneously, the practices clustered around the production, distribution, and interpretation of such representations provide the material and cognitive infrastructure that make archaeological theory possible.

Within such a framework, the ability to see relevant entities is lodged not in the individual mind but instead within a community of competent practitioners. This has a range of consequences. First, the power to authoritatively see and produce the range of phenomena that are consequential for the organization of a society is not homogeneously distributed. Different professions – medicine, law, the police, specific sciences such as archaeology – have the power to legitimately see, constitute, and articulate alternative kinds of events. Professional vision is perspectival, lodged within specific social entities, and unevenly allocated. The consequences that this had for who was entitled to instruct the jury about what was happening on the Rodney King videotape support Foucault's (1981) analysis of how the discursive procedures of a society structure what kinds of talk can and cannot be heard, who is qualified to speak the truth, and the conditions that establish the rationality of statements.

Second, such vision is not a purely mental process but instead is accomplished through the competent deployment of a complex of situated practices in a relevant setting. An earlier generation of anthropologists, influenced by Saussure's notion of *langue*, brought precision and clarity to their analytic projects by focusing on the grammars of cultural phenomena such as category systems and myths while ignoring the courses of practical action within which categories and stories were articulated in the endogenous scenes of a society's everyday activities. The procedures investigated in this article move beyond the mind of the actor to encompass features of the setting where action is occurring. Through practices such as highlighting, coding, and articulating graphic representations, categories (post molds, aggression) are linked to specific phenomena in a relevant domain of scrutiny, creating a whole that is greater than the sum of its parts – for example, an actual instantiation of a post mold or a visible demonstration of aggression. As argued by Wittgenstein (1958), a category or rule cannot determine its own application; seeing what can count as a "change of slope" or "aggression" in a relevant domain of scrutiny is both a contingent accomplishment and a locus for contestation – even a central site for legal argument. Categories and the phenomena to which they are being applied mutually elaborate each other.[18] This process is central among those providing for ongoing change in legal and other category systems.

Third, insofar as these practices are lodged within specific communities, they must be learned (Chaiklin and Lave 1993; Lave and Wenger 1991). Learning was a central activity in both of the settings examined in this article, but the organization of that learning was quite different in each. Like students in an anthropology class being lectured about events in another culture, the jury at the Rodney King trial was instructed by an expert about what a police officer (someone who they would never be) could see in the events visible on the tape (see figure 19.9). On the other hand, the young archaeologist, crouching in the dirt and struggling to determine where in it to properly position one of the tools of her profession, was learning to be a competent practitioner. The dirt in front of her was a locus for embodied practice, not an object of contemplation.

Consistent with recent research in conversation analysis on the interactive organization of work settings (Drew and Heritage 1992), different ways of learning and their associated modes of access to the phenomena being scrutinized were constituted in each setting through the alternative ways that human interaction was organized. Though ultimately the jury decided the case, throughout the trial its members never had the chance to question the expert witnesses who were lecturing them, but instead sat week after week as a silent audience. They had the opportunity to use the tools relevant to the analysis that they were charged with performing – that is, the opportunity to play the tape themselves – only when they were alone in the jury room. By way of contrast, Ann, the senior archaeologist, was positioned to monitor not only the dirt her student was studying but also embodied actions of that student within a field of relevant action.[19] Instead of being positioned as an expert lecturing to an audience, Ann's own ability to perform a relevant next action was contingent on the competent performance of her student; Ann could not mark her map until Sue had produced a necessary measurement.

Figure 19.9 *Instruction by experts: Sergeant Duke showing police officer perspective; archaeologist showing measurement technique. Historical still of the Rodney King Beating courtesy of George Holliday © 1991 George Holliday. All rights reserved.* NO REPRODUCTION OF THIS STILL MAY BE MADE WITHOUT THE PRIOR WRITTEN CONSENT OF GEORGE HOLLIDAY.

Each was dependent on the other for the moment-by-moment accomplishment of a common course of action. To make that happen, Ann first provided Sue with successive descriptions of what to look for and then got down in the dirt to point to relevant phenomena, thus adjusting in detail to the problems her student was visibly facing. The necessity of collaborative action not only posed tasks of common understanding as practical problems but also exposed relevant domains of ignorance, a process crucial to their remedy. In brief, though instruction was central to what both the archaeologists and the expert witnesses in the courtroom were doing, within each setting learning processes, encompassing participation frameworks, and modes of access to relevant phenomena were shaped into quite different kinds of events by the alternative ways that interaction was structured.

Despite very marked differences in how each setting was organized, common discursive practices were deployed in both. There seem to be good reasons why the configuration of practices investigated in this article are generic, pervasive, and consequential in human activity. First, processes of classification are central to human cognition, at times forming the basic subject matter of entire fields such as cognitive anthropology. Through the construction and use of coding schemes, relevant classification systems are socially organized as professional and bureaucratic knowledge structures, entraining in fine detail the cognitive activity of those who administer them, producing some of the objects of knowledge around which the discourse in a profession is organized, and frequently constituting accountable loci of power for those whose actions are surveyed and coded. Second, though most theorizing about human cognition in the twentieth century has focused on mental events – for example, internal representations – a number of activity theorists, students of scientific and everyday practice, ethnomethodologists, and cognitive anthropologists have insisted that the ability of human beings to modify the world around them, to structure settings for the activities that habitually occur within them, and to build tools, maps, slide rules, and other representational artifacts is as central to human cognition as processes hidden inside the brain. The ability to build structures in the world that organize knowledge, shape perception, and structure future action is one way that human cognition is shaped through ongoing historical practices. Graphic representations constitute a prototypical example of how human beings build external cognitive artifacts for the organization and persuasive display of relevant knowledge. This article has investigated some of the ways in which relevant communities organize the production and understanding of such representations through the deployment of situated practices articulated within ongoing processes of human interaction.[20] Human activity characteristically occurs in environments that provide a very complicated perceptual field. A quite general class of cognitive practices consists of methods for highlighting this perceptual field so that relevant phenomena are made salient. This process simultaneously helps classify those phenomena, for example, as an archaeological feature rather than an irrelevant patch of color in the dirt, or as an aggressive movement. Practices such as highlighting link relevant features of a setting to the activity being performed in that setting.

In view of the generic character of the issues that these practices address, it is not surprising that they frequently work in concert with each other, as when Sergeant Duke's pointing finger linked a category in a coding scheme to specific phenomena visible in a graphic representation. The way in which such highlighting structures the perception of others by reshaping a domain of scrutiny so that some phenomena are made salient, while others fade into the background, has strong rhetorical and political consequences. By looking at how these practices work together within situated courses of action, it becomes possible to investigate quite diverse phenomena within a single analytical framework. As these practices are used within sequences of talk-in-interaction, members of a profession hold each other accountable for – and contest – the proper perception and constitution of the objects of knowledge around which their discourse is organized.[21]

NOTES

I am very deeply indebted to Gail Wagner and the students at her archaeological field school for allowing me to investigate the activities in which they were engaged. Without their openness and support, the analysis being reported here would not be possible. I owe a tremendous debt to Lucy Suchman for demonstrating to me how important the way in which participants tailor and reshape objects in work settings in order to accomplish local tasks is to any understanding of human cognition and action (see, for example, Suchman 1987). I wish to thank Christopher Borstel, Lisa Capps, Aaron Cicourel, Janet Keller, John Heritage, Bernard Hibbits, Cathryn Houghton, Hugh Mehan, Curtis Renoe, Lucy Suchman, Patty Jo Watson, and most especially Candy Goodwin for helpful and insightful comments on an earlier version of this analysis. I thank Court TV for granting permission to use the images from their broadcast.

An earlier version of this article was presented as a plenary lecture at the International Conference on Discourse and the Professions, Uppsala, Sweden, August 28, 1992, and in colloquia at UCLA, the University of California at Santa Barbara, the University of California at San Diego, and the University of South Carolina.

1 See Bourdieu 1977, Chaiklin and Lave 1993, Hanks 1987, and Lave and Wenger 1991 for contemporary work on practice theory. Analyses of how cognition makes use of phenomena distributed in everyday settings can be found in Lave 1988, Rogoff 1990, Rogoff and Lave 1984, and Suchman 1987. Hutchins (1993) provides a very clear demonstration of how cognition is not located in the mind of a single individual but is instead embedded within distributed systems, including socially differentiated actors and external representations embodied in tools. Dougherty and Keller (1985) demonstrate how cognitive frameworks and material features of a setting mutually constitute each other. Recent work by linguistic anthropologists on the discursive constitution of context can be found in Duranti and Goodwin 1992. Work on activity theory (Engestrōm 1987; Wertsch 1985) growing out of the pioneering work of Vygotsky (1978) has long stressed the mediated, historically shaped character of both cognition and social organization. Though focused on the organization of sequences of talk rather than tool-mediated cognition, the field of conversation analysis (Atkinson and Heritage 1984; Drew and Heritage 1992; Sacks 1992; Sacks et al. 1974) has developed the most powerful resources currently available for the analysis of the interactive organization of emerging action with actual settings (Goodwin 1990), including the way in which each next action relies on prior action for its proper interpretation while simultaneously reshaping the context that will provide the ground for subsequent action.

2 For example, see Ochs 1979 and Scheiffelin and Doucet 1994.

3 See Heritage 1984 and Sacks et al. 1974.

4 For further discussion, see Du Bois et al. 1993, Gumperz 1982, Sherzer and Woodbury 1987, and Tedlock 1987.

5 An elaboration of this system can be found in Sacks et al. 1974 on pp. 731–3.

6 See Haraway 1989, Latour 1987, Latour and Woolgar 1979, Lynch 1985, Lynch and Woolgar 1988, and Pickering 1992.

7 Archaeologists distinguish between post molds and post holes. In order to place a post that will support a roof or other structure, people frequently dig a pit substantially larger than the post itself. After the post is in place, dirt is packed around it to support it. The larger pit is called a post hole, while the hole created by the post itself is called a post mold.

8 See Garfinkel 1967, Goodwin 1992, and Heritage 1984.

9 For analysis of how graphic representations are articulated in the mist of scientific practice, see Goodwin 1990 and Ochs et al. 1994. The more general issue of graphic representations in the discourse of science has been an important topic in the sociology of scientific knowledge (for example, Lynch 1988 and Lynch and Woolgar 1988).

10 For analysis of how participants read the movement of another's body through socially defined space, see Duranti 1992.

11 For extensive analysis of the reflexive relationship between socialization and language, see the work of Ochs and Scheiffelin (for example, Ochs 1988; Ochs and Schieffelin 1986; Scheiffelin 1990; Scheiffelin and Ochs 1986).

12 The practices at issue here have consequences for not only the production of such maps but also their reading. Competent archaeologists know that the dots on a map, the only points in the landscape that have actually been measured, have a different status than the lines connecting the dots. Thus they will sometimes discard the lines and rely only on the dots for subsequent analysis.

13 See Drew 1992, pp. 472–4, and Shuy 1982.

14 I am deeply indebted to Lucy Suchman for bringing the phenomena discussed in this paragraph to my attention.

15 The prosecution arguments at the second trial noted here are drawn from my notes made at the closing argument and from newspaper reports.

16 The ability to record events on videotape and replay them in the court created baroque possibilities for layering and framing the perception of events. At the second trial, one of the defendants, Officer Briseno, chose not to testify. However, the prosecution received permission to play for the jury videotape of his testimony at the first trial in which he criticized the actions of the other defendants. "That placed jurors in the federal trial in the unusual position of watching a defendant on one videotape describe yet another videotape" (Newton 1993b: A25). The jury was able to watch "as the taped Officer Briseno spoke from the monitor accompanied by the word *Live*, while the real Officer Briseno sat passively with the other defendants, following his own year-old words on a transcript" (Mydans 1993a: A14).

17 The notion of what events constitute "clutter" to be eliminated is of course an important political decision being made by the party who reshapes the image for presentation to the jury.

18 See Goodwin 1992, Heritage 1984, and Keller and Keller 1993.

19 The most thorough analysis of how archaeology is learned as a mode of embodied practice can be found in Edgeworth 1991.

20 See also Goodwin 1990.

21 Professional settings provide a perspicuous site for the investigation of how objects of knowledge, controlled by and relevant to the defining work of a specific community, are socially constructed from within the settings that make up the lifeworld of that community – that is, endogenously, through systematic discursive procedures. This should not, however, be taken to imply that such processes are limited to professional discourse. The way in which we reify our realities through practices such as highlighting and coding are pervasive features of human social and cognitive life.

REFERENCES

Atkinson, J. Maxwell, and John Heritage, eds. (1984) *Structures of Social Action*. Cambridge: Cambridge University Press.

Bourdieu, Pierre (1977) *Outline of a Theory of Practice*. Richard Nice, trans. Cambridge: Cambridge University Press.

Chaiklin, Seth, and Jean Lave, eds. (1993) *Understanding Practice: Perspectives on Activity and Context*. Cambridge: Cambridge University Press.

Cicourel, Aaron V. (1964) *Method and Measurement in Sociology*. New York: Free Press.

Cicourel, Aaron V. (1968) *The Social Organization of Juvenile Justice*. New York: Wiley.

Dougherty, Janet W. D., and Charles Keller (1985) Taskonomy: A Practical Approach to Knowledge Structures. In *Directions in Cognitive Anthropology*. J. W. D. Dougherty, ed., pp. 161–74. Urbana, IL: University of Illinois Press.

Drew, Paul (1992) Contested Evidence in Courtroom Examination: The Case of a Trial for Rape. In *Talk at Work: Interaction in Institutional Setting*. P. Drew and J. Heritage, eds., pp. 470–520. Cambridge: Cambridge University Press.

Drew, Paul, and John Heritage, eds. (1992) *Talk at Work: Interaction in Institutional Settings* Cambridge: Cambridge University Press.

Du Bois, John, Stephen Schuetze-Coburn, Danae Paolino, and Susanna Cumming (1993) Outline of Discourse Transcription. In *Talking Data: Transcription and Coding Methods for Language Research*. J. A. Edwards and M. D. Lampert, eds. Hillsdale, NJ: Lawrence Erlbaum.

Duranti, Alessandro (1992) Language and Bodies in Social Space: Samoan Ceremonial Greetings. *American Anthropologist* 94(3): 657–91.

Duranti, Alessandro, and Charles Goodwin, eds. (1992) *Rethinking Context: Language as an Interactive Phenomenon*. Cambridge: Cambridge University Press.

Edgeworth, Matthew (1991) The Act of Discovery: An Ethnography of the Subject–Object Relation in Archaeological Practice. Doctoral thesis, Program in Anthropology and Archaeology, University of Durham.

Engeström, Yrjö (1987) *Learning by Expanding: An Activity-Theoretical Approach to Developmental Research*. Helsinki: Orienta-Konsultit Oy.

Foucault, Michel (1981) The Order of Discourse. In *Untying the Text: A Post-Structuralist Reader*. R. Young, ed., pp. 48–78. Boston: Routledge & Kegan, Paul.

Garfinkel, Harold (1967) *Studies in Ethnomethodology*. Englewood Cliffs, NJ: Prentice-Hall.

Goodwin, Charles (1990) Perception, Technology and Interaction on a Scientific Research Vessel. Paper presented at the Annual Meeting of the American Anthropological Association, New Orleans.

Goodwin, Charles (1992) Transparent Vision. Paper presented at the Workshop on Interaction and Grammar, Department of Applied Linguistics, UCLA, May 1, 1992. (*Interaction and Grammar*, Elinor Ochs, Sandra Thompson, and Emanuael Schegloff, eds., Cambridge: Cambridge University Press, 1997.

Goodwin, Charles (1993) The Blackness of Black: Color Categories as Situated Practice. In *Proceedings from the Conference on Discourse, Tools and Reasoning: Situated Cognition and Technologically Supported Environments*, Lucca, Italy, November 2–7. Lauren Resnick, Clotilde Pontecarvo, and Roger Saljo, eds.

Goodwin, Marjorie Harness (1990) *He-Said-She-Said: Talk as Social Organization among Black Children*. Bloomington: Indiana University Press.

Gumperz, John J. (1982) *Discourse Strategies*. Cambridge: Cambridge University Press.

Hanks, William (1987) Discourse Genres in a Theory of Practice. *American Ethnologist* 14 (4): 668–92.

Haraway, Donna (1989) *Primate Visions: Gender, Race, and Nature in the World of Modern Science*. New York: Routledge.

Heritage, John (1984) *Garfinkel and Ethnomethodology*. Cambridge: Polity.

Hutchins, Edwin (1993) Learning to Navigate. In *Understanding Practice: Perspectives on Activity and Context*. S. Chaiklin and J. Lave, eds., pp. 35–63. Cambridge: Cambridge University Press.

Keller, Charles, and Janet Dixon Keller (1993) Thinking and Acting with Iron. In *Understanding Practice: Perspectives on Activity and Context*. S. Chaiklin and J. Lave, eds., pp. 125–43. Cambridge: Cambridge University Press.

Latour, Bruno (1987) *Science in Action: How to Follow Scientists and Engineers through Society*. Cambridge, MA: Harvard University Press.

Latour, Bruno, and Steve Woolgar (1979) *Laboratory Life: The Social Construction of Scientific Facts*. London: Sage.

Lave, Jean (1988) *Cognition in Practice*. Cambridge: Cambridge University Press.

Lave, Jean, and Etienne Wenger (1991) *Situated Learning: Legitimate Peripheral Participation*. Cambridge: Cambridge University Press.

Lieberman, Paul (1993a) King Case Prosecutors Must Scale Hurdles of History. *The Los Angeles Times*, February 7, pp. A1, A26.

Lieberman, Paul (1993b) King Trial May Come Down to a Case of Expert vs. Expert. *The Los Angeles Times*, April 4, pp. A1, A32.

Lynch, Michael (1985) *Art and Artefact in Laboratory Science*. London: Routledge & Kegan Paul.

Lynch, Michael (1988) The Externalized Retina: Selection and Mathematization in the Visual Documentation of Objects in the Life Sciences. *Human Studies* 11: 201–34.

Lynch, Michael, and Steve Woolgar, eds. (1988) *Representation in Scientific Practice*. Cambridge, MA: MIT Press.

Mydans, Seth (1993a) Defendant on Videotape Gives Trial an Odd Air. *The New York Times*, April 7, p. A14.

Mydans, Seth (1993b) Prosecutor in Beating Case Urges Jury to Rely on Tape. *The New York Times*, April 21, p. A7.

Mydans, Seth (1993c) Prosecutor in Officers' Case Ends with Focus on Beating. *The New York Times*, April 9, p. A8.

Mydans, Seth (1993d) Their Lives Consumed, Los Angeles Officers Await Trial. *The New York Times*, February 2, p. A10.

Newton, Jim (1993a) "I Was Just Trying to Stay Alive," King Tells Federal Jury. *Los Angeles Times*, March 10, pp. A1, A16.

Newton, Jim (1993b) King Jury Sees Key Videotape; Prosecutors Rest. *The Los Angeles Times*, April 7, pp. A1, A25.

Ochs, Elinor (1979) Transcription as Theory. In *Developmental Pragmatics*. E. Ochs and B. B. Schieffelin, eds, pp. 43–72. New York: Academic Press.

Ochs, Elinor (1988) *Culture and Language Development: Language Acquisition and Language Socialization in a Samoan Village*. Cambridge: Cambridge University Press.

Ochs, Elinor, Patrick Gonzales, and Sally Jacoby (1994) "When I Come Down, I'm in a Domain State": Grammar and Graphic Representation in the Interpretive Activity of Physicists. In *Interaction and Grammar*. E. Ochs, E. A. Schegloff, and S. Thompson, eds. Cambridge: Cambridge University Press, 1997.

Ochs, Elinor, and Bambi B. Schieffelin (1986) *Language Socialization across Cultures*. New York: Cambridge University Press.

Pickering, Andrew, ed. (1992) *Science as Practice and Culture*. Chicago, IL: The University of Chicago Press.

Rogoff, Barbara (1990) *Apprenticeship in Thinking*. New York: Oxford University Press.

Rogoff, Barbara, and Jean Lave (1984) *Everyday Cognition: Its Development in Social Context*. Cambridge, MA: Harvard University Press.

Sacks, Harvey (1992) *Lectures on Conversation*. 2 vols. Gail Jefferson, ed. Oxford: Blackwell.

Sacks, Harvey, Emanuel A. Schegloff, and Gail Jefferson (1974) A Simplest Systematics for the Organization of Turn-Taking for Conversation. *Language* 50: 696–735.

Schegloff, Emanuel A. (1968) Sequencing in Conversational Openings. *American Anthropologist* 70: 1075–95.

Schieffelin, Bambi B. (1990) *The Give and Take of Everyday Life: Language Socialization of Kaluli Children*. Cambridge: Cambridge University Press.

Schieffelin, Bambi B., and Rachelle Charlier Doucet (1994) The "Real" Haitian Creole: Metalinguistics and Orthographic Choice. *American Ethnologist* 21(1): 176–200.

Schieffelin, Bambi B., and Elinor Ochs (1986) Language Socialization. In *Annual Review of Anthropology*. B. J. Siegel, A. R. Beals, and S. A. Tyler, eds., pp. 163–246. Palo Alto: Annual Reviews, Inc.

Sherzer, Joel, and Anthony C. Woodbury, eds. (1987) *Native American Discourse: Poetics and Rhetoric*. Cambridge: Cambridge University Press.

Shuy, Roger (1982) The Unit of Analysis in a Criminal Law Case. In *Analyzing Discourse: Text and Talk*. D. Tannen, ed. Washington, DC: Georgetown University Press.

Smith, Dorothy E. (1990) *Texts, Facts and Femininity*. London: Routledge.

Suchman, Lucy A. (1987) *Plans and Situated Actions: The Problem of Human Machine Communication*. Cambridge: Cambridge University Press.

Tedlock, Dennis (1987) Hearing a Voice in an Ancient Text: Quiché Maya Poetics in Performance. In *Native American Discourse: Poetics and Rhetoric*. J. Sherzer and A. C. Woodbury, eds., pp. 140–75. Cambridge: Cambridge University Press.

Vygotsky, L. S. (1978) *Mind in Society: The Development of Higher Psychological Processes*. Cambridge: Harvard University Press.

Wertsch, James (1985) *Culture, Communication, and Cognition: Vygotskian Perspectives*. Cambridge: Cambridge University Press.

Wittgenstein, Ludwig (1958) *Philosophical Investigations*. G. E. M. Anscombe and R. Rhees, eds. G. E. M. Anscombe, trans. 2nd edn. Oxford: Blackwell.

STUDY QUESTIONS

1 Define and explain the term "professional vision" as it is used by Goodwin.
2 Describe how the practices of (1) coding; (2) highlighting; and (3) producing and articulating material representations are used in the field school for young archaeologists documented by Goodwin.
3 How does Goodwin argue that the practice of employing "coding schemes" is an important way in which "nature is transformed into culture"?
4 How does Goodwin show that, although the videotape of the Rodney King beating was presented by the prosecutor as a "self-explicating objective record," it was "shown" to be otherwise by the defense?
5 How does Goodwin's notion of "professional vision" relate to the notion of language ideology discussed in other chapters in this book?

20

Language, Race, and White Public Space

Jane H. Hill

The Study of Racism in Anthropology

Anthropologists share a contradictory heritage: Our intellectual ancestors include both founders of scientific racism and important pioneers of the antiracist movement. After many years in which anthropologists have given far less attention to racism as an object of cultural analysis than have many of our sister disciplines, we are now returning to work that honors and advances our antiracist heritage.

Racism should be as central a question for research in cultural anthropology as "race" has been in biological anthropology. We have always been interested in forms of widely shared apparent irrationality, from divination to the formation of unilineal kin groups to the hyperconsumption of (or abstention from) the flesh of cattle, and racism is precisely this kind of phenomenon. Why, if nearly all scientists concur that human "races" are imaginary, do so many highly educated, cosmopolitan, economically secure people continue to think and act as racists? We know that "apparent irrationalities" seldom turn out to be the result of ignorance or confusion. Instead, they appear locally as quite rational, being rooted in history and tradition, functioning as important organizing principles in relatively enduring political ecologies, and lending coherence and meaning to complex and ambiguous human experiences. Racism is no different: As Smedley (1993: 25) has argued, "race ... [is] a world-view, ... a cosmological ordering system structured out of the political, economic, and social realities of peoples who had emerged as expansionist, conquering, dominating nations on a worldwide quest for wealth and power." Racism challenges the most advanced anthropological thinking, because racial formation processes (Omi and Winant 1994) are contested and contradictory, yet global in their scope. At the local level racial practices (Winant 1994) can be very complex. Yet emerging global "racialscapes" (Harrison 1995: 49, borrowing from Appadurai 1990) encompass even the most remote populations, as when the Taiap of the backwaters of the Lower Sepik River feel themselves to be "Black" as against "White" (Kulick 1993).

For permission to publish copyright material in this book, grateful acknowledgment is made to: J. H. Hill (1998), "Language, Race, and White Public Sphere," *American Anthropologist* 100: 680–9.

From "All Languages Are Equal" to the Study of Racializing Discourses

Like other anthropologists (and other linguists), linguistic anthropologists have made "education," with its implicit assumption of a confrontation with "ignorance," their central antiracist strategy. Attempts to inoculate students against beliefs in "primitive languages," "linguistic deprivation," or the idea that bilingualism (in certain languages) is inevitably seditious can be found in every introductory textbook in linguistics, and major scholars in the field have tried to spread the message not only as classroom educators, but as public intellectuals in a wide range of functions. And what have we to show for these efforts? "Official English" legislation on the books in many states, and, in the winter of 1996–97, a nationwide "moral panic" (Hall et al. 1978)[1] about whether "Ebonics" might be discussed in the classrooms of Oakland, California. In the case of the Ebonics panic, the nearly universal reaction among linguists[2] and linguistic anthropologists was "We must redouble our efforts at education! How can we make classroom and textbook units on the equality of all languages, let alone all varieties of English, more effective? How can we place opinion pieces to fight this nonsense?" The problem here, of course, is that such interventions not only neglect the underlying cultural logic of the stigmatization of African American English, but also neglect the much deeper problem pointed out by James Baldwin: "It is not the Black child's language which is despised: It is his experience" (Baldwin 1979, cited in Lippi-Green 1997) – and Baldwin might have added, had he not been writing in the *New York Times*, "and his body."

Antiracist education in linguistics and linguistic anthropology has centered on demonstrations of the equality and adequacy of racialized forms of language, ranging from Boas's ([1889]1982) demolition of the concept of "alternating sounds" and "primitive languages" to Labov's (1972) canonical essay on "The logic of non-standard English."[3] But until very recently, there has been little research on the "culture of language" of the dominant, "race-making" (Williams 1989) populations. New studies are beginning to appear, such as Fabian (1986), Silverstein (1987), Woolard (1989), and Lippi-Green (1997). Urciuoli's (1996) ethnography of speaking of Spanish and English among Puerto Ricans in New York City is perhaps the first monograph on the talk of a racialized population that foregrounds, and contributes to, contemporary theories of racial formation processes through her analysis of cultural phenomena such as "accent" and "good English."

A central theoretical commitment for many linguistic anthropologists, that "culture is localized in concrete, publicly accessible signs, the most important of which are actually occurring instances of discourse" (Urban 1991: 1), prepares us to contribute in new ways to the untangling of the complexity of racism. Furthermore, such study is an obvious extension of an active line of research on linguistic ideologies (Woolard and Schieffelin 1994). We can explore questions like: What kinds of signs are made "concrete and publicly accessible" by racializing discourses? What kinds of discourses count, or do not count, as "racist," and by what (and whose) cultural logic? What are the different kinds of racializing discourses, and how are these distributed in speech communities? What discourse processes socialize children as racial subjects?[4] What are the discourses of resistance, and what do they reveal about the forms of racism? What discourse processes relate the racialization of bodies to the racialization of kinds of speech? And all of these questions must, of course, be qualified by the question, in what kinds of contexts?

"Spanish Accents" and "Mock Spanish": Linguistic Order and Disorder in White Public Space

To illustrate a linguistic-anthropological approach to these issues, I build on an analysis by Urciuoli (1996), recentering it from her research on bilingual Puerto Ricans in New York City to a national community of Whites.[5] I have been looking at uses of Spanish by

Whites, both through on-the-spot observation of informal talk and through following as wide a range as possible of media and sites of mass reproduction such as advertising fliers, gift coffee cups, souvenir placemats, and greeting cards, for several years. First, I review Urciuoli's analysis of the racialization of Puerto Ricans through attention to their linguistic "disorder."

Puerto rican linguistic marginalization: disorderly order

Urciuoli argues that her consultants experience language as differentiated into two spheres. In an "inner sphere" of talk among intimates in the household and neighborhood, the boundaries between "Spanish" and "English" are blurred and ambiguous both formally and functionally. Here, speakers exploit linguistic resources with diverse histories with great skill and fluency, achieving extremely subtle interactional effects. But in an "outer sphere" of talk (and engagement with text) with strangers and, especially, with gatekeepers like court officers, social workers, and schoolteachers, the difference between Spanish and English is "sharply objectified" (Urciuoli 1996: 2). Boundaries and order are everything. The pressure from interlocutors to keep the two languages "in order" is so severe that people who function as fluent bilinguals in the inner sphere become so anxious about their competence that sometimes they cannot speak at all. Among the most poignant of the intricate ambiguities of this duality are that worries about being "disorderly" are never completely absent from the intimacies of the inner sphere, and people who successfully negotiate outer-sphere order are vulnerable to the accusation that they are "acting White," betraying their friends and relatives.

Urciuoli observes that a (carefully managed) Spanish is licensed in the outer sphere in such contexts as "folk-life festivals," as part of processes of "ethnification" that work to make difference "cultural, neat, and safe" (Urciuoli 1996:9).[6] But Whites hear other public Spanish as impolite and even dangerous. Urciuoli (1996: 35) reports that "nearly every Spanish-speaking bilingual I know ... has experienced complaints about using Spanish in a public place." Even people who always speak English "in public" worry about their "accents." While "accent" is a cultural dimension of speech and therefore lives largely in the realm of the imaginary, this construct is to some degree anchored in a core of objective phonetic practices that are difficult to monitor, especially when people are nervous and frightened. Furthermore, it is well-known that Whites will hear "accent" even when, objectively, none is present, if they can detect any other signs of a racialized identity.[7] Speakers are anxious about far more than "accent," however: they worry about cursing, using vocabulary items that might seem uncultivated, and even about using too many tokens of "you know." Mediated by cultural notions of "correctness" and "good English," failures of linguistic order, real and imagined, become in the outer sphere signs of race: "difference as inherent, disorderly, and dangerous" (Urciuoli 1996: 9).

The main point for my argument is that Puerto Ricans experience the "outer sphere" as an important site of their racialization, since they are always found wanting by this sphere's standards of linguistic orderliness. My research suggests that precisely the opposite is true for Whites. Whites permit themselves a considerable amount of disorder precisely at the language boundary that is a site of discipline for Puerto Ricans (and other members of historically Spanish-speaking populations in the United States) – that is, the boundary between Spanish and English in public discourse. I believe that this contrast, in which White uses of Spanish create a desirable "colloquial" presence for Whites, but uses of Spanish by Puerto Ricans (and members of other historically Spanish-speaking groups in the United States) are "disorderly and dangerous," is one of the ways in which this arena of usage is constituted as a part of what Page and Thomas (1994) have called "White public space": a morally significant set of contexts that are the most important sites of the practices of a racializing hegemony, in which Whites are invisibly normal, and in which racialized populations are visibly marginal and the objects of monitoring ranging from individual judgment to Official English legislation.

White linguistic normalcy: orderly disorder

While Puerto Ricans are extremely self-conscious about their "Spanish" accents in English, heavy English "accents" in Spanish are perfectly acceptable for Whites, even when Spanish speakers experience them as "like a fingernail on the blackboard." Lippi-Green (1997) points out the recent emergence of an industry of accent therapists, who offer their services to clients ranging from White southerners to Japanese executives working at American plant sites. But the most absurd accents are tolerated in Spanish, even in Spanish classes at the graduate level. I have played to a number of audiences a tape of a *Saturday Night Live* skit from several years ago, in which the actors, playing television news writers at a story conference, use absurdly exaggerated "Spanish" accents in names for Mexican food, places, sports teams, and the like. The Latino actor Jimmy Smits appears and urges them to use "normal anglicizations" (Hill 1993a). Academic audiences find the skit hilarious, and one of its points (it permits multiple interpretations) seems to be that it is somehow inappropriate for Whites to try to sound "Spanish."

While Puerto Ricans agonize over whether or not their English is cultivated enough, the public written use of Spanish by Whites is often grossly nonstandard and ungrammatical. Hill (1993a) includes examples ranging from street names, to advertising, to public-health messages. *Wash Your Hands/Lava sus manos*, originally reported by Peñalosa (1980) in San Bernardino Country, California, can be found in restrooms all over the southwestern United States. Peñalosa observed that this example is especially remarkable since it has as many grammatical errors as it has words.[8] An excellent case was the reprinting by the *Arizona Daily Star* (August 10, 1997) of an essay by the Colombian Nobelist Gabriel García Márquez that originally appeared in the *New York Times* (August 3, 1997). All of the diacritics on the Spanish words – and the problem of accent marks had been one of García Márquez's main points – were missing in the *Star* version. Tucson is the home of a major university and has a large Spanish-speaking population, and the audience for the piece (which appeared on the op-ed page of the Sunday edition) no doubt included many people who are literate in Spanish. Clearly, however, the *Star* was not concerned about offering this audience a literate text.

While Puerto Rican code switching is condemned as disorderly, Whites "mix" their English with Spanish in contexts ranging form coffee-shop chat to faculty meetings to the evening network newscasts and the editorial pages of major newspapers. Their "Mock Spanish"[9] incorporates Spanish-language materials into English in order to create a jocular or pejorative "key." The practices of Mock Spanish include, first, semantic pejoration of Spanish loans: the use of positive or neutral Spanish words in humorous or negative senses. Perhaps the most famous example is *macho*, which in everyday Spanish merely means "male." Equally important are Spanish expressions of leave-taking, like *adiós* and *hasta la vista*, used in Mock Spanish as kidding (or as serious) "kiss-offs" (Mock-Spanish "adios" is attested in this sense from the mid-nineteenth century). A second strategy borrows obscene or scatological Spanish words for use as Mock-Spanish euphemisms, as on the handwritten sign "Casa de Pee-Pee" on the door of the women's restroom in the X-ray department of a Tucson clinic, a coffee cup that I purchased in a gift shop near the University of Arizona Main Gate that bears the legend "Caca de Toro," and, of course, the case of *cojones*, exemplified below. In the third strategy, elements of "Spanish" morphology, mainly the suffix *-o*, often accompanied by "Spanish" modifiers like *mucho* or *el*, are borrowed to create jocular and pejorative forms like "el cheap-o," "numero two-o," or "mucho trouble-o." In a recent example, heard on PBS's *Washington Week in Review*, moderator Ken Bode observed that, had the "palace coup" in the House of Representatives in July 1997 not been averted, the Speaker of the House Newt Gingrich would have been "Newt-o Frito." The last major strategy of Mock Spanish is the use of "hyperanglicized" and parodic pronunciations and orthographic representations of Spanish loan words, as with "Grassy-ass,"

"Hasty lumbago," and "Fleas Navidad" (a picture of a scratching dog usually accompanies this one, which shows up every year on Christmas cards).

Mock Spanish is attested at least from the end of the eighteenth century, and in recent years it has become an important part of the "middling style" (Cmiel 1990), a form of public language that emerged in the nineteenth century as a way for elites to display democratic and egalitarian sensibilities by incorporating colloquial and even slangy speech. Recent relaxations of proscriptions against public vulgarity have made even quite offensive usages within Mock Spanish acceptable at the highest level of public discourse, as when the then-Ambassador to the United Nations Madeleine Albright addressed the Security Council after Cuban aircraft had shot down two spy planes manned by Cuban exiles: Cuban president Fidel Castro, she said, had shown "not *cojones*, but cowardice." Although many Spanish speakers find this particular usage exceptionally offensive,[10] Albright's sally was quoted again and again in admiring biographical pieces in the major English-language news media after she was nominated to be Secretary of State (e.g., Gibbs 1996: 33).

The Semiotics of Mock Spanish

In previous work (e.g., Hill 1995), I analyzed Mock Spanish as a "racist discourse." That is, I took its major functions to be the "elevation of whiteness" and the pejorative racialization of members of historically Spanish-speaking populations. Mock Spanish accomplishes the "elevation of whiteness" through what Ochs (1990) has called "direct indexicality": the production of nonreferential meanings or "indexes" that are understood and acknowledged by speakers. Speakers of Mock Spanish say that they use it because they have been exposed to Spanish – that is, they are cosmopolitan.[11] Or, that they use it in order to express their loyalty to, and affiliation with, the Southwest (or California, or Florida) – that is, they have regional "authenticity." Or that they use it because it is funny – that is, they have a sense of humor. In one particularly elaborate example, in the film *Terminator 2: Judgment Day*, Mock Spanish is used to turn Arnold Schwarzenegger, playing a cyborg, into a "real person," a sympathetic hero instead of a ruthless and terrifying machine. When Schwarzenegger, who has just returned from the future, answers a request with a curt Germanic "Affirmative," the young hero of the film, a 12-year-old White boy supposedly raised on the streets of Los Angeles, tells him, "No no no no no. You gotta listen to the way people talk!" He then proceeds to teach Schwarzenegger the Mock Spanish tags "No problemo" and "Hasta la vista, baby" as part of a register that also includes insults like "Dickwad."[12]

Analysis reveals that Mock Spanish projects, in addition to the directly indexed message that the speaker possesses a "congenial persona," another set of messages: profoundly racist images of members of historically Spanish-speaking populations. These messages are the product of what Ochs (1990) calls "indirect indexicality" in that, unlike the positive direct indexes, they are never acknowledged by speakers. In my experience, Whites almost always deny that Mock Spanish could be in any way racist. Yet in order to "make sense of" Mock Spanish, interlocutors require access to very negative racializing representations of Chicanos and Latinos as stupid, politically corrupt, sexually loose, lazy, dirty, and disorderly. It is impossible to "get" Mock Spanish – to find these expressions funny or colloquial or even intelligible – unless one has access to these negative images. An exemplary case is a political cartoon in my collection, showing a picture of Ross Perot pointing to a chart that says, among other things, "Perot for El Presidente." This is funny only if the audience can juxtapose the pompous and absurd Perot with the negative image of a banana-republic dictator, dripping with undeserved medals. It is only possible to "get" "Hasta la vista, baby" if one has access to a representation of Spanish speakers as treacherous. "Mañana" works as a humorous substitute for "later" only in conjunction with an image of Spanish speakers as lazy and procrastinating. My claim that Mock Spanish has a racializing function is supported by the fact that on humorous greeting cards (where it is fairly common) it is often accompanied by grossly racist pictorial representations of "Mexicans."

I have labeled Mock Spanish a "covert racist discourse" because it accomplishes racialization of its subordinate-group targets through indirect indexicality, messages that must be available for comprehension but are never acknowledged by speakers. In this it contrasts with "vulgar racist discourse," which uses the direct referential function in statements like, "Mexicans just don't know how to work," or hate speech ("Lazy greaser!"), which seems to operate through the performative function as a direct verbal "assault" (Matsuda et al. 1993). It is not exactly like the kind of kidding around that most Whites will admit can be interpreted as racist, as when David Letterman joked that the artificial fat olestra, which can cause abdominal pain and diarrhea, was "endorsed by the Mexican Health Department" (*New York Times*, August 24, 1997: F12). It also contrasts with the "elite racist discourse" identified by van Dijk (1993). Van Dijk pointed out that like Mock Spanish this type has as one function the presentation by the speaker of a desirable persona. Since "being a racist" is an undesirable quality, tokens often begin with qualifications like "I'm not a racist, but ... " and then continue with a racializing argument like "I really resent it that all these Mexicans come up here to have babies so that American taxpayers will support them." Such qualifications do not make sense with Mock Spanish: One cannot say, "I'm not a racist, but no problemo," or "I'm not a racist, but comprende?," or "I'm not a racist, but adios, sucker." The reason this frame does not work is because Mock Spanish racializes its objects only covertly, through indirect indexicality.

Mock Spanish sometimes is used to constitute hate speech (as in posters saying "Adios, Jose" held by demonstrators supporting anti-immigration laws in California), and co-occurs with racist joking and with vulgar and elite racist discourses as well. It is sometimes used to address apparent Spanish speakers; many of my consultants report being addressed as "amigo," and Vélez-Ibáñez (1996: 86) reports an offensive use of "comprende?" (pronounced [kəmprɛndiy]). However, it is found very widely in everyday talk and text on topics that have nothing to do with race at all. Because of its covert and indirect properties, Mock Spanish may be an exceptionally powerful site for the reproduction of White racist attitudes. In order to be "one of the group" among other Whites, collusion in the production of Mock Spanish is frequently unavoidable.

In my previous work, reviewed above, I have assumed that the "elevation of whiteness" and the constitution of a valued White persona was accomplished in Mock Spanish entirely through direct indexicality. However, in the light of Urciuoli's new work on the imposition of "order" on Puerto Ricans, I now believe that Mock Spanish accomplishes the "elevation of whiteness" in two ways: first, through directly indexing valuable and congenial personal qualities of speakers, but, importantly, also by the same type of indirect indexicality that is the source of its negative and racializing messages. It is through indirect indexicality that using Mock Spanish constructs "White public space," an arena in which linguistic disorder on the part of Whites is rendered invisible and normative, while the linguistic behavior of members of historically Spanish-speaking populations is highly visible and the object of constant monitoring.

Research on "whiteness" (e.g., Frankenberg 1993) has shown that Whites practice not only the construction of the domain of "color" and the exclusion from resources of those racialized as "colored," but also the constitution of "whiteness" as an invisible and unmarked "norm."[13] Like all such norms, this one is built as bricolage, from the bits and pieces of history, but in a special way, as what Williams (1989), borrowing from Gramsci, calls a "transformist hegemony": "its construction results in a national process aimed at homogenizing heterogeneity fashioned around assimilating elements of heterogeneity through appropriations that devalue and deny their link to the marginalized others' contribution to the patrimony" (Williams 1989: 435).[14]

Bits and pieces of language are important "elements of heterogeneity" in this work. Urciuoli (1996) has shown that precisely this kind of "heterogeneity" is not permitted to Puerto Ricans. What I have tried to show above is that linguistic heterogeneity and even explicit "disorder" is not only permitted to Whites, it is an essential element of a desirable White public persona. To be White is to collude in these practices, or to risk censure as "having no sense of humor" or being "politically correct." But White practice is invisible to the monitoring of linguistic disorder. It is not understood by Whites as disorder – after all, they are not, literally, "speaking Spanish" (and indeed the phenomena of public ungrammaticality, orthographical absurdity, and parodic mispronunciations of Spanish are evidence that they go to some lengths to distance themselves from such an interpretation of their behavior [Hill 1993a]). Instead, they are simply being "natural": funny, relaxed, coloquial, authentic.

I have collected some evidence that members of historically Spanish-speaking populations do not share Whites' understanding of Mock Spanish. For instance, the sociologist Clara Rodríguez (1997: 78) reports that she was "puzzled ... with regard to [the] relevance" of the Mock Spanish in *Terminator 2: Judgment Day.* Literate Spanish speakers in the United States are often committed linguistic purists, and Mock Spanish is offensive to them because it contains so many grammatical errors and because it sometimes uses rude words. They focus on this concern, but of course they have little power to change White usage.[15] It is clear that many Spanish speakers do hear the racist message of Mock Spanish. In an interview,[16] a Spanish-speaking Chicano high school counselor in Tucson said, "You know, I've noticed that most of the teachers never use any Spanish around here unless it's something negative." A Spanish-speaking Chicano businesswoman said, "When you first hear that stuff, you think, that's nice, they're trying, but then you hear more and more and you realize that there's something nasty underneath." In lecturing on Mock Spanish, I have found that Chicano and Latino people in my audiences strongly concur with the main outlines of my analysis, and often bring me additional examples. Chicano scholars, especially Fernando Peñalosa (cf. 1980), have long pointed out the racist implications of disorderly Spanish usage by Whites. Thus, for thoughtful Spanish speakers, the fact that disorderly Spanish and "Mock Spanish" constitute a "White public space" is not news. One of the dimensions of this space is that disorder on the part of Whites (including not only Mock Spanish, but also cursing and a variety of locutionary sins of the "you know" type) is largely invisible, while disorder on the part of racialized populations is hypervisible to the point of being the object of expensive political campaigns and nationwide "moral panics."

More Sources for Homogeneous Heterogeneity

The "incorporation"[17] of linguistic elements into the linguistic "homogeneous heterogeneity" of White public space draws on many sources. Perhaps the most important is what Smitherman (1994) calls the "crossover" of forms from African American English (AAE).[18] Gubar (1997) builds on the work of Morrison (1992) and others in a richly detailed study of very widespread and pervasive incorporative processes in the usage of White artists and writers. However, AAE and White English are so thoroughly entangled in the United States that crossover is extremely difficult to study. While obvious "wiggerisms" like "Word to your Mother"[19] or moth-eaten tokens of minstrelsy like "Sho' nuff, Mistah Bones" are easy to spot, many other usages are curiously indeterminate.[20] Even where an AAE source is recognizable to an etymologist, it is often impossible to know whether the usage indexes any "blackness" to its user or audience. One way of understanding this indeterminacy might be to see it as a triumph of White racial practice. New tokens of White "hipness," often retrievable as Black in origin only by the most dogged scholarship (although often visible to Blacks), are constantly created out of AAE materials.

An example of indeterminate crossover appeared in the "For Better or for Worse" comic strip published in the *Arizona Daily Star* (August 22, 1997). Two White Canadian lads discuss how Lawrence should deal with his partner's departure to study music in Paris. Bobby, who is straight, tries to reassure Lawrence, who is gay,[21] that falling in love is always worth it, even knowing the risk of loss. Lawrence jokes, "Let it be known that this speech comes from a guy who's in a 'happening' relationship." "Happening" in this sense comes from AAE "happenin," but it seems unlikely that here it is intended to convey anything more than the strip creator's alertness to "the speech of today's young people" (although the quotation marks around the form do suggest that she regards this register as not part of her own repertoire). Yet similar usages can be highly salient for Blacks: Lippi-Green (1997: 196) quotes an audience member on an episode of Oprah Winfrey: "This is a fact. White America use black dialect on commercials every day. Be observant, people. Don't let nobody tell you that you are ignorant and that you don't speak right. Be observant. They started off Channel 7 Eyewitness news a few years ago with one word: whashappenin. So what's happening, America?"

Now, contrast the episode of "For Better or for Worse" described above with another episode, published a couple of years ago. Here the young people are on a ski slope, and one boy, Gordon, "hits on" (I am sure Smitherman [1994] is correct that this is AAE, but in my own usage it feels merely slangy) a pretty girl with our now-familiar token, "What's happening?" She "puts him down" (probably also AAE, but not in Smitherman 1994)[22] with "With you? Nada." While probably few White readers of this strip sense "blackness" in "What's happening?", most will immediately detect "Nada" as "Spanish." That is, while the "Black" indexicality of "What's happening" is easily suppressed, it is virtually impossible to suppress the "Spanish" indexicality of "Nada," which has in "Mock Spanish" the semantically pejorated sense "absolutely nothing, less than zero." It seems likely that there are tokens that originate in Mock Spanish where the original indexicality is suppressable (the word *peon*, pronounced [piyan], which appeared in English by the seventeenth century, may be an example of this type), but in general tokens of this practice are relatively easy to spot and interpret.

Because of this relative transparency of Mock Spanish, it is a good choice for linguistic-anthropological research. However, precisely because it is narrower in its range of opacity and transparency than is AAE "crossover," it must function somewhat differently in White public space, an issue that needs investigation. Furthermore, African Americans themselves apparently use Mock Spanish; Terry McMillan's 1996 novel, *How Stella Got Her Groove Back*, is rich in attestations in the speech of Stella, a beautiful and successful African American professional woman from California. In contrast, as far as I know no members of historically Spanish-speaking populations use Mock Spanish, at least not in anything like the routine way that Whites do.[23]

The same question, of differential functions of such linguistic incorporations into White "homogeneous heterogeneity," occurs with borrowings from other languages. For instance, tokens of "Mock French" like "Mercy buckets" and "bow-koo" do occur, but they are relatively rare, especially in comparison with the very extensive use of French in advertising, especially in the fashion industry, to convey luxury and exclusivity. "Mock Italian" seems to have been relatively important in the 1940s and 1950s but is apparently on the way out; I have found very few examples of it. "Mock Yiddish" is common but is used by members of historically Yiddish-speaking groups as well as by outsiders. "Mock Japanese" "sayonara" is perfectly parallel to Mock Spanish "adios," but may be the only widely used token of this type.[24] In summary, "Mock" forms vary widely in relative productivity and in the kinds of contexts in which they appear. By far the richest examples of linguistic incorporations are Mock Spanish and AAE crossover.

Can Mock Forms Subvert the Order of Racial Practices?

A number of authors, including Hewitt (1986), Gubar (1997) and Butler (1997), have argued that usages that in some contexts are grossly racist seem to contain an important parodic potential that can be turned to the antiracist deconstruction of racist categorical essentializing.

Hewitt studied Black–White friendships among young teenagers in south London and found a "productive dialogue of youth" (1986: 99) in which he identifies antiracist potential. Especially notable were occasions where Black children would tease White friends as "nigger," and the White teens would reply with "honky" or "snowflake." Hewitt comments, "This practice ... turns racism into a kind of effigy, to be burned up in an interactive ritual which seeks to acknowledge and deal with its undeniable presence whilst acting out the negation of its effects" (1986: 238). Gubar (1997) suggests that posters by the artist Iké Udé (such as a famous image of Marilyn Monroe, but in "blackface," and a transformation of Robert Mapplethorpe's infamous "Man in a Polyester Suit" with white skin and a circumcised penis) may use the symbolic repertoire of racism as "a crucial aesthetic means of comprehending racial distinction without entrenching or denying it" (Gubar 1997: 256). An example in the case of Spanish might be the performance art of Guillermo Gómez Peña,[25] who creates frenzied mixtures of English and multiple registers and dialects of Spanish (and even Nahuatl). Butler (1997), writing in opposition to the proscription of racist vocabulary by anti-hate speech legislation, argues that gays and lesbians have been able to subvert the power of "queer," and that other "hate words" may have similar potential. The kinds of games reported by Hewitt, however, remain reserved to childhood, unable to break through the dominant voices of racism; Hewitt found that the kind of interracial friendship that permitted teasing with racist epithets essentially vanished from the lives of his subjects by the time they reached the age of 16. In the light of the analysis that I have suggested above, the "subversions" noted by Gubar and Butler can also be seen simply as one more example of "orderly" disorder that is reserved to elites in White public space, rather than as carnivalesque inversions. Or, perhaps we should say that carnivalesque inversions can be a "weapon of the strong" as well as a "weapon of the weak."[26] The art of a Gómez Peña, to the degree that it is acceptable to White audiences, may precisely "whiten" this performer and others like him.

An important possible exception is the phenomenon of "crossing," discussed by British sociolinguist Ben Rampton (1995), who reports extensive use of out-group linguistic tokens among British adolescents of a variety of ethnic origins, including strongly racialized populations like West Indians and South Asians as well as Whites. "Crossings," while they retain some potential to give offense, often seem simply to acknowledge what is useful and desirable in the space of urban diversity. Thus, working-class White girls learn the Panjabi lyrics to "bhangra" songs, and Bengali kids speak Jamaican creole (which seems to have emerged in general as a prestigious language among British youth, parallel to the transracial "hip-hop" phenomenon in the United States). Early reports by Shirley Brice Heath of new work with American adolescents has identified similar "crossing" phenomena.[27] However, only slightly more than a decade ago Hewitt (1986) found that such crossings did not survive the adolescent years. We cannot be sure that these phenomena are genuinely outside the linguistic order of racism until we understand dimensions of that order – within which age-graded cohorts may have a relatively enduring place. I have tried above to show how linguistic-anthropological attention to the history, forms, and uses of White language mixing can help us toward such an understanding.

NOTES

I would especially like to thank María Rodríguez, Bambi Schieffelin, and Kathryn Woolard, who have provided me with valuable material on Mock Spanish.

1 Hall et al. (1978) borrow the notion of "moral panic" from Cohen (1972).

2 In a survey of 34 entries, encompassing about 100 messages, under the heading "Ebonics" on Linguist, the list that probably reaches the largest number of linguists, I found only one explicit mention of "racism" by an author who used the expression "institutional racism." It is, perhaps, appropriate for linguists to focus on their special areas of scholarly

expertise, and it is certainly the case that there may be a linguistic dimension to the educational problems confronted by many African American children, but the neglect of racism on the list was quite striking. It was sometimes addressed obliquely and euphemistically, as with one author's proposal of the "special" situation of African Americans in the United States.

3 The "all languages are equal" argument continues in spite of a warning by Dell Hymes (1973) that this claim is technically incorrect in many subtle ways.

4 Hirschfeld (1996) documents the very early association between raced categories and an essentialized understanding of "human kinds" for young children in the United States.

5 I am mindful of Hartigan's (1997) argument that "Whites" are by no means a homogeneous population. Indeed, in other work (Hill 1995) I have suggested that working-class speakers are less likely to use "Mock Spanish" than are other Whites. Much of my material comes from mass media that are part of the homogenizing project of "whiteness," and there is no question that different "Whites" experience this project in different ways. I use "Whites" here (perhaps injudiciously) as a sort of shorthand required first by lack of space and second because the data required to precisely characterize the population I have in mind are not available. Certainly it includes White elites such as screenwriters and nationally syndicated columnists.

6 Urciuoli (1996: 16) points out that it is essential to use Spanish in the folklife festival context because to translate songs, the names of foods, and the like into English would render them less "authentic," this property being essential to claims on "ethnicity" that are one way to resist racialization.

7 Here the canonical study is the matched-guise test conducted by Rubin (1992). Sixty-two undergraduate native speakers of English listened to a brief lecture (on either a science or humanities topic) recorded by a native speaker of English from central Ohio. While they listened, one group of students saw a slide of a White woman lecturer. The other half saw a slide of an Asian woman in the same setting and pose (and even of the same size, and with the same hair style, as the White woman). Students who heard the lecture under the "Asian slide" condition often reported that the lecturer had an Asian accent and, even more interestingly, scored lower on tests of comprehension of the lecture.

8 It should be *Lavarse las manos*, the usual directive for public places being the infinitive (e.g., *No fumar* "No Smoking," *No estacionarse* "No Parking"), the verb being reflexive, and body parts are not labeled by the possessive pronoun *su* unless they are detached from the body of their owner.

9 In earlier publications (e.g., Hill 1993b), I referred to these practices as "Junk Spanish." I think James Fernandez for the expression "Mock Spanish" and for convincing me that "Junk Spanish" was a bad nomenclatural idea, and the source of some of the problems I was having getting people to understand what I was working on (many people, including linguists and anthropologists, assumed that by "Junk Spanish" I meant something like the "Border Spanish" of native speakers of Spanish, rather than jocular and parodic uses of Spanish by English speakers). The most extensive discussion of Mock Spanish available is Hill (1995).

10 I am indebted to Professor Raúl Fernández of the University of California-Irvine for a copy of a letter he wrote to the *Los Angeles Times* protesting the appearance of *cojones* in a film review. Ernest Hemingway is probably to blame for the widespread knowledge of this word among monolingual speakers of English.

11 While some Whites who use Mock Spanish have a classroom competence in that language (I was a case in point), most of the speakers I have queried say that they do not "speak Spanish."

12 An anonymous referee for the *American Anthropologist* argues that this analysis,

suggesting that the "elevation of whiteness" is accomplished through direct indexicality, is not exactly correct. Instead, the direct indexicality of Mock Spanish elevates the individual, conveying "I am a nice/easy-going/funny/locally-rooted/cosmopolitan person." The elevation of "whiteness" is then accomplished indirectly when combined with the indirectly indexed message "I am White." This is an interesting suggestion, but I think the *Terminator 2: Judgment Day* sequence argues that the indexicality is direct: Mock Spanish is precisely "the way people talk" – and "people" can only be that group that is unmarked and thereby "White." Thus positive individual qualities and "whiteness" are simultaneously indexed. (A direct version of this, perhaps mercifully obsolete, is the expression that applauds some act of good fellowship with "That's mighty White of you.")

13 As Harrison (1995) points out, a more explicit construction of whiteness often appears among marginalized Whites, as in the current far-right "White pride" movement. She notes that this "undermines whatever incipient class consciousness exists among poor Whites" (Harrison 1995: 63). Thus we can see such movements as part of the very large cultural formation wherein "race" may be the single most important organizer of relationships, determinant of identity, and mediator of meaning (Winant 1994).

14 Williams focuses her analysis on the "national process," the creation of what she calls the race/ class/nation conflation, but the construction of whiteness is probably a project of global scope, and in fact Mock Spanish seems to be widespread in the English-speaking world. Bertie, a character in the Barrytown novels (*The Commitments, The Snapper, The Van*, which depict life in working-class Dublin) by the Irish author Roddy Doyle, often uses Mock Spanish. For another example from outside the United States, I am indebted to Dick Bauman for a headline from the gardening section of a Glasgow newspaper, inviting the reader to "Hosta la vista, baby!" (that is, to plant members of the genus *Hosta* for their decorative foliage).

15 I have discovered only one case of apparent concern about Spanish-speaking opinion in reference to the use of Spanish in mass media. Chon Noriega (1997: 88) reports that when the film *Giant* was presented for review to the Production Code Administration in 1955, Geoffrey Shurlock, the head of the PCA, requested that the ungrammatical Spanish in the film (in which Spanish appears without subtitles) be corrected, apparently for fear of offending the government of Mexico, then seen as a "good neighbor."

16 Dan Goldstein and I have begun a project of interviewing members of historically Spanish-speaking populations about Mock Spanish. We have compiled a scrapbook of examples, and subjects are audiotaped as they leaf through these and comment on them.

17 I borrow this term from Raymond Williams (1977).

18 I do not include "Vernacular" (many scholars refer to "African American Vernacular English" or AAVE), because AAE has a full range of register ranging from street argot through middle-class conversational usage to formal oratory and *belles lettres*. Scholars like Smitherman (1988) and Morgan (1994) have criticized sociolinguists for typifying AAE only through attestations of street registers.

19 Smitherman (1994: 237) defines *wigger* as "literally, a white NIGGER, an emerging positive term for White youth who identify with HIP HOP, RAP, and other aspects of African American Culture." She gives the proper form of the affirmation as "Word to the Mother," but I first heard it (from a young White woman) in the form given.

20 In the lexicon of AAE provided by Smitherman (1994) I recognized many forms in my own usage that she does not mark as "crossovers" (to give only one example, "beauty shop" for a hair-and-nails salon was the only term I knew for such establishments as I was growing up,

and it was universally used by my grandmothers, aunts, and mother, all White ladies who would never have dreamed of essaying any "Dis and Dat" [Gubar's (1997) term for the adoption of AAE forms by White writers]). My grandfather, an egregious racist who grew up in southeastern Missouri, was very fond of "copacetic," which Smitherman attributes to the speech of "older blacks" and does not recognize as ever having "crossed over."

21 A number of US newspapers refused to publish the series of episodes in which Lawrence mourns his partner's departure.

22 The *American Heritage Dictionary of the English Language* (Third Edition) lists "put down" as "slang." Unsurprisingly, their sentence of attestation comes from the work of Dr. Alvin Poussaint, an African American.

23 Some Spanish speakers find some of the greeting cards in my sample funny. One woman said that she might send a "Moochos Smoochos" card (illustrating hyperanglicized parody and the use of Spanish morphology to be funny) to her husband; she said, "That one's kinda cute."

24 "Honcho," from Japanese *han* "Squad" and *chō* "chief" (*American Heritage Dictionary of the English Language*, Third Edition) seems to be etymologically inaccessible as Japanese except to specialists; many Whites probably think that it is Spanish.

25 See, for instance, his *Warrior for Gringostroika* (1993). However, Gómez Peña uses so much Spanish that one must be bilingual to understand him; his art seems to me to be addressed mainly to multilingual Spanish-speaking audiences. Woolard's (1988) study of a comic in 1970s Barcelona, who entertained audiences with jokes that code switched between Castilian and Catalan during a period of extreme linguistic conflict and purism, provides another example of this type of subversion.

26 "Weapon of the weak" comes, of course, from Scott (1985). Work on discourses of resistance by scholars like Scott (see also 1990) and Bhabha (1994) often seems to imply that parody and humor are primarily strategies of resistance. However, it is obvious that humor is an important part of racist discourse, and the accusation that antiracists "have no sense of humor" is an important weapon of racists.

27 In a colloquium presented to the Department of Anthropology, University of Arizona, Tucson, January 27, 1997.

REFERENCES

Appadurai, Arjun (1990). Disjuncture and Difference in the Global Cultural Economy. *Public Culture* 2: 1–24.

Bhabha, Homi K. (1994). *The Location of Culture*. New York: Routledge.

Boas, Franz ([1889] 1982). On Alternating Sounds. In *The Shaping of American Anthropology, 1883–1911: A Franz Boas Reader*, George W. Stocking (ed.), pp. 72–6. Chicago, IL: University of Chicago Press.

Butler, Judith (1997). *Excitable Speech*. New York: Routledge.

Cmiel, Kenneth (1990). *Democratic Eloquence*. New York: William Morrow.

Cohen, Stan (1972). *Folk Devils and Moral Panics: The Creation of the Mods and the Rockers*. London: MacGibbon and Kee.

Fabian, Johannes (1986). *Language and Colonial Power: The Appropriation of Swahili in the Former Belgian Congo, 1880–1938*. Cambridge: Cambridge University Press.

Frankenberg, Ruth (1993). *White Women, Race Matters: The Social Construction of Whiteness*. Minneapolis: University of Minnesota Press.

Gibbs, Nancy (1996). An American Voice. *Time* 149(1): 32–3.

Gómez Peña, Guillermo (1993). *Warrior for Gringostroika*. St. Paul, MN: Graywolf Press.

Gubar, Susan (1997). *Racechanges: White Skins, Black Face in American Culture*. Oxford: Oxford University Press.

Hall, Stuart, Chas Critcher, Tony Jefferson, John Clarke, and Brian Roberts (1978). *Policing the Crisis*. London: The Macmillan Press Ltd.

Harrison, Faye V. (1995). The Persistent Power of "Race" in the Cultural and Political Economy of Racism. *Annual Review of Anthropology* 24: 47–74.

Hartigan, John, Jr. (1997). Establishing the Fact of Whiteness. *American Anthropologist* 99: 495–505.

Hewitt, Roger (1986). *White Talk Black Talk: Inter-Racial Friendship and Communication among Adolescents*. Cambridge: Cambridge University Press.

Hill, Jane H. (1993a). Hasta La Vista, Baby: Anglo Spanish in the American Southwest. *Critique of Anthropology* 13: 145–76.

Hill, Jane H. (1993b). Is It Really "No Problemo"? In *SALSA I: Proceedings of the First Annual Symposium about Language and Society – Austin*, Robin Queen and Rusty Barrett (eds.), *Texas Linguistic Forum* 33: 1–12.

Hill, Jane H. (1995). *Mock Spanish: A Site for the Indexical Reproduction of Racism in American English*. Electronic document. University of Chicago Lang-cult Site. http://www.cs.uchicago.edu/ discussions/l-c.

Hirschfeld, Lawrence A. (1996). *Race in the Making*. Cambridge, MA: MIT Press/Bradford Books.

Hymes, Dell H. (1973). Language and Speech: On the Origins and Foundations of Inequality among Speakers. In *Language as a Human Problem*, Einar Haugen and Morton Bloomfield (eds.), pp. 45–72. New York: W. W. Norton and Co.

Kulick, Don (1993). *Language Shift and Cultural Reproduction*. Cambridge: Cambridge University Press.

Labov, William (1972). *Language in the Inner City*. Philadelphia: University of Pennsylvania Press.

Lippi-Green, Rosina (1997). *English with an Accent: Language, Ideology, and Discrimination in the United States*. London: Routledge.

Matsuda, Mari J., Charles R. Lawrence III, Richard Delgado, and Kimberlé Williams Crenshaw (eds.) (1993). *Words that Wound: Critical Race Theory, Assaultive Speech, and the First Amendment*. Boulder, CO: Westview Press.

McMillan, Terry (1996). *How Stella Got Her Groove Back*. New York: Viking.

Morgan, Marcyliena (1994). The African-American Speech Community: Reality and Sociolinguists. In *Language and the Social Construction of Identity in Creole Situations*, Marcyliena Morgan (ed.), pp. 121–50. Los Angeles: UCLA Center for Afro-American Studies.

Morrison, Toni (1992). *Playing in the Dark: Whiteness and the Literary Imagination*. Cambridge, MA: Harvard University Press.

Noriega, Chon (1997). Citizen Chicano: The Trials and Titillations of Ethnicity in the American Cinema, 1935–1962. In *Latin Looks*, Clara E. Rodríguez (ed.), pp. 85–103. Boulder, CO: Westview.

Ochs, Elinor (1990). Indexicality and Socialization. In *Cultural Psychology*, James Stigler, Richard A. Shweder, and Gilbert Herdt (eds.), pp. 287–308. Cambridge: Cambridge University Press.

Omi, Michael, and Howard Winant (1994). *Racial Formation in the United States* (2nd edn.). New York: Routledge.

Page, Helán E., and Brooke Thomas (1994). White Public Space and the Construction of White Privilege in U.S. Health Care: Fresh Concepts and a New Model of Analysis. *Medical Anthropology Quarterly* 8: 109–16.

Peñalosa, Fernando (1980). *Chicano Sociolinguistics*. Rowley, MA: Newbury House Press.

Rampton, Ben (1995). *Crossing: Language and Ethnicity among Adolescents*. London: Longman.

Rodríguez, Clara E. (1997). The Silver Screen: Stories and Stereotypes. In *Latin Looks*, Clara E. Rodríguez (ed.), pp. 73–9. Boulder, CO: Westview Press.

Rubin, D. L. (1992). Nonlanguage Factors Affecting Undergraduates' Judgments of Nonnative English-Speaking Teaching Assistants. *Research in Higher Education* 33: 511–31.

Scott, James C. (1985). *Weapons of the Weak: Everyday Forms of Peasant Resistance*. New Haven, CT: Yale University Press.

Scott, James C. (1990). *Domination and the Arts of Resistance: Hidden Transcripts*. New Haven, CT: Yale University Press.

Silverstein, Michael (1987). *Monoglot "Standard" in America*. Working Papers of the Center for Psychosocial Studies, 13. Chicago, IL: Center for Psychosocial Studies.

Smedley, Audrey (1993). *Race in North America: Origin and Evolution of a Worldview*. Boulder, CO: Westview Press.

Smitherman, Geneva (1994). *Black Talk: Words and Phrases from the Hood to the Amen Corner*. Boston: Houghton Mifflin Company.

Smitherman-Donaldson, Geneva (1988). Discriminatory Discourse on Afro-American Speech. In *Discourse and Discrimination*, Geneva Smitherman-Donaldson and Teun van Dijk (eds.), pp. 144–75. Detroit: Wayne State University Press.

Urban, Greg (1991). *A Discourse-Centered Approach to Culture*. Austin: University of Texas Press.

Urciuoli, Bonnie (1996). *Exposing Prejudice: Puerto Rican Experiences of Language, Race, and Class*. Boulder, CO: Westview Press.

Van Dijk, Teun A. (1993). *Elite Discourse and Racism*. Newbury Park, CA: Sage Publications.

Vélez-Ibáñez, Carlos G. (1996). *Border Visions: Mexican Cultures of the Southwest United States*. Tucson: University of Arizona Press.

Williams, Brackette (1989). A Class Act: Anthropology and the Race to Nation across Ethnic Terrain. *Annual Review of Anthropology* 18: 401–44.

Williams, Raymond (1977). *Marxism and Literature*. Oxford: Oxford University Press.

Winant, Howard (1994). *Racial Conditions: Politics, Theory, Comparisons*. Minneapolis: University of Minnesota Press.

Woolard, Kathryn A. (1988). Codeswitching and Comedy in Catalonia. In *Codeswitching: Anthropological and Sociolinguistic Perspectives*, Monica Heller (ed.), pp. 53–70. Berlin: Mouton de Gruyter.

Woolard, Kathryn A. (1989). Sentences in the Language Prison. *American Ethnologist* 16: 268–78.

Woolard, Kathryn A., and Bambi Schieffelin (1994). Language Ideology. *Annual Review of Anthropology* 23: 55–82.

STUDY QUESTIONS

1 In which ways is this chapter intended to be a study about and against racial stereotyping?
2 What are the attributes of "Mock Spanish" and why does Hill consider it an example of racist discourse?
3 What does Hill mean by "white linguistic normalcy" and "white public sphere"? How does she use these concepts to explain the differentiated meaning of language choice among whites and members of linguistic minority groups?
4 What are some other examples of ethnic stereotyping accomplished through the use of language that you are familiar with? Could you apply Hill's method of analysis to them?
5 Elaborate on the relationship between the themes of this chapter and the themes found in the chapter by Ochs and Taylor or the chapter by Irvine and Gal.

21

No

Don Kulick

Performativity as a theory is most closely associated with the American philosopher Judith Butler, who in a number of well-known books has developed what she calls a performative approach to language and culture. The cornerstone of this approach is of course J. L. Austin's concept of the performative, which is concerned with language as action, language that in its enunciation changes the world – it brings about a new social state. The archetypal performatives with which Austin begins his discussion are utterances like 'I bet' or 'I promise', [which are contrasted with utterances like "it's raining," which Austin calls "constatives"] However, by the conclusion of *How to Do Things with Words*, Austin has collapsed the distinction between performatives and constatives that he established at the beginning, and he declares that even constative utterances are in fact performatives: "there can hardly be any longer a possibility of not seeing that stating is performing an act," he wrote (Austin 1997: 139).

This collapse of the distinction between performative and constative was the dimension of Austin's theory that Butler developed in her work. Focusing on gender, Butler claimed that utterances like the "It's a girl" delivered by a doctor to a mother who has just given birth are not merely descriptive. Like the priest's "I now pronounce you man and wife," an utterance like "It's a girl" performs an act. It *does something* in Butler's analysis. That act of naming "initiates the process by which a certain girling is compelled," she wrote (Butler 1993: 232). It requires that the referent so designated act in accordance with particular norms and create, in doing so, the appropriate gender in every culturally legible act that the person so designated performs, from sitting in a chair, to expressing her desire, to deciding what she ought to eat for dinner.

The relevant part of this story for the argument I will develop here is what happened next. After the publication of Butler's 1990 book *Gender Trouble*, performativity suddenly became all the rage. It entered the lexicon of literary studies, history, sociology and anthropology, and it even merits a separate entry in Alessandro Duranti's recent collection *Key terms in language and culture* (Hall 2001). Now for sociolinguists and linguistic anthropologists, this might appear somewhat odd, because while "performativity" was busy

For permission to publish copyright material in this book, grateful acknowledgment is made to: D. Kulick (2003), "No," *Language and Communication* 1: 139–51.

hypercirculating in other disciplines, another, older, term that seemingly referred to precisely the same thing – or at least it sounded pretty similar – already existed. That term was "performance."

But performance is not the same as performativity. The difference is this: performance is something a subject does. Performativity, on the other hand, is the process through which the subject emerges (Butler 1993: 2, 7, 95). This is a crucial distinction that was completely missed by many critics of Butler's work. Early rejections of her framework were based on a reading of performativity as performance; on the idea of an entirely self-aware and volitional actor who could choose to put on or take off genders the way people put on or take off clothes (see e.g. Weston 1993). This is wrong. Performance is one dimension of performativity. But performativity theory insists that what is expressed or performed in any social context is importantly linked to that which is not expressed or cannot be performed. Hence, analysis of action and identity must take into account what is not or cannot be enacted. Furthermore, a performative approach to language interrogates the circulation of language in society – not so much who is authorized to use language (which was Austin's concern, as it was a major concern of Pierre Bourdieu, e.g. Bourdieu, 1991), as how particular uses of language, be they authorized or not, produce particular effects and particular kinds of subjects in fields or matrices of power.

Performativity is not a linguistic concept – Austin was not a linguist, he was a philosopher, as is Butler – and this may be one reason why there are really very few linguistic studies that might be said to be performative.[1] There are lots of studies of performance, but few of performativity. The difference between the two perspectives is something I hope to illustrate in this paper. I propose to do this through an examination of the linguistic token of rejection or refusal, the word "no." My interest is in how the enunciation (or not) of "no" in particular social situations works to produce those situations as sexual, even as it materializes particular subjects as sexual subjects. I am also interested in how the enunciation of "no" is structured by certain absences, certain other enunciations that cannot or must not be expressed. I will illustrate my arguments by discussing the occurrence of "no" in three seemingly very different contexts, which I will link. The three situations I will discuss are situations of (1) sexual harassment and rape, (2) instances where the so-called Homosexual Panic Defense, which I will explain shortly, is invoked, and, finally, (3) sadomasochistic sex.

Sexual Harassment and Rape

The foremost context for the analysis of "no" in sexual situations is research that examines the language of sexual harassment and rape. This important research focuses on the fact that a woman's "no" is constrained by cultural expectations and demands of femininity (Ehrlich 1998, 2001; Lees 1996; Kitzinger and Frith 1999; Matoesian 1993; McConnell-Ginet 1989). The strongest articulation of this position is the assertion that a woman's refusal of sex simply cannot be heard in patriarchal culture (MacKinnon 1993). In a culture that relentlessly objectifies and sexualizes women, the illocutionary force of a woman's "no" to sex is consistently thwarted and distorted to mean "keep trying," or even its inversion, "yes." Hence, men can claim that they misunderstood women's refusal, and women who are raped can be blamed for not having conveyed their refusal clearly enough. This is particularly the case when there is no physical evidence, such as bruises or broken bones, that the woman refused the man's advances.

Phrased in terms of performativity theory, what linguistic analyses of sexual harassment and rape trials demonstrate is that the subject position "woman" is produced in part by the normatively exhorted utterance "no" when encountering male desire for sex. This differs from the subject "man," who, in contrast, is normatively exhorted to *never* say "no" when confronted with female desire. Indeed, for a male to say "no" to female desire for sex would threaten to signify him as a homosexual. In order to block this signification, extenuating circumstances need to be asserted, such as extreme physical unattractiveness in the female. All of this configures a cultural grammar in which saying "no" is part of what produces a female sexual subject, and *not* saying "no" produces a male sexual subject.[2] "No" in both its present and absent manifestations facilitates the production of heterosexual subjectivities and heterosexual sexuality. Its utterance invokes a domain in which one interactant can performatively produce himself as a man by responding to it by prolonging the encounter and ideally finally transforming it into a 'yes', and the other interactant can performatively produce herself as female by facilitating – willingly or not – that extension and prolongation of the sexual scene.

Any performative approach to language will ask: where does a particular signifying system run up against its own limits? One place "no" meets its limits is when a woman does not utter it, and says "yes" without persuasion. Now, while Conversation Analysts have shown us that a "yes" is an interactionally preferred response,[3] as a woman's response to a sexual advance, it is culturally a *dispreferred* one. Accordingly, the sexual subjects produced through "yes" are *marked* in the linguistic, Jakobsonian sense; they are not just women; there are many other names for them, most of them pejorative. A "yes" to sex can also produce female subjects as being outside heteronormativity, when that "yes" occurs as a response to the advances of a woman (who, of course, is also marked in this discursive system). As an aside, I can also note that women who say "yes" to sex are also marked in our academic texts, in this case through their virtual absence – we have several excellent studies on how women say "no" to sex, but little information on how they say "yes." One paper we do have, interestingly enough, indicates that many women say "yes" to (hetero) sex precisely by saying "no". This was a questionnaire study done in the late 1980s, which asked 610 female undergraduate students if they had ever said "no" to sex, even though they "had every intention of and were willing to engage in sexual intercourse." It turns out that 68.5 percent of these women reported saying "no" when they meant "maybe", and 39.3 percent reported saying "no" when they meant "yes." When asked why they said "no" when they meant "yes", women answered either that they were afraid of appearing promiscuous, or they felt inhibited about sex, or they wanted to manipulate the male – they were angry with him, they wanted to make him more aroused, or more physically aggressive; see Muehlenhard and Hollabaugh 1988.

The field of sexuality produced by "no" also runs up against its limits when a man says "no" to a woman. As I have already mentioned, this appearance of "no" threatens to signify the subject as marked "gay." But interestingly, this "no," rather than quashing sexuality, also invites its prolongation. Movies like the 1998 *The Opposite of Sex* (in which the main female character plots to seduce her brother's boyfriend, who says "no" to her advances, telling her he is gay) make explicit and exploit this domain of possibility raised by a man's "no" to female desire.

The most striking place where this system of sexual positionings runs up against its own limits is in instances when a man is solicited by another man. The marked subjectivity here is not so much the man doing the pursuing – men are subjects who pursue others sexually, and cultural stereotypes insist that men who pursue other men are the most fully sexed subjects of all (hence the most repellent heterosexual men in the world feel no embarrassment announcing that homosexuality is "OK" with them, as long as the homosexuals don't try to seduce them . . .). In this particular erotic choreography, the marked subjectivity is the man who says "no." Precisely by saying "no," this speaker performatively materializes the position reserved in heteronormative praxis for women. By having to utter "no," the speaker produces a feminine subject; one that importantly does not reject sex so much as facilitate it, by invoking a matrix of persuasion. In other words, the "no" here ensnares and constrains the male speaker in the same bind that it raises for female speakers who produce it. The fact that "no" ensnares both women and men in this way is one reason why analysis should not concentrate, I think, on the *performance* of "no." What is important to interrogate is the way particular iterations of language *performatively* produce particular subject positions; positions which may in fact undermine the performance of a coherent gender identity.

The Homosexual Panic Defense

That "no" is precisely *not* just "no," and that the performative force of "no" facilitates, rather than ends, a sexual scene, is explicitly highlighted in the form of a phenomenon popularly known as the Homosexual Panic Defense. The Homosexual Panic Defense is the name of a legal defense invoked on behalf of men who have murdered other men who they claim made sexual advances towards them. In effect, the Homosexual Panic Defense argues that a sexual advance is in itself an act of aggression, and that the defendant was justified in responding to it with violence.

The Homosexual Panic Defense is based on something called "acute homosexual panic." This is a psychiatric condition that was first proposed in 1920. In its original formulation, "homosexual panic" did not refer to a fear due to advances by other men. Instead, it referred to cases where men who had been in intensively same sex environments became aware of homosexual desires that they felt unable to control, and unable to act on. The original formulation of the disorder was based on diagnosis of a small number of soldiers and sailors in a US government mental hospital after WWI (Kempf, 1920). These men were not violent – they were, on the contrary, passive. The disorder was characterized by periods of introspective brooding, self-punishment, suicidal assaults, withdrawal, and helplessness. So "homosexual panic" was generally understood not as a temporary, violent episode, but, rather as an ongoing illness that comprised severe bouts of depression. Patients suffering from it were catatonic, not violent. Basically, "homosexual panic" was the diagnosis given to men who we today would try to get to "come out" and accept their homosexuality. In fact, some early psychiatrists recognized that the best treatment for the disorder was for the patient to accept his homosexual desires and act on them.

What happened during the course of the 1900s is that the original understanding of this condition shifted, and it came to be applied even to men who reacted violently in situations where homosexual desire was made explicit. In other words, it became used to explain situations where a man allowed himself to be solicited or seduced by another man, but then suddenly turned on that man and beat or even murdered him. In the psychiatric literature, there is no consensus that "homosexual panic" should or can be used to explain sudden violent outbursts like these. But to the extent that the fury is identified as "homosexual panic," the violence is explained by latent homosexual cravings and a challenge to or collapse of a heterosexual self-image.[4]

The Homosexual Panic Defense builds loosely on this later understanding of homosexual panic. It argues that there is a scientific and medical reason for, and, hence, a justification of, the behavior of defendants who murder gay men. The literary scholar Eve Sedgwick (1990: 19) has noted that the very existence of such a category rests on an assumption that hatred of homosexuals is a private and atypical phenomenon. But think about it, she says. To what extent would anyone accept "race panic" as an accountability-reducing illness for a German skinhead who bludgeoned a Turk to death? Or "gender panic" for a woman who shot a man who made an unwanted advance to her? (Consider how many bodies would be swept out of bars and clubs every morning). The fact that the Homosexual Panic Defense exists at all indicates that far from being an individual pathology, hatred of homosexuals is actually more public and more typical than hatred of any other disadvantaged group.

The defense is applied in English speaking countries like the US, Australia and Canada in two ways. One is as an insanity defense – that is, a defense that argues that the accused is in a condition or state where they cannot tell right from wrong or not understand the character of their actions. Legal scholars have argued that in pure legal terms, the Homosexual Panic Defense should not qualify as an insanity defense at all, first of all because to the extent that individuals can be said to panic at homosexuality, they do so precisely because they believe that homosexuality is "wrong." Second, cases that invoke the Panic Defense do no assert that defendants do not realize the likely consequences of shooting their victims in the heart, hacking them with meat cleavers, jumping on their heads or beating them with clubs – to take some more charming examples of the cases where the defense has been invoked. It is never asserted that defendants who do these things are unaware that they may kill the victim.

The second way the defense is applied is as a response to provocation. This defense relies on and promotes a view that there is no difference between a sexual advance and a sexual attack. In fact, the Homosexual Panic Defense argues that a sexual advance from a homosexual male is definitionally a sexual attack, and that the accused is justified in responding violently to such an act of aggression.

In practice, the Homosexual Panic Defense is used in ways that often bear almost no resemblance to any version of the psychiatric disorder. For example, the psychiatric criterion that homosexual panic is related to latent homosexuality in the accused is often disregarded. The most famous case of the Homosexual Panic Defense in recent years was a man named Jonathan Schmitz. Twenty-six-year-old Schmitz was brought onto an American television program called the *Jenny Jones* show, which is a kind of *Ricki Lake* or *Jerry Springer* show where people surprise their friends, family and lovers by revealing unexpected and often scandalous secrets about themselves on national television. Jonathan Schmitz had been told by the *Jenny Jones's* show's producers that someone he knew was secretly in love with him, and would reveal this crush on the air. It turned out that the person who was secretly in love with Schmitz was a 32-year-old gay man named Scott Amedure. Amedure greeted Schmitz when he appeared on the television stage and professed his attraction. Three days after the taping of the show, Schmitz bought a shotgun, drove to Amedure's home and shot him twice through the heart.

In the subsequent trial, Schmitz blamed the murdered Amedure for his actions – and this is how the Homosexual Panic Defense is increasingly being used. In other words, Schmitz's lawyers did not claim that Schmitz is a latent homosexual who panicked at the collapse of his heterosexual self-image. Instead, they claimed that Scott Amedure's public revelation of his desire in itself constituted an "ambush."[5] Schmitz's lawyers argued that Amedure's public revelation of an infatuation with Schmitz was, in and of itself, an act of aggression that excused a violent retaliation. The jury agreed with this line of reasoning and found Schmitz guilty not of first-degree premeditated murder, but of the lesser charge of second-degree (i.e. not premeditated) murder.[6]

Now let's look for a moment at the Homosexual Panic Defense in relation to what I have already argued about "no" in cases of sexual harassment and rape. At first glance, the two kinds of cases seem very different, which may be one reason why I have not seen them discussed together in any detail. In the case of rape, the victim of violence is the woman who rejects the sexual advance of a man. In the case of Homosexual Panic, the victim of violence is the man who (is reported to have) made the sexual advance.

What links the two cases, I am arguing, is "no." In both cases, a sexual advance acts as an interpellation, a calling into being of a sexual subject. Like Louis Althusser's famous example of the policeman's call "Hey, you there!" that produces a subject in the person who turns around (Althusser 1971: 174) – a subject who did not pre-exist the call, but who becomes constituted as a subject upon responding to it – a sexual advance calls into being a sexual subject. And in the case of both rape and Homosexual Panic, from the perspective of performativity theory, a "no" is not just a refusal of that subjection. It is also an acknowledgement of it; a response to the interpellative call that even in disputing it affirms it. It is a "no" that says "I refuse to acknowledge that I am being called into being as a sexual subject." But a refusal to acknowledge something is already a form of acknowledgment. In structural terms, therefore, a "no" to a sexual advance is – must be – both a "no" and a "yes" at the same time.

This dual indexicality[7] of "no" is what allows men to claim that they misunderstood a woman's "no," even as it also facilitates their assertion that sexual solicitation by another man in itself was an act of violence that justified a violent response. Remember that part of what produces the masculine sexual subject is the "no" of the other. To have to utter that "no" oneself is to be forced to produce oneself as a non-masculine subject. I think that it is for this reason that in cases in which the Homosexual Panic Defense is invoked, there is often no evidence that any verbal refusal ever even occurred. The word "no" is not – in a sense, cannot be uttered. Instead, the sexual interpellation is acknowledged non-verbally, with vicious physical violence.

I hope it is becoming clear where this argument is leading. My point is that "no" is essential not so much for the production of a sexual scenario (after all, a "yes" can produce that), but for the materialization of *a particular kind of sexual scenario* in which the sexual subjects so produced are differentially empowered and differentially gendered. In other words, "no" produces a sexualized, gendered field of power. As a final empirical example, I offer a situation that crystallizes all this, namely sadomasochistic sex.

Sadomasochistic Sex

Sadomasochistic sex is an extremely straightforward example of a case where "no" is self-consciously used to constitute a sexualized, gendered field of power. To see this, it is important to understand that any description or analysis of S/M discusses what is called a "safeword." This is a word or phrase that is negotiated in advance of the sexual scene and used by either the submissive bottom or the dominant top whenever either of them wants to stop some activity. The most important dimension of this for us is the fact that one of the very few words which cannot function as a safeword is, precisely, "no".

"Consider ... this dialogue," readers are instructed by one S/M manual, in a section on safewords:

> Top: 'Seems to me you deserve a good spanking with this hairbrush, my little slut.' Bottom (in role as obedient slave): 'If it pleases you, sir or madam' – or bottom (in role as reluctant victim): 'No! Please! Not the hairbrush!'[8]

"In either case," the manual explains, "the top has no guide to the bottom's real feelings" (Easton and Hardy 2001: 39). Why is this? The same authors go on to explain:

> The reason we need [a safeword] is that lots of us like to pretend we don't want to have all these amazing things done to us, and we may pretend by joyously shrieking 'Nonononononono', so we need another word to mean that (Easton and Hardy 2001: 44).

Another S/M manual (Henkin and Holiday 1996: 89, italics in original) puts it like this:

> Words other than No, Stop, or Slow Down are usually designated [as a safeword] because SM is a *consensual* eroticism in the realm of *erotic theatre*. If a bottom could just say 'Stop' to end a [sexual] scene, the illusion that the Top has total control might be threatened. Besides, many bottoms enjoy the fantasy of nonconsenuality and scream 'No, no, please stop!' – or words to that effect – when the scene is going very well; they would be upset, confused, and even angry if a Top actually did stop in response to their outbursts.

Another S/M manual explains that "A plea to 'Stop beating me' may well mean 'I love it. Keep going'" (Lee 1983: 186).

It is clear that "no" in these situations means its inversion, "yes." For that reason, manuals explain that safewords should be anything other than words like "no," "stop," or "don't" – that is to say, any words other than negations or expressions of pain. Most manuals recommend either contextually jarring words like "PICKLE!" or "RADISH!," or words that invoke associations to traffic lights: "YELLOW," meaning "lighter or slower," and "RED" meaning "stop".

In any case, my point is that S/M sex self-consciously exploits the performative potential of "no" to facilitate and extend sexual scenes. It recognizes the dual indexicality of "no" and deploys it to produce a domain of sexuality; a domain of sexuality that is, moreover, saturated with power. Because whatever else it may be about, all practitioners and observers of S/M are agreed that it is an eroticization and staging of power. S/M manuals all discuss power. The title of one of the first and most famous S/M manuals ever published, by the lesbian-feminist S/M support group, Samois (1981), was the pun: *Coming to Power.*[9] A common definition of S/M is "consensual exchanges of erotic power" (e.g. Henkin and Holiday 1996: 72). One manual elaborates a distinction between "power-over," which is power obtained at the expense of others, and "power-with," which is "the idea that we can all become more powerful by supporting each other in being more powerful" (Easton and Hardy 2001: 24–5). S/M, this manual explains, is a play with power for the fun of it; hence, a "power-with" in which erotic pleasure is produced by skillful manipulations of forms of power that are invested with new content. This same manual proposes that all bottoms ought to see themselves as what it calls "full-power bottoms".

We can debate the extent to which concepts like "full-power bottoms" are reasonable ones. But even those who reject them – for example radical feminists who insist that S/M practitioners merely reinscribe the very structures of power they claim to transcend – do not contest that what happens in sadomasochistic sex is an erotic staging of power.

The central role that "no" plays in this staging is not fortuitous or arbitrary. On the contrary, the structuring role of "no" in the production of a sadomasochistic sex scene is a distillation and elaboration of "no"'s role in wider arenas of social life. And that role, as I have been arguing, is not so much about performance as it is production. "No" performatively materializes specific kinds of erotic domains, ones in which power is channeled through and constitutive of specific social positions. Those positions are gendered in the sense that they are differently positioned in relation to "no" – as I mentioned earlier, the subject position "woman" is produced in part by the normatively exhorted utterance "no" when encountering a sexual interpellation. This contrasts with the subject "man," who is normatively exhorted to *never* say "no" to sex, and whose position as masculine is produced in part through the "no" of the other. S/M sex invokes this plane in order to exploit the disruptive potential of the erotic to manipulate and invert these positionings. Hence, it provides a space for the male body to temporarily (and socially inconsequentially) inhabit the "no" that is otherwise disallowed it; just as it provides a space for the female body to inhabit the position that is materialized through the enunciation of the "no" of the other (It is no secret to anyone that the over whelming majority of submissive bottoms are males – frequently the same males who exercise a great deal of social power outside the dungeon. Nor is it a secret that the tops that these men pay a lot of money to dominate them are female dominatrixes – how's that for a linguistically *marked* category?). The erotic plane that S/M sex constructs for itself also recognizes the violence that inheres in sexual domains invoked by "no," and it produces that violence. But it produces it not as realism or tragedy, but, rather, as *melodrama*, a genre that is characterized by the exteriorization of conflict and psychic structures in dramatic excess (see Gledhill 1987: 31; also Nowell-Smith 1987; Williams 1987).

Conclusion

In Cameron and Kulick (2003), we briefly discuss the way in which issues of language and sexuality for the most part have been studied in terms of language and identity. We noted there that this perspective has regarded sexuality *not* as a set of dynamics or practices that are animated by fantasy, desire, repression and power, but, instead, as an identity that is either revealed or concealed by fully intentional subjects. This focus on identity has unnecessarily restricted the scope of enquiry, and it has made research in this area unable to address the broader semiotic processes through which sexuality is produced and disseminated in language.

One of the points of this essay has been to suggest what I see as a difference between performance and performativity, and the relationship of those two perspectives to language. At several junctures, I noted where I think that a performance perspective differs from a performativity perspective. But there is a particular difference, a crucial one in my view, with which

I would like to end – one that bring us back to the question of identity. That difference is this: whereas studies conceived of in a performance framework have a tendency to see language in relation to *identity*, research framed as performative will concentrate more on *identification*. The difference is between identity, which in sociolinguistic and linguistic anthropological work is conventionally presented as a more or less conscious claim-staking of a particular sociological position,[10] and identification, which is concerned with the operations through which the subject is constituted. A psychoanalytic truism about identifications is that they do not constitute a coherent relational system. Nor are they entirely conscious. On the contrary, identifications are just as much structured by rejections, refusals and disavowals as they are structured by affirmations. Because they are not the same thing, it is important to not collapse identification into identity. A performative approach to linguistic phenomena does not start or end with identity. Instead, a performative approach would examine the processes through which some kinds of identifications are authorized, legitimate and unmarked, and others are unauthorized, illegitimate, and marked. I have tried to do this here with "no," examining it not by asking: who says it? but, rather: what does saying it – or not saying it – produce? That question leads me to another, more consequential one, namely: instead of a sociolinguistics of identity, what would happen if we began imagining a sociolinguistics of identification?

NOTES

This paper was presented as a plenary lecture at the Sociolinguistics Symposium 14, Ghent, Belgium, 4–6 April 2002. I am grateful to Jan Blommaert and Stef Slembrouck for inviting me to Ghent, and hence providing me with the impetus to develop my ideas about "No," which first arose during discussion with Deborah Cameron during the writing of *Language and Sexuality.* Debbie has been a continual source of inspiration and criticism. Susan Ehrlich, Bambi Schieffelin, and Christopher Stroud also provided me with thoughtful feedback and criticism. Fred Myers helped me to articulate links between older work in linguistic anthropology and performative approaches to language. I am indebted to Steve Albert and Kathe Managan for patiently tracking down many of the sources I use throughout this text. Finally, this paper forms part of the research project "Heteronormativity: an interdisciplinary ethnographic approach," funded by the Bank of Sweden Tercentenary Foundation (grant nr. 99–5061). I gratefully acknowledge that support.

1 Earlier work on language and political economy (e.g. Myers and Brenneis, 1984), discursive regimes of speaking (e.g. Lindstrom, 1990), Bakhtinian dialogism (e.g. Hill and Hill, 1986; Tedlock and Mannheim, 1995), and, most recently, 'language ideology' (e.g. Schieffelin et al., 1998) shares many concerns with performativity theory in that it examines who is authorized or enabled to say what, and who is silenced. Where this work arguably differs from performativity theory is, first of all, in its inattention to issues of sexuality; secondly, in its relative lack of concern with the processes through which subjects and subjectivities are produced; and thirdly, in its lack of awareness of the complex role that *identifications* (refusals as well as affirmations) play in linguistic practice. There are of course exceptions to this generalization, such as Hill (1995a), which examines the production of a specific moral subject without using the metalanguage of performativity theory. Cameron (1997) is a good example of an empirically grounded performative studies of language (that do reference performativity theory), because interrogates how particular kinds of language enable or block particular kinds of identifications and subjectivities.

2 Please note the 'part of what . . . '. I am not claiming that 'no' is the only linguistic iteration that produces sexualized, gendered subjects. But I am claiming that 'no' works as a performative to produce situations as

sexual, and it simultaneously materializes sexualized, gendered subjects that are positioned in a specific relation of power.

3 See Kitzinger and Frith (1999) for a discussion of this in the context of sexual harassment and rape.

4 See the following sources on homosexual panic and the Homosexual Panic Defense: Bagnall et al. (1984), Comstock (1989), Freiberg (1988), Glick (1959), New South Wales Government (1998), Suffrendi (2001), Hart (1958).

5 Michigan Court of Appeals (1998). 586 N. W. 2d 766, 768.

6 For details about the Schmitz case, see http://www.courttv.com/trials/jennyjones/background.html

7 I am indebted to Jane Hill (1995b, p. 13) for this term, but I adopt it here to mean something different from what she proposes.

8 For the uninitiated, I should note that the terms "top" and "bottom" in S/M culture denote, respectively, the dominant and submissive partner in a sexual scene.

9 The name Samois was chosen because it evokes several lesbian episodes and the figure of a lesbian dominatrix in *Story of O*, probably the most famous S/M literary classic' (Samois 1979: 4). For a history of the group, see Califia and Sweeney 1996.

10 See Cameron and Kulick (2003), chapter 6, for a more detailed exposition of this assertion.

REFERENCES

Althusser, L., 1971. Ideology and Ideological State Apparatuses (Notes towards an Investigation). In: Althusser, L. (ed.), *Lenin and Philosophy and Other Essays*. London Monthly Review Press, pp. 127–88.

Austin, J. L., 1997 [1962]. *How to Do Things with Words*, 2nd edn. Cambridge, MA: Harvard University Press.

Bagnall, R.G., Gallagher, P.C., Goldstein, J.L., 1984. Burdens on Gay Litigants and the Bias in the Court System: Homosexual Panic, Child Custody and Anonymous Parties. Harvard Civil Rights-Civil Liberties *Law Review* 19 (2): 487–559.

Bourdieu, P., 1991. Authorized Language. In: Bourdieu, P. (ed.), *Language and Symbolic Power*. Cambridge, MA: Harvard University Press, pp. 107–16.

Butler, J., 1990. *Gender Trouble: Feminism and the Subversion of Identity*. New York: Routledge.

Butler, J., 1993. *Bodies that Matter: On the Discursive Limits of 'Sex'*. New York: Routledge.

Califia, P., Sweeney, R., 1996. Come Soon, Come in, and Come as You Are: An Introduction. In: Califia, P., Sweeny, R. (eds.), *The Second Coming: A Leatherdyke Reader*. Los Angeles: Alyson Publications, pp. xi–xvii.

Cameron, D., 1997. Performing Gender Identity: Young Men's Talk and the Construction of Heterosexual Masculinity. In: Johnson, S., Meinhof, V. (eds.), *Language and Masculinity*. Oxford: Blackwell, pp. 47–64.

Cameron, D., Kulick, D., 2003. *Language and Sexuality*. Cambridge Cambridge University Press.

Comstock, G.D., 1989. Developments: Sexual Orientation and the Law. *Haryard Law Review* 102, 1508–51.

Easton, D., Hardy, J.W., 2001. *The New Bottoming Book*. Emeryville, CA: Greenery Press.

Ehrlich, S., 1998. The Discursive Reconstruction of Sexual Consent. *Discourse & Society* 9 (2): 149–71.

Ehrlich, S., 2001. *Representing Rape: Language and Sexual Consent*. London and New York: Routledge.

Freiberg, P., 1988. Blaming the Victim: New Life for the 'Gay Panic' Defense. *The Advocate* May 24: 10–13.

Gledhill, C., 1987. The Melodramatic Field: An Investigation. In: Gledhill, C. (ed.), *Home is Where the Heart is: Studies in Melodrama and the Woman's Film*. London: British Film Institute, pp. 5–42.

Glick, B.S., 1959. Homosexual Panic: Clinical and Theoretical Considerations. *The Journal of Nervous and Mental Disease* 129: 20–8.

Hall, K., 2001. Performativity. In: Duranti, A. (ed.), *Key Terms in Language and Culture*. Oxford: Blackwell, pp. 180–183.

Hart, H.H., 1958. Fear of Homosexuality among College Students. In: Wedge, B.M. (ed.), *Psychosocial Problems of College Men*. New Haven: Yale University Press, pp. 200–13.

Henkin, W.A., Holiday, S., 1996. *Consensual Sadomasochism: How to Talk About It and Do It Safely*. Los Angeles: Daedalus.

Hill, J., 1995a. The Voices of Don Gabriel. In: Tedlock, D., Mannheim, B. (eds.), *The Dialogic Emergence of Culture*. Urbana and Chicago, IL: University of Illinois Press, pp. 97–147.

Hill, J., 1995b. *Mock Spanish: A Site for the Indexical Reproduction of Racism in American English*. Available from http://www.language-culture.org/colloquia/symposia/hill-jane.

Hill, J., Hill, K., 1986. *Speaking Mexicano: Dynamics of a Syncretic Language in Central Mexico*. Tuscan: University of Arizona Press.

Kempf, E.J., 1920. *Psychopathology*. St Louis: C.V. Mosby Company.

Kitzinger, C., Frith, H., 1999. Just Say No? The Use of Conversation Analysis in Developing a Feminist Perspective on Sexual Refusal. *Discourse & Society* 10 (3): 293–316.

Lee, J.A., 1983. The Social Organization of Sexual Risk. In: Weinberg, T., Kamel, G.W. L. (eds.), *S and M: Studies in Sadomasochism*. New York: Prometheus Books, pp. 175–93.

Lees, S., 1996. *Carnal Knowledge: Rape on Trial*. London: Hamish Hamilton.

Lindstrom, L., 1990. *Knowledge and Power in a South Pacific Society*. Washington, DC, and London: Smithsonian Institution Press.

MacKinnon, C.A., 1993. *Only Words*. Cambridge, MA: Harvard University Press.

Matoesian, G.M., 1993. *Reproducing Rape: Domination Through Talk in the Courtroom*. Chicago, IL: University of Chicago Press.

McConnell-Ginet, S., 1989. The (Re)production of Sexual Meaning: A Discourse Based Theory. In: Frank, F., Treichler, P. (eds.), *Language, Gender and Professional Writing*. New York: Modern Language Association, pp. 111–34.

Muehlenhard, C. L., Hollabaugh, L. C., 1988. Do Women Sometimes Say No when They Mean Yes? The prevalence and correlates of women's token resistance to sex. *Journal of Personality and Social Psychology* 54(5): 872–9.

Michigan Court of Appeals, 1998. 586 N.W. 2d 766, 768.

Myers, F.R., Brenneis, D.L., 1984. Introduction: Language and Politics in the Pacific. In: Brenneis, D.L., Myers, F.R. (eds.), *Dangerous Words: Language and Politics in the Pacific*. New York: New York University Press, pp. 1–29.

New South Wales Government, 1998. *Homosexual Advance Defence: Final Report of the Working Party*. Available from http://lawlink.nsw.gov.au/clrdl.nsf/pages/had.

Nowell-Smith, G., 1987. Minelli and Melodrama. In: Gledhill, C. (ed.), *Home is Where the Heart is: Studies in Melodrama and the Woman's Film*. London: British Film Institute, pp. 70–4.

Samois (ed.), 1979. *What Color is Your Handkerchief: A Lesbian S/M Sexuality Reader*. Berkeley, CA: Samois.

Samois, 1981. *Coming to Power: Writings and Graphics on Lesbian S/M*. Boston: Alyson Publications.

Schieffelin, B.B., Woolard, K.A., Kroskrity, P.V. (eds.), 1998. *Language Ideologies: Practice and Theory*. Oxford and New York: Oxford University Press.

Sedgwick, E.K., 1990. *Epistemology of the Closet*. Berkeley and Los Angeles: University of California Press.

Suffrendi, K.S., 2001. Pride and Prejudice: The Homosexual Panic Defense. *Boston College Third World Law Journal* 21 (2): 279–314.

Tedlock, D., Mannheim, B. (eds.), 1995. *The Dialogic Emergence of Culture*. Urbana and Chicago, IL: University of Illinois Press.

The Opposite of Sex, 1998. Roos, D. (Director), Kirkpatrick, D., Besman, M. (Producers), SONY Pictures Classic Release.

Weston, K., 1993. Do Clothes Make the Woman? Gender, Performance Theory, and Lesbian Eroticism. *Genders* 17: 1–21.

Williams, L., 1987. 'Something else Besides a Mother': *Stella Dallas* and the Maternal Dilemma. In: Gledhill, C. (ed.), *Home is Where the Heart is: Studies in Melodrama and the Woman's Film*. London: British Film Institute, pp. 299–325.

STUDY QUESTIONS

1 What is the difference between performance and performativity?
2 How does the use of "no" participate in the construction of the identity of "woman" in the context of male demands for sexual intercourse and how is the same cultural logic reversed in the case of a man who says "no" to another man's request for sex?
3 How did the understanding of the "homosexual panic defense" change over time and how has it been used in courts in the USA, Australia, and Canada?
4 How does Kulick see "no" as the link between the case of so-called "homosexual panic" and the previously discussed cases of sexual harassment and rape?
5 In what ways, according to Kulick, do Sadomasochistic (S/M) sex practices (as described in the S/M manuals) illustrate the performative force of "no"?
6 Can you think of other speech exchanges that are understood to have different meanings depending on the gender of the speaker and hearer?

Index